CW00821930

THE MUGHAL EMPIRE, c.1595
Ṣūba and Sarkār boundaries
based on the Ā'īn-i-Akbarī
LEGEND
A LUCKNOW
B HANDIA
C JAUNPUR
D BIRŪN PANJNAD
E LAKHNAUTI
F SATGAON
G BANARAS
Ṣūba capital
Sarkār headquarters
50 0 100 200 Km
80°
84°
88°
92°
32°
28°
24°
20°
16°
MAUN
BHAL
BUDAUN
KHAIRABAD
BAHRAICH
AWADH
LUCKNOW
AWADH
GORAKHPUR
KANAUJ
MANIKPUR
JAUNPUR
KORA
KARA
KALPI
ALLAHABAD
GHAZIPUR
CHUNAR
KALINJAR
ALLAHABAD
BATTHA
RACH
ROHTAS
CHAMPARAN
SARAN
TIRHUT
HAJIPUR
BIHAR
BIHAR
BIHAR (UNMEASURED)
MONGHYR
KOKHRA
GAHORA
GARHA
PURNEA
TAJPUR
PANJRA
KUCH BIHAR
LAKHNAUTI
GHORAGHAT
BARBAKABAD
BAZUHA
SYLHET
BENGAL
TANDA
MAHMUDABAD
SONARGAON
SHARIFABAD
SULAIMANABAD
MADARAN
FATEHABAD
SATGAON
KHALIFATABAD
BAKLA
CHATGAON
JALESAR
ORISSA
BADHRA
KATAK
PUNAR
ALAM
ANIKDRUG
RAMGIR
BAY OF BENGAL

THE ECONOMY OF THE MUGHAL EMPIRE *c.* 1595

A Statistical Study

Revised and Enlarged Edition

SHIREEN MOOSVI

SPECIMEN COPY
NOT FOR SALE

OXFORD
UNIVERSITY PRESS

OXFORD
UNIVERSITY PRESS

Oxford University Press is a department of the University of Oxford.
It furthers the University's objective of excellence in research, scholarship,
and education by publishing worldwide. Oxford is a registered trademark of
Oxford University Press in the UK and in certain other countries

Published in India by
Oxford University Press
YMCA Library Building, 1 Jai Singh Road, New Delhi 110001, India

© Shireen Moosvi 2015

The moral rights of the author have been asserted

First Edition published in 1987

All rights reserved. No part of this publication may be reproduced, stored in a retrieval system, or transmitted, in any form or by any means, without the prior permission in writing of Oxford University Press, or as expressly permitted by law, by licence, or under terms agreed with the appropriate reprographics rights organization. Enquiries concerning reproduction outside the scope of the above should be sent to the Rights Department, Oxford University Press, at the address above

You must not circulate this work in any other form
and you must impose this same condition on any acquirer

ISBN-13: 978-0-19-945054-1
ISBN-10: 0-19-945054-4

Typeset in Times New Roman 10/12
by Zaza Eunice, Hosur, India
Printed in India by Rakmo Press, New Delhi 110 020

To the memory of

Shahenshah Husain Musavi
Uncle, guide, guardian

Contents

List of Maps and Figures

Maps

Figures

Preface to This Edition

In the preface to the first edition of this book published in 1987, I sought to define the objective, scope, and methodology of the work. The objective was to examine the main features of the Indian economy, *c.* 1595, and compare these to conditions in 1900–1. The reasons behind this were twofold. In order to understand how colonial rule had changed Indian economy, it was important to compare India of the time when colonial control had reached its apex with an earlier situation well before the onset of colonial conquest. Secondly, owing to the richness of the statistics contained in Abū'l Faẓl's *Ā'īn-i Akbarī*, 1595 happens to be the only year of the pre-colonial era where economic data are available in adequate profusion to enable us to construct a quantitative portrayal of the economy, while in the later period, 1900–1 is the year by which official statistics had been gathered and critically appraised sufficiently to enable us to be confident about the picture built on their basis: Fred J. Atkinson had attempted in 1902 an estimate of India's national income of the year 1895; and S. Sivasubramonian's standard calculations of Indian's national income (revised, 2000) begin with 1900–1.

As far as possible, I sought in my book to apply modern statistical methods to analyse the data contained in the *Ā'īn-i Akbarī*, along with those in other sources including numismatic evidence. As far as the *Ā'īn-i Akbarī* is concerned, I had to go to its early manuscripts to establish the original figures in the text, so as to avoid the effects of misprints or tabular misrepresentations in the printed versions. I also did my best to explain the arithmetic involved at each stage of my calculations.

As a result of this work, I was able to build up estimates of the size of agricultural and craft production, the pattern of distribution of surplus among various classes, the total value of external trade, the structure of wages and trends of price movements, and, finally, the size of population.

When my book came out, it received many reviews from scholars, both peers and seniors. By and large, there was approval of my textual research and arithmetic. There were also criticisms on several matters, which, to the best of my ability, I have considered in my revision of the book. Dr Najaf Haider has more recently shown that the name of *tanka* was not transferred to the *dām* after 1605, as I, along with other historians, had taken to be the case; and this has naturally led to my reframing the presentation of data on copper values.

A matter of greater weight has been my recalculation of the value of manufactures, which has caused me to reshape Chapter 13 and substantially revise Chapter 16. The basis for the fresh estimate has been laid out there and partly in the new Chapter 18, so I need not spell it out here.

Finally, after much thought and after publishing a paper (which I would now entirely recast!), I have decided to take the plunge and add a final chapter (18) devoted to the task of estimating the GDP *c.* 1595. A reviewer had taxed me for not attempting a conclusion in my first edition; I hope my chapter on GDP will now meet this objection.

For transliteration I have generally, but not exclusively, followed the system of spelling and diacritical marks adopted by Steingass for his *Comprehensive Persian-English Dictionary.* For geographical names I have followed Irfan Habib's *Atlas of the Mughal Empire*; I have dispensed with the diacritical marks in place names, since these are provided in the index to the *Atlas.*

In my revision and enlargement of the book I have continued to draw on the advice and counsel of my original Supervisor, Professor Irfan Habib. Professor Ishrat Alam and Dr S. Nadeem Rezavi have also been of help to me in various ways.

I am grateful to the staff of the library of the Department of History, especially Mr Bansidhar Sharma and Mr Javed Akhtar, successive librarians, for their ready and courteous assistance all the time. Ms Joytsna Arora and her colleagues at the splendid library of the Indian Council of Historical Research, New Delhi, have also been most helpful to me. The reproduction of part of a statistical table in the *Ā'īn-i Akbarī* from a manuscript in the Maulana Azad Library, AMU, was made possible by the courtesy of Ms Shayista Khan and Mr Asrar Ahmad Khan.

My text has been processed by Mr Muneeruddin Khan and, at a later stage, by Ms Nazima and Mr Zeeshan Khan. Mr Faiz Habib has redrawn afresh the map on the inner cover and two other maps within the volume and has also drawn a graph.

I have received constant assistance of all kinds from the staff of the office of the Aligarh Historians Society, Mr Arshad Ali, Mr Idris Beg, and Ms Ashma Khan.

July 2014 Shireen Moosvi
Aligarh

Note on Abbreviations: The reader is reminded that the list of abbreviations appears on pp. 434–6 and all abbreviated titles in my footnotes conform to this list.

Excerpt from the Preface to the First Edition (1987)

This book first took shape as a doctoral thesis under the supervision of Professor Irfan Habib. He went through the final typescript of the book, though he is, of course, not responsible for any errors that remain. My gratitude to him is far beyond the reach of expression.

I owe much to Professor S. Nurul Hasan who, by appointing me Statistician in the Department of History over sixteen years ago, was responsible for changing my research interests from Mathematics to Economic History. I have also received constant encouragement from Professor Rais Ahmad all these years.

Mr Faiz Habib and his senior colleague, Mr Zahoor A. Khan, Cartographer of the Department of History, have drawn all the maps; and I am grateful to both of them for bearing with patience my constant alterations and revisions.

Among my colleagues, Dr S.P. Gupta generously placed at my disposal his knowledge of Rajasthani material; Professor M. Athar Ali and Professor Iqtidar Alam Khan have always been ready to discuss with me (often to clarify) the various complexities of Mughal administration and political history; and Dr S.P. Verma and Dr B.L. Bhadani gave me assistance in correcting the proofs.

I am indebted to Mr S.A.I. Tirmizi, then Director, National Archives, for much help at the Archives, and to Dr A.K. Srivastava, Numismatic Officer, State Museum, Lucknow (presently Director, Mathura Museum), for giving me access to coin-find reports.

I should like to thank Mr Jalal A. Abbasi and his colleagues, Mr Aijaz M. Khan, Mr Arshad Ali, Mr M. Yusuf Siddiqi, Mr Noor Ahmad, and Mr Irfan Khan at the Research Library, C.A.S. in History, where most of my work has been done. Miss Maureen L. Patterson, Head, South Asia Section of the University of Chicago Library, gave me ungrudging assistance in using that splendid library. I am indebted also to the authorities and staff of the Maulana Azad Library (Aligarh), the British Museum, the India Office Library, and the Library of the School of Oriental and African Studies (London), and the Bodleian Library (Oxford) for all kinds of assistance.

A Senior Fulbright Fellowship enabled me to visit Chicago and to have the pleasure of working with Professor Robert W. Fogel, one of the 'fathers' of cliometric history (to which genre this book has no pretensions to belong) in 1984.

The Indian Council of Social Science Research gave me financial assistance to enable me to work at libraries in England, and I am indebted to Professor D.D. Narula for making the grant possible.

Mrs Marilyn Coopersmith, Deputy Director, Centre for Population Economics, University of Chicago, befriended me beyond any possible expectation, and even typed two chapters of my book. Mr M.A. Khan Afridi typed the final copy so clearly as to earn commendation from my publishers (not easily obtained, I believe).

To the Oxford University Press go my earnest thanks for agreeing to publish my book, even before the Centre of Advanced Study had agreed to subsidize its publication.

September 1986 — Shireen Moosvi
Aligarh

INTRODUCTION

CHAPTER 1

The Statistics and Their Sources

I

This study is an attempt to examine in quantitative terms the economic structure of the Mughal Empire about the close of the sixteenth century. That the attempt can be made at all is almost entirely due to the rich statistical material contained in Abū'l Faẓl's *Ā'īn-i Akbarī*, which is unique in a number of ways: its author deals with aspects that for other historians did not merit even passing notice; he revels in offering us quantitative data—an unusual trait for the period, and surely unexpected in a writer of so notably majestic a literary style. Any study of his statistics must begin with a grateful tribute to his vast endeavour.

The *Ā'īn-i Akbarī* is part of a large work that Abū'l Faẓl undertook upon the orders of the emperor Akbar.[1] The two volumes of his *Akbarnāma* record the events of Akbar's reign, preceded by an account of the reigns of Bābur and Humāyūn, his grandfather and father. The 'third volume' of what was ostensibly a single work, was devoted exclusively to recording the *Ā'īnhā-i Muqaddas-i Shāhī* ('the Sacred Imperial Regulations').[2] The separate title, *Ā'īn-i Akbarī* has been given to the volume through a consensus among readers at least from the seventeenth century. It certainly has, for all practical purposes, a distinct entity of its own, and its extant manuscript copies universally treat it as an independent work. The subject matter here is the organization of Akbar's court, administration and army, the revenues and geography of his Empire, and the traditions and culture of the people he governed.

The *Ā'īn-i Akbarī* contains five books (*daftars*): the first three give a detailed description of the administration—'the secular side of the Emperor'.[3] The first book (*Manzil-ābādī*, 'the Palace Establishment')

[1] *Akbarnāma*, I, 9.

[2] *Ā'īn*, II, 257.

[3] Ibid., 255.

deals with the emperor's household, covering a wide range of aspects, from the treasury to the prices of various commodities, and from the regulations of the 'Animal Stables' to the management of the 'Building Establishment'. The second book (*Sipāh-ābādi*, 'the Military Establishment') covers the military and civil administration and the establishments of officials and servants. Along with the nobles (*manṣabdārs*), learned men, poets, artists, physicians, and others also find notice here.

The third book (*Mulk-ābādī*, 'the Government of the Country') gives comprehensive information on the system of taxation, including detailed tables of revenue rates (*dastūru'l 'amal*) followed by the 'Account of the Twelve *Ṣūbas* (provinces)'. The last has a separate chapter on each *ṣūba*, describing its geography and resources; this textual portion is followed, under each *ṣūba*, first, by statistical tables, and then by brief dynastic annals of the region. Owing to the enormous significance of this portion of the *Ā'īn* for our study, the next section in this chapter is entirely reserved for a discussion of its data.

The concluding books deal with the sciences, religions, and culture of the Indian people, and also contain a collection of Akbar's 'auspicious sayings'.

Abū'l Faẓl in his conclusion[4] to the *Ā'īn* tells us of the way he collected the material for his work. He says that his information was based on the testimony of contemporaries and eyewitnesses after a critical assessment of whatever they had said. All the records of the State too had been put at his disposal. It seems that for the narrative history of the *Akbarnāma*, at least for the earlier years of the reign, he had to rely upon oral evidence (or, at best, memoirs recorded for him).[5] But for the *Ā'īn-i Akbarī*, he relied practically entirely upon state papers, and his statistical data were naturally supplied by government departments. But even here Abū'l Faẓl has not simply reproduced the official reports or documents; he has rearranged them, replacing the officialese of the bureaucratic originals with text refashioned in his own polished style. He tells us that he revised the text five times and was intending to undertake a sixth revision when the Emperor's insistence on getting the work completed, forced him to abstain from it.[6] Internal evidence suggests, as we will presently see, that he made additions even after the last day of the 42nd

[4] Ibid., 245–57. The conclusion is followed by a biography of the author's father together with a brief autobiography.

[5] See Bāyazīd Bayāt's statements as to how his memoirs came to be written down for the use of Abū'l Faẓl, *Tārīkh-i Humāyūn-o-Akbar*, ed., M. Hidayat Hosain, Calcutta, 1941, 1–2.

[6] *Ā'īn*, II, 256.

regnal year (20 March 1598), which is the date of the formal conclusion of the work.[7]

In view of the rigorously logical arrangement of its contents, the author's obvious concern with the maintenance of precision and accuracy and the manifest imprint of Abū'l Faẓl's literary style that the text bears, it is difficult to accept Moreland's description of the *Ā'īn* as a 'hastily edited collection of official papers'.[8] In actual fact, we have constant indication of the extreme care taken by Abū'l Faẓl in presenting his information, especially quantitative data. All numbers are expressed in words, a system clearly adopted to minimize the chances of transcriptional errors, for which there would have been much greater chance in Arabic numerals as well as the *raqam* notation. That the latter is eschewed, though it was the usual bureaucratic vehicle for conveying figures, is yet another proof of a deliberate avoidance of mere reproduction of official papers.[9]

The period to which the different statistical data in the *Ā'īn-i Akbarī* belong is not usually explicitly indicated, though there are important exceptions. One exception is offered by the '19-year rates' (*Ā'īn-i Nauzdah Sāla*), where the revenue rates for each regnal year are punctiliously given in tabular form. More to our purpose, the *jama'* statistics of the 'Twelve *Ṣūbas*' and the list of the *manṣabdārs* are both expressly assigned to the 40th regnal year.[10] On the strength of this ascription of two very important parts of statistical material, it is perhaps a matter of convenience to treat 1595–6 as the year to which the *Ā'īn*'s statistics may, in general, be assigned. But it is obvious that some information (apart from the 19-year rates) relates to a date earlier than this; and some of it must belong to later years. One has, therefore, to consider the limits of the period within which the *Ā'īn*'s information may be placed; and this can perhaps be done best by examining the evidence as to when (and, partly, how) the *Ā'īn*'s materials were collected.

In both the *Akbarnāma* and the *Ā'īn-i Akbarī*, Abū'l Faẓl refers to an imperial order issued to him to write an account of the life and achievements of his sovereign. One MS of the *Akbarnāma*[11] mentions the dates

[7] Ibid., 278.

[8] W.H. Moreland, *Agrarian System of Moslem India*, 81.

[9] The Arabic numerals used in Blochmann's printed text of the *Ā'īn*, are not justified by the texts of the MSS, which give all the figures in words.

[10] The Regnal or *Ilāhī* year began with the Nauroz (falling on 20 or 21 March) every year. The 40th Regnal Year thus began on 9 Rajab 1003 or 20 March 1595 (*Akbarnāma*, III, 667).

[11] H. Beveridge's introduction to his translation of the *Akbarnāma*, Vol.I, Calcutta, 1897, 33; the MS cited is RAS 17.

of the two decrees to this effect, the first being 22nd Isfandārmuz, 33rd regnal year (12 March 1589) and the second 26th Ardī Bihisht, 34th regnal year (18 May 1589). Elsewhere Abū'l Faẓl gives the last day of the 42nd regnal year (20 March 1598) as the date of completion of the *Ā'īn-i Akbarī*. He adds that it took him seven years to complete the work, during which he prepared five drafts of the text.[12] Counting seven years from the stated date of completion of the *Ā'īn*, the work of compilation should have started by the end of the 35th regnal year (March 1591) and not the 33rd regnal year. But since Abū'l Faẓl assigns two important portions of the *Ā'īn* (the list of the *manṣabdārs* and the *jama'* figures) to the 40th regnal year (1595–6), indicating that this was the year in which the *Ā'īn* was in the main completed, the seven years should really be counted back from that year. In that case, the initial year for the compilation would, indeed, be the 33rd regnal year (1588–9), precisely the year in which the decrees for its compilation had been issued.

Abū'l Faẓl must obviously have begun his work with the process of collecting information and it is possible that much of this information was received by him before 1589. He says in the chapter *Ā'īn-i Ābdārkhāna* that 'nowadays, Lahore is the capital'[13] (a fact true for the period, 1586–98);[14] but in another chapter, the *Ā'īn-i 'Imārat*, he refers to Fatehpur as the imperial seat,[15] which suggests that this particular portion of the text (and the documents on which it was based) had been prepared before 1586 (the year Fatehpur ceased to be the capital).[16]

Other internal evidence also suggests the use of other information coming down from a date before the initial year of compilation of the work. Abū'l Faẓl assigns his *jama'*-statistics to the 40th regnal year (1595–6); but the total *jama'* that he records (363 crore *dāms*)[17] is less than the figure of 440 crore *dāms* given in the *Ṭabaqāt-i Akbarī*,[18] which was completed in 1593. If we add Abū'l Faẓl's own totals for the original twelve *ṣūbas* (except Kabul), the grand total comes to 404 crore *dāms*.

[12] *Ā'īn*, II, 256.

[13] Ibid., I, 51.

[14] *Akbarnāma*, III, 494 & 748.

[15] *Ā'īn*, I, 168. It is significant that in the *Akbarnāma* Abū'l Faẓl denies to Fatehpur Sikri the designation of *Daru'l Khīlāfa* when Lahore was the capital (*Akbarnāma*, III, 581); but he applies this designation to it as soon as Akbar left Lahore (ibid., 722).

[16] *Akbarnāma*, III, 494.

[17] *Ā'īn*, I, 386.

[18] *Ṭabaqāt*, III, 546. Apparently by mistake, the *Ṭabaqāt* gives this figure not in *dāms* but in *tankas* or double-*dāms*.

Quite obviously, in stating the total as only 363 crore *dāms* for the twelve *ṣūbas*, Abū'l Faẓl has inadvertently allowed the total for the empire gathered from an earlier record to remain in his text. It has been suggested with some reason that the figure of 363 crore *dāms* actually belonged to the year 1580–1 when the *jama'-i dahsāla* was first established.[19]

Abū'l Faẓl assigns the list of his *manṣabdārs* to the 40th regnal year;[20] but this list too seems to have been completed much earlier. It was already available to the author of the *Ṭabaqāt-i Akbarī* who closed his work in 1593.[21] Even at that time the *Ā'īn*'s list was perhaps partly out-of-date, since Niẕāmuddīn Aḥmad made several additions and changes in the list. The *Ṭabaqāt*'s list gives fifteen names that are not mentioned in the *Ā'īn*, while for forty-eight *manṣabdārs* the *manṣabs* recorded in the *Ṭabaqāt* are higher than those given in the *Ā'īn*. Abū'l Faẓl does seem to have added some new names to his earlier list, partly at least to accommodate new appointments and promotions; but he seems to have failed to incorporate all the *manṣab* promotions given between the time of the original list and the 40th regnal year. No *manṣab* granted after the 40th year is incorporated, although Abū'l Faẓl formally completed the work two years later.[22]

The 40th regnal year also seems to form the end-line for some other data. For example, the *Ā'īn* omits any reference to the revised schedule of the monthly *barāwurdī* rates, issued in the 40th regnal year and duly recorded in the *Akbarnāma*.[23]

The *Ā'īn-i Akbarī*, however, did not fully close with the 40th regnal year or even the 42nd. The three new *ṣūbas*, Berar (annexed, 41st regnal year), Khandesh and Ahmadnagar (annexed, 45th), make their appearance in the 'Account of the Twelve *Ṣūbas*', raising the total number of *ṣūbas* from twelve to fifteen. Yet the old heading, '*Ā'īn-i Aḥwāl-i Doāzdah Ṣūba*' was retained (perhaps overlooked). In the notice of Khandesh (Dandesh) in the *Ā'īn*, Abū'l Faẓl himself mentions the 45th regnal year (1600–1) as the year in which the annexation occurred.[24] Not only were the accounts of these three *ṣūbas* inserted after the 45th regnal year, there are signs that additions were made elsewhere too in the 'Account of the Twelve *Ṣūbas*'. Malwa was one of the old twelve

[19] Irfan Habib, *Agrarian System*, 399 and *n.*15 (rev. ed. 454 & *n.*15).

[20] *Ā'īn*, I, 222.

[21] See the explicit acknowledgement in the *Ṭabaqāt*, II, 425.

[22] Cf. Irfan Habib, 'The *Manṣab* System, 1595–1637', *PIHC*, 1967, 243.

[23] *Akbarnāma*, III, 671–2. cf. I. Habib, '*Manṣab* System', 234.

[24] *Ā'īn*, I, 476. The fall of Asirgarh which may symbolize the final annexation of the Khandesh kingdom took place in 45th R.Y. (1600–1). (*Akbarnāma*, III, pp.780–1).

provinces but in the text preceding its tables, Abū'l Faẓl refers to his own passage through the province in the 43rd regnal year, when he was on his way to the Deccan.[25]

Similarly, in the account of the camel stables, Abū'l Faẓl records that in the 42nd regnal year, the allowance sanctioned for the camels' apparel was enhanced.[26] At another place, while describing the imperial horse stables, he reports that the horses belonging to Prince Murād were after his death transferred to the emperor's stables.[27] Since Prince Murād died in the 44th regnal year (May 1599),[28] this chapter was evidently revised after or during that year, and the insertion is thus subsequent to even the formal date of the completion of the *Ā'īn*.

Such additions do not modify the conclusion derived from the statements made by Abū'l Faẓl himself that the compilation of the *Ā'īn* was mainly carried out between 1589 and 1595–6. Since the collection of the information began in 1589, it is possible that the documents now obtained gave data for still earlier years. At the same time we may be justified in treating 1595–6 as the year after which very few statistics (apart from those for the newly annexed *ṣūbas*) were admitted into the body of the work. It is therefore more than a convenient convention to take the *Ā'īn*'s evidence as true for 1595–6. But the possibility that much of the statistical material relates to earlier years has to be constantly borne in mind, when dealing with any particular set of figures.

Though quite a few MSS of the *Ā'īn* survive, a new critical edition is greatly needed. H. Blochmann's text (in two volumes),[29] so far the standard edition and a product of considerable labour, was not unfortunately based on the best or earliest MSS and so is not free from errors. His edition, therefore, needs to be checked all the time with the MSS. The other two editions (Saiyid Ahmad's edition, Delhi, 1855, and the Nawal Kishore edition, Lucknow, 1869) are in every respect inferior to Blochmann's edition. The Nawal Kihsore edition of 1882 (in 3 vols.) is really a fairly faithful reprint of Blochmann's text, but with the addition of some errors. Blochmann also translated a portion designated by him as Vol.I (revised by D.C. Phillott, Calcutta, 1927 and 1939), while H.S. Jarrett translated the remaining portion (divided into Vols. II and III). For serious research neither translation is of much use; Jarrett's translation, in

25 *Ā'īn*, I, 455.

26 Ibid., I, 145.

27 Ibid., I, 148.

28 *Akbarnāma*, III, 754.

29 2 vols., Bib. Ind., Calcutta, 1867–77.

particular, contains an unduly large number of inaccuracies, which Sir Jadunath Sarkar in his revision (Calcutta, Vol.II, 1949, and III, 1948) leaves largely uncorrected.

The British Museum (now, the British Library) contains two very accurate seventeenth-century MSS of the *Ā'īn-i Akbarī* (Add. 7652 and Add. 6552).[30] In view of the inaccuracies in Blochmann's text and tables, I have collated the entire statistics (as well as text, whenever used) in his edition with these two MSS. I have ordinarily accepted the figures which the two MSS agree upon, irrespective of whether they accord or not with those of Blochmann's edition. But in cases of disagreement in the MSS, I have always checked with the Blochmann edition and generally accepted the reading of either MS which happens to be identical with Blochmann's text. Besides collation of this kind, I have tried to identify transcriptional errors in the revenue rates (*dastūrs*) by hypothesizing a restated schedule of conversion of the original rates.[31] The problem of establishing textual accuracy in the very important statistical tables of the *Aḥwāl-i Doāzdah Ṣūba*—'The Account of the Twelve *Ṣūbas*'—requires treatment at some length, to which the next section is devoted.

II

In the *Aḥwāl-i Doāzdah Ṣūba*, Abū'l Faẓl offers detailed descriptions of the various *ṣūbas* (provinces) along with statistical information appended to the account of each and set out in tabular form. As we have noted already, the actual number of *ṣūbas* is fifteen, owing to the insertion of the accounts of three provinces, Berar, Khandesh (Dandesh) and Ahmadnagar, annexed after the 40th regnal year (1595–6).

Abū'l Faẓl first gives a description of the geography and economic features of each province (*ṣūba*). At the end of this account, he gives us the numbers of *sarkārs* and *parganas* (or *maḥals*, the two terms being practically synonymous)[32] that the province contained; the total measured area (*zamīn-i paimūda*); the expected net revenue (*jama'*) and the

[30] I have consulted the British Library MSS, but have mostly worked with the microfilms of the two MSS in the Department of History, Aligarh.

[31] See Chapter 4 of this book.

[32] *Parganas* are essentially territorial divisions; *maḥals*, revenue-units. All *parganas* were *maḥals*; but the word *maḥal* was, in addition, applied to certain specified sources of revenue, such as port or markets. Thus there might be a *pargana* formed by a city and its environs; and, in addition, a *maḥal-i sā'ir* comprising revenues from its markets. The word *pargana* is never applied to the latter unit.

amount alienated out of it in 'charity' grants (*suyūrghāl*); the strength of the *zamīndārs*' troops (*būmī*), enumerating separately the horsemen (*sawār*) and foot-soldiers (*piyāda*), along with the number of elephants. The number of cannon pieces and boats (of *zamīndārs*) are given, but only under the *ṣūbas* of Bengal and Bihar.

After setting forth the totals of statistics for a province in this fashion, Abū'l Faẓl goes on to provide the tables of statistics for each of the *sarkārs* in the *ṣūba*. The tables consist of eight columns[33] bearing the headings (i) *pargana/maḥal;* (ii) *qilā'*, forts;[34] (iii) *ārāẓī/zamīn-i paimūda*, measured area; (iv) *naqdī/jama'*, net revenue assessed in cash; (v) *suyūrghāl*, revenue alienated through grants; (vi) *zamīndār/būmī* (caste/castes); (vii) *sawār* (horsemen of *zamīndārs*); (viii) *piyāda* (*zamīndārs*' foot-retainers). The number of elephants, wherever recorded, is given in the column for *sawār*. The first row of the table under each *sarkār* sets out the totals for the whole *sarkār*, the first column (to the right) in the row giving the total number of *parganas*. From the second row downwards follow statistics for individual *parganas* of the *sarkār*; the *parganas* are alphabetically grouped but only by taking into account their initial letters.

Though Abū'l Faẓl has sought to ensure transcriptional accuracy by writing the figures in words, not digits, the statistics exhibit an elementary flaw since the totals stated in the text do not often accord with the totals of the detailed figures given for the respective *sarkārs* and *ṣūbas*. That is to say, the sum of the totals stated for the individual *sarkārs* in the tables of a *ṣūba* differ, in most cases, from the total stated for that *ṣūba* in the text; and the totals of figures given against the *parganas* under a *sarkār* often differ from the totals stated at the head of the same table for the entire *sarkār*.

Moreland was the first to notice these discrepancies, especially in regard to the figures of *ārāẓī* and *jama'*. But he attributed all these variations to simple transcriptional and printing errors in Blochmann's edition.[35] A collation with the MSS, it is true, does reveal a number of

[33] Blochmann, in his printed text, replaced the tabular form of representation by a continuous text, and in the process dropped the column headings. This defect and some of the misinterpretations it led to were pointed out by Irfan Habib, '*Zamīndārs* in the *Ā'īn-i Akbarī*', *PIHC, 1958*, 320–3.

[34] Besides short descriptions of forts (specifying whether these were of brick or stone, for example), Abū'l Faẓl sometimes enters incidental remarks here, referring, for example, to the geographical situation of a place (on a hill, or on a river) or the existence of mines in the vicinity.

[35] W.H. Moreland, 'The Agricultural Statistics of Akbar's Empire', *JUPHS*, Vol.II, part I, 1919, 9.

inaccuracies in Blochmann's tables. I have closely checked the figures in the two early British Museum MSS,[36] and, as explained in the previous section, have usually accepted the reading which is common to both the MSS. But in addition, in the statistics of the 'Account of the Twelve *Ṣūbas*', I have accepted the reading in the MSS or in Blochmann's text which brings the actual worked-out total closer to the stated one. An illustration of how Blochmann's text can be corrected is offered by one example.

The *ārāẓī* figures as given in Blochmann and in the MSS for three *sarkārs* of Malwa are as follows:

Sarkār	Total stated in Blochmann's edition	Total stated in MSS	Total calculated from figures for *parganas*
Handia	89,573 *bīghas*, 11 *biswas*	2,89,573 *bīghas*, 15 *biswas*	2,89,573 *bīghas*, 15 *biswas*
Nandurbār	20,59,604 *bīghas*	8,59,604 *bīghas*	8,59,604 *bīghas*
Kotri Pirāwa	1,90,039 *bīghas*	1,92,839 *bīghas*	1,92,821 *bīghas*

The MS readings in all three cases accord fully or fairly closely with the actual totals worked out from the *pargana* figures. Moreover, the stated *sarkār* totals for *ārāẓī* as given in the MSS add up to the total stated for the whole *ṣūba*. The figures in Blochmann's text are, therefore, certainly incorrect and the source of error in at least the figures for two out of the three *sarkārs* can easily be discerned. In the case of *sarkār* Handia, there is an obvious printing error—the digit 2 at the extreme left has been omitted in print; and in Nandurbār, *bīst* (20) has been read for *hasht* (8). (The source of Blochmann's error in the figures for Kotri Pirāwa is not easily discoverable.) In these cases, then, the MS readings must be accepted without reservation, and the figures in Blochmann's text for all the three *sarkārs* should be corrected accordingly.

In addition to the mistakes in Blochmann's text that can be eliminated through a critical comparison with the MSS, we come across errors in figures in the MSS themselves arising out of simple mistranscriptions in either the original or its early copies. For instance, the stated total of the *jama'* of *sarkār* Munghyr in *ṣūba* Bihar in the MSS (as well as Blochmann)

[36] Add.7652, and Add.6552.

is 10,96,25,981, while the *pargana* figures add up to 2,96,22,181 *dāms*. Evidently the scribe misread the word *do* (two) for *dah* (ten), an error quite common in Persian. In *sarkār* Bhakkar, the stated *ārāẓī* total is 2,82,013, while the actual total is 10,82,013 *bīghas* and 15 *biswas*. Again, the confusion between *dah* (10) and *do* (2) is plain to see. Similar common errors that can be rectified by checking with actual totals are the misreadings of *sih* (3) for *nuh* (9); *yāzdah* (11) for *pānzdah* (15); *sīzdah* (13) for *hīzdah* (18); *hasht* (8) for *bīst* (20) or *shist* (60); *haftād* (70) for *hashtād* (80); *sih-sad* (300) for *shash-sad* (600); and *vice versa*.

In addition to errors arising out of misreadings of the number-words, there are some figures which betray obvious omissions or slips even in the earliest MSS. For instance, the *suyūrghāl* stated for *Doāba* Sindh Sagar of *ṣūba* Lahore is 4,680 *dāms*, while the actual total of the *maḥals*' figures come to 94,680 *dāms*. Here, then, we have a clear case of the omission of the initial *nawwad* (90) in the words making up the sum for the *Doāba*. To take another instance: for the *sarkār* of Badaun, *ṣūba* Delhi, the stated area of *ārāẓī* is 80,93,850 *bīghas*, and 10 *biswas*, while the *ārāẓī* figures given for the *parganas* of that *sarkār* add up to 18,93,756 *bīghas*. The latter brings the total of the stated figures for the *sarkārs* closer to the *ṣūba* total, since the total of the stated *sarkār* figures, with the stated *sarkār* total for Badaun is 3,47,96,495 *bīghas*, 7 *biswas*; with the actual total for *sarkār* Badaun replacing the stated total, the aggregate for *ṣūba* Delhi amounts to 2,85,96,495 *bīghas*, as against the stated total *ārāẓī* for the *ṣūba*, 2,85,46,816 *bīghas*, 16 *biswas*. It seems obvious that in transcribing the *sarkār* total for Badaun, confusion occurred between *hīzdah* (18) and *hashtād* (80). This is a rather unusual slip, since the words have different forms in Persian writing; but it could well have arisen if the figures were being transferred at some stage by dictation when *hīzhdah* was wrongly heard as *hashtād*.

By considering alternative readings for resolving such possible confusions, and restoring the few figures where omissions are obvious, a large number of differences between the stated and actual totals can be fully reconciled, or reduced to marginal variations. We may then at last claim to have the text of the tables as close as possible to the text as Abū'l Faẓl left it in his original copy.

But it is apparent that even in the text so restored, there remain numerous discrepancies between the stated totals and the actual totals. Most of these discrepancies are, however, only marginal (within a range of 2 per cent). Many of these too can be removed by accepting alternative readings; a course which I have not followed either because there is more than one option open to us in selecting the means of correction, or the mistranscription cannot be pinpointed definitely, or, finally, because it would necessitate no less than three or four 'corrected' readings (i.e., assuming a series of mistranscriptions). In any case, such differences between stated and actual totals are usually so minor that they do not affect analysis at any level.

There are still other variations which cannot be explained away as mere scribal slips; they are occasionally substantial enough to force themselves upon our notice. Of the 70 *sarkārs* for which we have two sets of *ārāẓī* totals (viz., stated and actual), in only four (Kalpi, Ahmadabad, Bari Doāb and Multan) does the difference between the two totals exceed 2 per cent. In the case of the *jama'*, out of 82 *sarkārs* (excluding the *sarkār* of Qandahar where the *jama'* is not stated in the same monetary unit), the difference is significant only in five (Baitalwadi, Ahmadabad, Rachnao, Multan and Diplapur). In the columns of the *suyūrghāl*, *sawār* and *piyāda* the number of inconsistent totals, is, however, larger across the board: of the totals of the *suyūrghāl* of 66 *sarkārs*, those of 17 differ substantially; of 58 *sarkārs* for which both the stated and actual totals for the *sawār* and the *piyāda* are available, the number of those differing significantly is 7 and 16 for *sawār* and *piyāda* respectively.

One possible source of these variations could be errors of calculation committed in Abū'l Faẓl's own secretariat. It seems very unlikely that Abū'l Faẓl received the *pargana* statistics in the form in which they appear in the *Ā'īn*, that is, arranged semi-alphabetically, with the figures written out in words. It is thus probable that after reaching him, the data were not only transferred from the records but were also rearranged, or even recalculated, so that there was now considerable room for errors of a purely clerical kind being introduced.

An illustration of such errors is offered by the figures of *ṣūba* Multan. In this *ṣūba* two of the three *sarkārs* are divided into *doābas* (each subdivided into *parganas*); and here, therefore, the totals in the various columns are given at three levels, *ṣūba*, *sarkār* and *doāba*, besides the primary figures for *parganas*. The *ṣūba*-level totals, viz., the stated *ṣūba* figures, and the totals respectively of the *sarkārs*, the *doābas* and the *parganas*, are as follows:

	Stated *ṣūba* total	Total of stated figures for *sarkārs*	Total of stated figures for *doābas*	Actual total of figures for *parganas*
Ārāẓī	32,73,932	30,74,432	30,74,452	32,51,698
Jama'/Naqdī	15,14,03,619	20,09,75,418	20,07,28,799	15,62,53,243

It can be seen that the total *ārāẓī* and the total *jama'* stated for the *ṣūba* largely differ from the sums of the stated totals for the *sarkārs* and the *doābas*, the two latter are close to each other, while the stated *ṣūba* total is much closer to the actual totals of *pargana* figures. Why this discrepancy should have occurred can be precisely located. The stated *ārāẓī* total for *doāba* Bet Jalendhar of *sarkār* Multan is 52,090 *bīghas*, while the *pargana* figures total 2,52,274 *bīghas*. Obviously the digit 2 at the extreme left in the *doāba* total was dropped by oversight at an early stage; the total for the *sarkār* was then calculated from the figures for the *doābas* which contained this error, so that the error was carried on to the stated *sarkār* total. The *ṣūba* total which was perhaps received independently from the official records (where it must have been calculated directly from the *pargana* figures), however, remained unaffected. The difference in *jama'* totals, on the other hand, is apparently due to a misreading of the total for *doāba* Bet Jalendhar of *sarkār* Dipalpur. Here the stated total is 8,88,08,955 *dāms*, while the totals of *pargana* figures is only 3,88,08,755 *dāms*. It would seem that the original figure being in the *raqam* notation, Abū'l Faẓl's assistants read 'three'  of the *raqam* in 'three cores' as 'eight'  the *raqam* signs for the two numbers being very similar in appearance. The *sarkār* total must have been worked out afterwards from the *doāba* figures so read, and thus carried a fictitious enhancement of five crores. But the *ṣūba* total remained unaffected, having been presumably derived from the *pargana* figures directly.

A similar mistake, detected in the *jama'* statistics of Bengal and Orissa, can also be ascribed to Abū'l Faẓl's own staff. He states the *jama'* of the *ṣūba* of Bengal and the sub-*ṣūba* of Orissa (attached to Bengal) to be 59,84,59,319 *dāms*. But the stated totals for the *sarkārs* yield a sum of 42,51,03,099 *dāms*; that is, the stated total for the two regions is 17,33,56,220 *dāms* in excess of the *jama'* based on the *sarkār* totals. The actual total of the *pargana* figures too is broadly in conformity with the aggregate of *sarkār* totals, being 43,07,94,875 *dāms*. The excess in the *Ā'īn*'s stated total for Bengal and Orissa is almost straightaway explained by the fact that the *jama'* for the five *sarkārs* of Orissa, grouped together in the *Ā'īn* with a separate subsection, add up to 17,07,32,638 *dāms*. This is remarkably close to the amount of excess; and the inference is irresistible that a clerk in Abū'l Faẓl's office, unclear as to whether the *ṣūba* total received for Bengal included the figure for Orissa, added the latter's figure again to the received figure for Bengal. The detection of this error is important, because, as corrected, the *Ā'īn*'s figures suit the subsequent statistics much better.[37]

One other possible source of error leading to inconsistencies between the stated and actual totals has also to be considered. It may be that the total as stated had been correctly calculated, but wrong figures have been put against *parganas* in the process of rearranging them alphabetically. For such an error to affect totals (which would remain unaffected if figures of *maḥal* A are simply assigned to B and vice versa), one should expect figures against some *parganas* to be repeated (i.e. where those of *maḥal* A are assigned to A as well as to B, whose actual figures do not appear). But such cases of duplication are not, in fact, found anywhere in the statistics except in *ṣūbas* Lahore and Gujarat. However, as will be seen in Chapter 2, the repetitions in *ṣūba* Lahore are not really transcriptional mistakes at all. All the *parganas* bearing the common figures are situated in hilly tracts and their *ārāẓī* figures appear to be fictitious, not having been obtained through actual measurement but calculated from the *jama'* (fixed in round numbers) at the arbitrary ratios of 1:41.2 and 1:39.86 *dāms* per *bigha*. There are other *maḥals* too, each with an *ārāẓī* that bears either of the same two ratios to the *jama'*, in all the four *doābas* of the *ṣūba*.

In *ṣūba* Gujarat one comes across the lone repetition that could be a transcriptional error perpetrated at a very early stage in the compilation of the figures; the *jama'* recorded for *pargana* Godhra *bā ḥavelī* and Kokana, the *pargana* immediately following it, is exactly the same but no other details given against the former *pargana* are repeated against the latter. The mistake seems real because the stated figure of the *jama'* for *sarkār* Godhra falls short of the total of the *parganas* by as much as 2,36,140 *dāms*, a difference that can best be ascribed to the hypothetical substitution of the larger figure of the *ḥavelī maḥal* for the much smaller one of an ordinary *pargana*.

[37] Thus the *Iqbālnāma-i Jahāngīrī* (Or. 1834, ff. 231b–232b) gives 41,91,07,870 *dāms* for Bengal and Orissa at Akbar's death. This matches well with the *pargana* total in the *Ā'īn* (43,07,94,875 *dāms*), the total of stated *sarkār* figures (42,51,03,099 *dāms*) and the stated figure in the *Ā'īn*, less the *jama'* for the Orissa *sarkārs* (42,77,26,681 *dāms*). Otherwise one would have to postulate an enormous decline in the *jama'* within ten years. Similarly, 25,43,70,461 *dāms* as the *jama'* for Bengal would eliminate the impression of decline in the *jama'* in Bengal between 1595–6 and 1632, as appears from the table in Irfan Habib, *Agrarian System*, first ed., 400. The figure 42,77,26,681 *dāms* under Bengal should be altered to 25,43,70,461 *dāms*; and the table on p. 328 of his book need correction accordingly. (These corrections have been carried out in his revised ed., 1999, 375, 456.)

The fact, however, that there should be only one such definitely established error of misalignment in the entire body of statistics should assure us that the transcription and reorganization of data at Abū'l Faẓl's secretariat was done with considerable care; and one may assume, on the whole, that the rows in the tables are set correctly against the appropriate *maḥals*.

Finally, there remain some variations in the stated and actual totals that cannot be attributed either to simple slips of arithmetic or to mistranscription by Abū'l Faẓl's assistants. For instance the stated *ārāẓī* for *sarkār* Kalpi in *ṣūba* Agra is 3,00,029 *bīghas*, 9 *biswas*, but the *pargana* figures aggregate to 17,36,107 *bīghas*, 12 *biswas*. The *ārāẓī* making up the latter total is well spread out among the *parganas* and the difference could not therefore be due to mistranscriptions of one or two figures. Moreover, for *ṣūba* Agra the stated total of the *ārāẓī* is over 30,00,000 *bīghas* higher than the total obtained by adding up the stated *sarkār* totals. One may, therefore, suggest that here the difference is a genuine one, caused probably by the partial incorporation of subsequent revision: it is possible that there was an extension of measurement in the various *parganas* of the *sarkārs* after the original statistics had been received. The revised *pargana* details as received subsequently were then incorporated, but the *sarkār* totals were left uncorrected, though the *ṣūba* total was apparently changed to accord with the enhancements of the *ārāẓī* in *sarkār* Kalpi as well as other *sarkārs*.

It is interesting that the variations which can be explained by revisions alone, are found in the two *ṣūbas* containing the capital cities, namely, Lahore and Agra. Possibly, being the 'core areas' of the empire, these were subjected to more frequent revisions which could not be incorporated fully or consistently in the *Ā'īn*'s statistics. Some revisions were introduced only in the totals without altering the *pargana* details; in other cases, the *pargana* figure were updated, but the totals (all or some of them) remained unchanged. In *ṣūba* Agra the recorded *jama'* for the *ṣūba* exactly matches the total of the figures stated for the *sarkārs*, but the *jama'* worked out from the *pargana* is a little less (0.23 per cent). Here, then, while the *ṣūba* and *sarkār* figures were changed according to later revisions, some *pargana* figures were obviously left unaltered.

We have already noticed that for the *ārāẓī* and the *jama'*, the totals are, by and large, consistent, but that the differences are more frequent and pronounced in the totals of the figures for *suyūrghāl*, *sawār*, and *piyāda*. In the case of *zamīndārs*' retainers (*sawār* and *piyāda*), a number of the differences in the recorded and calculated totals can be removed by assuming transcriptional errors (sometimes, even sets of such errors). However, the *suyūrghāl* totals cannot be made consistent with each other as easily. Significant differences in totals exist, where in as many as thirteen cases the actuals based on the *pargana* figures are lower than the stated *sarkār* totals. In *ṣūba* Agra the total of *suyūrg͟hāl* stated for the *ṣūba* is only 57 per cent of the total of the figures recorded for the individual *sarkārs*, which in turn is lower (by 4,49,866 *dāms*) than the actual total of the *pargana* figures. Could one suggest that a substantial reduction in the *suyūrg͟hāl* occurred in the *ṣūba* of Agra, so that the *ṣūba* figure was heavily brought down? A substantial reduction of this kind would be in line with what we know of Akbar's policy of resuming and restricting revenue grants in his later years.[38] The reductions were, however, only partly taken into account for correcting *sarkār* figures, and might possibly have been ignored at the level of *parganas*, where the figures received previously were allowed to stand.

Another fact that strengthens the impression of frequent though partial revision in the *ṣūba* of Agra is that against some *sarkārs* the total number of *parganas* is not specified; and the stated number of *parganas* for the *ṣūba* falls considerably below the actual number of *parganas*. In other *ṣūbas* too the stated number of *parganas* for the entire *ṣūba* does not exactly match the number actually listed. The differences in the numbers of *maḥals* (a) stated for *ṣūbas*, (b) stated for *sarkārs*, and (c) actually listed will appear from Table 1.1.

The incorporation of subsequent revisions may then well be responsible for most of the differences in totals at various levels that remain after MS variants are collated and the *Ā'īn*'s own transcriptional errors corrected. Since it is likely that the stated *ṣūba* totals are in accord with the revised figures, it does not mean that the *sarkār* or *pargana*-level figures are necessarily unreliable; what we are faced with is only the fact that they may belong to years that are different from those of the stated totals. In any case, it is best to recall that the differences between the actual totals from figures for *pargana* and the stated *sarkār* and *ṣūba* totals are mostly negligible or quite marginal in respect of the *ārāẓī* and the *jama'* statistics. These differences should always be borne in mind, of course, especially where they are of a magnitude larger than, say, ± 2 per cent. No interpretations or conclusions of this study would be more than marginally affected if one possible alternative figure is substituted for the other. Where, however, such a range of possible variations is larger, as in the case of figures of *suyūrg͟hāl* or *zamīndārs'* retainers (*sawār* and *piyāda*), this will be noted, and the use of *pargana* statistics circumscribed accordingly.

[38] Irfan Habib, *Agrarian System*, p. 310 and *n.* (rev. ed., 355–56*n*).

Table 1.1

Number of *Maḥals*

Ṣūba	(a) Stated total for the *ṣūbas*	(b) Total of stated totals for *sarkārs*	(c) Actual number of *maḥals* listed
Bengal & Orissa	787	781	779
Bihar	199	200	200
Allahabad	177	181	178
Awadh	138	133	131
Agra	203	252	257
Malwa	301	302	277
Berar	142	242	231
Gujarat	198	199	196
Ajmer	197	197	190
Delhi	232	237	237
Lahore	234	235	229
Multan (excluding Thatta)	88	88	87
Thatta (sub-province)	53	53	51
Kashmir (sub-province)	—	—	37
Kabul	—	—	22

In Appendix 1. A, I have set out the corrected totals for the *sarkārs* and *ṣūbas*, established through MSS collation, re-totallings of *pargana* figures and other arithmetical devices discussed above. The figures so established by me for *ārāẓī*, *jama'*, *suyūrghāl*, *sawār*, and *piyāda* will henceforth be used in this study: even when pages of Blochmann's edition are cited for the statistical tables, the figures used will be as read or corrected by me, and not those given by Blochmann, unless this is explicitly stated.

III

Though the *Ā'īn-i Akbarī* must form the bedrock of any quantitative study of the economy of the Mughal empire, one cannot do without a large amount of other contemporaneous material. For one thing, the *Ā'īn* itself cannot be interpreted in isolation. Its terminology can often be understood only by reference to other sources where definitions or illustrative uses of the terms occur. For matters of chronology and political geography, essential for comprehending the *Ā'īn*'s statistics, we have often to consult the histories of the period. Many administrative measures, basic to our understanding of why and how the statistics came to be compiled or what they denote, also happen to be described in the conventional historical sources.

For all these purposes the *Akbarnāma* of Abū'l Faẓl [39] must be considered to be the major source complementing the *Ā'īn-i Akbarī*, as Moreland has so strongly urged.[40] The *Akbarnāma* is the most detailed account of Akbar's reign. It not only gives considerable space to administrative measures, but also reproduces or summarises official documents. One MS of the work even gives us the original text of Todar Mal's memorandum on revenue administration.[41]

Besides Abū'l Faẓl's own work other histories like Bāyazīd Bayāt's memoirs,[42] the *Ṭabaqāt-i Akbarī* of Niẓāmuddīn Aḥmad[43] and the *Muntakhabu-t Tawārīkh* of Badāūnī,[44] help us in elucidating problems encountered in quantification. For instance, the working of the *manṣab* system, knowledge of which is essential for us to determine the income of the ruling class, becomes clear only through the accounts offered by Bāyazīd, Badāūnī and Mu'tamad Khān's *Iqbālnāma-i Jahāngīrī*.[45] The last, by often restating Abū'l Faẓl's stately narrative in simpler language, enables us to understand better the significance of particular terms and phrases.

Furthermore, though the *Ā'īn-i Akbarī* remains the only work that offers a comprehensive range of statistical information, it is not the sole source of quantitative data for its time. The *Ṭabaqāt-i Akbarī*, written *c.*1593, offers revenue statistics as well as a list of *manṣab*-holders. Firishta gives us figures for wealth, treasure, and numbers of animals left

[39] *Akbarnāma*, Bib. Ind. Text, 3 Vols., Calcutta, 1873–87. The translation by H. Beveridge, Calcutta, 1897–1921, though painstaking, is not of much use for interpretation of technical matters.

[40] W.H. Moreland, *Agrarian System of Moslem India*, 80–2.

[41] Br. Mus. Add. 27,247: The memorandum is reproduced on ff. 331b–332b. The MS apparently represents an early draft of the *Akbarnāma*.

[42] *Taẓkira-i Humāyūn-o-Akbar*, ed. M. Hidayat Hosain, Bib. Ind. Calcutta, 1941.

[43] Ed. B. De, Bib. Ind., 3 vols. (Vol.III revised and partly edited by M. Hidayat Hosain), Calcutta, 1913–35.

[44] Ed. Aḥmad Ali and W.N. Lees, Bib. Ind., Calcutta, 1864–9.

[45] The *Iqbālnāma-i Jahāngīrī* is in three volumes. Vol.I covers the reigns of Bābur and Humāyūn, and II that of Akbar; Vol.III is devoted to that of Jahāngīr. The work was originally written in Jahāngīr's time, partly to supersede the *Akbarnāma* by offering an account in more simple language and removing references unfavourable to Jahangir. I have used the Nawal Kishore ed., lithographed, Lucknow, 1870, for Vols.I and II. Vol.III, also published in Bib. Ind. Series, ed. Abdul Hai and Ahmad Ali, Calcutta, 1865, was written after Jahāngīr's death, and is not of much use for our purpose.

by Akbar.[46] A manuscript of Mu'tamad Khan's *Iqbālnāma* gives us important data such as revenue statistics and salary scales of the *manṣabdārs* at the time of Akbar's death.[47] These Persian works can be supplemented by some statistics preserved in near-contemporary European sources. John Hawkins (1608–11) and Francisco Pelsaert in his 'Chronicle' give us particulars of Akbar's treasure, animals, and army, the details being obviously derived from Persian documents.[48]

European literature of about this time also begins to furnish information about manufactures and trade, gathered mainly from the viewpoint of Dutch and English commerce with India. Closest to the period with which we are concerned and the most valuable for a general as well as statistical study of the Mughal Indian economy, is Pelsaert's *Remonstrantie*, written *c.*1626.[49] The data it gives on indigo production, prices of individual commodities, the mode of life of artisans and of the ruling class, are all of exceptional value. From the early years of the seventeenth century begin the English commercial records, from which pieces of relevant information can be extracted. The records have been published in two series, *Letters Received by the East India Company from its Servants in the East* and *the English Factories in India*.[50] A large number of European travellers have also left their journals or 'relations';

[46] Abū'l Qāsim 'Firishta', *Tārīkh-i Firishta*, ed. Nawal Kishore, Kanpur, 1874. Firishta says that his information came from an official (?) paper which had come into his possession. He himself was writing *c.*1606–7.

[47] See Br. Mus. MS. Or. 1834. This MS contains Vol.II of the *Iqbālnāma* and the statistics in question occur at the end of the volume. So far as is known, this MS is unique in reproducing them. Internal evidence (such as the inadvertent use of the term *tanka* for *dām*) suggests that it is no late insertion, although the MS itself was transcribed rather late, probably early in the nineteenth century.

[48] The 'Journal' of Hawkins was published by Purchas in his *Purchas his Pilgrimes;* it may be read in MacLehose's edition of that work, Glasgow, 1905, Vol.III, 1–50. W. Foster has published it with some annotation in his *Early Travels in India*, 60–121. Pelsaert's 'Chronicle', originally in Dutch, has been translated by B. Narain and S.R. Sharma as *A Contemporary Dutch Chronicle of Mughal India*, Calcutta, 1957 (printed in D.H.A. Kolff and H.W. van Santen, *De Geschriften van Francisco Pelsaert over Mughal India, 1627: Kroniek en Remonstrantie 'S-Gravenhage,* 1979). Its language and Hijra dates proclaim its dependence on a Persian original.

[49] Dutch text, ed. Kolkff and van Santen, op.cit., English translation, with annotation, by W.H. Moreland and P. Geyl, *Jahangir's India*, Cambridge, 1925.

[50] The *Letters Received*, 6 vols., London, 1896–1902, were edited by F.C. Danvers (Vol.I) and W. Foster (Vols.II–VI); the six volumes cover the period 1602–17. The 13 volumes of the *English Factories* were edited by Foster, 1906–27, and cover the period 1618–69.

many of these belonging to the sixteenth and early seventeenth century found a place in the great collection of travellers' accounts compiled by Samuel Purchas under the title *Purchas his Pilgrimes*, London, 1625.[51]

Recent researchers have succeeded in assembling dispersed statistics of European commerce in the latter half of the sixteenth century and the early years of the seventeenth century; and these can, therefore, be used by students of Indian economic history. Earl J. Hamilton undertook a fundamental study of the quantities of silver and gold that flowed in from the Americas to Spain during the sixteenth and seventeenth centuries.[52] Portuguese records have been explored extensively by Vittorino Magalhaes-Godinho, so that Indo-Portuguese trade of the sixteenth century can now be studied in quantitative terms.[53] The Venetian records have been used by Frederic C. Lane and Fernand P. Braudel to establish the quantities of Eastern goods that entered the Mediterranean through the Levant in the sixteenth century.[54] These works have been made use of, along with much direct investigation of statistical material from Portuguese and Italian sources, by Niels Steensgaard in his *Asian Trade Revolution of the Seventeenth Century*. In spite of the title, Steensgaard's main concern is with the period *c.*1585–1620.[55] The material brought to light makes it possible for us to supplement our statistical study of the internal economy of the Mughal empire with a quantitative appraisal of at least some important elements of India's overseas trade.

Finally, there is material of a quite different kind which lends itself to quantification and makes possible a statistical study of money supply within the Mughal empire. It was Aziza Hasan who first suggested that surviving Mughal coins, which contained both the name of the issuing

[51] The edition I have used is that of MacLehose, Glasgow, 1905. Many (but by no means all) these travellers' journals are included in W. Foster (ed.), *Early Travels in India (1583–1619)*, London, 1927.

[52] *American Treasure and Price Revolution in Spain, 1501–1650*, Cambridge (Mass), 1934.

[53] *L'economie de l'empire Portugais au XVe et XVIe Siecles*, Paris, 1969.

[54] The two basic articles by Lane have been published by Brian Pullan in *Crisis and Change in Venetian Economy in the Sixteenth and Seventeenth Centuries*, London, 1968, 25–58. Braudel's classic work is the *Mediterranean and the Mediterranean World in the Age of Philip II*, 2 vols., London, 1972–3. The eastern trade, with its statistics, is studied by Braudel in Vol.I, 542–70.

[55] Steensgaard's work first appeared under the title *Carracks, Caravans and Companies*, Copenhagen, 1973. I have however used the University of Chicago Press edition, 1974, under the changed title.

mint and the year of issue, can be counted and made to yield a currency-output curve.[56] The method adopted by her to count the coins has been criticized by John S. Deyell;[57] but, as will be seen in Chapter 15, such force as Deyell's criticism has can be met by using records of the hoards and stray finds instead of (or, in addition to) the catalogued museum collections. The number of Mughal coins whose finds have been recorded in U.P. alone are then large enough to justify quantification with a considerable degree of confidence.[58]

Appendix 1.A

Abstract of *Ā'īn*'s Statistics ('Account of the Twelve *Ṣūbas*')

(Figures as established after MSS collation and correction of clerical errors)

ĀRĀẒĪ (in *bīghas and biswas*)

	Totals stated for *sarkārs*	Totals of figures for *parganas*	Total stated for the *ṣūba*
BENGAL	No *ārāẓī* figures		
ORISSA	No *ārāẓī* figures		
BIHAR			
Bihar	9,52,590	9,52,588–4	
Monghyr	—	—	
Champaran	85,711–5	85,711–5	
Hajipur	4,36,952–15	4,36,951–7	
Saran	2,29,052–15	2,29,052–3	
Tirhut	2,66,464	2,66,881–2	
Rohtas	4,73,340–12	4,73,331–1	
Total for the *ṣūba*	(24,44,111–7)	24,44,515–2	24,44,120
ALLAHABAD			
Allahabad	5,73,615	5,73,585	
Ghazipur	2,88,780–7	2,88,780–12	
Banaras	1,56,863–12	1,54,702–12	

(*Continued*)

[56] 'The Silver Currency Output of the Mughal Empire and Prices in India during the 16th and 17th centuries', *IESHR*, VI (1969), pp.85–116; and 'Mints of the Mughal Empire: a Study in Comparative Currency Output', *Proc. I.H.C.*, Patiala Session (1968).

[57] *IESHR*, XIII (3), 393–401.

[58] Cf. S. Moosvi, 'The Silver Influx, Money Supply, Prices and Revenue Extraction in Mughal India', *JESHO*, XXX (1987), pp.47–94.

Appendix 1.A (*Continued*)

ĀRĀẒĪ (in *bīghas and biswas*)

	Totals stated for *sarkārs*	Totals of figures for *parganas*	Total stated for the *ṣūba*
Jaunpur	8,70,265–4	8,70,707	
Manikpur	6,66,222–5	6,66,919–12	
Chunar	1,06,270	1,06,269–16	
Kalinjar	5,08,273–12	5,08,273–12	
Kora	3,41,170–10	3,41,167–3	
Kara	4,47,556–12	4,50,487–15	
Battha Gahora	—	—	
Total for the *ṣūba*	(39,59,017–2)	(39,60,893–2)	39,68,000–3
AWADH			
Awadh	27,96,206–19	27,99,973–17	
Gorakhpur	2,44,283–13	2,44,289–8	
Bahraich	18,23,435–8	18,23,435–3	
Khairabad	19,87,000–6	19,88,024–6	
Lucknow	33,07,426–6	33,02,640	
Total of the *ṣūba*	(1,01,58,352–12)	(1,01,58,362–14)	1,01,71,180
AGRA			
Agra	91,07,622–4	91,82,258	
Kalpi	3,00,029–9	17,36,107–12	
Qanauj	27,76,673–16	27,76,673–16	
Kol	24,61,731	24,58,431	
Gawalior	15,46,465–6	15,46,465	
Erach	22,02,124–18	22,02,136–18	
Payanwan	7,62,014	7,62,014	
Narwar	3,94,350	3,94,358	
Mandlaer	65,346	65,321	
Alwar	16,62,012	16,30,368	
Tijara	7,40,001–5	7,40,001–6	
Narnaul	20,80,046	20,81,346	
Sahar	7,63,474	7,63,474	
Total for the *ṣūba*	(2,48,61,889–18)	(2,63,38,954–12)	2,78,62,189–2
MALWA			
Ujjain	9,25,322	9,25,622	
Raisen	(1,68,617)	1,68,617	

(*Continued*)

Appendix 1.A (*Continued*)

ĀRĀẒĪ (in *bīghas and biswas*)

	Totals stated for *sarkārs*	Totals of figures for *parganas*	Total stated for the *ṣūba*
Chanderi	5,54,277–17	5,54,277	
Sarangpur	7,06,202	7,06,204	
Bijagarh	2,83,277–13	2,83,277–13	
Mandu	2,22,969–15	2,23,009	
Handia	2,89,573–15	2,89,573	
Nandurbår	8,59,604	8,59,604	
Mandasor	—	—	
Gagraun	63,529	63,529	
Kotri Priawa	1,92,839	1,92,821	
Garh	—	—	
Total for the *ṣūba*	(42,66,212)	(42,66,533–13)	42,66,221–6
KHANDESH	No *ārāẓī* figures		
BERAR	No *ārāẓī* figures		
GUJARAT			
Ahmadabad	80,24,153	84,19,201	
Patan	38,50,015	38,50,909–16	
Nadaut	5,41,317–16	5,40,425	
Baroda	9,22,212	9,22,212	
Broach	9,49,771	9,49,731	
Champaner	8,00,337–11	8,00,328	
Surat	13,12,815–16	13,09,614	
Godhra	5,35,255	5,34,815	
Saurath	—	—	
Total for the *ṣūba*	(1,69,35,877–3)	(1,73,27,235–16)	1,69,36,377–3
AJMER			
Ajmer	56,05,487	56,92,850	
Chittor	16,78,800	16,87,794	
Ranthambhor	60,24,196	60,28,374	
Nagaur	80,37,450–14	80,36,893	
	No *ārāẓī* in remaining *sarkārs*		
Total for the *ṣūba*	(2,13,45,933–14)	2,14,45,911	2,14,35,941–7

(*Continued*)

Appendix 1.A (*Continued*)

ĀRĀẒĪ (in *bīghas and biswas*)

	Totals stated for *sarkārs*	Totals of figures for *parganas*	Total stated for the *ṣūba*
DELHI			
Delhi	71,26,107–18	71,24,097–3	
Badaun	18,93,850–10[a]	18,93,756	
Sambhal	40,47,193–2	40,15,101–3	
Saharanpur	35,30,379	35,30,679	
Rewari	11,55,001	11,55,011	
Hissar Firuza	31,14,497	31,14,497	
Sirhind	77,29,466–17	77,32,256	
Kumaun	—	—	
Total for the *ṣūba*	(2,85,96,495–7)	(2,85,65,397–6)	2,85,46,816–16
LAHORE			
Bet Jalendhar *Doāb*	32,79,302–17	32,96,668	
Bari *Doāb*	45,80,002	44,07,980	
Rachnao *Doāb*	42,53,148	42,66,560	
Chanhat *Doāb*	26,33,210	26,29,040	
Sindh Sagar *Doāb*	14,09,979	13,88,744	
Bairun Pajnad	—	—	
Total for the *ṣūba*	(1,61,55,641–17)	(1,59,88,992)	1,61,55,643–3
MULTAN (excluding Thatta)			
Multan	5,58,651–4	7,54,638–11	
Dipalpur	14,33,767–8	14,15,046–9	
Bhakkar	10,82,013[b]	10,82,013–15	
Total for the *ṣūba*	(30,74,431–12)	32,51,698–15	32,73,932
THATTA	No *ārāẓī* figures		
KASHMIR	No *ārāẓī* figures		
KABUL	No *ārāẓī* figures		

[a] The figure in the MS is 80,93,850–10.

[b] The figure in the MS is 2,82,013.

Appendix 1.A (*Continued*)

JAMA' (*NAQDĪ*) (in *dāms*)

	Total stated for *sarkārs*	Total of figures stated for *parganas*	Total stated for *ṣūbas*
BENGAL			
Tanda	2,40,78,700½	2,40,53,271	
Gaur	1,88,46,967	1,62,69,493	
Fatehabad	79,69,568	79,76,837	
Mahmudabad	1,16,10,256	1,27,06,178	
Halifatabad	54,02,140	54,00,318	
Bakla	71,31,641	71,31,440	
Purnea	64,08,793	64,08,633	
Tajpur	64,83,857	94,62,846	
Ghoraghat	89,83,072	86,41,941	
Panjra	58,03,275	57,97,475	
Barbakabad	1,74,51,532	1,74,50,351	
Bazuha	3,95,16,871	3,94,66,643	
Sonargaon	1,03,31,333	1,34,16,513	
Silhat	66,81,308	70,56,608	
Chatgaon	1,14,24,310	1,14,23,510	
Sharifabad	2,24,88,750	2,24,74,402	
Sulaimanabad	1,76,29,964	1,76,63,969	
Satgaon	1,67,24,724	1,67,03,515	
Madaran	94,03,400	93,80,042	
Total for Bengal	25,43,70,461½	(25,88,83,985)	
ORISSA			
Jalesar	5,00,52,738	5,00,45,684	
Bhadrak	1,86,87,170	1,86,86,170	
Katak	9,14,32,730	9,26,19,036	
Kaling Danpat	55,60,000	(55,60,000)	
Raj Mahendra	50,00,000	(50,00,000)	
Total for Orissa	17,07,32,638	17,19,10,890	
Total for Bengal and Orissa	(42,51,03,099½)	(43,07,94,875)	59,84,59,319

(*Continued*)

Appendix 1.A (*Continued*)

*JAMA*ʿ (*NAQDĪ*) (in *dāms*)

	Total stated for *sarkārs*	Total of figures stated for *parganas*	Total stated for *ṣūbas*
BIHAR			
Bihar	8,31,96,390	8,32,65,491	
Monghyr	2,96,25,981½[c]	2,96,22,181½	
Champaran	55,13,420	55,13,420	
Hajipur	2,73,31,030	2,73,36,635	
Saran	1,61,72,004½	1,61,72,304½	
Tirhut	1,91,89,777½	1,91,20,826½	
Rohtas	4,08,19,493	4,08,79,201	
Total for the *ṣūba*	(22,18,48,096½)	(22,19,10,059½)	22,19,19,404
ALLAHABAD			
Allahabad	2,28,31,999	2,28,31,599	
Ghazipur	1,34,31,325	1,37,29,622	
Banaras	88,60,318	88,60,618	
Jaunpur	5,63,94,927	5,60,02,527	
Manikpur	3,39,16,527	3,39,06,527	
Chunar	58,10,604	58,10,954	
Battha Gahora	72,62,780	(72,62,780)	
Kalinjar	2,38,39,470	2,38,09,087	
Kora	1,73,97,567	1,73,96,561	
Kara	2,26,82,048	2,26,54,068	
Total for the *ṣūba*	(21,24,27,565)	(21,22,64,343)	21,24,27,819
AWADH			
Awadh	4,09,56,347	4,09,56,147	
Gorakhpur	1,19,26,790	1,19,26,290	
Bahraich	2,41,20,525	2,41,20,519	
Khairabad	4,36,44,381	4,36,49,761	
Lucknow	8,07,16,160	8,07,47,220	
Total for the *ṣūba*	(20,13,64,203)	(20,13,99,937)	20,17,58,172

(*Continued*)

[c] The figure in MSS is 10,96,25,981½.

Appendix 1.A (*Continued*)

JAMA' (*NAQDĪ*) (in *dāms*)

	Total stated for *sarkārs*	Total of figures stated for *parganas*	Total stated for *ṣūbas*
AGRA			
Agra	19,17,19,265	19,05,25,826	
Kalpi	4,94,56,730	4,94,65,947	
Kanauj	5,25,84,620½	5,25,84,620½	
Kol	5,40,92,943	5,40,92,955	
Gawalior	2,96,83,649	2,96,83,348	
Erach	3,77,85,421	3,77,44,407	
Payanwan	84,59,296	84,58,596	
Narwar	42,33,322	42,33,320	—
Mandlaer	37,38,084	37,38,084	
Alwar	3,98,32,234	3,97,82,529	
Tijara	1,77,00,460½	1,77,00,466½	
Narnaul	5,10,46,711	5,10,41,881	
Sahar	59,17,569	59,17,569	
Total for the *ṣūba*	(54,62,50,305)	(54,49,69,548)	54,62,50,304
MALWA			
Ujjain	4,38,24,960	4,38,25,960	
Raisen	(1,39,92,792)	1,39,92,792	
Garh	1,13,77,080	1,14,32,025	
Chanderi	3,10,37,783	3,07,49,790	
Sarangpur	3,29,94,880	3,29,95,180	
Bijagarh	1,22,49,121	1,22,49,789	
Mandu	1,37,88,994	1,37,88,994	
Handia	1,16,10,969	1,13,10,969	
Nandurbar	5,01,62,250	5,01,62,250	
Mandasor	67,61,396	67,61,396	
Gagraun	45,35,794	45,36,094	
Kotri Pirawa	82,31,920	82,32,920	
Total for the *ṣūba*	(24,05,67,939)	(24,00,38,159)	24,06,95,052

(*Continued*)

Appendix 1.A (*Continued*)

JAMA' (*NAQDĪ*) (in *dāms*)

	Total stated for *sarkārs*	Total of figures stated for *parganas*	Total stated for *ṣūbas*
KHANDESH[d]	30,32,03,112	(30,32,03,112)	30,35,29,488
BERAR			
Gavil	13,46,66,140	13,46,66,140	
Punar	1,34,40,000	1,34,40,000	
Kherla	1,76,00,000	1,76,00,000	
Narnala	13,09,54,476	13,10,41,076	
Kalam	3,28,28,000	3,28,28,000	
Basim	3,26,25,250	3,26,25,250	
Mahur	4,28,85,440	4,28,85,440	
Manikdurg	1,44,00,000	1,44,00,000	
Pathri	8,07,05,954	8,03,05,954	
Telingana	7,19,04,000	7,23,04,096	
Ramgir	96,00,000	96,00,000	
Mehkar	4,51,78,000	4,51,76,000	
Baitalwadi	1,91,20,000	1,85,60,000	
Total for the *ṣūba*	(64,59,07,260)	(64,54,31,956)	64,26,03,270

(*Continued*)

[d]The stated *jama'* of Khandesh (no *sarkārs* within it) in the *Ā'īn* (I, p.474) is 1,26,47,062 *tanka-i Berārī*, also called *tanka-i* Dāndesh. The *pargana* figures add up to 1,26,33,463 of the same coinage. The *tanka* being equal to 16 *dāms* (*Ā'īn*, I, p.478), the stated *jama'* should be equal to 20,23,52,992 *dāms* and the *pargana* total to 20,21,35,408 *dāms*. But Abū'l Faẓl says that after the capture of Asirgarh (1601), Akbar increased the *jama'* of Khandesh by 50 per cent; and the *tanka* was therefore reckoned at 24 *dāms*. His editor (Blochmann) however gives the *jama'* as 45,52,94,230 *dāms* in parenthesis (*Ā'īn*, I, 474). But this is what one gets (with an error of 2!), if one converts the *jama'* (by *pargana* total) into *dāms*, taking the *tanka* as equal to 24 *dāms*, and yet again enhances it by 50 per cent. The double-enhancement, however, is an obvious mistake. The *jama'* should in fact have been enhanced to 30,32,03,112 *dāms* only, in conformity with the increased value of the *tanka*. This is borne out by the fact that the *jama'* of Khandesh in 1605 was set at 29,70,18,561 *dāms* (*Iqbāl Nāma*, II, Or. 1834, f.232b) and the *Bayaz-i Khushbu'i*, (ff.180–1) whose figures relate to 1628–32, gives 29,70,16,586 *dāms*.

Appendix 1.A (*Continued*)

JAMA' (*NAQDĪ*) (in *dāms*)

	Total stated for *sarkārs*	Total of figures stated for *parganas*	Total stated for *ṣūbas*
GUJARAT			
Ahmadabad	20,83,06,994	21,80,51,765	
Patan	6,03,25,099	21,80,51,765	
Nadaut	85,97,596	85,97,596	
Baroda	4,11,45,895	4,11,45,895	
Broach	2,18,45,663	2,18,00,653	
Champaner	1,05,09,884	1,05,08,479	
Surat	1,90,35,180	36,54,469	
Godhra	34,18,329	36,54,469	
Saurath	6,34,37,366	6,34,33,187	
Port revenues (in *sarkār*/Saurath)	18,01,048	26,02,060	
Total for the *ṣūba*	(43,66,22,006)	(44,83,39,676)	43,94,24,361
AJMER			
Ajmer	6,21,53,390	6,11,75,917	
Chittor	3,46,37,649	3,46,55,649	
Ranthambhor	8,98,64,576	8,95,44,576	
Jodhpur	1,45,28,750	1,45,35,750	
Sirohi	4,20,77,437	4,20,77,437	
Nagaur	4,03,89,830	4,03,05,696	
Bikaner	47,50,000	47,50,000	
Total for the *ṣūba*	(28,84,01,632)	(28,70,45,025)	28,84,557
DELHI			
Delhi	12,30,12,596	12,38,84,848	
Badaun	3,48,17,063	3,47,96,159	
Kumaun	4,54,37,700	4,54,37,700	
Sambhal	6,69,41,431	6,65,90,020	
Saharanpur	8,78,39,850	8,78,36,099	
Rewari	2,88,07,718	2,88,07,718	
Hissar Firuza	5,25,54,905	5,25,45,305	
Sirhind	16,07,90,549	16,07,89,948	
Total for the *ṣūba*	(60,02,01,812)	(60,06,87,797)	60,16,15,550

(*Continued*)

Appendix 1.A (*Continued*)

JAMA' (*NAQDĪ*) (in *dāms*)

	Total stated for *sarkārs*	Total of figures stated for *parganas*	Total stated for *ṣūbas*
LAHORE			
Bet Jalendhar *Doāb*	12,43,65,212	12,41,04,520	
Bari *Doāb*	14,28,08,183	14,28,17,025	
Rachnao *Doāb*	17,20,47,391	17,96,67,816	
Chanhat *Doāb*	6,45,02,394	6,44,99,335	
Sindh Sagar *Doāb*	5,19,12,201	5,16,48,708	
Bairun Panjnad	38,22,740	38,22,740	
Total for the *ṣūba*	(55,94,58,121)	(56,65,60,144)	55,94,58,423
MULTAN			
Multan	5,32,16,318	5,92,66,006	
Dipalpur	12,93,34,153	7,85,62,285	
Bhakkar	1,84,24,947	1,84,24,952	
Total for the *ṣūba*	(20,09,75,418)	(15,62,53,243)	15,14,03,619
THATTA			
Thatta	2,59,99,991	2,55,54,171	
Chachgan	1,17,84,586	1,17,84,586	
Sehwan	1,55,46,808	1,55,47,407	
Nasarpur	78,34,600	78,34,600	
Chakarhala	50,85,408	50,85,408	
Total for the *ṣūba*	(6,62,51,393)	(6,58,05,172)	6,61,52,393
KASHMIR	6,21,13,045	6,21,13,045	
KABUL			
(Excluding Kashmir and Qandahar)	8,05,07,465	8,05,07,465	

Appendix 1.A (*Continued*)

SUYŪRGHĀL

BENGAL	No *suyūrghāl* figure		
ORISSA	No *suyūrghāl* figures		
BIHAR			
Bihar	22,72,147	22,71,642	
	No *suyūrghāl* in remaining *sarkārs*		
Total for the *ṣūba*	(22,72,147)	(22,71,642)	22,72,147
ALLAHABAD			
Allahabad	7,40,021½	7,40,021½	
Ghazipur	1,31,825	1,21,837	
Banaras	3,38,184	3,38,084	
Jaunpur	48,17,654	30,55,181	
Manikpur	24,46,173	24,46,183	
Chunar	1,09,065	1,08,660	
Kalinjar	6,14,580	14,47,280	
Kora	14,98,360	13,57,120	
Kara	4,69,350	4,69,315	
Battha Gahora	—	—	
Total for the *ṣūba*	(1,11,65,212½)	(1,00,83,681½)	1,11,65,417
AWADH			
Awadh	16,80,248	16,80,165	
Gorakhpur	51,235	51,235	
Bahraich	4,66,482	4,66,482	
Khairabad	17,13,862	16,75,140	
Lucknow	45,72,526	45,84,712	
Total for the *ṣūba*	(84,84,353)	84,57,734	85,21,658
AGRA			
Agra	1,45,66,878	1,43,49,526	
Kalpi	2,78,292½	10,58,292½	
Qanauj	11,74,655	11,82,655	
Kol	20,94,840	20,94,799	
Gawalior	2,40,350	1,18,120	
Erach	4,56,493	4,56,493	
Payanwan	82,660	82,666	
Narwar	95,994	95,694	
Alwar	6,99,212	6,99,215	

(*Continued*)

Appendix 1.A (*Continued*)

SUYŪRGHĀL

Tijara	7,31,761½	7,31,760½	
Narnaul	7,75,103	7,75,083	
Sahar	1,09,447	1,09,447	
Mandlaer	—		
Total for the *ṣūba*	(2,13,05,685)	(2,17,54,751)	1,21,05,703½
MALWA			
Ujjain	2,81,816	2,81,816	
Chanderi	26,931	26,931	
Sarangpur	3,24,461	3,24,461	
Bijagarh	3,574	4,187	
Mandu	1,28,732	1,28,032	
Handia	1,57,054	1,57,053	
Nandurbår	1,98,428	1,98,478	
Mandasor	29,387	29,387	
	No *suyūrghāl* in remaining *sarkārs*		
Total for the *ṣūba*	(11,50,383)	(11,50,345)	11,50,433
KHANDESH	No *suyūrghāl* figures		
BERAR			
Gavail	1,28,74,048	1,12,73,348	
Narnala	1,10,38,422	1,05,85,174	
Basim	18,25,250	18,25,250	
Mahur	97,844	97,844	
Pathri	1,15,80,954	1,02,85,943	
Telingana	66,00,000	66,00,000	
Mahkar	3,76,000	3,76,000	
	No *suyūrghāl* in remaining *sarkārs*		
Total for the *ṣūba*	(4,43,92,518)	(4,10,43,559)	
GUJARAT			
Ahmadabad	65,11,441	66,65,528	
Patan	2,10,627	10,10,547	
Nadaut	11,328	(11,328)	
Baroda	3,88,358	3,88,358	
Broach	1,41,820	1,41,520	
Champaner	1,73,730	1,73,730	

(*Continued*)

Appendix 1.A (*Continued*)

SUYŪRGHĀL

Surat	1,82,670	1,80,630	
Godhra	—	—	
Saurath	—	—	
Total for the *ṣūba*	(76,19,974)	(85,71,941)	4,20,274
AJMER			
Ajmer	14,75,714	14,72,714	
Chittor	3,60,737	3,60,737	
Ranthambhor	1,81,834	74,499	
Nagaur	3,08,051	2,58,915	
	No *suyūrghāl* in remaining *sarkārs*		
Total for the *ṣūba*	(23,26,336)	(21,66,865)	23,26,336
DELHI			
Delhi	1,09,90,260	1,10,00,460	
Badaun	4,57,181	4,57,181	
Sambhal	28,92,394	28,92,093	
Saharanpur	6,91,903	50,22,485	
Rewari	7,39,268	7,38,968	
Hissar Firuza	14,06,519	12,98,214	
Sirhind	1,16,98,330	1,18,18,250	
Kumaun	—	—	
Total for the *ṣūba*	(2,88,75,855)	(3,32,27,651)	3,30,75,739
LAHORE			
Bet Jalendhar *Doāb*	26,51,788	27,29,019	
Bari *Doāb*	39,23,922	39,17,888	
Rachnao *Doāb*	26,84,134	26,48,216	
Chanhat *Doāb*	5,11,070	5,11,070	
Sindh Sagar *Doāb*	(9)4,680[e]	94,680	
Bairun Panjnad	—	—	
Total for the *ṣūba*	(98,65,594)	(99,00,873)	98,65,594

(*Continued*)

[e]The figure in the MS is 4,680 *dāms*.

Appendix 1.A (*Continued*)

SUYŪRGHĀL

MULTAN			
(excluding Thatta)			
Multan	54,94,236	3,36,694	
Dipalpur	20,79,170	21,58,168	
Bhakkar	6,00,419	6,03,419	
Total for the *ṣūba*	(81,73,825)	(30,98,281)	30,59,948
THATTA	No *suyūrghāl*		
KASHMIR	No *suyūrghāl*		
KABUL			
Kabul	1,37,178	(1,12,710)	

AGRICULTURAL PRODUCTION

CHAPTER 2

Extent of Cultivation

I

At first sight, the detailed *ārāẓī* (area) statistics in the *Ā'īn-i Akbarī* ought to provide us with adequate means of estimating the extent of cultivation at the close of the sixteenth century. The primary requirement for this, however, is an assurance of precisely what the term represented. The word '*ārāẓī*' itself simply means land (as well as area in the literal sense). The *Ā'īn* uses it as the heading for the column giving figures in terms of units of area (*bīgha* and *biswa*) in the 'Account of the Twelve Provinces'. When stating the *ṣūba* totals in the text, the *Ā'īn* also uses the words *zamīn-i paimūda*, 'measured land', for the same category of figures.

It seems a safe assumption that land-measurement was undertaken by the Mughal administration basically for purposes of revenue assessment. It is, therefore, quite likely that the crop-land was measured separately during the *kharif* and *rabi* seasons:[1] If so, the area sown or cropped in both seasons must have been combined to produce the figure for cultivated area included in the *ārāẓī*. The double-cropped area is, then likely to have been counted twice over. Moreland accordingly suggested that we have here the equivalent of the 'gross-cropped area' rather than the 'net cropped area' of modern statistics.[2]

We do not have any of the actual survey papers of the *Ā'īn*'s time by which this supposition can be tested. But we have in the later *Raqbabandī*

[1] *Dastūr-ul 'Amal-i 'Ilm-i Navīsandagī* (post-1676) (Br. Mus. Add.6599, ff.182–4, 185) sets out the measured area under *rabi* crops separately from the area covered by *kharif* crops.

[2] Moreland, 'The Agricultural Statistics of Akbar's Empire', *JUPHS, II* (I), 1919, 16.

Table 2.1

		(*bīghas*)
Total area (*raqba*)		3,50,011
Less *kallar* (saline) & *sīr* (revenue-free)		21,777
Total cultivable area		3,28,234
Less area of land grant		10,370
Net cultivable area, comprising		
Kharif	1,87,549	
Rabi	41,323	
Uncultivated	88,992	
		3,17,864

documents from Eastern Rajasthan an illustration of how *ārāẓī* figures included a double-count of the double-cropped area. This is clearly displayed in the area figures given in a survey of 146 villages of *pargana* Lalsot, of v.s. 1783 (AD 1726–7), contained in our Table 2.1.[3] Here the cultivated area, which amounts to just over 65 per cent of the total area measured, is expressly built up of the area cropped in kharif and rabi harvests, and is thus equal to the gross-cropped area precisely as Moreland had hypothesized.

The inclusion of gross-cropped area in the *ārāẓī* figures is confirmed by a peculiar feature of the *Ā'īn*'s statistics that cannot be explained on any other basis. In the case of certain divisions (*dastūr*-circles), the *ārāẓī* figures exceed the map-area. Three such *dastūr*-circles that we have found are Agra and Etawa in *sarkār* Agra, and Meerut in *sarkār* Delhi. The excess may be compared with the size of the double-cropped area of these divisions in 1909–10. The latter is, of course, given only for modern districts in the official *Agricultural Statistics*, but it has been adjusted to the limits of *dastūr*-circles by a simple device. We have first selected the district or districts which in whole or part contain the larger portion of the *dastūr*-circle. Totalling the double-cropped area (DC) and the map-area (M) of these sets of districts we have calculated the ratio DC:M for the aggregate. This ratio we have then applied to the *dastūr*-circles, whose map-area is established from Irfan Habib's *Atlas of the Mughal Empire:* what we get thus would be the DC in 1909–10 within the territory

[3] I am grateful to the late Dr S.P. Gupta for guiding me to this document which is preserved in the Rajasthan State Archives, Bikaner.

assigned to the particular *dastūr*-circle in Akbar's time. Table 2.2 presents the results of these calculations for the three *dastūr*-circles in question. These figures show a surprising degree of correspondence between the excess of *ārāẓī* over the map area and the size of the double-cropped area.

Table 2.2

Dastūr-circle	Excess of *ārāẓī* over map area (%)	Double-cropped area as % of map area (1909–10)
Ḥavelī Agra	2.08	6.41
Etawa	10.98	8.91
Meerut	11.12	18.94

Moreland must, therefore, be right in his view that the *ārāẓī* covered the gross, and not the net cultivated area. But the very fact that the *ārāẓī* exceeded the map area also suggests that he was in error in equating the *ārāẓī* with the gross-cropped area only, since the latter, even in recent times, is substantially smaller than the map area in most localities. In the three *dastūr*-circles in Table 2.2, the *ārāẓī* recorded in the *Ā'īn* (converted into percentage of map area) exceeds the gross cultivated area (GC) of the corresponding districts in 1909–10 by a large margin, amounting to 137 per cent of the latter in *dastūr*-circle Agra, 150 per cent in Etawa and 115 per cent in Meerut.

There is, moreover, the further phenomenon of very low figures being obtained when the *Ā'īn*'s *jama'* figures of certain *parganas* are divided by the *ārāẓī* figures, giving us the average *jama'* per *bīgha-i ilāhī* of measured land. In Middle *Doāb*, along the Yamuna, while the rate is as high as 33 *dāms* in Mahaban, it falls to just 6 *dāms* per *bīgha-i ilāhī* in the large *pargana* of Sahar across the Yamuna.[4] Clearly, much untaxed land (and, therefore, large areas of uncultivated waste) must have been included in *ārāẓī* in the latter *pargana* (and in other *parganas* with similar low rates).

For covering such an excess of the *ārāẓī* over the extent of gross cultivation in 1909–10, the *ārāẓī* could not only have comprised the entire gross-cropped area but must also have included, to varying extents, current fallows and portions of cultivable waste, and some part of uncultivable

[4] See Irfan Habib and Faiz Habib, 'The Political and Economic Geography of Braj Bhum' in: *Papers from the Aligarh Historians Society* for Indian History Congress, 73rd session (Mumbai, 2012), pp.258–60, esp. Map 2 on 258.

waste, which, together with habitational areas, make up the difference between the net cultivation and the map area in modern statistics.

This inference is corroborated by the break-down of figures we have already used from the records of *pargana* Lalsot, 1726–7. As we have seen, the cultivated area comprised about 65 per cent of the total measured area in the document in question, while the uncultivable waste together with *sīr* amounted to 6 per cent and the cultivable waste to a little over 25 per cent. Similar corroboration is forthcoming from earlier seventeenth-century documents as well. The specimen *taqsīm* document found in an administrative manual, the *Dastūr-ul 'Amal-i 'Alamgīrī*, written in Aurangzeb's reign, gives the following details of land surveyed in five villages:[5]

	bīghas	% of total area
Total measured area	2,943	100.00
Cultivable land[6]	2,612	88.75
Cultivable waste	200	6.80
Uncultivable waste, land under habitation, etc.	131	4.45

The inclusion as well as the low proportion of both cultivable waste (6.80 per cent of the measured area) and area not available for cultivation (4.45 per cent) may be noted.

Nainsi's *Vigat*, giving statistical information down to 1664, furnishes the following figures for the area surveyed in *pargana* Merta, *sarkār* Nagaur. (This *pargana* had been under Mughal imperial administration, and did not belong to the state of Marwar proper).[7]

[5] Br. Mus. MS, Add. 6598, f.36b. For dates, see Habib, *Agrarian System*, 412, rev. ed., 470. However, there appear some place names in the text that suggest a later date within Aurangzeb's reign.

[6] Here this category seems to cover land actually cultivated and current fallows. But where 'cultivable waste' is not recorded separately, it should have been included within 'cultivable land'.

[7] *Marwar ra Pargana ri Vigat*, ed. N.S. Bhati, Jodhpur, 1969, Vol.II, 77, Nainsi ascribes the survey to v.s. 1630 (AD 1572–3). This would, of course, suit my argument still better. But I have adopted the more conservative view that the figures themselves are based on a survey subsequent to that undertaken in Akbar's time, i.e., any time in or before Samvat 1721 (AD 1664), the last year mentioned in the *Vigat*.

	bīghas	% of total area
Total measured area	26,15,956	100.00
Cultivable land	23,96,425	91.61
Unassessed land	2,19,531	8.39

The 'unassessed land' must have included some uncultivable waste, comprising village habitation sites, nullahs, etc. The small percentage of the total unassessed area suggests that not the whole, but only a part of the actual waste, was measured. It is certainly difficult to believe that the uncultivable waste in *pargana* Merta set on the fringe of the Thar Desert was only a little over 8 per cent of the total area.[8]

In area statistics from Eastern Rajasthan[9] the different categories of measured area are often not indicated in any detail. For example, for eleven villages of *pargana* Antela Bhabhera of *sarkār* Alwar for the year 1649 we have the following data:

	bīghas	% of total area
Total measured area	61,180	100.00
Cultivable land	39,822	65.09
Unassessed land: *sīr* land, river, hills, *nullah*	21,358	34.91

Here since the unassessed land includes *sīr* which was unassessed though cultivated, it is not clear how much of the unassessed land was actually uncultivable. Similarly, the percentage of the cultivable waste out of the total cultivable area cannot be established, though its inclusion, within the measured area, seems certain.

A rather late *taqsīm* document of 157 villages in *pargana* Amarsar of *sarkār* Nagaur (AD 1758), gives the following figures for surveyed land:

	bīghas	% of total area
Total measured area	1,20,610	100.00
Cultivable land	1,07,693	89.29
Unassessed land (*erigauti, kharera, nullah*)	12,917	10.71

[8] Even in 1898–9 the proportion of land not available for cultivation in the district was 14.7% of the total area (*Agricultural Statistics*, 1897–8 to 1901–2, Part II, 18).

[9] I owe guidance on this material to Dr S.P. Gupta.

Here again the uncultivated area and cultivable waste are lumped together. Though it is difficult to be certain about the significance of some of the terms used for categories belonging to unassessed land, it can perhaps be assumed that it here covered only uncultivable land. The area of measured land that was not available for cultivation in these villages could thus have hardly exceeded 10 per cent of the total measured area and might possibly have been much less.

The documents then confirm Irfan Habib's suggestion that the *ārāẓī* of the Mughal surveyors comprised not only gross cultivation, but also included cultivable waste and a part of uncultivable land.[10] Beyond this it is difficult to extract any precise conclusion from these scattered examples. One can perhaps say that it must have been rare for the surveyors to have measured an area of uncultivable waste amounting to more than 10 per cent of the total. In the documents, the range is about 5 to 10 per cent, except for one locality only where (but for the uncertainty as to the exact size of *sīr* land) it could have been higher than 10 per cent. For our purposes, then, 10 per cent may be a safe allowance for uncultivable waste in the *Ā'īn*'s *ārāẓī* statistics.

For cultivable waste, however, it is not possible to place a uniform limit in this manner. Still, the ratio between the cultivable waste and cultivable land in the same localities in modern times (say, 1909–10) may be used as a rough index for 1595.[11] At first sight this suggestion seems rather bold, for one would think that with the extension of cultivation the size of cultivable waste would have contracted so that its ratio to the gross cropped-area would be much higher in 1595 than in 1909–10. But some reflection would show that there is nothing or, rarely, anything like absolutely uncultivable land. At any time the land deemed cultivable is one which, at that time, is likely to offer acceptable returns if

[10] Habib, *Agrarian System*, 7 (rev. ed., 6). An interesting description of the system of measurement taken over from Tipu Sultan's administration by the English, and in operation in 1800, corroborates these conclusions. Buchanan writes: 'The principal native officer here says that people are now employed in measuring the lands which belong to all the villages in this lately acquired division of Major Macleod's district. The measurement, however, will be by no means complete; as large hills and wastes are not included within the boundaries of any village and will not be comprehended in the accompts. Even within the village it is only the lands that are considered arable, or as capable of being made so, that are actually measured, steep and rocky places are taken by conjecture'. (Francis Buchanan, *A Journey from Madras through the Countries of Mysore, Canara and Malabar & c.*, II, 211–12).

[11] The figures for 1909–10 are drawn from the *Agricultural Statistics*, 1909–10.

cultivated; that is, it only includes that land which by fertility (and location) lies on the margin of cultivation. As with every increase in population inferior land is brought under the plough, some of the land which was previously considered uncultivable, because of the quality of its soil, lack of irrigation or difficulty of access, passes into the category of cultivable waste. In other words, the strip of cultivable waste shifts outwards as the circle of cultivation expands: as it shifts, its area too should expand since the outer circumference becomes larger. The total area of cultivable waste should accordingly increase and not decline, with any increase in cultivation.

Our hypothesis inspires confidence when we compare the ratio of cultivable waste to gross cultivation between 1909–10 and 1946–7 in those districts of U.P. where cultivable land (area under cultivation, current fallows and cultivable waste) was below 50 per cent of the total area in 1909–10 (Table 2.3).

Table 2.3

	Cultivable land as % of map-area		Cultivable waste as % of gross cultivation	
District	1909–10	1946–7	1909–10	1946–7
Dehradun	25.21	38.54	62.66	76.34
Mirzapur	48.87	76.42	65.81	102.23
Almora	9.74	16.74	12.80	13.04
Garhwal	9.44	9.23	22.19	22.23
Nainital	27.02	32.22	48.63	146.35

The theory, then, is reinforced by statistics. There is, however, an important reservation to be made. Where the physical limits to extension in cultivation have been reached, where, that is, the crop-land already covered a large portion of the total area, further increase in cultivation may fail to transfer a proportionate area from uncultivable to cultivable waste. This is demonstrated when we compare the change in the area of cultivable waste relative to gross cultivation in those districts of U.P. where cultivable land was already 90 per cent of the total area in 1909–10 (Table 2.4). In these districts, except for Bareilly and Shahjahanpur, the cultivable waste as percentage of gross cultivation shows a decline, although usually a small one, just as we had expected.

Table 2.4

	Cultivable land as % of total map area	Cultivable waste as % of total gross cultivation	
District	1909–10	1909–10	1946–7
Mathura	92.58	22.52	14.87
Etah	90.03	31.70	27.23
Bareilly	90.14	11.47	14.98
Badaun	92.18	16.12	14.88
Moradabad	92.94	19.90	18.15
Shahjahanpur	91.79	25.16	29.29
Banda	91.32	82.56	57.70
Sitapur	90.02	20.93	19.54

Considering the possible situation in 1595, when cultivation was presumably much less extensive than in 1909–10 in most areas, one would suppose that in the area covered in Table 2.4 the ratio of cultivable waste to gross cultivation was higher than in 1909–10; on the other hand, in areas covered in Table 2.3, the ratio in 1595 should have been lower than in 1909–10. But one must modify these conclusions by the consideration that whereas modern statistics are comprehensive, Mughal surveyors are likely to have excluded cultivable waste that was situated at a distance from the limits of villages surveyed by them. I have, therefore, assumed that within the *Ā'īn*'s *ārāẓī*, the cultivable waste as percentage of gross cultivation was about the same as early in this century within the corresponding area, except for tracts where cultivation was excessively low in 1909–10. The margin of error involved in accepting this assumption is probably not large, except perhaps in some cases where the *Ā'īn*'s *ārāẓī* comprises an exceptionally large portion of the map area.

A major issue still remains unsettled. Did the *ārāẓī* statistics cover the entire gross-cropped area in all localities for which they are offered in the *Ā'īn*? This was Moreland's view. He was prepared to accept a forty-fold extension of cultivation in some tracts between Akbar's time and his own, simply because this was the proportion the *ārāẓī* bore to the contemporary gross cultivation in the area in question.[12] This hypothesis can be tested from the data found in the *Ā'īn* itself. We may, first, compute the *jama'*/*ārāẓī* (J/A) rates for different *dastūr*-circles, by dividing the total

[12] *JUPHS*, II (i), 20.

jama‘ or the recorded net revenue-income of all the *parganas* within a *dastūr*-circle, by the total of their respective *ārāẓī* figures. These may be compared with the *dastūrs* or cash revenue rates of major crops for these circles. The results for some circles within the present state of U.P. are shown in Table 2.5.

Table 2.5

			Rates (Agra rate=100)		
Dastūr-circle	J/A *dāms*/*bīgha*	J/A Agra=100	Wheat	Rice	Cotton
Agra	28.09	100.00	100.00	100.00	100.00
Etawa	11.25	40.05	89.98	74.02	102.75
Delhi	22.65	80.63	93.70	91.58	102.57
Meerut	11.12	39.59	86.70	79.66	102.57
Awadh	12.87	45.82	81.69	72.23	95.28
Bhadoi	50.22	178.78	96.66	70.38	105.14
Jaunpur	64.71	230.37	96.66	81.51	110.28
Chunar	54.68	194.66	96.66	81.51	110.28
Ghazipur	47.59	169.42	96.66	81.51	110.43
Rae-Bareilly	53.35	189.93	93.32	77.80	107.71

It can be seen at once that the variation in the incidence of *jama‘* per *bīgha* of *ārāẓī* in the various *dastūr*-circles is considerable, ranging from 11.12 to 64.71 (or, when indexed to the J/A of Agra as 100, from 39.59 to 230.37). The differences among the *dastūr*-rates of these circles have, however, a far more limited range of variation (being, as indexed: wheat, 81.69 to 96.66; rice, 70.38 to 91.58; and cotton 95.28 to 110.43). Moreover, the rates sometimes display change in an opposite direction to that of the J/A, being occasionally lower in areas where the J/A is quite high. This is illustrated in the table by only three rates (for wheat, rice and cotton); but these rates are fairly representative of the *dastūr*-rates for the various crops in general. There can, therefore, be little doubt that the variations in J/A are due to the varying extents to which the assessed land was measured in the different localities. This explains the high J/A in eastern U.P. where measurement was apparently very incomplete. The exceptionally low J/A in some circles, on the other hand, can be attributed to an unusually high proportion of waste included in the surveyed area.

Our conclusion, then, would correspond to Irfan Habib's view that the measurement in 1595 while complete or nearly complete in some areas had only been partially carried out in others. For this he had adduced the evidence of the statistics of Aurangzeb's reign,[13] but, as has been shown above, a close study of the *Ā'īn*'s figures themselves would lead one to the same result.

To arrive at the extent of gross cultivation in 1595 the *ārāẓī* figures ought then to be scaled down to allow for uncultivable land as well as cultivable waste included in the measured area. We have suggested that 10 per cent of the total *ārāẓī* may be taken as the maximum limit for uncultivable waste; and that for allowing the cultivable waste, the *ārāẓī* should be reduced by applying the ratio of cultivable waste to cultivable land in the corresponding districts in 1909–10 (with the exception of some areas of extremely low cultivation). Where measurement had been undertaken on a very limited scale in Akbar's time, and so the extent of measured area recorded in the *Ā'īn* is very small, I have used the *jama'* figures and *dastūr* rates to calculate the gross-cropped area of the *Ā'īn*'s time, but this device has been very sparingly employed, as will be seen from the details furnished in the following sections of this chapter.[14]

[13] Habib, *Agrarian System*, 4 rev. ed., 4, reproduces these statistics. The number of measured and unmeasured villages is separately given. The figures for the *ṣūbas* of Agra, Delhi, Awadh, Allahabad, Gujarat and Lahore are as follows:

Villages

Ṣūba	Total Number	Measured	Unmeasured	Measured as % of total
Agra	30,180	27,303	2,877	90.47
Delhi	45,088	43,512	1,576	96.50
Awadh	52,691	33,842	18,849	64.23
Allahabad	47,607	45,345	2,262	95.25
Gujarat	10,370	3,924	6,446	37.84
Lahore	27.761	24,569	3,192	88.50

[14] This may be the point where a few words may be spared for an alternative mode of estimating the extent of cultivation on the basis of the *Ā'īn*'s data. K.K. Trivedi and Shaukatullah Khan argue in *Studies in History*, NS, Vol.14, No.2, 301–23, that the *Ā'īn-i Akbarī* area statistics were compiled not under any fiscal design, but under the impulse to work out the pattern of land-use. In the criticism that Trivedi offers of his predecessors' lack of comprehension, I pass by such small matters as Trivedi's own definition of "double-cropped" as land that produces a single crop in two seasons (303 & *n.*), or his assertion that Abū'l Faẓl had endorsed the *chaknama* of Navasari of 1596 which Irfan Habib had deciphered, translated, and analysed (p.303). The practical device offered by him is to forget the *ārāẓī* figures altogether and simply divide the *jama'/naqdī* figures by 40, whereafter, presto!, you will have the exact figure of gross cultivation in *bīgha-i ilāhī*. This flat rate (of tax per *bīgha*) overlooks all variations of crops sown, taxation rates, etc., and produces the result that the hilly south-western portion of *ṣūba* Berar comes out as one of the most highly cultivated

To be able to use data from modern statistics one ought to be definite about the limits of Mughal territorial divisions. As mentioned earlier, practically all the *parganas* situated within U.P. have been firmly identified; this can also be said for Gujarat and Haryana. Such identifications give weight to boundaries of *dastūr*-circles and *sarkārs* traced on the map. In the Panjab the number of identified *parganas* is admittedly rather small, but the limits of the *doābs*, being set by the rivers (or their old courses that are still traceable), are more or less well established.[15]

An attempt can thus be made to estimate the extent of cultivation, in—(a) those portions of Akbar's empire that fell within U.P. (comprising the entire *ṣūbas* of Awadh and Allahabad, except the *sarkār* of Battha Gahora, most of *ṣūba* Agra and parts of *ṣūba* Delhi); (b) the portion of the present state of Gujarat that corresponded to the *ṣūba* of Gujarat, but excepting *sarkār* Saurath (Saurashtra) in both cases; and (c) the British province of the Panjab, which was covered by parts of *ṣūba* Delhi, the whole of *ṣūba* Lahore and parts of *ṣūba* Multan.

II

Starting with U.P., I have based my figures primarily on statistics at the level of *dastūr*-circles, each of which comprised a group of *parganas*. The *dastūr*-circles are the smallest units for which limits are fairly well established and the map areas can be determined. I have then followed the method for which justification has been offered in the preceding section. The *ārāẓī* given in the *Ā'īn* for the *parganas* comprising a circle has first been scaled down by 10 per cent to allow for the portion of uncultivable waste. I have then estimated the cultivable waste for each *dastūr*-circle by calculating the ratio of cultivable waste to total cultivable land in 1909–10, in the sets of various districts within which the *dastūr*-circle lay, and then applying this ratio to the *ārāẓī* of the *dastūr*-circle to obtain an estimate of cultivable waste within it. The figure of *ārāẓī* that we now get (A′) should represent the area of gross cultivation in 1595. But this can only be true for the *dastūr*-circles where measurement was complete. Since, as we shall see in Chapter 5, 50 *dāms* represented the maximum

tracts, and Bengal among the least cultivated (as would appear from our Map IV, based on the ratio of *jama'*: map-area). The editor of the volume, Neeladri Bhattacharya builds on the result of such an innovative device (pp. 169–70), by comparing all-India data that includes the Himalayas, Baluchistan, Deccan, etc., with data that supposedly apply to the Mughal Empire which did not include these large mountains and hilly territories.

[15] As already indicated, I have used the boundaries as marked in Habib's *Atlas of the Mughal Empire*, New Delhi, 1982.

incidence of land-revenue per *bīgha* of cultivation in this region, measurement can be taken to be more or less complete in *dastūr*-circles where J′ (*jama‘* as stated by the *Ā’īn* enhanced by 23.3 per cent = the gross average collection of revenue)[16] divided by A′, was below 50 *dāms* (per *bīgha*). For these *dastūr*-circles A′ should be taken to be approximately the same as the gross cultivation of 1595.

On the other hand, where the revenue incidence exceeds 50 *dāms* per *bīgha* of A′, we must assume that measurement was incomplete and A′ represents only a portion of the gross cultivation of 1595. In such cases, I have divided J′ by 35, since the average rate of revenue-incidence in this region was about 35 *dāms* per *bīgha* (Chapter 5). The result may be taken as the approximate area of land (in *bīghas*) under gross cultivation.

These figures for the gross cultivation of 1595 can now be compared with the gross cultivation of 1909–10. I have calculated the latter for the limits of *dastūr*-circles in the following manner: first of all, the entire gross cultivation of the district in which each *dastūr*-circle lay (either wholly, or in the large part) has been obtained. Then the ratio of such cultivation to the total area of the district has been calculated. This ratio has then been applied to the map area of the *dastūr*-circle, in order to yield the estimated gross cultivation for the area of that circle in 1909–10 (tabulated in Appendix 2.A). For convenience of comparison, the figures given in acres in modern statistics have been converted into those in *bīgha-i ilāhī.*[17]

Certain *dastūr*-circles are too small for us to be reasonably sure of the accuracy of their map area. There is naturally a smaller margin of error when determining the map area of a larger territory; most inaccuracies resulting from a possibly inaccurate delineation of the limits of individual *dastūr*-circles are mutually cancelled if we combine adjoining *dastūr*-circles into bigger blocks. I have accordingly grouped the *dastūr*-circles lying in U.P. into twelve blocks (Table 2.6). (The *dastūr*-circles within each block are listed in Appendix 2.A).

Table 2.6 suggests that cultivation in 1595 was almost as high as in 1909–10 around Agra; about three-fourths of what it was in 1909–10 in the upper and middle parts of the *Doāb*; about two-thirds in Lower *Doāb* and some adjoining tracts; and about half or a little more in central U.P.

[16] The *jama‘* is reduced first by 10% to make allowance for taxes other than land revenue and then enhanced by 37% for allowances and payments made from gross revenue collection (see Chapter 5).

[17] One *bīgha-i Ilāhī* has been taken to be 0.6 acre, on the basis of the evidence offered in Irfan Habib, *Agrarian System*, 354–62, rev. ed., 409–15.

Table 2.6

(a) Blocks	(b) Assumed G.C. 1595 *bīgha-i Ilāhī*	(c) G.C. 1909–10 *bīgha-i Ilāhī*	(b) as % of (c)
North-west U.P.	63,75,289	78,45,901	81.26
Delhi	32,68,876	46,28,332	70.63
Rohilkhand	19,03,330	69,04,087	27.57
Middle *Doāb*	21,57,448	28,90,488	74.64
Agra	21,25,267	21,62,269	98.29
Lower *Doāb* (Yamuna)	25,57,334	30,73,838	83.20
Lower *Doāb* (Ganga)	21,01,513	35,13,665	59.81
Lucknow	54,37,029	92,72,934	58.63
North-east U.P.	12,67,719	28,90,255	43.86
Gorakhpur	5,41,024	96,13,041	5.63
South-east U.P.	34,09,939	79,88,890	42.68
Allahabad	35,67,268	49,15,193	72.57
Total	3,47,12,036	6,56,98,893	52.84

But cultivation was much less extensive in Rohilkhand (below 28 per cent); it was less than half of the gross cultivation of 1909–10 in north-east and south-east U.P. as well. In Gorakhpur, the figure is abnormally low (barely 6 per cent); but one may fairly doubt the accuracy of the *Ā'īn*'s *jama'* here.[18]

When put on the map (see Map I) these estimates do not appear improbable. The areas where cultivation is low are precisely the areas in which forests were reported in Mughal times or which are shown as forested by Rennell in 1780, or are those where cultivation is known to have progressed substantially during the intervening period.[19]

[18] This doubt is reinforced by later revenue-statistics. Considered as percentage of the total *jama'* of Awadh, the *jama'* of Gorakhpur was 5.7% in the *Ā'īn*. But it amounts to 11.85% of the total *jama'* of the *ṣūba* in the *Dastūr-ul 'Amal-i 'Alamgīrī*, f.114a–b, and 16.06% in the *Chahar Gulshan*. It is possible that part of the relative increase in *jama'* was due to an increase in cultivation but it is more likely that the *jama'* was substantially understated in the *Ā'īn*. If the latter is the case, we should perhaps assume that the actual extent of cultivation here was twice or thrice the extent deduced from our Table 2.6. In other words, the GC in 1595 was probably about 15% of what it was in 1909–10.

[19] See the two maps in *Cambridge Economic History of India*, I, 5. See also the depiction of forest areas in Irfan Habib, *Atlas of the Mughal Empire*, Sheet 8B, with notes for sources used.

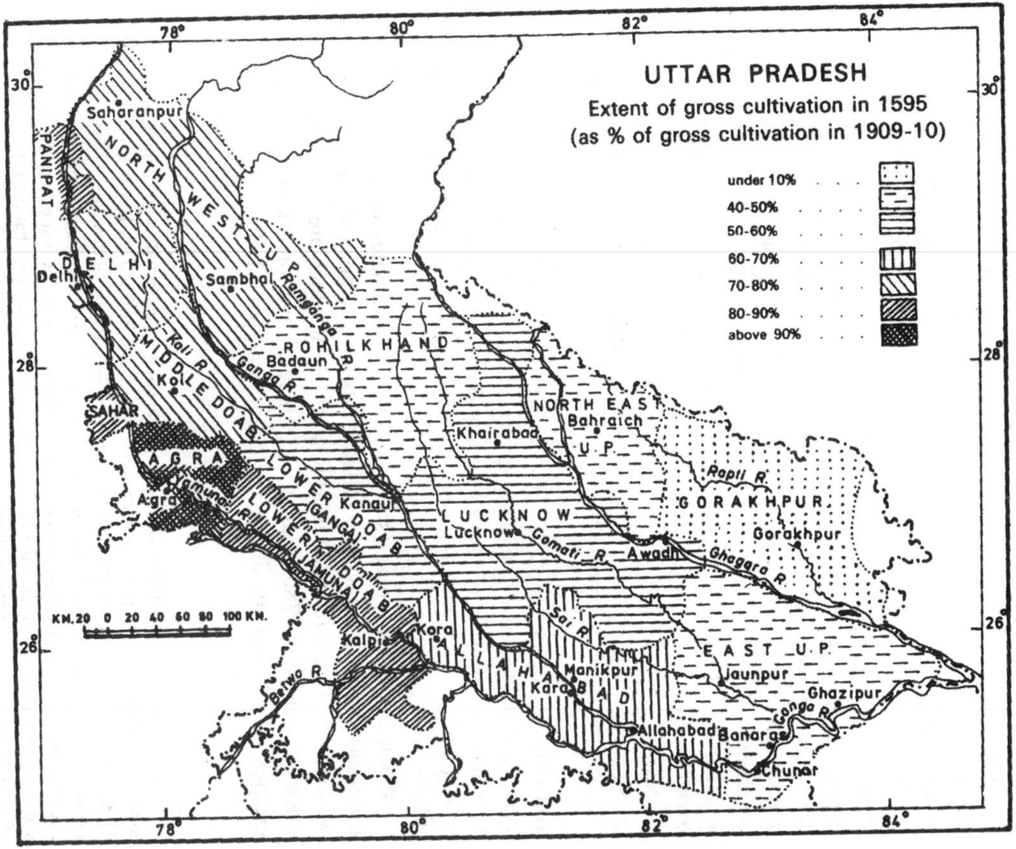
UTTAR PRADESH
Extent of gross cultivation in 1595
(as % of gross cultivation in 1909-10)
under 10%
40-50%
50-60%
60-70%
70-80%
80-90%
above 90%
NORTH WEST U.P.
DELHI
MIDDLE DOAB
ROHILKHAND
LOWER DOAB (GANGA)
LOWER DOAB (JAMUNA)
AGRA
SAHAR
PANIPAT
LUCKNOW
NORTH EAST U.P.
GORAKHPUR
EAST U.P.
ALLAHABAD
Saharanpur
Delhi
Sambhal
Badaun
Koil
Agra
Kanauj
Kalpi
Kora
Khairabad
Lucknow
Bahraich
Awadh
Gorakhpur
Manikpur
Kara
Jaunpur
Ghazipur
Allahabad
Banaras
Chunar
Ramganga R.
Ganga R.
Kali R.
Jamuna R.
Gomati R.
Ghagara R.
Rapti R.
Sai R.
Betwa R.
KM.20 0 20 40 60 80 100 KM.
78°
80°
82°
84°
30°
28°
26°

Map I

The gross cultivation of all the blocks in 1595 may probably give a false sense of precision. But it is difficult to resist the general conclusion that gross cultivation in 1595 over the entire region of Uttar Pradesh was probably only a little over half of what it was in 1909–10. This estimate is higher than that of Moreland, but accords broadly with that of Irfan Habib.[20]

III

From U.P. we pass on to Gujarat. For this province, except for the *sarkār* of Saurath and the tracts of Kachchh and Lesser Kachchh (Jamnagar), the *Ā'īn*'s record of *ārāẓī* is strikingly complete. The *ārāẓī* is recorded against all the *parganas* under the *sarkārs* of Patan, Nadaut, Baroda, Champaner, Surat and Godhra. In the *sarkār* of Bharuch, it is not recorded in two *parganas*, viz., *Bandar* (Port) Gandhar and the seat of the headquarters, Bharuch itself. It is possible that in both cases, the *pargana*, or rather *maḥal*, was purely urban, and there was no agricultural land to be brought under measurement. Finally, in *sarkār* Ahmadabad, of a total of twenty-eight *parganas*, five have no *ārāẓī* mentioned against them; but of these five one is definitely a port (*Bandar* Ghogha).[21]

The total *ārāẓī* as recorded in the *Ā'īn* is 47.60 per cent[22] of the map area of the corresponding portion of the *ṣūba*. It amounted to 85.62 per cent of the gross cultivation in the corresponding territory at the beginning of this century as calculated from modern official statistics (for which see below).

In spite of its extensive *ārāẓī* statistics, the *Ā'īn*-declares that Gujarat was mostly '*nasaqī*' and measurement was rarely undertaken.[23] But this

[20] Moreland, *India at the Death of Akbar*, 20–2; Habib, *Agrarian System*, 12–15, rev. ed., 12–15.

[21] *Bandar* Ghogha is wrongly read '*Bandar* Sola' in Blochmann's text, as well as MSS, the *kāf*-strokes having been omitted probably in the original by scribal error.

[22] As explained in Chapter 1, I have used the totals of the *Ā'īn*'s figures for individual *maḥals*, which here (and quite often elsewhere) are different from the *Ā'īn*'s *sarkār* totals, which again differ from its own recorded total for the *ṣūba*. The differences for Gujarat as a whole are, however, not substantial:

Stated *ṣūba*; total	Total of recorded *sarkār* figures	Total of *maḥal* figures
1,69,36,377–3	1,69,35,877–3	1,73,27,235–16

[23] *Ā'īn*, I, p.556.

statement may mean only that the figures of land once measured continued to be accepted in subsequent years (a practice that was a recognized form of *nasaq*[24]) without recourse to annual measurement. Since we are not in any case considering annual fluctuations in cultivation, this does not deprive the Gujarat figures of their value for the purpose of comparing them with figures of three hundred years later.

It has, however, to be established how far measurement in Gujarat covered the cultivated area. Gujarat had no *dastūrs* for various crops, so that the kind of check these make possible in the territory of U.P. is not available for Gujarat. One can, however, test the degree of completeness of the coverage by working out the ratios of *jama'/ārāẓī* (J/A) and *jama'/* map area (J/M) as well as the ratio of *ārāẓī* (A) to map area (M), for the different *sarkārs*. The results of these simple calculations are given in Table 2.7. Note that the map area has been converted from modern units into *bīgha-i ilāhī*, to be made comparable to *ārazī*.

Table 2.7

Sarkār	J/A *dāms* per *bīgha*	J/M *dāms* per *bīgha*	A as % of M
Ahmadabad	25.90	14.90	57.55
Patan	15.17	7.29	48.04
Nadaut	16.28	4.53	27.85
Baroda	44.63	32.97	73.83
Bharuch	22.95	9.42	41.02
Champaner	13.13	2.58	19.62
Surat	14.53	8.38	57.69
Godhra	6.83	2.00	29.24

The key figures in this table are those of *sarkār* Baroda, where A (*ārāẓī*) approaches three-fourths of M (total map area). In this *sarkār* J/A amounted to 44.63 *dāms* per *bīgha*, and J/M too is very high, viz., 32.97 *dāms*. *Sarkār* Baroda contained an extremely fertile tract, with high productivity. But even making allowances for it, one would expect that in other *sarkārs* too where the *ārāẓī* was substantially less than the cultivated area, J/A could not have been very much less than 32.97 *dāms* as this represented the possible minimum rate for Baroda, had the *ārāẓī* been equal to the map area. In other words, we should infer that in all *sarkārs*, where J/A is lower than even 32.97 *dāms*, the measured area must have been much larger than the taxed cultivated area. Since in fact

[24] Habib, *Agrarian System*, 225 (rev. ed. 255–7).

J/A is lower in all the other *sarkārs*, we must suppose that the cultivated area in the various *sarkārs* had been almost fully brought under measurement.

Applying the same assumptions now that we have ventured for U.P., we can work out the gross cultivation in Gujarat at the end of the sixteenth century. The assumptions are that (a) up to 10 per cent of the *ārāẓī* comprised land not then available for cultivation; and (b) the percentage of cultivable waste and current fallows in the total *ārāẓī* (less 10 per cent) was about the same as the proportion the two categories bore to the aggregate of cultivated and cultivable area at the beginning of the twentieth century (we have used the 1903–4 figures for Gujarat for this purpose).[25]

To apply the second assumption, I have followed a procedure which requires some explanation. The *Ā'īn*'s *sarkārs* do not correspond to the British districts and 'native states'. Therefore to get the ratio of cultivable land within the territory of a *sarkār*, I have first measured the part of a district which fell within that *sarkār*. Then its ratio to the total area of the district has been obtained. Thereafter, the figures of total cultivable land and cultivable waste for the whole district have been reduced in the proportion which the part of the district covered by the *sarkār* in question bears to the total area of the district. Proceeding in this way for the portions of all the districts which together constitute one whole *sarkār*, we get the cultivated land and cultivable waste for the entire territory of the *sarkār* in 1903–4. These figures enable us to work out the percentage of cultivable waste to the total area available for cultivation in that *sarkār*, which, under our assumptions, could stand for 1903–4 as well as *c.*1595.

The *ārāẓī* (less 10 per cent) of the *sarkār* can now be scaled down by the percentage so determined, to get the gross cropped-area (A′) for *c.*1595. Table 2.8 gives the *ārāẓī* recorded in the *Ā'īn* and the estimated gross cultivation for 1595 (A′).

The estimated gross-cropped area in all the *sarkārs* of Gujarat except Saurath thus amounts to 67.67 per cent of the total measured area: by our calculations, so that 32.33 per cent of the total measured area (*ārāẓī*) must have been covered by waste, cultivable as well as uncultivable.

While adopting this conclusion, one encounters an apparently discordant note in the *Mir'āt-i Aḥmadī*. This work states that in Akbar's time

[25] Since during the British period large areas of Gujarat were under princely states, which did not offer the necessary returns, the *Agricultural Statistics* are not complete in early years. I have supplemented their information by estimates found in the *Imperial Gazetteer*, Oxford, 1910, whose evidence relates to 1903–4.

Table 2.8

Sarkār	A *Ārāẓī* (*bīghas* & *biswas*)	A′ Gross cultivation *c.*1595 (*bīghas*)
Ahmadabad	84,19,201	56,77,404
Patan	38,45,909–16	22,99,932
Nadaut	5,40,425	4,28,951
Baroda	9,22,212	7,10,103
Bharuch	9,49,731	7,97,403
Champaner	8,00,328	4,60,269
Surat	13,09,614	9,99,301
Godhra	5,34,815	3,49,223
Total	1,73,22,235–16	1,17,22,046

the total measured area of Gujarat (excluding the *sarkārs* of Saurath and Godhra) was 1,23,60,594 *bīghas*, 9 *biswas* of which 83,47,498 *bīghas*, 3 *biswas* were cultivable.[26] The figures imply that of the total measured area, 67.53 per cent was cultivable and 32.47 per cent uncultivable. The attribution of these figures to Akbar's time is probably a mistake; the figures (if deemed to be in terms of *bīgha-i daftarī* not *bīgha-i ilāhī*) accord more with those of Auragnzeb's time when a large number of villages in Gujarat had not yet been surveyed.[27] Even so the evidence is quite puzzling, for it is hard to believe that the Mughal surveyors measured such a big portion of uncultivable land that was unassessable and useless for their purpose.

On the other hand, if we assume that the *Mir'āt* has erroneously used the word 'cultivable' for land actually cultivated it would offer surprisingly close support to our estimate of the size of cultivated land within the *Ā'īn*'s *ārāẓī*: we have found that the proportion of gross cropped-area to the total *ārāẓī* in the *Ā'īn* should have been 67.67 per cent and the *Mir'āt*, assuming the supposed error in categorization, would put it at 67.53 per cent.

[26] *Mir'āt-i Aḥmadī*, ed. Nawab Ali, Vol.I, Baroda, 1927, 25.

[27] In Aurangzeb's reign, of a total of 10,370 villages only 3,924 were measured, and the measured area amounted to 1,27,49,374 *bīgha* (*daftarī*), equal to 84,99,582 *bīgha-i Ilāhī* (Fraser 86, ff.57b–60b). The *Ā'īn*'s measured area for all the *sarkārs* (excluding Saurath) was 1,73,27,235 *bīghas*; excluding *Sarkār* Godhra as well, it was 1,68,62,925 *bīghas*.

Table 2.9

Sarkār	(a) G.C. *c.*1595 (*bīgha-i Ilāhī*)	(b) G.C. 1903–4 (*bīgha-i Ilāhī*)	(c) (a) as % of (b)
Ahmadabad	56,77,404	83,33,534	68.13
Patan	22,99,392	50,14,571	45.85
Nadaut	4,28,951	5,30,173	80.91
Baroda	7,10,103	8,04,229	88.30
Broach (Bharuch)	7,97,403	18,59,194	42.89
Champaner	4,60,269	16,12,665	28.54
Surat	9,99,301	11,34,406	88.00
Godhra	3,49,223	9,40,820	37.12
Total	1,17,22,406	2,02,29,592	57.945

(GC=Gross Cultivation)

There is another interesting piece of information from *pargana* Bharuch in 1776.[28] This comes from the report of the English Revenue Collector sent to collect revenue during a temporary cession of the *pargana* to the English by the Marathas. According to this report, 50.69 per cent of the total measured area within the *pargana* was actually cultivated. The low percentage might have been due to the abnormal conditions then obtaining in the area; the Collector, in any case, speaks of the year as one in which much less had been produced than in the preceding year.[29]

There is thus independent evidence to reinforce our inference that in Gujarat about two-thirds of the total *ārāẓī* was actually cultivated. The gross cropped-area of different *sarkārs* at the close of the sixteenth century calculated on this basis can now be compared with the gross cultivated-area in 1903–4.

To get the gross cultivation in 1903–4 in the regions of different *sarkārs*, I have proceeded in the same way as for estimating the cultivable waste and gross cultivation. The figures of gross cultivation for

[28] *Selections from the Letters, Despatches and Other State Papers, Preserved in the Bombay Secretariat*, ed. George W. Forrest, Vol.II, Bombay, 1887, 179–85.

[29] In this *pargana* according to the same Collector, even in this very year, a much higher proportion of the measured land was actually cultivated in lands held revenue-free or on special tenures. The percentage was as high as 83.18% in the 'Garshiya' lands, 74.01% in the 'Germia' and 'Valluddenrial' lands and 85.67% in the 'Pusayta' lands (ibid., 183–5).

the various districts have been reduced in the proportion which the area of the part of each district coming under a *sarkār* bears to the total area of the district. Building up figures for all the parts of different districts that make up the whole or large part of one *sarkār*, we get the ratio of the gross cultivation in 1903–4 to the total area of the *sarkār*. Since some small areas within the *sarkār* lie outside the districts/states for which we have information, we have taken the ratios of gross cultivation to the total area in the reporting territory within each *sarkār*, and have applied it to the map area of the whole *sarkār*, to obtain our estimate of gross cultivation for 1903–4. Acres have been converted into *bīgha-i ilāhī*, to complete our Table 2.9.

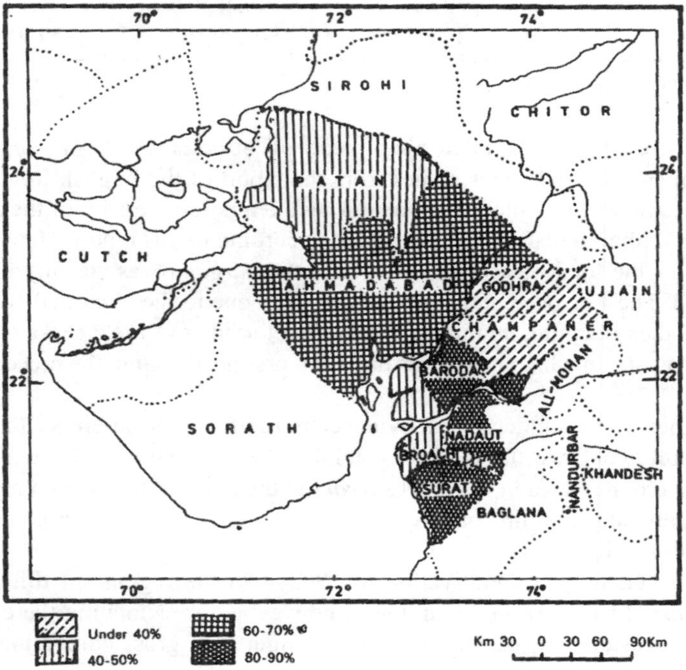

Map II GUJARAT
Extent of gross cultivation in 1595 as % of gross cultivation in 1909–10

The table shows that the ratio of gross cultivation in 1595 to gross cultivation in 1903–4 varies considerably from tract to tract (Map II). In Baroda and Surat the gross cultivation in 1595 approximates nine-tenths of that of 1903–4; but it is only about one-third in Godhra and a little over a quarter in Champaner. Such variations are plausible in that both the *sarkārs* of Champaner and Godhra contained hilly territory, then covered by forests. The high level of cultivation in 1595 in *sarkār* Surat is a little surprising since it contained timber forests famous for long afterwards for the teak used in building ships. The general conclusion that emerges from these figures is that the relative extent of the area under cultivation in Gujarat *c.*1595 in comparison with the gross cultivation during the first decade of this century was a little above that in U.P., but within the same range—i.e., between one-half and three-fifths.[30]

IV

Another region for which *ārāẓī* statistics are given in the *Ā'īn* in sufficient detail for us to attempt a comparison with modern land-use data, is the old British province of the Panjab (excluding, however, the Panjab Hill States). This corresponded roughly to portions of the Mughal *ṣūba* of Delhi lying west of the Yamuna; *ṣūba* of Lahore (excluding the hill territories) and the *ṣūba* of Multan (excluding the *sarkār* of Bhakkar).

The extent of measurement in the *ṣūba* of Delhi, west of the Yamuna (henceforth designated 'East Panjab' by us), can be judged from the ratios of *jama'*:*ārāẓī* and *ārāẓī*:map area worked out below:

Sarkār	A as % of M	J/A (in *dāms* per *bīgha*)
Rewari	90.16	24.94
Hissar Firuza	22.09	17.15
Sirhind	62.22	20.79
Delhi (west of Yamuna)	89.49	14.46

Since the *ārāẓī* in *sarkār* Rewari exceeded 90 per cent of its total area, it follows that measurement here should have been practically complete.

30 This is at variance with Habib's finding relating to Gujarat in *Agrarian System*, 19, rev. ed. 18, that 'when we compare the *Ā'īn*'s area with modern returns of cultivable area from the corresponding territory, the difference in favour of the latter is found only to be slight.' Presumably this is due to some undercalculation on his part of the modern area figures.

The *jama':ārāẓī* of this *sarkār* (24.94 *dāms*/*bīgha*) can therefore be taken to represent the normal level for areas where measurement was complete. Hence in any *sarkār* where the *jama':ārāẓī* is about or less than 25 *dāms* per *bīgha*, measurement of the assessable land may be considered to have been complete. Significantly, this is the case in all the *sarkārs* comprising our 'East Panjab' and we can thus assume with a reasonable degree of confidence that in this area, little cultivated land was left unsurveyed in the time of the *Ā'īn*.

To keep to a minimum the chances of error arising out of matching the British districts and native states with the individual Mughal *sarkārs*, it is better to treat the whole of East Panjab as one block for working out the gross cultivation for 1595 from the *ārāẓī* figures. For this, the ratios of the gross cropped-area to the total map area (GC/M) and of cultivable waste to the total cultivable land (CW/C) in 1909–10 have been calculated for all the corresponding districts together. From this we can get the gross cropped-area in 1595, according to assumptions already explained. Since the limits of the Mughal *ṣūba* of Delhi west of the Yamuna do not exactly correspond to the British East Panjab (excluding hill states), the gross cultivation of 1909–10 for the Mughal limits has been estimated by multiplying the latter's map area by the GC/M of the British limits. The final results are as follows (in *bīgha-i Ilāhī*):

(a) GC. 1595	(b) GC 1909–10	(c) (a) as % of (b)
1,22,49,686	2,74,01,085	44.705

The *ṣūba* of Lahore (excluding the northern hilly tracts), constituting the second block ('West Panjab', comprising all territory west of the Sutlej) displays a far more complex situation than 'East Panjab', and the comparative data for each of the five *doābs* comprising it have to be examined separately.

For the territories of the British districts roughly corresponding to each *doāb*, the CW/C and GC/M have been worked out for 1909–10. Following our standard assumptions, I have allowed 10 per cent for uncultivable waste and then reduced the remaining *ārāẓī* of each *doāb* by the CW/C of 1909–10 in the corresponding British districts.

If measurement was then complete, this modified *ārāẓī* (A′) should be equal to the gross cropped-area in 1595. On the other hand, by applying the GC/M of the corresponding British districts to the map area of each *doāb*, we get the estimated gross cropped-area of the latter for 1909–10. If the gross land revenue (J′)[31] of each *doāb* is now divided by A′ we should get the gross revenue realization per *bīgha* of actual cultivation (Table 2.10).

Table 2.10

Gross Revenue Realisation per *bīgha*

*Doāb**	A′ 1595	GC 1909–10	A′ as % of GC 1909–10	J′/A′
Bet Jalandhar	30,12,640	33,47,546	90.00	57.10
Bari	28,32,560	34,82,323	81.34	67.67
Rachnao	22,74,563	59,41,830	38.28	104.37
Chanhat	12,57,143	27,47,143	45.76	68.31
Sindh Sagar	5,22,262	1,65,14,975	3.16	129.82

* The Himalyan tract have been excluded from all the Doābs.

In the Bet Jalandhar *doāb*, A′ in 1595 was 90 per cent of GC in 1909–10; in the Bari *doāb*, it was 81 per cent. It is a fair assumption, then, that in both these *doābs* measurement was more or less complete in 1595. The incidence of land-revenue per *bīgha* of cultivation is nearly 57 *dāms* in Bet Jalandhar and about 68 *dāms* in Bari. These figures would give us the range expected wherever A′ represented the gross cropped-area of 1595. But in those *doābs* where J′/A′ is substantially above these figures, A′ cannot possibly be taken as representing the entire gross cultivation. Such is the position in the Rachnao and Sindh Sagar *doābs*. For these *doābs* the gross cropped-area must then be worked out by dividing the total land revenue (J′) by 57.10 (this being the J′/A′ in Bet Jalandhar).

The range for J′/A′, as well as its lower limit (57.10), in West Panjab is higher than in U.P. This seems plausible since even the gross land revenue per *bīgha* of map area was higher in this region than in U.P.[32]

That the J′/A′ of the Bet Jalandhar *doāb* can be used for this purpose is supported by the existence of a curious fact, viz., the use of a certain ratio of J′/A′ by the Mughal administration for filling in *ārāẓī* figures for certain *maḥals*. In 16 *maḥals* in Bet Jalandhar, 5 in Rachnao, 3 in

[31] As worked out in Chapter 5.

[32] See Chapter 5.

Chanhat, and 15 in Sindh Sagar *doāb*, round figures of *jama'* are accompanied by detailed *ārāẓī* figures. Closer scrutiny reveals that the *ārāẓī* figures are not the results of measurement, but are simply determined by dividing the *jama'* figures by 39.8 (and in the case of Sindh Sagar *doāb*, uniformly, by 41.2).[33] Clearly then the Mughal officials thought that every 40 *dāms* or so of *jama'* presupposed a *bīgha* of *ārāẓī* in the Panjab *doābs*. This happens to be surprisingly close to the actual simple J/A in the Bet Jalandhar *doāb*, which works out at 37.6, the J′/A′ being naturally higher (57.10).

We can, therefore, take it that the ratio of J′ to A′ in the Bet Jalandhar *doāb* (plains-*maḥals*) can be used with some confidence to work out the A′ of those portions of the Panjab where the Mughal survey was manifestly incomplete.

Our estimates of gross cultivation in 1595 recalculated on the above basis for the various *doābs* are set out in Table 2.11.

Table 2.11

Gross Cultivation 1595

Doāb	(a) GC 1595	(b) GC 1909–10	(c) (a) as % of (b)
Bet Jalandhar	30,12,640	33,47,546	90.00
Bari	28,32,506	34,82,323	81.34
Rachnao	41,64,715*	59,41,830	70.09
Chanhat	12,57,143	27,47,058	45.76
Sindh Sagar	12,87,847*	1,65,14,975	7.80
Total	1,25,54,851	3,20,33,732	39.19

*Gross cropped-area calculated from gross land-revenue.

While the results for all the *doābs* lie within the range of probability, the Sindh Sagar *doāb* forms an exception with an impossibly low figure for the gross cultivated area. There might be two reasons for this: either most of the area was really uninhabited and uncultivated or the zone was left largely to chiefs from whom only nominal tribute was demanded: the *jama'* assigned was so inordinately low. The second alternative seems more likely since this was the region of the powerful Ghakkar *zamīndārs*. Significantly enough, the *jama'* in 17 out of a total of 39 *parganas* is in round figures (rounded to a thousand and above) suggesting a fixed

[33] See Appendix 2.B for an examination of these statistics.

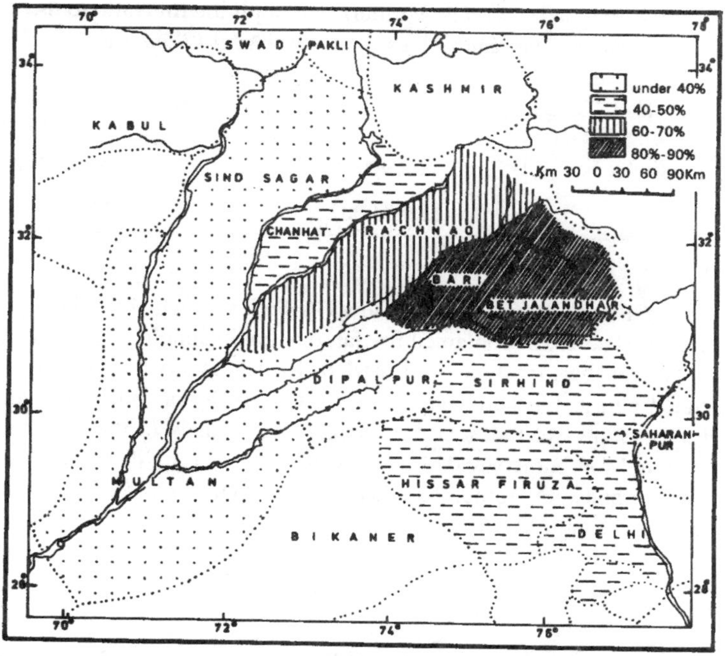

Map III PANJAB
Extent of gross cultivation in 1995 as % of gross cultivation in 1909–10

revenue claim, presumably fixed low as a concession to the Ghakkar chiefs or the *jāgīrdārs* to whom the area was assigned.

In the two *sarkārs* of Multan and Dipalpur belonging to *ṣūba* Multan and comprising our third block, 'South Panjab', the *ārāẓī* is only 4.5 per cent of the map area. Even if we exclude the Bairūn Panjnad and Sindh Sagar *doāb* of the Multan *sarkār*, the measured area of the block comes to less than one-tenth of the map area. This means that the *ārāẓī* here can be of little help in estimating the extent of cultivation. However, the gross cropped-area may possibly be estimated from the *jama'* statistics. It is difficult to get the incidence of land revenue in this region; nevertheless we can perhaps apply the limit that we have set for the adjoining block of West Panjab, i.e., 57.10 *dāms* per *bīgha*. The gross cropped-area of 1909–10 can then be estimated by calculating the GC/M for districts covering the bulk of the area of the two *sarkārs* (excluding Sindh Sagar and Bairun Panjnad of *sarkār* Multan), and applying this ratio to the map area of the block. The resulting estimates in *bīgha-i ilāhi* are:

(a) GC 1595	(b) GC 1909–10	(c) (a) as % of (b)
27,82,953	1,09,74,007	25.36

This indicates an exceptionally low GC for 1595, which is not entirely surprising. The block contained the famous Lakhi Jungle,[34] and it is also possible that the irrigation from modern British canals has considerably extended cultivation here. Indeed, according to the official *Agricultural Statistics,* 1909–10, the area now irrigated by canals in the districts of Ferozepur, Montgomery and Multan (corresponding roughly to the Mughal territory in question) amounted to as high a proportion as 52.3 per cent of the total gross cultivation.

V

An estimation of the extent of cultivation in other parts of Akbar's empire does not seem immediately possible. For large areas, the *Ā'īn* offers no *ārāẓī* statistics at all, as in the case of the *ṣūba* of Bengal and parts of Bihar[35] and Ajmer. In other territories the *ārāẓī* recorded is so

[34] For which see Sujān Rā'i Bhandārī, *Khulāṣtu't Tawārīkh* (written 1695), ed. Zafar Hasan, Delhi, 1918, 63.

[35] The *Ā'īn* offers *ārāẓī* statistics for all *sarkārs* of Bihar except Monghyr but they are uniformly low and in most cases, nominal. Under the *sarkār* of Monghyr, no *ārāẓī* figures are furnished for any *pargana* whatsoever. It is, therefore, rather surprising that there should exist 'Raqba-bandi documents of Akbar's Reign' from *pargana* Bhagalpur of this *sarkār*, which B.R. Grover has introduced in *Indian Historical Records Commission, Proceedings,* Volume XXXVI, Part ii, 35–60. It seems from Grover's own description that the documents belong to that class of 18th century revenue-literature where everything was ascribed to Todar Mal. The documents are entitled '*Raqba-bandi Todar Mali 1001 Fasli wa Tappah-bandi*'. Todar Mal had died three years before 1001 *Fasli* and so the ascription of the figures to him is simply out of ignorance. The name of some *tappas* like Azimnagar, Shujanagar and Azimabad also suggest a later date since these places were obviously named after Princes Shuja' and Aẓīmush Shān. Satisfaction is expressed by Grover that this document (allegedly of 1593) and another of 1771 'enumerate the same tappahs along with their respective mauzas, even though with a gap of 178 years of record (*sic*)' (ibid., p.55). The identity of contents surely proves, if nothing else, that the 'gap of 178 years' is illusory.

small (e.g. hardly 12 per cent of the map area in Malwa) that the measured area could have covered only a small fraction of the area under cultivation.

Even to work out a rough estimate on the basis of *jama'* figures only, dispensing with the *ārāẓī* altogether, as we have done for certain limited areas within U.P. and the Panjab, would be too risky an exercise. The incidence of *jama'* must have varied largely from region to region depending upon the price level, productivity of land, crop pattern and degree of Mughal administrative control. Some areas too might have been held on concessional rates as was probably the case, for example, with the *dastūr*-circle of Amber in *ṣūba* Ajmer.[36] In some tracts, again, the gross cultivation in the early years of the present century in the corresponding territory is not easy to establish, due to the problem of identification of the *Ā'īn*'s *parganas* and the resulting difficulty in using modern land-use statistics. Outside U.P., Gujarat and the Panjab, then, it is not possible to form any estimates of the extent of cultivation.

However, it may not be very wrong to generalize from the results we have obtained for the three regions where some means of estimation have been available. These together covered about 31 per cent of the total area and might well have contained about 32 per cent of the population (going by the 1911 census) of the territories of the Mughal empire (excluding the *ṣūba* of Kabul, but including the *sarkār* of Kashmir).

Quite naturally, within these regions, the relative extent of cultivation varied: at one extreme (the Agra block) cultivation in 1595 reached 98 per cent of that of 1909–10; at the other extreme (Rohilkhand), it was around 27 per cent. (In Gorakhpur block, it was as low as 6 per cent, but the figures are somewhat dubious.) But when larger areas are considered, the range is between two-fifths and three-fifths of the gross cultivation of the early years of this century.

If, then, we take U.P., Gujarat and Panjab together and compare the gross cultivation *c.*1595 with that of *c.*1910, we get the following picture (figures in *bīgha-i Ilāhī*).

	(a) GC *c.*1595	(b) GC *c.1910*	(c) (a) as % of (b)
U.P.	3,47,12,036	6,56,98,893	52.84
Gujarat	1,17,22,604	2,02,29,592	57.95
Panjab	2,75,87,490	7,04,08,824	39.19
Total	7,40,22,130	15,63,37,309	47.35

[36] See Chapter 4.

One may therefore hazard the conclusion that at the close of the sixteenth century the area of gross cultivation in Akbar's empire was approximately half of what it was at the beginning of this century.

There is, however, one important reservation. We have assumed, while arriving at our figures, that Mughal officials included uncultivable waste to the extent of 10 per cent of the entire measured area; and that they measured as much of cultivable waste in proportion to gross cultivation as has been done by modern surveyors. The assumptions probably overstate the coverage of these categories in Mughal statistics. Our estimate of gross cultivation for 1595 may then be an underestimate in the same proportion. It is, therefore, likely that the actual gross cultivation in 1595 was higher than 50 per cent of the gross cultivation in 1909–10. It could, for example, well reach 53 to 55 per cent, if we set the possible margin of error at 10 or 15 per cent over the total given above (47.35 per cent). It is unlikely, however, that it could have gone up much beyond these levels.

APPENDIX 2.A
Gross cropped-area, by *dastūr*-circles

Calculations of gross cropped-area have been made according to methods explained in Chapter 2.

			Gross Cropped-Area (*bīgha-i ilāhī*)	
Dastūr-circle	*Sarkār*	*Ṣūba*	1595	1910–10
North-West U.P.				
Deoband	Saharanpur	Delhi	20,34,333	22,29,465
Sardhana	,,	,,	5,90,602	6,12,370
Chandpur	Sambhal	,,	10,31,021	10,87,223
Sambhal	,,	,,	19,74,562	26,03,658
Lakhnaur	,,	,,	5,26,579	11,72,209
Kairana	Saharanpur	,,	2,18,192	1,40,976
Total			63,75,289	78,45,901
DELHI				
Delhi	Delhi	Delhi	14,80,307	24,50,073
Meerut	,,	,,	11,96,158	13,10,590
Baran	,,	,,	5,92,411	8,67,669
Total			32,68,876	46,28,332

(*Continued*)

APPENDIX 2.A (*Continued*)

Dastūr-circle	*Sarkār*	*Ṣūba*	Gross Cropped-Area (*bīgha-i ilāhī*) 1595	1910–10
ROHILKHAND				
Badaun	Badun	Delhi	13,62,064	50,05,895
Bharwara	Khairabad	Awadh	19,752	4,06,174
Pali	,,	,,	5,21,514	14,92,018
Total			19,03,330	69,04,087
MIDDLE DOĀB				
Thana Farida	Kol	Agra	5,71,831	13,20,210
Akbarabad	,,	,,	3,55,714	4,49,354
Kol	,,	,,	6,73,556	8,08,113
Marahra	,,	,,	3,14,067	2,42,588
Sikandarpur Atreji	Kanauj	,,	2,42,280	70,223
Total			21,57,448	28,90,488
AGRA				
Agra	Agra	,,	21,25.267	21,62,269
LOWER DOAB (Yumuna)				
Etawa	Agra	Agra	13,15,155	10,88,003
Phaphund	Kanaun	,,	2,21,952	2,69,460
Kalpi	Kalpi	,,	10,20,227	17,16,375
Total			25,57,334	30,73,838
LOWER DOAB (Ganga)				
Sakit	Kanauj	Agra	3,32,824	5,69,992
Bhogaon	,,	,,	11,35,451	16,68,350
Kanauj	,,	,,	6,33,238	12,75,323
Total			21,01,513	35,13,665
LUCKNOW				
Khairabad	Khairabad	Awadh	8,34,522	20,48,825
Unam	Lucknow	,,	5,42,901	8,67,395
Lucknow	,,	,,	19,50,369	37,33,943
Ibrahimabad	Awadh	,,	14,040	78,000
Awadh	,,	,,	20,40,478	25,20,718
Kishni	,,	,,	54,719	24,053
Total			54,37,029	92,72,934

(*Continued*)

APPENDIX 2.A (*Continued*)

Dastūr-circle	*Sarkār*	*Ṣūba*	Gross Cropped-Area (*bīgha-i ilāhī*) 1595	1910–10
NORTH-EAST U.P.				
Bahraich	Bahraich	Awadh	11,60,319	26,08,842
Firuzabad	,,	,,	1,07,400	2,81,413
Total			12,67,719	28,90,255
GORAKHPUR				
Gorakhpur	Gorakhpur	Awadh	4,87,295	90,97,370
Khuronsa	Bahraich	,,	53,729	5,15,671
Total			5,41,024	96,13,041
SOUTH-EAST U.P.				
Jaunpur	Jaunpur	Allahabad	22,49,549	53,33,617
Banaras	Banaras	,,	3,62,020	5,39,938
Chunar	Chunar	,,	2,37,419	14,15,454
Ghazipur	Ghazipur	,,	5,60,953	6,99,881
Total			34,09,939	79,88,890
ALLAHABAD				
Jajmau	Kora	Allahabad	2,05,523	2,47,158
Kara	Kara	,,	8,54,489	11,19,832
Kutia	Kora	,,	78,766	1,92,307
Korra	,,	,,	4,26,485	5,92,832
Rai Bareily	Manikpur	,,	3,71,189	5,63,956
Manikpur	,,	,,	9,94,115	14,22,047
Ghiswa	Jaunpur	,,	42,641	31,532
Bhadoi	Allahabad	,,	5,94,060	7,45,529
Total			35,67,268	49,15,193
Grand Total			3,47,12,036	6,56,98,893

APPENDIX 2.B

Certain ārāẓī statistics from ṣūba Lahore

The *jama'* and *ārāẓī* statistics of *ṣūba* Lahore contain a curious peculiarity, viz. in a number of *maḥals* belonging to the *doābs* of Bet Jalandhar, Rachnao, Chanhat and Sindh Sagar the *ārāẓī* stands in a practically fixed ratio to the *jama'*. In the case of *maḥals* in the first three *doābs* it is around 39.8 *dāms* and in the Sindh Sagar *Doāb*, it is exactly 41.2 (barring the *maḥal* of Bel

Ghazi Khan where the J/A is 41.32). Against most of these *parganas* (31 out of a total of 39) the *jama'* is given in round numbers (rounded to 1000 and above). *Suyūrghāl* figures are not entered against any of these *maḥals*.

One can see from Table A.1 that in these *parganas* the *ārāẓī* was not actually measured but has been worked out from the *jama'* figures by assuming a fixed incidence of the *jama'* per *bīgha* of *ārāẓī*. It is, of course, inconceivable for the reverse to have happened, i.e., for the *jama'* to have been worked out from the *ārāẓī* on the basis of the same fixed ratio: for in that case, the *jama'* attained could not possibly have been in round numbers. The *jama'* for these *parganas* seems, for the same reason, to have been the result of a more or less arbitrary estimate. Practically all these *parganas* were situated in the Himalayas or the Salt Range controlled by hill-Rajput *zamīndārs* and the Ghakkars and Januha (*Janjua*) chiefs (This cannot be definitely said, however, of those two *parganas* (both in Bet Jalandhar, whose geographical location has not been traced, and for which the *Ā'īn* enters no *zamīndārs*.) The absence of *suyūrghāl* figures strengthens the assumption that these areas were outside the limits of full-fledged Mughal administration. The nominal nature of Mughal control is also reflected in other limitations of the *Ā'īn*'s information: the *zamīndārs*' castes and the numbers of their retainers (*sawār* and *piyāda*) are not provided in as many as eight of these *parganas*.

It would seem, then, that for some reason which is not easy to establish, either Abū'l Faẓl or the officials who supplied information to him wanted to furnish *ārāẓī* figures for these *maḥals*, although no survey had taken place here. The rate of 40 *dāms* to the *bīgha* was applied to the *jama'* figures in order to obtain a theoretical *ārāẓī*, which was increased further by a minute fraction, so that the ratio fell below 40 *dāms* to about 39.8. In the Sindh Sagar *Doāb*, a rate of 41 *dāms*, 5 *jītals* to the *bīgha* was uniformly used for the same purpose.

The fact that the rate approximated to 40 *dāms* leads one to offer one possible suggestion for the two ratios. To begin with, what the officials had in mind was clearly the rate of one rupee per *bīgha*. Since the *jama'* was stated in *dāms*, the rupee needed to be converted into *dāms*. Since the rupee–*dām* rate fluctuated around 40 *dāms*, as stated by Abū'l Faẓl himself,[37] different rates might have prevailed if the calculations for the Sindh Sagar *doāb* and the other *doābs* were made at different times. Suppose that when the officials were recording the returns of the Sindh Sagar *doāb*, the prevailing value of the rupee was 41 *dāms*, 5 *jītals*, it would have been natural for them to use this rate to obtain the *ārāẓī*. In case the returns of the other *doābs* were prepared at some other time, when the rate was 40 *dāms* or just

[37] *Ā'īn*, I, p.27.

three or four *jītals* short of it, this rate would be applied to the *jama'* of the *parganas* lying within these *doābs*. At the moment, this seems the most plausible explanation for the two variant but closely approximate rates.

Table A.1

Pargana	*Ārāẓī* (*bīgha biswa*)	*Jama'* (*dāms*)	J/A	Geographical
BET JALANDHAR DOĀB				
Bhalwan	32,761	13,05,000	39.83	Not traced; but *zamīndār* Hill Rajput (Dudhwal)
Jaswan Balkoli	15,054	6,00,000	39.86	Himalayas
Dada	30,218	12,00,000	39.71	Himalayas
Dardhi	15,054	6,00,000	39.86	Not traced; but *zamīndār* Hill Rajput (Bansi)
Doon Nakur	11,430	4,55,870	39.88	Not traced
Sukat Mandi	42,150	16,80,000	39.86	Himalayas
Seba	20,114–8	8,00,000	39.77	Himalayas
Kotla	42,152	16,80,000	39.86	Not traced; but *zamīndār* Hill Rajput (Jasrotia)
Kotkher	32,932–16	13,10,847	39.80	Himalayas
Khewan Khera	6,021–6	2,40,000	39.86	Not traced; but *zamīndār*, Hill Rajput (Jaswal)
Kankot	6,021–6	2,40,000	39.86	Not traced; but *zamīndār* Hill Rajput (Jaswal)
Khera	6,021–6	2,40,000	39.86	Not traced; but *zamīndār* Hill Rajput ('Suraj Bansi')
Nakrok	32,642	13,00,061	39.83	Not traced; but *zamīndār* Hill Rajput (Jaswal)
Nandun	1,33,439	53,00,000	39.72	Himalayas
Kharak Dhar	12,043	4,80,000	39.86	Not traced, and no *zamīndār* caste entered
RACHNAO DOĀB				
Bhalot	20,612	8,18,182	39.69	Not traced; but *zamīndār* Hill Rajput ('Malanhas', mod. Manhas)
Bhilaura	6,021	2,40,000		Himalayas
Bhotiyal	2,407–18	96,000	39.86	Himalayas

(*Continued*)

Table A.1 (*Continued*)

Pargana	*Ārāẓī* (*bīgha biswa*)	*Jama'* (*dāms*)	J/A	Geographical
Jari Jana	6,021–6	2,40,000	39.86	Not traced; but *zamīndār* Hill Rajput ('Gawalyari', mod. Goleri)
Hiantal	6,021–6	2,40,000	39.86	Himalayas
CHHANHAT DOĀB				
Akhandui	9,866–5	3,92,000	39.73	Himalayas
Bhadu	4,817	1,92,000	39.86	Not traced; but *zamīndār* Hill Rajput ('Bhadwal')
Magli	10,839	4,32,000	39.86	Himalayas
SINDH SAGAR DOĀB				
Awan	10,096	4,15,970	41.20	Salt Range
Bel Ghazi Khan	17,426	7,20,000	41.32	Locations as given in Irfan Habib's Sheet 4A, *An Atlas of the Mughal Empire*, doubtful; *zamīndār*-caste Januha (Janua), whose *maḥals* are situated entirely in the Salt Range.
Thirchak Dhamir	6,082	2,50,575	41.20	Not traced; but *zamīndār* Ghakkar, and so probably in the Salt Range.
Dharab	2,330	96,000	41.20	Salt Range
Dodot	2,330	96,000	41.20	Not traced; but *zamīndār* Januha of the Salt Range
Kahwan	4,660	1,92,000	41.20	Not traced; but *zamīndār* Samker of the Salt Range
Kanbat	2,330	96,000	41.20	Not traced; no *zamīndār* caste entered
Langa Hatiyar	2,330	96,000	41.20	Not traced; no *zamīndār* caste entered
Makhiala	9,320	3,84,000	41.20	Salt Range
Maral	5,825	2,40,000	41.20	Salt Range
Malot	3,233	1,33,233	41.21	Salt Range

(*Continued*)

Table A.1 (*Continued*)

Pargana	*Ārāẓī* (*bīgha biswa*)	*Jama‘* (*dāms*)	J/A	Geographical
Hathiyar Lang	7,281	3,00,000	41.20	Not traced; but *zamīndār* Ghakkar (Salt Range)
Hazara Gojran	6,575	2,70,896	41.20	Salt Range
Himamat Khan Karamu	1,165	4,80,000	41.20	Not traced; but *zamīndār* Ghakkar (Salt Range)
Patala	15,146	6,24,000	41.20	Not traced; but *zamīndār* Januha (Salt Range)

CHAPTER 3

Agricultural Productivity

Crops and Yields

I

On agricultural productivity the *Ā'īn-i Akbarī* provides us direct information in the form of schedules of crop-yields and revenue-rates. These, so far as one can judge from Abū'l Faẓl's words, represent the *'rai's'* prepared by Sher Shāh's administration.[1] The yields are given for land under continuous or practically continuous cultivation (*polaj* and *parauti*). For each crop three estimates of yields per *bīgha* are furnished, namely, for: high (*gazīda*, *a'lā*), middling (*miyāna*) and low (*zubūn*). An average is then struck by simply dividing by three the total of the three yields. The land-revenue, purporting to be a third of the produce, is worked out by dividing this average again by three. Thus at the end we get the amount of the produce of each crop per *bīgha* claimed by the State by way of land revenue.

Abū'l Faẓl does not mention the basis on which the three categories of land (good, middling and bad) were distinguished. The classification could have been made either according to soil fertility or availability of irrigation, or both. It would perhaps be a fair assumption that the 'low' yield was that of unirrigated land, while the 'high' and 'middling' were those of irrigated land. In modern official returns too, beginning at least with 1892, estimates are provided separately for unirrigated and irrigated lands. It is therefore possible to compare the yield of the 'low' category of lands in Sher Shāh's schedule with modern estimates of yields of

[1] *Ā'īn*, I, 298. See W.H. Moreland, 'Sher Shāh's Revenue System', *JRAS*, London, 1926, 447–59, for an interpretation of the *rai'*-schedule.

unirrigated lands. Similarly, the high and middling yields of Sher Shāh's schedule may be compared with modern estimated yields for irrigated lands.

A question more difficult to answer is, how far the simple average of the three yields taken by Sher Shāh's (and Akbar's) officials can be held to represent the average overall yield of each crop. For it to so serve, one would have to make the naïve assumption that the area with each level of yield (good, middling, bad) under each crop was exactly one-third of the total land under that crop. This would of course, be far from reality. Some crops require more irrigation than others and are raised to a larger extent in irrigated lands. Other crops are almost exclusively grown on unirrigated lands, so much so that even estimates of yields on irrigated lands are not furnished for them in modern statistics.[2] It follows that the average yield calculated by Sher Shāh's officials must have exceeded the real average yield quite considerably in the case of inferior crops raised on indifferently-watered lands, while it was possibly lower than the real average in that of high-grade crops, normally requiring much artificial irrigation.

The area to which Sher Shāh's schedules applied is not defined. But one can reasonably suppose that they applied mostly to Delhi, the Doāb region and Haryana. It is also not made clear whether the units of area and weights used here are those in force at the time the *rai's* were framed by Sher Shāh or those prevalent *c.*1595, when Abū'l Faẓl incorporated the data into the *Ā'īn*. Since many figures are in complete *mans*, it is probable that the figures are not converted, i.e., they are in terms of the original units used in Sher Shāh's time. At the beginning of Akbar's reign (and so presumably under Sher Shāh), the *man* was based on a *ser* equal to 28 *dāms*' weight and not 30 (the standard set for the *ser* of *man-i Akbarī*).[3] Similarly the *bīgha* under Sher Shāh was based on the *gaz-i Sikandarī* which was 39/41 of *gaz-i Ilāhī*,[4] implying that the earlier *bīgha* was 37/41 of *bīgha-i Ilāhī*. Now, since both the units of weight and area were smaller than the corresponding units, *c.*1595, the former by only 6.7 per cent, the latter by 9.5 per cent, the figures of yields would increase only very marginally (by 2.8 per cent), if one were to restate the yields in terms of *man-i Akbarī* per *bīgha-i Ilāhī*. I have therefore ignored the difference.

[2] In the official *Agricultural Statistics,* the yields of many crops are given only for irrigated land, such as of sugarcane, while for bajra and jowar the yields are recorded for dry land only.

[3] Habib, *Agrarian System*, 367–8 (rev. ed. 420–21).

[4] Ibid., 353–6 (rev. ed., 406–9).

II

Reliable modern estimates of agricultural productivity are obtainable from the second half of the nineteenth century. They are in the first stage found mainly in Settlement Reports and District Gazetteers, while the official *Agricultural Statistics,* begun in 1884–85, give five-yearly estimates of yields from 1892 onwards. These are furnished district-wise and have separate figures for irrigated lands. From 1893 the crop-cutting method was introduced to determine the yields; until 1892 the estimates were 'based on the then available material, namely, the various statistical publications, such as the periodical agricultural and settlement reports, crop forecasts, replies received in response to enquiries from the Famine Commission and other *ad hoc* bodies.'[5]

The 1892 estimates seem the most suitable for comparison with the *Ā'īn*'s figures, since this would meet the possible objection that crop-cutting yields are too sophisticated to be set alongside the estimates made by Mughal officials.[6] Without entering into a discussion of how far this is a tenable objection, one would expect in any case that the estimates by Mughal and British officials (before the crop-cutting method came into use), were made under similar compulsions (revenue assessment), and by similar methods, and thus are broadly comparable, the margin of exaggeration, if any, being the same in both cases. But it is worth noting that a comparison of the yields of 1892 and 1908 in the *Agricultural Statistics* reveals hardly any change, at least in the areas covered by us, so that it would have mattered very little if the estimates based on 'crop-cutting' had been used by us in our comparisons.

Table 3.1 (a) below gives the yields of six major crops from irrigated lands for the districts of the Doāb and Delhi alongside the averages of Sher Shāh's 'high' and 'middling' yields. Table 3.1 (b) shows the yields of unirrigated land for the same districts and Sher Shāh's 'low' yields. Table 3.1(c) and 3.1 (d) offer similar comparative data for a set of Haryana and eastern Panjab districts. All modern quantities are converted into *man-i Akbarī* per *bīgha-i Ilāhī*.

The tables suggest that the mean of the *Ā'īn*'s high and middling yields is only slightly higher than the 1892 estimates for the Doāb districts for irrigated lands in the case of wheat, barley and gram; but it is much lower for sugarcane. In unirrigated lands the approximation of the *Ā'īn*'s low yields with modern estimated yields of wheat, barley, bajra

[5] *Agricultural Statistics*, part 1, 18th issue, 1904, xxiii.

[6] Cf. A.W. Heston, 'The Standard of Living in Akbar's Time—A Comment', *IESHR*, Vol.XIV, No.3 (July–September 1977), 391–6.

Table 3.1(a)

Crop Yields from Irrigated Lands (Doāb and Delhi) (*man-i Akbarī* per *bīgha-i Ilāhī*)

	Wheat	Barley	Gram	Bajra	Jowar	Cotton	Sugarcane	Mustard	Sesame
Ā'īn (Mean of high and middling yields)	15.00	15.25	11.75	9.0	11.75	8.75	11.75	9.5	·7.0
1892									
Delhi	12.13	10.41	—	—	—	—	15.62	6.1	—
Agra	10.67	14.32	10.67	—	—	—	—	—	—
Aligarh	16.01	14.23	10.67	—	—	6.13	22.23	—	—
Bulandshahr	14.21	14.23	10.67	—	—	6.13	22.23	—	—
Etawa	13.34	14.23	—	—	—	5.25	26.68	—	—
Etah	13.34	14.23	10.67	—	—	—	22.23	—	—
Muttra	14.21	14.23	8.89	—	—	5.52	17.79	—	—
Saharanpur	13.34	14.23	10.67	—	—	6.13	17.79	—	—
Muzaffarnagar	13.34	14.22	10.67	—	—	6.13	22.23	—	—
Mean, 1892	13.40	13.81	10.42	—	—	5.93	20.85	6.10	—

Table 3.1(b)

Crop Yields from Unirrigated Lands (Doāb and Delhi) (*man-i Akbarī* per *bīgha -i Ilāhī*)

	Wheat	Barley	Gram	Bajra	Jowar	Cotton	Sugarcane	Mustard	Sesame
Ā'īn (low yields)	8.87	8.12	7.5	7.50	5.02	5.0	7.5	5.13	4.0
1892									
Delhi	5.29	5.60	3.84	3.64	3.84	3.68	—	2.0	—
Agra	5.34	7.11	5.33	6.20	—	—	—	—	4.45
Aligarh	10.67	9.78	7.11	8.89	7.11	3.68	—	5.34	3.80
Bulandshahr	9.76	9.78	7.11	7.11	6.23	3.68	—	5.34	3.80
Etawa	6.23	7.11	5.34	—	—	—	—	—	4.45
Etah	6.23	7.12	7.00	7.00	—	—	—	4.45	
Muttra	9.76	9.78	4.45	6.23	5.34	—	—	—	4.45
Saharanpur	8.89	9.78	7.11	—	4.89	3.68	—	4.66	3.47
Muzaffarnagar	8.89	10.85	7.11	6.67	4.89	3.68	—	5.34	3.80
Mean, 1892	7.90	8.54	6.04	6.55	5.61	3.68	—	4.54	4.08

Table 3.1(c)

Crop Yields from Irrigated Lands (East Panjab and Haryana) (*man-i Akbarī* per *bīgha-i Ilahī*)

	Wheat	Barley	Gram	Bajra	Jowar	Cotton	Sugarcane	Mustard	Sesame
Ā'īn (mean of high and middling yields)	15.00	15.25	11.75	9.00	11.75	8.75	11.75	9.5	7.0
1892									
Hissar	6.31	5.20	—	2.60	3.47	—	—	3.62	—
Rohtak	10.91	10.84	12.15	4.53	8.68	—	27.77	—	—
Gurgaon	10.15	13.02	—	—	—	—	—	—	—
Karnal	9.09	9.26	3.90	4.97	3.90	—	16.49	5.64	—
Ambala	10.15	8.70	6.59	5.31	5.31	—	—	4.06	—
Ludhiana	11.76	10.98	—	—	—	—	—	8.42	—
Mean, 1892	9.72	9.70	7.55	4.35	5.34	—	22.13	5.44	—

Table 3.1(d)

Crop Yields from Unirrigated Lands (East Panjab and Haryana) (*man-i Akbarī* per *bīgha -i ilāhī*)

	Wheat	Barley	Gram	Bajra	Jowar	Cotton	Sugarcane	Mustard	Sesame
Ā'īn (low yields)	8.87	8.12	7.5	5.02	7.5	5.0	7.5	5.13	4.0
1892									
Hissar	4.75	5.18	5.27	2.56	2.75	—	—	1.26	—
Rohtak	6.25	10.84	7.98	3.47	5.29	—	—	—	—
Gurgaon	6.44	7.03	6.66	4.77	6.77	—	—	—	—
Karnal	5.40	4.90	7.81	2.99	2.52	—	7.81	5.12	—
Ambala	5.29	5.60	2.52	3.84	3.64	—	—	3.19	—
Ludhiana	6.05	3.95	5.03	—	4.49	—	—	3.68	—
Mean, 1892	5.70	6.25	5.87	3.53	4.24	—	7.81	3.32	—

and gram is quite striking. In Modern returns, estimates for jowar and bajra are not given for irrigated lands; and it is, on the other hand, assumed that sugarcane is not raised on unirrigated land. Modern (1892) yields for the Haryana districts are much lower than the yields in Sher Shāh's schedule, for both irrigated and unirrigated lands (see Tables 3.1(c) and (d)). It is possible, therefore, that Sher Shāh's schedule of yields was fixed more with an eye to the Doāb than to Haryana or the Panjab.

The comparison of yields from irrigated and dry land thus shows that, if the ratio of irrigated to dry land has remained the same, the average yield per unit of area about 1595 was probably the same as or a little above what it was in 1892. But if the proportion of irrigated land to dry land has in fact substantially risen, the modern average yield could well be higher than the average yield of Sher Shāh's time.

No information is forthcoming about the extent of irrigation in the sixteenth century, but what we know of the changes in irrigation in the second half of the nineteenth century could provide us with the means of judging how far, if at all, the ratio of irrigated to dry land has altered. The new factor during this period was almost entirely that of canals.

Table 3.2 shows the extent of total irrigated land, as well as canal-irrigated land, as a percentage of the total cultivated area during the early 1870s and the first decade of the twentieth century, in some districts of western U.P.[7]

In the 1870s then, irrigation covered between 31 to 80 per cent of the total cultivated land in the six districts, while canal irrigation was nowhere over 20 per cent of the total cultivated area. The area irrigated by canals increased markedly in the subsequent period, but the relative extent of irrigated area declined in four out of the six districts. Indeed, by and large, in western U.P. canal irrigation tended to replace well irrigation, rather than alter, in the net, the ratio of irrigated to dry land under cultivation. Not only is this fact borne out by the statistical evidence as it stands,[8] but it was also widely noted in official reports of the time.[9] The

[7] The figures for the 1870s are from Atkinson, II, 381–3; III, 23–4; IV, 21, 256, 508, 510; and for the 1910s from Nevill, IV, V, & VI (Appendix V in each vol.).

[8] The decline was not always only in relative proportion, but at times in absolute extent as well. For example, in the Bulandshahr district in 1865 the total irrigated area was 320,426 acres, of which 36,754 acres were irrigated by canals (i.e., 11.47%); in 1870 the land under irrigation had declined to 288,249 acres in absolute terms, while the area irrigated by canals increased to 121,968 acres, i.e., to 42.31% of the total irrigated area (Atkinson, Vol.III, 221–2).

[9] See W.H. Moreland, *Notes on the Agricultural Conditions of the United Provinces and of its Districts*, Allahabad, 1913.

Table 3.2

District	Total irrigated land as % of cultivated area		Canal irrigated area as % of cultivated area	
	1870s	1910s	1870s	1910s
Mainpuri	80.17	45.79	2.88	20.06
Etah	30.94	54.95	3.91	24.16
Etawa	48.29	41.67	19.13	29.80
Bulandshahr	36.98	48.35	15.61	24.06
Aligarh	72.32	47.84	10.16	16.45
Meerut	55.32	50.44	17.10	31.25

major reason for this phenomenon was that much of the irrigation before the canals came was from unlined or *kachcha* wells; and canals, by interfering with natural drainage lines, disturbed the water table and adversely affected well irrigation in many tracts.[10]

It can, therefore, be assumed that canal irrigation had not altered the relative extent of irrigation substantially in most of this region by early twentieth century. It follows that there was probably no major increase in the relative extent of irrigation between the end of the sixteenth and the close of the nineteenth century in western U.P. and the Delhi tract.

Given this as a fairly firm conclusion, it now seems possible to compare the average sixteenth-century yields with those of the nineteenth century. As has already been noted, the average yields set out in the *Ā'īn* are based on the assumption that two-thirds of the land under every crop was irrigated ('high' and 'middling') land. The assumption of a flat proportion of this kind for all crop is, of course, untenable. Irrigation must have covered varying proportions of area under different crops. Unfortunately, information about the ratios of irrigated to dry land under each crop is difficult to come by, even for the late nineteenth century. Nevertheless, it seems probable that a large part of wheat and, a lesser portion, of barley was grown on irrigated land. Irrigation would not have covered more than half of the area under gram, while bajra and jowar were mostly grown on dry land.[11]

[10] In 1870 in District Aligarh, 467,148 acres were irrigated by *kachcha* wells (Atkinson, Vol.II, p.381; *Settlement Report*, 83). In 1315 *Fasli* (1906–7), the area irrigated by wells (masonry and *kachcha*) had fallen to 282,425 acres (Nevill, Vol.VI, Appendix V).

[11] In 1871 in the district of Shahjahanpur, where only 20.2% of the total cultivated area was irrigated (the reason for this low extent of irrigation was most probably high rainfall,

As for cash crops, it seems a reasonable assumption that cultivation of indigo and sugarcane was confined to irrigated land only. Cotton, which is a *kharif* crop, needed artificial irrigation to a far smaller extent. Modern returns furnish estimates for yields of cotton on both dry and irrigated lands and one may perhaps legitimately assume that in the Delhi–Doāb area at least one-fifth of the land under cotton was irrigated. The other cash crops, mustard and sesame, mainly depended upon rainfall.[12] The *Agricultural Statistics* too give estimates of their yields on dry lands only.

Keeping in mind these facts about the degree of the major crops' dependence upon irrigation, we can attempt an estimation of the average yield for the whole of the cultivated land from the crop schedule ascribed to Sher Shāh, by simply giving different weights to the different categories of yields. For wheat, for example, we may assign 75 per cent to the mean of the high and middling yields (representing yield on irrigated land), and 25 per cent to the yield on dry land. In the case of barley, we may give equal weights to all the three yields; that is, we may assume that about 67 per cent of the land under that crop was irrigated. For gram equal weights may be given to the yield on irrigated and dry land. The estimates of yields on dry land alone should be accepted as normal yields for jowar and bajra, mustard and sesame. On the other hand, the average of the two yields on irrigated land should be taken as the standard for sugarcane. For cotton we should give to the mean of high and middling yields a weight equal to 20 per cent and to the low yield, a weight equal to 80 per cent.

The average yields from the sixteenth century, computed in this manner, can now be compared with the normal yields of the nineteenth century.

For the nineteenth century, official sources furnish estimates of normal or average yields for various crops for the Delhi and Doāb districts, for two sets of years, viz. 1841–2 and *c.*1870. For the productivity per acre of different crops in the districts of Agra, Bulandshahr, and Meerut, we have Mansel's estimates for 1841; and for Muzaffarnagar, Thornton's

which averages 39" per annum in this district), the proportion of irrigated land for various crops was as follows: wheat, 38%; barley, 27%; gram, 3%; jowar and bajra, less than 1%; indigo, 46%; sugarcane, 60%; and cotton, 39% (Atkinson, Vol.IX, 44). While this was the situation in a district where irrigation covered only a fifth of the total cultivation, in districts like Mainpuri and Aligarh, where irrigation respectively exceeded 72 and 80%, the percentage of irrigated land under wheat out of the total under the crop could hardly have been less than 75%; under other crops too it should have been correspondingly higher.

[12] Atkinson, Vol.IV, part I, 253.

estimate for 1842. These have been reproduced in Smith's *Final Settlement Report* of Aligarh.

For the years around 1870, Atkinson's volumes give the estimates of yields for certain districts. In some cases they are given straightaway for a particular district. These can, of course, be used directly. But in other cases separate estimates are offered for subdivisions, while in others still the yield of each crop is estimated separately for different soils. In these cases wherever possible, a simple mean has been taken. But it is obvious that these estimates leave much to be desired. For one thing, they are sometimes so close to, or are even higher than, the 1892 estimates for irrigated lands, that one begins to suspect that for the higher grade crops like wheat the official estimators often had in their minds crops raised on irrigated lands only.

The average yields in 1841–2 are not very different from those of *c.*1870, though the districts covered by the two sets of estimates are different, except for Agra (in whose case the two estimates are very close). Both sets of districts belong to the Delhi–Doāb region, to which Sher Shāh's *rai's* or crop-schedules may reasonably be held to apply. As such, both sets of estimated yields can be compared with the average yields deduced from Sher Shāh's *rai'*. The estimates are set out in Table 3.3.

We may now examine for each crop the data we have assembled on overall average yields for the 1540s, 1841–2, and *c.*1870 (Table 3.3), together with those on yields of irrigated and unirrigated lands in the 1540s and 1892, already set out above (Tables 3.1a and b).

Here we find that of wheat the average productivity was almost the same in the 1540s and 1841–2, but the estimated yield for 1540 is a little higher than the general estimated yield for *c.*1870.[13] The subsequent fall is more distinct still when compared with our 1892 data: furthermore it is more substantial in the case of irrigated lands, though less pronounced in that of yield on unirrigated land.

Of barley the average modern yield in 1841–2 as well as *c.*1870 is a little higher than that worked out for the 1540s; but the yield from irrigated land was higher in the sixteenth century. For unirrigated land, the yields of the two periods (1540s and 1892) are strikingly close.

[13] This is based on what Table 3.3 tells us of undifferentiated average output for 1870. For approximately that time, for the district of Etawa (Atkinson, Vol.IV, p.251), we have three estimates of wheat 'output', 18.77, 15.64, and 12.40 *man/bīgha-i Ilāhī*, on soils of different qualities. Sher Shāh's three estimates are 18, 15, and 8.87 *man/bīgha-i ilāhī.* While the first two match very well, the third as given in Sher Shāh's *rai'* is exceptionally low. This reinforces our view that Sher Shāh's low yield is not given for inferior soil but for unirrigated land.

Table 3.3

Average Crop Yields *(man-i Akbarī per bīgha-i Ilāhī)*

	Wheat	Barley	Gram	Bajra	Jowar	Cotton	Sugarcane	Mustard	Sesame
Ā'īn	13.49	12.93	9.71	5.02	7.57	5.75	11.75	5.13	4.0
1841–2									
Agra	13.33	13.07	5.17	5.42	7.87	—	—	—	—
Bulandshahr	16.26	15.89	12.58	—	—	—	—	—	—
Muzaffarnagar	8.61	9.74	6.77	3.85	4.57	—	—	—	—
Meerut	15.88	15.29	15.55	—	5.66	—	—	—	—
Mean, 1841–2	13.52	13.50	10.02	4.64	6.03	—	—	—	—
1870s									
Agra	13.13	12.34	7.69	4.23	7.12	6.15	13.39	—	—
Delhi	12.60	10.90	9.00	7.20	7.50	—	—	—	—
Aligarh	15.18	13.88	7.38	7.59	9.11	5.70	17.14	3.72	0.89
Etawa	14.06	—	—	10.85	10.85	4.78[a]	26.82	—	—
Saharanpur	15.32	20.23	16.96	7.66	4.02	6.26	18.89	10.71	4.02
Mean, 1870s	14.06	14.34	10.26	7.51	7.72	5.72	19.06	7.22	2.46

[a] The estimate for irrigated land is 6.65 and for dry 2.91.

In the case of gram, the average yield of the 1540s is slightly lower than the modern (1841–2 and *c.* 1870); but comparison with separate modern estimates for irrigated and unirrigated lands suggests a higher yield in the 1540s than in 1892.

In the case of bajra, it has been assumed that it was cultivated on unirrigated land alone. The estimated yield from the 1540s of the lowest category of land, is a little higher than the average estimate for 1841–2, but is much lower than the average worked out for *c.*1870. The estimates separately made for irrigated and unirrigated land in 1892 are also higher than the comparable yields derived from Sher Shāh's schedule in the *Ā'īn*.

For *jowar* too, the assumption is that its cultivation was confined to unirrigated land. Here we find a close approximation in the estimates for the 1540s and those of *c.*1870 and 1892. But the normal yield as estimated in 1841–2 is less than that of the 1540s.

On the whole, therefore, one can say that no major change in the productivity per acre of the major food crops seems to have occurred between the middle of the sixteenth and the end of the nineteenth century.

For sugarcane, one detects a marked increase in the productivity per acre between Sher Shāh's time and the nineteenth century.[14] The estimated yield of the irrigated land (average of 'high' and 'middling') for the 1540s is much lower than the average yield estimated for the 1870s. It is lower than the estimated yields in each one of the four districts for which estimates have been obtained for the 1870s. In fact even the *Ā'īn*'s 'high' yield (viz., 13 *man/bīgha*) is markedly lower than the average estimated in the 1870s (19.06 *man/bīgha*). The comparison with the estimates for 1892 indicates a yet greater increase by the latter year. The rise in the yields of sugarcane may possibly be attributed to the introduction of metal cane-crushers, resulting in an extraction of larger amounts of juice.[15] One can also suggest as contributory factors the introduction of new varieties of cane, and the larger supply of water through canal irrigation.

While the estimated overall averages of cotton yields for the 1540s and 1870s are about the same, the productivity separately estimated for

[14] The yield in *Ā'īn* is stated in terms of *qand-i siyāh* (lit. black sugar) and in nineteenth century statistics in terms of *gur* (jaggery).

[15] See Watt, VI, part II, 257. The iron 'Beheea mill' was introduced in 1873–4 and was soon adopted in U.P. Writing in 1893 Voelcker remarks, 'It is in the North-West Provinces (U.P.) that most advance has been made, and iron mills are almost general' (Voelcker, 276–7).

irrigated and unirrigated lands in 1892 suggests a decline for each category between 1545 and 1892.

Standard indigo yields are not stated in Sher Shāh's schedules, although it was very widely cultivated at that time. But in the 1620s, the careful Dutch factor Pelsaert made two statements, which when combined may give us an estimate of its yield in the celebrated Bayana tract close to Agra. He says, first, that the 'yield' (i.e., leaf and stalk) of one *bīgha* was put in one *put* or vat at a time and that the contents of each *put* varied from 12 to 20 *ser* of the dye, subject to a further loss of weight of about one-eighth through further drying in the course of subsequent handling.[16] Given the size of the local *bīgha* as defined by Pelsaert,[17] the average yield of the dye should have amounted to 16.59–27.66 pounds per *bīgha-i daftarī* at the vats, and 14.52–24.20 pounds after transportation.

Unluckily, this estimate cannot be compared with many modern estimates where the yield is stated in terms of the green plant. Even where we get the estimates in terms of the dye, as in the *Agricultural Statistics* for 1892, these figures are not directly comparable due to the change in processes of manufacture from the Indian method of natural evaporation (so well described by Pelsaert himself) to the boiling method adopted initially by the European indigo planters and then widely followed by 'native factories' during the latter half of the nineteenth century. The boiling method produced indigo of a much higher concentration but of far less weight in relation to the green plant from which it was extracted.[18]

According to Smith's *Final Settlement Report* for Aligarh (1872–3; published 1882), an acre yielded 42 maunds of green plant per acre.[19] Atkinson estimates the yield as ranging from 78.75 to 105 maunds per acre in the Etawa district.[20] If one accepts Hadi's ratio between the yield of evaporation ('*kachcha*' indigo) and boiling methods ('*pakka*' indigo) as inferred from his relative prices for both categories (viz., 1.8:1), we obtain the following figures of yield of dye by the evaporation method:

[16] F. Pelsaert, *Remonstrantie*, 255–7, tr. W.H. Moreland and P. Geyl, *Jahangir's India*, 10–11.

[17] This was identical with, or close to, the later *bīgha-i daftarī* (Habib, *Agrarian System*, 364 rev. ed. 416–17). The *man* and *ser* in the indigo trade were of *Akbarī* weight throughout the 17th century.

[18] Cf. S. Muhammad Hadi, *A Monograph on Dyes and Dyeing in the North-West Provinces and Oudh*, Allahabad, 1896, 76; Watt, IV, 408–9 (where the yield by evaporation is given under the designation *gad*).

[19] Smith, *Final Settlement Report*, 37.

[20] Atkinson, Vol.IV, 251.

District	Yield during 1860s and 1870s maunds/acre	Yield in 1892[a] maunds/acre
Agra (1871)	14.81[b]	12.96
Etawa (1864)	14.31–19.43[c]	13.68
Aligarh (1872–3)	7.62[c]	13.68

[a] All the figures in this column are based on the estimates in the *Agricultural Statistics* for the dye from irrigated land.
[b] Atkinson, Vol.VII, 455. In case of Agra there is an obvious misprint: The amount of dye per acre is given as 2¼ mds, and the total value of out-turn as Rs 24.36, which gives the value of dye as Rs 10.83 per maund—an impossibility. The figure '2' in the quantity of the dye seems superfluous and the correct figures should probably be ¼ md only, which I have adopted.
[c] In the case of Aligarh (*Settlement Report*, 37) and Etawa (Atkinson, Vol.IV, 251), where the yields are stated in terms of the green plant, the ratio between plant and dye has been taken as 325:1, following Smith, *Final Settlement Report*, 37. This falls within the range of estimated ratios, 300:1 to 333:1, given in Watt (Vol.IV, 408–9).

From the figures above it appears that the yield of dye from the evaporation method in 1892 was lower than the floor of the estimate for the 1620s (16.59 or 14.52 pounds), though the difference is not very large. The 1871 estimate for Agra and 1864 estimate for Etawa are almost the same as the lower limit of estimate for Bayana in the 1620s. But in the case of Aligarh, the estimate for 1872–3 is about half of the lower yield in the 1620s. This low yield has been ascribed to the introduction of a different strain of indigo producing a more concentrated dye;[21] but it is probable that, as Smith himself suspects, the Aligarh yield given for 1872–3 is an underestimate.

It seems, then, that Pelsaert's estimates of yield for the Bayana indigo in the form of manufactured dye is slightly above the level of the estimated yield of the better quality of the dye obtained through the 'native' process of evaporation in the nineteenth century. This may have been because the Bayana plant was of an especially high quality, and perhaps yielded, weight for weight, a larger amount of dye through evaporation than indigo crops cultivated in the adjoining Doāb tracts.

[21] K.K. Trivedi, 'Movement of Relative Value of Output of Agricultural Crops in the Agra Region, 1600–1900', read at IHC, 1975. Trivedi is, however, of the opinion that in the second half of the nineteenth century the yields in general were as low as those of Aligarh, a conclusion which is not borne out by the evidence for other districts in earlier years as well as in 1892.

On the whole, then, one would be inclined to conclude that indigo plant production per acre was probably about the same in 1600 as in the latter half of the nineteenth century, though the yield in the form of dye is not comparable to the modern concentrated dye that was obtained through the use of boilers.

The estimates of average yields from the 1870s usually omit oilseeds altogether; but, as noticed above, these crops were confined to dry lands, and modern statistics give us their estimated yields on dry lands for 1892. These are fairly close to the lowest yield in the *Ā'īn*. Any substantial change in the productivity per acre of these crops, is, therefore, unlikely.

III

From such evidence as we have, it may be held that between 1540–5 and *c.*1870, the yields per acre remained practically the same in the case of the major food crops; if any change occurred, it was barely marginal. On the whole, too, no great change is discernible in those cash crops for which we have evidence.

But all this does not *ipso facto* mean that overall agricultural productivity per acre has remained the same. One might still argue that given stable productivity for each crop, productivity in agriculture may have risen owing to an extension in the proportion of area sown with crops giving an out-turn of higher value. For example, a relative increase in area under 'high grade' crops like sugarcane, cotton, and wheat might lead to a general rise in the value of agricultural produce per acre, though productivity per acre of these and other crops might remain unaltered.

In order to consider this possibility, we should, ideally, have statistics for the area under various crops in the sixteenth century as well as in 1900. But since we do not have the former, we may think of other devices to substitute for this kind of direct evidence.

One possible pointer to whether the pattern of distribution of crops has changed since the sixteenth century may be found in changes in the value of output of various crops in relation to wheat between the sixteenth and the nineteenth centuries. If the relative value of output of the various crops has remained broadly the same, one can legitimately infer that the share of these crops in total production has also remained by and large constant. One may consider the possibility as extremely remote that though the share in the total production of a crop has substantially altered, its relative value might yet remain unaffected.

The value of output for the sixteenth century can be computed for Agra by multiplying the 'standard' average yields for the 1540s, by the prices given in the *Ā'īn*, and for other districts by the *Ā'īn*'s prices modified according to the price difference between these districts and Agra (deduced from the price data in the official *Prices and Wages* for the decade 1860–70).[22] We do not have prices of cotton and sugarcane for the sixteenth century, and therefore, the relative value of out-turn in the case of these two crops cannot be calculated. However, for these crops one can consider the demand in cash per unit of area (*dastūru-l 'amal*) in relation to the demand on wheat as broadly representing the relative value of their output. For *c.*1870 we have accepted the estimated value of output as given in the *District Gazetteers* and *Settlement Reports*.[23]

It appears from Table 3.4 (see next page) that relative to wheat, the value of output of food grains, in general remained more or less the same in the sixteenth and the latter half of the nineteenth century. Though there are individual cases of major variations, no large shift is deducible. But the position is quite different in the case of cash-crops; here we find a definite decline in the relative value of their output per acre which is strikingly large in cotton and indigo and noticeable in sugarcane.

For the major oilseeds modern information is, rather surprisingly, scarce. We have information for one district only (Aligarh). It will be unsafe to say anything on the strength of this solitary piece of evidence, since the yield reported for the district is exceptionally low, viz., 0.89 *man*/*bīgha* for mustard, while for 1892 the corresponding estimate given in the *Agricultural Statistics* is 5.34 *man*/*bīgha* and Watt's estimate for U.P. is 3.72 to 5.4 *man*/*bīgha*.[24] Such as they are, these yields match those inferable from the *Ā'īn* fairly well.

From all this we may draw two conclusions: first, the area under various food crops relative to the area under wheat did not probably alter very much between 1600 and 1870; secondly, the area under sugarcane, cotton and indigo probably declined relatively.

Since the largest amount of change during the three centuries is most likely to have occurred during the second half of the nineteenth century, marked by canal construction and railways, it would be interesting to see if the two broad inferences we have made are borne out by actual changes in crop-distribution during this period.

[22] I have used the *Prices and Wages* volume published in 1892. The prices in the decade 1861–70 are preferred because the effects of railways on prices were yet to be fully felt. Cf. Zahoor Ali Khan, 'Railways and the Creation of National Market in Foodgrains', *IHR*, Vol. IV, No.2, 178.

[23] Atkinson, Vol.III, 227, 470; Vol.IV, 251; Vol.VII, 43, 444–5.

[24] G. Watt, *The Commercial Products of India*, 177.

Table 3.4

Relative Value of Output per Acre of Various Crops (Wheat = 100)

	Agra		Kol (Aligarh)		Meerut		Etawa		Kanauj (Farrukhabad)		Sardhana (Muzaffarnagar)		Delhi	
	1545–95	1870–1	1545–95	1874–5	1545–95	1870	1545–95	1871–2	1545–95	1870	1545–95	1871–2	1545–95	1870
Wheat	100.00	100.00	100.00	100.00	100.00	100.00	100.00	100.00	100.00	100.00	100.00	100.00	100.00	100.00
Barley	63.90	70.24	71.40	65.32	71.84	100.00	75.65	43.63	69.60	75.00	64.37	48.48	64.77	66.61
Gram	47.99	40.65	55.34	48.57	62.34	88.89	58.09	32.14	52.20	N.A.	50.48	39.99	54.09	76.58
Jowar	46.76	41.14	47.32	42.86	62.01	66.67	52.11	48.50	54.14	52.50	43.78	38.02	42.03	56.93
Bajra	24.81	28.61	24.92	41.61	33.38	38.89	25.87	N.A.	25.45	N.A.	35.08	N.A.	25.51	49.98
Cotton	129.99	66.67	148.40	78.57	153.61	72.22	144.54	63.06	154.91	100.00	153.61	96.96	—	—
Sugarcane	219.80	197.56	222.65	217.86	211.71	—	222.65	227.02	269.56	160.00	211.70	116.42	—	—
Indigo	249.70	78.35	268.99	45.00	277.11	—	264.92	62.41	217.39	40.00	277.11	—	—	—
Sesame	—	—	45.93	28.57	—	—	—	—	—	—	—	—	—	—
Mustard	—	—	69.60	11.00	—	—	—	—	—	—	—	—	—	—

Sources for modern data: see footnotes 22 and 23 on page 89.

Table 3.5 gives the distribution of area under some selected crops in districts of western U.P. *c.*1870, 1884–5, 1897–8 and 1910–11, the area under each crop being shown as percentage of area under gross cultivation.

The data brought together show that no large increase in the percentage of area under wheat took place during this period. A sharp fall appears in the relative extent of area sown with *jowar*, but there is a corresponding increase in the area under gram. Since the values of out-turn of these two crops are of the same magnitude, these shifts should have left the general productivity unaffected. The cultivation of barley too shows a general tendency towards increase, while the relative extent under bajra remained more or less the same. Maize is a new crop not found in the *Ā'īn-i Akbarī* schedules; it generally shows a larger extent in 1897–8 than in 1910–11 when it rarely exceeds 5 per cent of the total cropped area. Its cultivation is therefore unlikely to have affected the general pattern of crop-distribution to any marked degree between the time of the *Ā'īn* and the beginning of the twentieth century.

It appears, then, that no substantial change occurred during the period 1870–1911 in the relative extent of area under the major food-crops, though there might just have been a slight increase. But this cannot be said of the area sown with cash crops. Table 3.5 (see next page) reveals a distinct tendency towards contraction in the area sown with cotton, with indigo too displaying a similar trend, while the relative area under sugarcane fluctuated considerably. The extent of land under tobacco (which, in any case, is insignificant) remained almost unchanged in relative terms. Only with oilseeds was there an increase in relative extent. But the percentage of area under oilseeds is so small that the change should hardly have made much difference to average productivity. There is one interesting development: the percentage of area under fodder crops showed a definite tendency towards increase during 1870–1911. This is surely to be attributed to the extension of cultivation and the contraction of natural grazing grounds, which would lead to a greater demand for fodder crops. But being of low value, they should have tended to pull down rather than raise the average productivity per acre of cultivation.

The two inferences made earlier were that in western U.P. the relative area under food-crops remained almost unchanged during the seventeenth to the nineteenth centuries and that some contraction occurred within this period in the area sown with cash crops. These inferences are corroborated by the more direct and detailed evidence for the railway period (1870–1911), which should have been the period of greatest change

Table 3.5

Distribution of Area under Various Crops, 1870–1 to 1910–11 (% of gross cultivation)

	Agra				Aligarh				Etawa			
	1870–1	1884–5	1897–8	1910–11	1872–3	1884–5	1897–8	1910–11	1870	1884–5	1897–8	1910–11
Wheat	15.26	8.41	10.25	10.80	20.58	16.29	22.96	17.97	10.00	13.36	14.50	12.28
Barley	3.40	—	13.32	16.31	10.57	—	14.94	18.32	2.44	—	11.71	15.13
Gram	7.70	—	16.50	30.33	6.36	—	11.74	18.31	3.94	—	14.42	18.41
Jowar	21.06	—	11.06	6.06	17.99	—	10.57	6.49	18.63	—	9.18	5.93
Bajra	17.44	—	22.07	15.21	7.96	—	8.37	8.79	14.31	—	9.52	18.38
Maize	0.82	—	1.58	0.13	0.41	—	8.57	3.93	2.68	—	8.24	2.98
Sugarcane	0.71	0.53	0.19	0.37	0.18	18.32	0.36	1.11	4.11	0.94	1.16	2.45
Cotton	14.08	16.82	7.15	0.39	13.54	12.84	5.99	8.83	14.06	1.27	6.30	6.40
Indigo	0.40	1.00	0.56	—	3.28	5.99	3.95	0.26	1.34	6.85	6.60	0.37
Oil seeds	—	0.42	0.42	2.11	0.04	12.84	0.07	2.43	—	0.06	0.02	0.37
Tobacco	—	0.10	0.20	0.40	—	0.40	0.40	0.50	—	0.30	0.50	0.20
Fodder crops	—	0.39	2.30	3.10	—	1.20	3.70	5.10	—	1.00	1.40	1.90

Sources: Atkinson's *Gazetteers* for years 1870–3; and *Agricultural Statistics of India* for all other years.

(*Continued*)

Table 3.5 (*Continued*)

	Muzaffarnagar				Farrukhabad			
	1860–1	1884–5	1897–8	1910–11	1870	1884–5	1897–8	1910–11
Wheat	31.6	31.14	29.26	36.90	31.10	14.91	16.89	22.65
Barley	3.1	—	4.09	4.91	20.35	—	16.92	15.68
Gram	4.3	—	12.44	17.33	3.46	—	8.67	11.37
Jowar	4.4	—	3.81	0.35	15.16	—	10.75	7.93
Bajra	5.2	—	2.57	6.22	13.01	—	5.12	12.68
Maize	2.7	—	5.63	4.19	0.20	—	12.83	5.63
Sugarcane	6.2	6.85	9.36	4.80	3.64	1.78	1.60	2.79
Cotton	4.1	3.69	2.55	3.57	5.14	5.82	3.74	0.14
Indigo	—	0.12	—	—	0.11	4.02	1.79	0.08
Oil seeds	—	3.69	0.09	0.09	—	0.02	0.06	0.18
Tobacco	—	0.08	0.20	0.20	—	0.70	0.60	0.60
Fodder crops	—	0.80	1.20	13.40	—	2.30	2.50	2.60

during the entire span of time.[25] This gives us confidence in restating our major conclusions in a more specific form.

To take, first, agricultural productivity between 1540 and 1900, in the region around Agra and Delhi: while the average output of foodgrains stayed unchanged until *c.*1900, in the major cash crops such as cotton and sugarcane the increase in yield has been accompanied by a fall in value (relative to wheat) and perhaps in relative extent. In the case of indigo no change in productivity can be established, largely because of a change in the process of manufacture, while a contraction in the area cultivated is possible. A slight increase in the relative area under oilseeds cannot have off-set the general contraction in the area under the major cash crops. The extension of fodder crops would be a factor in pulling down the average value of output of cultivated land. If we thus go simply by our statistics, overall productivity would appear to have either remained broadly stationary or, as is more probable, marginally declined between the sixteenth century and the last years of the nineteenth century.

Obviously these inferences are based on data available for one region only, though this was the core region of the Mughal empire. In other areas, were the evidence available, the result might possibly be widely different. It is possible, for example, that cotton cultivation increased in Gujarat during the closing decades of the nineteenth century; and that in Bengal jute cultivation expanded phenomenally during the same century. Such changes could have affected overall productivity in complex ways. But such an effect was, on balance, probably always marginal; and unless specific evidence turns up to alter it, the results we have derived from the detailed examination of evidence for the central region, could, in their broad features, be held to apply to the country as a whole.

[25] My inference would be that while there was a contraction in non-food crops in this area, there was an expansion in other areas more suited to their cultivation, as a result of railway construction. MacAlpin, however, finds on the basis of statistics of a very large area comprising Berar, Bombay Presidency, Central Provinces, Madras Presidency and the Panjab, that 'railroads construction in India does not appear to have been accompanied by a decrease in the absolute amount of land planted with foodgrains' (*IESHR*, Vol.XII, No.1, 58). But 'food-grains' is a very broad category: wheat (an export crop) expanded at the cost of inferior grains between 1875 and 1895 in 'British India'. Among non-food crops, the area under cotton increased from 3.72 to 4.52 per cent of the total cropped area in the same period, and that under jute from 0.48 to 1.05 per cent (Irfan Habib, *Indian Economy, 1858–1914*, (New Delhi, 2007), 56–7.

LAND REVENUE

4

Land-Revenue Demand

Land revenue was at the base of the vast structure of the Mughal empire; and much attention has naturally been paid in modern studies to its size and mode of assessment and collection.

It has been recognized that Akbar's administration achieved a remarkable degree of standardization of the land-revenue system over a fairly large region. The evolution of Akbar's land-revenue policy has been studied in detail by W.H. Moreland, R.P. Tripathi, and Irfan Habib.[1] But important as their interpretations are, a number of their hypotheses have yet remained untested by actual recourse to the *Ā'īn*'s statistics; and there appear to be certain loose ends, too, in their arguments that the statistics could have conceivably tied up. In this chapter an attempt is first made to check every existing assumption or inference with the *Ā'īn*'s text and statistics, and to see whether the received picture of the evolution of Akbar's revenue policy can be made more precise and, wherever necessary, modified. Much of this is relevant for us in so far as it helps to take us nearer towards an elucidation of what to the economic historians appears a far more crucial question: the magnitude of the part of gross agricultural product alienated from the producer through payment of revenue.

I

The region where the systematized land-revenue administration of Akbar functioned comprised the larger portion of Northern India, the territory extending from the Salt Range to the river Son and contained within it eight *ṣūbas* (provinces) after their creation in 1580. The standard mode

[1] W.H. Moreland, *Agrarian System of Moslem India*, 82–92; R.P. Tripathi, *Some Aspects of Muslim Administration*, (first published), Allahabad, 1936 (reprinted, 1956) 308–38; Habib, *Agrarian System*, 190–256 (rev. ed. 230–97).

of revenue assessment followed here was known as *ẕabṭ*. The term *ẕabṭ* signified assessment of revenue by the application of standard rates, fixed in cash, to the area under each crop. The rates annually fixed from the 6th to the 24th regnal year are recorded in the *Āʼīn* in a set of tables titled *Āʼīn-i Nauzdahsāla* ('The *Āʼīn* of Nineteen Years').[2] In these tables the *dastūrs* are given province-wise, in single rates or pairs (lowest and highest).[3] In the first four years, from the 6th to the 9th regnal year the crops are given a single rate throughout each province; indeed, in many cases the same rate prevails in almost all the eight provinces. Since the rates for all the provinces (except Malwa) were practically the same during these years, one would infer that uniform productivity as well as uniform prices had been assumed at least on paper. From the 10th year a change appears: the rates are much lower than those during the previous three years and for most crops two rates, the maximum and the minimum, are entered (except in the *ṣūbas* of Lahore and Malwa). The rates now vary from province to province. It is difficult to say how this change was brought about, whether, that is, this was done by assuming different prices or by estimating different yields for different localities, or both.[4]

The rates from the 15th (in some cases the 14th) to the 24th regnal year on which the final cash-rates were supposedly based, were still lower than the rates of previous years: the rates for inferior crops show a marked decline, and the variations from province to province and year to year also become more pronounced.

Under the heading '*Āʼīn-i Dahsāla*' ('*Āʼīn* of Ten Years'),[5] Abū'l Faẓl sets out in detail the cash rates (*dastūru-l ʻamal*) in force in the eight

[2] *Āʼīn*, I, 303–47.

[3] The *ṣūbas* themselves were formed in 1580, and Abū'l Faẓl, or his source, must have had first to assign the rates fixed for the previous divisions of varying sizes to the corresponding *ṣūbas* in order to compile the 19-Year Rate Tables. The question also arises as to whether the earlier rates were fixed for the same circles for which the final *dastūrs* were separately formulated. It is unlikely that this was so; the rates might well have been fixed for entire *sarkārs* (the earlier larger ones, as listed, for example, in the *Bāburnāma*, Haidarabad Codex, ff.292a–3a). Since some of the later *ṣūbas* corresponded to single *sarkārs* of the earlier period, this may explain why even after the 10th regnal year, only a single rate continues to appear under a *ṣūba*. The variations and range might have increased with the 15th year, because the rates were retrospectively calculated for the new *dastūr*-circles formed as part of the 'Karori Experiment' of that year.

[4] Abū'l Faẓl (*Āʼīn*, I, 347) tells us that in the 11th R.Y. the *taqsīm* papers were collected to revise *jama'* figures. But while the papers called *taqsīm* gave data about the revenue and area, they did not ordinarily contain information on yields and prices (cf. Irfan Habib, *Agrarian System*, 203 *n*.35; rev. ed. 243 & *n*.35). The *taqsīm* papers, therefore, might have been used to revise the *jama'*; but, of themselves, they could not have been of much help in revising the *dastūrs*.

[5] *Āʼīn*, I, 348–85.

provinces at the time the *Ā'īn* was written (*c.*1595). From these tables it clearly emerges that the crops were not normally rated uniformly within a province, but the province was divided into circles comprising groups of *parganas*, each circle having a separate schedule containing single cash rates for individual crops. Each circle was named after a *pargana* lying within it. The *Ā'īn* provides, separately for each province, lists of *parganas* constituting the various *dastūr* circles within the province; these lists precede the *dastūr* tables themselves. Usually a *dastūr* circle does not cross the boundaries of a *sarkār*; in some cases the limits of a circle coincide with those of a single *sarkār*. But a few circles comprise groups of *parganas* drawn from more than one *sarkār*. The *parganas* constituting a circle were normally contiguous, but in exceptional cases, isolated blocks of them also occur. The circles varied in size: while some might contain two or three *sarkārs*, others comprised just one *pargana*.

While the figures in the '*Ā'īn* of Nineteen Years' are generally given in *dāms* only, the final cash-rates are usually given in *dāms* with complex fractions expressed in *jītals* (1 *dām* = 25 *jītals*). This seeming exactness tends to give the impression that the rates must have been determined by a very close calculation based on revised crop rates and new data on prices. But from a scrutiny of the tables it appears that in actual fact the same figures (i.e., the same fractions, in *jītals*, accompanying the same whole numbers) recur many times over under different crops in different circles. Such repetition would, of course, be very rare if the rates had been individually calculated on the basis of varying crop-rates and freshly compiled local prices. In fact, the reason why the figures go into fractions lies not in any excessive anxiety for exact computation but in the standard enhancement of about 11 per cent on the rates that were themselves originally fixed in whole numbers. This uniform enhancement was on account of the larger size of *bīgha* as a consequence of the introduction of the *gaz-i Ilāhī*, as we can establish by considering the evidence of the *Ā'īn* itself and some administrative documents.

The *gaz-i Ilāhī* was introduced in 1586,[6] and Abū'l Faẓl gives minutely detailed figures showing how the area of the old *bīgha* was successively restated, after the introduction of (a) bamboo rod, and (b) the *bīgha-i Ilāhī*, the second diminution amounting to 2,93,364/27,84,000 or 10.5376 per cent.[7] This diminution implies that the *bīgha-i Ilāhī* was 11.7787 per cent larger than the superseded *bīgha*. Table 4.1 shows how in the grants this official rate was implemented.

[6] *Ā'īn*, II, 297.

[7] *Ā'īn*, II, 297. Cf. Habib, *Agrarian System*, 354–5 (rev. ed. 408–9).

Table 4.1

	(a)		(b)		(c)		(d)	(e)
	Total original area		Deduction		Net Area		(b) as % of (a)	(b) as % of (c)
Locality of grant	*bīghas*	*biswa*	*bīgha*	*biswa*	*bīgha*	*biswa*		
Jakhbar (Panjab)[a]	10	0	1	2	8	18	11.00	12.360
Allahabad (U.P.)[b]	20	0	2	4	17	16	11.00	12.360
Batala (Panjab)[c]	30	0	3	3	26	17	10.500	11.732
Batala (Panjab)[d]	70	0	7	7	62	13	10.500	11.732
Batala (Panjab)[e]	90	0	9	9	80	11	10.500	11.732
Mathura (U.P.)[f]	100	0	10	11	89	9	10.550	11.794
Batala (Panjab)[g]	104	6	10	19	93	7	10.499	11.730
Batala (Panjab)[h]	120	0	12	12	107	8	10.500	11.732
Jakhbar (Panjab)[i]	170	0	17	19	152	1	10.559	11.805
Banaras & Chunar (U.P.)[j]	200	0	22	0	178	0	11.000	12.360
Bahraich (U.P.)[k]	240	0	27	16	212	4	11.583	13.101
Bahraich (U.P.)[l]	400	0	42	8	357	12	10.600	11.850

a. B.N. Goswamy and J.S. Grewal, *The Mughal and the Jogis of Jakhbar*, Simla, 1967, Doc.III (80).
b. M. Azhar Ansari (ed.), *Administrative Documents of Mughal India*, Delhi, 1984, Doc. No.33. The grant size is 20, not 200 *bīghas* as read by the editor.
c. I.O. 4438:11.
d. Ibid:25
e. Ibid., 7.
f. I. Habib, *Agrarian System*, rev. ed., 408*n*.
g. I.O. 4438: 55
h. Ibid., 7. This is the total of No.3 & 5 in the same document.
i. Goswamy and Grewal, op.cit., Doc.II (60).
j. M.A. Ansari, op.cit., Nos.6–7.
k. U.P. Record Office, Allahabad, No.1177.
l. Ibid.

Column (d) in Table 4.1 gives the rate by which the deduction was made in the existing figure of *bīghas* to restate the same areas in the larger *bīgha-i Ilāhī*: column (e) gives the rate of increase in the size of *bīgha* implied by that reduction in grant. They all approximately conform to a rate of 10.5 per cent, a rate slightly lower than that of the actual increase in the *bighas*' size: The rate of reduction seems to have been put at 11 per cent in grants at the very bottom (10 or 20 *bīghas* in original area), or at 200 *bīghas* and above, but tending to return to proximity with the real rate in grants that were still larger[8] (as for the one of 400 *bīghas*).

An enlargement of the area of the *bīgha*, assumed to be about 11.8 per cent, would naturally have necessitated an enhancement of the *dastūrs* in the same proportion. In order to carry out this enhancement the Mughal administration appears to have adopted a conversion schedule, which we propose by a simple device to reconstruct.

When we tabulate all the final rates (*dastūrs*) in an ascending order, it soon transpires that between every two consecutive rates the difference normally amounts to one *dām*, 3 *jītals*, and occasionally to one *dām*, 2 *jītals*. One conjectures easily that in the conversion table one *dām* of the pre-1586 schedules was ordinarily deemed equal to one *dām*, 3 *jītals* (representing an initial enhancement of 12 per cent) in the new schedules; the occasional smaller equivalent (one *dām*, 2 *jītals*) of an additional *dām* in the old schedule is clearly designed to keep the cumulative enhancement to below 12 per cent. The smaller equivalent is first put against the 14th *dām* of the pre-1586 schedule and recurs at an interval of usually 20 *dāms*, e.g., at 33rd, 53rd, 74th, 93rd and 114th, 140th, 153rd, 210th, and 219th (the positions of 93rd, 210th and 219th are not precisely fixed). In our reconstructed conversion schedule, 100 *dāms* of the old scale correspond to 111 *dāms*, 20 *jītals* of the *dastūrs*. For 200 *dāms* the corresponding figure (drawn from the *dastūrs*) is exactly double (223 *dāms*, 15 *jītals*). The increase in both cases is 11.8 per cent. But in other cases the increase can be as low as 10.28% as in the case of the *dastūr* rate 107 *dāms*, 8 *jītals*. Obviously the schedule was constructed by following some rules of the thumb, permitting deviations from arithmetical exactitude. We have set out the conversion schedule as reconstructed by us in Appendix 4.A.

Our reconstructed schedule obtains a particularly direct corroboration from the rates stated for the water-plant, *singhāra*. This crop has the same rate, 100 *dāms*, in all *ṣūbas* under the '*Ā'īn-i Nauzdahsāla*' Tables; and the final *dastūrs* too happen to be uniform, being 111 *dāms*, 20 *jītals*.[9] Clearly the latter is a flat enhancement of the former. Moreover, the figure in the final *dastūrs* is precisely the one worked out by us for the conversion schedule.

[8] One may, by way of speculation, suggest that in the case of smaller grants 11% was a convenient standard rate, while it was resorted to in the case of grants in the range of 200–40, perhaps because here a very large number of grants were involved and a higher rate of reduction would have been beneficial for the administration.

[9] Such variations as 115 *dāms*, 8 *jītals*, for 111 *dāms*, 20 *jītals*, are due to misplacings of dots, substituting *pānzdah* for *yāzdah*, and *hasht* for *bīst*.

Only a few among the final cash-rates fall outside the rates based on our conversion schedule, some being in whole numbers. These, if they do not arise from errors of transcription, may suggest that here the converted rate was replaced by a fresh estimate, which would naturally tend to be in a whole number.

The extent to which such revisions might have occurred may be judged from Table 4.2, in which the number of rates based on the conversion table as against the total number of all rates is given for some major crops.

Table 4.2

Province	Total number of *dastūrs*	Number of *dastūrs* corresponding to the 'conversion Table'				
		Wheat	Barley	Jowar	Sugarcane	Indigo
Agra	28	25	24	28	24	18
Delhi	27	22	24	25	24	23
Allahabad	15	13	13	13	7	13
Awadh[a]	12	—	—	—	11	—
	6	5	6	6	—	5
Lahore[a]	8	6	5	—	7	—
	6	—	—	5	—	6
Ajmer	9	9	9	9	9	8
Multan	3	1	2	2	3	3
Malwa	1	1	1	1	1	1

[a] For certain crops, the *dastūrs* are not recorded under some circles. So two totals are shown under the *ṣūbas* affected.

Even if we assume that all the rates which do not conform to the 'conversion schedule' were the result of a revision, it is obvious that relatively very few rates were in fact revised after the converted rates had been scheduled in 1586. We must then take it that most of the final *aastūrs* in the *Ā'īn* are the same as were laid down during the five years, 1581–6.

To judge from Abū'l Faẓl's statements,[10] these cash rates (as established in 1581–6) should have been averages of the rates fixed for the period from the 15th to the 24th regnal years. The exceptions were rates on high-grade crops (*jins-i a'lā*) which are said to have been formulated

[10] *Ā'īn*, I, 348; *Akbarnāma*, III, 282–3.

on the basis of the highest rates imposed during the decade (regnal years 15–24).[11] If therefore we re-convert them, by using our conversion table, to the rates in force before the *bīgha-i Ilāhī*, we can test whether these could be simple averages of the rates entered for the 15th to the 24th regnal years, or in the case of high-grade crops, be equal to the highest reached during that period.

Owing to the fact that the rates in the '*Ā'īn* of Nineteenth Years' are not given for different *dastūr*-circles, a direct check is not possible. But even so, a simple device might be used.[12] The Rates of 'Nineteen Years' are given province-wise; and though the rates for individual *dastūr* circles are not furnished, the range of rates for different circles for any year is indicated by the lowest and highest rates. Now, if the final *dastūrs* are averages of the rates of the regnal years 15 to 24, no rate under any *dastūr* circle could possibly have exceeded the average of the highest rates of ten years in the province, nor could any *dastūr* be less than the average of the lowest rates during the ten years. Table 4.3 sets out the highest and lowest rates amongst the *dastūr* circles for each crop, along with the averages of the highest and lowest rates in the 15th–24th regnal years.

We find that in four provinces (Agra, Delhi, and Allahabad), the highest and lowest of the final *dastūrs* fall well within the range of the ten years' rates. Out of nine crops (other than high-grade crops), which we have taken into account, the only exceptions are rice in Agra and Delhi, barley in Allahabad, and mustard in Delhi, where the highest final *dastūrs* exceed the average of maximum rates of the ten years.

The probability that the final *dastūrs* were mostly averages of the rates of the decennial period, regnal years 15–24, is reinforced by the *dastūrs* for the circle *Ḥavelī* Agra. This circle has the highest *dastūrs* among all circles of the Agra *ṣūba*, for gram, barley, jowar, bajra and mustard (see Appendix 4.B). It may be assumed that the same circle, containing the capital, contributed the highest rates on these crops in the *ṣūba* during most of the ten years (15th–24th R.Y.) as well. We discover that, in fact, the averages of all the maximum rates during this period is strikingly close to the rates in this circle for the five crops mentioned. On the other hand, in the case of peas, for which the rate for the *dastūr*-circle *Ḥavelī* Agra is lower than the rates in seven other circles of the *ṣūba*, the average of the maximum rates for the decade considerably exceeds that of the Agra circle.

[11] *Ā'īn*, I, 298–300. For the interpretation given in our text, see Habib, *Agrarian System*, 209–12, *n* (rev. ed., 250–2).

[12] Cf. Habib, *Agrarian System*, 211 (rev. ed., 251).

Table 4.3

Crops	Rates, 15th–24th R.Y.		Final Dastūrs	
	Average of		Converted to pre-1586 figures	
	Maximum rates	Minimum rates	Highest	Lowest
Agra				
Wheat	68.4	42.4	62	52
Gram	41.9	22.6	40	30
Barley	45.7	25.6	44	34
Mustard	31.6	21.7	30	26
Peas	32.0	17.5	30	20
Rice	53.3	35.2	57	40
Jowar	39.5	25.6	40	29
Bajra	28.4	19.3	28	21.5
Cotton	85.4	65.1	84	76
Allahabad				
Wheat	75.4	45.2	58	52
Gram	49.2	26.2	37	34
Barley	56.5	30.9	60	36
Mustard	44.6	25.2	36	25
Peas	41.5	16.6	36	20
Rice	58.0	35.5	44	40
Jowar	36.9	26.2	36	31
Bajra	36.8	20.3	—	—
Cotton	112.0	71.3	86	80
Awadh				
Wheat	53.4	42.4	40	24
Gram	39.3	25.8	26	22
Barley	41.4	28.2	34	22
Mustard	30.6	23.6	22	18
Peas	—	—	—	—
Rice	39.9	29.7	39	24
Jowar	35.7	25.3	29	22
Bajra	—	—	—	—
Cotton	95.9	69.7	—	—

(*Continued*)

Table 4.3 (*Continued*)

Crops	*Rates, 15th–24th R.Y.* Average of		*Final Dastūrs* Converted to pre-1586 figures	
	Maximum rates	Minimum rates	Highest	Lowest
Delhi				
Wheat	63.0	37.09	58	45
Gram	38.8	20.0	33	26.5
Barley	38.6	20.3	38	23
Mustard	29.4	18.6	32	17
Peas	30.9	15.9	28	18
Rice	54.7	31.2	57	30
Jowar	34.1	21.9	34	24
Bajra	25.3	18.5	26	19
Cotton	97.0	67.6	96	80
Lahore				
Wheat	46.7	39.1	50	30
Gram	30.4	25.5	32	28
Barley	32.0	25.3	42	28
Mustard	27.6	23.6	28	24
Peas	24.5	19.6	—	—
Rice	41.9	32.9	44	30
Jowar	35.8	28.2	36	28
Bajra	26.0	21.5	28	21
Cotton	89.2	79.5	82	68
Multan				
Wheat	45.5	37.5	50	48
Gram	33.7	22.3	—	—
Barley	34.1	24.8	44	27
Mustard	33.4	23.8	40	26
Peas	20.4	19.2	—	—
Rice	41.0	36.9	44	44
Jowar	34.9	29.1	34	32
Bajra	28.0	23.4	40	26
Cotton	89.5	71.8	84	78

The position in the *ṣūbas* of Lahore, Multan, and Awadh as depicted in Table 4.3 is, however, different. Here the highest among the final *dastūrs* in all the crops considered (except for jowar in Lahore) exceed the average of maximum rates of the '*Ā'īn* of Ten Years'. In Lahore, the lowest rates for wheat, rice and cotton fall far below the average of the minimum rates for the years 1570–80.

In the case of *ṣūba* Lahore, one could perhaps attribute the excess of the highest final rates over the arithmetic mean of the earlier maximum rates, to the enhancement in tax assessments after the Court shifted to Lahore in 1586.[13] But there would be two objections to this. The Lahore *dastūrs* are not ordinarily higher than those of the other provinces; indeed, these usually appear to be in a lower range (see Appendix 4.B). It is therefore difficult to assume that these represent a 20 per cent increase over previous rates. Secondly, if we lower the Lahore rates by one-sixth, the lowest rates in the final *dastūrs* would, in the case of all the crops selected for our table, be much less than the mean of the lowest rates for the ten years. There is, lastly, the crucial point that the final *dastūrs* in the Lahore province accord with the main steps in the conversion table for the 1586 enhancements. A 20 per cent increase subsequent to 1586 would most certainly have ruled out such conformity.

For high-grade crops, given Abū'l Faẓl's statements, our test is more direct and definite: In each province the highest among the maximum rates of the years 1570–1 to 1579–80 should be equal to the highest rate on the crop among *dastūr*-circles of the same province (converted to pre-1586 figures).

For this test, I have treated as high-grade crops those whose rates are higher than 100 *dāms* per *bīgha* in the final *dastūrs*, and I have then picked the highest rates from amongst the rates for the 15th–24th R.Ys. as well as the final *dastūrs*, for poppy, *paunda* sugarcane, ordinary sugarcane and indigo. Cotton has been treated here as an ordinary crop, though in *ṣūba* Delhi the maximum *dastūr* on cotton exceeds 100 *dāms*. The final *dastūrs* are scaled down to the pre-1586 figures by using our conversion schedule (Appendix 4-A).

We find that the highest *dastūrs* exceed the highest rates from the regnal years 15–24 for most crops: poppy, in all provinces except Agra and Lahore; indigo, in all provinces, except Allahabad; and *paunda* sugarcane in all provinces without exception. Only in the case of ordinary sugarcane are the highest *dastūrs* lower than the highest rates during the ten years; but here again *ṣūba* Lahore is an exception.

[13] *Akbarnāma*, III, 748.

Table 4.4

Crop	15th–25th R.Y.·	Final *dastūr* converted to pre-1586 figures
	Highest maximum rate	Highest *dastūr*
Agra		
Poppy	130	130
Sugarcane (*Paunda*)	200	214
Sugarcane (*Sāda*)	174	166
Indigo	140	146
Allahabad		
Poppy	130	140
Sugarcane (*Paunda*)	200	215
Sugarcane (*Sāda*)	180	128
Indigo	180	146
Awadh		
Poppy	130	140
Sugarcane (*Paunda*)	200	215
Sugarcane (*Sāda*)	144	120
Indigo	136	146
Delhi		
Poppy	130	138
Sugarcane (*Paunda*)	200	225
Sugarcane (*Sāda*)	164	124
Indigo	150	148
Lahore		
Poppy	130	116
Sugarcane (*Paunda*)	200	215
Sugarcane (*Sāda*)	120	132
Indigo	134	142

Our general conclusions, then, are that in the case of ordinary crops, the final *dastūrs* could possibly have been simple averages of the rates sanctioned for regnal years 15–24 in all but two *ṣūbas*; but in the case of high-grade crops, the final *dastūrs* are not only not averaged from the rates for the 15th–24th years, but are not even identical with the highest rates sanctioned during those ten years, though they approximate to them, or rather slightly exceed them, in most cases.

II

The next question concerns the share of agricultural produce that the *dastūr-ul 'amals* represent. From Abū'l Faẓl's formula for the calculation of the revenue rates on the basis of Sher Shāh's *rai 's*, it has been assumed that Akbar's *dastūrs* too were designed to represent one-third of the yield per *bīgha*, and that the rates so fixed in kind were commuted into cash at prices prevailing in the rural localities,[14] exceptions being offered only by certain cash crops.[15] However, there is no plain, direct statement to this effect in Abū'l Faẓl. Neither the officially determined crop-yields nor the prices current in the various *dastūr*-circles at the time the *dastūrs* were formulated, or were in force, are known. It is therefore not possible to check directly the assumptions that have so far been generally accepted. However, certain available data can still be used to test whether the assumptions are plausible.

The *Ā'īn* reproduces the revenue rates in kind worked out by Sher Shāh's administration; these were fixed expressly on the basis of the tax being set at one-third of an estimated rate of produce, averaged from yield estimates for three kinds of land, all of which are set out in tabular form.[16] The prices prevalent at the imperial camp are also furnished in the *Ā'īn*.[17]

In Table 4.5 we attempt an estimate of the value in *dāms* per *bīgha* of various crops, by multiplying the yields adopted in Sher Shāh's schedule by the prices recorded in the *Ā'īn* for the imperial camp. This value would be the maximum possible for the crops of the locality, since the prices are not country prices, but those of the imperial camp. Now we can perhaps determine what proportion of the total value Akbar's final *dastūrs* represented. Since the prices were presumably those of Agra,[18] we may initially determine the magnitude of demand for the Agra circle.

Column (a) in Table 4.5 gives the value in *dāms* per *bīgha* of different crops (*rai'* multiplied by camp prices); column (b) the *dastūr-ul 'amals* of Agra circle; and column (c) the proportion of the value of produce represented by the *dastūrs*.

It is remarkable that even with the 'average yields' adopted by Sher Shāh's officials, and the prices given for the Imperial Camp, the *dastūrs*

[14] Moreland, *Agrarian System of Moslem India*, 83, and Habib, *Agrarian System*, 201 (rev. ed. 240–41).

[15] *Ā'īn*, I, 230. Cf. Habib, *Agrarian System*, 208 (rev. ed. 248).

[16] *Ā'īn*, I, 297–300.

[17] Ibid., 53–60.

[18] See Chapter 14 for a discussion of this question.

Table 4.5

Dastūr Rate as % of Crop Values, Agra

Crops	(a) Value of yield	(b) *Dastūr*	(c) (b) as % of (a)	Crops	(a) Value of yield	(b) *Dastūr*	(c) (b) as %
Rabi				*Kharif*			
Wheat	155.52	67.08	43.13	Mung	139.50	49.50	35.48
Barley	103.44	49.20	47.56	Maash	124.00	40.24	32.45
Gram	82.80	44.02	53.16	Moth	61.92	29.08	46.96
Lentil	75.60	29.08	38.47	Jowar	103.50	44.72	43.21
Arzan	48.25	24.38	50.53	Shamakh	48.24	15.68	32.50
Mustard	96.84	33.60	34.70	Kodron	90.72	31.32	34.52
Peas	63.48	31.32	49.34	Sesamum	120.00	44.72	37.27
Fenugreek	116.40	44.72	38.40	Bajra	64.60	31.32	48.48
				Lobiya	93.00	31.32	33.68
Average			44.41	Average			38.28

for *rabi* crops range from 34.70 to 53.16 per cent of the total value, giving a mean of 44.41 per cent; the *dastūrs* for the *kharif* crops range from 32.45 to 48.48 per cent, the mean being 38.28 per cent. Since the camp (Agra) prices must have been substantially higher than the rural prices at which the peasant actually sold his produce, the real ratio of the *dastūr* to value of yield (which in reality was much less than is shown in Table 4.5) should have been substantially higher than what we get in our Table 4.5.

While there seems no means of determining the difference between rural and urban prices in 1595, it might not be far wrong to assume that with the then available means of transport, the difference in the two sets of prices must have amounted to at least 10 per cent. If we make allowance for such a difference between rural and urban prices, we would have to assume that the *dastūrs* represented about a half of the average produce (48.85 per cent for *rabi*, 42.11 per cent for *kharif*, going by the mean figures). It is then quite probable that one-half and not one-third was actually set as the share of produce for formulating the *dastūrs* whatever the nominal modes of calculation.

However, there is still another possibility, that Akbar's administration had altogether ignored the average yields prepared by Sher Shāh's officials. The latter were based upon the rather improbable assumption that the area of all the three kinds of land, whether under *kharif* or *rabi*, was equal: as a result of this premise, the 'average yields' for all *kharif* crops had been invariably over-estimated, while the yields of certain high-grade *rabi* crops were underestimated.[19] We find, in fact, that the *dastūrs* represent a lower share of the value of the 'total produce' in the *kharif* crops than in the *rabi* as calculated on the basis of Sher Shāh's *rai's*. If the inflated yields of Sher Shāh's *rai's* were scaled down, the total share of the produce claimed in revenue should have been around a half; and one is therefore tempted to conclude that Akbar's administration in framing its *dastūrs* flatly laid claim to one-half of the total produce.

That the Mughal claim was laid not on one-third of the value of the produce but on a much higher share can be shown by still another means that does not oblige us to make any assumption about the use of Sher Shāh's *rai'* by Akbar's administration. Official estimates of the value of output per unit of area of various crops are furnished for Agra, 1870.[20] Had the *dastūrs* approximated to one-third of the value of produce, they should also have approximated to a third of the value of the officially estimated yield in 1870, after adjustments to allow for the rise in prices. The scale of the rise in prices between 1595 and 1870 can be worked out from the prices in *Ā'īn* and from the prices for the decade 1866–75 reported from Agra. The rise in rural prices must have been greater than that in market prices, since with improved means of communication and transport, the margin of difference between rural and urban prices must, if anything, have contracted during the nineteenth century.

Table 4.6

Crops	(a) *Dastūrs*	(b) Value of Output 1870 (*dāms/bīgha-i Ilāhī*)	(c) 1/3 × (b)/(a)	(d) ½ × (b)/(a)	(e) 1870 price, divided by *Ā'īn*'s price
Wheat	67.08	835.20	4.1	6.2	5.0
Barley	49.20	418.40	2.8	4.3	6.0
Gram	44.72	300.00	2.2	3.3	5.2
Jowar	44.72	422.40	3.1	4.7	4.6
Bajra	31.32	451.68	4.8	7.2	6.0
Average			3.40	5.14	5.36

Column (a) in Table 4.6 gives the *Ā'īn*'s *dastūr* for certain crops for the Agra-circle, while column (b) gives the value of output per unit of

[19] See Chapter 3.

[20] Atkinson, IV, part II, 368.

area (here converted into *dāms* per *bīgha-i Ilāhī*, from rupees per acre), as estimated in 1870.[21] Columns (c) and (d) show the result, respectively, of one-third and one-half of (b) divided by (a). Column (e) exhibits the 1870 market prices divided by the *Ā'īn*'s prices.

It can now be seen that while on average market prices went up 5.36 times from 1595, the value of one-third of the produce in 1870 amounted, on average, to only 3.54 times the *dastūr* for Agra. On the other hand, the value of half the produce as estimated in 1870 was 5.14 times the *Ā'īn*'s *dastūrs*. In other words, the increase in the value of yield kept pace with the rise in prices only if it is assumed that the *dastūrs* represented a half and not a third of the produce. Indeed, since harvest prices are likely to have risen rather more than urban market prices, the relative difference between *dastūrs* and the average estimated value of the crops for 1870 divided by 2, should be expected to exceed the rise in market prices between 1595 and 1870. This is practically what we get from Table 4.6.

III

We have been concerned uptil now with the share of the produce represented by the *dastūrs* of the Agra circle. The next question is whether the Mughal administration was intent on claiming an equally high share of the produce in other localities as well. For this, we have to study the trends and ranges in variation of the *dastūrs* for various crops, compared with the *dastūrs* for the circle of *Ḥavelī* Agra.

I have made such calculations for eleven major crops: wheat, gram, barley, mustard, peas, jowar, bajra, rice, sugarcane, cotton, and indigo (Appendix 4B). I have found that apart from a few exceptions the range of variation for most crops is not very wide. In nine out of the eleven crops considered, the *dastūrs* for Agra circle are usually the highest. The main exceptions are cotton and indigo, where most of the *dastūrs* in provinces other than Lahore and Ajmer are higher than those of Agra.

If we arrange the *dastūrs* of major crops, with *dastūrs* for Agra as 100 indexed into intervals (Table 4.7, see next page) it becomes clear that the *dastūrs* of all the provinces except Ajmer tend to form clusters, under most of the crops.

For wheat the range within which the *dastūrs* are concentrated is 81–100 in Agra, Allahabad, Awadh and Lahore; but in Delhi the range is a little wider, i.e., 71–100. For barley too the range in Agra and Allahabad is 81–100; in Awadh and Lahore, 71–80. In Delhi it is substantially wider,

[21] Ibid.

Table 4.7

Ranges of *Dastūr* Rates (*Ḥavelī* Agra = 100)

Dastūr	Agra	Delhi	Allahabad	Awadh	Lahore	Ajmer
WHEAT						
101–10	2		1			2
91–100	20	6	8	1		1
81–90	6	13	6	5	5	3
71–80		6			1	2
61–70		1			1	
51–60					1	
41–50						1
BARLEY						
101–10			1			2
91–100	7	2	5	1	1	1
81–90	19	11	8	1		
71–80	2	10		4	5	1
61–70		3			1	4
51–60						
41–50						1
RICE						
101–10	9	2				
91–100	6	3				
81–90	4	6	4		3	2
71–80	9	12	9	7	2	4
61–70		2		5	2	
51–60		1			1	1
41–50						1
GRAM						
101–10						2
91–100	4		4			1
81–90	20	7	8	2	4	1
71–80	4	14	2	4	3	3
61–70		6				1
51–60						
41–50						1
JOWAR						
101–10						
91–100	2					1
81–90	20	12	8	6	7	1

(*Continued*)

Table 4.7 (*Continued*)

Dastūr	Agra	Delhi	Allahabad	Awadh	Lahore	Ajmer
71–80	6	13	6	6	1	2
61–70			1			3
51–60			1			1
41–50						
31–40						1
BAJRA						
101–10						
91–100	2		3		5	1
81–90	19		11	4	1	1
71–80	6		12	8	2	2
61–70			1			2
51–60						2
41–50						
31–40						1
SUGARCANE						
101–10	2					
91–100	4	4	3	2	5	
81–90	15	23	6	10	2	
71–80	7		3			6
61–70						
51–60						2
COTTON						
101–10	26	9	12	10	2	
91–100	2	18		2	4	1
81–90					2	3
71–80						2
61–70						2
51–60						
41–50						1
INDIGO						
101–100	26	23	14	6	1	
91–100	2	4			5	
81–90					2	5
71–80						2
61–70						
51–60						
41–50						2

viz., 61–100. For ordinary food crops, viz., gram, jowar and bajra, the *dastūr* indices in all the provinces except Ajmer are close to each other and are within the range 71–90. For rice, the *dastūr* indices fluctuate most sharply; even in the Agra province the range is as wide as 71–110, while Delhi, as usual, offers the widest range, 51–110; in Allahabad and Awadh the fluctuations are moderate, falling within 71–90 and 61–80, respectively. For cash crops, the *dastūr*-indices make close clusters, ordinary sugarcane in the Agra province being the lone exception. The modal class for sugarcane is 81–90; for cotton and indigo, it is 90–110, though here Ajmer offers an exception.

Furthermore, it seems that there were blocks of contiguous *dastūr*-circles where the range of variations in *dastūrs* for different crops was very narrow. It would appear, then, that while sanctioning the *dastūrs* for different localities, *dastūrs* within a region were considered in relation to a regional standard, which they either equalled or around which they clustered.

The variations being as they are, we may see if these were intended to conform to the difference in productivity and levels of prices, this being what we may infer from some of Abū'l Faẓl's statements.[22] Since we have neither contemporary estimates of yield nor prices for localities other than Agra, we can only invoke help from nineteenth-century statistics. There are, it is true, certain difficulties in using modern data. First, there is the likelihood of the effects of the railways on prices.[23] From nineteenth-century statistics, therefore, one should use prices for the period 1861–70, the earliest decade for which they are available, and which are least likely to have been affected by the railways. Yields for the same period are difficult to come by; the official *Agricultural Statistics* begin to give yield estimates only from 1892, and even then general estimates are not available, since the estimates are furnished separately for irrigated and unirrigated lands. For certain districts, however, we have estimates for 'normal yields' in the *Settlement Reports* and in Atkinson's *Statistical Account* for various districts of the North-Western Provinces (U.P.). These general yields are based on older methods of estimation and so are more likely to conform to Mughal methods (see Chapter 3). From these data I have constructed hypothetical rates for wheat and barley by multiplying the yields by average prices for 1861–70, and then indexing

[22] *Akbarnāma*, III, 282–3; *Ā'īn*, I, 348. Cf. Habib, *Agrarian System*, 201–9 (rev. ed. 240–49).

[23] How the railways tended to have a levelling effect on prices between the 1860s and 1890s is shown by Zahoor Ali Khan in *IHR*, Vol.IV, No.2, 1978.

them, with the hypothetical rate at Agra as 100. In Table 4.8 these are compared with actual *dastūr*-indices of the circle to which the modern districts correspond. Columns (b) and (c) give prices and yields indexed by taking those of Agra as 100.

It is apparent from Table 4.8 that variations in *dastūrs* do not generally correspond to modern yields, nor to modern yields multiplied by modern prices.

Table 4.8

Districts	(a) *Dastūr* indices	(b) Price indices	(c) Yield indices	(d) Hypothetical rates (yield × price)
Wheat				
Agra	100.00	100.00	100.00	100.00
Bulandshahr	86.70	75.51	123.80	93.56
Meerut	86.70	78.70	120.94	94.61
Delhi	93.92	92.54	95.96	88.29
Aligarh	89.98	87.21	120.94	100.71
Etawa	89.98	88.61	107.06	94.72
Saharanpur	83.36	86.72	116.68	101.13
Barley				
Agra	100.00	100.00	100.00	100.00
Bulandshahr	77.24	94.48	128.79	121.54
Meerut	77.24	87.14	123.91	109.15
Delhi	86.34	93.20	88.33	69.17
Aligarh	81.79	125.17	112.45	140.77
Saharanpur	72.76	105.44	163.94	171.93

All the *dastūr*-circles in Table 4.8 are confined to a limited geographical region (Delhi and Western U.P.). Even in modern *Agricultural Statistics* from 1897 onwards the yield estimates are not given for individual districts but only for big blocks consisting of many districts. It would be unrealistic to expect from Mughal officials a more detailed estimation of yields. However, since we do not have 'average yields' for other regions we can only get some broad hints from the yield estimates for irrigated and unirrigated lands given in the *Agricultural Statistics* for 1892. As a sample, we can consider Haryana. We, have already noticed that in this region the yields were much lower than in U.P. for irrigated as well as unirrigated lands.[24] The low *dastūrs* for this region seem to reflect these low yields.

The extent to which local variations in *dastūrs* might have been affected by prices can be studied rather more definitely. The prices of wheat, barley and *jowar* for the decade 1861–70 are available for almost all districts of U.P. and the Panjab; the comparison of *dastūr* and price indices can therefore be extended to all *dastūr*-circles falling within U.P. and the Panjab.

In making this comparison, a word is necessary about the choice of the index-base. While Agra was the capital and the largest city of the empire in 1600, it was reduced to the position of an ordinary town by 1872 (population, 1,63,935). It is, therefore, obvious that the relative price-levels at Agra would have been much higher in 1600 than in 1861–70. In any comparison of the *dastūrs* with modern prices, Agra, being so altered in its position, can hardly serve as a satisfactory index-base. Delhi seems a much better one, since it was a *ṣūba*-capital, but not a large town by any means, in 1595. ('The city is in ruins, but the grave-yards are well populated', says Abū'l Faẓl.[24a]) After 1857, it was similarly a small decaying town (population in 1882: 1,73,393). I have therefore taken the *dastūrs* and prices at Delhi as base, equalling 100 for my Table 4.9. Since the index figures for Agra follow in the next line, the reader can easily convert the *dastūrs* and prices set against any circle into what they would have been, with Agra as base, by dividing them by the figure set out for Agra and shifting two decimal places. *Dastūr*-circles for localities within which modern price data have not been available are omitted.

For localities falling within U.P. Table 4.9 shows a fairly close relationship between the revenue rates and price indices for wheat. There are only a few exceptions, of which again some can be explained. For example, the price index for Allahabad and neighbouring circles is higher than the *dastūr*-index. This is to be expected since in 1586 Allahabad was yet to emerge as an important city. In Haryana and Punjab the *dastūr* indices are generally lower than price indices. This is again what we should have expected in a region where rainfall was low and canal irrigation had not yet developed, even by 1892.[25] In the case of barley and *jowar* the correlation is not so obvious; but the trends in a very large number of localities coincide.

[24] See Chapter 3, Table 3.1(c) & (d).

[24a] *Ā'īn*, I, 514.

[25] See Chapter 3, Table 3.1(c) & (d).

Table 4.9

	Wheat		Barley		Jowar	
Dastūr-circle	*Dastūr*	Price 1861–70	*Dastūr*	Price 1861–70	*Dastūr*	Price 1861–70
Delhi	100.00	100.00	100.00	100.00	100.00	100.00
UTTAR PRADESH						
Agra	106.48	108.71	115.82	107.29	93.33	121.10
Etawa	95.81	96.33	94.73	112.51	89.99	119.55
Kanauj	100.00	98.03	94.16	104.96	—	119.60
Bhogaon	93.32	92.98	89.45	94.48	83.31	119.54
Phaphund	101.14	96.33	94.73	112.51	100.36	119.55
Kol	95.81	94.80	94.73	104.69	109.77	106.96
Thana Farida	93.32	91.54	89.4	105.99	109.77	104.61
Akbarabad	101.14	94.80	100.00	93.28	100.00	106.96
Meerut	93.32	92.07	89.45	94.72	100.00	126.04
Baran	93.32	82.02	89.45	107.29	100.00	106.96
Badaun	79.87	88.85	107.82	102.50	112.28	107.99
Deoband	88.76	94.28	84.27	115.58	78.90	133.63
Sardhana	93.32	98.22	81.64	99.73	100.00	149.25
Tihara	93.65	82.30	77.97	83.65	100.00	85.01
Sambhal	88.63	82.38	79.47	89.12	109.89	104.50
Chandpur	86.95	88.34	84.27	98.79	115.38	111.76
Allahabad	95.80	111.62	95.10	120.09	103.33	132.65
Jalalabad	92.32	115.70	95.29	126.38	106.67	137.07
Bhadoi	102.92	116.49	—	124.74	—	126.31
Banaras	101.65	117.29	113.18	134.23	119.90	110.86
Jaunpur	101.65	100.32	157.91	117.34	106.67	116.63
Mongera	92.37	102.55	95.29	109.98	119.90	116.24
Jajmau	96.70	103.08	94.35	109.97	97.14	119.24
Manikpur	92.37	89.40	100.00	92.29	105.24	95.41
Rae Bareilly	99.37	95.30	107.91	126.38	113.23	105.32
Awadh	86.98	92.70	92.90	99.41	106.67	104.01
Kishni	92.37	91.60	100.00	101.65	105.24	112.20
Bahraich	86.98	75.81	89.45	68.06	113.23	71.78
Faizabad	88.76	78.26	84.27	74.56	100.00	71.78
Khoransa	88.57	65.79	89.45	67.23	113.23	68.34

(Continued)

Table 4.9 (*Continued*)

	Wheat		Barley		Jowar	
Dastūr-circle	*Dastūr*	Price 1861–70	*Dastūr*	Price 1861–70	*Dastūr*	Price 1861–70
HARYANA AND PANJAB						
Panipat	93.32	95.70	95.10	100.00	100.00	104.32
Jhajhar	95.58	96.35	97.36	102.26	100.00	105.87
Rohtak	93.32	96.35	81.64	102.26	106.67	105.87
Hissar	99.94	103.35	95.10	99.50	113.23	105.95
Gohana	93.32	99.85	100.00	100.87	113.23	105.91
Sirsa	93.32	103.35	100.00	99.50	113.23	105.95
Indri	81.65	95.70	86.95	100.00	100.00	107.86
Thanesar	81.65	92.23	75.04	105.43	103.37	104.12
Lahore	80.19	97.96	108.29	93.28	119.90	111.40
Parasrur	85.20	84.30	89.45	78.17	113.23	112.97
Haibatpur	85.20	100.18	89.45	93.24	113.23	104.78
Jalandhar	85.20	87.78	—	—	106.67	—
Sialkot	53.65	84.30	89.45	78.17	113.23	112.97
Hazara	88.76	100.64	89.45	99.29	113.23	130.36

Note: Rates for these crops are not given under six *dastūr*-circles of *ṣūba* Awadh (Khairabad, Pali, Bharwara, Gorakhpur, Lucknow and Unam).
Nineteen *dastur*-circles for which modern price-data are not available have not been listed: Bayana, Sakit, Sinkandarpur Atreji, Marahra, Palwal, Rewari, Taru Sohna, Sirhind, Samana, Lakhnaur, Chunar, Kara, Ghazipur, Kora, Kutia Ibrahimabad, Rohtas, Batala.

On the whole, one can suggest that alterations in the *dastūrs* were made mainly to allow for local price variations, while single standard yields were assumed for large geographical blocks. This, at first sight, might seem impracticable,[26] but, as a matter of fact, even in the estimated yields in the modern official *Agricultural Statistics*, the variations are not substantial, at least in U.P. For all the districts of U.P. that we have considered, the range of such estimates for wheat from irrigated lands in 1892 was 1,476 to 1,120 lb/acre, implying that the variations were confined to a margin of ±13.7 per cent from the mean (1,298 lb).

[26] For this view see Habib, *Agrarian System*, 201 (rev. ed. 240).

For certain *dastūr*-circles like Amber, Rohtas and Sialkot, the *dastūrs* are exceptionally low, while for Jodhpur and Nagaur these are as exceptionally high. The nineteenth-century data for prices and yields fail to justify these abnormalities. It is possible that the low rates were the result of political concessions. This in the case of the Kachhwaha territory (Amber) seems quite probable, the purpose being to rate Kachhwaha *parganas* at a low *jama'* in order to entitle the Amber rulers to lay claim to *jāgīrs* elsewhere. On the other hand, the high rates for Jodhpur and Nagaur could be attributed either to high prices prevailing there in the sixteenth century, or to an attempt to inflate the *jama'*, for the purpose of awarding higher *mansabs* to Rajput chiefs than could be justified by the actual income of their territories.[27]

There are other sets of variations and correspondences in the *dastūrs* which also suggest that the formulation of *dastūrs* for some circles was independent of local yields and price levels, owing to some administrative bias. There are some small *dastūr*-circles comprising only single *parganas*, such as Kishni and Ibrahimabad, which, though situated inside the *dastūr*-circle of Awadh, had their separate sets of revenue rates. These rates are quite different from those sanctioned for Awadh, but identical for almost all crops with those sanctioned for Manikpur and Rae Bareilly respectively. It is a reasonable deduction that these *parganas* were included in the *jāgīrs* of some big nobles who held the other circles as well and wished to have identical *dastūrs* in various parts of their *jāgīrs*. This might also have been the case with the *dastūr* circle of Kairana which consisted of only two *parganas* and had practically the same rates as Panipat. The only difference here is that unlike Kishni and Ibrahimabad, Kairana was contiguous to Panipat. The reason for recording it as a separate *dastūr*-circle could be that while the *dastūr* circle of Panipat belonged to *sarkār* Delhi, the two *parganas* of the Kairana circle lay in *sarkār* Saharanpur.

Such considerations of political favour, administrative convenience or regard for single-*jāgīr* jurisdictions might have introduced departures

[27] It is interesting to note that the '19-year Rates' for *ṣūba* Ajmer are not given in the *Ā'īn*. Probably these were disregarded in framing the final *dastūrs* for Jodhpur and Nagaur. The Rathor ruler Mota Raja Udai Singh was restored to his principality in 1583 (*Vigat*, I, 76; *Vir Vinod*, Vol.2, part II, 815), Jodhpur having come previously under Mughal occupation. Since the final *dastūrs* for Jodhpur and Nagaur are detailed figures (in *dāms* and *jītals*), it could be assumed that the inflated *dastūrs* for Jodhpur were promulgated immediately after 1583; and that after 1586 these were increased according to the schedule, to allow for the larger *bīgha* (*Ilāhī*) promulgated in that year.

elsewhere too from the standard yield and prices formally adopted as a basis for formulating the *dastūrs*. But there are not many cases where such extraneous considerations can be inferred; and we can feel confident that normally Akbar's administration went by its own view of the yield and price levels in different regions and localities.

We see, then, that the actual rates of *dastūrs* suggest that the land revenue assessed on most food and other ordinary crops (including wheat) was equal to about half the value of the produce, as estimated for certain localities. For the higher-grade crops (sugarcane, indigo, etc.), it is difficult to be sure if all the *dastūrs* approximated to half the value of the produce; they were in any case not fixed in accordance with estimates of crop yields, and comparisons of *dastūrs* of these crops with modern data cannot be meaningfully made. They seem to have been fixed so as to allow the cultivator some concession as an incentive, while also striving to claim as land revenue a substantially larger impost than could be levied on other crops. But it is unlikely that these concessions on a few crops modified the main fact; and this was that the land revenue was generally expected to amount, in value, to that of about half of the total agricultural produce.[28]

APPENDIX 4.A

Reconstructed schedule of conversion of earlier rates into final *dastūrs*

OLD	NEW		OLD	NEW		OLD	NEW	
dām	*dām*	*jītal*	*dām*	*dām*	*jītal*	*dām*	*dām*	*jītal*
1	1	3	10	11	5	19	*21	6
2	2	6	11	*12	8	20	*22	12
3	3	9	12	*13	11	21	*23	15
4	4	12	13	14	14	22	*24	18
5	5	15	14	*15	16	23	*25	21
6	6	18	15	16	19	24	*26	24
7	7	21	16	*17	22	25	*27	2
8	8	24	17	*19	0	26	*29	5
9	10	2	18	*20	3	27	*30	8

* Rate actually found in *dastūrs*.

(*Continued*)

[28] Abū'l Faẓl expressly commends his patron for setting the land-revenue at just half the produce in Kashmir (*Ā'īn*, I, 570).

Appendix 4.A (*Continued*)

Reconstructed schedule of conversion of earlier rates into final *dastūrs*

OLD *dām*	NEW *dām*	NEW *jītal*	OLD *dām*	NEW *dām*	NEW *jītal*	OLD *dām*	NEW *dām*	NEW *jītal*
28	*31	11	62	*69	8	96	*107	8
29	*32	14	63	70	11	97	108	11
30	*33	17	64	*71	14	98	109	14
31	*34	20	65	*72	17	99	110	17
32	*35	23	66	73	20	100	*111	20
33	*36	0	67	*74	23	101	*112	23
34	*38	3	68	*76	1	102	114	1
35	*39	6	69	*77	4	103	115	4
36	*40	9	70	*78	7	104	*116	7
37	*41	9	71	79	10	105	117	10
38	*42	12	72	80	13	106	118	13
39	43	15	73	*81	16	107	*119	15
40	*44	18	74	*82	18	108	120	19
41	*45	21	75	*83	21	109	121	22
42	*46	24	76	*84	24	110	*123	0
43	*48	2	77	*86	2	111	*124	3
44	*49	5	78	*87	5	112	*125	6
45	*50	8	79	88	8	113	*126	9
46	*51	11	80	*89	11	114	*127	11
47	*52	14	81	90	14	115	*128	14
48	*53	17	82	*91	17	116	*129	17
49	*54	20	83	92	20	117	130	20
50	*55	23	84	*93	23	118	*131	23
51	57	1	85	*95	1	119	133	1
52	*58	4	86	*96	4	120	*134	4
53	*59	6	87	97	7	121	135	7
54	*60	9	88	98	10	122	*136	10
55	*61	12	89	99	13	123	137	13
56	*62	15	90	*100	16	124	*138	16
57	*63	18	91	101	19	125	139	19
58	*64	21	92	*102	22	126	140	22
59	65	24	93	103	24	127	142	0
60	*67	2	94	105	2	128	*143	3
61	68	5	95	*106	5	129	*144	6

* Rate actually found in *dastūrs*.

(*Continued*)

Appendix 4.A (*Continued*)

Reconstructed schedule of conversion of earlier rates into final *dastūrs*

OLD	NEW		OLD	NEW		OLD	NEW	
dām	*dām*	*jītal*	*dām*	*dām*	*jītal*	*dām*	*dām*	*jītal*
130	*145	9	154	172	4	178	199	22
131	146	12	155	173	7	179	200	3
132	*147	15	156	174	10	180	201	6
133	*148	18	157	175	13	181	202	9
134	149	21	158	176	16	182	203	12
135	150	24	159	177	19	183	204	15
136	152	2	160	178	22	184	205	18
137	153	5	161	180	0	185	206	21
138	*154	8	162	181	3	186	208	24
139	155	11	163	182	6	187	209	27
140	*156	13	164	183	9	188	*210	5
141	157	16	165	184	12	189	211	8
142	*158	19	166	185	15	190	212	11
143	159	22	167	186	18	191	213	13
144	*161	0	168	187	21	192	214	16
145	*162	3	169	188	24	193	215	19
146	163	6	170	*190	2	194	216	22
147	164	9	171	191	5	195	218	1
148	165	12	172	192	8	196	*219	3
149	166	15	173	193	10	197	220	6
150	167	18	174	194	14	198	221	9
151	168	21	175	195	13	199	222	12
152	169	24	176	196	16	200	*223	15
153	171	2	177	197	19			

* Rate actually found in *dastūrs*.

Appendix 4.B

Dastūr indices with Agra = 100

	Wheat	Gram	Barley	Mustard	Peas	Jowar	Lahdhra	Rice	Sugarcane	Cotton	Indigo
AGRA											
1. *Ḥavelī* Agra	100.00	100.00	100.00	100.00	100.00	100.00	100.00	100.00	100.00	100.00	100.00
2. Etawa	89.98	80.05	81.79	93.33	92.85	80.05	78.54	74.02	90.89	102.75	102.15
3. *Ḥavelī* Biana	100.00	94.99	90.81	100.00	107.15	89.98	—	96.36	100.73	102.57	101.43
4. Mandawar	100.00	89.98	90.89	100.00	103.58	80.05	85.70	105.57	90.89	102.57	102.86
5. Alwar	100.00	89.98	90.91	100.00	103.58	80.05	85.70	105.50	90.89	102.57	102.86
6. Bachhera	96.66	82.56	86.34	93.33	101.53	80.05	76.12	105.57	84.85	102.57	102.86
7. Mubarakpur	94.51	80.32	84.07	93.33	92.85	80.05	85.70	105.50	85.70	91.28	100.13
8. Erach	94.93	77.55	93.50	96.66	71.39	85.60	85.70	77.80	117.29	105.13	104.14
9. Tijara	96.66	82.56	86.34	93.33	100.00	80.05	85.70	105.57	125.50	102.57	102.86
10. Khora *ka* Thana	100.00	89.98	90.81	100.00	103.58	80.05	85.70	105.50	90.89	102.57	102.86
11. Besru	100.00	82.56	86.34	93.33	100.00	82.56	85.70	96.36	93.93	108.99	104.29
12. Sahar	100.00	82.56	86.34	93.33	100.00	92.56	85.70	96.36	92.57	108.94	104.14
13. Pahari	96.66	82.56	96.34	93.33	100.00	80.05	85.70	105.57	84.85	102.57	102.86
14. Nonehra	101.49	89.98	90.81	100.00	104.09	80.05	83.14	105.50	84.12	102.57	102.86
15. Kanauj	90.70	84.08	81.30	94.87	92.85	72.90	82.12	77.80	89.38	107.71	104.29
16. Sakit	96.66	87.48	86.34	97.14	101.53	87.48	85.70	81.51	93.33	107.71	102.30
17. Bhogaon	86.70	75.04	77.24	89.99	78.54	80.05	77.27	74.09	98.80	97.43	101.43
18. Sikandarpur Atreji	89.98	84.97	81.79	96.66	92.85	87.48	85.70	81.51	100.03	107.71	102.86

(*Continued*)

Appendix 4.B (*Continued*)

Dastūr indices with Agra = 100

	Wheat	Gram	Barley	Mustard	Peas	Jowar	Lahdhra	Rice	Sugarcane	Cotton	Indigo
19. Phaphund	94.99	77.55	81.79	96.66	71.39	85.60	85.70	77.80	77.80	96.96	105.14
20. Gawalior	103.34	97.23	81.79	100.00	100.00	100.00	100.00	92.45	100.00	100.00	102.30
21. Kalpi	94.99	94.99	81.79	97.14	71.39	85.60	85.70	77.80	96.88	105.14	104.22
22. Kol	89.98	80.05	81.79	86.65	85.70	79.96	78.29	77.80	90.89	102.75	104.22
23. Thana Farida	86.70	77.55	77.24	89.99	92.85	75.04	78.54	77.53	90.89	107.71	102.84
24. Akbarabad	94.99	80.05	86.34	86.65	92.85	79.96	78.54	77.80	90.89	102.75	102.84
25. Marehra	89.98	84.97	81.79	96.66	92.85	88.01	85.70	81.51	93.93	107.71	102.84
26. Narnaul	93.32	82.47	84.07	93.21	89.14	79.96	89.14	100.00	90.89	102.57	105.80
27. Baroda Rana	94.99	80.05	84.07	93.33	92.85	80.05	85.70	105.57	86.34	102.57	99.67
28. Chalkalana	91.65	80.05	84.07	93.33	85.70	74.15	85.70	88.93	84.85	102.57	102.86
29. Kanoda	—	—	—	—	—	—	—	—	—	—	—
DELHI											
1. *Ḥavelī Qadīm*	93.92	82.56	86.34	86.41	92.85	75.04	85.70	91.58	86.34	102.57	102.86
2. Panipat	86.70	82.56	81.79	86.65	85.70	75.04	85.70	74.09	83.33	105.14	102.86
3. Meerut	86.70	89.98	77.24	94.76	78.67	75.04	71.39	79.66	83.33	102.57	102.86
4. Baran	86.70	72.54	77.24	104.89	92.85	75.04	78.03	77.53	90.89	107.57	102.86
5. Jhajhar	91.65	75.04	84.07	93.33	85.70	75.04	85.70	88.93	84.85	102.57	102.86
6. Palwal	96.66	75.04	86.34	93.33	101.53	59.93	85.70	97.02	93.79	108.99	102.86
7. Rohtak	86.70	66.28	70.49	90.35	85.70	80.05	92.85	81.51	86.56	103.03	102.53
8. Badaon	75.01	67.53	93.09	78.31	—	84.26	71.39	60.64	84.85	110.28	103.22

(*Continued*)

Appendix 4.B (*Continued*)

Dastūr indices with Agra = 100

	Wheat	Gram	Barley	Mustard	Peas	Jowar	Lahdhra	Rice	Sugarcane	Cotton	Indigo
9. *ḥavelī* Hissar	93.32	65.03	81.79	94.76	93.74	84.97	89.40	85.22	84.85	102.57	105.72
10. Gohana	85.21	66.28	86.34	86.65	93.74	84.97	89.27	—	86.37	102.57	105.72
11. Sirsa	86.70	67.53	86.34	86.65	93.74	84.97	85.70	75.94	86.37	102.57	105.72
12. Maham	86.70	79.96	86.34	89.99	85.70	78.26	92.85	80.84	86.15	102.57	99.67
13. Rewari	94.99	80.05	84.07	93.33	82.85	80.05	92.27	105.57	86.34	102.57	99.75
14. Tarau	96.12	69.50	—	93.33	92.85	80.05	69.73	105.57	84.85	102.57	102.86
15. Sahra	51.94	78.26	86.34	—	101.53	82.56	85.70	96.37	93.93	108.99	104.29
16. Kohana	100.00	75.04	90.89	100.00	99.23	80.05	85.70	55.86	90.95	102.57	102.86
17. Deoband	83.36	75.04	72.76	88.92	103.58	60.02	71.39	70.38	83.33	102.57	100.00
18. Sardhana	86.70	77.55	77.24	94.76	96.42	75.04	71.39	80.12	83.33	102.57	102.86
19. Kairana	86.46	78.98	81.79	81.79	85.70	75.04	85.70	74.09	83.33	105.14	102.86
20. Indri	76.68	82.56	75.04	79.98	65.01	75.04	78.54	70.38	80.30	123.07	102.86
21. *Ḥavelī* Sirhind	76.68	78.26	71.14	79.98	71.39	75.04	80.33	70.38	82.57	123.07	102.86
22. Thanesar	88.25	71.29	64.80	75.45	70.63	77.55	78.54	74.09	81.54	120.78	102.86
23. Tihara	76.68	74.06	79.51	77.47	72.80	75.04	78.54	74.09	80.03	123.02	102.86
24. Samana	76.68	75.04	68.21	79.98	79.82	75.04	78.54	82.17	80.27	120.50	102.86
25. *Ḥavelī* Sambhal	83.24	75.04	68.21	86.65	96.42	82.47	78.54	70.38	87.86	117.94	104.29
26. Chandpur	81.69	80.05	72.76	83.31	96.42	86.58	78.54	68.52	88.62	111.70	100.00
27. Lakhnaur	75.01	80.05	72.76	78.31	—	82.56	71.39	70.38	81.82	110.73	103.22

(*Continued*)

Appendix 4.B (*Continued*)

Dastūr indices with Agra=100

	Wheat	Gram	Barley	Mustard	Peas	Jowar	Lahdhra	Rice	Sugarcane	Cotton	Indigo
ALLAHABAD											
1. *Ḥavelī* Allahabad	89.98	84.97	81.79	106.67	78.54	77.55	—	40.95	—	102.57	104.29
2. Jalalabad	86.70	87.48	82.28	80.93	92.85	—	—	—	—	—	—
3. Bhadoi	96.66	—	—	—	—	80.05		70.38	85.61	105.14	103.58
4. Banaras	96.66	92.23	97.72	119.90	128.48	89.98	—	81.51	83.33	110.28	103.58
5. *Ḥavelī* Jaunpur	96.66	92.49	136.34	119.90	128.48	89.98	—	81.51	83.33	110.28	103.58
6. Mongera	86.70	87.48	86.34	83.31	92.85	80.05	—	70.38	85.60	105.14	103.58
7. Chunadh	96.66	92.49	95.69	119.90	128.48	89.98	—	81.51	110.68	110.28	103.58
8. Ghazipur	96.66	92.49	97.24	119.90	128.48	89.98	—	81.51	110.43	110.28	103.58
9. Kara	89.62	84.97	—	105.24	78.54	76.39	—	74.09	71.31	102.57	104.27
10. Korra	103.93	77.55	81.46	94.87	71.39	74.42	—	77.80	96.96	105.14	104.29
11. Kutia	89.62	84.97	81.46	105.24	76.63	77.55	—	74.09	70.24	102.06	104.29
12. Jajmau	90.82	82.73	81.46	84.87	64.11	72.54	—	72.83	96.96	106.79	104.29
13. Kalinjar	94.81	77.55	81.46	96.66	65.01	83.36	—	77.80	97.34	105.14	104.29
14. Manikpur	86.70	87.48	86.34	115.73	92.85	78.98	—	70.38	85.53	105.14	103.65
15. Rae Bareilly	93.32	87.48	93.17	115.73	121.33	84.97	—	77.80	83.33	107.71	104.22
AWADH											
1. *Ḥavelī* Awadh	81.69	77.55	79.51	89.99	92.85	80.05	78.54	72.23	81.03	95.28	104.22
2. Ibrahimabad	93.32	87.48	93.17	113.23	121.33	84.97	82.12	77.80	83.33	107.71	103.58

(*Continued*)

Appendix 4.B (*Continued*)

Dastūr indices with Agra=100

	Wheat	Gram	Barley	Mustard	Peas	Jowar	Lahdhra	Rice	Sugarcane	Cotton	Indigo
3. Kishni	86.70	87.48	86.34	83.31	92.85	78.98	78.54	70.38	85.37	105.14	103.58
4. Bahraich	81.69	75.04	77.24	86.65	82.38	84.97	74.97	66.67	83.33	102.57	104.29
5. Firuzabad	83.36	72.54	72.76	86.65	78.54	75.04	78.54	68.52	90.89	105.57	104.29
6. Kharonsa	83.18	75.04	77.24	86.65	82.12	84.97	74.97	66.67	83.33	102.57	103.65
7. *Ḥavelī* Khairabad	—	—	—	—	—	75.04	78.54	68.52	90.89	102.57	—
8. Pali	—	—	—	—	—	72.54	82.12	77.80	89.38	107.71	—
9. Bhurwara	—	—	—	—	—	80.05	78.80	72.37	81.03	96.15	—
10. Gorakhpur	—	—	—	—	—	84.97	74.97	66.67	83.33	102.57	—
11. Lucknow	—	—	—	—	—	78.26	80.33	74.09	86.45	107.43	—
12. Unam	—	—	—	—	—	72.54	82.12	77.80	89.38	107.71	—
LAHORE											
1. Lahore	81.99	80.05	93.50	93.33	—	89.98	99.87	81.51	98.48	92.59	100.26
2. Parasroor	80.02	80.05	77.24	93.33	—	84.97	96.42	66.67	98.24	100.00	100.00
3. Patti Haibatpur	80.02	75.04	77.24	93.33	—	84.97	92.85	77.14	90.89	100.00	100.00
4. Jalendhar	80.02	—	—	—	—	80.05	85.70	70.38	83.33	102.75	100.00
5. Rohtas	66.67	70.04	63.66	79.98	—	70.04	78.54	55.60	83.33	87.39	85.74
6. Siyalkot	50.21	80.05	77.24	93.33	—	84.97	73.69	68.52	—	88.53	86.07
7. Hazara	83.36	77.55	77.24	106.79	—	84.97	100.00	81.51	100.00	105.14	101.43
8. Battala	73.34	75.04	72.76	86.65	—	80.14	95.15	81.51	92.41	97.48	100.00

(*Continued*)

Appendix 4.B (*Continued*)

Dastūr indices with Agra = 100

	Wheat	Gram	Barley	Mustard	Peas	Jowar	Lahdhra	Rice	Sugarcane	Cotton	Indigo
AJMER											
1. *Ḥavelī* Ajmer	73.35	75.04	68.21	133.25	84.16	55.01	64.24	74.22	75.75	69.49	85.71
2. Amber	46.69	44.72	40.89	79.98	64.24	34.97	39.34	38.10	58.29	46.15	54.59
3. Jodhpur	150.03	125.04	136.34	166.63	—	70.04	57.09	74.22	75.42	76.93	85.71
4. Chittor	83.36	70.04	68.21	79.97	71.39	65.04	71.39	88.93	75.42	87.20	71.43
5. Ranthambor	83.36	70.04	68.21	79.97	71.39	65.92	71.39	83.96	75.42	87.20	71.43
6. Chatsu	80.08	84.97	77.24	73.30	—	82.47	82.12	111.13	80.89	89.72	85.71
7. Delhwara	100.00	94.99	100.00	83.31	—	94.99	100.00	77.80	75.75	94.86	85.71
8. Toda	70.01	62.52	65.93	54.95	—	67.17	60.66	51.89	55.31	61.93	57.14
9. Nagur	150.03	125.04	136.34	166.63	—	70.04	57.09	74.09	75.75	76.83	85.71
MULTAN											
1. Multan	79.84	—	100.00	133.25	—	94.99	142.78	81.51	90.89	107.71	92.87
2. Dipalpur	66.67	—	61.38	86.65	—	80.05	92.85	82.17	85.61	100.00	101.43
3. Sadghara	82.65	—	72.76	92.61	—	84.97	99.23	81.51	96.96	102.57	102.15
MALWA											
1. Ujjain	—	—	..	—	—	—	—	—	—	—	—
2. Raisen	104.05	94.99	95.45	—	100.00	100.00	—	—	100.00	100.00	—
3. Mando	—	—	—	—	—	—	—	—	—	—	—

CHAPTER 5

Land-Revenue Realization

I

While *dastūrs* represented the tax claim laid on the peasant, the *jama'* or *naqdī* of the *Ā'īn-i Akbarī* represented revenue realization. In the Mughal administration, the system of assignment of *jagīrs* required that the *jama'* (or, as it was later styled, the *jama'-dāmī*) of the territory be exactly equal to the *ṭalab* or pay due to the assignee.[1] Abū'l Faẓl's own words imply such an equation.[2] The *jama'* could not, therefore, be an estimate of the total amount of assessed taxation, but the net income (i.e., gross realization less expenses on collection, including allowances from collection drawn by others) which, in the administration's view, the *jāgīrdār* could obtain from the territory in question.[3]

In the *ẓabṭī* provinces at least, the peasant had to part with about half his produce to satisfy the land-revenue demand. In these provinces, the *dastūrs*, multiplied by cultivated area, should have equalled the gross realization, provided the collection fully matched assessment. The proportion that the net realization bears to the gross collection can then theoretically be determined by finding the difference between the *dastūrs* multiplied by the gross cropped-area (worked out from *ārāẓī* figures), and the *jama'* (or *naqdī*) set out in detail in the *Ā'īn*'s 'Account of the Twelve *Ṣūbas*'.

[1] Cf. Habib, *Agrarian System*, 261 (rev. ed. 302).

[2] *Ā'īn*, I, 347.

[3] The definition of *jama'* (= *jama'-dāmī*) is at variance with that of Habib (*Agrarian System*, 1st ed., 261, but see rev. ed., 302) and other historians who appear to have assumed that it was an estimate of gross realization.

To clear a minor point: Abū'l Faẓl, while giving the *ṣūba* totals, uses the word *jama'*; but in the table where he sets out the *pargana*-wise break-up of his information, he puts the corresponding figures under the column heading, *naqdī*. It therefore appears that despite its other connotations,[4] the word *naqdī* is here synonymous with *jama'*.

Since the *jama'* was the estimate of net income from all sources of revenue which the assignee, or, in the unassigned areas, the king's establishment (*k͟hāliṣa sharīfa*), expected to receive, it must also have included taxes other than land revenue. This is not expressly stated in the *Ā'īn*, but it can be inferred from its statistics. While setting out the *pargana*-wise figures in the 'Account of the Twelve *Ṣūbas*', Abū'l Faẓl records the *jama'* against *maḥals* comprising only cities. In certain cases, the *maḥals* of *balda* (city) and *ḥavelī* (environs) bearing the same name are separately mentioned, no *ārāẓī* being recorded against the *balda*. In such a *maḥal*, therefore, the *jama'* could only be made up of the expected revenue from taxes other than land revenue. For example, for the city of Ahmadabad a substantial amount is entered as *jama'*, while no *ārāẓī* is recorded. More direct evidence is available from Bengal and in a stray case from Gujarat. Here the *jama'/naqdī* figures against certain *maḥals* are expressly stated to consist of income from taxes other than land revenue (Table 5.1, see next page).

The inclusion of taxes other than land revenue in the *jama'* is thus quite well established. There is, however, no easy way of determining the proportion, within the *jama'*, of the total amount derived from such taxes; what we have are only rough indicators. Assuming that taxes collected in the large towns accounted for the bulk of taxes other than land revenue, we can consider the *jama'* figures recorded for certain towns. Of the total *jama'* of 19,05,25,826 *dāms* for Agra *sarkār*, the *jama'* of the town of Agra with *ḥavelī* (rural district) was 4,49,56,450 *dāms*. This gives the Agra *pargana* a share in the *jama'* of the *sarkār* amounting to 23.60 per cent. The *pargana* of Agra, however, contained a large rural district, its measured area amounting to 9.76 per cent of the total measured area of the *sarkār*. Supposing that the rural area of *ḥavelī pargana* Agra contributed its share of land revenue in proportion to its area (nearly 10 per cent of the total *jama'* of the *sarkār*), the share of its urban district in the total revenue of the *sarkār* should have been about 14 per cent. For some *parganas* in *ṣūba* Gujarat containing sizeable cities, we have the following figures (Table 5.2, see next page).

[4] For these other connotations, see Habib, *Agrarian System*, 175–7, 258 (rev. ed. 215–17, 299).

Table 5.1

Specification of *jama'*	*Mahal*	*Sarkār*	*Ṣūba*
Sā'ir ẕakāt	Narainpur	Sonargaon	Bengal
,,	Gora	Ghoraghat	,,
Sā'ir	Harnagar	Silhat	,,
,,	Sakhu	Sonargaon	,,
Ḥāṣil ẕakāt	Dilwarpur	,,	,,
Sāi'r jalkar	Sali Sari	,,	,,
,,	—	Bazuha	,,
Ḥāṣil-i dukānha	Chaukhandi	Sonargaon	,,
Ẕakāt	—	Purnea	,,
Sā'ir az namaksār	—	Chatgaon	,,
Maḥsūl sāi'r-jihāt	*Maḥsūl*		
Sā'ir-jihāt	*Sā'ir-jihāt*	Surat	Gujarat

[a] *Ẕakāt* meant not the canonical duty of charitable gifts enjoined on Muslims, but a road-toll; *sāi'r* and *sāi'r-jihāt* signified market and transit dues; *jalkar*, tax on water-produce; *ḥāṣil-i dukānha*, tax on shops; *sā'ir az namaksār*, tax on salt-pans.

Table 5.2

Pargana	*Sarkār*	(a) *Jama'* of *pargana* as % of *jama'* of *Sarkār*	(b) *Ārāẕī* of *pargana* as % of *ārāẕī* of *sarkār*	(c) Inferred income from taxes other than land-revenue as % of total (a) minus (b) in *sarkār* as a whole
Baroda	Baroda	65.61	54.32	11.29
Surat	Surat	29.07	3.87	25.20
Ahmadabad	Ahmadabad	7.57	—	7.57
City & the Port of Ghogha		1.16	—	1.16
Patan	Patan	1.64	—	1.64

Though the share of urban taxes seems to vary a great deal, the figure for Agra can perhaps be taken as the maximum limit for urban taxation in any large territory of the Mughal empire. Agra was probably the biggest city in the empire, being not only its capital, but also its largest commercial centre. There was hardly any other large town in the Agra *sarkār* with the possible exception of Mathura and Bayana. The share of urban taxation in the total taxation-revenue of *sarkār* Agra could not therefore have been substantially above 14 per cent. In Gujarat the portion of urban taxes in Surat appears to be extraordinarily high; but Surat was a big port, while the agricultural zone in the *sarkār* contained large forested and hilly areas.

As a sample, representing the average rather more accurately in geographical terms, we can take later taxation statistics from eastern Rajasthan, which have the further merit of directly distinguishing between land revenue (*māl-o-jihāt*) and other taxes, which together formed the *mwāfiq jama‘ bandi* (revenue realized according to assessment). Taking the statistics for four *parganas*, *c.*1690, we get the figures set out in Table 5.3.[5]

Table 5.3

Pargana	Year	(a) *Māl-o-jihāt*	(b) *M. Jama‘ bandi*	(a) as % of (b)
Bahatri	1691	17,659	19,076	92.57
Malarna	1690	11,550	12,331	93.66
Lalsot	1687	35,035	37,433	93.59
Amber	1690	88,725	1,03,073	86.08

These figures inspire respect, since *pargana* Amber, which contained the capital town of the Kachhwahas, gives the lowest percentage share for land revenue. There being other adjacent *parganas* whose revenue figures for corresponding years are not available, a general average for the Amber territory cannot be attempted. But we may reasonably assume that the share of taxes other than land revenue did not normally exceed 10 per cent.

Let us, therefore, take it that the land revenue accounted for at least 90 per cent of the total *jama‘*. Given this assumption, the *jama‘* should ordinarily be reduced by 10 per cent, if we wish to estimate the net expected realization from land revenue only.

In his *jama‘/naqdī* Abū'l Faẓl also includes revenue income alienated under *suyūrghāl*,[6] the amount of which is specified by him separately as well. But since the income alienated under *suyūrghāl* too was a part of

[5] Papers from the Rajasthan State Archives. I am indebted to Dr S.P. Gupta for guidance on this evidence.

[6] See Chapter 6.

net realization by revenue receivers, and, because the *ārāẓī* figures presumably include areas granted in *suyūrghāl*, the *Ā'īn*'s *jama'* figures in so far as they include *suyūrghāl*, remain valid for any calculation of land revenue realization per unit of area.

Deducing from the *jama'* our estimated figure of net land revenue realization, we might go on to determine the gross land revenue collection if we could establish the sanctioned or allowed payments, commissions, remissions and exemptions that comprised the difference between gross and net realizations.

One important claim on land revenue was that of the *zamīndārs* and local officials and village headmen. An extended consideration of this claim is reserved for Chapter 7, but some discussion of the matter is here inescapable. In the seventeenth century the *zamīndār*'s share of authorized land-revenue in northern India was nominally set at 10 per cent.[7] It seems at first sight, from a tradition preserved in the *Mīr'āt-i Aḥmadī*, that the *zamīndārs*' share in Gujarat amounted to a quarter of the total revenue since the time of the Sultans, this right being duly confirmed by Akbar.[8] But it is not clear if the *zamīndārs* in Gujarat obtained a quarter of the revenue of the entire territory, or only of their own ancestral domain within it, there being also a peasant-held (*ra'iyatī*) zone in Gujarat, over which their claims did not extend. Should the latter have been very large, the *zamīndārs*' actual share might well have been substantially less than 25 per cent of the entire land revenue.

Evidence for the shares of local officials is partly found in the *Ā'īn*, but it has to be supplemented by sixteenth- and seventeenth-century documents. Their total share seems to have amounted to 7 per cent, the break-up being as follows:[9]

	%
Muqaddam (village headman)	2.5
Chaudhurī (*pargana*-level tax collector)	2.5
Qānūngo (*pargana*-level record keeper)	1.0
Patwārī (village accountant)	1.0

[7] Habib, *Agrarian System*, 146 (rev. ed., 182).

[8] *Mi'rat-i Aḥmadī*, I, 173–4. Cf. Habib, *Agrarian System*, 142 (rev. ed., 176).

[9] *Ā'īn*, I, 288, 300. See also Habib, *Agrarian System*, pp.131 & *n*, 135 & *n*, 294 & *n* (rev. ed., 162, 163&*n*, 169, 337).

While it is difficult to find how much the *jāgīrdār* was expected to spend on revenue collection, we are told that in the *khāliṣa* the amount allowed to the *karorī* (revenue-collector) for the costs of collection (*ḥaqq-i taḥṣīl*) was 20 per cent of the total collection in Akbar's time.[10] This proportion was allowed to the *karorī* while he was responsible for assessment as well as collection. It seems a fair assumption, therefore, that the *jāgīrdār* too must have spent about as much of the total towards the cost of tax collection within his assignment.

Adding all these different charges together, that is, taking 10 per cent for the *zamīndārs*' share, 7 per cent for that of local officials and 20 per cent for the permitted costs of collection, we should have to allow for 37 per cent as the normal total cost of collection of land revenue in northern India in Akbar's later years.

If one now wishes to get an estimate of the total gross land revenue collection from the net land revenue realization (= 90 per cent of the *jama'* in the *Ā'īn*), the latter figure should be so raised that the addition is 37 per cent of the sum obtained.

This would put the gross land revenue realization in the *ẕabṯi* provinces at about 159 per cent of the net land-revenue realization, or 143 per cent of *jama'* as set out in the *Ā'īn* (assuming the net land-revenue realization to be 10 per cent less than the *jama'*). We must remember that in working out these calculations we are ignoring many possible significant local variations, but our assumptions could still serve us for the general standard.

Let us now designate the gross land revenue realization so fixed as J′ (*jama'* raised by 43 per cent). If we divide J′ by A′ (the gross cropped area, for which see Chapter 2), we should get the gross land revenue realized per *bīgha*. Before making our detailed calculations on this basis, it is worth noting that Abū'l Faẕl provides us with a standard J′ per *bīgha*. He expressly gives us an estimate of *ḥāṣil* (or realization) from a *bīgha* of land as forty *dāms*. He regards this as the minimum, saying however, that the actual realization varied with each locality (*qaṣba*, i.e., *pargana*).[11] This statement occurs in his chapter on the *suyūrghāl* grants;

[10] *Khulāṣatu-s Siyāq*, Br. Mus., Add. 6588, f.79a, collated with Or 2026, f.34a. Habib suggests that 20 (*bīst*) is an error for 8 (*hasht*) (*Agrarian System*, 279; rev. ed. 322). But it is not possible to accept this suggestion since the same source goes on to say that the amount was first *reduced* to 10% in the reign of Shāhjahān, upon the transfer of the work of assessment from the work of *karorī* to *amīn*, and then further to 5% upon the loss of *faujdārī* (military) jurisdiction by the *karorī*.

[11] *Ā'īn*, I, 199. *Qaṣba* was used both as a synonym for *pargana* and as meaning a township.

and the context shows that he had in mind the income that a grantee was likely to derive from a *bīgha* of cultivated land. The grantee's income consisted of the land revenue and other fiscal claims due to the King. But the grantee was further exempted from all requisites of officials, expressly including the '5 per cent' cess of the *muqaddam* (and *chaudhurī*) and the '2 per cent' allowance of the *qānūngo* (and *patwārī*).[12] It seems, however, that he yet had to pay the *zamīndār*'s share (*ḥaqq-i milkiyat*).[13] In other words, the gross income of the grantee was likely to consist of our J′, less 10 per cent. Given 40 *dāms* as the grantee's income per *bīgha*, one would expect J′ per *bīgha* to have averaged 44.44 *dāms*.[14]

While, as we have seen, the *jama'/naqdī* in the *Ā'īn*, when scaled up by 43 per cent, gives us an estimate of gross land revenue realization, the gross cropped-area (A′) can be worked out by reducing the *ārāẓī* first by 10 per cent to exclude the uncultivable waste and, then, by the ratio of cultivable waste to cultivable land (i.e., gross cultivation plus cultivable waste) in the corresponding area in 1909–10.[15] The gross cropped-area can thus be determined for the regions for which modern land-use statistics are available, and where the identifications of the *Ā'īn*'s *parganas* are comparatively firm and complete.

We can accordingly work out the J′/A′ for those regions of the Mughal empire that comprise the modern states of U.P., Haryana and the Panjab—that is, the entire *ẓabṯ* region except for the Malwa and Ajmer provinces.

Since measurement might not have covered the entire assessed land, J′/A′ (gross-revenue collection divided by gross cultivation, 1595) should give us the maximum limit for revenue incidence in terms of *dāms* per *bīgha*. On the other hand, dividing J′ by gross cultivation figures for 1909–10 (designated C) will give us the minimum limit, since it can be assumed that gross cultivation in 1909–10 must have been considerably in excess of the actual gross cultivation in 1595.

Table 5.4 sets out J′, A′, and C and the ratio J′/A′ and J′/C for each *dastūr*-circle situated within U.P. Since within each *dastūr*-circle the cash rate on each crop was the same in all *parganas*, it would be possible

[12] Habib, *Agrarian System*, 131*n* (rev. ed. 162–3*n*).

[13] Ibid., 300–1 (rev. ed. 344–5).

[14] This suggests a refinement of our calculations of J′. To get J′ one should not just multiply J by 143/100, but take (with S = *Suyūrghāl*), J′ = (J – S) × 143/100 + S × 111/100. However, the difference would be trifling, and it can be argued that S is really J alienated (see Chapter 6) and thus not J′ – 10/100 J′ at all.

[15] See Chapter 2.

Table 5.4

Dastūr circle	J′ (*dāms*)	A′ (*bīgha-i Ilāhī*)	C (*bīgha-i Ilāhī*)	J′/A′	J′/C
1. Deoband	8,71,74,382	20,34,333	22,29,465	42.85	39.10
2. Sardhana	2,06,71,085	4,01,913	6,12,370	51.43	33.76
3. Chandpur	3,60,85,738	4,54,665	10,87,223	79.37	33.19
4. Sambhal	4,63,61,930	19,74,562	26,03,658	23.48	17.81
5. Lakhnaur	87,00,560	5,26,579	11,72,209	16.52	7.42
6. Kairana	76,36,719	1,36,800	1,40,976	55.82	54.17
7. Delhi (East of Yamuna)	6,91,80,480	14,80,307	24,50,073	46.73	28.24
8. Meerut	2,60,40,839	11,96,158	13,10,590	20.14	19.87
9. Baran	1,55,87,726	5,92,411	8,67,669	26.31	17.97
10. Badaun	4,97,87,399	13,62,064	50,05,895	36.55	9.95
11. Bahrwara	6,91,336	5,973	4,06,174	115.74	1.70
12. Pali	3,13,24,494	5,21,514	14,92,018	60.06	20.99
13. Thana Farida	2,71,40,755	5,71,831	13,20,210	47.46	20.56
14. Akbarabad	1,20,94,751	3,55,714	4,49,354	34.00	26.92
15. Kol	2,59,61,501	6,73,556	8,08,113	38.54	32.13
16. Marahra	1,18,69,924	3,14,067	2,42,588	37.79	48.93
17. Sikandarpur Atreji	3,85,559	2,42,280	70,223	1.59	5.49
18. Agra	10,76,60,225	21,25,267	21,62,269	50.66	49.79
19. Etawa	3,10,34,066	13,15,155	10,88,003	23.59	28.56
20. Phaphund	77,68,319	69,147	2,69,460	112.34	28.83
21. Kalpi	7,07,36,304	10,20,227	17,16,375	69.33	41.21
22. Sakit	1,21,65,207	3,32,824	5,69,992	36.55	21.34
23. Bhogaon	3,19,02,733	11,35,451	16,68,350	28.10	19.12
24. Kanauj	2,21,63,330	3,59,466	12,75,323	61.66	17.38
25. Khairabad	3,04,03,327	8,34,522	20,48,825	36.43	14.84
26. Unam	2,46,89,865	5,41,901	8,67,395	45.56	28.46
27. Lucknow	9,07,78,659	19,50,369	37,33,943	46.54	24.31
28. Ibrahimabad	6,36,948	14,040	78,000	45.37	8.17
29. Awadh	4,27,86,378	20,40,478	25,20,718	20.97	16.97
30. Kishni	19,15,179	20,083	24,053	95.36	79.62
31. Bahraich	2,96,10,143	11,60,319	26,08,842	25.52	11.35
32. Firuzabad	30,01,684	1,07,400	2,81,413	27.95	10.67
33. Gorakhpur	1,70,55,310	1,84,309	90,97,370	92.54	1.87
34. Khuransa	18,80,523	20,817	5,15,671	90.34	3.65

(*Continued*)

Table 5.4 (*Continued*)

Dastūr circle	J′ (*dāms*)	A′ (*bīgha-i Ilāhī*)	C (*bīgha-i Ilāhī*)	J′/A′	J′/C
35. Jaunpur	7,87,34,154	6,18,520	53,33,617	127.29	14.76
36. Banaras	1,26,70,684	1,57,273	5,39,938	80.56	23.47
37. Chunar	83,09,664	78,456	14,15,454	105.91	5.87
38. Ghazipur	1,96,33,359	2,13,114	6,99,881	92.13	28.05
39. Jajmau	71,93,288	70,856	2,47,158	101.52	29.10
40. Kara	2,99,07,117	3,43,401	11,19,832	87.09	26.71
41. Kutia	27,56,813	26,748	1,92,307	103.07	14.34
42. Korra	1,49,26,991	2,31,626	5,92,832	64.44	25.18
43. Rai Bareilly	1,29,91,606	1,13,469	5,63,956	114.49	23.04
44. Manikpur	3,47,94,028	3,35,091	14,22,047	103.83	24.47
45. Ghiswa	14,92,451	14,189	21,532	105.18	69.31
46. Bhadoi	2,07,92,093	1,75,859	7,45,529	118.23	27.89
47. Allahabad	1,02,30,869	—	—	—	—

Note: *Dastūr* circles Nos. 1–10 belong to *ṣūba* Delhi; 11, 12, and 25–34 to Awadh; 13–24 to Agra; and 35–47 to *ṣūba* Allahabad.

to compute, as we shall see, the average cash revenue-rate for each circle (by applying weights based on the distribution of crops cultivated in these localities during the nineteenth century). Moreover, the *dastūr*-circle happens to be the smallest unit for which J′/C can be calculated, since for the present the map area can be measured only for the *dastūr*-circles, since their limits alone (and not those of *parganas*) are shown in Irfan Habib's maps. Moreover, with the *dastūr*-circles each embracing a number of known places, the margin of error in measuring the area is greatly reduced.

In certain *dastūr* circles, J′/C is very close to J′/A′, in other words the difference between the upper and lower limits of gross land-revenue incidence is very small. These circles present us with a correspondingly narrow margin within which the average land revenue collected per unit of assessed area may be placed. In the *dastūr*-circle of Agra, the difference between the two limits is less than one *dām* per *bīgha*, while its J′/C is the highest in U.P. The gross cultivation (A′) in the territory of the Agra circle in 1595 was 98 per cent of what it was in 1909–10. This means that A′ here included almost the entire assessed area, and there is little possibility that the actual incidence was less on account of any unsurveyed revenue-paying land being excluded from the *Ā'īn*'s figure of *ārāẓī*. It is possible, Agra being the capital and the biggest city of the empire, that the surrounding districts experienced high prices and maintained an extensive cultivation of market crops, which generally yielded high revenue. But this very fact also suggests that no other *dastūr*-circle could have had such a high incidence of revenue upon assessed land. In turn, we are led to a further inference: in the *dastūr*-circles where J′/A′ is higher than in Agra, i.e., where it exceeds fifty *dāms* per *bīgha*, the high rate must be due to incomplete measurement, A′ there representing only a fraction of actual gross cultivation of 1595. From our own calculations of A′ and C, in Table 5.4, this seems invariably to be the case.

The land-revenue incidence in the Agra *dastūr*-circle cannot serve as an index of the average revenue burden per *bīgha*, since because of the likelihood of higher prices prevalent here, it really sets the maximum limit. Now among the *dastūr* circles in U.P., J′/A′ has a wide range of variations, the lowest being barely two *dāms* (Sikandarpur Atreji) and the highest 127 *dāms* (Jaunpur). Even if we omit those which exceed fifty *dāms* as non-actuals, the variations would still be too wide to lead us to a convincing average. One alternative then is to work out a modal index.

For this purpose, we have arranged the *dastūr* circles according to their J′/A′ into classes with a class length of 10 (Table 5.5).

Table 5.5

J′/A′	Number of *dastūr* circles	J′/A′	Number of *dastūr* circles
0–10	1	70–80	1
10–20	1	80–90	2
20–30	8	90–100	4
30–40	6	100–10	5
40–50	6	110–20	4
50–60	3	120–30	1
60–70	4		

If mode is any index of incidence, it would seem that the revenue burden mainly ranged between 20 and 50, since the three classes have the highest number of *dastūr*-circles (twenty in all, out of forty-six). Taking the mean between the extremes of the three classes, one gets thirty-five.

Arranging J′/C similarly we get Table 5.6 (next page).

The class with the highest number of circles is 20–30 (with 17 out of 46 *dastūr*-circles), followed by class 10–20 (11 *dastūr*-circles). Since

Table 5.6

J′/C	Number of *dastūr* circles	J′/C	Number of *dastūr* circles
0–10	8	40–50	4
10–20	11	50–60	1
20–30	17	60–70	0
30–40	4	70–80	1

J′/C represents the floor for revenue incidence, one should infer that the average revenue-incidence was not likely to be lower than 30 *dāms* per *bīgha-i Ilāhī*. This supports the figure of 35 *dāms* for the average incidence of gross land-revenue collection per *bīgha* of assessed land deduced from Table 5.5.

If we take the figures for J′ and A′ for all those circles where J′/A′ is below the J′/A′ for Agra,[16] the J′/A′ comes to 35.80 *dāms* per *bīgha*; a figure that further strengthens our estimate of 35 *dāms*/*bīgha* as the average incidence of estimated gross collection in the U.P. plains, *c.*1595.

However, the above estimate is that of average revenue-burden and does not exclude the possibility of substantial variations in individual localities within U.P. We have seen that the *dastūr* circle of Agra had a higher revenue incidence (around 50 *dāms*/*bīgha*) while there are four *dastūr*-circles with J′/A′ lower than 25 *dāms*/*bīgha*.

Since the *dastūrs* represented different rates for different crops, they cannot be converted into an average rate per *bīgha* of cultivation without some system of weighting. Since we do not know what area was under which crop in 1595, we can only draw upon information derived from modern statistics. Although crop distribution could not have remained the same in the intervening period, the use of modern information for the purpose of giving weights to the *dastūrs* of individual crops might still lead us to useful results. This can be seen from the evidence for Aligarh District. We have statistics for crop distribution for two years, namely 1872–3 and 1909–10.[17] The cropping pattern in 1872–3, when the impact of the railways was still only partly felt is naturally different from that of 1909–10. Even so, if we apply to the *dastūrs* the two different systems of weighting based on crop-distribution in 1872–3 and in 1909–10, the

[16] Only circles where J′/A′ is of this magnitude should be taken for the reason (discussed earlier in this chapter) that wherever J′/A′ is higher than for Agra, A′ cannot simply be taken to represent the total gross cultivated area.

[17] Smith, *Final Settlement Report*, 44–5; Nevill, *Aligarh Dist. Gaz.*, App.VI.

result is little affected. Weights based on 1872–3 give us 50.69 *dāms*; those on 1909–10 give 49.73 *dāms* per *bīgha-i ilāhī*.

By recourse to modern crop-area statistics for assigning weights to the various crops, we offer in Table 5.7 the estimated average *dastūr* per *bīgha* of cultivation (R) for certain *dastūr* circles, together with J′, J′/A′ and J′/C for the same circles. For assigning weights, the modern crop-statistics used are those given for each *taḥṣil* in Nevill's *U.P. District Gazetteers* for the first decade of the twentieth century. Crops whose *dastūrs* have been used to calculate the average weighted rates throughout covered more than 80 per cent of the sown area according to Nevill's statistical tables.

Multiplying the average *dastūr* or revenue rate (R) by gross cultivated area (A′), worked out from the *ārāẓī* figures, we get the *dastūr*-based total assessed revenue, which, if the *dastūrs* were faithfully enforced, the peasants should have paid to satisfy the land-revenue demand. As against this, J′/A′ should represent the actual estimated gross revenue realization per *bīgha*. A comparison of R and J′/A′ should therefore show us the gap that might have existed between the land revenue claimed and what was actually obtained from the peasant.

Table 5.7

Dastūr-circle	J′/A′	J′/C	R	J′/A′ as % of R
Delhi				
(East of Yamuna)	46.73	28.24	59.08	79.10
Meerut	20.14	19.87	44.40	45.36
Baran	26.31	17.97	51.50	51.09
Kol	38.54	32.13	49.70	77.55
Agra	50.66	49.79	52.00	97.42
Deoband	42.85	39.10	53.26	80.45
Awadh	20.97	16.97	45.10	46.49
Bahraich	25.52	11.35	43.20	59.07
Ghazipur	92.13	28.05	55.00	167.51
Unam (Unao)	45.56	28.46	47.60	95.71

Note: J′/A′ and J′/C are taken from Table 5.4.

In all the *dastūr* circles covered in Table 5.7, J′/A′ is invariably lower than R. The only exception is Ghazipur, where A′ happens to be only a fraction of gross cultivation; so the exception it offers is of no importance. In two of the 10 *dastūr* circles the revenue incidence is even less than half the *dastūr* incidence, and in most others the difference between the two is substantial. Only in the *dastūr* circle of Agra is the difference as slight as 2.58 per cent. Otherwise J′/A′ as percentage of R ranges from 45.36 to 95.71. Nowhere is R less than 40 *dāms/bīgha*.

The average J′/A′ in all the ten *dastūr* circles, barring Ghazipur, comes to 34.98 *dāms* per *bīgha*—a figure that once again reinforces our estimate of 35 *dāms* per *bīgha* for average revenue-incidence. The average *dastūr* for these circles is 49.19 *dāms* per *bīgha*. This average has been calculated by multiplying A′ by R for each *dastūr* circle and then dividing the result by the total A′ of all the circles; it is, therefore, not a simple but a weighted average. We may then consider 50 *dāms* per *bīgha* to be a fair approximation to the average *dastūr* or revenue rate for the entire region of plains in U.P.

If we are right in this assumption, it follows that here the actual revenue incidence was only 70 per cent of incidence implied by the *dastūrs*.

One should remember that we have calculated J′ by so increasing the *jama*ʻ (*naqdī*), as to accommodate other claims on land revenue, such as those of *zamīndārs*, local officials and headmen, and the cost of collection. It is, therefore, all the more striking that the gulf between the land revenue claimed (R) and actual revenue realization (J′/A′) should be so large in U.P. which comprised two entire *ṣūbas* (Awadh and Allahabad) and large portions of the *ṣūbas* of Agra and Delhi. We may now try to see whether this was the situation in other regions as well.

II

Turning to Haryana and the Panjab, we can follow the same assumptions about the ratio between *jama*ʻ and gross realization and between *ārāẓī* and gross collection as we have done for U.P. I have, accordingly, scaled up the *jama*ʻ by 43 per cent to obtain gross land-revenue collection (J′) and the *ārāẓī* figures have been converted into those of gross cultivation (A′) by reducing them first by 10 per cent to allow for uncultivable waste and further by the percentage of cultivable waste to total cultivable area at the beginning of the present century, to allow for cultivable waste.

To calculate the average *dastūr* or revenue-rates (R), weights have been assigned on the basis of early twentieth-century crop area statistics, for individual *taḥṣīls* in the *Panjab District Gazetteers*,[18] the *taḥṣīls* being grouped to correspond as nearly as possible with *dastūr* circles. Once these are assembled, it appears that the *dastūr* circles situated in this region can be combined into four distinct blocks, on the basis of contiguity and statistical similarities. See Table 5.8.

[18] *Panjab District Gazetteers*, Lahore, 1913, Parts B of Volumes XII to XXVII.

Table 5.8

	J′/A′	J′/C	R	A′ as % of A	A′ as % of C	J′/C as % of R	J′/A′ as % of R
South Haryana							
Jhajhar	37.03	12.87	36.93	34.24	34.76	34.85	100.27
Hissar	15.08	11.00	43.08	56.47	72.97	25.53	35.00
Sirsa	35.64	23.45	36.57	50.16	65.81	64.12	97.46
Samana	22.51	8.93	30.82	31.58	39.67	28.97	73.04
Gohana	77.66	22.87	45.56	8.45	29.46	50.20	170.46
Total	23.23	10.96	36.45	36.18	48.53	30.07	63.73
Delhi–Sirhind							
Delhi (west of Yamuna)	67.79	53.38	43.65	41.52	78.74	122.29	155.23
Panipat	55.81	37.71	50.33	41.01	67.55	74.93	110.89
Thanesar	77.86	58.72	46.88	49.24	75.42	125.26	166.08
Sirhind	38.71	37.53	46.63	85.11	96.95	80.48	83.02
Total	51.00	43.54	46.79	54.22	85.39	93.05	109.00
Lahore–Jalandhar							
Jalandhar	54.52	41.10	46.79	58.55	75.38	87.84	116.52
Haibatpur	33.66	35.91	44.09	78.59	106.69	81.45	76.34
Lahore	73.49	17.88	53.72	1.62	17.23	33.28	136.80
Batala	63.38	62.46	52.20	81.79	98.53	119.66	121.42
Barasur	88.98	54.63	55.00	46.84	61.39	99.33	161.78
Sialkot	77.63	51.96	45.81	57.52	67.34	113.42	169.46
Total	57.96	45.61	49.43	54.15	71.39	97.05	114.83
Total[a]	55.21	46.66	48.08	64.66	81.87		
Hazara	129.77	18.52	48.46	5.53	14.27	38.22	267.79
Rohtas	72.63	26.96	46.91	14.58	37.11	57.47	154.83

[a] Excepting Lahore.

The South Haryana block displays features similar to those of the U.P. *dastūr* circles. Though the J′/A′ here varies from 15.08 to 77.66, the average for the block comes to 23.23 *dāms*/*bīgha*. One new feature is that unlike the *dastūr* circles in U.P., the average *dastūr* (R) in the South Haryana block is below 40 *dāms*/*bīgha*. Moreover in Jhajhar and Sirsa, the average *dastūr* is almost equal to or even slightly lower than J′/A′. But the average J′/A′ for the whole block is less than two-thirds of the average R, i.e., the difference between the revenue claimed and gross collection is a little larger than in U.P.

In the Delhi–Sirhind block we have a radically different picture. Here, though the R is never less than 40 *dāms/bīgha*, the J′/A′ in three out of four *dastūr* circles is substantially higher than R. Since A′ is about three-fourths of the gross cultivation *c.*1910–11, the high value of J′/A′ cannot be attributed to incomplete measurement. In two cases even the J′/C, which sets the lower limit of land-revenue incidence, is higher than R. Over the entire block J′/A′ is 9 per cent in excess of the average R and J′/C is 93.05 per cent of R, a situation so very different from U.P. where even J′/A′, the maximum limit, was only 70 per cent of R. This difference in pattern is well illustrated by the figures for the portion of the *dastūr*-circle of Delhi lying on either side of the river Yamuna. The revenue incidence on the eastern (U.P.) side works out at two-thirds of the average *dastūr* (R). But in the western (Haryana) portion, the actual revenue incidence (J′/A′) is 55 per cent higher than the average *dastūr*; here even J′/C is 22 per cent above R. This is chiefly because J′/A′ in the western portion is nearly 170 per cent of the J′/A′ in the eastern portion of the *dastūr* circle.

The Lahore–Jalandhar block similarly gives a high revenue incidence while the average *dastūr* (R) is of the same magnitude as in U.P. Here, barring Haibatpur, J′/A′ for all the circles is higher than R, and the average J′/C is almost equal to the average *dastūr*.

It is thus evident that from Delhi westwards to beyond Lahore, the incidence of land-revenue collection was higher than in U.P. Not only is J′/A′ higher here than in U.P., but even J′/C is appreciably higher than the J′/C in *dastūr* circles within U.P. In the two blocks (Delhi–Sirhind and Lahore–Jalandhar) realization seems, indeed, to exceed the revenue claimed under the *dastūrs*.

An interesting feature—possibly of some significance—is that the *dastūr* circles where J′/A′ is the highest are ranged along the route from Delhi to Lahore.

In the *dastūr* circles of Hazara and Rohtas measurement was probably incomplete, because while J′/A′ is as high as 129.77 *dāms* per *bīgha*, A′ amounts to only 14 per cent of the gross cultivation in 1910–11 and 5.5 per cent of the map area. Little definite can therefore be said about these two *dastūr* circles.

III

Another region for which J′/A′ and J′/C can be computed is Gujarat. For this province no *dastūrs* were formulated, and so one cannot compare the J′/A′ with R. But one can still compare the J′/A′ in Gujarat with J′/A′ in the two regions (U.P. and the British 'Panjab') already covered.

We may argue that for determining J′ or gross land-revenue collection for Gujarat, the *jama*ʻ needs to be raised by a higher percentage than that we have allowed for in U.P., Haryana and the Panjab. In Gujarat the *zamīndār*'s share was 25 per cent of the revenue of his *zamīndārī* territory, and not 10 per cent as noted already. But the *zamīndārī* areas only formed a part of the whole; and the relative size of the area under the *zamīndārī* and the *raʻiyatī* zones is not known. I have therefore allowed 10 per cent of gross collection as the *zamīndārs*' average share here as well. Since there are no *dastūr* circles, I have taken the *sarkārs* as units; and, to work out gross cultivation or A′, I have followed the same assumption as for U.P., Haryana and the Panjab.

Table 5.9

Sarkārs	J′/A′	J′/C	A′ as % of C
Ahmadabad	54.92	37.42	68.15
Patan	36.27	16.63	45.85
Nadaut	29.33	23.73	80.91
Baroda	82.88	73.17	88.30
Bhroach	39.09	16.77	42.89
Champaner	32.65	9.32	28.54
Surat	27.22	23.98	88.00
Godhra	14.96	5.55	37.13
Average	46.91	26.95	57.945

We can see from Table 5.9 that J′/A′ in the various *sarkārs* of Gujarat ranged, in terms of *dāms* per *bīgha*, from 14.96 (Godhara) to 82.88 (Baroda); for all the *sarkārs* put together the J′/A′ is 46.91 *dāms*/*bīgha*. This shows an incidence which is much in excess of our average for the U.P., but still keeps largely within Abū'l Faẓl's limit of 40 *dāms* per *bīgha* or rather 44.4 *dāms*, if we add the *zamīndārs*' share of one-tenth.

The higher incidence is perhaps partly to be explained by the fact that prices in Gujarat appear to have been higher than inland. Gujarat was a large importer of foodstuffs,[19] and as such the food prices in Gujarat ought to have been relatively high. Another possible reason for the high incidence of *jama*ʻ in Gujarat could be a higher claim for tax in the produce. Seventeenth-century evidence supports this assumption. Geleynssen

[19] Gujarat is said to have imported wheat and other food grains from Malwa and Ajmer, and rice from the south (*Āʼīn*, I, 485). See also Habib, *Agrarian System*, 73–4 (rev. ed. 80–1).

and De Laet suggest that in Gujarat the demand was closer to three-fourths instead of one-half, the norm in northern India.[20]

Another factor still for high revenue-incidence could have been the superior cropping pattern, especially manifested in extensive cultivation of cotton,[21] a crop for which *dastūrs* in the *ẓabti* provinces are 25 to 40 per cent higher than for wheat. In Baroda the revenue incidence seems extraordinarily high, even allowing for a different price-level. Here even J′/C, which represents the floor, is 73.17 *dāms* per *bīgha*. This may possibly be attributed to the great fertility of the tract. In 1938–9, in Baroda district of the Sate of Baroda, cotton covered 42.74 per cent of the entire sown area, while in the Ahmadabad district, in the same year, it covered only 23.32 per cent.[22] On the other hand, in both these districts a far higher proportion of land was under cotton than anywhere in U.P. at that time.[23]

These statistics of land-revenue realization form an interesting geographical pattern. In one large block comprising U.P. and parts of Haryana, the realization seems to fall much short of the standard demand, for the average revenue-incidence (J′/A′) is only slightly more than two-thirds of the average *dastūr* (R). In these regions the average revenue-incidence is also far lower than the floor-limit of 40 or 44.4 *dāms* per *bīgha* set by Abū'l Faẓl. In other parts of Haryana and eastern and central Panjab, however, the realization slightly exceeds the standard, and the incidence of gross realization (J′/A′) is about 51 per cent higher than in U.P. It may be noted that while demand as represented by the average *dastūr* (R) does not alter very much from area to area, the incidence of gross collection (J′/A′) generally shows great variations, which are responsible for the great difference between U.P. and the Panjab–Haryana region.

In Gujarat the revenue realized per cultivated *bīgha* was substantially higher (by 40 per cent) than in U.P., but lower (by 8 per cent) than in the Panjab. Since Gujarat was a province for which *dastūrs* were not set, we cannot naturally say how far the actual realization approximated to standard demand.

To what factors can one ascribe the lower revenue incidence in U.P.? The gross collection here sometimes even fell to less than half the claimed land-revenue (Table 5.4). Meerut, for example, has J′/A′=20.14

[20] Habib, *Agrarian System*, 194 (rev. ed. 234).

[21] See Salbancke's account relating to 1609 in *Purchas*, III, 82, and Pelsaert, *Remonstrantie*, 254; tr. 9, for cotton cultivation in Gujarat.

[22] *Agricultural Statistics*, Vol.2, 1938–9. Unfortunately, I am unable to obtain earlier figures for Baroda state.

[23] In 1938–9 Mathura had the highest proportion of sown land under cotton (9.95%) in U.P. Cotton occupied only 1.45% of the sown land in the entire province.

and J′/C = 19.87; we may infer that the actual incidence of revenue in that circle was about 20 *dāms* per *bīgha*. The average *dastūr* (R) for the circle was 44.40 *dāms* per *bīgha*, i.e., the gross collection per *bīgha* of actual cultivation was only 45 per cent of the demand (Table 5.4). Similar large gaps are seen in the corresponding figures for Baran, Awadh and Bahraich, besides other circles.

It seems that in these areas there were either some losses from revenue that we have not taken into account, or that we have gravely underestimated the proportion of uncultivated land included in the *ārāẓī*. As far as the latter possibility is concerned, we have a suggestion from Desai that *ārāẓī* was not the gross cultivated area, but arable land, some of which was cultivated only 'occasionally'.[24] On detailed scrutiny, however, this thesis of 'shifting cultivation' runs into some insurmountable obstacles.

For one thing, plotted on the map the *dastūr* circles with low J′/A′ are so interspersed with circles of high revenue incidence that one would be forced to believe that the phenomenon of 'shifting cultivation' was confined to some scattered non-contiguous pockets which were not geographically or ecologically distinct in any sense from the tracts around them. Some of these pockets such as Meerut and Baran were situated in the Doāb region. These two circles adjoined Thana Farida, with J′/A′= 47, Delhi J′/A′=39.99, and Sardhana, J′/A′=51. Similarly, the *dastūr* circles situated around Awadh, with J′/A′=21, had much higher J′/A′. Moreover, according to Desai, it was the 'selection of land for cultivation', rendered possible by the low intensity of cultivation that was responsible for higher yields.[25] In the South Haryana block, A′ (gross cultivation in 1595) amounts to about half of the map-area and comes to around 55 per cent of what it was *c.*1910. In this block, however, J′/A′ (23.23 *dāms*/*bīgha*) is much less than the average J′/A′ for U.P. Thus while South Haryana seems a fit case for the existence of 'shifting' cultivation, the yields, to judge from the *dastūrs*, were lower than in U.P. Apart from the low *dastūr* for individual crops (Chapter 4), the average weighted *dastūr* (R) here is only 36.45 *dāms*/*bīgha*, i.e., considerably lower than the average R for U.P.

The low revenue-incidence in U.P. cannot, therefore, be explained by assuming a very high component of fallows or abandoned lands in the *ārāzī*. The remaining possibility is that the loss of revenue in U.P. was more than we have allowed. We felt fairly certain about the allowances sanctioned for the local village officials (*muqaddam*, *chaudhrī*, *qānūngo*

[24] Ashok V. Desai, 'Population and Standard of Living in Akbar's Time—A Second Look', *IESHR*, Vol.XV, No.1, January–March 1978, 74 & 76.

[25] Ibid., 76.

and *patwārī*), since these are specified in the *Ā'īn*. Evidence about the amount allowed for the cost of collection, though late, is sufficiently circumstantial to invite trust. No direct information about the proportion of the *zamīndārs*' share is, however, forthcoming from the *Ā'īn* or any other source belonging to the sixteenth or even the early seventeenth century. But one way of checking the different magnitude of the *zamīndārs*' share of revenue consists in estimating the *zamīndārs*' expenditure by the help of the *Ā'īn*'s information about their retainers and horses. The method used for attempting these estimates is explained in Chapter 7.

Table 5.10 gives the *zamīndārs*' expenditure (ZE) and J′/A′ for some *dastūr* circles and *sarkārs* in U.P.

Table 5.10

Dastūr circle	*Sūba*	ZE as % of J	J′/A′
Deoband	Delhi	4.92	42.85
Lakhnaur	Delhi	62.29	16.52
Delhi	Delhi	3.80	39.99
Meerut	Delhi	48.69	20.14
Awadh	Awadh	14.99	20.97
Khairabad	Awadh	7.32	36.43
Kol	Agra	22.00	38.54
Kanauj	Agra	23.00	61.66
Kalpi	Agra	10.00	69.33
Agra	Agra	16.53	50.66

The general correlation between the high expenditure of *zamīndārs* as percentage of *jama*ʿ and the low incidence of gross collection is noteworthy. We infer that it was not really the actual amount of land revenue extracted from the peasant which was low in U.P., but that the Mughal administration often conceded an exceptionally large share to *zamīndārs* or local potentates in many localities.

This unevenness of the *zamīndārs*' share was not confined to the inland provinces. In *ṣūba* Gujarat again we find an obvious inverse relation between the *zamīndārs*' expenditure and incidence of gross-revenue collection.

Sarkār	ZE as % of J	J′/A′	J′/C
Godhra	44	14.96	5.55
Baroda	4	82.88	3.17

Our figure (35 *dāms* per *bīgha*) for incidence of gross collection in U.P. may therefore be an underestimate only because we have assumed the *zamīndārs*' share at a uniform 10 per cent of revenue. If we take the *zamīndārs*' share to average roughly somewhere between 15 and 20 per cent of gross land-revenue, the incidence of gross collection for U.P. would rise to between 38 and 42 *dāms* per *bīgha*. This estimate too is rather arbitrary; but it does not seem to be far wrong, keeping in view the fact that there is a cluster of twelve *dastūr* circles with revenue rates varying between 30 and 50 *dāms* per *bīgha* of cultivation (see Table 5.5).

IV

For the other parts of the Mughal Empire (other than U.P., Panjab and Gujarat), it does not seem possible to determine the revenue incidence per unit of area of cultivated land on similar lines. In the remaining *ṣūbas* either the measurement of land was not undertaken by Akbar's administration (as in Bengal, Berar, Khandesh and parts of Ajmer, Malwa and Bihar) so that no *ārāẓī* figures are available; or the measurement was so incomplete that the *ārāẓī* figures cannot be used for forming any estimate of the gross cropped-area (as for large parts of *ṣūbas* Malwa, Bihar and Ajmer). These areas (except for portions of Malwa and Ajmer) were not under the *ẓabṭ* system of assessment; thus here also we do not have *dastūrs* for the various crops.

In the absence of the *ārāẓī* statistics we are left with the map-area (M) in *bīgha-i ilāhī* as the only means of studying comparative revenue-incidence. I have computed the *jama*' incidence per *bīgha* of map area (J/M) for all the *sarkārs* of the Empire (see Map IV).[26] The *ṣūba* figures are set out in Table 5.11 (see next page).

As might be expected, the ratio of the *jama*' to map area varies from province to province. The range of variations is quite wide, from 24.13 (Khandesh) to 1.96 (Malwa). Clearly the primary factor to consider, in explaining the variations, is the varying extent of gross cultivation in relation to the map area. In regions where the cultivated area constituted a larger portion of the map area we should expect the J/M to have been high; and, conversely, in sparsely cultivated regions the J/M should have been low. When we compare the J/M of certain *ṣūbas* with the ratios of gross cultivation to the map area in modern territories roughly corresponding to

[26] The map area is based on Irfan Habib's *Atlas of the Mughal Empire* and the *jama*' figures are as calculated by me after collating the MSS and verifying the totals of *parganas*. They do not necessarily conform to *sarkār*/*ṣūba* totals given by Abū'l Faẓl himself.

Table 5.11

Ṣūba	J/M	*Ṣūba*	J/M
Bengal	2.69	Gujarat	7.91
Orissa	7.84	Ajmer	2.24
Bihar	4.34	Delhi	8.43
Allahabad	5.76	Lahore	9.76
Awadh	7.14	Multan	2.23
Agra	5.56	Thatta	2.24
Malwa	1.96	Kashmir	5.19
Malwa (without *Sarkār* Garh)	4.31	Kabul	2.01
Berar	8.23	Khandesh	24.13

them, there is a striking correlation between the two. This can be seen from Table 5.12 (see p. 151), where the area of gross cultivation is taken from the *Agricultural Statistics* for the year 1897–8.

We thus find that the incidence of *jama'* is invariably low where the modern gross cropped-area forms a proportion of the map area lower than 40 per cent; in such cases J/M never exceeds 2.4. Where GC exceeds 50 per cent of the map area, J/M does not fall below 5.8. All this suggests that in these regions, the extent of cultivation was the major factor in determining variations in the incidence of *jama'* per unit of map area.

But in some other *ṣūbas* positive correlation with GC/M is not obtained. For example, while GC forms 67 per cent of the map area of Bengal and 68.4 per cent of Bihar, the J/M of the two *ṣūbas* is respectively only 2.69 and 2.34. Here some other factors seem to be at work. The most obvious is the price level: Abū'l Faẓl tells us quite expressly that Bengal was marked by constant prevalence of low prices (*arzānī*).[27] The low J/M in Bengal and probably Bihar could, therefore, be best ascribed to the lower price-levels prevailing in the eastern regions. It is noteworthy that the J/M was below 5 *dāms* in 14 of a total of 19 *sarkārs* in Bengal; while in the *sarkārs* around Hugli River (Lakhnauti, Barbakabad, Tanda, Sharifabad and Sulaimanabad) it exceeded 5 *dāms*. One may explain this, again, by suggesting that a slightly higher price-level prevailed in this commercially-oriented region. We have already seen that the high revenue-incidence in Gujarat is probably to be ascribed

[27] *Ā'īn*, I, 389.

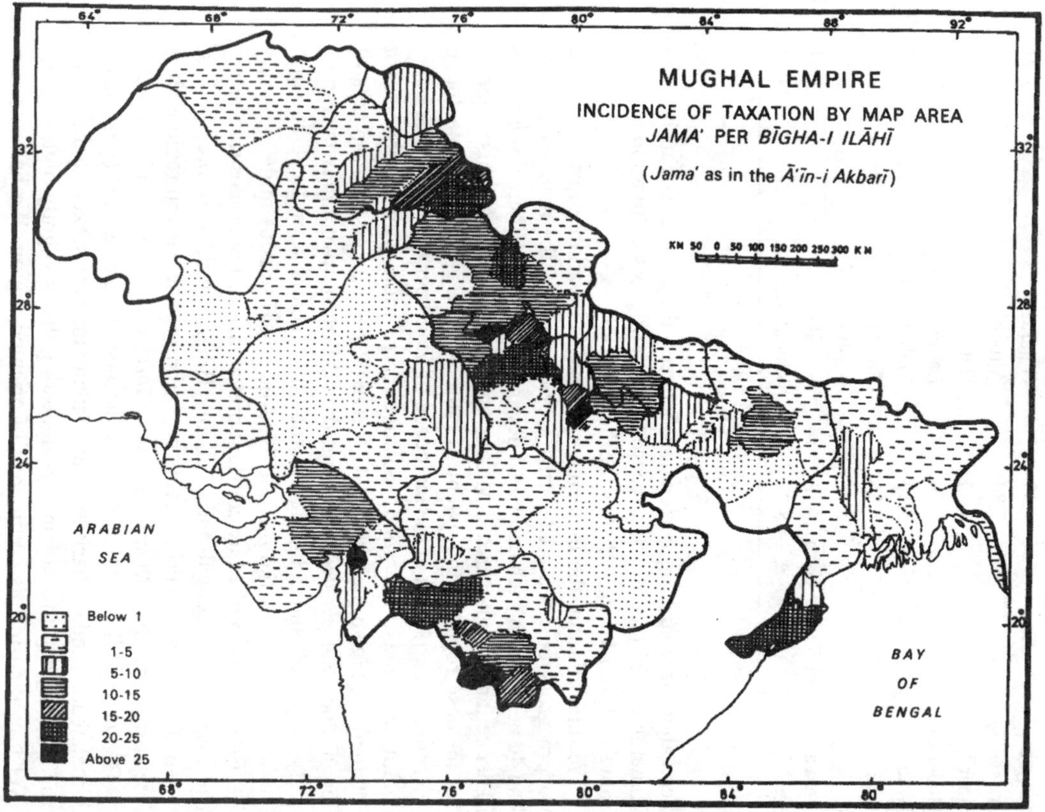
MUGHAL EMPIRE
INCIDENCE OF TAXATION BY MAP AREA
JAMA' PER *BĪGHA-I ILĀHĪ*
(*Jama'* as in the *Ā'īn-i Akbarī*)
KM 50 0 50 100 150 200 250 300 KM
ARABIAN SEA
BAY OF BENGAL
Below 1
1-5
5-10
10-15
15-20
20-25
Above 25
64°
68°
72°
76°
80°
84°
88°
92°
32°
28°
24°
20°

Map IV

Table 5.12

	J/M (*dāms/bīgha*)	GC as % of M
Ṣūbas with J/M above 5.		
Khandesh	24.1	60.2
Gujarat	7.9	56.7
Berar	12.2	58.6
Agra	11.1	
Allahabad	5.8	61.3
Awadh	7.1	
Delhi	8.4	54.3
Lahore	9.6	
Ṣūbas with J/M below 3.		
Ajmer	2.2	24.6
Thatta	2.4	36.4
Multan	2.2	19.9
Malwa	1.9	33.9

partly at least to its high prices, in turn caused by its great commercial orientation and relatively high level of urbanization.

Large 'leakages' from gross realization too could furnish another reason for the low J/M in certain areas. In such cases, high gross-realization might yet be accompanied by low net revenue-realization. The *jama'* might have been low, if the subordinate claims on the agrarian surplus, notably the *zamīndārs*' share, were large. We have already noted the inverse relationship between the *jama'*-incidence and the *zamīndārs*' share in several areas. The low J/M for Bihar could in the same way be partly attributed to the fact that here the administration had to concede a larger share to the local potentates (in Bihar: *zamīndārs*' expenditure (ZE) equalled 22 per cent of the *jama'*).[28] An analysis of the figures at the *sarkār* level makes this even more obvious (Table 5.13).

For certain other regions we could confidently say that the J/M was low simply because of lax administrative control; the *jama'* here more or less represented tribute, and was not fixed according to the actualities of revenue realization. If the *jama'* is stated in round figures, one could fairly presume that it was not based on actual assessment. In *sarkār* Garh of *ṣūba*

[28] See Chapter 7.

Table 5.13

	J/M	ZE as % of J
Bihar (unmeasured *maḥals*)	0.75	32
Champaran	1.50	67
Tirhut	2.80	45
Bihar (measured *maḥals*)	13.29	3
Hajipur	10.33	4

Malwa the *jama'* for all the *parganas* is in round numbers, while the J/M amounts to a trifling 0.16 *dāms* per *bīgha*. The low J/M here is obviously due to lack of administrative control, accentuating the already low ratio of gross cultivation to the map area owing to the Central Indian forests.

We come across an interesting situation in *ṣūba* Berar. Here the *jama'* is stated all through in round figures, but the J/M is comparatively high, viz., 12.16 *dāms*. Of a total of 13 *sarkārs*, J/M either exceeds, or is around, 10 *dāms* in seven *sarkārs*. This is partly explained by a fairly high ratio of gross cultivation to map area, to judge from modern figures. In the *sarkārs* of Kherla and Narnala where Abū'l Faẓl mentions strong Gond *zamīndārs*,[29] the J/M falls to 2.2 and 2.6 respectively: for this fall, the hilly terrain of these *sarkārs*, as well as the *zamīndārs*' larger share in the surplus must also be held mainly responsible.

It appears, then, that the incidence of *jama'* not only varied according to the extent of cultivation,[30] but also through other factors such as the price level, the *zamīndārs*' share in gross revenue-realization, and, finally, the degree of administrative control.

In all this we assume that the magnitude of land-revenue demand in relation to produce was uniform in all regions. But that varied as well: in coastal Gujarat, for example, it seems to have represented a higher share of the produce than in other parts of the empire, while in parts of Rajasthan lower proportions prevailed. We must keep in mind the fact that in *jama'* after all, we do not have the total obtained through uniform shares of the surplus among different claimants, but that absolute portion of the total agricultural (and non-agricultural) product of the country which the

[29] *Ā'īn*, I, 477.

[30] A possible factor we have ignored is the pattern of cropping: an area growing higher-priced market crops might have had a larger *jama'*. At a regional level, such a pattern would have made for a higher price-level; and thus the price-factor should probably cover its influence.

Mughal ruling class was able to appropriate for its own use and consumption. If its share of the net land-revenue collected was high, the *jama'*, in so far as it could represent physical quantities of the produce, would be high; but, in money terms, this would be moderated by the varying local price-levels. In other words, the unknown complexities underlying our hypotheses are very many; but we have to learn to live with such unresolved difficulties in any analysis seeking to cover the whole of the Mughal empire.

LOCAL CLAIMS TO AGRARIAN SURPLUS

CHAPTER 6

Revenue Grants

A part of the imperial tax-claim was transferred to individuals by way of *suyūrghāl*.[1] The nature of *suyūrghāl* is described in a chapter in the *Ā'īn-i Akbarī*, titled '*Ā'īn-i suyūrghāl*.'[2] Here Abū'l Fazl tells us that the grants the Emperor made in cash were known as *waẓīfa*, while those given in land were designated *milk* or *madad-i ma'āsh*. It may be inferred from this that the land and cash grants taken together were comprehended under the term *suyūrghāl*.[3] But Abū'l Fazl himself used the word *suyūrghāl* quite loosely, making it at times a synonym of *madad-i ma'āsh*, as when he says, 'the *suyūrghāl* of the Afghans and the *Chaudhurīs* was converted into *khāliṣa*'; or when he speaks of the *suyūrghāl* land (*zamīn-i suyūrghāl*). The use of the term by other writers in India is very rare, though when employed it is always a mere synonym of *madad-i ma'āsh*.[4] In any case, land grants must always have formed the bulk of *suyūrghāl* grants.[5]

In using the word '*suyūrghāl*' Abū'l Fazl not only defied ordinary technical usage, but the unit in which he has stated it was also rather unusual. *Madad-i ma'āsh* grants were normally made in terms of area

[1] *Ā'īn*, II, 348–90.

[2] Ibid., 198–9.

[3] Cf. Moreland, *Agrarian System of Moslem India*, 277; and Habib, *Agrarian System*, 313 (the statement is missing in the rev. ed.).

[4] As in Bābur's *farmān*, I.O. 4438: (1), and *Maẓhar-i Shāhjahānī*, ed. Husamuddin Rashidi, Karachi, 1962, 73.

[5] There is to my knowledge only one statistical statement, which brings out the relative sizes of land and cash grants: The *Mir'āt-i Aḥmadī*, I, 25–6, puts the total *jama'* alienated through *madad-i ma'āsh* in Gujarat at 1,20,00,000 *dāms*, while it puts the total amount of cash grants (*in'ām*) in the *ṣūba* at Rs 40,000 per annum. Since nominally 40 *dāms* went to the rupee, the cash grants seem to have amounted to only 13.33% of the estimated income from the land grants.

and the *farmāns* or other deeds of the original grants almost invariably made provision for a specified area to be assigned out of land excluded from assessment (*khārij-i jama'*).[6] However, in his 'Account of the Twelve *Ṣūbas*' Abū'l Faẓl not only specifies the grants in terms of money (*dāms*), but also definitely states that these figures formed part of the *jama'/naqdī* figures. When giving the totals for each *ṣūba*, he records, first, the total *jama'* of the *ṣūba* and then 'from out of it' (*as-ān miyān*), the *suyūrghāl* of the *ṣūba*.[7]

His words are consistently supported by his figures. In no single *pargana* do the *suyūrghāl* figures exceed the *jama'*. The only exception is the statistics for a *pargana* in *ṣūba* Berar which is probably due to a clerical error.[8] What decisively supports our inference is another feature of the statistics: when we subtract the *suyūrghāl* from the *jama'* we get round figures for a number of *parganas*, rounded, in fact, to thousands and, in many instances, to lakhs. Table 6.1 contains the figures given against a few such *parganas* picked at random.

Table 6.1

(a) *Pargana*	*Sarkār*	(b) *Ṣūba*	(c) *Naqdī (Jama')*	(d) *Suyūrghāl*	(c) *minus* (d)
Wazirpur	Agra	Agra	20,09,255	9,255	20,00,000
Meerut	Delhi	Delhi	49,91,996	3,41,096	46,50,900
Kheri	Khairabad	Awadh	32,50,522	50,522	32,00,000

In Appendix 6.A, I have set out all such cases found in the *Ā'īn*'s statistical tables. The total number of entries, where the net *jama'* (that is,

[6] Habib, *Agrarian System*, 303 (rev. ed. 34*n*).

[7] See e.g., *Ā'īn*, I, 417, 424, 434, et passim.

[8] Blochmann's edition enters the figure of 3,60,000 *dāms* for the *jama'* of *pargana* Jintur, *sarkār* Pathri, while recording 12,00,000 *dāms* for *suyūrghāl*. But Br. Mus. MSS Add.6552 and Add.7652 show no such discrepancy in the case of this *maḥal*, reading the respective figures as 16,00,000 and 4,00,000. These MSS, on the other hand, have four such cases of excess of *suyūrghāl* in the same *sarkār*. But three of these are explained by the misplacing of the figures in the *naqdī* column owing to the omission of a *pargana* (Kosri, which is duly recorded in Blochmann), which should have been placed just after the eleventh entry. When the figures are adjusted accordingly, the excess disappears in three out of the four cases. Only the *pargana* of Kosri would remain (after our adjustment), with *naqdī* at 36,00,000 and *suyūrghāl* at 64,00,000 *dāms*. But it is probable that 64,00,000 is an error for 24,00,000 (*bīst* incorrectly written as *shist*). The stated total for the *suyūrghāl* of the *sarkār* would be closer to the actual if this reading is assumed. (The stated total, 1,15,80,954 compares with 1,63,36,154 if we read *shīst*, but with 1,23,36,154 if we read *bīst*.)

gross *jama'* less *suyūrghāl*) for *pargana* turns out to be in round figures, is 71, out of 781 entries under all the *ṣūbas*, excluding Kabul and Berar; of these 71, as many as 31 are rounded to lakhs.

Among exact (unrounded) figures a number can ordinarily be in full lakhs (with five zeroes) only in one case out of 100,000. In Abū'l Fazl's tables, however, the actual frequency of such roundings to lakhs is nearly one out of only twenty-five. It is thus an inescapable conclusion that the *jama'* figure was determined first, and being an estimate, was often in the round; the *suyūrghāl* figure, being usually a precise one, was then added to it to give the gross *jama'* or *naqdī* figure for each *pargana*.

The other possible view that the *suyūrghāl* is excluded from *naqdī*, is not supported by the results of adding *suyūrghāl* and *naqdī* (*jama'*) figures. No more than two roundings result; and these are to a hundred only. In other words, while an accidental rounding to hundreds is theoretically possible in one out of every hundred entries, here in 781 entries we have no more than two cases (instead of a possible seven or eight) of such rounding (Chandaus in *sarkār* Kol, *ṣūba* Agra, and Jais in *sarkār* Manikpur, *ṣūba* Allahabad).

We have also alluded to the fact that out of 781 entries in the column of *suyūrghāl*, only two are rounded to thousands, and nine to hundreds, while all the remaining 770 are carried to the last digit. But of the *jama'* figures for the corresponding *parganas* six are already in the round; and in seventy-one cases detected, there is concealed rounding, that is, they were originally round and have become exact only due to the addition of *suyūrghāl*. The estimate of income from *suyūrghāl* lands therefore seems to have been based on a more detailed assessment than was the estimate of tax-realization from the general revenue-paying lands. It is indeed possible that since the latter category had to be assigned in lieu of *manṣab* salaries, the net *jama'* figures were often rounded simply for the convenience of assigning the lands against salary claims which were normally stated in round figures.[9]

The question naturally arises as to how the Mughal administration obtained estimates for the revenue-paying capacity of *suyūrghāl* lands, when it neither collected the land revenue on those lands, nor stood in need of the figures for formulating the *jama'* or estimated revenue-income for assigning *jāgīrs*. Since the *suyūrghāl* figures themselves are not in the round (except for *pargana* entries in Berar), we must suppose that they are not rough estimates, but are built up of exact totals from detailed figures. Even if we assume that these figures are originally those of *jama'*,

[9] See the pay schedules in the *Ā'īn-i Akbarī*, I, 180–6.

being the estimate of revenue that the land paid when it was granted, our difficulties are not over. When the grants were made, the land assigned in grants had to be at least half in uncultivated waste,[10] while, in fact, in most cases it was given entirely in waste and unassessed land (*khārij-i jama'*).[11] It is therefore unlikely that the amount stated under *suyūrghāl* is the amount of revenue alienated when the grant was originally conferred.

One possible explanation remains. By a *farmān* issued in 1578, whose text has fortunately survived, Akbar ordered the consolidation of scattered holdings of grants in a few select villages in each *pargana*.[12] This was done ostensibly to protect the grantees from oppression by *jāgīrdārs* and revenue collectors,[13] but really, perhaps, to prevent fraud on the part of the grantees.[14] At any rate, it is said to have caused them much distress.[15]

This process of concentrating all grant lands in a few earmarked villages involved an exchange of existing grant lands with lands that had hitherto been paying revenue. The exchange must have involved valuation of the lands on either side. If lands yielding a certain amount of revenue were being transferred to the grantees, it must have been important for the administration to ensure that the grantees relinquished lands that could yield comparable revenue, that is, be capable of being assigned the same *jama'* as was borne by the lands transferred in return. The measure thus required the Mughal administration to estimate the revenue-paying capacity of the lands already held in each of the grants, and then to transfer lands, yielding identical *jama'*, to the grantees. Our suggestion, then, is that the *Ā'īn*'s *suyūrghāl* statistics were based on *jama'* figures standing in the records against lands given to grantees in the course of implementing the *farmān* of 1578.

[10] *Ā'īn*, I, 199.

[11] Cf. Habib, *Agrarian System*, 303 (rev. ed., 347).

[12] Allahabad, 24. I have used a transcript of the document in the Department of History, Aligarh.

[13] An incident described by 'Abdu's Sattār (*Majālis-i Jahāngīrī*, pp.207–8) illustrates how such oppression could occur if the *suyūrghāl* land was not separated. An old man holding a small *suyūrghāl* land complained to Jahāngīr (22 April 1611) that the local *jāgīrdār* had deprived him of three years' income from his *suyūrghāl* despite his producing all the requisite documents. Jahāngīr ordered the lost income to be paid out of the treasury, while an *aḥdī* (imperial horseman) was to be sent to the locality to obtain double payment from the erring *jāgīrdār*.

[14] Abū'l Faẓl (*Akbarnāma*, III, 240; *Ā'īn*, I, 198) in fact says that dishonest grantees used to hold lands at more than one place on the basis of the same deed of grant.

[15] Badāūnī, *Muntakhabu-t Tawārīkh*, II, 254.

This is corroborated by the fact that *suyūrg͟hāl* figures are not recorded in the *Ā'īn* for regions such as Bengal, Kashmir, Sind, Qandahar and Khandesh, which were not under Akbar's effective control in 1578. There are only two exceptions, namely, Kabul and Berar.

Though Kabul was outside Akbar's empire in 1578, we have five entries for *suyūrg͟hāl* in its tables. None of these figures is rounded; nor do any round figures result if the *suyūrg͟hāl* is subtracted from the *jama'*. It is, however, possible that some concentration of land grants took place in Kabul subsequent to the annexation, and that the *suyūrg͟hāl* figures are a result of that process. But there is no documentary support for this supposition.

Berar was also not subjugated until 1596. Blochmann's figures for this *ṣūba* are in many cases not supported by two of the best surviving MSS of the *Ā'īn*,[16] which themselves do not give identical readings. However, we can still attempt an analysis of the Berar statistics on the basis of a collation of figures given in Blochmann's text with the two MSS. We find that for Berar, there are 46 *suyūrg͟hāl* entries in all. Of these, 33 are in round numbers and only 13 are exact. It would thus seem that the *suyūrg͟hāl* figures in Berar were rough aggregate estimates rather than the totals of detailed assessments of individual *suyūrg͟hāl* grants. They are, therefore, on a different plane altogether from the *suyūrg͟hāl* statistics of other *ṣūbas*.

Indeed, Abū'l Faẓl's words preceding the statistical tables of Berar indicate that a very summary procedure had been adopted in that *ṣūba*. The revenue figures were taken from the records of the previous administration, being stated originally in Berari *tankas*. These were converted into *dāms*, by multiplying the original figures by 16. We might assume that the *suyūrg͟hāl* figures were also similarly dealt with. Taking the round figures for *suyūrg͟hāl*, we find that of the 33 round figures, all except 3 are divisible by 16. But when we take the exact figures, only one out of 13 is divisible by 16. It seems, then, that except for a few *parganas*, Abū'l Faẓl simply borrowed summary estimates for land grants from the previous administration and transferred them to his statistics, through a mere conversion into *dāms*.

On the whole, then, it would seem to be reasonable to take the *suyūrg͟hāl* figures (except in the *ṣūbas* of Kabul and Berar) as derived from the measures of 1578. For that very reason we may use them with some confidence for estimating the amount of revenue alienated in the form of grants. One should, however, remember that these figures

[16] Br. Mus. Add. 6552 and Add 7652.

represent only grants made by the emperor. The *jāgīrdārs* themselves made separate grants, which were temporary, being valid only for the terms of the *jāgīrdārs*' own assignments. The kind of grantees, on the other hand, that we are considering were those called *makhādīm-i 'uẓẓām*, or imperial grantees.[17]

II

This class of grantees, according to Abū'l Faẓl, was made up of four categories of persons, namely, seekers after true knowledge; devout persons who had abandoned the world; destitutes not possessing the capacity of earning their livelihood; and persons of noble lineage who would not, 'out of ignorance', take to any employment. Women of respectable lineage, as members of the last category, were also recipients of *suyūrghāl*: Abū'l Faẓl specifically mentions land grants held by 'Irani and Turani' women.[18] It seems that the grants were largely meant for people falling into any of the four above mentioned categories, since Abū'l Faẓl informs us in the same chapter that the *suyūrghāl* lands of *chaudhurīs* (hereditary local officials), who obviously did not belong to any of these categories, were converted into *khāliṣa*. Elsewhere he adds that lands were liable to be confiscated if the grantees were found to be 'in service' (*naukar*).[19]

The proportion of total revenue-income this class of grant-holders appropriated can be estimated broadly from the ratio which the *suyūrghāl* bore to the gross *jama'* recorded in the *Ā'īn*. The *suyūrghāl* statistics as given in the *Ā'īn* pose some difficulties, which we have dealt with already in Chapter 1. The totals stated for *sarkārs* differ significantly from the actual totals based on *pargana*-level figures in 17 out of 66 *sarkārs* where *suyūrghāl* is recorded. Again, the *suyūrghāl* figures given for *ṣūbas* are not in agreement with the totals of those given at the *sarkār* and *pargana* levels in five out of 10 *ṣūbas* for which figures are provided at all three levels.

Since these inconsistencies cannot always be attributed to transcriptional or other errors and could possibly be the result of revisions,[20] the *suyūrghāl* statistics have to be scrutinized at all three levels. In Table 6.2 are exhibited the proportions of *suyūrghāl* out of *jama'* for the different *ṣūbas*, based on the three sets of totals obtained.

[17] *Ā'īn*, I, 196.

[18] Ibid., 198–9.

[19] Ibid., 197.

[20] Excluding Berar and Kabul where the *ṣūba* totals are not recorded.

Table 6.2

Suyūrghāl as percentage of *jama'* (Based on Appendix, Chapter I)

Ṣūba	Based on *pargana* figures	Based on *sarkār* figures	Based on *ṣūba* figures
Bihar	1.024	1.024	1.024
Allahabad	4.750	5.256	5.256
Awadh	4.199	4.213	4.224
Agra	3.992	3.900	2.216
Malwa	0.479	0.478	0.478
Berar	6.359	6.873	—
Gujarat	1.969	1.745	0.096
Ajmer	0.755	0.807	0.807
Delhi	5.497	4.811	5.498
Lahore	1.748	1.763	1.763
Multan	1.983	4.067	2.021
Kabul	0.140	0.170	—
All *Ṣūbas*	3.376	3.442	2.379

The amount of revenue alienated through *suyūrghāl* seems to be quite modest, at whatever level we take the figures. For the twelve *ṣūbas* tabulated it amounts to a little over 3 per cent at *pargana* and *sarkār* levels. Taking the stated *ṣūba* totals, the figure is even lower, about 2.4 per cent. There is, however, no *ṣūba*-level figure given for Berar, where the *suyūrghāl* was above 6 per cent, going by *pargana* and *sarkār* totals. Besides Berar, it is only in Allahabad and Delhi that the *suyūrghāl* exceeds 5 per cent of the *jama'* at any level. For Agra and Gujarat the percentage is considerably lower if we take the stated *ṣūba* figures. As suggested earlier this might be the result of an actual reduction that Abū'l Faẓl had incorporated in *ṣūba* figures while leaving the detailed figures unrevised.[21]

Considering the entire empire, the share of *suyūrghāl* in the *jama'* is at best a mere 3.4 per cent. It was not uniformly distributed over the empire either. The four *ṣūbas*, Agra, Delhi, Awadh and Allahabad, for example, together contained more than 50 per cent of the total amount of *suyūrghāl*.

In the *ṣūba* of Agra, in *pargana* Santhavari of *sarkār* Tijara, as much as 65.79 per cent of the *jama'* is accounted for by *suyūrghāl*. But this is an isolated instance: among all the 243 *parganas* of the *ṣūba*, only in 7 does the share exceed 10 per cent of the *jama'*. In Delhi, while the

[21] See Chapter 1, Sec.II.

maximum found is 36.88 per cent in *pargana* Shakarpur of *sarkār* Delhi, there are only 20 *parganas* out of 213 where the *suyūrghāl* exceeds 10 per cent of the *jama'*. In Awadh and Allahabad, the maxima reached are not so high, being 23.31 per cent (*pargana* Ibrahimabad, *sarkār* Awadh) and 21.30 per cent (*pargana* Mahoba, *sarkār* Kalinjar); but there are more instances of appreciable alienation of *jama'* in *suyūrghāl*: in Awadh, in 9 out of 128 *maḥals*, and in Allahabad in 13 out of 120 *maḥals*, the proportion of revenue claimed by the grantees exceeds 10 per cent.

Plotted on a map, the *parganas* representing high and low *suyūrghāl* can be shown in two ways. One is by providing symbols (by size) for the absolute figures of *suyūrghāl* for each *pargana*. This, however, may give a false impression for *parganas* where the *suyūrghāl* figure was high merely because the area of the *pargana* (and so its *jama'* as well) was large. This, for example, is the case with Badaun, Bahraich and Kalpi. The other method would be to assign symbols by the size of *suyūrghāl* as a percentage of *jama'* in each *pargana*. Here, while we might have a better picture of the relative amount of *suyūrghāl*, there is still the danger of misrepresentation of an opposite kind. A small *pargana* may contain a small amount of *suyūrghāl* in absolute terms, and yet the *suyūrghāl-jama'* ratio may be very high, just because its *jama'* is also low. On the other hand, large areas given in *suyūrghāl* in a large *pargana* could escape notice. In order to have a more reliable view of the distribution of *suyūrghāl*, it seemed best to use both methods and then to cross-check. Maps V and VI depict the results based on these two methods.[22]

A comparison of the two maps shows that there were certain regions of high concentration of *suyūrghāl*. It is possible to identify these blocks as follows:

> Block A: The region from Sirhind extending towards the upper Doāb, and including the cis-Yamuna region, northern Doāb and the adjacent trans-Ganga tract, covering parts of the Rohtak, Gurgaon and Rewari districts in Haryana and the Saharanpur, Muzaffarnagar, Meerut, Bulandshahr, Bijnaur, Moradabad and Badaun districts in U.P.
>
> Block B: Agra. This region though small in size is quantitatively quite important. The districts involved are Agra and Mathura. The peculiarity here is that except for a very high figure of *suyūrghāl* in the *ḥavelī* (headquarters) *pargana* of Agra, the size of the *suyūrghāl* in the whole *sarkār* is not impressive, so much so that the *suyūrghāl* for the

[22] These maps are based, for their boundaries and *pargana* locations, upon sheets 4A, 6A and 8A of Irfan Habib's *Atlas of the Mughal Empire*.

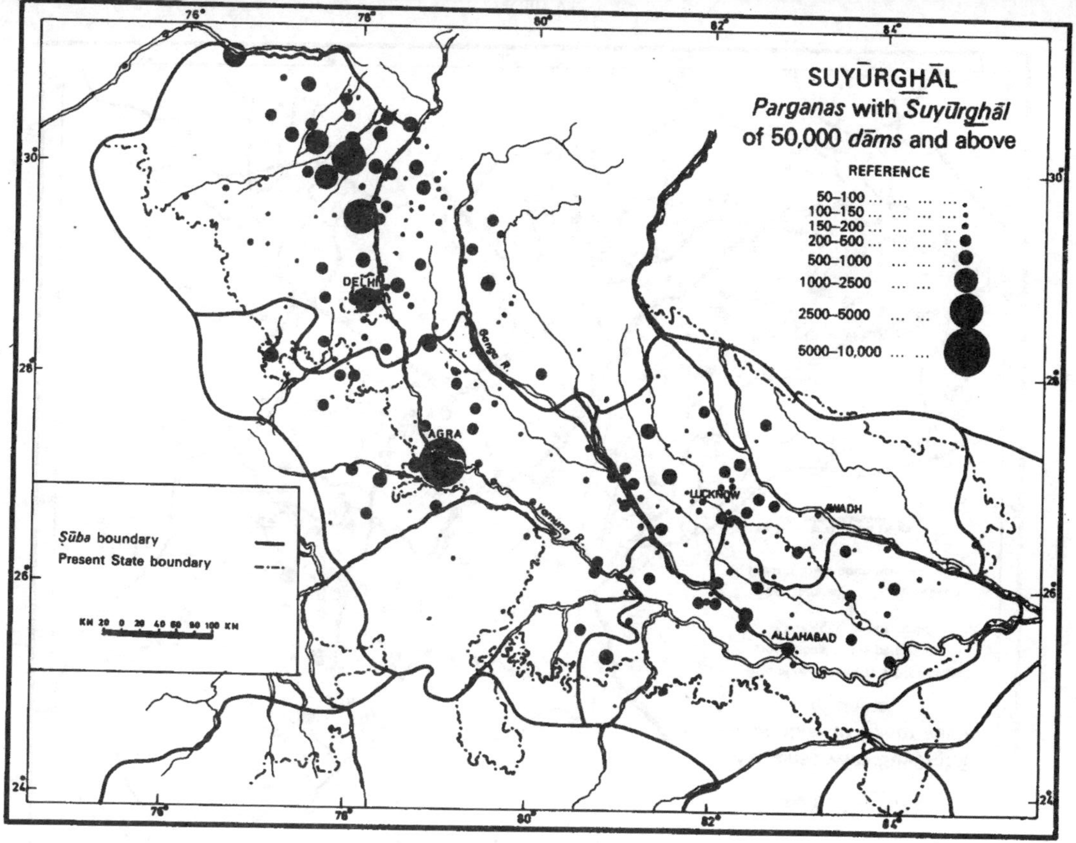
SUYŪRGHĀL
Parganas with *Suyūrghāl*
of 50,000 *dāms* and above
REFERENCE
50–100
100–150
150–200
200–500
500–1000
1000–2500
2500–5000
5000–10,000
DELHI
AGRA
LUCKNOW
AWADH
ALLAHABAD
Ganga R.
Yamuna R.
Ṣūba boundary
Present State boundary
KM 20 0 20 40 60 80 100 KM
76°
78°
80°
82°
84°
30°
28°
26°
24°

Map V

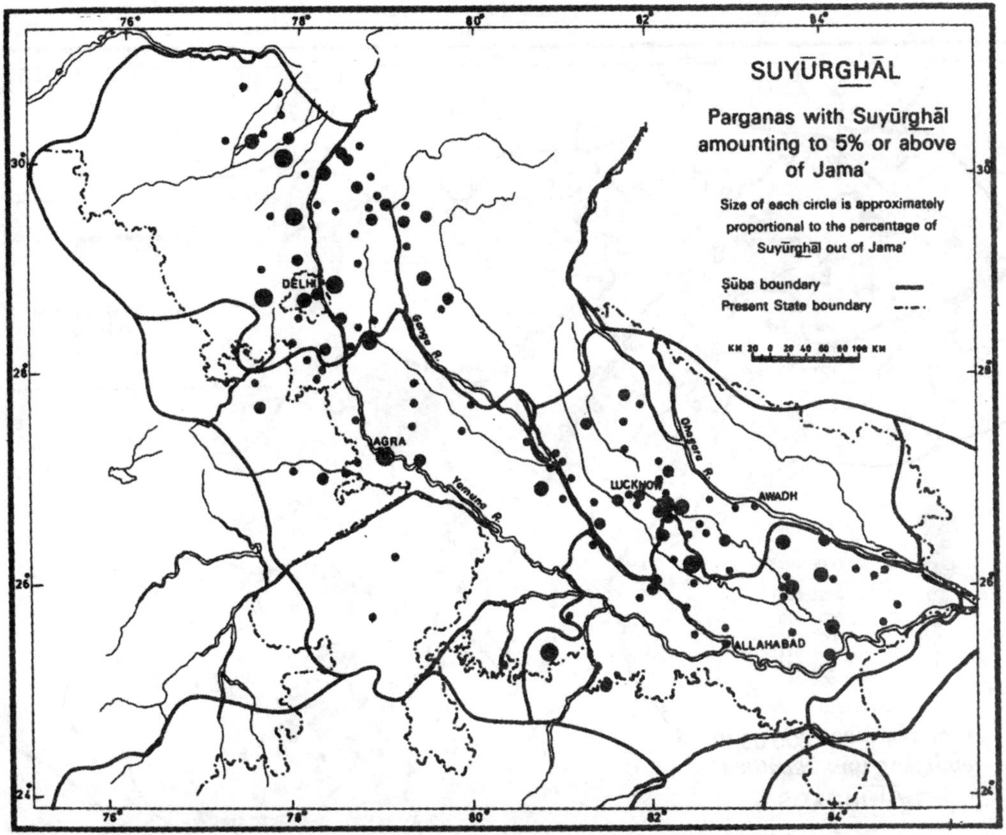
SUYŪRGHĀL
Parganas with Suyūrghāl amounting to 5% or above of Jama'
Size of each circle is approximately proportional to the percentage of Suyūrghāl out of Jama'
Ṣūba boundary
Present State boundary
KM 20 0 20 40 60 80 100 KM
76°
78°
80°
82°
84°
30°
28°
26°
24°
DELHI
AGRA
LUCKNOW
AWADH
ALLAHABAD
Ganga R.
Yamuna R.
Ghagara R.

Map VI

ḥavelī-pargana amounts to 60.61 per cent of the *suyūrghāl* of the entire *sarkār* of Agra.

Block C: A region extending from around Kanauj to Ayodhya (Awadh) towards the east and to Kara–Manikpur in the south-east. This very large block covers the districts of Hardoi, Sitapur, Lucknow, Unnao, Faizabad, Rae-Bareilly, Kanpur and Fatehpur.

Block D: High *suyūrghāl* figures also appear in the region extending from Banaras (Varanasi) northwards up to the river Ghagara, containing Jaunpur, Azamgarh and Partapgarh districts and part of Faizabad district.

One possible explanation for a distinct pattern of such concentrations is that the *suyūrghāl* area was large wherever the urban population was more numerous. Map VII depicts the distribution of urban population by showing all towns with populations of 10,000 or above at the time of the 1881 Census.

A comparison of Map VII with Maps V and VI shows that while our blocks A and B of *suyūrghāl* concentrations match fairly well with the areas of urban concentration (1881) reflected in high percentages of urban population or concentrations of big towns, the *suyūrghāl* concentrations of the central-eastern blocks C and D are not matched by any corresponding urban concentration in the same districts in 1881. High *suyūrghāl* figures in such isolated localities as Lucknow, Banaras and Allahabad are however reflected in high urban-concentration in 1881.

Since it is possible that shifts of urban population took place between the beginning of the seventeenth century and the closing years of the nineteenth, I have tried yet another device to check the hypothetical correspondence between high *suyūrghāl* and urban concentrations.

The archaeological remains of Mughal times (sixteenth and seventeenth centuries) can be taken as evidence for urban sites and, with much reservation, for comparative sizes of towns. Map VIII is based on a map of sixteenth-and-seventeenth-century monuments and archaeological remains in U.P., listed in Fuhrer's *Monumental Antiquities etc. in North Western Provinces* (Allahabad, 1891), prepared by Zahoor Ali Khan.[23]

A comparison of Maps, V, VI and VIII shows that our Block A (excluding the areas outside U.P.) accords well with a distinct region of high concentration of monuments in Map VIII as well. Block B too matches well with the high density of monuments in this region. However,

[23] Cf. also Zahoor Ali Khan, 'Medieval Archaeological Remains in Uttar Pradesh—A Geographical Study', paper presented at IHC, 1975 (cyclostyled).

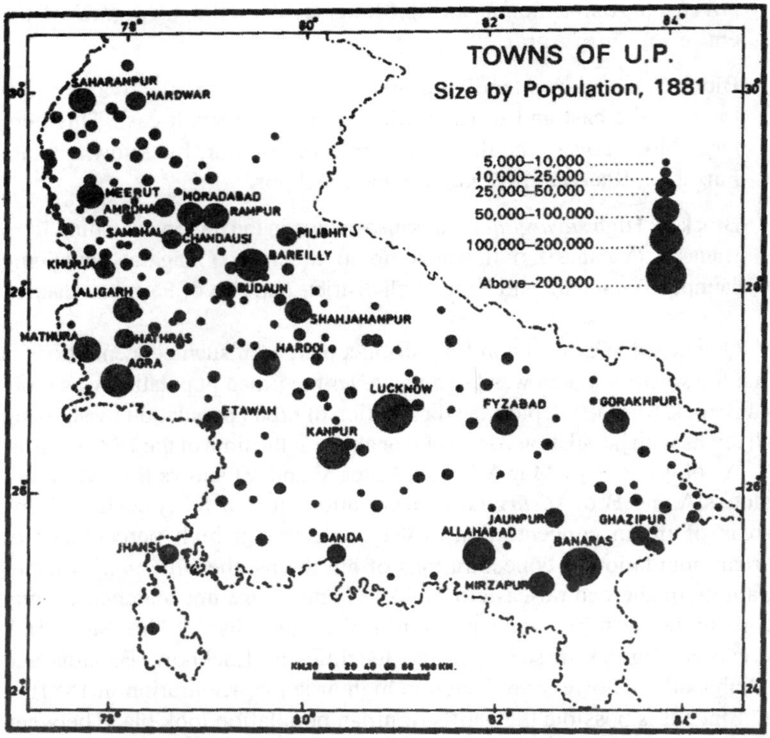

Map VII

the area covered by Block C in Maps V and VI does not appear as a single region of concentration; there are two distinct clusters lying within this region. One cluster comprises Kanauj and the trans-Ganga tract from Shahjahanpur to Bilgram, and extending further eastwards from this line. The other comprises the lower Doāb with the adjoining trans-Ganga tract. In the remaining part of the region of *suyūrghāl* concentration, Map VIII shows normal spread with no distinguishable cluster. The high figures of *suyūrghāl* in Block C accord, broadly speaking, with the density of archaeological remains in that area.

In addition to this, there are some interesting instances of correlation. The isolated *pargana* of Kalinjar with high *suyūrghāl*, for example, corresponds with the large complex of monuments at that important fortress.

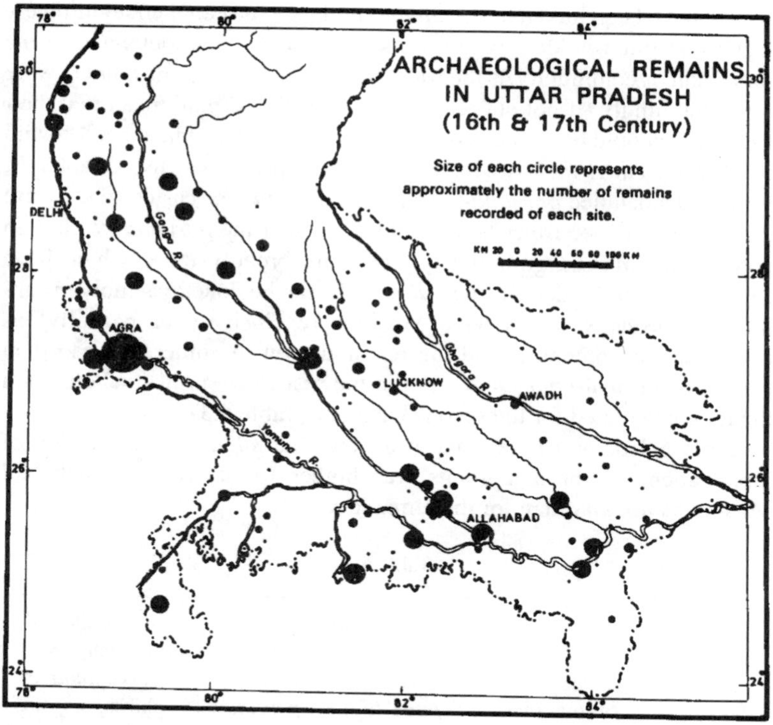

Map VIII

On the other hand, the area with low *suyūrghāl* figures in the Rohilkhand tract south-east of Bareilly and extending westward between Badaun and Sambhal up to the Ganga, has very few archaeological remains listed. Similarly, the entire region east of the Ghagara, comprising the districts of Lakhimpur, Bahraich, Gonda, Basti, Gorakhpur and Deoria, has very low *suyūrghāl*. It has also very few urban sites established by archaeological evidence.

On the whole, the pattern of *suyūrghāl* corresponds to a noticeable extent with the pattern of urban distribution indicated by archaeological remains of the sixteenth and seventeenth century. This makes it strongly probable that the grantees were in large part a town-based class.

The opposite view, that land grantees were essentially a rural class, can be tested by a device entirely based on the *Ā'īn*'s own evidence. If the grantees were rural in character, it should reasonably follow that they should have been linked to the *zamīndār* class. One can then legitimately argue that grant-holders within a locality should have belonged to the same clan or community as the *zamīndārs*. Now since grant-holders were overwhelmingly (if not entirely) Muslims,[24] this should mean that their *suyūrghāl* should have been concentrated in *parganas* which had Muslim *zamīndārs*. The *Ā'īn*, as we have noticed (Chapter 1; see also Chapter 7), furnishes a detailed *pargana*-wise record of *zamīndār* castes; and we are thus enabled to see from its own tables whether the *parganas* with high percentages of *suyūrghāl* out of *jama'* are broadly those which have Muslim clans recorded as *zamīndārs*. This can be done by simply grouping all *parganas* which have Muslims (exclusively or partially) as *zamīndārs*, on one side, and the remainder on the other; we can then compare the *suyūrghāl-jama'* ratio in the first category as a whole, with the ratio calculated for the second category (Table 6.3).

Table 6.3 demonstrates that in all the four *ṣūbas* the proportion of *jama'* alienated through grants was higher for *parganas* which had Muslim *zamīndārs* than for the remainder.

Table 6.3

Ṣūba	Total *suyūrghāl* as % of total *jama'*	Total *suyūrghāl* of *parganas* with Muslim *zamīndārs* as % of *jama'* of these *parganas*	*Suyūrghāl* of other *parganas* as % of *jama'* of those *parganas*
Agra	3.992	4.465	3.887
Delhi	5.843	9.181	5.105
Awadh	4.309	8.762	3.701
Allahabad	5.013	5.335	4.953

This tendency emerges also from figures at the *sarkār* level. In Appendix 6.A, are set out figures for various *sarkārs*. In seven *sarkārs* of nine in Agra *ṣūba* the percentage of *suyūrghāl* in *jama'* is higher for *parganas* with Muslim *zamīndārs*. In Delhi, again, the *suyūrghāl*, as percentage of *jama'*, is higher in *parganas* with Muslim *zamīndārs* in six out of seven *sarkārs*. In Awadh only three out of five *sarkārs* have Muslim *zamīndārs* recorded against their *parganas*. In all three *sarkārs* the percentage of *suyūrghāl* out of *jama'* is, again, higher in *parganas* with Muslim *zamīndārs* than in others. The corresponding

[24] Habib, *Agrarian System*, 310. The flat statement is missing in the revised edn., but see pp. 355–7.

figures for *sarkārs* in *ṣūba* Allahabad are, however, four out of seven *sarkārs*.

Parganas with Muslim *zamīndārs* thus consistently account for a larger proportion of the total *suyūrghāl*. In other words, Muslim *zamīndārs* appear to have attracted land-grantees to a recognizably greater degree than non-Muslim *zamīndārs*. The difference is, however, by no means dramatically large.

From this one might deduce that the sites of grants were affected by the composition of *zamīndārs*. But it may merely reflect that land-grantees, being Muslims, sought grants in *parganas* with Muslim *zamīndārs*. It does not imply that the grantees were of the same clans as Muslim *zamīndārs*. Indeed an overwhelmingly large proportion of *suyūrghāl*, ranging from 71.57 per cent in *ṣūba* Delhi to 82.50 per cent in *ṣūba* Allahabad, lay in *parganas* without any recorded Muslim *zamīndārs*.

Furthermore, in certain *sarkārs* a situation opposite to the general tendency is also discernible. In *sarkār* Sirhind which has a high amount of *suyūrghāl* relative to *jama'* (8.34 per cent), the percentage of *suyūrghāl* out of *jama'* in *pargana* with Muslim *zamīndārs* is substantially lower (5.42 per cent) than in *parganas* without Muslim *zamīndārs*.[25]

In a number of *parganas* in *ṣūba* Allahabad, Brahmans are entered as *zamīndārs* (with no Muslim clan recorded alongside). Yet the percentage of *suyūrghāl* out of *jama'* is usually higher in those *parganas* than in others. Within *sarkār* Kara, for example, in *parganas* with Brahman *zamīndārs*, the percentage of *suyūrghāl* out of *jama'* ranges from 8.63 to 13.42, as against the general *sarkār* percentage of 6.50.

Any correlation between higher *suyūrghāl* and Muslim *zamīndārs* at *pargana* level that we can detect, shows at best that Muslim grantees tended to harbour a preference for localities with Muslim *zamīndārs*. But this by no means implies a rural origin for their class. Indeed, the fact that the bulk of grantees had their lands in areas of non-Muslim *zamīndārs* would rule out affiliation with any *zamīndār* group or clan.

[25] I have put the Ranghar caste among non-Muslims, on the strength of Jalaluddin Thanesari's statements in his *Risāla Taḥqīq-i' Ārāẓī Hind*, written in Akbar's reign (MS Maulana Azad Library, Shaifa Coll. Fiqh Arbiya, 24/26, f.10b). But present tradition (cf. Ibbetson, *Panjab Castes*, Lahore, 1916, 139; Elliot, *Memoirs of the Races of North-Western Provinces and c.*, ed. J. Beams, London, 1869, I, 47), declares them to be Rajputs converted to Islam. It would seem more reasonable to rely on contemporary authority than on later tradition. But if we suppose the Ranghars to have been Muslims in Akbar's time, the percentage of *suyūrghāl* out of *jama'* in *parganas* with Muslim *zamīndārs* in *sarkār* Sirhind would come to 8.51%. Conversely, the percentage of *suyūrghāl* in *parganas* with non-Muslim *zamīndārs* would decline to 8.21. In this case, then, *sarkār* Sirhind would not offer an exception to the general rule.

APPENDIX 6.A

Concealed Rounding of Net *Jama'* Figures in the *Ā'īn-i Akbarī*

Pargana	*Jama'*	*Suyūrghāl*	*Jama'* less *Suyūrghāl*
***Ṣūba* Agra**			
Sarkār Agra			
Udai	28,84,365	78,165	28,06,200
Bhosawar	55,05,460	2,55,460	52,50,000
Wazirpur	20,09,255	9,255	20,00,000
Sarkār Kalpi			
Rath	92,70,894	2,70,894	90,00,000
Sarkār Kanauj			
Patti Nakhat	5,66,997	10,497	5,56,500
Chabramau	15,22,128	22,128	15,00,000
Sarkār Kol			
Atrauli	54,54,459	54,459	54,00,000
Tappal	18,02,571	2,571	18,00,000
Sarkār Erach			
Khaksis	13,43,073	7,673	13,35,400
Sarkār Alwar			
Baroda Fateh Khan	2,01,059	1,059	2,00,000
Sarkār Sahar			
Bhadouli	4,41,840	6,840	4,35,000
Nonera	6,18,115	17,515	6,00,000
***Ṣūba* Delhi**			
Sarkār Delhi			
Jhinjhina	17,00,250	1,00,250	16,00,000
Jalalpur Sarot	10,01,875	1,775	10,00,100
Meerut	49,91,996	3,41,096	46,50,900
Sarkār Sambhal			
Islampur Dargu	4,29,375	675	4,28,700
Bachhraon	8,28,322	3,632	8,24,700
Kundarki	6,74,936	74,936	6,00,000
Gunnaur	2,67,919	17,919	2,50,000
Sarkār Saharanpur			
Bidauli	31,15,125	1,40,025	29,75,100
Chhartawal	16,68,882	68,882	16,00,000
Rampur	17,78,597	78,597	17,00,000

(*Continued*)

Appendix 6.A (*Continued*)

Concealed Rounding of Net *Jama'* Figures in the *Ā'īn-i Akbarī*

Pargana	*Jama'*	*Suyūrghāl*	*Jama'* less *Suyūrghāl*
Rurkee	16,28,861	8,861	16,20,000
Sikri Bukhari	33,10,615	1,10,615	32,00,000
Sarasawa	26,16,165	16,165	25,00,000
Sambhalera	10,11,078	11,078	10,00,000
Sarkār Rewari			
Kot Kasim Ali	33,57,930	1,10,330	32,47,600
Sarkār Hissar Firuza			
Jamalpur	42,87,461	87,461	42,00,000
Sarkār Sirhind			
Dahot	16,01,346	1,646	15,99,700
Deorana	5,80,985	17,385	5,63,600
Sunam	70,07,696	7,696	70,00,000
Ludhiana	22,94,633	44,633	22,50,000
Machiwara	6,53,552	28,552	6,25,000
***Ṣūba* Awadh**			
Satrikh	11,26,292	92,692	10,23,600
Sarkār Khairabad			
Basara	2,76,066	4,566	2,71,500
Kheri	32,50,522	50,522	32,00,000
Laharpur	30,29,479	2,09,079	28,20,400
Nimkhar	35,66,055	66,055	35,00,000
Sarkār Lucknow			
Sarausi	12,39,767	1,567	12,38,200
Fatahpur	31,61,440	2,61,440	29,00,000
Kakori	14,34,430	1,34,430	13,00,000
***Ṣūba* Allahabad**			
Sarkār Allahabad			
Saraon	32,47,527	1,61,527	30,85,000
Sarkār Ghaziabad			
Sarkār Total	1,34,31,325	1,31,825	1,32,99,500
Sarkār Kalinjar			
Mandaha	29,98,062	1,54,062	28,44,000

(*Continued*)

Appendix 6.A (*Continued*)

Concealed Rounding of Net *Jama‘* Figures in the *Ā’īn-i Akbarī*

Pargana	*Jama‘*	*Suyūrghāl*	*Jama‘* less *Suyūrghāl*
***Ṣūba* Lahore**			
Bait Jalandhar Doāb			
Miyani Nuriya	21,06,156	6,156	21,00,000
Hadiabad	5,19,467	5,17,400	5,17,400
Bari Doāb			
Bholra	24,13,268	13,268	24,00,000
Paithan	72,97,015	97,015	72,00,000
Khokharwal	34,75,510	3,510	34,72,000
Rachnao Doāb			
Hafizabad	45,48,000	48,000	45,00,000
Mahrur	30,05,602	6,602	29,99,000
Chhant Doāb			
Gujrat	82,66,150	66,250	81,99,900
Hazara	46,89,136	2,19,536	46,69,600
Sindh Sagar Doāb			
Nandanpur	24,110	4,110	20,000
Hazara	18,05,342	5,342	18,00,000
***Ṣūba* Multan**			
Sarkār Dipalpur			
Baba Ghoj	20,20,256	20,256	20,00,000
Jhain	12,00,600	600	12,00,000
Firuzpur	1,14,79,404	1,99,404	1,12,80,000
Sarkār Bhakkar			
Alor	11,32,150	20,550	11,11,600
***Ṣūba* Ajmer**			
Harsor	12,00,926	926	12,00,000
Sarkār Chittor			
Phulia	28,43,470	43,470	28,00,000
Sarkār Ranthambhor			
Delwara	4,09,260	9,260	4,00,000
Kankhara	11,11,994	11,994	11,00,000
Sarkār Nagor			
Bhundana	12,71,960	70,460	12,01,500

(*Continued*)

Appendix 6.A (*Continued*)

Concealed Rounding of Net *Jama'* Figures in the *Ā'īn-i Akbarī*

Pargana	*Jama'*	*Suyūrghāl*	*Jama'* less *Suyūrghāl*
***Ṣūba* Malwa**			
Sarkār Ujjain			
Budhnawar	30,56,195	1,095	30,55,100
Ashta	30,00,790	790	30,00,000
Karhli	74,47,906	80,506	73,67,400
***Ṣūba* Gujarat**			
Sarkār Patan			
Pattan	9,57,462	1,43,862	8,13,600
Bijapur	60,01,832	2,832	59,99,000
***Ṣūba* Bihar**			
Biswak	27,06,530	1,70,630	25,35,900
Bhulwari	18,560	9,41,160	9,22,600

APPENDIX 6.B

Sūyūrghāl as percentage of *Jama'*

Ṣūba/Sarkār	All *Parganas*	*Parganas* with Muslim *zamīndārs*	Other *Parganas*
Ṣūba Agra	3.995	4.465	3.887
Agra	7.631	5.638	7.843
Kalpi	2.135	2.619	1.810
Kanauj	2.284	5.980	1.812
Kol	3.772	16.962	2.811
Gwalior	0.586	—	0.586
Erach	1.196	3.972	0.196
Payanwan	0.977	—	0.977
Narwar	2.268	—	2.268
Mandlaer	0.000	—	0.000
Alwar	1.543	2.788	0.083
Tijara	4.065	4.183	0.286

(*Continued*)

Appendix 6.B (*Continued*)

Sūyūrghāl as percentage of *Jama'*

Ṣūba/*Sarkār*	All *Parganas*	*Parganas* with Muslim *zamīndārs*	Other *Parganas*
Narnaul	1.519	0.930	1.720
Sahar	1.984	2.096	1.962
Ṣūba Delhi[a]	5.843	9.181	5.105
Delhi	8.879	16.257	6.581
Badaun	1.314	3.919	0.581
Sambhal	4.443	14.238	3.034
Saharanpur	5.653	6.634	5.313
Rewari	2.565	5.229	0.737
Hissar Firuza	2.677	4.509	2.406
Sirhind[b]	8.339	5.415	9.069
Kumayun	0.000	—	—
Ṣūba Awadh	4.306	8.762	3.701
Awadh	4.684	6.894	4.677
Gorakhpur	0.430	0.496	0.420
Bahraich	1.934	—	1.934
Khairabad	3.837	—	3.837
Lucknow	5.673	9.896	4.497
Ṣūba Allahabad	5.015	5.335	4.953
Allahabad	6.482	3.972	6.708
Ghazipur	0.887	—	0.887
Banaras	3.816	—	3.816
Jaunpur	5.446	10.715	4.388
Manikpur	7.180	9.490	6.909
Chunar	1.879	1.016	2.020
Kalinjar	3.497	2.428	3.623
Korra	2.698	4.505	2.305
Kara	6.489	7.134	6.416

a. Counting the Ranghars as Muslims, figures for the *ṣūba* in the last two columns would be 9.708% and 4.619% respectively.

b. Counting the Ranghars as Muslims, the figures in the last two columns would be 8.512 and 8.213 respectively.

CHAPTER 7

The *Zamīndārs*' Share in the Surplus

Zamīndārs in Mughal India were socially a heterogeneous group and there is little doubt that their rights, as well as obligations, varied a great deal according to localities. In the 'directly' administered areas, they were a major support of the Mughal land-revenue machinery, while in other regions they were little more than tribute-payers and collected land tax from the peasantry mainly for their own coffers.[1]

We have already seen that the wide difference between the land-revenue claim, represented by the revenue-rates (*dastūrs*), and the estimated net realization (*jama'*)[2] of the Mughal ruling class suggests that it was unable to collect a large part of the surplus claimed by it; and much of this could well have been appropriated by the *zamīndārs*. No information about the size of the *zamīndārs*' share in the revenue is forthcoming from any sixteenth- or early seventeenth-century source. The *Ā'īn-i Akbarī* does not provide us with a direct statement on this matter. There is one statement, it is true, which might possibly refer to a *zamīndār*: The *ra'is-i dih* (lit. village chief) was to be allowed to have one-fortieth of the land, revenue-free, after the full revenue had been collected through his endeavours.[3] This 2½ per cent allowance, however, could hardly be the one paid to the *zamīndār* in satisfaction of his claims by virtue of his prescriptive right. It is much more likely that it represents the headman's or *muqaddam*'s share in the allowance known as *dahnīmī-i (o) muqaddamī* (a '5 per cent' allowance), mentioned in *madad-i ma'āsh* documents.[4]

[1] Cf. Habib, *Agrarian System*, Chapter V; and S. Nurul Hasan, '*Zamīndārs* under the Mughals' in *Land Control and Social Structure in Indian History*, ed. R.E. Frykenberg, London, 1969; and Irfan Habib, '*Zamīndārs* in the *Ā'īn-i Akbarī*', *Proceedings of Indian History Congress*, 1958, pp.320–3.

[2] See Chapter 5.

[3] *Ā'īn*, I, 285.

[4] Habib, *Agrarian System*, 131 & *n*. (rev. ed. 162 & n).

While exempted from making this payment, the *madad-i ma'āsh* holders had still to pay the *ḥaqq-i milkiyat*, or the *mālik/zamīndār*'s claims on the land.[5] This makes it still more definite that the *zamīndārs*' intrinsic claim was distinct from the headman's allowance of 2½ per cent (or 5 per cent.), which was dependent upon his actual performance in collecting the revenue.

Eighteenth-century sources contain statements to the effect that the *zamīndār*'s claim (*mālikāna*) could be compounded at just 10 per cent of the land-revenue[6] (25 per cent in Gujarat),[7] whenever he abandoned his obligation to help in the collection of revenue. This together with the *nānkār*, or allowance for service in collecting the land-revenue, which is set in these sources at 5 to 10 per cent of the revenue, would suggest an absolute minimum of 15 to 20 per cent of land revenue for the *zamīndārs*' gross income in northern India (30 to 35 per cent in Gujarat). But it is not certain, first, whether these standards applied to the earlier (sixteenth and seventeenth) centuries as well; secondly, how far the *zamīndārs*' actual income was higher than these standards in different localities; and, thirdly, what factors caused those variations.

One kind of evidence from the earlier two centuries, viz., the ratio between the prices of *zamīndārī* and actual land-revenue, would suggest that the *zamīndār* expected his own net income (let alone gross income) to be much more than 15 per cent of the revenue in northern India. The *zamīndārī* prices in a locality within *sarkār* Bahraich in the province of Awadh during Aurangzeb's reign work out at about 228 per cent of the average annual land-revenue.[8] If the purchaser expected a full return of the investment within as many as ten years, his *net* income should have been 23 per cent of the land revenue. The *gross* income should, of course, have been much larger. Even if the expectation was that the investment would be recovered within 15 years, the net annual income should have been 15.2 per cent of the land revenue. In fact, with the average rate of interest in commerce approximating to 1 per cent per month (=12 per cent p.a.) if not more,[9] one would rather think that *zamīndārs* must have

[5] Ibid., 143 (rev. ed., 179–80).

[6] Yāsīn's Glossary, Br. Mus. Add. 6603, f.79a.

[7] *Mir'āt-i Aḥmadī*, I, 173–4. This is, however, true only for *zamīndārī* lands (see below).

[8] Cf. Habib, *Agrarian System*, 152–3 (rev. ed. 188–9), where, however, the point of distinction between net and gross income of the *zamīndār* is not raised.

[9] Irfan Habib, 'Usury in Medieval India', *Comparative Studies in Society and History*, Vol.VI, No.4, 1964, 397.

expected a return of capital invested in the land, wherever purchased, within ten years of the purchase rather than fifteen. The revenue:price ratio in another document from Shamsabad (U.P.) belonging to 1530, is almost identical,[10] indicating accordingly a similar size of the *zamīndārs*' net income compared with land revenue in the sixteenth century as well. Rather late documents (1772), again from Awadh, offer still more explicit evidence in that they show the right to land revenue as having a sale-value of fifteen rupees, while the *zamīndārī* right for the same land had a value of six rupees.[11] This suggests that the ratio of the *zamīndār*'s net income to net land-revenue realization here was as high as 40:100.

While this evidence enables us to have some notion of the *zamīndār*'s *net* income in terms of the share in the peasant's surplus, what is of relevance is not so much the *zamīndār*'s net income as his gross revenue, i.e., not what he retained *after* meeting the expenses (on his retainers, fort, etc.) necessary for the collection of his share from land revenue, as well as for collecting his own imposts, perquisites, customary claims, etc., but the total amount he obtained from the peasants by all these means.

An estimate of the magnitude of the *zamīndārs*' gross share can be hazarded if, with an estimate of *zamīndārs*' net income, we could also frame an estimate of the *zamīndārs*' expenditure on retainers and other items.

Now Abū'l Faẓl in his statistics for the 'Twelve *Ṣūbas*'[12] provides us with detailed information on the castes and retainers (*sawār* or cavalry, *piyāda* or infantry, elephants, guns and boats) of *zamīndārs*. The information on castes has already been subjected to some analysis.[13] But the possibilities of utilizing the information on *zamīndārs*' retainers must also be explored. If, from the number of retainers one was able to make an estimate of the *zamīndārs*' military expenditure, one could establish a minimum level for their total income in different areas.

Abū'l Faẓl puts the total strength of *zamīndārs*' troops at more than 44,00,000 for the whole empire,[14] and sets out figures for the provinces

[10] Irfan Habib, 'Aspects of Agrarian Relations and Economy in a Region of U.P. during the 16th Century', *IESHR*, Vol.IV, No.3 (1967).

[11] Allahabad documents, 355, and 457. (Prof. Z.H. Jafri drew my attention to this evidence).

[12] *Ā'īn*, I, 303–595.

[13] B.S. Cohn, 'Structural Changes in Rural Society', in *Land Control and Social Structure in Indian History*, ed. R.E. Frykenberg, London, 1969; K.K. Trivedi, 'Changes in Caste-Composition of the *Zamīndār* Class in Western Uttar Pradesh, 1595–circa 1900', *IHR*, Vol.II, No.1, 1975, 47–8.

[14] *Ā'īn*, I, 175.

and their divisions and sub-divisions in his statistical tables of the 'Account of the Twelve *Ṣūbas*'.[15] In the textual portion preceding the statistics of each province, he states the total number of *zamīndārs*' horsemen and infantry, prefacing the number by the word *būmī*. In two provinces alone, Berar and Dandesh (Khandesh), are the total numbers of *zamīndārs*' retainers for the province not stated. In Berar, *sawārs* and *piyādas* are entered against some of the *parganas* of *sarkārs* Punar, Kherla and Basim; but the *sarkār* totals even in such cases are not given. In the tables for Khandesh no entry is made at any level.

In the remaining provinces the Mughal administration seems to have collected fairly detailed information about the strength of the *zamīndārs*' armed followers. Excepting Bengal, Bihar and Ajmer, details are given against *parganas* in most of the *sarkārs* of the provinces. We have such entries against the *parganas* of all the *sarkārs* of Awadh, Lahore, Multan and Kabul. In *ṣūba* Allahabad, *sarkār* Battha Ghora has no *pargana* details, and in *sarkār* Chunar the entire cavalry and infantry are ascribed to one *pargana*, namely, Chunar *bā ḥavelī*; but otherwise full *pargana* details are provided. In Delhi, only the outlying *sarkār* of Kumaun has no *pargana* figures. Out of the 13 *sarkārs* of Agra, only under two, Narwar and Mandlaer, are *pargana* entries not recorded. In Gujarat, *sarkār* Nadaut has no entries for retainers, while under Surat, Godhra, and Saurath the information does not go beyond the *sarkār* totals; all other *sarkārs* have *pargana* details. For the province of Malwa detailed statistics are provided under all the *sarkārs*, excepting the *sarkārs* of Nadurbar and Gagraun, under which neither the castes of *zamīndārs* nor the number of their retainers is recorded. For *sarkār* Mandu and Handia the Mughal administration does not seem to have collected information for *zamīndārs*' castes, since the provincial tables leave the *pargana* spaces for *zamīndār* caste completely blank; and at the *sarkār*-level, the vague entry, 'various castes' (*aqwām-i mukhtalifa*) is resorted to. In Orissa all the *sarkārs* except Kaling Dandpat and Raj Mahendra (not yet subjugated) have *pargana* details. In the provinces of Bihar and Ajmer, only the *sarkārs* of Bihar and Sirohi, respectively, have *pargana* entries.

It would seem, then, that Akbar's administration usually failed to obtain detailed statistics from areas having tributary or recalcitrant *zamīndārs*. Otherwise, full particulars were collected, with just a small number of exceptions.

The data provided by the *Ā'īn* suggest that the census, where it was enforced, demanded severe exactitude. The figures for elephants seem

[15] Ibid., 303–494.

exact and are rarely in the round, even if we take endings in 5 (five) as round figures; cavalry too is not always given in round numbers, and we get many detailed figures. For infantry on the other hand, the figure is usually rounded except once, viz., 56 *piyādas* for *pargana* Niman of *sarkār* Handia in Malwa. There is no *sarkār*-wise breakdown for cannon (Bengal) and boats (Bengal and Bihar).

The figures then were not rough estimates; and it appears that local officials like *qānūngos* or *chaudhurīs*, and, possibly, the *zamīndārs* themselves, were made to furnish precise information about the *zamīndārs*' retainers. It further suggests that the maintenance of retainers, if not an obligation for the *zamīndārs*, was at least an established right, recognized as such by the Mughal administration.

The data on retainers may have a statistical significance as well. Could these be used for making at least a rough estimate of the *zamīndārs*' minimum 'necessary' expenditure, if one could estimate the average expenditure on a *sawār* and a *piyāda*? Though immense variety must have existed in the manner of payments by individual *zamīndārs* to individual retainers, it is possible that some customary standards prevailed in different localities. The *Ā'īn* gives us no information on this; Abū'l Faẓl, however, sets out the amounts that the imperial exchequer sanctioned for different breeds of horses and elephants, as well as the salaries paid to different types of troopers. These figures are always given with a detailed breakdown of costs of fodder, equipment, etc.[16] Naturally, it cannot be assumed that *zamīndārs* paid their retainers at the same rates; but these rates can still serve as a basis for establishing a range of the expenses of *zamīndārs* on horses and elephants.

The amount sanctioned for the most inferior horse (*jangla*) in the imperial establishment was 240 *dāms* per month. This included the allowance for grass, *ghī*, etc. It could be assumed that *zamīndārs* paid their retainers only for the bare essentials. The amounts under heads which may be deemed essential, are: grain fodder (*dāna*), 45 *dāms*,[17] saddle (*zīn-o-lajām*), 10 *dāms*, shoeing (*na'l*), 2 *dāms*, groom (*sāi's*), 45 *dāms*. In total we get 102 *dāms* per month, i.e., 1,224 *dāms* per year. To make an allowance for the difference in payment by the royal exchequer

[16] *Ā'īn*, I, 177–88. See Chapter 10.

[17] Akbar's administration, making a provision for the horses of revenue-survey officials, allowed just 6 *sers* of grain-fodder (*dāna*) per horse per day, it being rated at 12 *dāms* per *man* (Todar Mal's memorandum, original text in *Akbarnama*, Br. Mus. Add. 27247, ff.331–2b, and Abū'l Faẓl's polished version in ibid., Bib. Ind., II, 381–3). I have, however, allowed 5 *sers* of *dāna* at the price of 12 *dāms* per *man*, for expenditure on a *zamīndār*'s horse. The *Ā'īn* allows 5 *sers* daily to the *jangla* horse.

and the *zamīndārs*, even these essentials may be scaled down by 20 per cent to take 1000 *dāms* per annum as the likely minimum limit of expenses on a cavalryman by the *zamīndār*.

The amount sanctioned for the most inferior elephant (*phun-darkiya*) in the imperial establishment was 300 *dāms* per month.[18] This covered expenditure on grain and keeper (*mahāwat*) only; and it seems reasonable to accept it as the *zamīndārs*' average expenditure on an elephant.

The lowest paid foot-soldier in the imperial establishment got 240 *dāms* per month.[19] This amount seems too high to be applicable to the *zamīndārs*' foot soldiers. The amount paid by the *zamīndār* to his foot-retainers is difficult to determine since it seems natural that *zamīndārs* maintained only 'part-time' or seasonal retainers. They might not have been required all the time, and were probably kept in reserve to be called on when needed. One extreme suggestion could be that service as a foot-soldier was an obligation for the peasant, and therefore, was obtained *gratis* by *zamīndārs*. However, this is unlikely since the relatively small infantry figures cannot possibly represent the total number of the able-bodied rural male population. If the obligation was imposed on some special clan or caste of the peasantry, such peasants must have been granted some benefits, e.g., lower revenue-rates or revenue exemptions; and this would represent one form of payment. In most cases, perhaps, the *zamīndār* paid his retainers in cash or (by alienation of revenue) in land. I have taken 100 *dāms* per annum as the minimum cost of maintaining one foot-soldier. This is a purely arbitrary figure; but it is so low that it is surely difficult to conceive of a lower rate of payment or expenditure per retainer.

There is one valid objection to this method. We have estimated the cost incurred by the *zamīndār* on his retainers, horses, and elephants by assuming and then scaling down the prices and costs that prevailed in the imperial camp. But can any rates uniformly apply to all regions since in actual fact the rural price levels must have varied very greatly from region to region? For example, it is very probable that the cost levels in Gujarat were much higher than those in U.P. while those in Bengal must have been much lower.[20] Our analysis thus becomes subject to a wider margin of error as we go further away from the capital cities of Agra and

[18] *Ā'īn*, I, 177–8.

[19] Ibid., 188.

[20] Habib, *Agrarian System*, 71–3 (rev. ed. 78–9). One explanation of the high rates of revenue incidence in Gujarat could be that prices were high there relative to the *ẓabṭī* provinces (see Chapter 5).

Lahore. The best we can do, however, is to keep this source of possible error always in mind while assessing our results.

The minimum expenditure incurred by *zamīndārs* on their retainers (*būmī*, *ulūs*) is henceforth designated ZE (*zamīndārs*' expenditure). As a percentage of the *jama'*, ZE naturally varies considerably from province to province. Indeed, the margin of variation is appreciably large for different *sarkārs* within a province; even within a *sarkār* the proportion of ZE out of the *jama'* for individual *parganas* varies a great deal.

Taking first the empire as a whole, we find that in the entire empire, ZE, as we have calculated it, was about 16 per cent of the total *jama'*. The province-wise break-up in an ascending order is given below, being based on the *sarkār*-level data given in Appendix 7.A).

Table 7.1

Province	ZE as % of *jama'*	Province	ZE as % of *jama'*
Gujarat	8	Agra	19
Delhi	9	Bihar	22
Allahabad	12	Multan	23
Awadh	12	Malwa	32
Lahore	17	Ajmer	42
Bengal	18		

To avoid a false impression of precision, I have rounded off the decimal fractions all through.

It will be seen from Table 7.1 that in Agra and Lahore, the provinces that contained the two capital cities, and where the administration might be assumed to have been the strongest and most efficient, ZE reaches 19 per cent and 17 per cent respectively. But the *sarkār*-wise figures modify this general picture (see Appendix 7.A and Map IX, which depicts ZE as percent of the *jama' sarkār*-wise). ZE in *sarkār* Agra was around 10 per cent while in the adjacent areas of Kol and Kanauj it was above 20 per cent of the *jama'*. In *sarkār* Mandlaer, it works out as 2.4 times the *jama'*! In no *sarkār* of Agra province was ZE less than 10 per cent of the *jama'*. Within the *ṣūba* of Lahore, in the peripheral area of Bairun Panjnad, ZE was the highest, viz., 36 per cent of the *jama'*. In Bet Jalandhar, which had cash revenue-rates and where measurement was almost complete, it was less than 10 per cent.

Sandwiched between the provinces of Lahore and Agra, the province of Delhi presents a different picture. Here ZE was exceptionally low: in 3 out of 8 *sarkārs* it was below 10 per cent, *sarkār* Delhi itself yielding

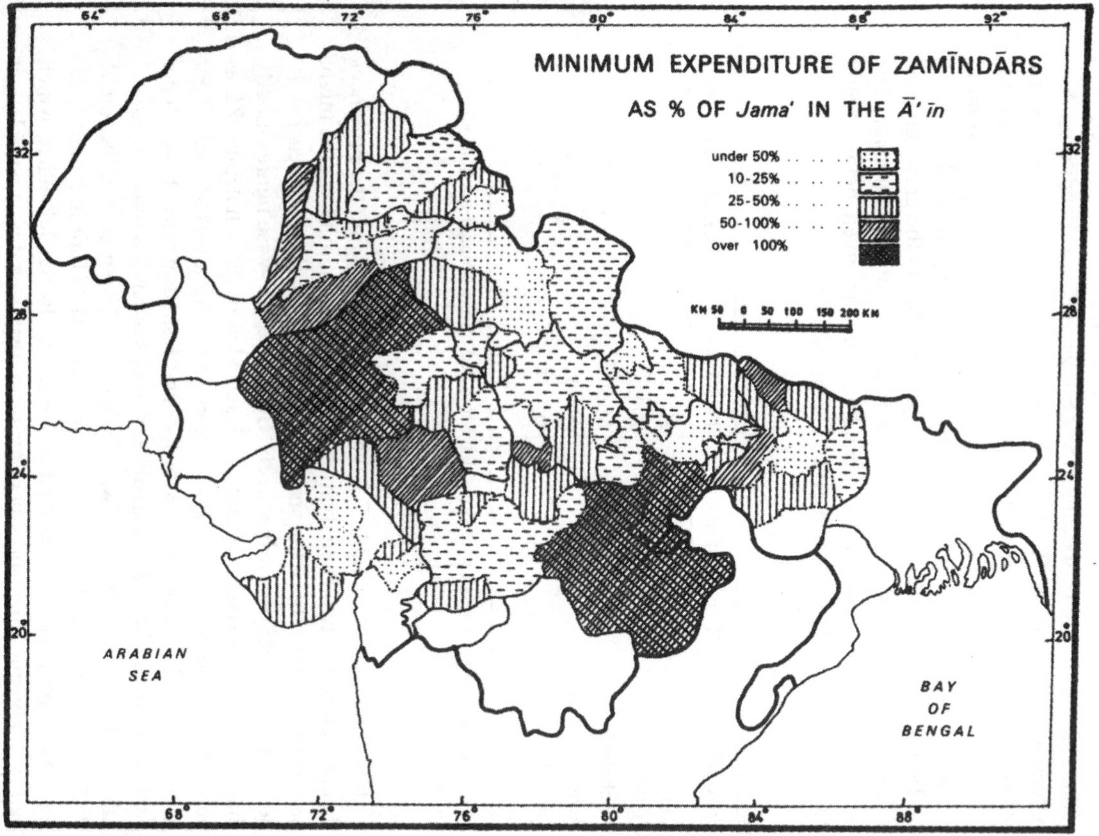

MINIMUM EXPENDITURE OF ZAMĪNDĀRS
AS % OF *Jama'* IN THE *Ā'īn*
under 50%
10-25%
25-50%
50-100%
over 100%
KM 50 0 50 100 150 200 KM
ARABIAN SEA
BAY OF BENGAL

Map IX

the lowest ZE of all (4 per cent). The only *sarkār* in this province where ZE exceeded 20 per cent was Hissar Firuza.

As one would perhaps expect, the proportion was the highest (42 per cent) in the Ajmer province which consisted largely of the dominions of Rajput chieftains. In *sarkār* Bikaner, comprising the two principalities of Bikaner and Jaisalmer, effective ZE works out at almost 3.6 times the *jama'*. In Jodhpur too it exceeds the *jama'*.

The *zamīndārs*' expenditure was, surprisingly enough, lowest (8 per cent of the *jama'*) in Gujarat though it has been held that there the *zamīndārs* appropriated 25 per cent of the revenue (but within their lands only?).[21] In most *sarkārs* of the province (6 out of 9) ZE is much below 10 per cent of the *jama'*. In Godhra and Saurath (Saurashtra) which had large areas under chieftains, however, it reaches very high percentages, 44 and 33, respectively. The low ZE in this *ṣūba* may partly be explained by the fact that the price level was higher in Gujarat than Agra, so that we should allow for a higher factor than the standard accepted by us in order to obtain the true level of minimum expenditure incurred by *zamīndārs*. But even a doubling of ZE in Gujarat would only put it at 16 per cent of the *jama'*. This strongly confirms the suspicion that the *zamīndārs*' nominal share of 25 per cent came only out of *zamīndārī* lands, and that in the large *ra'iyatī* tracts, he was not allowed such a large allowance.[22]

The other province which is known to have been under powerful *zamīndārs* was Bengal; but here again ZE does not appear to be very high and amounts to about 18 per cent of the *jama'*. In 7 *sarkārs* out of its total of 19 it is below 10 per cent and only in 6 does it exceed 20 per cent of the *jama'*. The maximum attained is, however, 87 per cent (Silhat), while the minimum is as low as 2 per cent (Chatgaon). If cost levels were especially low in Bengal, the true ZE in Bengal might have been much less than even 18 per cent. But the Mughal conquest of Bengal was still in progress in 1595, and the entire statistics of Bengal are, on those grounds, a little suspect. Certainly for Chatgaon, at least, the *Ā'īn*'s information for both the *jama'* and ZE must have been either fictitious or simply inherited from the obsolete records of the Sultans of Bengal.

From the detailed *sarkār*-level figures we can draw certain inferences: the *zamīndārs*' expenditure was generally higher in regions which were not closely administered or in peripheral areas where the chiefs were

[21] Irfan Habib, 'Social Distribution of Landed Property in Pre-British India', *Essays in Indian History*, p.102.

[22] This is indeed implied in Irfan Habib's interpretation of the *Mir'āt-i Aḥmadī*'s passage (*Agrarian System*, 112; rev. ed. 124–5).

Table 7.2

Sarkār	*Ṣūba*	ZE as % of *jama'*
Bhattha Ghora	Allahabad	138
Garh	Malwa	271
Bairun Panjnad	Lahore	61

allowed a semi-tributary status. This can be seen in the high ZE in the following territories (Table 7.2).

One can illustrate this relationship between high ZE and lax Mughal control if we were to make one reasonable assumption. Wherever the land had been extensively surveyed in the time of the *Ā'īn*, we may take the area to have been under close administrative control; conversely, where, in the *ẕabṯi* provinces, the *ārāẓī* figures (A) in the *Ā'īn* form a very low proportion of the map area (M), the Mughal administration's control over the area is more likely to have been lax. The figures in Appendix 7.A show, indeed, that, as a rule, there is an inverse relationship between the extent of measurement and size of ZE. A few examples follow (Table 7.3). To cite yet another example, and this from Bihar, we find that ZE was as low as 3 per cent in the measured *parganas* of the *sarkār* of Bihar, and as high as 11 per cent in the unmeasured *parganas*.

Table 7.3

	Ṣūba	*Sarkār*	Map area as times *arāẓī*	ZE as % of *jama'*
A.	Awadh	Gorakhpur	37.34	27
	"	Awadh	1.17	11
B.	Agra	Mandlaer	53.15	241
	"	Agra	1.04	11
C.	Delhi	Hissar Firuza	4.26	26
	"	Delhi	1.19	4

But such correlation cannot be looked for in other provinces where measurement was yet to be completed. In such regions, the *jama'* per *bīgha* of map area might, however, serve as an index of the degree of administrative control. This would call for allowance to be made for three factors: (a) extent of cultivation at that time; (b) productivity of soil; and (c) price-level. Broadly speaking, one can detect a general tendency of low ZE with high J/M (*jama'* divided by map area). This tendency is most pronounced in portions of Bihar and, excepting certain *sarkārs*, is present in Lahore, Multan, and Gujarat. Malwa and Allahabad, however, do not exhibit such a correlation (see Appendix 7.A). Still, these checks largely reinforce our hypothesis that the size of ZE varied in an inverse ratio to the degree of Mughal administrative control.

The one problem which remains arises out of our assuming uniform cost-levels. We have seen that this is a questionable assumption in so far as regions like Gujarat or Bengal are concerned. The only way to avoid possible major pitfalls would be to take a homogeneous block for scrutiny.

A detailed examination of *pargana*-level statistics in the *Ā'īn* has been attempted for the area broadly corresponding to the present state of U.P., where the assumption of uniform cost-levels should cause only marginal deviations from the actual.

I began by plotting on the map every *pargana* with its ZE as a percentage of *jama'*. I have then grouped the *parganas* into three zones, viz. (1) where ZE is less than 10 per cent of the *jama'*, (2) where it ranges from 10 to 40 per cent and (3) where it is over 40 per cent (Map X).

The result broadly confirms what we have inferred from our *sarkār*-level study of the empire, that ZE is higher in the outlying and forested areas. But there are certain pockets with a relatively high ZE. One such pocket is south of Lucknow along the Ganga river. A pocket of moderate ZE is situated in Middle Doāb (around Agra and Aligarh). In general, in central and western U.P., especially in *sarkār* Delhi, low ZE is accompanied by a high degree of measurement; but in central Doāb, and especially Allahabad province, low ZE coexists with high J/A (*jama'* divided by measured land or *ārāẓī*), i.e., with incomplete measurement.

Another interesting feature is that if *parganas* assigned to the Rajputs, Brahmans or Muslims as *zamīndārs* are separately considered, no consistent correlation with the ZE is obtained. But if one takes single castes such as Bachgotis, Bais and, in certain *sarkārs*, Chauhans, among the Rajputs, one finds that relatively high ZE is often assigned to *parganas* with them as *zamīndārs*. One is therefore tempted to infer that even within the closely administered zones ZE varies considerably, and that the *zamidars*' caste-position could have been a factor behind this variation. This leads us to a further possibility: ZE was probably high or at least moderate where the peasant communities were weak, and where the land was controlled by small corporate bodies of *zamīndārs* or *muqaddams* (e.g. in middle Doāb and Baiswara); conversely, it was low where peasant communities were strong, e.g. Upper Doāb. Can we then infer that peasant communities were also strong in eastern U.P. (*sarkār* Jaunpur), where too ZE is low over an extensive area (see Map X)?

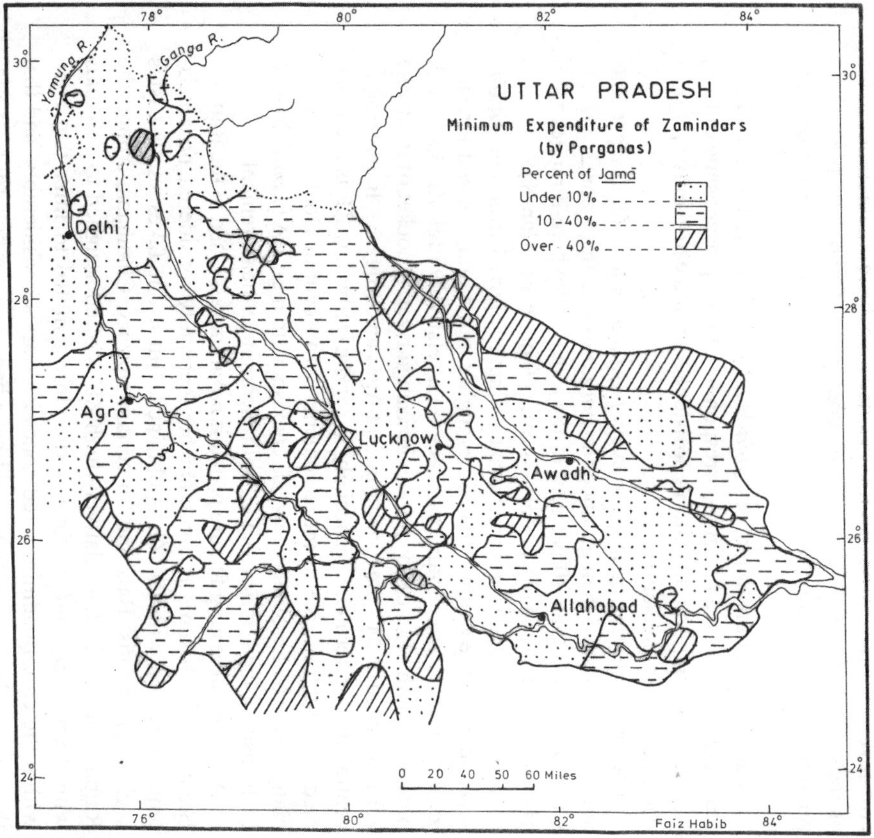
UTTAR PRADESH
Minimum Expenditure of Zamindars
(by Parganas)
Percent of Jamā
Under 10%
10–40%
Over 40%
Yamuna R.
Ganga R.
Delhi
Agra
Lucknow
Awadh
Allahabad
0 20 40 50 60 Miles
Faiz Habib

Map X

The high range of variations in the *zamīndārs*' expenditure from region to region makes it hazardous to work out any general tendency. However, in most of the *sarkārs* of Agra, Delhi, Lahore, Awadh, and Allahabad (where the expenses worked out on the basis of the *Ā'īn*'s standard allowances seem most applicable), ZE mostly falls between 10 to 25 per cent of the *jama'* (in 23 out of 43 *sarkārs*); that is, one can roughly take the average as 17 per cent of the *jama'*. This is a tempting figure since ZE over the entire empire amounted to a little over 16 per cent of the *jama'*.

An attempt like this to use the *Ā'īn*'s great census of *zamīndār* castes and retainers for the purpose of defining the *zamīndārs*' share in the surplus extracted from the peasantry must obviously be pursued with considerable caution. Yet in the absence of any other direct source of information, the data as worked out here appear to be the only means of shedding light on this important question. The mode of calculating the *zamīndārs*' military expenditure (ZE) is based on such conservative criteria that it must represent the minimum expenditure rather than the normal. Moreover, the *zamīndārs*' income must have substantially exceeded their military expenditure. Keeping both these considerations in mind, we may set the *zamīndārs*' gross income at about twice the amount of ZE. If, therefore, ZE over the entire empire amounted to a little over 16 per cent of the *jama'*, the *zamīndārs*' income must have approximated to nearly a third of the *jama'*. We have suggested in Chapter 5 that taking the *jama'* to represent the net income of the *jāgīrdārs* (and *k͟hāliṣa*) only, we may estimate the total land-revenue realization (J′) at 142.857% of the *jama'*. But in the latter we have allowed 10 per cent for the *zamīndār*'s share, but we are here, of course, concerned with the size of the *zamīndār*'s income, or his share in the total surplus and not in the gross revenue claim (J′) alone. We must, then, first deduct 10% of J′ from J′, to get (142.857 *minus* 14.286=) 128.571% of J, and then add to it 33.33% of J (one-third of stated *jama'*) to get 161.901% of J, which should represent the entire agricultural surplus (S). This would mean that at 33.33% of J, the *zamīndārs*' share amounted to nearly a fifth of the surplus.

These very rough estimates do not negate the general hypothesis that the *zamīndārs*' role in the system of agrarian exploitation was a secondary one, though their share of the surplus so deduced is much more than what has been hitherto supposed. Moreover, one must remember that averages are deceptive; detailed *pargana*-level scrutiny reveals the existence, in the very middle of strongly-administered areas, of pockets where ZE was exceptionally high and where, therefore, the existence of an economically dominant *zamīndār* class must be assumed.

APPENDIX 7.A

Sarkārs	Minimum ZE as % of *jama'*	*Jama'/ārāẓī* (*dāms/bīgha-i Ilāhī*)	*Jama'*/map-area (*dāms/bīgha-i Ilāhī*)
AGRA			
Mandlaer	241	57	1
Narwar	59	11	3
Erach	35	17	6
Payanwan	34	11	2
Alwar	27	24	14
Kol	23	22	17
Gawalior	23	19	9
Narnaul	22	26	11
Kanauj	22	19	9
Sahar	20	8	6
Tijara	12	24	21
Agra	11	21	20
Kalpi	10	29	16
DELHI			
Hissar Firuza	26	17	4
Kumaun	18	N.A.	2
Badaun	16	18	3
Rewari	13	26	22
Sambhal	11	16	11
Sirhind	9	21	13
Saharanpur	7	25	24
Delhi	4	17	15
AWADH			
Gorakhpur	27	49	1
Lucknow	14	24	13
Awadh	11	13	13
Bahraich	11	13	5
Khairabad	9	26	8

(*Continued*)

Appendix 7.A (*Continued*)

Sarkārs	Minimum ZE as % of *jama'*	*Jama'/ārāẓī* (*dāms/bīgha-i Ilāhī*)	*Jama'*/map-area (*dāms/bīgha-i Ilāhī*)
ALLAHABAD			
Batta Gahora	138	N.A.	1
Chunar	40	55	8
Manikpur	19	51	12
Banaras	17	43	13
Ghazipur	14	48	8
Kalinjar	13	47	4
Korra	11	51	12
Jaunpur	8	64	9
Allahabad	7	40	8
Kara	6	41	12
BIHAR			
Champaner	67	64	2
Rohtas	51	86	6
Tirhut	45	81	3
Saran	37	57	4
Bihar (unmeasured)	32	N.A.	1
Munger	24	N.A.	3
Hajipur	4	61	10
Bihar (measured)	3	83	13
AJMER			
Bikaner	358	N.A.	6
Jodhpur	138	N.A.	2
Chittor	87	N.A.	6
Ajmer	39	N.A.	1
Sirohi	28	N.A.	4
Nagaur	17	N.A.	3
Ranthambor	13	N.A.	0.1
GUJARAT			
Godhra	44	7	2
Saurath	33	N.A.	4
Surat	14	15	9
Broach	8	23	10

(*Continued*)

Appendix 7.A (*Continued*)

Sarkārs	Minimum ZE as % of *jama'*	*Jama'*/*ārāẓī* (*dāms*/*bīgha-i Ilāhī*)	*Jama'*/map-area (*dāms*/*bīgha-i Ilāhī*)
Champaran	6	13	3
Baroda	4	44	32
Ahmadabad	3	38	22
Pattan	2	15	7
Nadaut	N.A.	16	5
MALWA			
Garh	271	N.A.	0.2
Chanderi	41	56	3
Kotri Pirawa	36	46	4
Bijagarh	30	87	5
Mandasor	24	N.A.	2
Raisin	22	83	1
Handia	16	39	2
Saranpur	16	54	6
Mandu	10	62	5
Ujjain	10	47	8
Nadurbar	2	58	2
Gagraun	N.A.	71	2
LAHORE			
Bairun	36	N.A.	9
Bari	31	31	19
Sindh Sagar	30	37	2
Chanhat	12	25	10
Rachnao	10	41	14
Bet Jalendhar	8	31	18

THE DISTRIBUTION OF THE SURPLUS AMONG THE RULING CLASS

CHAPTER 8

Imperial Finance

Total Income and Accumulation

I

Until now we have concerned ourselves principally with the realization of the state's claim to the agricultural surplus under the name of land revenue, which was naturally subject to deductions on account of the claims of other right holders and the cost of revenue collection. Our estimate is that after these had been allowed for, the Mughal administration aimed at realizing in the net about 60 per cent of the total claimed land revenue.[1] With such a large share of the surplus appropriated by the apparatus of the State, its distribution among the ruling class necessarily constituted a major element in the economy of Mughal India.

The income of the empire was represented by the *jama'* (or, in the seventeenth-century terminology, the *jama'-dāmī*). To recapitulate our earlier conclusions, the *jama'* represented a standard estimate of the net revenue realization (i.e., gross realization *less* charges of collection and other allowances left to subordinate right-holders). The *jama'* statistics for the whole empire are set out along with other data in the 'Account of the Twelve *Ṣūbas*' in the *Ā'īn*.[2] In the body of this chapter Abū'l Faẓl subsequently added some material (notably the sections on Berar and Khandesh) coming down to as late as the 45th regnal year (1600–1). But his remarks at the beginning of that chapter suggest that his information applied in general to the 40th regnal year (1595–6), and this should,

[1] See Chapters 5 and 7.

[2] *Ā'īn*, I, 386–595.

therefore, be taken to be the year of statistics of all the *ṣūbas*, except where a subsequent insertion can be detected.[3]

Abū'l Faẓl states that the *jama'-i dahsāla* of the entire empire amounted to 3,62,97,55,246 *dāms*.[4] It has been suggested by Irfan Habib that this figure is probably the total fixed at the conclusion of the *Dahsāla* experiment, that is in 1584–5.[5] The total *jama'* calculated by us from *pargana* figures in the *Ā'īn*'s own statistics comes to 5,06,76,49,932 *dāms*.[6]

There is good reason to fix the 40th regnal year as the standard year for our data. The *manṣabdārs'* share should be the largest in the net income of the empire, and this can be calculated principally from Abū'l Faẓl's list of *manṣabdārs*. This he assigns explicitly to the 40th regnal year. We should, therefore, establish as nearly as possible what the total *jama'* of the empire was in this year, that is, 1595–6. To obtain the income of the empire in 1595–6, we have to subtract the *jama'* of Berar and Khandesh from our total of 5,06,76,49,932 *dāms*. Berar was subjugated just after the close of the 40th year, within 1596, and the *manṣab* promotions granted to Zain Khān Koka and Ṣādiq Khān in the beginning of the 41st year,[7] obviously for services rendered in the Berar campaign, are not incorporated in the *Ā'īn*'s record of ranks of *manṣabdārs*.[8] The *jama'* of Berar ought therefore to be excluded from any total for the empire designed for comparison with expenditure estimated on the basis of the *Ā'īn*'s *manṣab* lists. Khandesh, annexed as late as the 45th regnal year, will obviously have to be excluded.

The *jama'* of the empire (less that of Berar and Khandesh), adds up to 4,11,86,88,488 *dāms*.[9] The total is in broad agreement with the figure of 4,40,06,00,000 *dāms* given in the *Ṭabaqāt-i Akbarī*,[10] which having been completed in 1593–4, could not have possibly included either of the two Deccan provinces.

In eastern India certain large tracts in the *ṣūbas* of Bengal and Orissa, whose *jama'* is formally included in the *Ā'īn* (and also presumably in the

[3] See Chapter 1, Sec. II.

[4] *Ā'īn*, I, 386.

[5] Habib, *Agrarian System*, 399 & *n*. (rev. ed. 454–5&*n*)

[6] This total differs from the *jama'* calculated by Habib (*Agrarian System*, 399) (rev. ed. 454–5), which is based on the *ṣūba* totals stated in the *Ā'īn*.

[7] *Akbarnāma*, III, 770.

[8] *Ā'īn*, I, 223.

[9] This is arrived at by deducting from the grand total of 5,06,76,49,932 *dāms* given above, the totals of 64,54,31,956 *dāms* for Berar and 30,35,29,488 *dāms* for Khandesh.

[10] *Ṭabaqāt*, III, 54. The amount is stated in terms of *tanka-i murādī*, or double *dāms*, but this must be a mistake for *dām*.

Ṭabaqāt-i Akbarī), had not been subjugated.[11] 'Īsā Khān still occupied the larger portion of the Bhati region in eastern Bengal.[12] The Mughals had nevertheless succeeded in seizing large parts of Bhati west of the Brahmaputra; and Sherpur Murcha (Salimnagar), in *sarkār* Bazuha, was established as their important garrison town.[13] Towards the north the *sarkār* of Ghoraghat had been occupied as well, since the Mughals were able to compel Kuch Bihar to submit to them by the 41st regnal year.[14]

The parts of Bengal and Orissa which were still not in fact under Mughal control and could not have been available for assignment in *jāgīrs* may accordingly be listed as follows:

Sarkār	*Jama'* in *dāms*
Ṣūba Bengal	
Bakla	71,31,440
Chatgaon	1,14,23,510
Sonagaon	1,34,16,513
Fatehabad	79,76,837
Silhat	70,56,608
Orissa	
Kaling Dandpat	55,60,000
Raj Mahendra	50,00,000
Total	5,75,64,908

If we deduct the *jama'* figures for these *sarkārs*, the total *jama'* for the empire in 1595–6 would come down to 4,06,11,23,580 *dāms*. The *Ā'īn*'s *jama'* figures included too the revenue alienated in the form of revenue-grants (*suyūrghāl*). Since this amount was not really part of the *jama'* against which *jāgīrs* were assigned, and, as we have shown (Chapter 7), was simply added to the *jama'* figures by Abū'l Fazl, the amounts shown

[11] *Akbarnāma*, III, 259, 263, 432-3. In Orissa Raj Mahendra and Kaling Dandpat had not been subdued; and no *pargana*-wise statistics are furnished for them in the *Ā'īn*. One assumes that Bengal had been formally annexed to the Mughal empire much earlier, since the *Ṭabaqāt-i Akbarī*'s figure for the revenues of the empire also included these paper estimates.

[12] *Ā'īn*, I, 387. For the limits of the country known as Bhati, see Habib, *Atlas of the Mughal Empire*, 45 and 104.

[13] *Akbarnāma*, III, 697.

[14] Ibid., III, 243 and 716–17.

in *suyūrghāl* columns in the *Ā'īn*'s table must be subtracted from the total *jama'*. The total of *pargana* figures for *suyūrghāl* (excluding *ṣūba* Berar) works out at 10,07,96,474 *dāms*. Subtracting these figures as well, the effective *jama'* of the empire in 1595–6 comes to 3,96,03,27,106 *dāms*.

The *jama'* comprised land revenue as well as taxes other than land revenue,[15] and therefore represented practically the entire income of the empire. Certain other sources of income for the emperor, which were not covered by the *jama'* were the gifts received (and sometimes imposed), fines, and the property acquired in escheat, at least in the case of those nobles who died without leaving heirs.[16] There does not appear to be any means of determining the actual size of income so obtained; Monserrate does suggest that it was not inconsiderable.[17] We have not added anything on their account to the total figure of the *jama'*; but we shall have to make some allowance for this income while estimating expenditure on various heads and also while discussing the size of the annual savings.

While the major part of the *jama'* was alienated in the form of territorial revenue assignments (*jāgīrs*) to *manṣabdārs*, the remainder belonged to the *khāliṣa* (or properly *khāliṣa sharīfa*), where the revenue was collected directly for the Imperial Treasury.[18] Even out of the revenues of the *khāliṣa*, a portion must have again been claimed by such *manṣabdārs* as were designated *naqdī*, i.e., receiving pay in cash from the Imperial Treasury.[19] The imperial establishment was maintained mainly out of the balance of the *khāliṣa* revenues.

Keeping in view the division of the *jama'* under the *jāgīr* and *khāliṣa*, we can fix a minimum limit for the expenses incurred on the nobles' salaries: since *jāgīrs* were given in lieu of salaries, the portion of the *jama'* accounted for by *jāgīrs* represented the minimum level of the share of revenue alienated to nobles; but the actual amount disbursed on salaries must have been larger, since many of the *manṣab*-holders also received their pay in whole or in part in cash out of the revenues of the *khāliṣa*.

The extent of the *khāliṣa*, or conversely, of the *jāgīrs*, in the year 1595–6 is, however, difficult to estimate directly. In his 31st regnal year Akbar remitted one-sixth of the *jama'* of the *khāliṣa* in the provinces of Awadh, Allahabad and Delhi, and the remission amounted in absolute

[15] See chapter 5.

[16] Monserrate, p.207, for gifts and escheat; and for fines, *Ā'īn*, I, 163–4. For a detailed discussion of escheat, see M. Athar Ali, *Mughal Nobility under Aurangzeb*, 63–8.

[17] Monserrate, 207.

[18] Habib, *Agrarian System*, 259 (rev. ed. 300).

[19] Ibid., 258.

figures to 4,05,60,596 *dāms*.[20] This in turn gives us 24,33,63,576 as the total *jama'* of the khāliṣa in the three provinces. The total *jama'* of these provinces given in the *Ā'īn* is 1,01,43,52,077 *dāms*; and so the *jama'* of the *khāliṣa* in the 31st year was about 23.99 per cent of the total *jama'* within this region, as it was in the 40th year. Though it cannot be assumed that the extent of the *khāliṣa* in all the provinces was the same, what we find to have been its extent in the three provinces should offer us a fair sample, because these exclude Agra and Lahore where the *khāliṣa* might well have been larger, as well as such provinces as Bengal, Ajmer and Bihar, where it is likely to have been smaller.

In the Jesuit accounts, we come across another estimate:[21] 'For all the kingdoms and provinces which he [Akbar] conquers he holds as his own, appointing his captains over them. From these he takes a third portion of the revenues, the remainder being for their personal needs, and the maintenance of the soldiers, horses, and elephants which each of them is bound to keep.' The only meaning this passage will bear is that *jāgīrs* normally accounted for two-thirds of the *jama'*, and the *khāliṣa* for a third.

From this rather limited evidence it would appear that during Akbar's reign the *khāliṣa* accounted for anything between 24 per cent and 33 per cent of the total *jama'*; and the *jāgīrs*, conversely, for between 67 and 76 per cent. This gives a floor of 2,65,34,192 *dāms* for payment of salaries; and a ceiling of 1,30,69,079 *dāms* for expenditure on the imperial establishment. In the latter case the actual expenses must have been much smaller because, as we must remember, a part of the nobles' pay-claim had to be met in cash out of the *khāliṣa* revenues.

For more precise limits and more detailed indications of break-up of the expenditure we have to examine the large amount of data in the *Ā'īn*.

While Abū'l Faẓl deals with revenue resources of the empire in Book III (*Ā'īn-i Mulkābādī*) of the *Ā'īn*, the first two books, namely, *Ā'īn-Manzilābādī* (Camp) and *Ā'īn-i Sipāhābādī* (Army) give details of the expenditure of the emperor's own establishment. The headings are a little misleading since Abū'l Faẓl includes animal stables, arsenal, army and artillery under *Manzilābādī*, along with the harem, kitchen, wardrobe and library, while the hunting animals, pigeons, etc., along with slaves, are put by him under *Sipāhābādī*.

Undoubtedly, for interpreting certain statements of Abū'l Faẓl's, particularly his reference to the total expenditure on the *buyūtāt* or imperial

[20] *Akbarnāma*, III, 494. Cf. Habib, *Agrarian System*, 272 & *n.* (rev. ed., 314 & *n.*)

[21] *Akbar and the Jesuits*, tr. C.H. Payne, 5–6.

household, his own classification must be kept in mind. But a more logical division of the imperial expenditure would be one under three heads, viz. (i) the salary bill of the *manṣabdārs*; (ii) expenditure in the imperial military establishment; and (iii) expenses of the imperial household. The detailed examination in the succeeding chapters will follow this division.

II

There were numerous channels through which the revenue collected in the empire flowed out into the hands of the recipients of the surplus; but a significant portion of the revenues was excluded from the process of distribution, being reserved for the imperial hoard. Besides the growing store of precious stones and ornaments, a separate cash treasury used to be maintained.[22] At Akbar's death, according to the details given by Pelsaert, professedly copied from the royal account books, the cash treasury contained 69,70,000 gold *muhrs*, 10 crore silver rupees, and 23 crore copper *dāms*.[23] These figures get some support from Firishta's account. While he does not offer us any tally of gold and copper specie, he does give the number of silver rupees as 10 crore.[24] In addition, he specifies quantities of gold and silver bullion as well as uncoined copper.

Qazwīnī, the first official historian of Shāhjahān, while criticizing the extravagance of Jahāngīr, says that Akbar had left behind seven crore of rupees (apparently besides what he had left in gold), out of which Jahāngīr spent six crores, so that only one crore remained in the treasury at his death.[25] Qazwīnī thus gives a figure for rupees which is much smaller than the one offered by both Pelsaert and Firishta. This seems all the more puzzling since in the context it would have suited Qazwīnī's purpose not to understate the amount left behind by Akbar. It is practically impossible to give preference to one over the other figure, and I have assumed a range of seven to ten crores of rupees for the silver-coin hoard left by Akbar.

For the rest, proceeding on Pelsaert's figures, whose general reliability is discussed in Chapters 10 and 11, the amount hoarded in the form of specie in the imperial treasury in 1605 can be computed as follows:

[22] *Ā'īn*, I, 30.

[23] Pelsaert, *Kronick* 117; *Chronicle* tr., 33.

[24] Firishta, I, 272.

[25] Qazwīnī, *Pādshāhnāma*, Br. Mus. MS Add 20,734, 444–5, Or. 173f. 221a–b.

Muhrs 69,70,000	worth	2,50,92,00,000 *dāms*
Rupees 7 to 10 crores	"	2,80,00,00,000 to 4,00,00,00,000 *dāms*
Dāms		23,00,00,000
	Total	5,53,92,00,000 to 6,73,92,00,000 *dāms*

Since in 1605 a *muhr* fetched nine silver rupees and forty *dāms* went to a rupee, we have here made the conversion of *muhrs* and rupees into *dāms* at these rates, and not at those which Pelsaert, taking the quotations of his own time, adopted.

In order to estimate the entire amount 'withdrawn from circulation' we may also add the amount of bullion and uncoined copper recorded by Firishta. While the price of uncoined copper is directly given by Abū'l Faẓl as 1044 *dāms* per *man*,[26] the price of gold and silver bullion in terms of *dāms* can also be worked out from the detailed data given in the *Ā'īn*.[27] Assuming the *man* given by Firishta to be the *man-i Akbarī* we may first convert the quantity of gold into grains troy: $10 \times 55.32 \times 7000 = 38{,}72{,}400$ grains troy. Since one *muhr* weighed 169 grains,[28] a quantity of 38,72,400 grains of gold would have been equal, weight for weight, to 22,913.6 *muhrs*. But since the seigniorage and minting costs too had to be taken into account (working out at about 5 per cent),[29] the actual number of *muhrs* minted from 10 *mans* of gold should have been 21,767.93. This at the rate already noted, would be equal to $(21{,}767.93 \times 9 \times 40 =)$ 78,36,455 *dāms*.

Similarly since a rupee weighed 178 grains troy,[30] 70 *mans* of silver should have yielded $(70 \times 55.32 \times 7000 \div 178)$ 1,52,285.39 rupees in weight. The seigniorage and minting costs in the case of silver being 5.6 per cent,[31] the actual number of rupees minted from this quantity would have been 1,43,757.41, which in turn should have been worth 57,50,296 *dāms*.

According to Abū'l Faẓl one *ser* of copper yielded 26 *dāms* and 2 *jītals* (26.08 rounded to 26.1 *dāms*). Therefore, 60 *mans* of copper should have yielded 62,640 *dāms*.[32]

[26] *Ā'īn*, I, 31.

[27] Ibid., 31–2.

[28] Irfan Habib, 'Currency System of the Mughal Empire', *Medieval India Quarterly*, IV, nos.1–2, 9.

[29] Ibid.

[30] Ibid., 3.

[31] Ibid.

[32] *Ā'īn*, I, 31. The *Ā'īn* also gives the price of one *man* of copper as 1044 *dāms*; and this exactly accords with the yield of coined *dāms* per *ser*.

Adding these amounts to the estimate of cash worked out above, the total value of coin and bullion in the imperial cash treasury in 1605 may be put at between 5,55,28,61,574 and 6,75,28,61,574 *dāms*.

The hoard so accumulated must have been built up through additions made over the entire reign (1556–1605). It is logical to assume that the size of the annual transfer to the hoard increased in proportion to the extension of the empire. Since Akbar's effective dominions at the time of his accession at Kalanaur barely comprised the Panjab, the annual savings in the early years could only have fraction of what they were when the empire approached its zenith, around the close of the sixteenth century. Thus, hypothetically, the amount transferred to the hoard must have stepped up every year. Assuming that the hoard Akbar inherited in 1556 was practically negligible we may postulate a simple annual increase in the savings in regular 'arithmetical progression' from zero at the time of the accession.

Using this method, we can calculate the amount that went into the hoard in the 40th regnal year (1595–6).[33] Given our two figures for the total value of the hoard in 1605, the estimates for savings (transfers to hoard) in the 40th regnal year work out at 18,13,17,920 *dāms* (accepting Qazwīnī) or 22,05,01,600 *dāms* (accepting Pelsaert and Firishta).

A considerable part of this amount must have come from sources not covered by the *jama'*. The major source of income outside the *jama'* was probably war booty: Large amounts were seized from the treasuries and hoards of rulers of conquered provinces.[34] While the actual size of the contribution of such booty to the hoard cannot be determined, one may arbitrarily accept some proportion; and I have assumed that out of the total hoard, 10 per cent was gained from this source. We have to make some further allowance for cash presents received regularly on New Year's Day,[35] upon the weighing ceremony[36] and numerous other

[33] $$S = \frac{n}{2}(2a_1 + n - 1)\,d$$

$$a_i = a_1 + (i - 1)\,d$$

Where—

S denotes total savings
n denotes total number of years, i.e., 50 years (1556–1605)
a_i denotes savings in the ith year
d denotes common difference

[34] *Akbarnāma*, II, 138, 142–3, 214; *Ṭabaqāt*, II, 152–3, 155; Badāūnī, II, 47–8; *Akbarnāma*, III, 296.

[35] *Akbarnāma* (the *Takmila*), 803, 836.

[36] Tavernier, I, 301. One may expect that the tradition went back to Akbar's time.

occasions;[37] and also for amounts coming from fines and escheats. From such inflow of cash we have to deduct the amount the emperor gave-away in gifts, including charity. The *Ā'īn* says one crore of *dāms* were kept ready all the time for this purpose.[38] Making allowance for this outflow, we may take gifts to the Emperor as contributing one-twentieth of the total savings. Making our deductions accordingly, we can take it that in 1595–6, an amount of about 15,50,26,829 to 18,85,28,870 *dāms* was probably drawn from the *jama'*-based income, for transfer to the imperial hoard.

With the imperial 'savings' behind us, we may now pass on to different items of 'expenditure'. Chapters 9, 10, and 11 will be wholly devoted to its estimation for 1595–6. We hope to be able thereafter to see also whether our estimate for the transfer to the hoard accords with the difference between the total income of the *k͟hāliṣa* and the total expenditure estimated by us.

[37] *Akbarnāma*, II, 149; *Ṯabaqāt*, II, 155.

[38] *Ā'īn*, I, p.11.

CHAPTER 9

The Salary Bill of the *Manṣabdārs*

The *ṭalab* or pay claim of the Mughal *manṣabdār* was determined by his *manṣab* (numerical rank).[1] An understanding of some features of the *manṣab* system is thus necessary before one can attempt an estimate of the total expenses incurred by the Mughal administration on the emoluments of the *manṣabdārs*.

It has been supposed that from the 18th regnal year of Akbar, Mughal nobles were assigned numerical ranks (*manṣabs*), consisting of a pair of numbers, the first designating *ẕāt* (setting personal rank and salary) and the second *sawār* (setting size of cavalry contingent and payment thereof).[2] However, before 1595, we have no actual reference to the paired ranks, and in the two lists of Akbar's nobles, prepared until 1595, only a single rank is recorded.[3] The existence of two ranks before the 40th regnal year thus becomes rather suspect. This impression is reinforced by the fact that the text of the *Ā'īn-i Akbarī* seems to speak of only a single rank; and neither the term *ẕāt* nor *sawār* is employed in the sense of either of the two ranks. Since the *Ā'īn-i Akbarī*'s text mainly pertains

[1] It is generally held (Moreland, 'Ranks (*manṣab*) in the Mughal State Service', *JRAS*, London, 1936, p.650; and Abdul Aziz, *Mansabdari System and the Mughal Army*, London, 1945, pp.147–9) that the recipient of high ranks—500 under Akbar, and 1,000 under Shāhjahān—were designated *umarā'* while the word *manṣabdār* was used for those holding lower ranks (below 500 or 1,000). However, Abū'l Faẓl (*Akbarnāma*, III, 671; *Ā'īn*, I, pp.187, 188, 190) and Mu'tamad Khān (*Iqbālnāma*, II, p.288) use the term *manṣabdār* for all rank-holders without any distinction. It is true, on the other hand, that to judge from the *Ṭabaqāt-i Akbarī*, p.456, the word *umarā'* was reserved under Akbar to those holding *manṣabs* exceeding 500.

[2] A.J. Qaisar, 'Note on the Date of Institution of *Mansab* under Akbar', *Proc. I.H.C.*, 24th Session, 1961, pp.155–7 (read 18th regnal year for the 20th). See also M. Athar Ali, *Mughal Nobility under Aurangzeb*, Bombay, 1966, p.39.

[3] *Ā'īn*, I, pp.222–32; *Ṭabaqāt*, II, pp.425–56.

to the 40th regnal year, the existence of the paired ranks prior to this date cannot legitimately be taken for granted.

According to Abū'l Faẓl, it was in the 18th regnal year (1573–4), that the *dāgh* (system of branding horses) was introduced, and the ranks of the imperial officials were fixed.[4] These innovations were actually put into effect the next year (1574–5).[5]

Mu'tamad Khān giving the details of the measure says:

> 'The *manṣabs* were fixed according to the capacity for maintaining and organizing a contingent… *Manṣabs* from *dahbāshī* (10) to *panjhazārī* (5,000) were established and the salary for each was fixed. A regulation to the effect that the *manṣabdārs* would separately bring their personal horses and elephants for branding (*dāghs*) was imposed. A trooper, if capable of being a *sih-aspa* ('horseman with three horses'), would bring three horses; if capable of being a *do-aspa* ('with two horses'), two horses; and if capable of a *yak-aspa* ('with one horse'), he should bring one horse for the *dāgh*. In this way the pay ('*alūfa*) for everyone was fixed.'[6]

Thus, in addition to refraining from any suggestion that there were two (*ẕāt* and *sawār*) ranks, Mu'tamad Khān indicates that the single rank he is referring to represented the size of the contingents maintained by the *manṣabdār*. He is, of course, writing after Akbar's death, but contemporaries are no less explicit. The earliest direct contemporary reference to *manṣabs* so far traced occurs in Abū'l Fatḥ Gīlānī's letters (February–March, 1581), and the statements made clearly imply that the *manṣab* was single, and directly related to the military obligation.[7]

Badāūnī too relates the *manṣabs* directly to the number of *manṣabdārs'* troopers (*tābīnān*) in a striking passage.[8] Most important of all, Abū'l Faẓl not only says that the *manṣabs* were fixed on the basis of the capacity for organizing (*sarkardan*) a contingent,[9] but makes it plain that the number of the single rank represented directly the size of the contingent. He says that the troops (*sipāh*) of nobles did not exceed 5,000, while the

[4] *Akbarnāma*, III, p.69.

[5] Ibid., p.117.

[6] *Iqbālnāma*, II, p.288.

[7] *Ruq'āt-i Abū'l Fatḥ Gīlānī*, ed. M. Bashir Husain, Lahore, 1968, pp.15–16, 20–1 and 27. The Hindi word *pūra* (full) is used for sanction of the full pay due on a *manṣab*.

[8] *Badāūnī*, II, p.190.

[9] *Akbarnāma*, III, p.117.

ranks (*manṣabs*) of princes were fixed at higher figures: the words *sipāh* and *manṣab* appear here as interchangeable.[10]

Statements by Niẕāmuddīn Aḥmad and Bāyazīd Biyāt also show beyond dispute that the single rank which was in vogue up till the 40th regnal year was directly related to the size of the military contingent. In the concluding remarks to his list of Akbar's nobles, Niẕāmuddīn Aḥmad says: 'Let it be known that such of the Imperial servants as maintain only 500 retainers (*naukar*) are not counted among the *umara'* (plural of *amīr*)'.[11]

Here again the parity of the number of retainers (*naukar*) with the number of the *manṣab* is assumed. Niẕāmuddīn adds that he has only given in his list such nobles as had the rank (*palla*) of over 500. He acknowledges that he has used the list of the nobles given by Abū'l Fazl.[12] This list again gives only one rank;[13] and one can deduce that contrary to the general assumption,[14] the *manṣabs* given in the *Ā'īn*'s list are not *ẕāt* ranks, but the single comprehensive ranks that represented the number of troopers (as well as the personal pay). Finally, Bāyazīd records that he was made a *do-ṣadī*, i.e., held the rank of 200 (in later parlance *do-ṣadī* would always mean 200 *ẕāt*), and then goes on to account for the actual two hundred *sawārs* that he was obliged to maintain.[15]

A change is noticeable, first of all, in the 40th regnal year itself; the paired rank now makes its first (and very uncertain) appearance. It occurs in the following passage of the *Akbarnāma*:

> During this year the *manṣabdārs* were grouped into three categories. First, those whose *sawārs* (*sawārān*, horsemen) are equal to their *manṣabs*; second, one half or more; the third less than that (one half of their *manṣabs*), as is described in the last volume [*Ā'īn-i Akbarī*].[16]

The *Ā'īn-i Akbarī* practically reproduces this text.[17] The description of this measure, read with the passages from Badāūnī and Bāyazīd,

[10] Ibid., III, p.219.

[11] *Ṭabaqāt*, II, p.456.

[12] Ibid.

[13] *Ā'īn*, I, pp.222–32.

[14] Abdul Aziz, *Mansabdari System*, p.110; M. Athar Ali, *Mughal Nobility*, p.8; A.J. Qaisar, *Proc. I.H.C.,* 1961, p.156; and Irfan Habib, 'The *Manṣab* System (1595–1637)', *Proc. I.H.C.*, 29th Session, p.212.

[15] Bāyazīd Biyāt, *Taẕkira-i Humāyūn-o-Akbar*, ed. H. Husain, RAS Calcutta, 1941, pp.373–4.

[16] *Akbarnāma*, III, p.671.

[17] *Ā'īn*, I, p.179: 'A difference in monthly pay was instituted to accord with the *sawār* (cavalry). [The Emperor] gave him who has cavalry (*sawār*) equal to his *manṣab*, the first

implies that while *manṣabdārs* were expected to maintain horsemen equalling their *manṣab* number, this expectation was not fulfilled by many of them. The Mughal administration had ultimately to acknowledge the force of reality and modify the system. From now on the number of *sawārs* that were actually expected to be maintained, became distinct from the *manṣab* number. The single *manṣab* now became valid for the payment of salary for the person (*z̤āt*) of the *manṣabdār* only, while a new *sawār*-number was suffixed, against which the *barāwurdī* or partial rates were paid.[18]

The origin of the name *z̤āt* for the first rank and *barāwurdī* for the second (or *sawār*) rank lies here. The terms were clearly in the final stage of evolution (but not yet established completely) when the main text of the *Ā'īn* was being drafted (in or about the 40th regnal year). Even in the 41st year the distinction was not complete: Shāhrukh was granted 5,000 *z̤āt*, half the *sawār* being *barāwurdī*.[19] This means that 5,000 *z̤āt* still implied a theoretical strength of 5,000 (cavalry), though only half thereof (2,500) were paid for at *barāwurdī* rates. Soon afterwards this would be spoken of simply as 5,000 *z̤āt*, 2,500 *sawār*. Another reference to the two ranks occurs soon afterwards in the same year—5,000 '*z̤āt* and *sawār*'[20] meaning 5,000 *z̤āt* and 5,000 *sawār*. Here the two ranks are at last given full recognition.

Henceforth *z̤āt* determined the personal pay and the number of *khāṣa* (personal) animals to be maintained according to the schedule in force. The *sawār* rank indicated the number of horsemen the *manṣabdār* was required to maintain. The pay due against the *sawār* rank would be worked out from the rank-numbers by use of separate schedules sanctioned for the purpose.[21]

It is thus clear that the *z̤āt* and *sawār* ranks made their appearance in the regnal years 40–1 (1595–7), though not immediately with firm separate designations. When the *Ā'īn* was completed, the separate *z̤āt* and *sawār* ranks were still in effect in an embryonic form. As is evident from Mu'tamad Khān's account of the introduction of the (single) *manṣabs* in the 19th regnal year (1574–5), the payment for *tābīnān* (the *manṣabdār*'s troopers) was from the beginning distinct from the personal pay of the *manṣabdār*. The regulations given in the *Ā'īn* again confirm that the

grade (*pāya*); to him who has half or more, the second, and he put him who has less than that, into the third'.

[18] For the significance of the term *barāwurdī*, Habib, 'The *Manṣab* System', p.233.

[19] *Akbarnāma*, III, p.717.

[20] Ibid., p.721.

[21] Habib, 'The *Manṣab* System', pp.233–4.

payment for the *ẕāt* or 'person' (in the literal sense) of the *manṣabdār* was separate from that for his horsemen. It was laid down that when a promotion in *manṣab* was given, the increased pay for his person (*ẕāt*) was allowed immediately on the enhanced rank, but the amount for the additional troopers implied by the increase in rank was paid only after the *dāgh* (brand).[22] The rule shows that, when it was formulated, the *manṣab* was still a single, not dual, rank; yet the payment for the person and for the cavalry of the *manṣabdār* was separately made.

Therefore, though the *ẕāt* and *sawār* ranks were not distinguished until the 40th/41st regnal year, and then also not without ambiguity, the actual situation prevailing immediately earlier was not very different. But already the contingent which the noble might actually present, or for which *barāwurdī* payment might be made in anticipation, was much smaller. This situation provided the basis for the formula for the three scales of 'personal' pay of *manṣabdārs*, based on the ratio of the contingent to the total *manṣab*, spelled out in the 40th regnal year. This 'contingent' was really the future second or *sawār* rank.[23]

In the following sections, not only is the separate existence of the two ranks assumed for 1595–6 (this would in any case be in accordance with fact), but for convenience of exposition the designations *ẕāt* and *sawār* are also employed for them, though, strictly speaking, this anticipates later terminology.

II

The *Ā'īn-i Akabrī* sets out the schedule of pay, as well as the detailed requirements of horses, elephants and beasts of burden which were to be maintained by *manṣabdārs* as their personal contribution (*khāṣa*). Since the schedules give the pay separately for each of the three grades of ranks created in the 40th regnal year, it follows that the pay schedule of the *Ā'īn* cannot be of a date earlier than 1595–6.

The *manṣabs* listed in the schedule start from 10,000 and come down to 10. According to Abū'l Faẓl there were in all 66 ranks, equalling the numerical value of the letters in the name of God (Allah).[24] Blochman's text and the British Museum MS Add 7652, however, list only 65 ranks, while against the rank of 600 two sets of figures specifying salary and

[22] *Ā'īn*, I, pp.191–2.

[23] My own reading of the evolution of the *manṣab* system under Akbar is set out in 'Evolution of the *Manṣab* System under Akbar', *JRAS*, No.2, 1981, pp.173–85.

[24] *Ā'īn*, I, 179.

animals are given. The schedule is given correctly in British Museum MS Add. 6552, which records the rank 1,250, omitted in the other MSS. It is assigned the pay that is given in the printed text and other MSS against 1,200. Then onwards, the pay of each rank in Add. 6552 is the one which is given in the printed text to the next lower rank; so it continues down to 600, against which the second of the pair of figures in the printed text is entered. Thus Add. 6552 enables us to restore the correct original form of the schedule, with 66 ranks in all.

The schedule provides the salaries for all three grades against each rank; no such grades are however supposed to exist above 5,000, and for the three ranks above 5,000 the salary is given only for the first grade. While the *z̤āt* salary varies among the remaining ranks according to the grades, the number of animals remains the same for all the three grades of each rank.

Abū'l Faẓl says that in the 18th regnal year, alongside the institution of *dāgh* or branding, a classification of animals was laid down, and schedules of the sanctioned 'average' costs of maintenance of various breeds of horses, elephants, camels, oxen, mules and carts were issued.[25] By the time the schedule actually reproduced in the *Ā'īn* had been formulated, this classification seems to have undergone some changes. The *Iqbālnāma-i Jahāngīrī*, giving the earlier classification, records five categories or breeds of horses,[26] while the *Ā'īn-i Akbarī* gives seven classes.[27]

The *Ā'īn* sets out the costs of maintenance of the animals with a detailed breakdown of sanctioned expenses.[28] We here get the cost calculated originally and the subsequent enhancements. In the case of horses three increments were granted. The first is said to have been granted simply out of the emperor's concern for the comfort and welfare of the army. Thereafter, the rise in copper price of the rupee from 35 to 40 *dāms* in the 29th–30th regnal year,[29] compelled the emperor to sanction another enhancement in the rates. This suggests that though the costs were calculated in *dāms*, these were commuted into rupees at the time of actual payment. The reason for the third enhancement is not specified, it being simply stated that next an additional allowance of 'Rs 2 was granted on

[25] Ibid., p.176.

[26] *Iqbālnāma*, II, p.288.

[27] *Ā'īn*, I, p.176.

[28] Ibid., pp.176–8. The most superior breed ('*arabī*') was not included among the horses required to be maintained as *khāṣa* (*Ā'īn*, 180–6); nor is the salary of horsemen with an Arab horse set out in the *'dāghī'* rates (p.188).

[29] *Ā'īn*, I, p.28.

all breeds except the *jangla* horse.'[30] For elephants it is specifically stated, obviously by way of exception, that the payment remained fixed in *dāms*, and was unaffected by changes in the copper value of the rupee. One enhancement in the rates for elephants was indeed sanctioned, but the reason is not recorded.

These rates (*Ā'īn-i Jāndārān*) were apparently sanctioned for payment for the animals, carts, etc., of *manṣabdārs* to be maintained as their *kh̲āṣa* (directly under their own establishment) and for those maintained by their troopers, after they had been actually branded (*dāg̲h*). This is evident from Abū'l Faẓl's language as well as from the context. The rates precede the chapter on *manṣabdārs* which gives their *ẕāt* obligations and salaries. On the other hand, they follow the chapter entitled '*Ā'īn-i Sipāh-ābādī*, giving the *barāwurdī*-rates,[31] and details of muster and brand. The columns of animals and carts in the *manṣab* pay-schedules are arranged in exactly the same order as in the *Ā'īn-i Jāndārān*. The decisive piece of evidence is to be found in Abū'l Faẓl's statement concluding the chapter on *Ā'īn-i Jāndārān* to the effect that elephants and carts were allowed only to *manṣabdārs*, and superior troopers (*gazin-sawār*) were to bring only camels and oxen for the brand.[32] This means that the rates applied both to the animals maintained by *manṣabdārs* under what subsequently were termed their '*ẕāt*' ranks, and to those maintained by their troopers in fulfillment of the obligation against the *manṣabdārs*' '*sawār*' ranks.

To determine the actual expenditure against what later was called the *ẕāt* rank, it has to be decided whether the maintenance cost of animals was paid over and above the stated salary or was included in it. Abdul Aziz has assumed that the *manṣabdārs* were obliged to maintain these animals out of their own salaries, and the animals belonged to the State.[33] But it is not possible to accept this premise in view of the evidence of the *Ā'īn* itself.

[30] Ibid., pp.176–7.

[31] Ibid., pp.175–86.

[32] Ibid., p.178. It is possible to read *juz-manṣabdār* to mean small *manṣabdārs*, so that the meaning would be that elephants and carts were not allowed to small *manṣabdārs*: in the pay-schedule elephants and carts are not indeed assigned to the *dah-bāshī* (p.185). The conjunction *wa* in the words *gazīn- sawār wa shutr* in the text is an obvious slip, and ought to be omitted, as in MS Add. 6552. Abū'l Faẓl says (p.188) that troopers having more than one horse (*g̲hair-i yak aspa*) were given an additional allowance for ox and camel (to meet the costs of ox and camel transport presumably) at 50% or 40% of the sanctioned allowance assigned to the *yak-aspa*. Apparently, the allowance is included in the rates for the *yak-aspa* which Abū'l Faẓl then sets out.

[33] Abdul Aziz, *The Mansabdari System*, pp.48–9.

The detailed specifications of average expenses in the *Ā'īn-i Jāndārān* could only be relevant if the Mughal administration had to use them to make payments at some stage. If it was obligatory for each *manṣabdār* to maintain the animals out of his own salary as fixed by the *manṣab* pay-schedule, there would not be any need for the imperial administration to make these meticulous calculations, especially since for the imperial stables such details are in any case separately furnished.[34] To work out the salaries, only rough estimates would have sufficed, and these need not have been stated in the *Ā'īn*. Furthermore, the *Ā'īn* says that for elephants the payment was always made in *dāms*. If it was not a separate payment it would have been difficult to assimilate it to the salaries which are given in rupees.

The crucial evidence is Abū'l Faẓl's statement that certain enhancements in the sanctioned costs of maintenance were made to provide relief 'to the army,' i.e., the *manṣabdārs*. This could hardly have been the case if payments for these animals were made by *manṣabdārs* out of their own resources. Clearly, it was the *manṣabdārs* themselves who must have received the enhanced rates, if they were to draw any benefits from the enhancements.[35]

There is yet one more argument for refuting Abdul Aziz's hypothesis: if the monthly salaries stated in the schedules include the allowances for animals, then, on subtracting the expenses on these obligations from the stated salaries, we should have the net salaries. But we find that calculations on this basis give us impossibly low net salaries for some ranks. For example, the holder of rank 20 in category I would have had a net salary of Rs 21.50 per month; category II, Rs 11.50; and category III, Rs 1.50 only. But the pay of even a *yak-aspa* (trooper with one horse), with the most inferior horse (*jangla*) was Rs 12 a month. Further, if on the basis of Abdul Aziz's hypothesis we make a calculation of the net salary for the rank of 10, it would turn out to be higher than that for 20; and the net salary for the rank of 300 would be slightly higher than that for 350! Moreover, there would hardly have been any difference between the net salaries for the ranks (category I) of 3,500 and 3,000; 800 and 700; and 200 and 150.[36]

[34] *Ā'īn*, I, pp.133–44.

[35] To anticipate a suggestion that these enhancements might have been assimilated through increase in *ẓāt* (personal) pay, we should remember that (i) there is no statement in the *Ā'īn* to justify the supposition of such a second round of adjustments; and (ii) the adjustments for enhancements in maintenance costs would have resulted in detailed figures for *manṣab*-pay whereas the pay figures are invariably (with only one or two exceptions) in round numbers or, in case of low ranks, with 5 as the last digit.

[36] These calculations are made by simply deducting the figures for allowance of animals in Table 9.1 (below) from the sanctioned monthly salaries.

One must therefore accept what the *Ā'īn* plainly implies, viz., that the allowances for animals and carts were in addition to the personal (*zāt*) salaries, and were not assimilated to them.[37]

It is also not possible to assume with Abdul Aziz that the animals maintained by the nobles according to the pay schedule of *manṣabdārs* were those of the imperial stables, lent to them for maintenance and use. The *Iqbālnāma* giving the account of the 19th regnal year explicitly refers to the *manṣabdārs'* own 'personal' elephants and horses (*fīl-o-asp-i khāṣa-i khwud*),[38] which were to be brought for muster and brand. According to Abū'l Faẓl, the practice of *manṣabdārs*' bringing elephants to the brand was discontinued some time before the 40th regnal year,[39] a thing hardly possible if these were imperial elephants.

It seems that the practice of assigning imperial elephants to *manṣabdārs* and obliging them to maintain these out of their own salary (*khwūrāk-i dawābb*) was a later development, though its origin might be traced to Akbar's time. Abū'l Faẓl does say that the imperial elephants, herded into *ḥalqas*, were placed under different nobles; but he explicitly adds that fodder (*khwūrash*) for them was supplied by the state.[40] For horses too there were similar arrangements; the fodder (*'alīq-o qaẓīm*) was again supplied by the imperial establishment.[41]

Thus, for determining the expenses against the '*ẓāt*' rank one has to add the allowances sanctioned for the animals to the salaries recorded in the schedule. The *Ā'īn*'s detailed breakdown of costs and specification of animals and carts to be maintained makes it possible to calculate the amount paid for them which may then be added to the *ẓāt* salaries. The total payments so worked out are given in Table 9.1. Figures here are worked out only for those ranks that were actually held (and not all the

[37] In a paper in *IESHR*, Vol.24.4 (1987), 411–21, K.K. Trivedi contests the view here put forward, but avoids considering the many facts that had been given in the first edition. He does not care to explain why the costs of maintenance of animals should have been so meticulously laid out in the *Ā'īn-i Akbarī* if these were to be met by the *manṣabdārs* themselves; or why it should be mentioned that the costs of elephants were paid out in copper currency by the treasury, if the treasury had no obligation to pay them; or, again, why an increase in the calculated cost of maintenance of horses should have benefited the officers, if it is the latter who had to meet it. There is also some woolly-headedness about 'economies of scale' (Trivedi, 419), when the cost-rates are in fact uniform, irrespective of size of contingents.

[38] *Iqbālnāma*, II, p.288.

[39] *Ā'īn*, I, p.128.

[40] Ibid., p.135.

[41] Ibid., p.141.

Table 9.1

Manṣab	Monthly salary (rupees) I	II	III	Allowance for animals and carts (rupees)
10,000	60,000	—	—	20,849.00
8,000	50,000	—	—	16,992.75
7,000	45,000	—	—	14,643.63
5,000	30,000	29,000	28,000	10,703.50
4,500	26,000	25,800	25,700	9,416.88
4,000	22,000	21,800	21,600	8,422.88
3,500	18,600	18,400	18,300	7,702.13
3,000	17,000	16,800	16,700	6,568.25
2,500	14,000	13,800	13,700	5,254.75
2,000	12,000	11,900	11,800	4,219.13
1,500	9,000	8,900	8,800	3,431.40
1,000	7,700	7,400	7,100	2,838.50
900	5,000	4,700	4,400	2,464.88
800	4,000	3,700	3,600	1,968.13
700	3,500	3,200	3,000	1,486.00
600	2,800	2,750	2,700	1,314.25
500	2,500	2,300	2,100	1,144.75
400	2,000	1,700	1,500	726.50
350	1,450	1,400	1,350	612.50
300	1,400	1,250	1,200	561.00
250	1,150	1,100	1,000	485.50
200	975	950	900	448.50
150	875	850	800	354.50
120	745	740	730	329.00
100	700	600	530	302.50
80	410	380	350	241.00
60	300	285	270	186.50
50	250	240	230	186.50
40	223	200	185	164.00
30	175	165	155	121.50
20	135	125	115	113.50
10	100	82.5	75	44.00

66 ranks given in the Schedule), such being specified authoritatively in the *Ā'īn*'s own list of *manṣabdārs*.[42]

Once we determine the number of *manṣabdārs* in each rank at a particular point of time, we can compute the total amount required to meet the entire pay-claim against the '*ẕāt*' ranks, as well as the proportion that it bore to the expected net revenue-income or the *jama'* of the empire.

As mentioned earlier, two lists of Akbar's *manṣabdārs* have come down to us. The first is given by Abū'l Faẓl in his *Ā'īn-i Akbarī*.[43] This list contains the names of all *manṣabdārs* of 500 and above, whether dead or alive at the time it was compiled. Abū'l Faẓl also gives the names of *manṣabdārs* holding *manṣabs* below 500 but not less than 200, confining this list professedly to those alive in the 40th regnal year. As for *manṣabdārs* of below 200, he contents himself with providing the number of recipients in each rank in that year.[44]

According to Abū'l Faẓl, the list was completed in the 40th regnal year (1595–6), but it seems to have been partially out-of-date even before this year. Though the *Ṭabaqāt-i Akbarī*, which closed in 1593 and which contains the second list, refers to Abū'l Faẓl's list, it shows some significant changes.[45] It adds fifteen new names of those alive, while for twenty-eight *manṣabdārs* it gives *manṣabs* higher than those recorded in the *Ā'īn*. Evidently, the *Ā'īn*'s list was originally compiled some time before 1593; and though additions were undoubtedly made to it by Abū'l Faẓl himself in order to include promotions or new appointments, these additions were not comprehensive enough. The *Ṭabaqāt* renders us further service by omitting to assign any *manṣab* to those whom Abū'l Faẓl has awarded fictitious 'posthumous' *manṣabs*.[46] It also takes care to specifically record deaths of the nobles who were no longer alive.

Supplementing and correcting the *Ā'īn*'s list through use of the *Ṭabaqāt*'s information, one can determine with fair accuracy the number of *manṣabdārs* of each rank alive in 1595.

Though the *manṣabs* given in these two lists are formally single *manṣabs*, determining personal salaries as well as the size of contingent, these *manṣabs* afterwards continued in the shape of *ẕāt* ranks (see Section I) and can be used to compute the total payment both on account of the personal monthly salaries and allowances for animals. Here the only

42 The number of the ranks actually given was 32 only.

43 *Ā'īn*, I, pp.222–31.

44 Ibid., p.223.

45 *Ṭabaqāt*, pp.425–56. Cf. Habib, 'The *Manṣab* System, pp.228–49.

46 A.J. Qaisar, *Proc. I.H.C.,* 1961, pp.155–7.

difficulty is that since the size of contingent maintained by each *manṣabdār* is not known, it is not possible to work out the number of *manṣabdārs* in each of the three categories (based on the ratios of size of contingent to number of rank) in which every rank was subdivided. Thus one cannot determine the exact amount of total pay against the *z̤āt* ranks. However, the category-wise variations in the pay schedule are marginal; the range in any case can be worked out by assuming two extreme possibilities: that all *manṣabdārs* belonged to the first category; or that, alternatively, all belonged to the third category. We can also assume that they all belonged to the second category and treat the result as the mean. Table 9.2 gives these calculations, with (a) and (c) the extremes, and (b) the mean.

Placing all the *manṣabdārs* in each of the three categories by turn, three different sums have been worked out for the total salary and allowances for animals against *zāt* ranks. The pay schedule in the *Āʼīn* records the salaries in terms of rupees per month. These have been converted into *dāms* per annum, at the *Āʼīn*'s own rate of 40 *dāms* to the rupee. We get a minimum of 78.68 crore *dāms* per annum if all *manṣabdārs* belonged to category III, and a maximum of 87.16 crores, if all were in category I. Perhaps the total based on caregory II, viz., 82.75 crores, is likely to have been closest to the actual salary bill for the *z̤āt* ranks. The total allowance for animals works out at 37.14 crores. This remains constant for all the three categories. Adding this to the expenditure on salaries we have a maximum of 124.30 crore and a minimum of 115.82 crore *dāms* per annum; but the mean would be 119.89 crore *dāms*.

Since the effective *jama'* of the empire as calculated by us was 3,96,03,27,106 *dāms* for 1595–6, expenditure on the '*z̤āt*' salary should have been between 29.25 and 31.39 per cent of the expected net income of the empire; more precisely, it should have been 30.27 per cent had all *manṣabdārs* belonged to the middle category.

III

Fixing the amount to be paid for the cavalry (*sawārs*) maintained by *manṣab*-holders was a complex process, both before the emergence of a separate *sawār*-rank and afterwards. The process was initially carried out in two stages.[47] At first, while a person was awarded a '*sawār*' rank (either at the first appointment or by way of promotion), he was paid in anticipation at a uniform rate per unit of '*sawār*' rank. This rate was

[47] Cf. Habib, 'The *Manṣab* System', p.227.

Table 9.2

Manṣab	No. of holders	Total *z̲āt* salary (rupees)			Total Allowance for animals
		(a)	(b)	(c)	
10,000	1	60,000	(60,000)	(60,000)	20,849.00
8,000	1	50,000	(50,000)	(50,000)	16,992.75
7,000	1	45,000	(45,000)	(45,000)	14,643.63
5,000	9	270,000	261,000	252,000	96,331.50
4,500	1	26,000	25,800	25,700	9,416.88
4,000	3	66,000	65,400	64,800	25,268.64
3,500	2	37,200	36,800	36,600	15,404.26
3,000	4	68,000	67,200	66,800	66,273.00
2,500	3	42,000	41,400	41,100	15,764.25
2,000	9	108,000	107,100	106,200	37,972.17
1,500	7	63,000	62,300	61,600	24,019.80
1,000	16	123.200	118,400	113.600	45,416.00
900	12	60,000	56,400	52,800	29,578.56
800	2	8,000	7,400	7,200	3,936.26
700	16	56,000	51,200	48,000	23,776.00
600	4	11,200	11,000	10,800	5,257.00
500	31	77,500	71,300	65,100	35,487.25
400	17	34,000	28,900	25,500	12,350.50
350	19	27,550	26,600	25,650	11,637.5
300	32	44,800	40,000	38,400	17,952.00
250	12	13,800	13,200	12,000	5,826.00
200	81	78,975	76,950	72,900	36,328.50
150	53	46,375	45,050	42,400	18,788.50
120	1	745	740	730	329.00
100	250	175,000	150,000	132,500	75,625.00
80	91	37,310	34,580	31,850	21,931.00
60	204	61,200	58,140	55,080	38,046.00
50	168	4,000	3,840	3,680	2,984.00
40	260	57,980	52,000	48,100	42,640.00
30	39	6,825	6,435	6,045	4,738.50
20	250	33,750	31,250	28,750	28,375.00
10	224	22,400	18,480	16,800	9,855.00
Total		18,15,810	17,23,865	16,39,225	7,73,793.45
Total (*dāms*/year)		87,15,88,800	82,74,55,200	78,68,28,000	37,14,20,856

known as *barāwurdī*.[48] It was an ad hoc payment to be adjusted after the recipient presented his men and horses for inspection and *dāgh*.[49] The final salary was fixed on the basis of the contingent of troopers (*tābīnān*) actually brought to the brand.[50] The pay sanctioned upon branding was determined by such factors as the number of horses per trooper, the breeds of the horses and the race to which the *manṣabdār* belonged.[51]

The *Akbarnāma* gives the *barāwurdī* rates as revised in the 40th regnal year. The new schedule allowed 1,000 *dāms* a month for a *sih-aspa* ('with three horses'), 800 *dāms* for a *do-aspa* ('with two horses'), and 600 *dāms* a month for a *yak-aspa* ('with one horse'). For Rajput *manṣabdārs* the rates were lower: 800 *dāms* a month for a *sih-aspa* and 600 *dāms* a month for a *do-aspa*.[52]

The need to fix rates separately, for horsemen with three, two and one horse each, seems to have arisen out of the requirements, separately fixed, of different numbers of each category of troopers in each contingent of ten horsemen (lit. the contingent maintained by a '*dahbāshī*'). At an earlier stage the formula for such composition was 2 *chahār-aspas* (4-horse troopers), 3 *sih-aspas*, 3 *do-aspas*, and 2 *yak-aspas*. But by the time the *Ā'īn* was compiled, the standard requirement had been altered to 3 *sih-aspas*, 4 *do-aspas* and 3 *yak-aspas*.[53] On the basis of this formula, given the *Akbarnāma* rates of the 40th regnal year, the average rate per unit of *tābīnān* (=subsequent '*sawār*' rank) works out at 800 *dāms* or Rs 20 per month.[54]

[48] *Ā'īn*, I. 176.

[49] Ibid., I, p.176. If a *manṣabdār* found it difficult to muster horsemen, he was given some enrolled ('branded') troopers (*naqsh-pizīr-raftagān*), as part of his contingent. But he was not paid any allowance for them. These troopers, designated *dā<u>kh</u>ilī*, obtained their salaries directly from the imperial treasury on verification by the *manṣabdārs* to whom they were assigned (ibid., p.191). See note on *Dā<u>kh</u>ilis* at the end of chapter.

[50] *Ā'īn*, I, pp.176, 191.

[51] The rates varied according to the *manṣabdārs*' race and not to that of the cavalry troopers. Cf. Habib, '*Mansab* System', p.233.

[52] *Akbarnāma*, III, p.672. We come across another schedule in a MS of *Iqbālnāma-i Jahāngīrī* (Br. Mus. Or. 1834), allegedly in force in 1605; the rates given are 1000, 800, and 400 *tankas* respectively (cf. Habib, '*Mansab* System', p.235); The *tankas* here seem to be a mistake for *dāms*, though in the case of *yak-aspa*, the rate would be too low. Even for the maintenance of the *jangla* horse the sanctioned amount was 240 *dāms* a month (*Ā'īn*, I, p.177); the amount left for the trooper would be a mere 160 *dāms* per month, if the *Iqbālnāma* rates were followed.

[53] *Ā'īn*, I, p.188.

[54] See Moreland, 'Rank (*manṣab*) in the Mughal State Service'. Cf. also Habib, '*Mansab* System', pp.234–5, though the interpretation offered of this passage by the latter seems rather forced.

This rate of Rs 20 a month obtains confirmation from the earlier *barāwurdī* rates recorded in the *Ā'īn*. That schedule which is professedly for *barāwurdī* payments, allows Rs 25 a month for (horsemen serving) Iranis and Turanis, Rs 20 for Indians and Rs 15 for revenue collectors of the imperial establishment (*'amal pardāz-i khaliṣa*).[55] It seems therefore that in the *Akbarnāma*'s schedule of 1595 the standard amounts had not been revised (since 1,000 *dāms*=Rs 25; 800 *dāms*=Rs 20; 600 *dāms*=Rs 15). What was now altered was the basis on which the rates were sanctioned, being henceforth fixed on the more reasonable ground of the number of horses per trooper. However, the revision did place Rajput *manṣabdārs* in a less advantageous position, since for them the average rate per unit of '*sawār*' rank would have been only 660 *dāms* a month.

The *Ā'īn-i Akbarī* also gives the rates of pay of *yak-aspas*, varying according to horses of various breeds.[56] The amount allowed for the trooper in each case can be calculated by subtracting the cost of maintenance of horses of different breeds, as given at another place in the *Ā'īn* (Table 9.3).[57]

Table 9.3

	Pay of *yak-aspa* (rupees)	Sanctioned rate for horse (rupees)	Balance theoretically left with the trooper (rupees)
'Irāqī	30	17	13
Mujannas	25	14	11
Turkī	20	12	8
Yābū	18	10	8
Tāzī	15	8	7
Jangla	12	6	6

To judge from the documentary evidence of Shāhjahān's time, the horses most commonly in use were Turkī and Yābū.[58] It would be a fair assumption to take Rs 8 per month as the amount normally allowed for the trooper's personal subsistence, this being the minimum allowed to the horseman irrespective of the allowance for his horse or horses.[59] It

[55] *Ā'īn*, I, p.175.

[56] Ibid., p.188.

[57] Ibid., pp.176–7.

[58] R.A. Alavi, 'New Light on Mughal Cavalry', *Medieval India—A Miscellany,* Vol.II, p.98. In a sample of 1750 troopers with 1775 horses. Turkī horses numbered 981 (55.3%), Yābū 422 (23.8%) and Tāzī 340 (19.2%). There were only 31 Jangla horses, or less than 2%. No horse superior to Turkī was recorded.

[59] In 1577 Akbar fixed Rs 10 a month as the maximum authorized pay for a cavalry trooper which the Governor could engage in Gujarat. This provoked a revolt from the

then becomes evident that for calculating the *barāwurdī* rate, the Mughal administration allowed only the most inferior horse, that is, jangla with its monthly maintenance cost at Rs 6. The rate for a standard contingent of 10 may then be determined as follows:

3 *sih-aspas*	Rs 3 × (6 × 3 + 8) = 78
4 *do-aspas*	Rs 4 × (6 × 2 + 8) = 80
3 *yak-aspas*	Rs 3 × (6 × 1 + 8) = 42
Total, 10 horsemen	Rs 200

A total of Rs 200 allowed for 10 horsemen gives us a monthly rate of Rs 20 or 800 *dāms* per unit of cavalry or *sawār* rank (*tābīnān*), and this happens to be exactly the rate which we have derived from the *Akbarnāma*'s *barāwurdī* rates for the 40th year.

While the *barāwurdī* payment was sanctioned at the same rates as for the most inferior horse, enhanced payment on account of horses of superior breed was made when such horses were actually brought for the *dāgh*.[60] The *dāgh* rate therefore might change for a *manṣabdār* at each *dāgh-i mukarrar* (subsequent brand), though his rank remained the same.

It does not therefore seem possible to calculate the exact imperial expenditure on the *manṣabdārs'* cavalry. Nevertheless, one may place a lower and upper limit for such expenditure. The minimum expenditure can be worked out by assuming that payment was made according to *barāwurdī* rates against the entire '*sawār*' rank. The maximum *dāghi* payments can be estimated on the assumption that all the horses brought to the brand were of a superior quality, say, Turkī (whose sanctioned maintenance cost was Rs 12 a month). To take them all as 'Irāqī or Mujannas, the two most superior categories would, of course, be unreasonable.

The monthly *dāghi* rate per unit of *sawār* rank, if all the horses were Turkī, may be worked out as follows (calculating for the standard contingent of ten-horsemen):

3 *sih-aspas* = 3 troopers + 9 horses: Rs 3 × 8 + 9 × 12 = 132
4 *do-aspas* = 4 troopers + 8 horses: Rs 4 × 8 + 8 × 12 = 128
3 *yak-aspas* = 3 troopers + 3 horses: Rs 3 × 8 + 3 × 12 = 60

'Mughal' troopers who had apparently received much higher pay under the preceding Governor. (Shaikh Sikandar, *Mir'āt-i Sikandarī*, ed. S.C. Misra and M.L. Rahman, Baroda, 1961, p.459).

60 *Ā'īn*, I, pp.189, 191: *Akbarnāma*, II, p.147.

This would give Rs 320 per month or Rs 3,840 per annum for ten horsemen, or Rs 384 (15,360 *dāms*) per annum for every unit of *sawār* rank.

Now, with the *barāwurdī* and *dāghi* rates at hand, as the floor and ceiling of expenditure per unit of '*sawār*' rank we can go on to compute the minimum expenditure on the *manṣabdārs*' cavalry by treating the total '*sawār*' rank as *barāwurdī*, and to compute the maximum by assuming that the payment against the entire *sawār*-rank was made according to the *dāghī* rates for Turkī horses.

As noted earlier, there is no list of Akbar's *manṣabdārs* specifying *sawār* ranks. It is, therefore, not possible to determine the actual number of *sawār* ranks with a firm degree of precision. An attempt at rough estimation can, however, still be made.

The *sawār* rank begins to be mentioned in the *Akbarnāma* from the 41st regnal year, though only occasionally. It is in the account of the closing years of Akbar's reign contained in the *Iqbālnāma* that *sawār manṣabs* are recorded quite frequently. By assembling the recorded pairs of *ẕāt* and *sawār* ranks for the last years of Akbar's reign in this work, we can work out the average ratio between the number of *ẕāt* and *sawār* ranks on the basis of a fairly large sample.

Taking into account only those *manṣabdārs* (47 in all) for whom both the *ẕāt* and *sawār* ranks are recorded in the *Iqbālnāma* from the 47th to 50th regnal years, the total of *sawār* numbers awarded amounts to 59.15 per cent of the *ẕāt* ranks. This ratio of *sawār* to *ẕāt* rank is corroborated by the information for the early years of Jahāngīr. During the second and third years of his reign the ratio of *sawār* to *ẕāt* rank worked out from all the references to ranks given in the *Tuzuk-i Jahāngīrī* comes respectively to 100:64.42 and 100:57.95.[61] It should then be reasonable to take the total of '*sawār*' ranks as amounting to 60 per cent of the *ẕāt-manṣabs* for the year 1595 as well.

Given this ratio, the total number of *manṣabs* against which cavalry was required in 1595–6 should have been 1,88,070 being six-tenths of the total of *manṣabs* (3,13,450) as indicated by Abū'l Faẕl's list and statistics corrected by information from Niẕāmuddīn Aḥmad. This should have included both cavalry which had been inspected and branded and paid for at *dāghī* rates, and cavalry that was due to be maintained, but not yet brought to the brand, and paid for at *barāwurdī* rates. It may be assumed, then, that while the maximum number of cavalry that Akbar's

[61] I have derived the data from *Tuzuk-i Jahāngīrī*, ed. S. Ahmad, Aligarh, 1864, pp. 41–73.

manṣabdārs would have maintained was 1,88,070, it must in actual fact have been much smaller. This fits pretty well with what we know of the size of the Mughal army in Shāhjahān's time (1646–7). According to Lāhorī's estimate based explicitly upon an application of the 'Rule of One-fourth' to the total of '*sawār*' *manṣabs* held at that time, the total number of cavalry was 185,000.[62] Since the empire had expanded by that time, the proximity of actual numbers of cavalry under Shāhjahān to the maximum size under Akbar seems quite reasonable. This, then, is a fairly good confirmation of our supposition that the ratio between the *manṣab* and the equivalent of *sawār* rank in 1595–6, was 10:6.

To apply the *barāwurdī* rates for calculating the pay claim (*ṭalab*), we should in addition know the total *sawār* ranks of the Rajputs, since they were assigned lower *barāwurdī* rates. From the *Ā'īn*'s list supplemented by the *Ṭabaqāt*, we can see that the total number of Rajput *manṣabs* was 29,650, while the total *manṣabs* listed were 2,41,250.[63] That is, the Rajputs' share in the *ẕāt* ranks held by holders of 200 and above was 12.29 per cent. Assuming that this was approximately the percentage in '*sawār*' ranks and taking the total of '*sawār*' ranks as 1,88,070 (60 per cent of 3,13,450, the total *manṣabs,* based on the *Ā'īn*'s figures), the total *sawār–manṣabs* of the Rajputs may be estimated at 23,114.

Proceeding from these figures, the estimation of minimum and maximum expenditure on *manṣabdārs*' cavalry is a matter of simple arithmetic. Multiplying the total '*sawār*' ranks for the non-Rajputs (1,64,956), by the *barāwurdī* rate of 9,600 *dāms* per annum and the '*sawār*' ranks of Rajputs (23,114), by 7,920 *dāms*, and adding the two products we get the floor for the total pay sanctioned for *manṣabdārs*' cavalry, as 1,76,66,43,811 *dāms* per year. This is 44.61 per cent of the total *jama'* calculated from the *Ā'īn*.

The maximum limit can be obtained by multiplying the total estimated '*sawār*' rank (1,88,070) by the hypothetical *dāghī*-rate of 15,360 *dāms* per unit of *sawār* rank per year. This yields a total of 2,88,87,55,200 *dāms* or 72.94 per cent of the total *jama'* of the empire.

We have here the minimum and maximum limits on expenditure against *sawār* rank salaries. The actual level of expenditure that lay in between can be estimated if we can determine the portion of the total '*sawār*' rank on which only *barāwurdī* payments had been made, whereby

[62] Lāhorī, II, p.719.

[63] Hindus other than Rajputs are not included among the Rajputs by us.

we might make separate calculations for the total *barāwurdī* and *dāghī* payments. For this we have no direct evidence whatsoever. But it seems certain that the proportion of *sawār* rank on which *dāghī* payments were made could not have been very high. *Manṣabdārs* did not always maintain many horses and men as were required under their '*sawār*' rank. A despatch by Abū'l Faẓl from the Deccan suggests that even bringing one-half the required number to the brand was not usual.[64] We can then hardly assume that the *dāghī* payments accounted for more than a fourth of the '*sawār*' ranks. Moreover, even when the full number was brought to the brand, additional payment on *dāghī* rates was not always made. This is the burden of Bāyazīd Biyāt's complaints.[65] Finally, if six years elapsed after the last muster (renewal of the *dāgh* was due every three years),[66] a deduction of 10 per cent was made on '*sawār*' rank payments, and this continued until the horses and men were presented for the *dāgh* and muster afresh. If a promotion was granted and three years passed after the last brand no payment (even on *barāwurdī* rates) was made for the additional '*sawār* rank', pending the actual presentation of men and horses at the brand.[67]

It should, therefore, be an acceptable assumption that the '*sawār*' ranks against which *dāghī* rates were paid did not exceed one-third of the '*sawār*' *manṣabs*. We may, therefore, proceed on the hypothesis that '*sawār*' ranks were divided in a 3:1 ratio, into those (a) against which only *barāwurdī* payments had been made and (b) against which *dāghī* payments had also been made. On this basis, the total expenditure on the '*sawār*' rank payments can be estimated at 2,03,89,33,800 *dāms*, that is, at 51.49 per cent of the total effective *jama'* of the empire in 1595–6.

We may now recall our estimate for payments against '*ẓāt*' ranks, viz., 82,74,55,200 *dāms*. Total payment against *manṣabs* (both '*ẓāt*' and '*sawār*' ranks), can be estimated at 323.78 crore *dāms*.[68] One can

[64] *Ruqa'āt-i Abū'l Faẓl*, lithograph, p.45. This collection of letters, however, contains some material that seems to have been interpolated later.

[65] Bāyazīd Biyāt, p.373.

[66] *Ā'īn*, pp.191–2.

[67] Ibid., I, p.192.

[68] In actual practice, the salary for eleven months in a year was calculated, and paid for in money or through *jāgīr*-assignment or in cash; the salary for the twelfth month was paid in horses and other goods called *armās* (*Ā'īn*, I, p.196; for *armās* see *Selected Documents of Shāhjahān's Reign*, pp.1–21). What Abū'l Faẓl says here means that the twelfth month's salary was also stated in cash, and met by the grant of horses and other articles, at valuation. He admits that the recipients could suffer because the valuation of horses had been enhanced, but argues that since there had been greater scrutiny into the quality of horses, they obtained better material. This practice is well borne out by the documents belonging to the early years of Shāhjahān, with the only difference that the pay for the twelfth month is not stated at all.

therefore infer that 81.76 per cent of the effective *jama'* in 1595–6 was alienated in payments to *manṣabdārs*.

V

We have suggested that the total income of all the *manṣabdārs* accounted for about 82 per cent of the total *jama'*. Putting it differently, we may say that 82 per cent of the entire net revenue resources of the empire were appropriated by just 1,671 persons. This concentration of revenue resources becomes still more pronounced when we analyse the pattern of distribution among various ranks of *manṣabdār*. Table 9.4 gives the total expenditure (separately against '*z̤āt*' and '*sawār*' ranks) on different ranks as percentages of the total expenditure on *manṣab* salaries. The mode of calculation of expenditure against *sawār* ranks is the same as has been followed above in calculating the entire expenditure on the total *manṣabs* (i.e., assuming a ratio 3:1 between the *manṣabs* covered by *barāwurdī* and *dāg͟hī* payments).

Table 9.4

Manṣabs	No. of *manṣabdārs*	Salary as % of *jama'*
5,000–10,000	12	18.590
2,500–4,500	13	11.714
500–2,000	97	21.579
100–400	365	13.812
10–80	1,184	16.464

The class of *manṣabdārs* displayed a very high degree of concentration of resources at the higher levels. The top twelve controlled 18.59 per cent of the total *jama'*. Furthermore, as much as 51.88 per cent of the total *jama'* was required to meet the pay claims of only 122 *manṣabdārs* holding the ranks of 500 and above. On the other hand, as many as 1,184 *manṣabdārs* in the lowest ranks controlled only a little over 16 per cent of the *jama'*.

These figures give us a measure of the immense concentration of revenue resources in the hands of a very small number of persons constituting the core of the ruling class under Akbar.

This concentration of wealth and power seems to have continued under Akbar's successors. For Jahāngīr's reign we do not have the necessary data; but from Shāhjahān's reign we have lists of *manṣabdārs* at the end of the 10th and 20th regnal years in Lāhorī,[69] and at the end of the 30th regnal year in Waris.[70] These lists give the ranks of all *manṣabdārs* holding *z̤āt manṣabs* of 500 and above. The pay schedules in force under Shāhjahān have also survived.[71] Lāhorī gives the *jama'* of the empire for 1646–7.[72] On the basis of these data, Qaisar has worked out the distribution of revenue resources for the year 1646–7.[73] According to his calculations, 445 *manṣabdārs* holding *z̤āt* ranks of 500 and above, claimed 61.54 per cent of the total *jama'*. We have seen (Table 9.4) that under Akbar the top 487 *manṣabdārs* controlled 66.69 per cent of the revenue, implying almost the same, if not a higher, degree of concentration. Indeed, the higher strata under Akbar seem to have taken a distinctly larger share of the total revenue than under Shāhjahān. The top twenty-five *manṣabdārs* under Shāhjahān controlled 24.3 per cent of the *jama'*; but under Akbar the pay claim of the top twenty-five accounted for as much as 30.29 per cent of the *jama'*.

Note on *Dākhilīs*

Dākhilīs formed a category of trooper maintained by Akbar's administration. If any *manṣabdār* holding the rank of 500 or above found it difficult to muster horsemen, he was assigned horsemen from amongst the *dākhilīs*, who were paid directly by the imperial treasury.[74] The number of *dākhilīs* so assigned did not exceed one-tenth of a *manṣabdār's* rank, the exception being the *manṣabdār* of 500, who could have up to 100 *dākhilīs*, i.e., up to 20 per cent of the rank.

Along with the *dākhilī* horsemen there were also assigned to *manṣabdārs*, some *dākhilīs* foot-retainers numbering half the assigned *dākhilī* horsemen.[75] The prescribed composition for foot-retainers in turn was one-fourth *bandūqchī* (musketeers) and the remainder *tīrandāz* (archers), with a few others such as carpenters, ironsmiths, water-carriers

[69] Lāhorī, *Bādshāhnāma*, Bib. Ind., pp.717–52.

[70] Moḥammed Wāriṣ, *Bādshāhnāma*, Br. Mus. Add 6556, ff.523–530a; Or 1675, 200a–214a.

[71] *Selected Documents of Shāhjahān*'s *Reign*, pp.79–84.

[72] Lāhorī, II, p.729.

[73] A.J. Qaisar, *Proc. I.H.C.*, 1965, pp.240–3.

[74] The term *dākhilī* seems to have been used primarily for the 'transferred' troops. For such use, see Bāyazīd Bayāt (pp.373–4) where he designates as *dākhilī* troopers transferred from his deceased son to himself. From this it was natural to apply the same words to troopers transferred from the imperial contingent to *manṣabdārs*.

[75] *Ā'īn*, I, p.175.

and spademen. The captain (*sargaroh*) of musketeers was allowed a monthly pay of 160 *dāms*; ordinary musketeers were paid 140 *dāms*. A captain-of-ten (*mīrdah*) of archers was allowed 120 to 180 *dāms* a month; the ordinary archers, 100 to 120 *dāms*.[76]

Dākhilī troopers, horsemen as well as foot-retainers, obtained their salaries from the imperial treasury, on verification by the *manṣabdārs* whom they were assigned to.[77] However, the amount paid to the *dākhilīs*, although given directly to the horseman, was still a part of the *manṣabdārs*' salary against *sawār* rank. This payment is, therefore, covered by the expenditure on *sawār* rank calculated by us.

The practice of maintaining *dākhilīs* did not perhaps survive the measures of the 40th regnal year.[78] It would have become redundant once the practice of two-stage payment against *manṣabs* came to an end with the dual (*ẕāt* and *sawār*) rank; and when *barāwurdī* payment became the uniform, final payment on the *sawār* rank. Accordingly, the term *dākhilī* in the sense in which Abū'l Faẕl uses it is not to be found in documentary sources of Jahāngīr's reign and later.

[76] Ibid., p.190.

[77] Ibid., p.175.

[78] See *JRAS*, 1981, pp.180–3.

CHAPTER 10

Expenditure on the Imperial Military Establishment

In addition to *manṣabdārs* and their troopers, the Mughal administration maintained imperial horsemen (*aḥadīs*), auxiliaries (*kumakī*), infantry (*piyādagān*) and artillery.[1] The large number of war animals and beasts of burden (horses, elephants, camels, mules and oxen) would have required for their acquisition and maintenance a considerable proportion of the total revenue resources of the empire. Finally, there were the expenses incurred on the imperial arsenal, armoury and fire-arms.

On the basis of information given in the *Ā'īn*, one may attempt an estimate of the expenses incurred on these items. While the information is not sufficiently detailed to lead us to a precise calculation of the amount of expenses, the extreme limits can perhaps be determined with some assurance.

I

According to Abū'l Faẓl some military men were not awarded a *manṣab*; but neither were they placed under anyone's command. They were counted among the imperial servants (*bandagān-i khāṣ*) and paid directly from the imperial treasury. Such troopers were known as *aḥadīs*, as if, that is, their *manṣab* was one (*aḥad*).[2]

The *Ā'īn* tell us that Akbar set fresh regulations (*dastūrs*) for the gradation of *aḥadīs* and laid down the procedure for their recruitment and salary. Separate *diwāns* and *bakhshīs* were appointed for them.[3] These

[1] *Ā'īn*, I, 175. [2] Ibid., 175 and 187. [3] Ibid., 187.

measures were most probably a part of his general attempt at administrative and military reorganization, undertaken about the 19th regnal year (1575–6). The *aḥadīs* seem to have formed the lower ranks of the imperial service; they were also employed in various imperial *kārkhānas*. It is a little difficult to determine their precise number. Abū'l Faẓl says, under the 22nd regnal year, that the number of imperial horsemen (*sawarān-i khāṣa*), 'who are now known as *aḥadīs*', had been fixed at 12,000.[4] But this figure seems suspect since much lower numbers for the *aḥadīs* are reported for the time of Akbar's death and the early part of Jahāngīr's reign. Pelsaert, giving the number of those 'from the highest to the lowest who, after Akbar's death, entered Jahāngīr's service' counts 741 *chahār aspa* (4-horse troopers); 1,322 *sih-aspa* (3-horse troopers); 1,428 *do aspas* (2-horse troopers); and 950 *yak-aspas* (1-horse troopers), i.e., 4,441 *aḥadīs*, in all.[5] Hawkins, writing in the early years of Jahāngīr (1608–13), puts the number of 'haddies' at 5,000; but his 5,000 included horsemen with six horses as well.[6] By Shāhjahān's time the number of *manṣabdārs* had increased considerably; yet Lāhorī, in 1647, gives the number of 7,000 for the *aḥadīs* and *barq-andāz sawār* (mounted musketeers).[7]

Moreover, the very context in which Abū'l Faẓl has mentioned the number of *aḥadīs* in 1577–8 suggests the possibility of overstatement. He tells us that the number of troops of any noble did not exceed 5,000; and the number of *sawarān-i khāṣa* called *aḥadīs* had been fixed at 12,000. He then gives the ranks awarded to the princes, which ranged from 6,000 to 10,000.[8] It seems that Abū'l Faẓl here is treating the number of *aḥadīs* as equivalent, in a sense, to the rank of the emperor himself, since at that time the number of the rank indicated the number of troopers that had to be maintained.[9] He could, therefore, hardly have admitted that the actual number of the emperor's own troopers was less than 10,000—the contingent the eldest prince was expected to maintain.

We may therefore take Pelsaert's figures of *aḥadīs* at Akbar's death to be the more plausible. An interesting point is that his breakdown of *aḥadīs* into *chahār-aspas, sih-aspas, do aspas* and *yak-aspas* in ratios of 1.7:3:3:2 practically conforms to the standard formula of composition

[4] *Akbarnāma*, III, 219.

[5] Pelsaert, *Kroniek*, 120; *Chronicle*, tr., 35.

[6] *Early Travels*, 99.

[7] Lāhorī, II, 715.

[8] *Akbarnāma*, III, 219.

[9] See Chapter 9.

(2:3:3:2) prescribed for the *manṣabdārs*' contingents, when the *manṣabdār* was required to maintain the *chahār-aspa* as well.[10]

Abū'l Fazl says that a number of *aḥadīs* received more than 500 rupees per month, though this included expenditure on his mounts. Such cases must have been very exceptional, since even the personal monthly *ẕāt* pay of a *dah-bāshī* (commander of 10 troopers), exclusive of expenditure on his cavalry, was Rs 100.[11] On the other hand, Badāūnī gives the *barāwurdī* (or provisional, advance) pay (*'alūfa-i barāwurdī*) as only six rupees for a single *yak-aspa* trooper.[12] The rate for advance pay quoted by Badāūnī seems rather low, since the *barāwurdī* rate for a *manṣabdār*'s *yak-aspa* trooper was as high as 600 *dāms*, or Rs 15 a month.[13]

Whatever the amount allowed to an *aḥadi*, it is quite evident from the *Ā'īn-i Akbarī*'s description that the pay was fixed in two stages, in the same manner as was the *manṣabdār*'s *ṯalab-i tabīnān* (pay against the *sawār*-rank). At the time of appointment, payment was made at the provisional (*barāwurdī*) rates; and these were afterwards enhanced by two and a half to seven times (*az nīm sawāi tā dah-haftād*).[14] The total salary consisted of his personal allowance (*rozgār*) and allowance for his horse (*kharch-i-satūr*).[15]

Though one has to assume a wide disparity in the rates paid to *aḥadīs* the average scale of pay may be worked out on the basis of allowances sanctioned by the imperial administration for horses of various breeds and the pay allowed for a *yak-aspa* trooper with different breeds of horses,[16] following the same procedure as the one we have followed for working out the *daghī*-rate for *manṣabdārs*' troopers.

A *dahbāshī* was required to keep Turki and Yābū horses in even proportions against his personal rank,[17] and these were the two breeds that were also maintained by the *manṣabdārs*' *tābīnān* or cavalry troopers.[18] One may, therefore, assume that the *aḥadīs* too maintained horses of

[10] *Ā'īn*, I, 187–8.

[11] Ibid., 186.

[12] Badāūnī, II, 191. He says disparagingly that *do-aspas*, *yak-aspas* and *nīm-aspas* were enrolled as *aḥadīs*, and that in the case of the last meaning '½ horse', two troopers (*sawārs*) shared a single horse as well as the *barāwurdī* pay for it.

[13] *Akbarnāma*, III, 671–2.

[14] *Ā'īn*, I, 187.

[15] Ibid.

[16] Ibid., 188.

[17] Ibid., 186.

[18] See Chapter 9.

these two breeds. Moreover, except for the first horse, all subsequent horses were provided to *aḥadīs* in part-payment of their salaries by the administration;[19] so that the *aḥadīs*' horses should generally have been of superior breeds. We may then allow the same amount for the *aḥadīs*' personal subsistence as was sanctioned for the horsemen maintaining Turkī and Yābu horses, namely Rs 8 a month.

Proceeding on these assumptions, the stipends of *aḥadīs* with different number of horses may be worked out (Table 10.1).

Table 10.1

Category	(a) Turkī	(b) Yābū	(c) Personal Rs.	Total (a+b+c) Rs.
Chahār-aspa	2 × 14	2 × 12	8	60
Sih-aspa	1 × 14	2 × 12	8	46
Do-aspa	1 × 14	1 × 12	8	34
Yak-aspa	Nil	1 × 12	8	20

If we now multiply the number of *aḥadīs* in different categories with these rates, we may get an estimate for their total monthly salary bill in rupees (Table 10.2).

Table 10.2

(a) Category	(b) Monthly Salary Rs.	(c) Number	Monthly Expenditure (b × c) Rs.
Chahār-aspa	60	741	44,460
Sih-aspa	46	1,322	60,812
Do-aspa	34	1,422	48,348
Yak-aspa	20	950	19,000
Total			Rs 1,72,620

This (multiplied by 40 and the result by 12) would give us 8,28,57,600 *dāms* per annum for the total expenditure on the salary bill of the *aḥadīs*.

[19] *Ā'īn*, I, 187.

II

A large category of imperial servants is grouped by Abū'l Fazl under the designation '*piyādagān*' (foot-retainers). In his chapter bearing this heading, Abū'l Fazl deals with clerks, musketeers, gate-keepers, palace-guards, couriers, swordsmen, wrestlers, slaves, palanquin-bearers and the infantry component of the *dākhilī* retainers.[20] He thus appears to have included among the *piyādagān* all such imperial servants (other than officials) as were not horsemen.[21]

The *Ā'īn*'s chapter on *piyādagān* gives the pay-scales for all the categories of foot retainers described; for some categories it also mentions the total number of employees. Since the numbers are not given for all the categories, it is not possible to compute the expenditure on all 'foot-retainers'. Nevertheless, the amount spent on some major categories of *piyādagān* can be estimated with some degree of confidence.

First of all, there were a sizable number of musketeers (*bandūqchīs*). Abū'l Fazl gives their number as 12,000 and devotes a separate chapter (*Ā'īn-i māhwāra-i bandūqchī*) to the pay scales sanctioned for them.[22] Since the musketeers belonged to the category of *piyādagān,* the same pay scales are repeated in the chapter on foot retainers.

Musketeers were divided into various grades; and their pay scales varied accordingly. There were four grades of *mīr-dahs* (captains of 10 musketeers) with monthly salaries of 300; 280; 270; and 260 *dāms*. For the ordinary musketeer, there were five grades, each of which was subdivided into three classes: the rates for all these ranged from 250 to 120 *dāms* a month.[23]

While we have no means of finding out the precise number in each grade, it seems reasonable to assume that of the 12,000 musketeers the number of *mīr-dahs* was 1,090; and that the remainder (10,910) were

[20] Ibid., 190.

[21] When the source is not otherwise indicated, it should be assumed that the information from the *Ā'īn* used in this section is drawn from the chapter on foot-retainers (*piyādagān*) (*Ā'īn*, I, 188-90).

[22] *Ā'īn*, I, 127. Shāhjahān's official historian, Lāhorī, gives 40,000 as the number of unmounted musketeers, gunners, cannoniers, and rocket-throwers, of whom 10,000 were in attendance at the court and the remainder ('3,000' in the text being an obvious error for 30,000) posted 'in the provinces and forts' (Lāhorī, II, 715). Presumably, the number of musketeers and foot-soldiers in the artillery increased substantially between 1595–6 and 1646–7, the year for which Lāhorī gives his figures.

[23] For the rates paid for *dākhilī* musketeers, see note on *Dākhilīs* at the end of Chapter 9.

ordinary musketeers, since this would give us the standard ratio of 1:10 between them.

As noted above, the rates were not uniform for all *mīr-dahs* and ordinary musketeers. We can best estimate the total expenditure by simply taking the average rates:

Mīr-dahs	1,090 × 277.5	=	3,02,475
Ordinary	10,910 × 180	=	19,63,800
	Total	=	22,66,275 *dāms*/month

The entire salary bill for the musketeers, was, therefore, about 2,71,95,300 *dāms* per year.

One thousand *darbāns* (gatekeepers) were employed to guard the royal palace. The pay of their *mīr-dahs* was specified in five grades, ranging from 200 to 120 *dāms* a month. Assuming that they were evenly divided among the various grades, the average monthly rate for *mīr-dahs* should have been 150 *dāms*. The maximum rate for an ordinary *darbān* was 120 *dāms*, while the minimum was 100; that is, on an average, the ordinary *darbān* probably received 110 *dāms* a month. There should have been about 90 *mīr-dahs* among the 1,000 *darbāns*. The salary bill for gate-keepers may, therefore, be estimated as follows:

Mīr-dahs	90 × 150	=	13,500
Ordinary *Darbāns*	910 × 110	=	1,00,100
	Total	=	1,13,600 *dāms*/month.
		=	13,63,200 *dāms*/year

There were a thousand guards known as *khidmatiyas* set to keep watch over the environs of the royal palace. These belonged to four ranks: the *panjāhī* and *bīstī* (captains over 50 and 20) received 200 *dāms* a month; *dah-bāshīs* (captains over 10), 180 to 140 *dāms*; and the rates for ordinary *khidmatiyas* varied from 120 to 110 *dāms* a month. There is no indication of the number of persons in each rank. However, taking the average salary of the *dah-bāshī* to be 160 *dāms*, and of others 115 *dāms* a month (the means of the sanctioned rates), we get an estimate that would be on the lower side, since the rates for the *panjāhīs* and the *bīstīs* have not been taken into account. The estimated amount required for paying the *khidmatiyas* would then be:

Dah-bāshīs	90 × 160	=	14,400
Others	910 × 115	=	1,04,650
Total		=	1,19,050 *dāms*/month
		=	14,28,600 *dāms*/year

For supplying intelligence and conveying orders over distances, the Mughal administration employed runners called *mewrahs*; they worked as spies as well. Firishta says that 4,000 of them were employed in Akbar's service.[24] He also tells us that the *mewrahs* rode horses, but Abū'l Faẓl classifies them amongst the foot-retainers and gives their number as only 1,000. He adds that their grades and pay-scales were similar to those of the *khidmatiyas*. Accepting Abū'l Faẓl's figures rather than Firishta's, the expenditure on *mewrahs* may be put at 14,28,600 *dāms* a year.

The *Ā'īn* says that the number of swordsmen in the empire exceeded one hundred thousand, but that only 1,000 were employed in imperial service. The highest monthly pay allowed to them was 600 *dāms*, and the lowest 80 *dāms*. While there was thus great disparity among the rates of pay, we may take the mean of the two extreme limits for the purpose of estimating the total salary paid to the swordsmen. The annual expenditure would then have been (340 × 1000 × 12 =) 40,80,000 *dāms*.

Palanquin-bearers (*kahārs*) formed another class of *piyādas*; their leader (*sar-guroh*) received 192 to 384 *dāms* a month, while the others were paid from 120 to 160 *dāms*. The *Ā'īn* says 'some thousands' were in service. Taking 'some' to mean a figure above 2,000, we have arbitrarily taken the number to be 3,000; allowing 140 *dāms* a month as the average salary, we reach a rough estimate of expenditure on this head at (3000 × 140 × 12 =) 50,40,000 *dāms*/year.

The total expenses on the salaries of musketeers, gatekeepers (*darbāns*), palace-guards (*khidmatiyas*), runners (*mewrahs*), swordsmen (*shamshīrbāz*) and palanquin bearers (*kahārs*) that we have thus been able to estimate add up to 4,05,35,700 *dāms* a year.

Some categories of *piyādagān* or 'foot-retainers' still remain: clerks (placed in four grades with monthly scales of 500, 400, 300, and 240 *dāms*), who must have been very numerous; wrestlers (drawing a monthly

[24] Firishta, I, 272.

pay of from 70 to 450 *dāms*); and slaves (*chelas*), paid from 1 *dām* to Re 1 a day. *Dākhilī* troopers who were not horsemen are included by Abū'l Fazl among the *piyādagān*, and he also furnishes the rate of allowance paid for them to the *manṣabdārs* they were assigned to. But as argued in the note to Chapter 9, the payments made on *dākhilīs* are already absorbed in estimates of payments to *manṣabdārs*. There were other retainers, like blacksmiths, diggers, water-carriers, etc., working at the imperial camp (apart apparently from those employed in the building department or other departments of the imperial establishment, payment of whose staff is included in estimates offered in Chapter 11). These could be quite numerous: in setting up one encampment of the imperial camp on the march, 500 diggers, 100 water-carriers, 50 carpenters, 30 leather workers and 150 sweepers had to be employed.[25] For the categories of foot retainers in the *Ā'īn-i Piyādagān* that have been left out in our estimates as well as for those not covered by estimates in Chapter 11, we shall assume expenditure of about half of what was spent on the pay of categories already covered. The estimated sum of 4,05,35,700 *dāms* arrived may thus be increased to 6,00,00,000 *dāms* in the round so as to represent a comprehensive approximate figure for expenditure on all other staff than those covered in Chapter 11.

III

The elaborate account of the imperial establishment given by Abū'l Fazl tempts one to seek ways of offering an estimate of expenses incurred in the imperial stables. Abū'l Fazl devotes separate sections to classifying each species of war animals, their diet, apparel, trappings and attendants. Part of the expenses may be characterized as the cost of conspicuous consumption; but the major portion of these expenses must still be regarded as essentially military expenditure. The *Ā'īn* furnishes detailed descriptions of the stables of elephants, horses, camels, bullocks and mules.[26] These animals were kept not merely for display, but mainly for use in marches and battles, and for military transport. Game animals such as cheetahs, deer, pigeons, etc., are dealt with separately in the *Ā'īn*,[27] and will be treated under Household expenditure in Chapter 11.

Horses were the most important animals from the military point of view. These were broadly classified into khāṣagī, animals intended or

[25] *Ā'īn*, I, 42. [26] Ibid., 128–53. [27] Ibid., 205–14, 216.

available for the emperor's personal use, and *ghair-khāṣagī*, other horses in the imperial stables.[28] The *ghair-khāṣagī* horses were those kept in the stables of the royal princes,[29] stables of the *khānazād* (stud-bred) horses and the *rāhwār* (courier) horses. There were apparently two criteria by which the imperial stables were classified: by the number of horses in a stable—the largest stable was *chihal-aspī*, containing 40 horses, and the smallest *dah-aspī*, with 10 horses[30]—and by the price of the horse. Some stables were designated *haftād-muhrī*, because horses of the value of 70 *muhrs* each were kept there.

Both the quantity and quality of fodder per horse as well as the trappings, apparel and furniture varied from stable to stable. The stipends of various attendants also differed.

Horses belonging to *khāṣa* stables had a larger and more expensive diet; and the attendants' wages too were the highest here. The *Ā'īn* specifies the quantities of various articles of diet for different kinds of horses; but the price of the article or total expenses thereon are not furnished. Similarly, the expenditure on harnesses cannot be determined. For many of the offices in the imperial stables, it is simply stated that the incumbents were *manṣabdārs*, *aḥadīs* or *piyādas*; their emoluments or ranks are not given.[31] But their salaries are already covered in our estimates.

Thus, although the data provided are at first sight abundant, there are so many lacunae that the precise monthly expenditure on horses cannot be easily calculated. Even if some estimate could be worked out for a stable, there is the further difficulty that the number of stables of various kinds is not given.

One possible means of working out the expenditure on horses in imperial stables is by returning to our calculations for expenditure on *manṣabdārs'* horses. The *Ā'īn* provides us with the amount of individual

[28] Ibid., p.141. The emperor rode *ghair-khāṣagī* horses too, but only occasionally (p.145).

[29] These horses appear to be different from those which the princes were required to maintain against their *manṣabs*. Even a *dah-hazārī*, the holder of 10,000 (the *manṣab* held by Prince Salīm) had to maintain some horses of inferior breed, such as *tāzī* and *jangla* (*Ā'īn*, I, 180); but the imperial horses assigned to the princes' stables were of such superior breed and high value that they were regarded next only to the *khāṣa* horses. The general rule was to make good any deficiencies in the *khāṣa* stables from amongst the horses assigned to the princes' stables. After the death of Prince Murād, horses of his stables were incorporated into the *khāṣa* stables (ibid., 145).

[30] *Ā'īn*, I, 141.

[31] Ibid., 144. For our purpose here, this last is not a grave omission. The salaries of holders of these offices are covered by the estimates of salaries of *manṣabdārs*, *aḥadīs* and *piyādas* that we have already offered.

items of expenditure on those horses as well as the monthly allowances sanctioned for them.[32] By comparing the amounts and quantities allowed on similar items for horses of the imperial stables, we can estimate the difference in the scale of expenditure from that of *manṣabdārs'* horses. Since the actual expenditure on the latter is known to us, we can from this work out the probable expenditure incurred on imperial horses.

In the imperial stables the quantity and quality of diet varied according to the breed or value of the horse. However, grain fodder (*dāna*) was allowed at a uniform daily rate of 7½ *sers*. The quantity of sugar and *ghī*, for those to whom these were allowed, was ½ to 1½ *sers* and 30 to 50 *sers* a month respectively. Two *dāms* a day were sanctioned for hay.[33] The quantities sanctioned for *manṣabdārs*' horses were 5 to 6 *sers* of grain fodder per day, 30 to 60 *dāms* a month for sugar, 10 to 75 *dāms* a month for *ghī*, and 30 to 90 *dāms* a month for hay.

While the only attendant allowed for a *manṣabdār*'s horse was a groom (*sā'is*), the imperial stables were far more lavishly staffed. Besides the groom, there were eighteen other posts in each of the imperial stables. The *k̲h̲āṣa* stables even had a *sipandsoz*—a person whose duty was to burn certain seeds to guard against the evil eye. On the other hand, as we have noted, some of the functionaries were *manṣabdārs*, and quite a few attendants got their salaries on the rolls of *aḥadīs* or *piyādas*.[34] Attendants for imperial horses were not only more numerous than those permitted to *manṣabdārs* for their horses, but were also paid at higher rates. The wages of a groom tending one horse in the imperial stables ranged between 50 and 85 *dāms* a month, while the amount sanctioned for the groom attending a *manṣabdār's* horse was between 45 and 63 *dāms* a month.

The expenditure on harness, as mentioned earlier, is difficult to work out. The annual allowance on horse apparel (*harsāla-poshish*) for each horse ranged from 155½ to 227½ *dāms*.[35] This excluded the cost of ornaments and jewels. The amount sanctioned to *manṣabdārs* under the head *k̲h̲arch-i yarāq-i asp* was 8½ to 70 *dāms* a month. The upper limit of allowance to *manṣabdārs* on this account thus appears to be much higher than the 227½ *dāms* per annum allowed for even *k̲h̲āṣa* horses; but the *yarāq-i asp* included items which were not part of the horse apparel of

[32] Ibid., 176–7.

[33] Ibid., 141–2.

[34] Ibid., 143–4.

[35] Ibid., 142. These amounts (except 227½ *dāms*, for which no breakdown is offered) exactly equal the sums of the costs of different articles given under clothing; but the prices of items charged twice a year are not counted twice. The totals therefore appear to represent the value of the total outfit rather than the total annual expenditure on horse apparel.

imperial horses, namely, *pāy-band* (leg fastening), *mekh* (iron pegs), etc.[36] The cost of jewels and ornaments used in the imperial stables is not specified, though it must have been high.[37]

The precise difference between the maintenance costs of a horse in the imperial stables and that of a *manṣabdār*'s cannot be determined. But the disparity between the grooms' wages and the quantity of grain-fodder allowed serves as a rough index of the difference in the scale of expenditure. As we have seen, the grooms employed by the imperial establishment were paid 10 to 26 per cent more than those employed by *manṣabdārs*. Moreover, imperial horses were allowed 20 per cent more grain-fodder than the horses belonging to *manṣabdārs*. Keeping in view higher expenditure on all other heads (with the remote possible exception of harness) in the imperial stables, we may assume the imperial expenditure on a horse as at least 20 per cent more than that allowed for a *manṣabdār*'s horse.

If we could now work out the actual number of horses of various breeds in the imperial stables, we should be able to estimate their cost of maintenance by allowing for the horse of each breed an expenditure that is 20 per cent above what was sanctioned for *manṣabdārs*. Abū'l Faẓl says that the imperial stables were continually enlarged, while at the same time many horses were given away; the total number at a time remained at about 12,000.[38] This figure is strikingly corroborated by Hawkins, Firishta and Pelsaert (*c.*1626), all of whom say that Akbar had 12,000 horses in his stables at his death.[39]

But we also need a break-down according to breeds. Such a break-down is provided by Hawkins and Pelsaert, who give these rather divergent figures:[40]

Hawkins: Persian, 4,000; Turkish, 6,000; Kashmiri, 2,000.
Pelsaert: Persian, 3,200; Turkish, 5,970; Cutch, 2,540; Sind, 210; Mares, 120.

It will be seen that the two enumerations practically agree as to the number of Turkish horses, which comprised about half of Akbar's stables.

[36] *Ā'īn*, I, 176–7.

[37] I have considered the expenditure on jewels and ornaments and on gold-harness as more properly belonging to Chapter 11, where the emperor's store of precious stones and gold ornaments is discussed.

[38] *Ā'īn*, I, 140.

[39] *Early Travels*, 103; Firishta, I, 272; Pelsaert, *Kroniek*, 120, *Chronicle*, tr., 34–5.

[40] *Early Travels*, 103; Pelsaert, *Kroniek*, 120, *Chronicle*, tr., 34–5.

In respect of the Persian horses, the difference, though noticeable, is not very substantial, Hawkins setting their number at a third of the total and Pelsaert above a quarter. The main difficulty is about the identification and numbers of the remaining breeds. According to Hawkins, these horses numbering 2,000 were from Kashmir; but Pelsaert describes 2,540 of them as of 'Cutch'. The *Ā'īn*'s own testimony is not of any help, since it mentions horses of Kashmir as well as Cutch among the imperial horses.[41] For our present purpose, however, this last discrepancy is not very material, because in sanctioning the allowances for the maintenance of Indian horses no distinction was apparently made between Kashmir and Cutch horses.

Though the total expenditure, then, would not be very different on the basis of the numbers of horses of the different breeds given by either Hawkins or Pelsaert: the latter's figures being more detailed inspire greater confidence; and we are perhaps on stronger ground in making our calculations on their basis.

Among the seven classes into which the horses of the *manṣabdārs* were divided, three, namely, 'Arabi, 'Iraqi and Mujannas, came from Iran and the surrounding regions; and one may therefore take the average of the rates allowed for these three breeds as applicable to the category collectively designated 'Persian' by Hawkins and Pelsaert. There is, of course, no problem of identification involved in the case of 'Turki' or Turkish horses; in the classification given in the *Ā'īn*, they constitute a separate class. The two classes of superior Indian breeds were Yābū and Tāzī.[42] We may take Pelsaert's 'Cutch horses' to correspond to the Yābū and Tāzī categories. The rates allowed for *jangla* may be applied to the remaining categories (210 'Sind' horses and 120 'Mares') listed by Pelsaert.

Taking the rates on the different breeds as outlined above, and enhancing them by 20 per cent to convert the rates on *manṣabdārs*' horses into those on imperial horses, we get the figures (in *dāms*) given in Table 10.3.

The entire annual expenses on the imperial horses should have amounted to 8,56,78,080 *dāms*.

The imperial male elephants were divided on the basis of their physical characteristics and age into seven classes, viz., *mast*, *shergīr*, *sāda*, *karrah*, *manjhola*, *phundarkiya* and *muwakkil*. Female elephants were divided into four classes.[43]

[41] *Ā'īn*, I, 140.

[42] The use of the word *Tāzī* (lit. Arab horse) for an Indian breed which, judging from the sanctioned allowances, was not the most superior Indian breed either (the allowance for the 'Yābū' is higher) is a little puzzling. It is unfortunate that the problems regarding breeds of horses have not yet been elucidated in any modern work.

[43] *Ā'īn*, I, 133.

Table 10.3

	Rates per month (*dāms*)	Number of horses (Pelsaert)	Total expenditure in *dāms*/month
Persian	784	3,200	25,08,800
Turkish	576	5,970	34,38,720
Cutch	432	2,540	10,97,280
Sind and Mares	288	330	95,040
		Total	71,39,840

While the same kind of fodder was allowed for all the elephants except the *k͟hāṣa* elephants (deemed to be the emperor's 'personal' animals), the quantity varied from class to class. The number of attendants allowed too differed for various classes.[44] The data in the *Āʾīn* enable us to calculate the expenditure on fodder and attendants for each elephant under all the classes. But while Abū'l Faẓl describes the elephant trappings at length, he does not specify the cost of all the items.[45] Only the minimum cost of trappings can, therefore, be calculated.

Table 10.4 gives the average expenditure on diet,[46] wages of servants, and the minimum amount of expenditure is trappings in respect of each elephant of different categories.[47]

To work out the imperial expenditure on elephants, we should now have the number of elephants belonging to each class.

Abū'l Faẓl says that there were 5,000 imperial elephants in all, each having a separate name.[48] This accords with the number of 5,000 mentioned by Monserrate for the imperial elephants.[49] According to Firishta, the number of imperial elephants under Akbar was never below 5,000, and never exceeded 6,000.[50] Pelsaert gives a slightly higher figure, viz.,

[44] Ibid., 134.

[45] Ibid., 135–8.

[46] The grain-fodder (*dāna*) has been converted into money at the rate of 12 *dāms* per *man* (*Āʾīn*, I, 176).

[47] Among the articles included in the harness, Blochmann's text and Br. Mus. MSS 6552 give 'one *man* of grain-fodder and ten *sers* of iron' (*yak man dāna-o-dah-ser-i āhan*). The mention of grain-fodder is curious and quite out of context here. Br. Mus. MS. Add. 7652, reads 'one *man* and twelve *sers* of iron' (*yak man-o-doāzdah ser-i āhan*). I have accepted this reading, which certainly appears more reasonable. It seems that the scribe of some very early MS misread *dāna-o-dah* for *doāzdah*.

[48] *Āʾīn*, I, 161.

[49] Monserrate, 89.

[50] Firishta, I, 272.

Table 10.4

	Expenditure in *dāms*/month			
	Diet	Servants	Harness	Total
Male elephants				
Mast	891	887	183.5	1961.5
Shergīr	756	778	183.5	1717.5
Sāda	621	662	183.5	1466.5
Manjhola	540	550	136.0	1226.0
Karrah	441	437	136.0	1014.0
Phunderkiya	324	265	81.5	670.5
Muwakkil	216	215	81.5	512.5
			Average	1224.07
Female elephants				
Kalān	522	355	77.5	954.5
Miyāna	414	298	77.5	789.5
Khwurd	265.5	172.5	77.5	515.0
Muwakkil	145.8	172.5	77.5	395.8
			Average	663.8

6,751.[51] Unluckily, no break-down according to classes is provided in any of these sources. Abū'l Faẓl and Pelsaert agree, however, on the number of the *khāṣa* elephants: Abū'l Faẓl has 101,[52] and Pelsaert 100 (the latter describing them as elephants of extraordinary beauty and excellence).[53]

It seems reasonable to accept the lower figure of 5,000 given by Abū'l Faẓl for the total number of elephants and his figure of 101 for the *khāṣa* elephants. Since we have no means of finding out the number of elephants in each of the seven classes listed by Abū'l Faẓl, it is not possible to compute the expenses incurred on the imperial elephants with any degree of exactitude. However, to get a rough estimate, we may assume that the number of male elephants was equal to that of female elephants. This assumption seems fair keeping in mind the preference for tuskers and the more powerful male elephants which were better suited for war purposes. We may make a further assumption that the ordinary male elephants were evenly divided into all the classes and so work out the total amount of expenditure. It is not possible with the data provided by Abū'l Faẓl to

[51] Pelsaert, *Kroniek*, 120, *Chronicle*, tr., 5.

[52] *Ā'īn*, I, 138.

[53] Pelsaert, *Kroniek*, 120, *Chronicle*, tr., 35.

work out the cost of maintenance of a *khāṣa* elephant. Nevertheless, it will not be far wrong to assume that the expenses on a *khāṣa* elephant could not have been less than 10 per cent higher than those on a *mast* elephant.

Proceeding on the basis of these assumptions, the monthly imperial expenditure on elephants may be calculated as follows:

Khāṣa elephants	101 × 2,157.65	=	2,17,923
Male elephants	2,450 × 1,224.07	=	29,98,972
Female elephants	2,450 × 663.7	=	16,26,065
	Total		48,42,960 *dāms*/month

The minimum expenditure would then be 5,81,15,520 *dāms* per annum.

Since we have taken into account only a part of the expenditure on trappings and have assumed a rather inferior composition for the imperial elephants than what might actually have been the case, our total figure probably represents only the floor of expenditure on elephants.

The other transport animals in the imperial stables were camels, mules and oxen. Camels were used as courier-animals along with horses.[54] Though the *Ā'īn* gives a fairly detailed account of expenditure on these animals, it is silent about their numbers. Pelsaert, in his inventory of Jahāngīr's inherited possessions, however, provides us with the numbers of these animals. There were, he says, 6,223 camels in Akbar's stables.[55]

The quantity of grain-fodder (*dāna*) allowed varied according to the breed and age of the camel. The camels were divided into 'strings' or *qaṭārs* of 5 camels each; each *qaṭār* was under the charge of a *sārbān* (camel-driver). Abū'l Faẓl gives four rates for *sārbāns* without specifying the number in each grade. Over the *sārbān* were placed *bīstopanjīs* ('25-ers', each having charge of 5 *qaṭārs* and 4 *sārbāns*), the *panjāhī* ('50-ers', each commanding 10 *qaṭārs* and 9 *sārbāns*), and the *pānṣadī* ('500-ers', each supervising *over* 100 *qaṭārs* and 99 *sārbāns* under him). The

[54] *Ā'īn*, I, 146.

[55] Pelsaert, *Kroniek*, 121, *Chronicle*, tr., 35.

[56] *Ā'īn*, I, 148–9.

bīstopanjīs and the *panjāhīs* were placed under the *pānṣadī*.[56] The number of these officials are not given though their salaries are recorded. The *pānṣadīs* were usually *manṣabdārs*.[57]

The rates given here seem to be those worked out when the *ser* had the weight of 28 *dāms*: the quantity of grain-fodder is mentioned expressly in terms of a *ser* of this weight. Abū'l Faẓl says that these quantities were changed when the weight of the *ser* was raised to 30 *dāms*; but the revised quantities are not given.[58] This suggests that the amounts mentioned here were to some extent obsolete. The impression is further strengthened by the *Ā'īn*'s own admission that the amounts sanctioned for the harnesses of camels were so outdated that the contractors incurred losses, and these were therefore allowed to be calculated according to the prices currently prevailing.[59]

It is then not safe to estimate the imperial expenditure on camels on the basis of data provided in the *Ā'īn*. However, allowances sanctioned for *manṣabdārs*' animals could again provide us with a basis for estimating the expenditure on imperial camels.

The grain-fodder allowed to a full-grown Indian camel (*lok*) in the imperial stables was 7 *sers* a day (7½ *sers* in terms of a *ser* of 28 *dām*-weight); and 2 to 1½ *dāms* a day were allowed for hay for 8 months in a year.[60] The *manṣabdārs*' camel was allowed daily 6 *sers* of *dāna* and 1 *dām* for hay.[61] The average salary of a *sārbān* employed in the imperial stables was 63 *dāms* a month;[62] the *manṣabdārs* were given 60 *dāms* a month for the *sārbān*, the only attendant allowed.[63] In this way the imperial expenditure on these three essential heads works out at 161 *dāms* a month, while the corresponding figure for the *manṣabdārs*' camel was 144 *dāms*: the imperial expenditure on these heads, even on the basis of the obsolete rates, was therefore nearly 12 per cent higher than the amount sanctioned to the *manṣabdārs*. The expenditure on the salary of the other officials, viz., *bistopanjī*; *panjāhī* and *raibārī* (trainer), etc., was in addition to this, the *manṣabdārs* not being allowed any functionaries corresponding to these officials.

We would, therefore, not perhaps be far wrong in assuming that the imperial expenditure on a camel was at least 15 per cent higher than that allowed to *manṣabdārs*.

[57] Ibid., 149.
[58] Ibid., 147.
[59] Ibid., 148.
[60] Ibid., 147.
[61] Ibid., 178.
[62] Ibid., 149.
[63] Ibid., 178.

Pelsaert tells us that out of the 6,223 imperial camels, 523 were 'dromatae' (dromedaries or fast riding-camels) and the remaining 5,700 were 'camels of this country'.[64]

The amount sanctioned for the maintenance of a *manṣabdār's* camel was 240 *dāms* a month.[65] Enhancing it by 15 per cent, we get 276 *dāms*. If we further assume, rather arbitrarily, that the expenditure on dromedaries was 20 per cent higher than the allowance sanctioned for ordinary camels to the *manṣabdārs*, we can attempt the following estimate of monthly expenditure on the imperial camels:

	dāms
'Dromatae'	523 × 288 = 1,50,624
Other camels	5,700 × 276 = 15,73,200
Total	17,23,824

This gives us an expenditure on camels amounting to a total of 2,06,85,888 *dāms* per annum.

The oxen in the imperial establishment were classified on the basis of their functions. The diet allowed varied in accordance with this classification; the quantity of grain-fodder allowed was between 5 and 6¼ *sers*; 1 to 1½ *dāms* were given daily for hay.[66]

The wage sanctioned for the herdsman was 4 *dāms* a day. But 18 of the herdsmen were allowed the higher rate of 5 *dāms*. In the *kh̲āṣa* stables one herdsman was charged with the care of four oxen; in other stables, one was charged with six.[67]

On the basis of these data, the average expenses upon each ox in the imperial stables can be put at 107 *dāms* a month. The amount allowed to the *manṣabdārs* for an ox was, however, higher, being 120 *dāms* a month; though no allowance was made for the herdsman and the amount given for grain fodder and hay was only 66 *dāms* a month, as against 87.5 *dāms* allowed in the imperial stables for the same items. The rates allowed to the *manṣabdārs* were higher probably on account of the two increments, one of 38 *dāms*,[68] and the other of 10 *dāms* a month, which were

[64] Pelsaert, *Kroniek*, 121, *Chronicle*, tr., 35. The word 'dromedary' is now used for the single-humped Arabian (Indian) camel as against the Bactrian camel. But in the 17th century it was used for fast riding-camels.

[65] *Ā'īn*, I, 178.

[66] Ibid., 147.

[67] Ibid., 148–9.

[68] Ibid., 178.

apparently given to keep up with the change in prices between the 18th and 39th regnal years.

Since the amounts sanctioned for the imperial stables do not include such enhancements, they would seem to relate to an earlier date. As we have seen, the expenses on these animals were fixed when the *ser* was of 28 *dām*-weight,[69] and, on the *Ā'īn*'s own admission, were low and out-of-date.[70] To make the rates applicable to the 40th regnal year we may then allow the same enhancement in the case of imperial rates for oxen as sanctioned for *manṣabdārs*: this would mean a sum of 155 *dāms* a month for the average expenditure on each ox.

Pelsaert gives us the figures of 7,000 for oxen belonging to the imperial stables at Akbar's death. The *Ā'īn* says that 600 carts (*'arāba*) were employed to fetch fuel for the imperial kitchen, and 200 to transport material for the building establishment.[71] Since, as Abū'l Fazl tells us, one cart required four oxen, at least 3,200 oxen had to be employed on these 800 carts alone; and there must also have been other demands upon oxen,[72] as well as the need to keep a number of them in reserve; thus the figure of 7,000 given by Pelsaert seems by no means excessive.

Since Pelsaert does not offer any breakdown of the categories of oxen, we can only estimate the imperial expenditure on oxen by applying the rate worked out by us (viz., 155 *dāms*) uniformly to all the 7,000 oxen. This yields (7000 × 155 × 12=) 1,30,20,000 *dāms* per annum.

The *Ā'īn* suggests that mules in the imperial stables were native-bred as well as imported: the amount spent upon them varied according to whether they were indigenous or foreign. Pelsaert does not follow this or any other classification, while giving the number of mules. In any case, the number given by him is so small (260) that an attempt to compute the expenditure on them on the basis of the detailed data in the *Ā'īn* would seem to be an unnecessary refinement, especially when a simpler mode of calculation is available. Abū'l Fazl says that in fixing the allowance paid to *manṣabdārs* for animals kept by them, mules were reckoned formerly as equal to Tāzī horses, but now only as equal to *jangla* horses.[73] On this basis we may apply the rate for a *jangla* horse in the imperial

[69] Ibid., 147.

[70] Ibid., 148.

[71] Ibid., 151–2.

[72] For example, many oxen must have been needed for pulling the guns of the artillery of 'the Stirrup' or the imperial army (*Ā'īn*, I, 119).

[73] *Ā'īn*, I, 179.

stables as calculated earlier (viz. 264 *dāms* a month). The annual expenditure on mules by the imperial administration would then come to (260 × 264 × 12 =) 8,23,680 *dāms* per annum.

IV

In addition to the cost of maintenance the total imperial expenditure on animals should also have included the amounts spent on their purchase. Information on this matter is so scarce that only a very tentative estimate can be made.

Abū'l Faẓl tells us that merchants brought horses to the court from various countries, drove upon drove being brought from Iran and Central Asia.[74] From Abū'l Faẓl's description it appears that commerce in horses was conducted at least partly under state control. A place was assigned where, except for a few trusted or privileged merchants, all the horse-dealers were required to stay along with their horses; and an official, designated *amīn-i kārvānsarā*, was appointed to keep watch over them. Clerks were employed to keep records and experienced men to determine prices.[75] From Monserrate's account, it transpires that in spite of all these controls and restrictions, there was no state monopoly, and horses were sold through open auctions. The price money was counted in public to avoid any 'suspicion of oppression'. The emperor, or rather his officials, purchased horses in the same manner as private bidders.[76]

To compute the amount spent on the purchase of horses we should know the number of horses bought by the emperor in a year as well as the price of each of them. Since this information is not directly available, we may build up an estimate by indirect means.

The normal life-span of a horse in India was held to be thirty years;[77] but its working life, according to a seventeenth-century source, was twelve years.[78] Assuming that all the horses in the imperial stables when purchased were in their prime and that they thus spent no less than twelve years in the imperial stables, one would have to infer that, at the very least, one-twelfth of the horses needed to be replaced every year. If the horses, on average,

[74] Ibid., 140.

[75] Ibid., 141.

[76] Monserrate, 208.

[77] *Ā'īn*, I, 146.

[78] Anonymous, *Farasnāma* (MS Maulana Azad Library, AMU, Subhanullah Collection, 616/3, 3). It seems to have been written in the 17th century since it refers to Jahāngīr as *Jannat-Makānī*, and the use of this posthumous title suggests proximity to the reign.

spent less than twelve years in the imperial stables, as is rather more likely (being perhaps given away as gifts when they were past their prime), the proportion replaced every year should have been higher. On the other hand, the court received a number of horses as gifts and offerings, without having to pay anything. Therefore, the horses purchased every year might still be assessed as about a twelfth of the total. We would still be ignoring mortality in wars; but possibly by 1595–6, imperial horses were seldom involved in actual fighting. Since Akbar's stables contained about 12,000 horses, the number annually purchased should have been about 1,000.

In order to use this figure for making an estimate of the actual amount spent in purchasing horses, one would need information on the prices that different kinds of horses fetched. The *Ā'īn* rather unhelpfully gives the range of prices as from 2 (scribal error for 10?) rupees to 500 *muhrs*.[79] However, since the price of horses was also taken as a criterion for the classification of stables, we may roughly establish, from a reference to the stables, a narrower range of prices ordinarily paid for imperial horses.

We find that among the imperial stables there were stables containing *dah-muhrī* ('of 10 *muhrs*') as well as *haftād-muhrī* ('of 70 *muhrs*') horses. This suggests that the price of horses in the imperial stables varied normally from 10 to 70 *muhrs*. Since there seems no means of determining how many horses belonged to the various price-categories within this range, we can only resort to taking the mean between 10 and 70, namely 40 *muhrs*. This again has a lower bias since one would expect the imperial horses to be throughout of a superior breed.

With these assumptions, arbitrary but probably erring on the lower side, we may compute the annual imperial expenditure on the purchase of horses as follows: Since 9 rupees went to a *muhr*[80] and a rupee was equal to 40 *dāms*, the average price of a horse should have been $(40 \times 9 \times 40 =)$ 14,400 *dāms*. The price of 1,000 horses was therefore 1,44,00,000 *dāms*.

While this or a larger amount of money must have been spent annually on horses, a small part of the expenditure was recovered from stable employees. There were firm regulations about fines imposed on officials and attendants at the stables if a horse in their charge died.[81] The actual amounts so recovered cannot be worked out, and would not have amounted to more than a minute part of the cost of the horses.

[79] *Ā'īn*, I, 146.

[80] Ibid., 27.

[81] Ibid., 145, 164.

It seems that Akbar's administration did not spend much money on purchasing elephants. Elephants were either caught in organized hunts, or were received as tribute or war booty.[82] Even the 'land-revenue' was paid through delivery of elephants in parts of Central India.[83]

Abū'l Faẓl provides detailed prices for each breed of camel,[84] but since we do not know the breakdown of imperial camels under various breeds we may again take the unweighted average of these prices. The natural life of a camel was twenty-five years,[85] but their active life was only twelve years.[86] We may suppose that the Mughal administration had to purchase of 519 camels annually to maintain a corps of 6,223 camels. Taking 5.5 *muhrs* as the average price, the expenditure on purchase of camels would have been ($5.5 \times 9 \times 40 \times 519=$) 10,27,620 *dāms* per annum.

Though Akbar is said to have bought a pair of oxen at as high a price as Rs 500, the usual price of an ox around Delhi was Rs 10.[87] The active life of an ox too may be assumed to be twelve years.[88] To maintain the strength of 7,000 oxen in the imperial stables the administration must have had to add 584 oxen each year. The expenditure thus would have been about ($584 \times 10 \times 40=$) 2,33,600 *dāms* per annum.

For mules, Abū'l Faẓl gives the normal life-span as 50 years, and the price of the finest one in the imperial stables as Rs 100.[89] But neither the average price nor the working life is specified. In any case the number of mules is a trifling 260, so that the total amount spent on purchasing the beasts each year would hardly have affected the total expenditure on animals in the imperial stables. Table 10.5 sets out our estimates of the annual expenditure on animals.

[82] Ibid., 206. See also S. Moosvi, *Man and Nature in Mughal Era*, IHC Symposium No.5, Delhi, 1993, 21–3.

[83] Ibid., II, 456. There is a *farmān* of Shāhjahān of his 40th regnal year (Add. 3582, f.107a) in which the emperor granted concessions to certain merchants who brought elephants from Zerbād (south-east Asia) aboard ships to the ports of Bengal and Machhilipatam and then transported them overland for sale at the imperial camp. But the *Ā'īn* makes no reference to purchase of south-east Asian elephants by Akbar's officials.

[84] Ibid., I, 150.

[85] Ibid.

[86] Watt, *Dictionary of Economic Products of India*, Vol.II, 57 (c.219).

[87] *Ā'īn*, I, 150.

[88] Watt, V, 576, 667.

[89] *Ā'īn*, I, 152.

Table 10.5

	Maintenance (*dāms*)
Horses	8,56,78,080
Elephants (minimum)	5,81,15,520
Camels	2,06,85,888
Oxen	1,30,20,000
Mules	8,23,680
Total maintenance expenses (*dāms*/year)	17,83,23,168
Cost of purchase	*dāms*
Horses	1,44,00,000
Elephants	—
Camels	10,27,695
Oxen	2,33,600
Total cost of purchase (*dāms*/year)	1,56,61,295

Thus our estimate for the total annual expenditure on animals in the imperial stables is 19,39,84,463 *dāms*.

V

Of matchlocks, Abū'l Fazl says that these were manufactured in the imperial workshops (*kārkhāna-i khāṣa*) or were purchased; many were also received as presents.[90] This might also be true of other weapons and items of armour. Whatever be the value of the material received through gifts, the expenses incurred on the imperial arsenal and armour could not still have been inconsiderable. Though Abū'l Fazl devotes separate chapters to the arsenal, guns and matchlocks,[91] his data do not help us in estimating the annual expenditure on them. Fortunately, Pelsaert reproduces a translation of the statement which gives the value of pieces of artillery, armour, and hand-weapons which Akbar left behind at his death. According to this statement, the cannon, muskets, lead for shot, gunpowder and other munitions of war were valued at Rs 85,75,971; armour, shields, poniards, bows, arrows, and similar weapons, at Rs 75,55,525; and gold-embroidered

[90] Ibid., 126.

[91] Ibid., 118–27.

cloaks for all kinds of royal armour at Rs 50,00,000.[92] To calculate the actual costs incurred, a scaling down by 20 per cent would be necessary for the purchase or manufacturing costs would have been lower than the value now attributed to the materials. Since it is obvious from Abū'l Faẓl's account that the number of weapons given away as gifts was quite large,[93] I have assumed that the cost of presents distributed on behalf of the Emperor would counterbalance the value of those received by him in presents. The total value in 1605 (scaled down by 20 per cent.) may be converted into annual expenditure in the 40th year (1595–6) by the same formula that we have established for annual additions to the imperial hoard (Chapter 8), i.e., divide the total amount by 1225 and then multiply by 40 to get the annual figure for the 40th year. The resulting figure in rupees needs to be further multiplied by 40, to give us the expenditure in terms of *dāms* incurred on arsenal and armour in the 40th regnal year.[94] By this means we may estimate the entire imperial expenditure on weaponry at 2,20,80,257 *dāms* for the year 1595–6.

This estimate can be checked only very roughly from Abū'l Faẓl's statements. Of the total of 2,20,80,257 *dāms*, as much as 89,61,015 *dāms* should have been spent on cannon, muskets, etc., whose value Pelsaert has placed at Rs 85,75,971. Abū'l Faẓl's own account suggests a similarly heavy scale of expenditure on artillery. Rather frustratingly he confesses an inability to give any number for cannon pieces simply because the pieces, especially the *gajnāl* and the *narnāl*, were 'so numerous'.[95] In the case of matchlocks, of 'the thousands' manufactured, 105 were selected for the emperor's personal use (*k͟hāṣa*) and 31 kept in reserve (*kotal*) to replenish stocks on account of *k͟hāṣa* muskets being constantly given away by the emperor as presents.[96] One hundred and one matchlocks were kept in the harem.[97]

Many hand weapons were marked as *k͟hāṣa*, and several were distributed as presents; the number of *k͟hāṣa* swords was 30, and those kept in

[92] Pelsaert, *Kroniek*, 119, *Chronicle*, tr. 34 (the figure 50,000,000 in the transl. is a misprint for 50,00,000).

[93] *Ā'īn*, I, 118, 127.

[94] For this mode of calculation, see Chapter 8 f.n. 33.

[95] *Ā'īn*, I, 125. But Jahāngīr (*Tuzuk-i Jahāngīrī*, 10) in his first regnal year (1605–6) speaks of his ambition to have 3,000 carts in his artillery (*top-k͟hāna*). If each gun needed a cart, Akbar might have left behind at least 2,000 guns for Jahāngīr to have aimed at possessing 3,000.

[96] Owing to the frequency of presents, 31 kept in full reserve (*kotal*) were not deemed sufficient, and 27 more were marked for this purpose in 'partial reserve' (*nīm kotal*) (*Ā'īn*, I, 127).

[97] Ibid., 127.

reserve to make up the shortage (*kotal*), 40.[98] Abū'l Fazl gives a detailed account of the hand weapons kept for the emperor's personal use (*khāṣa*). These swords must have belonged to Abū'l Fazl's superior category of swords, whose price he sets at 15 *muhrs* each.[99] In addition to the *khāṣa* weapons, an entire arsenal used to accompany the emperor when he held court, or went on hunting expeditions or other excursions.[100] The best daggers cost 2½ *muhrs* each. Though the data provided by Abū'l Fazl cannot serve as a firm basis for quantification, the number and the price of hand-weapons given in the *Ā'īn* suggest that a total expenditure of 78,94,753 *dāms* per annum, derived from Pelsaert's figures, is, again, not unreasonable.

The total annual amount incurred on the entire imperial military establishment, *c.* 1595, may now be tabulated (Table 10.6).

Table 10.6

	dāms
Pay of *aḥadīs*	8,28,57,600
Pay of foot-retainers	6,00,00,000
Expenditure on animals	19,39,84,463
Artillery, arms and Armour	2,20,80,257
Total	35,89,22,320

In other words almost 9.06 per cent of the total *jama'* of the empire was spent on the maintenance of the emperor's personal military establishment. The only qualification that has to be made, is that many of the *aḥadīs* and some foot retainers (whose pay forms part of our estimates) worked in various departments of the household, though they drew their salaries from the army list.[101] Thus at least some of the expenditure on the military establishment was actually incurred for purely non-military purposes.

[98] Ibid., 118.

[99] Ibid., 119.

[100] Ibid., 118–19.

[101] On this see also the concluding paragraphs of Chapter 11.

CHAPTER 11

Expenditure on the Imperial Household

The imperial household establishment may be expected to have accounted for a considerable portion of imperial expenditure. The household, as described in Abū'l Faẓl's chapter, '*Manzil-ābādī*', consisted mainly of the harem, the kitchen and various other departments including the storehouses of precious stones and gold ornaments, the wardrobe and library. With the help of the data in the *Ā'īn* and some statistics in other sources, we hope to attempt estimates of the annual expenses on the individual departments which comprised the imperial household.

In the imperial household establishment, the harem not only constituted the largest department but also accounted for the heaviest expenditure. Abū'l Faẓl says that the female inmates of the imperial harem numbered over 5,000.[1] Stipends were paid in cash to the ladies in the harem, under a special seal; no paper drafts (*barāt*) were issued.[2] High-ranking ladies (*mahīn-bāno*) received stipends ranging from Rs 27 to 1,610 a month. The other female inmates were placed in two grades: the monthly stipends of those in Grade I ranged from Rs 20 to 51, and of those in Grade II, from Rs 2 to 40.[3]

Abū'l Faẓl does not give the number of those whom he styles 'high-ranking ladies' nor of those who were placed in either of the other two grades of other inmates. One may say that at least all the wives and female relations of the emperor would have belonged to the category of

[1] *Ā'īn*, I, 40.

[2] Ibid., 41.

[3] Ibid., 40. Blochmann's text and Add.7652 give Rs 2 to 40; but Add. 6652 reads Rs 10 to 40; '*dah*' (10) seems a possible error for '*do*' (2) here. The division of female-inmates of the harem (*mukhaddarāt-i iqbāl*) was first put into effect in the 19th year (*Akbarnāma*, III, 105). For a discussion on women attendants in the imperial harem see my 'Domestic Service in Precolonial India—Bondage, Caste and Market', *Domestic Service and the Formation of European Identity—Understanding the Globalization of Domestic Work*, 16th–21st Centuries, ed. Antoinette Fauve-Chaumoux, Bern, 2004, 556.

mahīn-bānos. Acquaviva in 1580 speaks of 'at least a hundred wives' of the emperor, and Monserrate puts their number at 300.[4] We do not know the number of other female relations (aunts, sisters, cousins, daughters, etc.), but to calculate the floor of expenditure, the number of all the high ranking ladies may at a minimum be put at 300. The range of their pay is too wide to give any workable average. We may, therefore, take Rs 100 rather arbitrarily as the probable average monthly pay per head of ladies in this category. This assumed average is on the lower side, since it implies that a large number of Akbar's wives and female relations received less than Rs 100 a month.

On this conservative basis the minimum annual expenditure on cash stipends to the high-ranking ladies can be set at 1,44,00,000 *dāms* (=300 × 100 × 40 × 12).

With at least 300 thus accounted for, the other female inmates should have numbered at the most 4,700. The designation used for them, *parastārān-i ḥuẓūr*, could cover anyone from a favoured concubine to an ordinary female servant or slave. We have no means of knowing for certain how many of these women were placed in Grade I and how many in Grade II. Grade I probably comprised concubines and holders of offices in the harem.[5] As such their number is not likely to have been less than 700, it being improbable that the ratio between them and the high-ranking women was much less than 1:2.5. The remaining 4,000 may then be taken to be female attendants and slaves, and to have formed Grade II.

Now, since the minimum monthly pay for Grade I is set at Rs 20 and the maximum at Rs 51, an assumed average pay of Rs 30 may not be far from the truth. For Grade II, comprising the attendants and slaves, the average might well have been closer to the minimum (Rs 2); and the assumption we may make, then, is that the female attendants received Rs 5 per month on an average—a salary about twice that of an unskilled workman, so that it may represent a reasonable average of salaries in the various scales in both grades ranging between the extremes of Rs 2 and Rs 51. On these assumptions, the annual expenditure in *dāms* could be computed as follows:

	dāms
Grade I: 700 × 30 × 40 × 12	1,00,80,000
Grade II: 4,000 × 5 × 40 × 12	96,00,000
Total for Grades I & II	1,96,80,000

[4] *Letters from the Mughal Court*, 59; Monserrate, 105.

[5] Such female officials are mentioned in the *Ā'īn*, I, 40; some seem to have been designated *urdū-begīān*, 41.

Adding to this the amount paid to the women of high ranks, the total annual expenditure on cash stipends in the harem should have amounted to 3,40,80,000 *dāms*.

This amount does not include the pay or cost of maintenance of the eunuchs who served in the harem.[6] Their actual number is not known. Presumably their pay was higher than that of ordinary male slaves. To allow for this additional expenditure, and keeping in view the generally conservative assumptions we have made, we may put the annual amount spent on cash stipends and wages in the harem at the round figure of 3,50,00,000 *dāms*.

The imperial kitchen was a very large establishment serving not only the emperor, but the entire harem. Since the time for the emperor's meals was not fixed, says Abū'l Faẓl,

> the officers (of the kitchen) so keep everything ready that a hundred dishes (*qāb*) can be served all at once upon the Emperor's desire. Whatever food (*rātiba*) has to be supplied to the inmates of the harem begins (to be prepared) from the morning and continues mostly into the night.[7]

This system at the imperial household was in conformity with the aristocratic practice of the day as may be seen from Pelsaert's description of the arrangements in a high noble's household:

> Each wife (of the noble) has separate apartments for herself and her slaves, of whom may be 10 or 20, or 100 according to her fortune. Each has a regular monthly allowance for her *gastos*… Their food comes from one kitchen, but each wife takes it in her own apartments.[8]

But from some other remarks made in the *Ā'īn*, it would seem that some of the high-ranking ladies of the imperial harem and the princes maintained their kitchens as well. Abū'l Faẓl says that Akbar marked the end of his long period of 'abstinence' by partaking of meat dishes sent from his mother's establishment, followed by dishes received from other principal wives (*begamān*), princes and some other 'near ones'.[9] The *Ā'īn* also says that the copper utensils in the imperial kitchen received a

[6] *Ā'īn*, I, 40.
[7] Ibid., 53.
[8] Pelsaert, *Remonstrantie*, 313; tr., 64.
[9] *Ā'īn*, I, 59.

tin coating (*qala'i*) every month, while those of the princes and others were tinned once in two months.[10]

These were, however, clearly 'private' kitchens, and the bulk of the 5,000 inmates of the harem received their food from the imperial kitchen. This is corroborated by the large quantity of firewood consumed in the imperial household, viz., 1,50,000 *man-i Akbarī* (3,766.5 quintals) a year.[11] Even if we assume that the number of those served by the imperial kitchen was 5,000 (all the inmates of the harem as counted by Abū'l Faẓl), the firewood consumption per head works out at 30 *mans* per annum or 3.3 *sers*, i.e., 2.06 kg a day). This seems rather high, particularly since the firewood supplied to the imperial kitchen must have been of a superior quality. Assuming that some firewood was also used for heating in winter and for providing hot water in the *ḥammām* (baths), the amount consumed was still high enough to suggest that the number of persons for whom food was cooked was more than 5,000. One should also keep in mind that so much food was cooked in the imperial kitchen that it used to supply a veritable market outside, as Bernier was to note sixty years later.[12]

Such large numbers fed from the kitchen meant that its staff would also have had to be very large. Even given five cooks and helpers to every 100 persons fed, there would have been at least 250 persons employed in the imperial kitchen to cater for the 5,000 inmates of the harem alone (excluding the staff employed in cooking for the emperor's table). The pay scale in the imperial kitchen for a *piyāda* varied from 100 to 400 *dāms* a month.[13] If we assume that their salary on average was 150 *dāms* a month, the expenditure on wages of cooks and helpers for the harem works out at ($150 \times 250 \times 12 =$) 4,50,000 *dāms* a year. Other members of the kitchen staff were *aḥadīs* and *manṣabdārs*, and their salaries are already included in our figures of expenditure under those categories.

Using the recipes given by Abū'l Faẓl, the value per *ser* (*Akbarī*) of various dishes (23 of the 30 for which complete details are provided) can be calculated on the basis of camp prices given in the *Ā'īn*. This will probably result in some overestimation, the camp prices being retail prices,[14] while the supplies for the imperial establishment came from various places all over the country,[15] and were therefore most probably equivalent to wholesale prices (after adding the cost of transport to prime costs).

[10] Ibid., 55.

[11] Ibid., 151–2. For conversion of *man-i Akbarī* into kilograms see Habib, *Agrarian System*, rev. ed. 421.

[12] Bernier, 251.

[13] *Ā'īn*, I, 60.

[14] See Chapter 14.

[15] *Ā'īn*, I, 53.

The weights and prices of various dishes described in the *Ā'īn* are given in Table 11.1. I have arranged these broadly in four groups, viz., rice preparations; wheat preparations; sweet dishes; and meat and vegetable preparations. An estimate of the cost of bread (*chapāttī*) is added at the end.

Table 11.1

	Value in *dāms*	Weight in *sers*	Value in *dāms* per *ser*
RICE PREPARATIONS			
Qubūlī	85.05	24.38	3.48
Qīma Pulāo	106.78	27.90	3.83
Wizobiryān	99.39	24.00	4.14
Khushka	22.70	10.50	2.16
Khichri	20.40	13.00	1.56
Shola	85.56	17.48	3.49
Average			3.58
WHEAT PREPARATIONS			
Qutab	77.20	17.92	4.31
Harīsa	74.62	17.56	4.25
Koshak	78.28	16.11	4.86
Ḥalīm	76.13	15.27	4.99
Average			4.58
Sweet Dishes			
Zard biranj	103.92	20.40	5.09
Shīr biranj	14.00	12.00	1.17
Ḥalwa	86.75	30.00	2.89
Average			3.28
MEAT AND VEGETABLE DISHES			
Do piyāza	5.95	14.58	5.21
Malghoba	73.53	22.42	3.28
Yakhni	66.70	11.50	5.80
Kabāb	73.70	11.75	6.27
Baghra	107.23	20.27	5.29
Qīma shorba	75.86	15.32	4.95
Mutbakh gosfand	76.11	13.05	5.83
Dampukht	92.56	15.65	5.91
Qaliya	77.82	13.26	5.87
Average			5.38
BREAD			
Chapāttī (bread)	0.55	0.07*	5.18

*15 *chapatis* to the *ser*; according to the *Ā'īn*: must have been excessively thin!

We further assume a uniform composition of food for all inmates of the harem. The composition of food would not have been the same for all the harem inmates, and the high-ranking ladies would have been served a larger variety of dishes, and better food, than the attendants and slaves; but since we are using unweighted averages of all the possible recipes, the number of dishes should not affect our estimates markedly.

Assuming the following composition of the diet per head, and multiplying these quantities with the average value per *ser* worked out by us for the four groups of dishes, we get the following estimate for the daily consumption per head.

Table 11.2

	Sers	*Dāms*
Wheat preparations	¼	1.15
Rice preparations	¼	0.86
Meat & vegetables	¼	1.30
Sweet dishes	¼	0.82
Chapāttī (bread)	½	0.27
Total	1½	4.40

At 1½ *sers* or nearly one kg of food consumed daily, the allowance per person is perhaps on the generous side, but we must remember that the diet is that of members of the imperial household, who are likely, in any case, to have been allowed a generous quantity.

The daily expenditure on food per head in the imperial establishment thus works out at 4.40 *dāms*, or more than double the total wage of an unskilled labourer.

To convert this into total expenditure per year on the female inmates only, one would need to multiply the estimated expenditure per head by the number of persons served and by the number of days in a year, to get $(4.4 \times 5000 \times 365 =)$ 80,30,000 *dāms*.

We must remember, too, that from the quantity of firewood consumed, the total number of persons fed by the imperial establishment seems to have considerably exceeded 5,000. Furthermore, this amount does not include expenditure on the royal table itself, which could not have been negligible.

As we have seen, 100 dishes were supposed to be kept in readiness round the clock, since Akbar used to eat once a day without previously fixing any time for it.[16] Monserrate tells us that forty courses were served at each meal.[17]

Of the numerous dishes prepared by expert cooks recruited from within India as well as from Iran, Turkey, and other countries, the recipes for thirty are given by Abū'l Faẓl. In these recipes Abū'l Faẓl seems to have taken 10 *sers* (6.2 kg) as the standard minimum unit. One might assume that these thirty dishes at least were served at each meal and the total weight of basic ingredients in all the dishes cooked was, at the minimum, 10 *sers* (6.2 kg).

The cost of the food served at each meal at Akbar's table, upon these assumptions, works out at 1,645.22 *dāms* (about Rs 41). This certainly involves some under-estimation, since instead of forty dishes reportedly served at the royal table, we can compute the costs only for twenty-three dishes. Moreover, the dishes served at the royal table would have richer ingredients than the ordinary ones described by Abū'l Faẓl. Since Akbar ate only once a day, the annual minimum expenditure works out at (1645.22 × 365 =) 6,00,505 *dāms*.

Since such a large number of dishes had to be kept ready round the clock, we may allow 100 cooks to cater especially to the needs of the royal table. According to Abū'l Faẓl, as we have seen, there were cooks from various countries,[18] and being expert cooks must have been highly paid. We may thus allow a high rate of, say, 300 *dāms* a month for them (the scale generally prescribed for all *piyādas* in the kitchen being 100 to 400 *dāms*).[19] The higher cooks' total wages thus work out at (300 × 100 × 12 =) 3,60,000 *dāms* a year. The superior officials should again be excluded since they must have been on 'army' rolls as *aḥadīs* and *manṣabdārs*.[20]

In estimating the cost of firewood we can use the prices given by Pelsaert. The latter says that the price of firewood at Agra varied from 12 to 18 pice per *man* of 60 lbs.[21] Allowing for the increased weight of the latter *man*,[22] and for the depreciation of *dāms* or pice (now 58 to the

16 Ibid., 52.

17 Monserrate, 199.

18 *Ā'īn*, I, 55. The Jesuit fathers reported that Akbar had a cook who could prepare dishes in the European style; the emperor sent them some delicacies prepared by the cook on Easter 1580 (*Letters from the Mughal Court*, 38).

19 Ibid., I, 60.

20 The entire kitchen establishment was headed by the *mīr bakāwal* or *bakāwal begī*. Bāyazīd Bayāt held the office of *bakāwalbegī*, while a *manṣab*-holder of 200; he dictated his memoirs to a scribe of Abū'l Faẓl, while simultaneously carrying out the duties of the kitchen (*bāwarchīkhāna*) (Bāyazīd, 2).

21 Pelsaert, *Remonstrantie*, 297; tr. 48.

22 For *man-i Akbarī*, see Habib, *Agrarian System*, 368 (rev., ed. 420–1).

rupee instead of 40) and then taking a lower rate within the range reported by Pelsaert, we may suppose the approximate price of firewood at 7 *dāms* per *man-i Akbarī*. The total expenditure on 1,50,000 *man-i Akbarī* would then have been 10,50,000 *dāms*.

The total imperial expenditure on food per annum may be summarized as follows:

	dāms
For harem inmates	
Kitchen ingredients	80,30,000
Cooks' and helpers' wages	4,50,000
For royal table	
Kitchen ingredients	6,00,505
Cooks' wages	3,60,000
Firewood	10,50,000
Total	1,04,90,505

The cost of utensils, tinning, polishing, etc., remains unknown. But such costs can be allowed for by rounding off kitchen expenditure to 1,15,00,000 *dāms*, i.e., allowing over 10,00,000 *dāms* on these heads.

The arrangements for drinking water were so elaborate that it required from Abū'l Faẓl a separate chapter (*Ā'īn-i Ābdār k͟hāna*) to describe them.[23] Akbar used to drink water brought from the river Ganga, whether he was at the capital or on the march; and even the water used for cooking contained some Ganga water. Special officials were appointed to arrange for the conveyance of water to the Imperial palace or camp.

Ice was used round the year; the cost of the ice brought from 'an average distance' is said to be 15 *dāms* per *ser*.[24] Water was also cooled by using saltpetre; 2.5 *sers* of saltpetre were needed to cool a *ser* of water, while the cost of saltpetre was 10 to 53 *dāms* per *man*.[25]

Since we have neither estimates for the amount of ice consumed nor of the water cooled, it seems difficult to estimate expenses on these heads. Nevertheless, we can at least fix some lower limit for the expenses. Even if we assume that only two *mans* of ice was consumed in the

[23] *Ā'īn*, I, 51–2.
[24] Ibid., 52.
[25] Ibid., 51.

imperial household daily over half the year, the amount spent on ice alone would have amounted to ($40 \times 15 \times 2 \times 182.5 =$) 2,19,000 *dāms* per year. Besides this the amount spent on cooling water, arranging for the supply of Ganga water, the wear and tear of utensils and the salary of employees in the department, should add up to a significant amount. One may, therefore, hazard the conjecture that at a minimum about 10,00,000 *dāms* must have been spent on the *ābdār-khāna*.

The price of a variety of fruits is set out in the *Ā'īn*, but we have no figures for the quantities consumed. Moreover, part of the fruits would surely have come from the imperial gardens and orchards. But orchards and gardens too would have required investment and recurring expenditure; the fruits from them must therefore also have represented a considerable expenditure.

Abū'l Faẓl treats betel leaves as 'fruits'.[26] Since these were also received in lieu of land revenue, the expenses on this item are difficult to compute.[27] We can suggest that the expenditure on fruits, etc., was one-tenth of the expenditure on food, that is 11,50,000 *dāms* per year.

The total expenditure on the kitchen, *ābdār-khāna* and fruitery should therefore have added up to 1,36,50,000 *dāms* per year.

In keeping with the time-honoured Mongol tradition, Akbar maintained a huge hunting department. According to Abū'l Faẓl one thousand cheetahs or hunting leopards (*yūz*) were maintained in the imperial parks.[28] Of these, 50 were selected as *khāṣa*,[29] and kept at the court. Two hundred servants were employed to look after the *khāṣa* animals.[30] Other cheetahs were allowed two or three attendants each: those carried on horses two; the remainder, carried on ox-drawn carriages three attendants each. The servants were divided into two categories; the superior received 180 to 300 *dāms* per month; the lower staff, from 100 to 160 *dāms*. The meat sanctioned for a cheetah varied from 2.57 *sers* to 5 *sers* a day.[31]

[26] Ibid., 80.

[27] Ibid., II, 424. Some 12,00,000 leaves were received in lieu of revenue from Allahabad province.

[28] *Ā'īn*, I, 208. Firishta (I, 272), however, records a tradition that it was Akbar's wish to possess 1,000 cheetahs; but whenever the number exceeded 900, some died, so that the number always remained below 1,000.

[29] *Ā'īn*, I, 208

[30] Ibid., 207.

[31] Ibid., 208.

If we allow the *khāṣa* beasts the maximum ration of meat, allow the highest wages to their attendants and further assume that the servants were evenly divided into the two categories, the expenditure works out as follows:

		dāms
Food	$(5 \div 40)\ (30 \times 50 \times 365)$*	68,438
Servants	$(100 \times 300 \times 12) + (100 \times 180 \times 12)$	5,76,000
	Total	6,44,438

* Quantity of meat per *man* multiplied by price per *man*, and, then by number of cheetahs and finally by days in the year.

Assuming that of the remaining 950 cheetahs, half were provided with two servants each and the other half with three each, and further that to each cheetah one of the attendants assigned was of the superior category, and allowing also average wages to servants and average ration of meat to animals, we may estimate the expenditure on the 950 animals as follows:

		dāms
Food	$(3.72 \div 40)\ (30 \times 50 \times 365 \times 950)$	9,67,433
Servants	$(950 \times 240 \times 12) + (2{,}375 \times 130 \times 12)$	49,59,000
	Total	59,26,433

The imperial expenditure on food and servants of both categories of cheetahs would then have been 65,70,871 *dāms* a year.

We have not considered the amount spent on carts (*'arāba*) and horses, because the carts for cheetahs were perhaps counted among those 1,750 for which the expenditure has already been estimated;[32] the horses might similarly have been accounted for among the 12,000 imperial horses. Abū'l Faẓl mentions expensive trappings for cheetahs, without mentioning their cost. The amount spent on these would have been a part of the total expenditure on trappings for imperial animals, which is estimated

[32] See Chapter 10.

separately in this chapter. However, we have to make some allowance for litters for the animals. The imperial expenditure on cheetahs may thus have been in the vicinity of 70,00,000 *dāms* a year.

Animals such as deer, dogs, panthers (*siyāh-gosh*) and hawks were also kept for hunting.[33] The *Ā'īn* gives the number of deer at 12,000 of which 101 were selected as *khāṣa* animals;[34] but no data for the costs of maintenance are furnished. For dogs, panthers and hawks the amounts of food allowed and the wages of servants (100 *dāms* a month for the attendants of dogs and panthers)[35] are recorded. But the number of animals is not specified. Besides hunting animals and hawks, a large number of pigeons were reared and kept. Abū'l Faẓl estimates the number at over 20,000. Of these, 500 were kept as *khāṣa*,[36] to be taken with the imperial camp, by bearers (*kahār*). All the servants attached to the pigeon house drew their salary on the army rolls.[37] Their wages ranged from 80 *dāms* a month to as high as 1,920 *dāms* a month.

Though the *Ā'īn* does not enable us to compute the expenditure on hunting animals other than cheetahs, it at least offers clues by giving the number of deer and pigeons and the wages of the attendants of animals. These figures suggest that expenditure on these animals could not have been less than 60,00,000 *dāms* a year. This estimate is arbitrary; but it could err only on the lower side.

In all, the expenditure on hunting animals, hawks and pigeons should have been around 1,30,00,000 *dāms* a year.

There were a number of other departments such as the wardrobe, library, encampment, and stores of precious stones, on which the imperial administration must have incurred considerable expenditure. But though the *Ā'īn* gives a fairly detailed description of these departments, the data it gives are inadequate for calculating the expenditure on them. Either there are no statistics or the information offered is so scanty or incomplete that no attempt at quantification is possible. We are, however, fortunate in possessing in Pelsaert (and, copying from him, de Laet)[38] a statement of

[33] *Ā'īn*, I, 208–12.

[34] Ibid., 165, 167; Firishta, I, 272, however, gives the number of the deer as 5,000.

[35] *Ā'īn*, I, 209–10.

[36] Ibid., 217. Monserrate in a letter of February 1580, tells us that Akbar used to keep deer, panthers, fighting cocks, vultures, eagles, pigeons, etc. (*Letters from the Mughal Court*, 37, also 81).

[37] *Ā'īn*, 218.

[38] Pelsaert, *Kroniek*, 116–21; *Chronicle*, tr. 33–5; de Laet, *The Empire of the Great Mogol*, tr. J.S. Hoyland, 107–10.

the value of different kinds of goods in the stores of the imperial establishment at the time of Akbar's death (1605); and from this we can attempt an estimate of the annual expenditure in these departments.

Pelsaert gives us to understand that his figures are drawn from account books maintained by the Mughal administration. In his inventory of Akbar's possessions, along with the stocks of specie, he records the value of cloth in the imperial wardrobe (the *Ā'īn*'s *tosha khāna*), tents and articles of furniture in the imperial stores (*farrāsh-khāna*), cannon, muskets, hand weapons and armour in the imperial arsenal (*qūr khāna*), books in the imperial library, rich trappings for animals, etc. He also furnishes us with the number of animals in the imperial stables. As we have seen in Chapter 10, Pelsaert's figures for horses, elephants, etc., are largely corroborated by the *Ā'īn* as well as by the account left by Firishta. Moreover, all the items for which the total values are given by Pelsaert also figure in the *Ā'īn*. To take just one instance, Abū'l Faẓl mentions the animal trappings and harnesses of gold and silver cloth studded with jewels which were used for the *khāṣa* animals;[39] their value is provided in Pelsaert's list.

Abū'l Faẓl says that all the cloth bought, woven to order or received in presents, was stored, and experienced men were appointed to enquire into the previous as well as the current prices of these articles.[40] Thus there must have been a standing official valuation of all goods in the imperial store houses; and Pelsaert's figures could very well have come from an official record of valuation, just as he says they do.

Before Pelsaert's Chronicle in the original Dutch was printed one had to rely on the translations of Pelsaert's *Chronicle* and de Laet's *De Imperio Magni Mogolis*, the figures contain some errors. Some misprints in Pelsaert's *Chronicle* can be corrected by referring to de Laet. Other errors, common to both, can be rectified by reconciling the different items of value with sub-totals and with the grand total given by Pelsaert. It was found that only three slight corrections are needed. Now, the Dutch text of the *Chronicle* has shown that the original figures bear out these corrections. The figures in that text are given in Table 11.3.

These figures provide us with the means of estimating the annual expenditure on various departments. We can perhaps best do so by venturing a few assumptions and then examining the results. It would, first, be a valid assumption that goods left by Akbar would have taken years to accumulate and the total value by Pelsaert would comprise the total of

[39] *Ā'īn*, I, 135–8, 142.
[40] Ibid., 101.

Table 11.3

CASH HOARD	
	Rupees
Muhrs worth	9,75,80,000¾
Rupees	10,00,00,000
Dāms worth	7,66,666
Total	19,83,46,666¾
PRECIOUS STONES, WROUGHT SILVER, GOLD, PORCELAIN, ETC.	
	Values in Rupees
Precious stones	6,05,20,521
Silver objects	22,25,838
Gold ornaments	1,90,06,745
Gold objects	95,07,992
Copper works	51,225
Porcelain	25,07,747
Total	9,38,20,068
OTHER ITEMS	
	Value in Rupees
Cloth	1,55,09,979
Woollen cloth	5,03,252
Tents, etc.	99,25,545
Books	64,63,731
Artillery	85,75,971
Armour & weapons	50,00,000
Animal harness	25,25,646
Special armours and muskets	50,00,000
Total	5,60,59,649
Grand Total	34,82,26,383

the costs annually incurred upon their acquisition. Since the empire constantly increased in extent, and the revenue-resources increased correspondingly, the scale of market purchases and domestic manufacture should have become greater in later years.

We must, therefore, make the same assumptions as for annual savings (Chapter 8), that the costs incurred every year were in arithmetical progression, and compute expenditure in the 40th year accordingly. This, as we have seen, may be done by dividing the value by 1225 and then multiplying the quotient by 40 (to account for a period of 40 years). The result, however, does not include the amount spent to cover loss and wear and tear. At the same time, the value of presents received appears here as part of expenditure, while the cost of articles given away as presents is not counted. Since it seems practically certain that the value of presents received exceeded those given away, this excess may be set off against the annual depreciation (through age, use and loss) of the value of the stored articles.

We must bear another factor in mind: from Abū'l Faẓl's account it seems that the valuation of goods in the imperial store-houses was made on the basis of prevailing market prices. Only this can explain the appointment of experienced men to enquire into previous and current prices.[41] This implies that the 'value' does not represent the actual cost of manufacture, whenever these were products of the imperial *kārkhānas*. Abū'l Faẓl gives an example of such a departure from cost: a carpet woven at the cost of Rs 1,802 (*ba kharch raft*) in the imperial *karkhānas* was valued at Rs 2,715 (*arj bar nihād*).[42] In other words, the price was fixed here at 50 per cent above cost. Such high valuation might be an exception, but generally speaking the value assigned to goods in the imperial storehouses were probably higher than the actual cost incurred on acquiring them. The scale of overestimation might reasonably be fixed at 25 per cent; that is, the actual amount spent on these goods was 20 per cent less than their recorded value. We could therefore scale down the value given by Pelsaert by 20 per cent to get the actual expenditure.[43]

The annual cost of acquisitions worked out in this way would include the wages of workmen and other employees as well as other expenses on the imperial workshops (*kārkhānas*) where perhaps most of the articles stored in the imperial storehouses were made. Thus no separate calculation for expenses in workshops need be made.

Based on our method of computation of cost for the year 1595–6, we may now offer some figures and comments on the annual imperial expenditure on different heads.

According to Pelsaert the value of the cloth in the imperial stores was Rs 1,60,13,231 (woollen articles valued at Rs 5,03,252; other kinds at Rs 1,55,09,279). Reducing the amount by 20 per cent to get the cost price,

[41] Ibid.

[42] Ibid., 51.

[43] Moreover, if the valuation kept on being revised, it might have been influenced by a rise in price levels which, though restrained in Akbar's time, must have resulted in inflating valuation of earlier purchases to some extent. This would have the result of increasing the annual expenditure calculated for the 40th R.Y. somewhat above the real figure.

and, after conversion into *dāms*, proceeding by the method of calculation already described, we obtain the figure of 1,67,32,193 *dāms* for the expenditure on cloth for 1595–6.

This amount is by no means excessive, since from the account given in the *Ā'īn*, one would certainly expect a large amount of expenditure on the wardrobe (*tosha-khāna*). In each half-year (*faṣl*) one thousand suits were made for the emperor, from different types of cloth. Of these, 120 were kept in readiness all the time.[44] Such a large number of garments were perhaps needed because of the practice of conferring robes of honour (*khil'at*) on favoured persons. That the robes were given out of the *khāṣa* dresses is evident from Abū'l Faẓl's statement that Akbar's clothes were found to fit everybody whether tall or short![45]

There is little specific information in Abū'l Faẓl's description to build up any kind of estimate of annual costs in this department. He says that in Lahore alone there were 1,000 *kārkhānas* making shawls.[46] But since the figure probably included the *kārkhānas* of nobles and even of merchants, it does not help us in estimating the imperial expenditure on shawls. Abū'l Faẓl does provide us with the prices for a variety of golden (*zarrīn*), silken (*abreshmī*) and cotton (*rīsmānī*) cloth.[47] He mentions woollen cloth too as being manufactured at the imperial *kārkhāna* but does not give the prices.[48] The tailoring costs of some dresses are given; but since the number of these is not recorded, one cannot estimate the expenses incurred in the *tosha-khāna*. One may, however, suppose that the actual expenditure was even higher than that arrived at from the value given by Pelsaert, since in the case of robes the value of material given away probably exceeded the value of those received in offerings or presents.

Pelsaert gives the value of gold pots, dishes, cutlery, figurines, silver utensils chandeliers, bedsteads, etc., copperware and porcelain crockery, as Rs 1,42,92,802; this should be scaled down by 20 per cent to give us approximate cost-prices. Following the method of calculation explained above, we get from this the figure of 1,49,34,520 *dāms* for expenses during the year 1595–6. We assume that the value of gifts received was offset by the loss through wear and tear which ought to have been high in the case of porcelain. There is little reason to believe that the emperor gave away articles of this kind in gifts to his nobles.

[44] *Ā'īn*, I, 102–3.

[45] Ibid., 103.

[46] Ibid., 104.

[47] Ibid., 106–11.

[48] Ibid., 104.

Abū'l Faẕl mentions rich trappings and pieces of harness that were used to decorate the *kh͟āṣa* animals (elephants, horses, camels, etc.) on ceremonial occasions; these were in addition to the usual harness which was changed periodically[49] (see Chapter 10). From Pelsaert's statistics the amount spent in 1595–6 on pieces of expensive harness can be calculated at 26,39,043 *dāms*.

Akbar had a remarkably rich library. Pelsaert says that there were 24,000 volumes, originals (authors' 'autographs'?) as well as copies, the estimated value being Rs 6,46,373. The high cost (more than Rs 259 per volume) seems justified because it is not only the high quality of handmade paper and splendid calligraphy that made the books precious, but they were often illustrated profusely by Akbar's painters. This can be seen from such MSS as have survived. One book, the *Qiṣṣa-i Ḥamza*, contained no less than 1,400 illustrations.[50] The costs might well have included payments made to calligraphers, as well as painters and even, perhaps to translators of Sanskrit texts which Akbar patronized.[51] A number of calligraphers and painters were on the imperial pay-rolls.[52]

Following the method we have so far adopted we may estimate expenses on the library in 1595–6 at 67,53,940 *dāms*. This estimate is possibly on the lower side since it does not include the amount spent on the library staff (the salary of *piyādas* appointed in the department ranged from 600 to 1,200 *dāms* per month)[53] and the payments made to readers who read books aloud to the emperor other than those who like Naqīb K͟hān held *manṣabs*.[54] It is to be noted that the books were not only given away as presents but were even given in *armās* (payment in kind to *manṣabdārs* presumably against cash valuation).[55] On the other hand, books were also acquired as war booty, as well as in offerings and presents, and possibly as part of property acquired in escheat. These acquisitions probably balanced the losses through imperial presents.

According to Pelsaert, the value of tents and other articles used in camps, as entered in the account books, was Rs 99,25,545. This gives us

[49] Ibid., 135–8, 142.

[50] Ibid., 117–18. 'Ārif Qandahārī, 45–6, says that each volume of the *Qiṣṣa-i Ḥamza*, prepared in two years, cost 20,00,000 *dāms*.

[51] Ibid., 115–16; Badāūnī, II, 336, 366.

[52] *Ā'īn*, 118.

[53] Ibid., 118.

[54] Ibid., 112.

[55] Badāūnī, II, 202.

an expenditure of 1,03,71,182 *dāms* for 1595–6. Abū'l Faẓl's detailed description of the layout and organization of the camp in his chapter on the *farrāsh khāna*, accords with the high value assigned in Pelsaert's record to tents and furniture. The *Ā'īn* says that one tent designated the *bārgāh* cost Rs 1,000; and there were eleven other kinds of tents, some double-storeyed, as well as folding.[56] The *sāyabāns* (hanging shades) of the tents were made of brocade and velvet, and embroidered with gold.[57]

Pelsaert valued the precious stones in the royal treasury at Akbar's death at Rs 6,05,20,521; and the gold ornaments, at Rs 1,90,06,745. These are very high values; yet the fact that they are not round but detailed, suggests that the figures are totals formed by actual or detailed valuations of individual pieces. Admittedly the valuation of the stones must have been a difficult task, and somewhat arbitrary.[58] But that the total value offered by Pelsaert is not excessive is supported by Abū'l Faẓl's statements in respect of individual stones and gems. He mentions rubies worth Rs 52,000 each and strings of pearls in which each pearl was valued at 30 *muhrs* (Rs 270).[59]

In trying to estimate the annual expenditure based on the total value of precious stones and ornaments in 1605, one has to remember that several of them were seized as booty from defeated chiefs and rulers.[60] Since precious stones and gold ornaments do not wear out, items reposing in the Mughal treasury in 1605 might have been in the possession of the Mughal imperial house for more than a generation; and there must have been a recognizable portion inherited from Humayun. It may, therefore, perhaps be reasonable to assume that about one-third of the total jewels in the imperial treasure at the close of Akbar's reign, were those acquired in booty or as heirlooms. We have also to make an allowance for presents (or rather the net value of presents, being the value of presents received less that of gifts awarded), which should have been considerable, since precious stones were the most acceptable items of gifts (*nazr/peshkash*) made to the emperor by high nobles.[61] There were, in addition, jewels

[56] *Ā'īn*, I, 49–50.

[57] Ibid., 49.

[58] See *Tavernier's Travels in India*, tr. Ball and Crooke, New Delhi, 1977, Vol.I, 112–13; Vol.II, 72–3, where it is related that only the deposed Emperor Shāhjahān was able to estimate the value of a particular diamond correctly.

[59] *Ā'īn*, I, 11–12. Compare Tavernier's prices for a ruby (Rs 95,000) and a 'large Topaz' (Rs 181,000) in the Mughal treasury (Vol.II, 100, 102).

[60] See, e.g., *Akbarnāma*, II, 214; & III, 836.

[61] *Early Travels* (John Mildenhall's account, 1599–1606), 55; *Akbarnāma*, II, 149; *Ṭabaqāt*, II, 155. Cf. Tavernier, II, 100–1.

acquired through escheat. We may, therefore, allow that at least 20 per cent of the gems and ornaments in Akbar's vaults in 1605 had been acquired through gifts and confiscations. A further scaling down by 20 per cent has to be made to allow for the excess of stated value above costs. With a net estimated total of values of precious stones and jewels actually purchased by the emperor, viz. 1,35,72,65,357 *dāms*, in our hands, we can now apply our simple formula for calculating the annual expenditure: it would give the total expenditure on precious stones and ornaments, in the 40th regnal year (1595–6), as 4,43,18,868 *dāms*.

This is a large figure, even after scaling down the original valuation so heavily. It might seem strange that the sum spent on acquiring gems and ornaments should have exceeded expenditure on the arsenal or, for that matter, on the entire harem. But this was in keeping with the Mughal emperors' intense interest in collecting all kinds of jewels and ornaments; and such heavy expenditure on these items is an economic fact of importance in its own right.

According to Abū'l Faẓl large sums were spent on the construction of forts, *sarāi's*, schools, houses of worship (*riyāẓat kada*), tanks, wells, etc.[62] He also records the wages of labourers and craftsmen, and the prices of building materials.[63] But these offer us little clue to the total expenditure on buildings. The reported costs of individual buildings erected by Akbar are perhaps better indicators: the Agra fort, taking fifteen or sixteen years to build, cost Rs 35,00,000 (=14,00,00,000 *dāms*);[64] the Fatehpur Sikri complex cost Rs 15,00,000 (=6,00,00,000 *dāms*);[65] the Allahabad fort, taking five years to build, cost Rs 12,00,000 (=4,80,00,000 *dāms*);[66] and according to an inscription in the Nagarnagar fort at Srinagar, the emperor sent 1,10,00,000 *dāms* to meet the costs of construction of that fort.[67]

Keeping these figures in mind, one may estimate the average annual expenditure on buildings at about one and a half crore *dāms*. This figure

[62] *Ā'īn*, I, 167. For *sarāi's* see also *Akbarnāma*, II, 262–3.

[63] *Ā'īn*, I, 167–71.

[64] *Haft Iqlīm*, II, p.493 gives the expenditure as 7 crore *tankas* (14 core *dāms*), and this is corroborated by *Tuzuk*, 2. Badāūnī, 74, puts the costs at '3,00,00,000 of money', presumably *tankas*, and so equal to 6 crore *dāms*. Pelsaert, *Kroniek*, 84; *Chronicle*, tr., 18, gives the cost at Rs 25,00,000 (=10 crore *dāms*). The *Haft Iqlīm*'s estimate being of 1593 and supported by the official estimate provided by Jahāngīr should be surely preferred.

[65] Pelsaert, *Kroniek*, 84; *Chronicle*, tr., 18. The Fatehpur Sikri mosque alone cost Rs 5,00,000 (*Tuzuk*, 262). See also Irfan Habib, 'Fatehpur Sikri—The Economic and Social Setting', *Fatehpur-Sikri* eds. Michael Brand and Glenn D. Lowry, Bombay, 1987.

[66] Pelsaert, *Kroniek*, 92; *Chronicle*, tr., 21.

[67] Inscription on the gateway of the Nagarnagar fort (personally seen).

is justified by the enormous building activity which occurred under Akbar. The construction of at least one large-scale fort of the kind, as at Allahabad, was in progress all the time; and the construction of buildings, renovations and maintenance[68] must surely have needed about half as much expenditure again as incurred on the Allahabad fort annually during its five years of construction.

The emperor granted cash allowances paid out periodically (daily, monthly, yearly) from the imperial treasury. These were called *waẓāi'f* (plural of *waẓīfa*) and were considered part of the *suyūrghāl*.[69] The *suyūrghāl* consisted, in bulk, of the land grants called *madad-i ma'āsh*.[70] We have argued in Chapter 6 that the figures in *dāms* that Abū'l Faẓl gives under the heading *suyūrghāl* in his 'Account of the Twelve *Ṣūbas*' consists of the estimated revenue alienated through land grants plus the total amount given in cash allowances. Abū'l Faẓl adds the total to the *jama'* to produce an enlarged *jama'*, styled *naqdī*; we had, therefore, deducted the *suyūrghāl* figures to restore the actual *jama'*. This, however, does not mean that the amount paid in cash allowances can be excluded from our estimates of expenditure out of the imperial treasury.

Unluckily, there is no means of judging from the *Ā'īn* the total amount that was claimed from the treasury in the form of such cash allowance.[71] Land grants must always have formed an overwhelmingly large portion of the total *suyūrghāl*. I have, as a measure of last resort, taken the amount of cash allowances to be about 10 per cent of the total *suyūrghāl*.

[68] *Ā'īn*, I, 170, gives the costs of cleaning wells in winter as well as summer.

[69] Ibid., I, 197. The Emperor also paid in cash on daily basis to those who were presented to him by officials, and to destitutes and needy who presented themselves. For this, special provisions were made at the imperial treasury so as to keep cash handy at the hall of audience while bags containing copper coins were carried by officials accompanying the emperor (whether at the capital or on his tours). Ibid., 11. Since this payment is reported to be mainly in copper coins, it is evident that the expenditure was not substantial. For a detailed discussion see my 'Charity objectives and Mechanism in Mughal India (16th and 17th Centuries)', *PIHC*, 73rd session (Mumbai), 2012, 335–46.

[70] Ibid.

[71] The only hint of a ratio between the total *suyūrghāl* and cash grants seems to come from the *Mir'āt-i Aḥmadī* (Vol.I, 26), which gives the following data for *madad-i ma'āsh* and *in'ām* in Gujarat: 1,20,00,000 *dāms*; 50,000 *bīghas* of *ārāẓī*; and 103 villages; and Rs 1,40,000 in cash from the treasury. The actual ratio cannot be worked out since the amount of revenue alienated through 50,000 *bīghas* of *ārāẓī* and 103 villages is not known. It is also possible that the total amount given in cash allowances might have increased under Aurangzeb as a result of the *jizya*, or poll tax on non-Muslims, whose yield was largely reserved, at least on paper, for this purpose.

Calculating on the basis of the entire *suyūrghāl* (excluding that of Berar) this would imply an expenditure of 1,01,01,643 *dāms* in 1595–6.[72]

To this should be added an amount of, say, 25 lakhs of *dāms* to cover (a) cash donations paid on daily basis to these who were presented to the King by officials, and to destitutes and beggars who presented themselves,[73] (b) free kitchens (*āsh khāna, langar*) providing free food for the poor run by the state permanently.[74] Alms in cash were distributed at the time of the weighing ceremony (*tūlādān*/*wazn-i muqaddas*).[75] If such alms needed a separate treasury, of which Abū'l Faẓl speaks,[76] the amount must have been considerable: a guesstimate of 25,00,000 *dāms* will probably err on the lower side. To avoid any false impression of precision, we may, therefore, round off the total amount spent on cash grants (*waẓāi'f*) and alms of the latter kind at 1,25,00,000 *dāms*.

There were two other departments belonging to the household establishment, viz., illumination (*chirāgh afrozī*) and the drum-house (*naqqār khāna*). The drums were used not only during military marches, but were also a time-announcing device.[77] Though the *Ā'īn* describes these departments,[78] it is not possible to work out annual expenditure on the basis of the data it provides for them.

Another head on which the expenditure would not have been inconsequential was the preparation of wines. Although Abū'l Faẓl describes the process of liquor distillation in detail,[79] he is silent about the preparation or provisioning of wine in the imperial household. In the seventeenth century, nobles as a matter of course maintained their own *sūchī khānas* or wine-provisioning establishments.[80] The imperial household must have had a much larger establishment of this kind than the one maintained by any noble.

[72] Chapter VI.

[73] *Ā'īn*, I,11, 197. For the disbursement of cash among the needy, special provisions were made at the imperial treasury so as to keep cash handy at the hall of audience while money bags were carried by officials accompanying the Emperor, whether at the capital or on his tours. See f.n. 69.

[74] Ibid. Badāūnī reports that in 1583–4 Akbar established two eating houses for feeding poor Muslims and Hindus designated 'Khairpura' and 'Dharampura'. Since large numbers of Yogis also flocked to these establishments, a third place was built for them, receiving the name 'Jogipura'. Badāūnī, II, 324.

[75] *Ā'īn*, I, 197.

[76] Ibd., 11.

[77] Ibid., 46.

[78] Ibid., 43–7.

[79] Ibid., 143.

[80] *Siyāqnāma*, 184.

There were other items too of expenditure such as perfumes and incense[81] and, occasionally, boats.[82] We have assumed that the annual expenses on all such miscellaneous items amounted to about 25,00,000 *dāms*.

We may now attempt to compute the entire expenditure on the imperial household establishments by bringing together in Table 11.4 the various estimates which we have offered above.

Table 11.4

Harem	3,50,00,000
Kitchen, *ābdār-khāna*, fruits	1,36,50,000
Wardrobe	1,67,32,193
Material for encampment	1,03,71,182
Utensils	1,49,34,520
Animals' trappings	26,39,043
Books and paintings	67,53,940
Ornaments and gems	4,43,18,868
Hunting animals	1,30,00,000
Building construction	1,50,00,000
Cash-allowances and alms	1,25,00,000
Miscellaneous	25,00,000
Total	18,73,99,746

Our conception of the imperial household is not the same as Abū'l Faẓl's since he included animals and the arsenal within it, while he has placed hunting animals and cash grants and alms under the rubric of 'Army'. According to him the total expenditure on the household (*buyūtāt*) in the 39th regnal year amounted to 30,91,86,795 *dāms*.[83] Taking all those items of expenditure that Abū'l Faẓl counts under the household, or *buyūtāt*, our estimated figures total 37,66,86,570 *dāms*[84] for the 40th regnal year. This is 6,74,99,775 *dāms* higher than the amount given by Abū'l Faẓl indicating an appreciable difference. The difference

[81] *Ā'īn*, I, 82.

[82] *Akbarnāma*, III, 716. In the 41st R.Y. Rs 16,338 (6,53,520 *dāms*) were spent on building a boat of a tonnage of more than 15,000 *mans*.

[83] *Ā'īn*, I, 9.

[84] This covers the expenses incurred on animals (19,38,58,567 *dāms*); arsenal (2,20,80,257 *dāms*); and the entire expenditure on the household calculated by us *less* the costs on hunting animals (1,90,00,000 *dāms*) and expenditure on cash grants and alms (1,25,00,000 *dāms*).

could, however, be partly explained since as Abū'l Faẓl says expressly, he does not count under *buyūtāt* the pay of 'most of the officials of the *buyūtāt*', who were put on the rolls of the 'Army'.[85] The pay of such officials as held *manṣabs* or were *aḥadīs* is also excluded in our figure, being included by us under *manṣabdārs* and the army establishment. But the large number of clerks, artisans and labourers who were, as Abū'l Faẓl explicitly tells us elsewhere, on the rolls of the Army,[86] appear under the household establishment in our estimates.[87] It is not unlikely that 'civil' or non-military lower staff (formally on 'Army' rolls) of the imperial establishment received an equal amount in wages and salaries, and that this is spread over in concealed form in our estimates of the expenses on various departments of the *buyūtāt*. If this were so, the difference between our estimate of expenditure and Abū'l Faẓl's figure for the expenses of the *buyūtāt* would become marginal (a matter of 74,99,775 *dāms*). If our figures had not been necessarily so often in the round and aspiring only to rough approximations, we could even have pleaded that such a difference could well occur between the expenses of one year and another: between, in the present case, the 39th, to which Abū'l Faẓl's figure for the *buyūtāt* expenditure refers) and the 40th, our own standard year.

Estimates of imperial expenditure on the three main heads, viz., the salary bill of the nobles, imperial military establishment, and the imperial household, are given in tabular form in Table 11.5. The entire expenditure is set against the total effective *jama'* of the empire to see what portion of the revenue income has been accounted for.

We find that the *manṣabdārs*' salary accounted for a very large part of the total effective *jama'*—81.76 per cent—while the amount for maintenance of the imperial household was a mere 4.73 per cent of it. The entire imperial expenditure, comprising the costs incurred on both military and household establishments, comes to 54,63,22,066 *dāms*, or 13.79 per cent of the effective *jama'*. We may recall that our minimum limit for the size of the *k͟hāliṣa*, out of which the imperial expenditure was met, was 24 per cent of the total effective *jama'*, that is 95,04,25,715 *dāms*.[88] Our estimate of the imperial expenditure is, therefore, well within the income of the *k͟hāliṣa*. From the remaining income of the *k͟hāliṣa,* the salaries of *naqdī manṣabdārs* must have been paid.

[85] *Ā'īn*, I, 9.

[86] Ibid., 190.

[87] We may recall that the estimate for the pay of foot retainers on the army rolls amounts to 6 crore *dāms*.

[88] See Chapter 8.

Table 11.5

Income		
Effective *jama'* in 1595–6		**3,96,03,27,106**
Expenditure		
Salary bill of *manṣabdārs:*		
Ẕāt salaries	82,74,55,200	
Sawār payment	2,03,89,33,800	
Allowances for animals under the *Ẕāt* establishment	37,14,20,856	
Total		3,23,78,09,856
Imperial military establishment		
Aḥadī	8,28,57,600	
Piyādagān	6,00,00,000	
Animals	19,39,84,463	
Arsenal and armour	2,20,80,257	
Total		35,89,22,320
Imperial household Harem	3,50,00,000	
Kitchen, *ābdār-khāna*, fruits	1,36,50,000	
Wardrobe	1,67,32,193	
Material for encampment	1,03,71,182	
Utensils	1,49,34,520	
Trappings of animals	26,39,043	
Books and paintings	67,53,940	
Ornaments and gems	4,43,18,868	
Building construction	1,50,00,000	
Hunting animals	1,30,00,000	
Cash allowances and alms	1,25,00,000	
Miscellaneous	25,00,000	
Total		18,73,99,746
Total expenditure		**3,78,41,31,922**
Balance (cash and assets in hand)		**17,61,95,184**
Grand Total		**3,96,03,27,106**

The expenses on all the three heads combined accounted for 3,78,41,31,922 *dāms*, while the effective *jama'* of the empire in 1595–6 was 3,96,03,27,106 *dāms*. In other words, after meeting all the salary claims and expenses as estimated by us, Akbar's administration should have been left with 17,61,95,184 *dāms*, to be transferred to the imperial hoard or cash reserves.

Since the range for the amount transferred in 1595–6 has been estimated by us (on the basis of the total amount held in cash and bullion in 1605), as 15,50,26,829 to 18,85,28,870 *dāms*,[89] we now find that the savings for 1595–6 (17,61,95,184 *dāms*), resulting from our item-wise estimates of expenditure are well within this range.

Here, then, we find one estimate corroborated by a series of other estimates, so that both are to some degree reinforced. A third source of corroboration, at least for the size of savings, comes from Shāhjahān's court historian, Qazwīnī, whose history closed in 1638. He says that the *khāliṣa* had been reduced under Jahāngīr, but that Shāhjahān (acc.1628) enlarged it considerably so as to yield a cash income of 60,00,00,000 *dāms*; at the same time the new emperor restricted annual expenditure from the imperial treasury to Rs 1,00,00,000 or, in years when military campaigns were undertaken, to Rs 1,20,00,000.[90] This gives us a range of annual expenditure of 40,00,00,000 to 48,00,00,000 *dāms*, and, therefore, savings of 12,00,00,000 to 20,00,00,000 *dāms* a year. The scale of annual saving which Shāhjahān was apparently able to achieve roughly corresponds to the level of savings we have estimated for 1595–6.

Our several leads, therefore, tie up. This does not, of course, mean that all our detailed estimates are of uniform reliability; but it does entitle us to say that, subject to adjustments of the more conjectural figures, the broad quantitative pattern of the imperial expenditure we have established from the large amount of direct and indirect data in the *Ā'īn* and other sources, is well within the realm of statistical probability.

[89] See Chapter 8.

[90] Qazwīnī, *Pādshāhnāma*, Br. Mus. MS Add 20,734, ff.444–5, Or 173, ff.221a–b.

CHAPTER 12

Diffusion and Consumption of the Surplus

The way the Mughal ruling class spent the large share of the agricultural surplus it appropriated, must naturally have been of crucial consequence for the whole economy. We have seen in Chapter 11 that the nobility probably claimed about 82 per cent of the effective *jama'*, which in its turn came overwhelmingly out of the agricultural surplus, with only a relatively small amount drawn from taxes on commerce and crafts. Of the remainder, the expenses of the emperor's personal establishment accounted for 13.79 per cent of the *jama'*, while 4.73 per cent according to our estimate, found its way into the imperial treasure-hoard.

In exploring the pattern of diffusion of the appropriated surplus, we have, theoretically, to consider two possibilities:

(A) If the major proportion of the total expenditure of the emperor and the nobles went to create and sustain a large, low-paid service sector, and promoted the employment of large classes of persons (and expenditure on numerous animals), such dependents would simply eat away the agricultural produce taken from the peasants to meet the revenue claims of the ruling class. This would conform to the conditions envisaged by Irfan Habib for a hypothetical 'Phase I' in the development of economies.[1]

(B) The other possibility would be that a substantial part of the income of the emperor and nobles drawn from the peasantry through tax, was spent on craft goods. This would imply that a large section of the urban population (though small in proportion to the rural population) was engaged in productive labour, so that the surplus obtained from the land and other natural resources was largely in the form of raw material for

[1] Irfan Habib, 'Potentialities of Capitalistic Development in the Economy of Mughal India', *Essays in Indian History—Towards a Marxist Perception*, 180–232.

manufactures, with a much smaller part (in terms of total value) consumed as food and fodder. This would conform to Irfan Habib's 'Phase II', in whose fully developed stage he places capitalism.

This classification appears to be a useful one.[2] We now venture a quantification on the basis of certain conclusions already reached and some hypotheses now offered, so as to discover which of the two economic forms—or 'Phases'—accords with the pattern of expenditure of the Mughal ruling class.

II

Since our most detailed information on the pattern of expenditure relates to the emperor's own establishment (*vide* Chapters 10 and 11), we may adopt it as our starting point for determining the direction in which the appropriated surplus was channelled in the initial stages of diffusion.

On the basis of estimates already arrived at, we can say that of the amount remaining with the emperor, estimated at 72,25,17,250 *dāms* (after meeting the cash pay claims of the *manṣabdārs*), about one-half (49.68 per cent) of the remainder was spent on the imperial military establishment, while the entire household expenditure accounted for 25.94 per cent; and the balance, 24.38 per cent, was transferred to the cash hoard.

As one would expect, war animals represented the heaviest charge upon the military budget, claiming 54.05 per cent of it. Imperial cavalry (*aḥadīs*) drew 23.08 per cent; foot-retainers, 16.72 per cent; and the remainder (a mere 6.15 per cent of the entire military expenditure) went towards additions to the arsenal and armour including cannon and muskets (*vide* Chapter 10).

The amount paid in salaries to foot retainers directly contributed towards maintaining a large population of the pure 'service' type. The majority of those employed in the military establishment obtained wages that seem to have been a little above subsistence level. Palanquin-bearers received monthly wages of 100 to 120 *dāms*; common gate-keepers, guards, *mewrahs* (runners), etc., 120 to 200 *dāms*; and musketeers, 110 to 300 *dāms*.[3] We may remind ourselves that the minimum wages paid by the imperial administration were 2 *dāms* a day (60 *dāms* a month), which, as we shall see in Chapter 14, through a study of prices, were barely sufficient

[2] Cf. V.I. Pavlov, *Historical Premises for India's Transformation to Capitalism*, Moscow, 1979, 53.

[3] *Āʾīn*, I, pp.188–90. See also Chapter 11.

to purchase the required minimum amount of inferior food grains for the wage earners' families and meet, at the same time, their minimum needs of clothing. Those paid at higher rates, palanquin-bearers, etc., must have had something left to spend on comforts or, perhaps, even to save.

The expenditure on animals, broadly speaking, can be divided into three categories: (1) expenses on animals' food and fodder; (2) the amount spent on saddles, trappings, utensils, etc.; and (3) payments to keepers of animals. Costs incurred on the purchase of horses, a large number of which were imported, were also considerable (1.44 crore *dāms* per annum). Evidently, a part of the expenditure on animals, in the form of allowances to keepers of animals, again went to enlarge the service sector. Here the wages were low: a groom received 45 to 63 *dāms* a month; a mahout, 45 to 120, and his assistant, 30 to 90 *dāms*.[4] The costs incurred on articles forming category (2) above (saddles, etc.) should have contributed to the craft sector by creating employment for craftsmen. Most of the sums spent on the purchase of horses too would have indirectly encouraged craft production since the horses were mostly imported from Persia and Central Asia, and the imports must have been paid for through exports of high-value goods.[5] Pelsaert's breakdown of the imperial horses indicates that over 76 per cent of the horses (Arabian, Persian and Turkish) were imported. Imported horses being more expensive, it may be reasonable to assume that at least 85 per cent of the total purchase cost of imperial horses must have been spent on acquiring imported animals. We may, therefore, say that a portion of the expenditure on animals was channelled into the service sector, and some part of it could even promote the craft sector. But the major part of it, the expenses on food and fodder, represented a direct consumption of the agricultural surplus in physical terms.

As for expenditure on the arsenal and armour, many weapons were manufactured in the imperial *kārkhānas*; others were purchased (such as were not received in gifts, whose production was, of course, independent of imperial expenditure). The amount spent on armour and the arsenal may, then, largely be credited to the craft sector.

[4] *Ā'īn*, I, 177–8.

[5] This argument would be modified if it could be shown that, as during the Sultanate period, the import of horses was at least partly paid for by an export of slaves to Central Asia and Iran (See Habib, 'Economy of the Delhi Sultanate', *IHR*, Vol.IV, part 2, 292–4). Craft production would then not have been benefited by imports of horses. But slave trade of such dimensions is not indicated by evidence from the Mughal period, and, indeed, was officially prohibited (*Tazkiratu'l Mulūk*, Add 23833 ff.231b–232a). See also Irfan Habib, 'Akbar and Social Inequities', *PIHC, 53rd session, Warangal, 1993*, 300–2.

The way the cavalry troopers' (*aḥadīs*) share of the surplus was further diffused will be discussed in a separate section of this chapter, together with the pattern of expenses of the cavalry employed by *manṣabdārs*. The amount spent on the pay of *aḥadīs* (8,28,57,600 *dāms*) is, therefore, treated separately from imperial establishment and appears in Section IV of this chapter and in Appendix 12-A.

On the whole, we may say that of the entire military budget (excluding the expenses on cavalrymen) 10,45,80,792 *dāms* went to the service sector (through the 6 crore *dāms* spent on foot-retainers, to which about one-fourth of the costs of the maintenance of animals may be added). Less than one-fourth (6,40,785 *dāms*) went directly or indirectly to sustain craft production (in the form of expenditure on the arsenal, 85 per cent of the costs of the purchase of horses, and, roughly, a sixth of the maintenance costs of animals). The remaining 10,74,43,143 *dāms* represented direct consumption of the agricultural surplus.

We then pass on to expenditure in the imperial household. These, as worked out in Chapter 11, are restated in Table 12.1 as percentages of the total expenditure on the household:

Table 12.1

Harem	18.68
Kitchen	7.28
Wardrobe	8.93
Building	8.01
Encampment material	5.53
Utensils	7.97
Trappings of animals	1.41
Books and paintings	3.60
Ornaments and gems	23.65
Hunting animals and pets	6.94
Miscellaneous	1.33
Cash grants	6.67
Total	100.00

Expenses on the wardrobe, encampment material, utensils and trappings of animals can be assumed to have been incurred largely on the procuring of craft products. In the case of books and paintings the line of demarcation between craft and art is exceptionally difficult to draw. For our present purpose, however, we have treated expenditure on these departments as expenditure on craft-goods.

The largest share in the expenses of the imperial household was on account of purchase of precious stones and ornaments. A part of this amount should have gone to create highly-specialized employment: artisans (or artists) in the jewellery trade were paid rather handsomely: for instance, the payment for boring a single pearl of class I was half a rupee.[6] The purchase of precious stones must also have encouraged mining within the Mughal empire and in the Deccan (especially diamond mining).[7] Even when stones and gems were imported, payments made for them should have induced exports of craft commodities in exchange for such high-value imports.

The pocket allowance paid to high-ranking ladies constituted 42 per cent of the total expenditure on the harem: since in most cases these allowances were in addition to the food supplied (which came under the kitchen, a separate item) and wages paid to attendants and slaves, it may be held that these allowances were spent at least partly on the purchase of luxuries turned out by craftsmen (e.g. high quality silken and cotton cloth, ornaments, etc.). A third of the total expenditure on the harem may then be taken as being channelled into the craft sector.

The building industry, accounting for a little over 8 per cent of the household budget, must have employed a sizeable labour force, the bulk of which was paid subsistence-level wages. A small section of workmen, for example, carpenters of Grade I, were among the better-paid workers (7 *dāms* a day),[8] and might have been able to have some extra amount for comfort goods or savings. But whatever the pattern of the secondary diffusion, the costs incurred on building construction may wholly be regarded as expenditure on the craft sector.

In this way, we find that about two-thirds of the imperial house-hold budget (i.e., 12,24,16,413 *dāms*) was so spent that it went to encourage the craft sector. The emphasis, however, would seem to have been on skill-consuming articles (small quantities of high value) or on rarities obtained (e.g., precious stones) or on buildings such as absorbed both skilled and unskilled labour.

The remaining amount was largely funnelled into the non-productive sectors. A relatively small part was in the form of direct consumption of surplus (e.g. grain and meat for the kitchen and fodder and meat for hunting animals). One-tenth of the total bill for the kitchen went towards cooks' wages; the costs incurred on the *ābdār-khāna* (water

[6] *Ā'īn*, I, 12.

[7] On the Deccan diamond mines, see Irfan Habib, *Atlas of Mughal Empire*, Notes to Maps 15B and 16B, 62 (col.b), 67 (col.a).

[8] *Ā'īn*, I, 170.

department) too were mainly in the form of payments to various employees. In this way only about one-fifth of the expenses incurred on the kitchen could have gone to the service sector. In the allowances budgeted for hunting animals, servants' salaries amounted to about 90 per cent of the total.

The 4,000 women belonging to the harem and getting, on average, a sum of Rs 5, or 200 *dāms* a month (in addition to food), could have only enlarged the army of servants employed unproductively. Over a quarter of the total amount laid out for paying allowances to the inmates of the harem should thus be categorized as expenditure on the service sector.

The share allotted to the head 'miscellaneous' in the imperial household budget comprises mainly the amount paid to servants in some minor departments and so was of the same kind, in economic terms, as the expenditure on the low-paid harem attendants—a primitive form of service-sector employment.

Cash allowances to the needy and devout, worth 6.67 per cent of the total household budget, cannot be easily categorized. One could, perhaps, say that it went to maintain an economically unproductive population: where the recipients lived at subsistence level, it did not do anything more; where the recipients had larger incomes, they might have spent them on comforts or on servants. But the generation of demand for craft goods through these charity-receivers' expenditure could not have been large. As a whole, therefore, imperial charity may be supposed to have sustained mainly the service sector.

Our estimate on the basis of these considerations is that about 3,81,80,000 *dāms*, forming about a fifth of the imperial household expenditure must have helped to sustain the service-sector. This leaves a balance of 2,68,03,333 *dāms* for direct consumption of rural produce.

According to our estimates, offered in Chapter 11, nearly a quarter of the emperor's share in the surplus was transferred to the cash treasury. Over 95 per cent of this hoard consisted of gold and silver, in coin as well as bullion. The hoarding of precious metals had its own implications for the economy. Additions to bullion within the Empire came only through imports, chiefly from Europe (through the Middle East or around the Cape of Good Hope), since the amount of gold collected from river sands was small and silver mines as of Panjshir had long been abandoned. Imports of bullion (including specie) had to be paid for through exports; and export commodities were mainly high-value goods, whether processed agricultural goods (like indigo, saltpetre, or silk) or craft products (like muslin and chintz). While the actual composition of exports from Mughal India is not easy to envisage, available data suggest, as we shall see in Chapter 16, that craft goods accounted for over three-fourths of the total value of exports. Any imperial hoarding of bullion through purchases on the market (and such hoarding according to our estimate should have amounted to 4.45 per cent of the *jama'*) must then have largely given a corresponding inducement to exports of craft goods. In other words, out of the 17,61,95,184 *dāms* that were transferred to the imperial hoard in the 40th regnal year, 13,21,46,388 *dāms* should have gone to support craft production.

III

The nobility claimed a large share in the extracted surplus: even the allowances paid for personal maintenance (the *z̲āt* salary), as distinct from the amount paid to meet military obligations (the pay against the *sawār*-rank), absorbed 20.89 per cent of the entire *jama'*. The amounts paid for the maintenance of animals under *z̲āt* were in addition to these two payments.

Our next concern is the manner in which this large share in the surplus (82,74,55,200 *dāms*, claimed as *z̲āt* salaries in 1595–6)[9] reaching the nobility and the lower officers of the army affected the economy. Except a few qualitative statements, no statistical data are forthcoming from our sources about the proportions in which *manṣabdārs* incurred expenses on different items of their personal establishments. We can, however, construct a hypothetical pattern on the basis of certain assumptions. First of all, we can take it that the nobles' life style mirrored, on a more moderate scale, the habits, fashions and traditions followed at the Imperial Court. For instance, the harem, the animals, the palace, the food, the employment of large retinues of servants and the propensity to hoard, were all features as prominent in the life style of the nobles as of the imperial court.[10] We can, therefore, infer that the major items of expenditure in the nobles'

[9] It may be noted that not only *sawār*-rank payments, but also payments on animals and carts required to be maintained by the *manṣabdārs* came under their *z̲āt* ranks.

[10] This may be seen from the very interesting account of the way the Mughal nobles lived, given in Pelsaert's *Remonstrantie* 1626, references that follow being in each case to printed text and English translation: the harem (313–14; tr. 64–6); animals (303; tr. 54); palace (316; tr. 66–7); kitchen and food (313–14; tr. 64–5, and 316; tr. 67–8); servants (310; tr. 61–3); hoarding (303–5; tr. 54–6). The description shows that in almost every particular, the noble's household presented a small replica of the imperial household as described by Abū'l Faẓl (especially in respect of hoarding, harem attendants, other servants, etc., for which see *infra*). See also Bernier, 213. The *Bayāẓ-i Khwushbūi'*, I.O. 828, a work written during the first two decades of Shāhjahān's reign, gives in detail all the requirements of an

households were identical with those of the imperial one:[11] only the ratios of expenses on each may have varied, for Engel's 'Law of Family Budgets' must have operated as much then as in modern societies.

Under this 'law' the proportion of income spent on necessaries declines with every increase in income, while that on comforts rises; at still higher levels the expenditure on luxuries tends to increase at a higher proportion than on comforts, with each rise in income. To apply Engel's law we have, thus, to divide all the heads of expenditure into three broad categories, namely, Necessaries (N); Comforts (C); and Luxuries (L). The significance of each of these terms is, of course, relative; and the boundaries between them tend to be blurred and to vary; the classification must, therefore, always be subjective in nature. If we suppose that Engel's Law operated from the emperor downwards, then we must also assume that, in spite of the emperor's life-style being the ideal of the entire nobility, the ratio of expenses on corresponding items could not have been the same, but must have varied, those on N and C rising in different proportions as the income decreased. In order to have such variations reflected in our estimates of the nobles' expenses, we must, therefore, first attempt a division of the corresponding imperial expenditure into N, C and L. The imperial expenditure taken into consideration must be that on the domestic establishment. This would include, besides what we have considered in Chapter 11 under imperial household, some other expenditure that formed part of the military establishment but was really domestic or personal in character. These items are brought together in Table 12.2 (see next page).

The amounts for items 2–4, 9–11 and 13–15 in Table 12.2 are those estimated for the imperial household in Chapter 10. These are directly reproduced. For the remaining items (1, 5–8 and 12) some explanation is necessary.

aristocratic household. Of special interest to us is the description of 'food and kitchen' (ff.96a–100b), buildings and orchards (ff.108a–110b), wardrobe and encampment material (ff.130b–134a), library (ff.137b–139a), animal stables (ff.126b–130a), and the arsenal (ff.135b–137a). The nobles seem to follow the life style of the emperor in every detail. The *Siyāqnāma*, 182–4, shows that the nobles too kept cheetahs, hunting birds and deer. They also maintained *ābdār-k̲h̲āna* (arrangements for water), and *mash'al-k̲h̲āna* (illumination department) as well as a *sūchī-k̲h̲āna* (wine-provisioning).

[11] The income out of which expenses were incurred on a noble's household was drawn against the *z̤āt* ranks. But out of this salary the nobles had to provide for certain items of expenditure which we have not included under the imperial household. The items on which the *z̤āt* income of *manṣabdārs* was spent did not thus totally correspond with the items of imperial household expenditure. In order to make them correspond, part of imperial expenditure on foot-retainers, armour and arsenal, beasts of burden, and display animals must be added to imperial household expenditure.

Table 12.2

	Expenditure	Amount as per cent of total expenditure	Estimated per cent of each item of expenditure			Per cent of total expenditure		
			N	C	L	N	C	L
1. Kitchen	1,60,74,000	7.04	50	20	30	3.5200	1.4080	2.112
2. Encampment material	1,03,71,182	4.54	15	35	50	0.6810	1.5890	2.270
3. Building	1,50,00,000	6.57	15	35	50	0.9855	2.2995	3.285
4. Wardrobe	1,67,32,193	7.32	10	45	45	0.7320	3.2940	3.294
5. Harem	3,25,60,000	14.25	5	45	50	0.7125	6.4125	7.125
6. Foot-retainers	1,92,60,400	8.43	5	45	50	0.4251	3.7935	4.215
7. Arsenal & armour	2,20,80,257	9.67	5	45	50	0.4835	4.3515	4.835
8. Beasts of burden	60,58,666	2.65		25	75		0.6625	1.987
9. Utensils	1,49,34,520	6.54		25	75		1.6350	4.905
10. Books & paintings	67,53,940	2.96		25	75		0.7400	2.220
11. Gems & ornaments	4,43,18,868	19.40		25	75		4.8500	14.550
12. Display animals	61,35,629	2.69			100			2.690
13. Trappings of animals	26,39,043	1.16			100			1.160
14. Hunting animals	1,30,00,000	5.69			100			5.690
15. Miscellaneous	25,00,000	1.09			100			1.090
Total	22,84,34,698	100.00						

Since a few of the high-ranking imperial ladies maintained a separate kitchen,[12] some of the total expenditure on food in the imperial household was exclusive of the expenditure we have estimated for the imperial kitchen, and belonged to expenditure in the harem. To account for this extra expenditure on food we may assume that the high-ranking women concerned spent about 10 per cent of their salaries on food and that 5 per cent of the low-grade female harem inmates were employed to serve in their kitchens. The total expenditure in the imperial household would then have been about 1,60,74,000 *dāms*, made up of 1,36,50,000 (expenditure on imperial kitchen); 14,40,000 *dāms* (10 per cent of the salary bill of the high-ranking ladies) and 9,84,000 *dāms* (5 per cent of the emoluments of the low-grade female inmates). The amount transferred from the harem to the kitchen (viz. 24,40,000 *dāms*) should be deducted from the expenditure on the imperial harem, which would be reduced to 3,25,60,000 *dāms*.

The expenditure on non-military foot-retainers is obtained by bringing together the expenses incurred on gate-keepers (13,63,200 *dāms*); guards (14,28,600 *dāms*); *mewrahs* (14,28,600 *dāms*); *kahārs* (50,40,000 *dāms*), and allowing 1,00,00,000 *dāms* for others, such as carpenters, blacksmiths, water-carriers and clerks. The total amounts to 1,92,60,400 *dāms* (see Chapter 10).

Item 7 (arsenal and armour) has been entirely transferred from imperial military expenditure to 'Domestic Establishment' to accord with such expenditure being made out of the *manṣabdārs*' *z̤āt* salaries.

As for item 8, there were 800 carts in use in the imperial household establishment, 600 carrying fuel for the imperial kitchen and 200 for the transport of building material.[13] One cart was pulled by four oxen, and so 3,200 oxen must have been required. The monthly expenditure on an ox being 155 *dāms*,[14] the annual expenditure on beasts of burden would work out at 60,58,666 *dāms*.

Item 12, imperial expenses on display animals, consisted of (i) imperial expenditure on *k͟hāṣa* elephants (26,14,800 *dāms*),[15] and (ii) expenses incurred on horses belonging to six *k͟hāṣa* stables of 40 horses each.[16] The monthly expenditure on a horse has been taken as 846 *dāms* (20 per cent higher than the allowance sanctioned to *manṣabdārs* for 'Irāqī, the

[12] See Chapter 11.

[13] *Ā'īn*, I, 151–2.

[14] See Chapter 10, Section III.

[15] Ibid.

[16] *Ā'īn*, I, 141.

most superior breed, which was 720 *dāms* per month).[17] These *khāṣa* horses are stated to have been worth more than 70 *muhrs* each.[18] Assuming their average price to be 100 *muhrs* and their working life twelve years,[19] the annual cost of purchase should be 7,20,000 *dāms*.

Taking 100 camels to belong to the *khāṣa* stables and allowing the sanctioned expenditure of 288 *dāms* a month (see Chapter 10), the maintenance cost of camels comes to 3,45,600 *dāms* a year. If the camel's average cost is taken to be twelve *muhrs* and active life-span twelve years (Chapter 10), the annual expenses on purchase of camels can be estimated at 36,000 *dāms* a year. The total on display animals is thus made up as follows:

	dāms
Elephants: Maintenance cost	26,14,829
Horses: Maintenance cost	24,19,200
Horses: Purchase cost	7,20,000
Camels: Maintenance cost	3,45,600
Camels: Purchase cost	36,000
Total	61,35,629

Charities forming part of the imperial household budget are here excluded.

The items that we have now brought together so as to let the imperial expenditure correspond with expenditure from the *manṣabdārs' ẕāt* pay, is divided into N, C and L, on the basis of what we know of the actualities of the expenditure (described in Chapters 10 and 11). They are considered entirely from the point of view of the imperial family (the emperor, his wives, concubines, princesses and other ladies). Obviously the 'family' here was of an extraordinarily large size; the average family size would naturally diminish with the diminishing income of *manṣabdārs*.

Table 12.2 thus gives us the following distribution for imperial domestic expenditure: N, 7.5 per cent; C, 31 per cent; and L, 61.5 per cent.

With these ratios forming the starting point, we offer in Fig.12.1 our reconstruction of N, C and L curves for different levels of income in the nobility, the cavalry and lower classes. The terminal points of the N: C: L ratios, for the two levels of the common people, are derived from data examined in Chapter 11.

[17] Ibid., 176.

[18] Ibid., 145.

[19] Chapter 10.

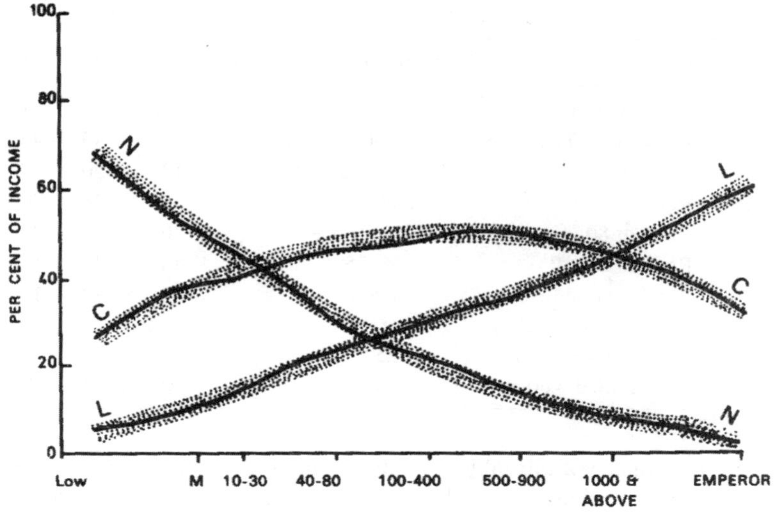

Figure 12.1

Assumed Pattern of Expenditure by Income Level

We have here followed a division of nobles, and others into seven classes adopted by Akbar's administration itself when it imposed a levy on marriages. *Manṣabdārs* were then divided into (i) those holding ranks of 5,000 to 1,000; (ii) those holding ranks below 1,000 down to 500; (iii) below 500 to a *ṣadī* (rank of 100); (iv) below 100 to the rank of 40; (v) from *tarkashbands* (*manṣabdārs* holding the rank of 30) to *dahbāshī* (holder of 10). The other two categories were: *miyāna mardum* (middle-class people) and *'āmma* (common men).[20] *Manṣabdārs* of ranks of above 5,000 were apparently exempted from the levy; but I have included these *manṣabdārs* (which included princes) in category (i). The actual income-levels of each category have been determined in categories (i) to (v) on the basis of the *ẕāt* salary-schedules of *manṣabdārs* in the *Ā'īn-i Akbarī*; those of category (vi), the 'middle class', on the pay scales sanctioned for *aḥadīs* and *tābīnān* (cavalrymen) (see Chapters 9 and 10); and of the 'common people' at two levels of pay (skilled and unskilled) on salaries and wages for employees and attendants in the *Ā'īn* (see Chapter 14).

The curves in Fig.12.1 are read in Table 12.3, which gives the classification of *manṣabdārs* and officials as well as the proportions of expenditure on N, C and L.

[20] *Ā'īn*, I, 180–6.

Table 12.3

		Income (Rs/month)	N	C	L
	The emperor	9,31,843	7.5	31	61.5
(i)	Rank of 1,000 and above	60,000–8,000	9	45	46
(ii)	Rank of 900–500	7,700–2,100	13	50	37
(iii)	Rank of 400–100	2,000–500	22	48	30
(iv)	Rank of 80–40	410–185	30	46	24
(v)	Rank of 30–10	175–75	45	40	15
(vi)	'Rank of middle class'	18–8.6	50	39	11
(vii)	'Common people'				
	I (skilled workers)	5.25	75	20	5
	II (unskilled workers)	1.50	90	10	0

In making use of this table for determining the nature of the diffusion of surplus, let us remember that we are concerned here only with the pattern of expenditure of those categories which were directly paid out of the imperial revenues. Thus the expenditure ascribed to the emperor comprehended, as we have seen, the expenditure on the imperial household and a small part of expenditure on the military establishment. The *manṣabdārs* received their pay directly from the imperial resources, by way of *jāgīr* and cash; and the *aḥadīs* and *tābīnān* from the imperial army establishment and the *sawār* payments to *manṣabdārs*. Those belonging to category (vii), 'Common people' are not involved in this distribution of surplus, and have been ignored for the purposes of this chapter.

Of the seven categories listed above, the incomes of the *manṣabdārs*, categories (i) to (v) have already been computed (Chapter 9, Table 9.2). We have now to estimate what proportions of these incomes were spent on the items considered in Table 12.2 and what were the other burdens, constant or varying, on their salaries. First, a substantial part of their income must have been saved and hoarded, notably in the form of coined and uncoined gold and silver. Transfers to the hoard accounted for 23.72 per cent of the total imperial household budget. The nobles, as Pelsaert tells us, were also great hoarders of wealth;[21] but, of course, the proportion of income available for addition to their hoard must have been

[21] *Remonstrantie*, 304; tr. 55. One gets an idea of how much was hoarded by the nobles from the fact that in 1645 the emperor acquired 60 lakh rupees in cash from a deceased noble's property, while another left behind 1 crore of rupees in cash and goods (1657). Cf. Habib, 'Potentialities of Capitalistic Development, etc', *Essays in History*, 208.

smaller. The proportions, for the five categories of *manṣabdārs*, have been assumed to be respectively 28, 18, 16, 14 and 12 per cent of the total personal salary. These assumptions are naturally arbitrary; but the fact of declining proportions should be incontestable.

Secondly, a part of all *manṣabdārs*' earnings was paid out in charity. We have assumed the traditional *zakāt* rate of 2.5 per cent (one in forty) for such expenditure.[22] Thirdly, we have allowed a very small percentage (1 per cent of the income) for presents and offerings (*naẕr*) made to the emperor. Since this amount has not been taken into account by us in the imperial budget, it has to appear here.

The total estimated net income for each class of nobles remaining after these deductions, is given in column 2 of Table 12.4 (next page), together with savings, charities and *naẕr* in columns 2–4 and 13. Thereafter, expenses out of the balance of income (column 5) divided into N, C, and L are set out in columns 6, 7 and 8 as computed on the basis of ratios fixed in Table 12.3.

With the ratios of various heads in N, C, and L in hand (Table 12.2), the total expenditure by *manṣabdārs* on various individual items can now be computed (using the proportions established for the various items of expenditure in Figure 12.1).

That is, expenditure on item number i

$$\frac{\mathrm{N}\times\mathrm{Ni}}{\sum_{i=1}^{15} Ni}+\frac{\mathrm{C}\times\mathrm{Ci}}{\sum_{i=1}^{15} Ci}+\frac{\mathrm{L}\times\mathrm{Li}}{\sum_{i=1}^{15} Ni}$$

where

N = Total expenditure on Necessaries
C = Total expenditure on Comforts
L = Total expenditure on Luxuries

and

N_i = Expenditure on item number i on Necessaries
C_i = Expenditure on item number i on Comforts
L_i = Expenditure on item number i on Luxuries

[22] In 1660 at the order of Mir Jumla, the government of Bengal, all, non-imperial grants were resumed and the grantees were asked to cultivate their lands and pay the revenue as ordinary land-holders. This measure caused much distress among the grantees, and the next governor (Shā'ista Khān) ruled that every *jāgīrdār* should reinstate the grants as long as the revenue lost to him did not exceed 2.5% of the total revenue (Shihābuddin Tālish, *Fatḥiya-i 'Ibriya*, Bodl. Or 589, f.51b).

Table 12.4

Category	1 Total Income	2 Savings	3 Charity	4 *Nazr*	5 Net income	6 N	7 C	8 L
Ranks of 1000 and above	45,13,92,000	9,02,78,400	1,12,84,800	45,13,920	34,53,14,880	3,10,78,339	15,53,91,696	15,88,44,845
Below 1000 to 500	9,47,04,000	1,70,46,720	23,67,600	9,47,040	7,43,42,640	96,64,543	3,71,71,320	2,75,06,777
Below 500 to 100	18,30,91,200	2,92,94,592	45,77,280	18,30,912	14,73,88,416	3,24,25,452	7,07,46,440	4,42,16,525
Below 100 to 40	7,13,08,800	99,83,232	17,82,720	7,13,088	5,88,29,760	1,76,48,928	2,70,61,690	1,41,19,142
Ranks of 30 to 40	2,69,59,200	32,35,104	6,73,980	2,69,592	2,27,80,524	1,02,51,236	91,12,210	34,17,079
Total	82,74,55,200	14,98,38,048	2,06,86,380	82,74,552	64,86,56,220	10,10,68,498	29,94,83,356	24,81,04,368

Table 12.5

	Items	Annual Expenditure	
1.	Kitchen	6,93,24,924	
2.	Encampment material	3,36,34,853	
3.	Building	4,86,74,427	
4.	Wardrobe	5,49,07,253	
5.	Harem	10,02,11,651	
6.	Foot-retainers	5,92,83,042	
7.	Arsenal & armour	6,80,03,062	
8.	Beasts of burden	1,44,20,240	
9.	Utensils	3,55,88,268	
10.	Books and paintings	1,61,07,373	
11.	Precious stones and jewellery	10,55,67,412	
12.	Display animals	1,08,64,738	
13.	Animals' trappings	46,85,203	
14.	Hunting and pet animals	2,29,81,411	
15.	Miscellaneous	44,02,364	
	Sub-Total		64,86,56,221
16.	Charity	2,06,86,380	
17.	*Nazr*	82,74,552	
18.	Savings	14,98,38,048	
	Total		82,74,55,201

The results of the calculations are given in Table 12.5 above where the amounts for items 16, 17 and 18 only are brought forward from Table 12.4.

Given this distribution of the *manṣabdārs*' income, we can derive certain inferences about the character of the diffusion of surplus that it points to. As suggested above, while discussing imperial household expenditure, the amounts incurred on the wardrobe, encampment material, building, arsenal and armour, gems and jewellery, utensils, books and paintings, trappings of animals, a third of the expenses on the harem[23] and one-sixth of the amount spent on beasts of burden and display animals—in all, 40,47,85,898 *dāms*—should have gone directly to promote craft production. The amount which was hoarded as well as that which, by way of presents to the emperor became a part of the imperial hoard, was kept in the form of gold and silver (coined and uncoined) and must

[23] Representing the amount spent by the ladies of the harem on craft-made articles (comforts as well as luxuries).

have been built up mainly by acquisition of bullion. Again, since gold and silver were largely imported, at least three-fourths of these must have been paid for by export of high-value craft goods.

Thus we find that in all 52,33,70,348 *dāms*, that is, 63.26 per cent of the entire amount paid as personal salaries to nobles, went in various ways to support the craft sector. This is certainly a larger proportion than one would have expected. But since the emphasis was on quality rather than quantity, the volume of production in physical terms might not have been large.

The proportion of nobles' income funnelled into the service sector seems to have sustained a large entourage of unproductively employed labour. In a noble's harem, says Pelsaert, every wife was attended upon by ten to 100 maidservants.[24] This duplicated, on a minor scale, the pattern of the imperial harem, where 4,700 women served 300 ladies of the imperial family. Pelsaert's description shows that the nobles' retinues, excluding the harem, also contained an exceedingly large number of servants. Some were employed simply for display, or to keep running before their master's horse; these were, in addition to the *farrāshs* (tent-pitchers), the *mash'alchīs* (torch-bearers), runners to convey messages, palanquin-bearers and numerous other attendants.[25] In addition, there were the keepers of animals. By and large we can assume that the service sector was supported by the same heads of expenditure of the nobles' household budget as that of the imperial household, estimated above by a scrutiny of the *Ā'īn*'s description of the imperial establishment.[26] The sum given away in charity representing, in part, payment to unemployed persons or gentlemen-idlers also maintained what was in essence an unproductive sector. On the whole, then, 15,02,94,198 *dāms*, i.e., 18.16 per cent of the nobles' total personal income may be supposed to have been channelled into the service sector. The proportion in terms of money was not high, but, as Pelsaert remarks, wages too were very low; the number of those employed out of a relatively smaller share of nobles' income could therefore still have been 'exceedingly numerous'.[27]

[24] *Remonstrantie*, 313; tr., 64.

[25] Ibid., 310; tr., 61–2.

[26] I have accordingly assumed that the following items went to support employment in service sector; (i) one-fourth of the expenses on the harem; (ii) nine-tenths of expenses on hunting animals; (iii) one-fourth of the costs incurred on display animals and beasts of burden; (iv) one-fifth of kitchen expenses; (v) the entire amount spent on 'miscellaneous' items; and (vi) the entire sum paid to the foot-retainers.

[27] Pelsaert's words (*Remonstrantie*, 310; tr., 61).

With the craft and service sectors accounted for, the balance, being 18.5 per cent of the *manṣabdārs*' personal salaries (i.e., 15,37,90,655 *dāms*), may be taken to have been spent on direct consumption of rural produce.

A part of the appropriated surplus received by *manṣabdārs* in allowances for animals maintained against the *ẕāt* rank was also partly drained into the service sector. A detailed breakdown of the sanctioned costs of maintenance provided by Abū'l Faẓl indicates that on average around a quarter of the allowance was set aside for salaries of the animal keepers.[28]

We can work out the number of employees paid out of this amount. According to the schedule given in the *Ā'īn-i Akbarī*, which sets out the number of horses, elephants, camels, mules, and carts to be maintained under the *ẕāt* requirements by *manṣabdārs* of various ranks,[29] the number of animals maintained by all the *manṣabdārs* in service in 1595–6, works out at 25,921 horses, 7,709 elephants, and 23,730 camels. There should in addition have been 10,400 carts. We may allow one groom to a horse and one sweeper and one water-carrier for the stable of, say, 20 horses; and as prescribed by the imperial administration, three attendants for each *shergīr*, *sāda* or *manjhola* elephant (such elephants numbered 5,164) and two for each *karra* or *phundarkiya* elephant (there being 2,545 such elephants); one keeper (*sārbān*) for a camel; one for a mule;[30] and one driver (*bahlīwān*) for each cart. The total number of animal keepers and cartmen employed by *manṣabdārs* would then add up to 84,390. The entire amount paid in their salaries being 9,28,55,214 *dāms* per annum, their wages on average should have come to about 92 *dāms* a month. The wages sanctioned in the *Ā'īn* varied as we have seen, from 45 to 120 *dāms* a month; and our average rate derived from our estimate of the number of persons employed happens to fall very reasonably within the range.

One-sixth of the total maintenance costs for the *manṣabdārs*' animals must have been directly spent on craft-produced commodities (saddles, reins, chains, buckets, etc.) while the costs incurred on the purchase of imported horses again can be regarded as an indirect inducement to

[28] *Ā'īn*, I, 176–8. In the case of horses the salary of grooms constituted, on an average, 17.6% of the total sanctioned expenditure, but the proportion was much higher for elephants, being over 31% of the total allowance.

[29] *Ā'īn*, I, 180–6.

[30] To provide one keeper for a mule may suggest an excessive degree of care for the animal; but see *Ā'īn*, I, 177, where this is recommended.

export of craft-goods. Assuming the working life of a horse to be twelve years[31] and the average price to be fifteen *muhrs* (ten *muhrs* being the minimum price of a horse belonging to the imperial stables), the total cost of replacement of horses annually should have been about 1,16,64,450 *dāms*. Since more than half of these were of high breeds brought form Persia and Central Asia, with prices much higher than those of Indian breeds, around 75 per cent of the total purchase cost may be assigned for the purchase of imported horses. That is, on the whole 6,87,07,401 *dāms* or about 20 per cent of the total allowances on animals must have gone towards purchasing craft-goods and horses.

The balance, 20,98,58,241 *dāms*, comprising the expenditure on fodder and grain, represented direct consumption.

IV

To get a complete pattern of diffusion of the surplus, we must enquire how the imperial cavalrymen (*aḥadīs*) and nobles' horsemen (*tābīnān*) consumed the income derived from the salaries paid to them.

Mughal cavalrymen were genetlemen-troopers having fairly large establishments with retinues of servants.[32] The *aḥadīs* and the *tābīnān* can, therefore, be taken to constitute Abū'l Faẕl's category of the 'middle-class' (Category VI). Applying the ratios worked out in Table 12.3 for this category, we can also reconstruct their pattern of expenditure. But while we may assume that all the *aḥadīs*, who were imperial servants, were paid in cash and were quartered in towns, this cannot be assumed for all the *tābīnān*, some of whom were paid by their aristocratic masters through sub-assignments of portions of *jāgīrs*.[33] They might well have 'lived off the land', their income representing a more or less direct consumption of the agricultural surplus. We can take it that perhaps not more than one-fourth of the cavalrymen could have held sub-assignments in this fashion: this is, of course an arbitrary, though not unreasonable, estimate.[34]

The amount received by all *aḥadīs* in 1595–6 as personal salaries works out at 2,66,28,240 *dāms*; the remaining 5,62,29,360 *dāms* were to be spent on their horses. The sum paid to all the *tābīnān* collectively in personal allowance was 66,35,13,312 *dāms*.[35] We have assumed above

[31] See Chapter 10.

[32] *Remonstrantie*, 310; tr., 61; Manucci, II, 75*n*.

[33] Cf. Habib, *Agrarian System*, 285–6, rev. ed. 329–30.

[34] Had a few sample studies of the size of the *jāgīrdārs*' own *k͟hāliṣa* within their *jāgīrs* been available, this point could perhaps have been elucidated much better.

that, at a minimum, three-fourths of them must have been stationed in towns. This implies that at least 49,76,34,984 *dāms* flowed into the urban economy through this channel. The total personal income of *aḥadīs* and that of three-fourths of the *tābīnān* adds up to 52,42,63,224 *dāms*. Assuming that these urban gentlemen-troopers saved 10 per cent of their income, gave 2.5 per cent in charity, and 1 per cent in *naẕrs* to their superiors, the balance spent by them would have been 45,34,87,689 *dāms*. Using the ratios for N, C, and L set out in Table 12.3, the expenditure on necessaries works out at 22,67,43,844 *dāms*; on comforts 17,68,60,199 *dāms*; and on luxuries 4,98,83,646 *dāms*. Proceeding in the same manner as for the *manṣabdārs*, we can now estimate the expenses incurred on various items by the cavalrymen (Table 12.6).

Table 12.6

Cavalrymen

	Items	Amounts	
1.	Food/kitchen	11,56,48,676	
2.	Encampment material	3,13,88,399	
3.	Building	4,54,23,477	
4.	Clothing/ wardrobe	4,34,70,682	
5.	Harem	6,37,66,178	
6.	Attendants/ foot-retainers	3,77,22,852	
7.	Weapons and armour	4,32,71,519	
8.	Beasts of burden	53,89,370	
9.	Utensils	1,33,00,507	
10.	Books, etc.	60,19,849	
11.	Gems and ornaments	3,94,53,964	
12.	Display animals	21,84,455	
13.	Animals' trappings	9,42,003	
14.	Hunting and pet animals	46,20,622	
15.	Miscellaneous	8,85,136	
	Sub-total		45,34,87,689
16.	Charity	1,31,06,581	
17.	*Naẕr*	52,42,632	
18.	Savings	5,24,26,323	
	Total		52,42,63,224

[35] For detailed calculations on which these estimates of personal salaries of *aḥadīs* and *tābīnān* are offered, see Appendix 12.A.

Taking Table 12.6 and using the same criteria for categorizing items of expenditure as for nobles, we find that as much as 28,90,39,811 *dāms*, that is, 55.13 per cent of the cavalrymen's personal income, is likely to have directly or indirectly supported craft production; 9,68,37,865 *dāms*, or 18.47 per cent went towards service-sector employment; and the remainder represented a direct consumption of the agrarian surplus.

The total amounts given as allowances for horses were: 5,62,29,360 *dāms* to *aḥadīs*, and 1,37,54,20,488 *dāms* to *tābīnān* (see Appendix 12-A). A part of these sums must have been spent on the purchase of horses, whether these were procured by the cavalrymen themselves or were provided, in the first instance, by their employer (the emperor, for the *aḥadīs*; the nobles, for the *tābīnān*), with deductions made later from their salaries.[36] If the working-life span of these horses was, on an average, ten years (lower than those of imperial horses and the *manṣabdārs*' horses since their mortality rate was probably higher on account of being used in action more often), then 29,284.2 horses must have had to be purchased every year. The average price of a cavalry horse may fairly be put at ten *muhrs*;[37] if so, 10,54,23,120 *dāms* must have been spent annually on procurement of horses. It is possible that many of the horses of this level of cavalry were not imported, but bred from imported horses, or procured from horse-breeding areas within the empire.[38] But even if the number of imported horses was fewer—about 60 per cent of the total[39]—the higher prices they fetched makes it unlikely that they accounted for less than three-fourths of the total cost of annual procurement of cavalry horses. For reasons already touched upon, this amount (7,90,67,340 *dāms*) must then have gone quite largely to promote the craft sector for whose products an external market was created by such imports.

After deducting the costs of purchasing horses the amount left for maintenance should have been 5,23,64,400 *dāms* for *aḥadīs* and 1,27,38,62,328 *dāms* for *tābīnān*. Of the latter, we have to allow up to one-fourth as going to cavalrymen feeding their horses in their rural sub-assignments. For maintenance of town-based cavalry, then, we are left with 1,00,77,146 *dāms*.

[36] *Ā'īn*, I, 187, 196.

[37] See Chapter 10. The quality of the imperial horses must, of course, have been greatly superior to the ordinary cavalry horses.

[38] For these see the *Ā'īn*, I, 140–1, 177.

[39] We may take 55 per cent of the horses belonging to the *tābīnān* as imported (cf. R.A. Alavi, 'New Light on Mughal Cavalry' (*Medieval India—A Miscellany*, IV, 74). The proportion should be even higher in the case of *aḥadīs* since they received at least their first horse from the imperial establishment (*Ā'īn*, I, 187).

According to the detailed breakdown of the allowances sanctioned for the maintenance of Turkī horses, which the *tābīnān* usually maintained, 60 per cent was to be spent on food and fodder, 20 per cent on payment to grooms and 20 per cent on saddles, trappings, etc.[40] On this basis, we can say that 20,15,52,229 *dāms* must have gone towards the wages of low-paid unskilled workers. About an equal amount was spent on craft products for the horses' equipage.[41] The expenses on grain and fodder would have been 60,46,56,688 *dāms*.

Table 12.7 (next page) presents detailed estimates of the portion of the appropriated surplus which went towards supporting employment in the service sector and the portion which was channelled into the craft-sector.

The estimated expenses on craft production thus amounted to 37.38 per cent of the *jama'*. The share that found its way directly into the service sector accounted for 17.28 per cent. The remaining 45.34 per cent seems to have taken the form of direct consumption of agrarian produce.[42]

This distribution of surplus might appear to suggest that the proportion of the *jama'* that went directly to create employment for unproductive labour was not very large, being a mere 17 per cent of the entire extracted surplus. We must, however, keep in mind the low wages paid when forming any impression of the numbers employed.

The part of the revenue income spent on craft products was considerable—more than one-third of the *jama'*. But while the investment on craft goods was rather larger than one would have expected, it did not necessarily contribute to the production of large quantities of commodities. Rather, the demand was for goods of high value (being products of high skill) or rarities (such as precious stones obtained from mines by the deployment of a large amount of labour). Putting it differently, we can say that there was yet no 'home-market', representing an effective demand for large amounts of manufactured goods of moderate values.[43]

The amount that went into the urban service-sector and the portion of the agricultural surplus consumed directly took, in all, about 63 per cent of the

[40] *Ā'īn*, I, 177. These horses were usually *yābū* and *tāzī* (see Chapter 10).

[41] Sometimes, however, a part of the salary was paid in the form of old trappings, etc., from the emperor's or noble's stables (*Ā'īn*, I, 187, 196; Pelsaert, *Remonstrantie*, 310–11; tr. 62–3).

[42] The share would, however, be smaller if we assume that less than 25% of the nobles' cavalry held rural sub-assignments.

[43] Such demand, making for product duplication, creates the ideal conditions for large-scale factory production. This is, of course, the Marxian, and not the popular, definition of the term 'home-market'. I know of no other term which can stand for the sense I have in mind here.

Table 12.7

	Total	Craft sector	Service sector	Direct consumption
Imperial Expenditure				
Army (excluding *aḥadīs*)	27,60,64,720	6,40,40,785	10,45,80,792	10,74,43,143
Household	18,73,99,746	12,24,16,413	3,81,80,000	2,68,03,333
Savings	17,61,95,184	13,21,46,388	—	4,40,48,796
Total	63,96,59,650	31,86,03,586	14,27,60,792	17,82,95,272
Nobles' Expenditure				
Personal pay	82,74,55,200	40,47,85,898	15,02,94,197	11,42,62,505
Nazr		62,05,914	—	20,68,638
Savings	14,98,38,048	11,23,78,536	—	3,74,59,512
Allowance for animals	37,14,20,856	6,87,07,401	9,28,55,214	20,98,58,241
Total	1,19,88,76,056	59,20,77,749	24,31,49,411	36,36,48,896
Cavalrymen's Expenditure				
Personal pay	69,01,41,552	24,57,88,096	9,68,37,865	28,98,46,634
Nazr		39,31,974	—	13,10,658
Savings		3,93,19,744	—	1,31,06,581
Allowance for horses	1,43,16,49,848	28,06,19,569	20,15,52,229	94,94,78,050
Total	2,12,17,91,400	56,96,59,383	29,83,90,094	1,25,37,41,923
Grand Total	3,96,03,27,106	1,48,03,40,718	68,43,00,297	1,79,56,86,091
Percentage		37.38%	17.28%	45.34%

jama'. This perhaps indicates that the conditions obtaining in the Mughal empire were more akin to 'Phase A' than to 'Phase B' of the hypothetical economic organization we had considered at the beginning of this chapter. In other words, the distribution of the surplus took place according to a pattern in which a major part of it took the shape of food-crops and fodder, and maintained a population unconnected with material production. The basis for any real accumulation of capital out of agriculture could not have arisen so long as this remained the dominant form of consumption of the surplus.

At the same time, our estimates offer us some indication of the size and character of the urban economy. In our estimates the service sector considered is totally urban, and so also, more or less, is the craft sector. We can thus say that at least 54.66 per cent of the entire *jama'* was directed to sustaining the urban sector.

APPENDIX 12.A

The total number of *aḥadīs* at Akbar's death according to Pelsaert was 4,441 of which 741 were *chahāraspa*, 1,322 *sih-aspa*, 1,428 *do-aspa* and 950 *yak-aspa* (see Chapter 10, section I). The horses maintained were Turkī and Yābū; the allowance sanctioned for the maintenance of a Turkī horse was 6,720 *dāms* and for Yābū, 5,760 *dāms* per annum. The *aḥadi's* personal allowance was 3,840 *dāms* a year in all the four categories, but savings on the first horse have been estimated at 5 per cent; on the second, 15 per cent; on the third, 25 per cent; and on the fourth, 30 per cent (see Chapter 10). The total of personal salaries computed accordingly are given below in *dāms*:

Personal salary in *dāms*	Number of *aḥadīs*	Total in *dāms*
8,688	741	64,37,808
6,672	1,322	88,20,384
5,216	1,428	74,48,448
4,128	950	39,21,600
Total	4,441	2,66,28,240

Since the total estimated expenditure on *aḥadīs* was 8,28,57,600 *dāms* per annum, the total allowance for horses would amount to 5,62,29,360 *dāms* (8,28,57,600 *less* 2,66,28,240).

For *tābīnān*, the total estimated *sawār* ranks against which salary was paid amounted to 1,88,070. A fourth of these have been assumed to be *dāghī* and three-fourths *barāwurdī*. This implies that the number of cavalrymen actually maintained was at least 1,41,053. The *tābīnān* usually maintained Turkī horses (Chapter 9). If we assume the standard composition of 3 *sih-aspa*, 4 *do-aspas* and 3 *yak-aspa*, then with same allowances and assumptions as for the *aḥadīs*, the *tābīnān*'s total personal incomes can be calculated as follows (in *dāms*):

	Number	Salary in *dāms*	Total income in *dāms*
sih-aspas	42,316	5,280	22,34,28,480
do-aspas	56,421	4,704	26,54,04,384
yak-aspas	42,316	4,128	17,46,80,448
Total			66,35,13,312

The total salary paid against *sawār* ranks in 1595–6 has been estimated at 2,03,89,33,806 *dāms* (Chapter 9). Deducting from it the personal allowance for the *tābīnān* calculated above, the balance constituting the maintenance allowance for horses would have amounted to 1,37,54,20,488 *dāms*.

THE URBAN ECONOMY

CHAPTER 13

The Extent of Urbanization

I

As is widely recognized, the Mughal ruling class was almost entirely town-centred. Though their income depended on the expropriation of a large portion of the agricultural surplus, the *jāgīrdārs* and their retinue only partly lived directly 'off the land'. *Jāgīrs*, being service assignments, were not hereditary and the system of transfer of posts and *jāgīrs* was deliberately designed to prevent the development of any local roots.[1] The relationship between the *jāgīrdār* and villages in his *jāgīr* revolved almost entirely around his claim to the bulk of the peasant's surplus in the form of land revenue. His own establishment, domestic as well as military, was usually quartered in the towns or in camps away from his *jāgīr*(*s*). The net revenue realized (the *jama'*) was thus in large part drained away from the countryside to maintain the Emperor's and *jāgīrdārs*' establishments and retinue in the towns.

Let us, first, begin with the expenditure incurred on urban craft production out of revenues received by the ruling class. As shown in Table 12.7 in Chapter 12 we have estimated that 1,19,64,96,050 *dāms* were spent net of savings on craft commodities, a portion whereof must have gone to maintain the producers at a subsistence level. It is naturally difficult to determine the precise portions contributed by raw material and labour to the total value of craft goods. Nevertheless, some rough indications can be used to work out an approximate ratio. Pelsaert tells us of

[1] The *waṯan jāgīrs* (and the *altūn-tamgha* grants instituted by Jahāngīr) were exceptions, and might be thought to represent a possible beginning of ruralization; but these assignments remained limited in extent. Cf. Habib, *Agrarian System*, rev. ed., 302&*n*.

articles made of silver and gold which were generally in demand (like bedsteads, fan-handles, dishes, cups, betel boxes), that, 'provided the workmanship is good, half the silver might be paid for manufacture.'[2] This implies that even in the case of high-value goods made of silver the cost of labour (in this particular case, of craftsmanship) could amount to a third of the total value. This may, by its context, be taken as the floor of the share of labour in the value of manufactures. For the ceiling, let us take coarse cloth. According to data collected by Buchanan early in the nineteenth century the cost of yarn accounted for 72.6 per cent of the total value of coarse cloth,[3] while the price of uncleaned cotton used in it amounted to 44.3 per cent of the total value of yarn.[4] In other words, the basic cost of raw material in cloth was 32.162 per cent of the value of the end-product; and that of labour, 67.838 per cent. This, since we are here speaking only of a low-priced product, may serve as the ceiling for the share of labour in the cost of manufactures. Thus, taking silverware and coarse cloth to set the two limits, the range of the share of craft labour would seem to have varied from about one-third to two-thirds of the total market value. Here we may note that in the case of silver the mining-labour costs are already embedded in the value of silver metal, just as in the price of raw cotton the cost of peasant-labour is included. The costs in agriculture are already included in our estimate of the value of total agricultural production; and for metals and precious stones the costs should be covered in our estimates of value of extractive industries (see Chapter 18). Keeping, therefore, to costs of what may be called post-raw-material labour, we should not perhaps be far wrong if we assume parity between the cost of labour and the value of raw material in manufactures generally, looking for a mean between labour-costs in silver and coarse cloth, although we may have to make exceptions where high-priced or inferior qualities of products might be involved.

Given the inferences, set out above, half of the amount spent by the emperor, ruling class and cavalry on craft commodities (viz. 59,82,48,025 *dāms*) as per Table 12.7 may, then, be assumed to have been spent on providing wages to the workmen.

To this figure we ought to add the demand for urban manufacture generated by staff engaged in urban and rural taxation. Now we have estimated that the *jama'* (J) of the Empire in its territories in 1595–6 was

[2] Pelsaert, *Remonstrantie*, 169, tr. 27.

[3] F. Buchanan, *An Account of the Districts of Bihar and Patna in 1811–1812*, Vol.II, Patna, 1928, p.774.

[4] Ibid., Vol.I, pp.536–7.

4,06,11,23,580 *dāms* (*vide* Chapter 8), from which 10 per cent should be deducted on account of urban taxation (*vide* Appendix 13B). We therefore get the figures of 3,65,50,11,222 *dāms* for agrarian and 40,61,12,358 *dāms* for urban taxation, both excluding costs of collection. In the agrarian taxation, we need to increase the amount (J) by 43 per cent to obtain the figure of gross taxation (J′) (*vide* Chapter 5), viz. 5,22,66,66,047 *dāms*. These estimates are important for us, since we will have occasions to refer to them frequently in our calculations below. For the moment, we need to work out from these figures the income of the staff that was employed in tax-collection, and see how much was spent out of it on urban manufactures. In Chapter 5 we found that in connection with land-revenue the expenditure on collection staff was held to be 20 per cent., or 1,04,53,33,209 *dāms*; for urban taxation, we have suggested that the expenditure on corresponding staff could have been 10 per cent of the gross collection. The gross urban taxation should, then, have amounted to (40,61,12,358 × 1.111 =) 45,11,90,830 *dāms*, of which the income of the collection staff should (at 10 per cent) have amounted to 4,51,19,083 *dāms*. Now while the collection-staff for urban taxation should have been entirely town-based, we can hardly assume this to have been the case with the land-revenue staff, of which the portion based in the towns could have hardly claimed more than a tenth of the collection costs. On this basis we may put the total expenditure on town-based revenue-collection staff at (10,45,33,321 + 4,51,19,083 =) 14,96,52,404 *dāms*. If at least 20 per cent of the income of this class of persons went into consumption of urban manufactures, we may put the value of such manufactures at 2,99,30,481 *dāms*, out of which the wage-costs would be 1,49,65,240 *dāms*.

Here a minor addition may also be made of the expenditure on crafts by the imperial land-grantees. Though they held land in the villages they were mainly a town-based class,[5] and their expenditure on urban craft products may therefore be assumed to have been at least about 25 per cent of their income, considering that for cavalrymen we have also estimated such expenditure at about 25 per cent of their income.[6] The *Ā'īn* puts the *jama'* alienated through land-grants (*suyūrghāl*), excluding Khandesh (which has no *suyūrghāl* figures) and Berar, at 10,07,96,474 *dāms*;[7] and this would mean, under our above assumption, an expenditure of 2,51,99,118 *dāms* a year on urban craft products. Assuming parity

[5] See our own discussion in Chapter 6, Sec.II.

[6] See Table 12.7, where the expenditure on craft-goods (*less* savings) amounts to 53,03,39,639 *dāms*, or 24.99 per cent of the cavalrymen's income.

[7] See Appendix I.A to Chapter 1, Table of *Suyūrghāl* statistics.

between material and labour costs, the value thus added to urban manufactures should have been 1,25,99,559 *dāms*.

The *zamīndārs* and village headmen too must have spent some amount on superior quality cloth, muskets, other weapons, ornaments and other luxury craft-goods, such as were mainly produced in the towns. (This should exclude savings, which if put in the hoard in the form of silver coins, would have mainly gone to induce production of urban manufactures, to pay for imported bullion). We assume that *zamīndārs* (who included the big territorial chiefs in their ranks), after paying for their retainers spent on goods drawn from towns about 25 per cent of their net income, the net income of the *zamīndārs* being 40,60,80,374 *dāms* (see Appendix 13.C), the amount spent on urban products comes to 10,15,20,094 *dāms*. Assuming that the headmen and local hereditary officials, out of their income of 36,58,66,232 *dāms* (assumed to be 7 per cent of J′) and *zamīndārs*' cavalry from the amount of 38,45,58,000 *dāms* they received from *zamīndārs* (*vide* Appendix 13.C), spent a much lower proportion, but not less than 5 per cent of their income on urban manufactures, their expenditure would have amounted to 3,75,21,212 *dāms*. Thus urban manufacture consumed by the *zamīndārs*, headmen, and *zamīndārs*' cavalry should have amounted in value to 13,90,41,306 *dams* yielding the figure of 6,95,20,653 *dāms* for value added in manufactures.

In Chapter 14, which is to follow the present chapter, we set forth reasons for inferring that in the central regions of the empire an ordinary family of 4–5 persons spent for bare subsistence 342.64 *dāms* on food, and 212.3 *dāms* per annum on clothing. If this ratio represented the expenditure of lower levels of ordinary townspeople on urban and rural products, then we may suppose that out of the 68,43,00,297 *dāms* spent by the ruling class and the cavalry on the service sector, which thereby constituted the income of the domestic and other servants and some professionals living in the towns (*vide* Table 12.7), 38.26 per cent thereof, viz. 26,18,13,294 *dāms*, was spent on urban manufactures. In addition we must consider the demand of a similar nature created by other servants being those of merchants, shopkeepers, and other individuals, not included among those directly maintained from the income of categories listed in Table 12.7. We have no means of knowing how many these were. If we take it that they could not have been more than a fifth of those maintained by the imperial establishment, officials and cavalrymen, as shown in Table 12.7, their income on that basis should have amounted to 13,68,60,059 *dāms*. If we allot 38.26 per cent of it for consumption of urban products, that amount would be 5,23,62,659 *dāms*. In other words, we would have a total expenditure on urban service sector amounting to 82,11,60,356 *dāms* and expenditure on urban manufactures, out of it, to 31,41,75,953 *dāms*. Since the urban manufactures consumed by these classes of persons are likely to have been of the inferior sort, the wage-component in the manufactures should have been around 67.838 per cent (see above), so that the total value added to urban manufactures from demand of the urban service sector should have amounted to about 21,31,30,683 *dāms*.

We have also to take into account separately the manufactured products consumed by urban merchants and tradesmen, including bankers and brokers, money-lenders, etc., who cannot simply be classed with the ordinary mass of servants. The miserliness of the Banya merchants was proverbial, so also that of the Armenians. But the Banyas also spent much on ornaments; and there were other communities of merchants too, like Muslim Bohras, Iranians, etc. who probably spent a higher proportion of their income on luxuries and consumer goods. It is true that perhaps a large amount of saving may be allowed for in the case of merchants than in that of other classes. This could take three possible forms: (a) bullion (b) stocks of grain and agricultural produce and (c) stocks of manufactured products, e.g. textiles, jewellery, etc. Since (a) was mainly accounted for by imported bullion, paid for by exports of manufactures (considered separately below), and (b) is already counted in agricultural produce, we are left largely with (c) as the form of saving that could have contributed to increase in manufactures. We may take merchants' savings at the high rate of 20 per cent of their income and take (c) to account for a quarter of the savings, or 5 per cent of their total income. To this we may add 25% of their income on urban manufactures for their own use or consumption, which, in case of larger merchants, could include not only houses but also ships, on the one hand, and high quality textiles and jewellery, on the other. The class, of course, also included smaller merchants (van Leur's 'pedlars'), agents of the bigger merchants, petty money-changers and shop-keepers, and so the consumption requirements would have varied greatly. It is in this light that our estimate of the percentage of total expenditure of this class being set at 25% should be judged. Keeping the estimated income of this class at 1,35,65,16,804 *dāms* (see Appendix 13B to this Chapter), we get the amount (at 30 per cent, comprising 5 per cent under saving and 25 per cent under consumption) the sum of 40,69,55,041 *dāms* for its expenditure on urban manufactures. This in turn would yield 20,34,77,521 *dāms* as the value added in urban manufacturer, taking labour costs as equal to the value of raw materials in these better-quality manufactures.

Alongside that of the urban merchant, we have to take into account the demand for urban manufactures generated by the rural merchants (including moneylenders and *banjārās*) whose total income we have estimated at 68,53,14,604 *dāms* per annum (see Appendix 13.B). If these merchants, who by the very nature of their business must have frequently come to the towns spent at least 10 per cent of their income on urban manufactures, this should have created a demand for 6,85,31,460 *dāms* of urban manufactures, yielding 3,42,65,730 *dāms* for value added.

There has been some controversy over how much the peasants could have spent on urban manufactures. Irfan Habib has held it to have been virtually negligible, while Raychaudhuri has thought that such expenditure cannot be disregarded.[8] We have, indeed, to consider the fact that while rural blacksmiths might have mended, repaired and even made some iron tools, it is likely that blades of spades, and steeled tips of coulters were initially made by urban blacksmiths, and that, similarly, town coppersmiths must have made the copper bowls in use in peasant huts. The stone sugar mills must also have been carved at quarries (like Chunar) or at townships. We may, therefore, suppose that a portion of the peasant's income must have been used to sustain the demand for some urban manufactures. We will see below (under 'Rural Manufactures') that the peasants' gross income came to about the same figure as J′, based on agrarian taxation i.e., 5,22,66,66,047 *dāms*. If no more than 2 per cent of this went into purchase of urban manufactures, and half of that counted as net addition to value by manufacture, the latter would amount to 7,83,99,991 *dāms*. A similar ratio of expenditure on urban products out of their income on the part of *zamīndars*' foot retainers would have further added 42,77,057 *dāms* to the value added in urban manufacture.

In addition to the value thus added by urban manufacture catering to domestic demand, we have to consider the value added in urban manufactures sent out to external markets. While we cannot directly estimate the total value of such exports, we can hazard a rough notion of the value of imports against which they were exported. In Chapter 16 we estimate that in *c.* 1595 imports of bullion amounted to Rs 2,04,71,768, and of horses to Rs 28,47,461; and since there were few other important items,

[8] Buchanan found that there was a group of blacksmiths in towns making swords, spears, knives and guns especially for rural markets (Montgomery Martin, *Eastern India,* Vol.II, Indian reprint, Delhi, 1976, pp. 260–6). For a similar report from the kingdom of Oudh, see Donald Butter, *Outlines of the Topography and Statistics of the Southern Districts of Oudh and the Cantonment of Sultanpur Oudh,* Calcutta, 1839, 79–81. The point about a rural market for urban products was theoretically raised by T. Raychaudhuri in *Enquiry,* N. S.II, (I), 92–121. See also *Cambridge Economic History of India,* Vol.I, 173–93. Irfan Habib, *Agrarian System*, 2nd ed., 89–90, recognises that demand for urban goods existed among 'prosperous *zamīndārs*', but doubts that demand for them existed among peasants 'to any recognisable extent'.

we may round off the total imports at Rs 2,60,00,000. Against this may be set off re-exports and capital transfers (the latter of which could have been responsible for the fall of interest rates in 1640s) and reduce the value of net imports that had to be paid for through exports, to Rs.2,30,00,000. We have then supposed that if around three-fourths of this amount was paid for by exports of textiles, their value would have been in a round number, Rs.1,75,00,000, equal to 70,00,00,000 *dāms*. Since the value of the material for the export goods would have been of a high quality, we may put the urban wage-share at 40 per cent of its value, or 28,00,00,000 *dāms*.

Table 13.1

Value Added in Urban Manufactures (in *dāms*)

1.	Emperial Establishment nobles, and *tābīnān*	59,82,48,028	
2.	Revenue-collecting staff	1,49,65,240	
3.	Revenue grantees	1,25,99,559	
4.	*Zamīndārs*, headmen, *zamīndārs*' cavalry	6,95,20,653	
5.	Domestic service sector	21,31,30,683	
6.	Urban merchants	20,34,77,521	
7.	Rural merchants	3,42,65,730	
8.	Peasants, Pastoral Sector	7,83,99,991	
9.	*Zamīndārs*' foot-retainers	42,77,057	
10.	Exports of urban manufactures	28,00,00,000	
	A. Total of items 1–10		1,50,88,84,462
11.	Urban artisans and 'industrial' labourers	39,16,28,228	
	B. Total of A and item 11		1,90,05,12,690

From Table 13.1, we can see that from our calculations above the total value added to manufactures should have been 1,50,88,84,462 *dāms*, which should also have been the income of all those engaged in urban manufactures as artisans and labourers. If we assume that this class of persons also spent as much as 38.26 per cent of their income on urban manufactures as did domestic servants, we get 57,72,99,195 *dāms* for the absolute amount so spent by them. Since the materials of their consumption would have been of the inferior sort, coarse clothing, etc., we should allow the same percentage for value added in manufacture as in the case of domestic servants, viz. 67.838 per cent of the market value, viz. 39,16,28,228 *dāms* (as is shown in the above Table). We forbear from considering the further demand created in turn from still other artisans, etc., serving to meet the demand for manufactured goods generated through this expenditure. Ignoring such infinitely extending multiplier effect should hopefully introduce a further air of moderation in our estimates!

The total of value added to urban manufactures, which may be taken as the wage-income of the towns' industrial population, thus amounts to 1,90,05,12,690 *dāms*. This has to be put side by side with the amount 82,11,60,356 *dāms* which constituted the income of the urban domestic service sector, as calculated by us above. In other words all in all 2,72,16,73,046 *dāms* went to maintain what may be called the working population of the towns and their dependents.

We may now turn to the amount that went to maintain the rural working population; and from that enquiry try to establish the relative size of the working populations of towns and villages in Mughal India. Here our task, to start with, seems simple. Given the conclusion we reached in Chapter 4 that the peasants had to part with half of the produce in tax and cesses, we should set their income as equal to J′ representing the gross agrarian part of taxation, which we have taken as equal to 5,22,66,66,047 *dāms*. This must have maintained the peasants as well as the agricultural workers, including the 'menial' village servants, paid through shares in harvests.

India's pastoral sector was largely an adjunct of agriculture, and we have followed economic historians in treating pastoral income, largely obtained by peasants, as a certain proportion of agricultural income. We have assumed this proportion to be a quarter, and on this basis held total pastoral income to be 2,61,33,33,024 *dāms* (see Appendix 13.B). Added to the peasants' agricultural income, this gives us a total of 7,83,99,99,071 *dāms* for the total income of peasants as both agriculturists and pastoralists.

Agriculture and pastoral pursuits had naturally to be supplemented by rural industry, a major part of which was directed towards processing material for urban manufactures. The latter related to both food and non-food products. Thus sugarcane, after being removed from the field, was crushed to produce juice, out of which *gur* or jaggery and varieties of sugar were made, which in turn served as necessary ingredients for sweet-meat manufacture in both towns and villages. Similarly, there was oil-milling, providing a necessary food-ingredient as well as fuel for lamps. Among non-food crops, the most prominent were cotton and indigo. Much of cotton processing, from seed-separation to spinning, even for the urban market, was probably carried out in villages. Indigo was extracted out of vats usually installed in the rural localities containing indigo-cropping.[9]

[9] A succinct description of 'agricultural manufactures' in Mughal times will be found in Habib, *Agrarian System*, 2nd ed., 62–7.

Now, in our estimates of values added to manufacture in the towns, which may be deemed equivalent to total urban wage-costs contained within urban manufactures, we had implicitly allowed for the value of raw material received in the towns, as portions of the total value of urban manufactures with reference to items exhibited in Table 13.1 in the following manner:

	A Labour-cost per cent of value	B Material-cost per cent of value	C B, converted to absolute figures
Item 5 and 11	67.383	32.617	29,27,19,705
Item 10	40.000	60.000	42,00,00,000
All other items	50.000	50.000	1,18,77,92,985
Total			1,90,05,12,690

From the above figures we can deduce that the processed or semi-processed materials annually received by the towns from the countryside need to be assigned a value of 1,90,05,12,690 *dāms*, based on our Table 13.1, and the assumptions on which it has been constructed. Now, of this total value, a part should have been contributed by agriculture in the form of the price of the crop removed from the field or threshing floor, that has already been counted in the value of agricultural produce above. The rest of the value of the material must have been added through labour, i.e., through wage-costs. As we have seen in the beginning of this chapter, in the case of coarse cloth, such labour contributed 67.838 per cent of the value of the product. While this could be true of a coarse material, such a high share of wage-cost might not have been present in material of better quality; and it may, therefore, be safe to take labour as contributing about half the value, viz. 95,02,56,345 *dāms* as the value added by rural manufacture in material supplied to towns.

We have now to consider the value added in such rural manufacture, as were directed to rural consumption. We have already estimated the peasants and agricultural labourers' annual income at 5,22,66,66,047 *dāms* and that of *zamīndārs*' foot-retainers at 42,77,05,700 *dāms* (Appendix 13.C), making a total of 5,65,43,71,747 *dāms*. Assuming that we are here dealing with the poorer strata of the population, it is best to take a cue from the pattern of expenditure which W. Crooke provided in his hypothetical reconstruction of a small peasant's family budget in Western

Uttar Pradesh in 1887–8. Out of net income of Rs 139 (gross, Rs 214 less rent, Rs 75), Rs 40 were spent on repair, hire and use of manufactured materials, in both agricultural operations and for consumption.[10] This gives us a rather high percentage of 28.78 per cent for expenditure on manufactures. We have already assigned a rather nominal expenditure of 2 per cent by the two classes above-mentioned on urban manufacture. If we now put their expenditure on rural manufactures at 20 per cent of their income, this would have amounted to 1,13,08,74,349 *dāms*. Considering that their demand would have been for inferior quality goods, the wage-content should have been higher in the products consumed, viz. 67.838 per cent, as deduced from data about coarse cloth. (We must remember that besides textiles, a significant part of rural manufacturing activity consisted of skinning animals and leather production carried out by low-paid 'menial' castes.) This would mean that the value added to rural manufacture under this category should have been 76,71,62,541 *dāms*.

One needs here to consider the demand for rural manufactures that arose out of pastoral income, estimated by us at 2,61,33,33,024 *dāms* (Appendix 13.B). The family budget, presented by Crooke, which we have used to estimate the portion of the peasant's income spent on manufactures, does *not* include, as Crooke himself notes,[11] the value of milk and milk products produced and consumed within the peasant households. Since much of the dairy produce was consumed in producers' households, only *ghī* or clarified butter, being the major market product, we cannot, therefore, assume that out of the pastoral income the same percentage was spent on products of manufacture as of earnings from agriculture, shown in Crooke's theoretical peasant family budget. It may, perhaps, be best to set it at 10 per cent of the pastoral income, 2 per cent spent on urban manufactures (see above) and 8 per cent on rural. The demand for rural manufactures out of this source would then amount to 20,90,66,642 *dāms*, within which the value added at 67.838 per cent of the latter, would be 14,18,26,629 *dāms*.

As for *zamīndārs* and headmen, as well as *zamīndārs*' housemen, we should recall that the total income of these categories has already been

[10] Crooke's important reports were published in the official *Inquiry into the Condition of the Lower Classes of the North-Western Provinces and Oudh (1887–88)*, issued, Naini Tal, 1890. William Crooke, in his note, drew an average small tenant's annual budget in Etah Distirct (*Inquiry, & c.*, 59–60). He placed the peasant's annual income net of rent, at Rs 139. In Crooke's estimate there would be no saving, but an annual deficit of Rs 5. We would also be right in assuming that in ordinary peasant's case in Mughal India too there would have been little or no saving, to go into any hoard.

[11] Ibid., 60.

estimated by us early in this chapter as follows:- *zamīndārs* (net income), 40,60,80,374 *dāms*; headmen, etc., 36,58,66,232 *dāms*; *zamīndārs*' cavalry, 38,45,58,000 *dāms*. This gives us a total of 1,15,65,04,606 *dāms*. Although, we had set different percentages of income for these classes' expenditure on urban manufactures, we would not be far wrong if we put their expenditure on rural manufactures at a higher proportion than that of peasants, say, 25 per cent of their income. This would mean an expenditure of 28,91,26,152 *dāms*. Since the demand in these categories would be for the better kinds of goods, we may here hold the labour component of the value of goods to be just half; and so the value added by rural manufacture here should be taken as 14,45,63,076 *dāms*.

In Appendix 13.B we estimate the income of the rural merchants, and Banjaras at about 68,53,14,604 *dāms*. We go on to presume that this includes the income of money-lenders as well. We have further presumed above that 10 per cent of the rural merchants' income went into acquisition of urban manufactures. It would not be unreasonable to put their expenditure on rural manufactures at 25 per cent of their income, as in the case of *zamīndārs*, etc., and apply the same proportion (50 per cent) to obtain wage-costs out of the total value of goods acquired. This would mean the rural merchants, etc., spent 17,13,28,651 *dāms* on rural manufactures, of which 8,56,64,326 *dāms* represented the value added.

Now we can construct our Table 13.2, in which we show the values added (=wage costs) under various categories of rural manufactures, according to sources of demand.

The Table shows the total value added under the categories, dealt with above, as 2,08,94,72,917 *dāms*. Now, as in towns, the artisans and others employed in production and obtaining this amount as their aggregate income would also themselves generate demand for rural manufactures. Suppose this amounted to about 25 per cent of their income (just above that of peasants, who, we suppose, spent 20 per cent on rural and 2 per cent on urban manufactures), then the total amount the artisans spent on rural manufactures would have amounted to 52,23,68,229 *dāms*. The goods involved being of the coarser sort, we may take the labour component to be 67.838 per cent of the total, amounting, therefore, to 35,43,64,159 *dāms*. We ignore here, as in case of the towns, the future multiplier effect this additional artisanal population generated. The grand total for the value added in all rural manufactures would, then, be 2,44,38,37,076 *dāms* (Table 13.2).

Among the category of rural society we have dealt with, it is the *zamīndār* foot-retainers only, who, with an estimated total income of 42,77,05,700 *dāms* and recorded number of 42,77,037—amounting with their dependants at 4.5 members per family, to a population of 19.25 million—appear

Table 13.2

Value Added in Rural Manufactures

	Source of Demand	*Dāms*	
1.	Urban demand	95,02,56,345	
2.	Peasants, agricultural labourers, *zamīndārs*' foot-retainers	76,71,62,541	
3.	Pastoral income	14,18,26,629	
4.	*Zamīndārs*, headmen, horsemen	14,45,63,076	
5.	Rural merchants, *Banjaras*	8,56,64,326	
	A. Total of items 1–5		2,02,94,72,917
6.	Persons employed in rural manufacture	35,43,64,159	
	B. total of A and item 6		2,44,38,37,076

to constitute a working low-level service-sector. They were obviously, given their low pay as part-time servants, being otherwise peasants of some sort. It is possible, seeing their large numbers, that these foot-retainers included also the domestic servants of the *zamīndārs*, many being essentially peasants either holding privileged tenures in lieu of service or being subject to *begār* or forced labour. In either case their main income has already have been computed under the category of peasants; and only the low rates paid to the 'foot-retainers' can be treated as remuneration for services, giving us the total that appears above in this paragraph.

We can now, perhaps, set out the total amount that annually went to maintain the rural working population under specific heads:

	dāms
Peasants and agricultural labourers	5,22,66,66,046
Pastoral income	2,61,33,33,024
Rural manufactures	2,44,38,37,076
Low level service sector	42,77,05,700
Total	10,71,15,41,846

If the above total is compared with the total amount of income of the urban working population (2,72,16,73,046 *dāms*) it amounts to 3.936 times the latter. In other words the amount of income of the urban working population was 20.26 per cent of the aggregate spent on the two (urban and rural) classes of working population.

Now, this proportion cannot be translated immediately into relative numbers of population, for two main reasons. Firstly, there are working populations left out in these calculations such as of miners, forest folk, and transport workers. Secondly, there was a difference between wage and price levels prevalent in the towns and the countryside, those in the country being much lower than those in the towns, as is, indeed, even the case today. What the different levels were in Mughal times, we do not know. But even if we allow a reduction by a quarter in the urban share of the total income of the working populations, to take into account the above two possible factors, we get 15.185 per cent which may, then, represent the actual share of the non-elite working population in the towns as of the total such population in the Mughal Empire in 1595. Our estimate thus coincides with that of Irfan Habib, who put the urban population of Mughal India at not much less than one-sixth (16.6 per cent) of the total population.[12]

The size of urban population we have postulated on the basis of our detailed estimates (where some links are undoubtedly weak) appears reasonable in the light of our knowledge of the demographic changes in the nineteenth century. A sample taken from the districts of eastern India showed that the fall of urban population in absolute figures was a little over 6 per cent between 1813 and 1872.[13] In the 1881 census the urban population was put at 9.3 per cent of the total. If we assume first that the population in India as a whole showed the same relative increase as that of the eastern districts in the same period of 1800–81, and secondly that the urban population in the country as a whole declined in the same ratio as in the eastern districts between 1813 and 1872, the urban population in 1800 should have been well in excess of 13 per cent of the total.[14] The estimated size of urban population in 1595–6 as about 15 per of the total population, does not, therefore, seem to be unreasonably high, particularly since it is quite possible that there had been some urban decline during the course of the eighteenth century as well.

[12] Irfan Habib, 'Potentialities of Capitalistic Development in the Economy of Mughal India' (1969), reprinted in his *Essays in Indian History: Towards a Marxist Perception* (New Delhi, 1995), 211–12.

[13] Irfan Habib, 'A Note on the Population of India, 1800–1872' (cyclostyled).

[14] In this calculation, the total population in 1801 has been taken to be 194,439,000, as suggested by M.D. Morris (*IESHR*, XI, Nos.2–3, 311). D. Bhattacharya offers a slightly higher estimate, viz. 207 million (*Report on Population of Eastern India*', Vol.III, New Delhi, 1985, 1811–20, cyclostyled). Kingsley Davis, *Population of India and Pakistan*, 127, offers an estimate of only 125 million. At the latter estimate, the urban population in 1800 would have been as high as 20.4%; but Davis's estimate for the total population in 1800 has been strongly criticized and may be ignored for our present purpose.

II

We have argued in Chapter 12, that 17 per cent of the income of the ruling class went directly towards maintaining unproductive labour; and this partially at least supports the picture of 'camp-cities', popularized from a reading of Bernier, as a specific feature of pre-industrial urbanization in India.[15] The bulk of the population of such 'camp-cities', given the prevalent low wages, could have contributed little to demand for goods beyond the very bare necessities. On the other hand, members of the nobility had the resources to purchase all kinds of luxuries and so could generate demand sustaining long-distance trade in high-value goods.

A number of towns which subsisted directly on the expenditure of the ruling class might thus have been essentially service-based, dependent upon supplies from surrounding villages while the higher grade craft-products came from distant centres. Thus, inherent in the existence of these 'camp-cities' was the existence of other towns as stable manufacturing centres, meeting the demand generated in the 'camp-cities'. Such manufacturing centres could theoretically exist even if no *jāgīrdār* established his household and quartered his retainers and attendants there. Many towns, of course, might well have had a dual character—but our argument is that even if there were cities created wholly by military and service-establishments, these had to be supplied with manufactured products from other towns, which were, conversely, firmly based upon craft production for distant markets.

Implicit in this hypothesis is the possibility that the degree of urbanization in a region need not have directly corresponded with the actual concentrations of members of the ruling class and their dependents. Regions where they resided in fewer numbers might still contain large towns sustained by markets provided by aristocratic demand elsewhere. Thus to study the degree of urbanization we need to do more than recite the names of capital cities. Unfortunately, except for fleeting statements, no detailed descriptions are available for late sixteenth-century towns to help us trace the pattern of urbanization in geographical terms.

In the absence of any straightforward demographic data, the only way sizes of various towns and regional levels of urbanization can be explored is by a device which gives us estimates of tax-income from various towns.

[15] See Bernier's description of the mud-walled and thatch-roofed huts of Delhi, in which lodged the common troops and all that vast multitude of servants and camp-followers who followed the court and the army (Bernier, *Travels*, 220).

The means by which the size of urban taxation may be determined is based on the assumption that since the *jama'* recorded in the *Ā'īn* included urban taxes as well, the *jama'/ārāẓī* (J/A) ratio for the *maḥal* comprising a large town should be higher than the J/A for the adjoining rural *parganas*. If we assume further that generally *parganas* containing large towns contributed their share of land revenue according to the recorded *ārāẓī*, the component of land-revenue in the *jama'* of these *parganas* can be worked out by multiplying the *ārāẓī* by the J/A calculated for the remaining *parganas* in the *sarkār* or the *dastūr*-circle (as the case might be). On subtracting the result (representing the estimated land-revenue) from the *jama'* of the urban *pargana* we should get the total amount realized from taxes collected in the towns situated within the *pargana*.

Underlying this device is the supposition that the efficiency of measurement was uniform in the whole of a *sarkār* or *dastūr*-circle. In most cases, the assumption of uniformity in the ratio of measured area to the total revenue paying area in the two kinds of *parganas* is not unreasonable, especially where measurement had reached high levels in the *sarkār* or the region as whole. But it would not hold good for those tracts where measurement was still in progress. In such localities there is a strong possibility that the *ārāẓī* was more fully measured in the *pargana* containing the *sarkār* headquarters or *ṣūba* capital than in other *parganas*. Here the J/A for the 'rural' *parganas* would consequently have been exceptionally high. This high J/A, when multiplied with the *ārāẓī* of the *pargana* containing the *sarkār* headquarters, where measurement might have covered the entire cultivated area, would certainly yield an inflated figure for the component of land revenue in the *jama'*, and this would result in our understating the size of urban taxes in that *pargana*.

The device we are speaking of can thus be used only for those regions where measurement had been widely undertaken and the *ārāẓī* figures are thus more or less complete. Within such regions a number of places which are described in literary sources as towns, manufacturing centres, ports, ferry points, junctions on important routes, etc., have been first selected; these are listed in Appendix 13-A.[16] The *parganas* which contain them have then been tested to show whether their J/A is higher than the J/A of adjoining *parganas*; and, if so, the absolute amount of difference is calculated that can be ascribed to urban taxation.

[16] Individual towns are discussed and listed under various heads in Hamida Khatoon Naqvi, *Urbanization and Urban-Centres under the Great Mughals, 1556–1707*, Simla, 1972. Her study may be consulted to check my own list, which has been made independently from contemporary sources.

In 72 of the 98 towns selected by us, the J/A of urban *parganas* is distinctly higher than the J/A of adjoining *parganas*. For all such urban *parganas*, I have calculated 'urban tax-indices', taking the hypothetical urban tax for Agra as 100. The figures are set out in Table 13.3.

We find that in certain cases the J/A in the rural *parganas* exceeds the J/A of the urban. Such *parganas* account for 26 of the 98 towns listed in Appendix 13.A. Almost all these places contained *sarkār* headquarters in regions where measurement was incomplete, being mainly situated in the *ṣūbas* of Allahabad, Malwa, and Bihar, and parts of *ṣūbas* Agra and Awadh.[17] For instance *pargana* Allahabad gives us a negative result. Here we find that the *ārāzī* recorded under this single *pargana* amounted to over 49 per cent of the total *ārāzī* of the entire *sarkār* of Allahabad. It is obvious that measurement in the *pargana* of the *sarkār* head-quarters was practically complete, while in all the other *parganas* it was in the process of being initiated. Moreover, it will be noticed that not only is Appendix 13-A overburdened with places which were *sarkār*-headquarters, but we have also no indication otherwise that they were towns of any significance. Quite possibly some of them were glorified villages or forts from which little was collected by way of non-agricultural taxation.

The size of urban taxation estimated by us (in the far more numerous cases with positive results) can serve as a very rough index of urbanization. Since unlike land revenue no fixed rates of urban tax to the total product can be propounded, the size of urban tax is, of course, no accurate indicator of the volume of urban commerce or value added by urban manufactures. Yet it can still indicate the capacity to bear tax and, therefore, may provide us with some clue as to the level of urbanization and urban income in different regions.

Map XI presents the geographical pattern contained in Table 13.3.

Table 13.3 demonstrates that Agra was indisputably the largest city in the empire, and the level of urbanization in Agra *ṣūba* was fairly high. A number of places (in all 15) appear to have been flourishing towns: some like Fatehpur Sikri, Bayana, Alwar, Gwalior, were manufacturing centres; while others, e.g. Chanwar and Dholpur, were commercial centres as they lay on trade routes.

The city of Ahmadabad accounted for the second-largest amount of urban tax. Some other towns in Gujarat also seem to have been large in size; moreover, the number of towns (13) in Gujarat is the largest for any *ṣūba* except Agra. The third *ṣūba* where the number of urban centres turns out to be large is Lahore (12 towns). Some of these (like Shamsabad, Dhangot and Makhiala) might have contributed large amounts of tax

[17] Vide Chapter 2.

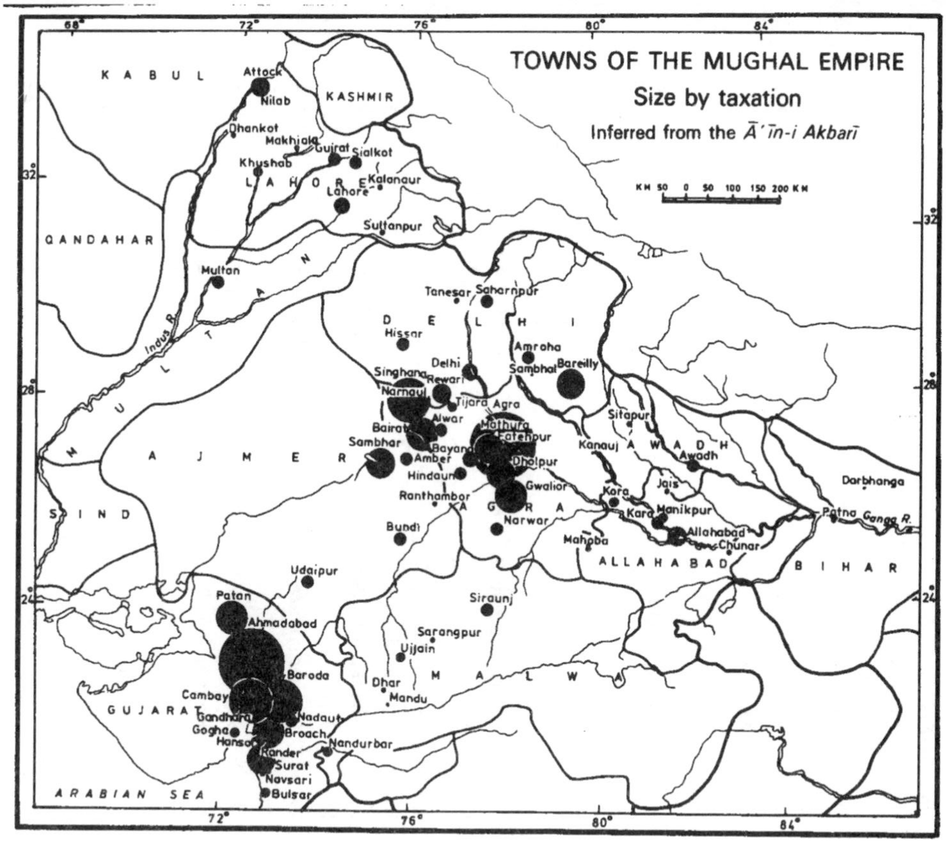
TOWNS OF THE MUGHAL EMPIRE
Size by taxation
Inferred from the Ā'īn-i Akbarī
KM 50 0 50 100 150 200 KM
68°
72°
76°
80°
84°
32°
28°
24°
KABUL
KASHMIR
QANDAHAR
LAHORE
MULTAN
DELHI
AJMER
AGRA
AWADH
ALLAHABAD
BIHAR
SIND
GUJARAT
MALWA
ARABIAN SEA
Indus R.
Ganga R.
Attock
Nilab
Dhankot
Makhiala
Gujrat
Sialkot
Khushab
Kalanaur
Lahore
Sultanpur
Multan
Tanesar
Saharnpur
Hissar
Amroha
Delhi
Bareilly
Sambhal
Singhana
Rewari
Narnaul
Tijara
Agra
Alwar
Mathura
Bairat
Fatehpur
Sambhar
Bayana
Amber
Dholpur
Hindaun
Gwalior
Ranthambor
Narwar
Bundi
Sitapur
Kanauj
Awadh
Jais
Kora
Manikpur
Kara
Allahabad
Chunar
Mahoba
Darbhanga
Patna
Udaipur
Patan
Ahmadabad
Sironj
Sarangpur
Ujjain
Baroda
Dhar
Mandu
Cambay
Gandhara
Nadaut
Gogha
Broach
Hansot
Nandurbar
Rander
Surat
Navsari
Bulsar

Map XI

Table 13.3

Size of Urban Tax

	Parganas	Amount of tax (deduced)	Index (No.1 as base, = 100)
Ṣūba AGRA			
1.	Agra *bā ḥavelī*	3,18,24,093	100.00
2.	Bayana	36,43,456	11.449
3.	Chanwar	54,39,987	17.094
4.	Dholpur	55,47,650	17.432
5.	Fatehpur Sikri	53,91,305	16.941
6.	Mathura	6,05,910	1.904
7.	Hindaun	19,05,258	5.987
8.	Qanauj *bā ḥavelī*	88,789	0.279
9.	Gawalior *bā ḥavelī*	75,32,255	23.668
10.	Narwar	12,44,602	3.911
11.	Alwar	10,08,004	3.167
12.	Bairat	67,24,859	21.131
13.	Tijara	5,42,225	1.7
14.	Narnaul *bā ḥavelī*	22,43,294	7.049
15.	Singhana	1,18,81,629	37.335
Ṣūba ALLAHABAD			
16.	Hadiabad	5,14,902	1.618
17.	Manikpur *ba ḥavelī*	2,02,866	0.637
18.	Jais	1,34,928	3.512
19.	Chunar *bā ḥavelī*	1,42,918	0.424
20.	Mahoba	2,63,423	0.449
21.	Kora *bā ḥavelī*	6,45,969	0.828
22.	Kara *bā ḥavelī*	11,17,732	2.030
Ṣūba AWADH			
23.	Awadh *bā ḥavelī*	14,67,507	4.611
24.	Chhitapur	2,97,850	0.936
Ṣūba DELHI			
25.	Delhi	37,41,494	11.757
26.	Bareilly	89,40,902	28.095
27.	Sambhal	95,468	0.300
28.	Amroha	11,21,112	3.523
29.	Saharanpur	20,24,253	6.361
30.	Rewari	28,43,075	8.934

(*Continued*)

Table 13.3

Size of Urban Tax

	Parganas	Amount of tax (deduced)	Index (No.1 as base, = 100)
31.	Hardwar (*pargana* Bhogpur)	44,275	0.139
32.	Hissar Firuza	11,24,659	3.534
33.	Thanesar	3,18,332	1.000
Ṣūba LAHORE			
34.	Lahore	32,64,848	10.259
35.	Kalanaur	2,55,007	0.801
36.	Sultanpur	3,52,248	1.107
37.	Sialkot	22,27,185	6.998
38.	Gujarat	14,49,838	4.556
39.	Attock Banaras	30,54,724	9.594
40.	Ruhtas *bā ḥavelī*	27,58,363	8.668
41.	Khushab	7,12,918	2.240
42.	Dhangot	2,43,016	0.764
43.	Shamsabad	63,63,085	19.995
44.	Makhiala	1,30,285	0.409
45.	Nilab	2,42,100	0.761
Ṣūba MULTAN			
46.	*Balda* Multan	15,56,196	4.890
Ṣūba GUJARAT			
47.	Ahmadabad	3,13,02,645	98.361
48.	Bandar Ghogha	6,00,000*	1.855
49.	Khambayat	1,73,27,855	54.449
50.	Patan *bā ḥavelī*	52,15,679	7.692
51.	Nadaut *bā ḥavelī*	24,48,001	31.976
52.	Baroda	1,01,76,136	31.976
53.	Broach *bā ḥavelī*	67,26,039	21.135
54.	Gandhar	2,40,000	0.754
55.	Hansot	13,36,875	4.201
56.	Bulsar	5,19,235	1.632
57.	Rander	7,339	0.023
58.	Surat *bā ḥavelī*	50,12,465	15.751
59.	Navsari	1,20,667	0.379
	Saurath Ports revenue	26,02,060	8.176

(*Continued*)

Table 13.3

Size of Urban Tax

	Parganas	Amount of tax (deduced)	Index (No.1 as base, = 100)
Ṣūba AJMER			
60.	Amber	22,50,435	7.071
61.	Sambhar	89,75,176	28.202
62.	Ranthambor	1,51,649	0.47
63.	Bundi	11,61,251	3.649
64.	Udaipur	11,20,000*	3.519
Ṣūba MALWA			
65.	Ujjain *bā ḥavelī*	7,21,863	2.268
66.	Sironj	10,47,051	1.084
67.	Mandu	23,254	0.073
68.	Jalalabad *bā ḥavelī*	17,687	0.056
69.	Handia	1,45,117	0.456
70.	Nadurbar	8,98,640	2.824
71.	Dhar	2,60,585	0.819
Ṣūba BIHAR			
72.	Patna	2,07,160	0.651

* Town/port revenue directly stated.

owing to manufacture or commerce in salt.[18] Yet, quite surprisingly, Lahore has a very modest size of urban taxation to offer; this appears to be quite contradictory to what Abū'l Faẓl's testimony and travellers' descriptions would lead us to expect from the size of Lahore city.[19] Certainly at this time one would have expected it to be larger than Agra, and very much bigger than Delhi.[20] In Ajmer *ṣūba* the high figure of urban taxation on *pargana* Sambhar reflects not the size of town but the revenue from salt collected in that *pargana* from the Sambhar Lake.

In *ṣūbas* Allahabad and Malwa, though the number of towns was not very small, the size of tax realized from individual centres was, on

[18] According to Abū'l Faẓl the merchants who bought salt at 2 *dāms* a *man* paid 40 *dāms* for every 17 *mans* to the State (*Ā'īn*, I, 539); that is, the State duty was 117.6 per cent of the prime cost.

[19] *Ā'īn*, I, 538; Monserrate, 159–60; Coryat in *Early Travels* 243 (he visited Lahore in 1615).

[20] Cf. Moreland, *India at the Death of Akbar*, 12.

average, small. Other *ṣūbas* (Awadh, Bihar, Multan and Ajmer) seem to have had only a small number of towns which yielded a significant size of taxation. In these regions, however, incomplete measurement in the rural *parganas* might, as suggested earlier, also be partly responsible for the low figures of taxation for the towns that we get by our method.

One objection to this method of estimating the relative size of towns can be that urban taxation might have varied not only according to varying kinds and rates of taxes, but also according to differences in price levels. One might argue, for example, that in Gujarat we have high figures because of higher prices prevailing there in relation to Agra; and that, conversely, low prices are responsible for the smaller size of urban taxation in Bihar. However, higher prices should also have generated a higher *jama'* per unit of gross cultivation. If so, while we cannot compare the taxable capacities and (still less) sizes of individual towns in relation to Agra, we can nevertheless determine the level of urbanization in each region worked out from the tax figures of towns in each *ṣūba* (from Table 13.3) set in relation to the total *jama'* of the *ṣūba*.

The ratios of urban taxation to the total *jama'*, as set out in Table 13.4, show Gujarat, again, to have been the most urbanized region: here urban taxation is strikingly high at 18.73 per cent of the *jama'*. This certainly suggests a high degree of commercialization in the economy of Gujarat.[21] In the Agra province urban tax is high enough, at 15.7 per cent of the total *jama'*, but is still distinctly below the ratio achieved in Gujarat. In the other *ṣūbas* the ratio does not even reach 5 per cent; only *ṣūba* Ajmer comes close to this level.

It is remarkable that, by and large, the ratios of urban tax to *jama'* revealed by Table 13.4 should conform to the situation existing in recent times. A glance at the map of urban population based on the 1961 Censuses of India and Pakistan,[22] shows Gujarat as the most highly-urbanized region within the areas covered by our statistics; and the territories corresponding to *ṣūbas* Bihar, Allahabad and Awadh appear in the 1961 map as the least urbanized. Rajasthan, like the Mughal *ṣūba* of Ajmer, shows a relatively higher degree of urbanization. The main difference is the position of districts forming the Mughal *ṣūba* of Agra; these

[21] Cf. Pearson who estimates the total value of sea trade at Rs 8,00,00,000 in 1572, which according to him was 2.42 times the total value of the agricultural produce of Gujarat (*Merchants and Rulers in Gujarat—The Response to the Portuguese in the Sixteenth Century*, California, 1976, 23–4). For a criticism of this calculation, however, see S. Moosvi, *Medieval India—A Miscellany*, IV, 217–20.

[22] See Fig.4.2 (Map) in O.H.K. Spate and A.T.A. Learmonth, *India and Pakistan*, 3rd edition, 1967, 126.

Table 13.4

Total Urban Tax (based on Table 13.1 as % of *Jama'* (in *dāms*)

Ṣūbas	(a) Urban tax	(b) *Jama'*	(a) as % of (b)
Bihar	2,07,160	22,19,10,059	0.093
Allahabad	30,22,738	21,22,64,343	1.424
Awadh	17,65,357	20,13,99,937	0.877
Agra	8,56,23,316	54,49,69,548	15.712
Malwa	31,14,197	24,00,38,159	1.297
Gujarat	8,36,34,996	44,83,39,676	18.730
Ajmer	1,36,58,511	28,70,45,025	4.758
Delhi	2,02,53,570	60,06,87,797	3.372
Lahore	2,10,53,617	56,65,60,144	3.716
Multan	15,56,196	15,62,53,243	0.996
Total	23,38,89,658	3,47,94,67,931	6.723

no longer appear as highly urbanized, whereas the districts of central Panjab show a higher level of urbanization.

A final note about the total extent of urban taxation in the empire as a whole: at 6.730 per cent of the *jama'*, it remains within the ceiling of 10 per cent we have allowed for non-agricultural taxation within the *jama'* of the Mughal empire in order to calculate the estimated gross-revenue realization (J′) from the empire. To this extent, these figures supply a welcome corroboration of an inference we had drawn from other evidence.

Appendix 13.A

	Ṣūba AGRA	
1.	Agra *bā ḥavelī*	The capital of the empire; major commercial centre; mint (*Ā'īn*, I, 27).
2.	Bayana	High quality indigo produced and manufactured; centre of indigo trade (*Ā'īn*, I, 422, Finch, 151–2, *Remonstrantie*, 259, tr., 13).
3.	Chanwar	Ferry point on the main route from Agra to Allahabad.
4.	Dholpur	On the route from Agra to Burhanpur; commanding the Chambal ferry.

(*Continued*)

Appendix 13.A (*Continued*)

	Ṣūba AGRA	
5.	Fatehpur Sikri	Well-known capital of Akbar; producing woollen carpets (*Ā'īn*, I, p.50; *Remonstrantie*, 257, tr., 9, Thevenot, 56); red sandstone quarries (*Ā'īn*, I, 422, Finch, 151–2); mint (*Ā'īn*, I, 27).
6.	Mathura	Pilgrim centre; on the Agra–Delhi route.
7.	Hindaun	Production centre for indigo (*Remonstrantie*, 259, tr., 14).
8.	Qanauj *bā ḥavelī*	*Sarkār*-headquarters; copper-mint.
9.	*Kol	*Sarkār*-headquarters; indigo manufacture (Finch, *Early Travels*, p.179; *Remonstrantie*, 260, tr., 15).
10.	Gawalior *bā ḥavelī*	*Sarkār*-headquarters; produced jasmine oil (Mundy, II, 62–3); copper-mint (*Ā'īn*, I, 27).
11.	*Earch	*Sarkār*-headquarters.
12.	*Payanwan	*Sarkār*-headquarters.
13.	Narwar	*Sarkār*-headquarters.
14.	*Mandlaer	*Sarkār*-headquarters.
15.	Alwar	*Sarkār*-headquarters, woollen carpets, glass (*Ā'īn*, I, 422–5), saltpeter (*Ā'īn*, I, 45); copper-mint (*Ā'īn*, I, 27).
16.	Bairat	Copper-mines (*Ā'īn*, I, 422).
17.	Tijara *bā ḥavelī*	*Sarkār*-headquarters.
18.	Narnaul *bā ḥavelī*	*Sarkār*-headquarters; later, mint.
19.	Singhana	Copper-mines (*Ā'īn*, I, 422, 454); copper-mint (*Ā'īn*, I, 27).
20.	Sahar	*Sarkār*-headquarters.
	ṣūba ALLAHABAD	
21.	*Allahabad	*ṣūba* and *sarkār* capital; mint (*Ā'īn*, 27).
22.	Hadiabas	Ferry point facing Allahabad across the Jamuna.
23.	*Ghazipur	*Sarkār*-headquarters, on Allahabad–Patna route.
24.	*Banaras	*Sarkār*-headquarters, copper-mint (*Ā'īn*, I, 27); muslin (*Ā'īn*, p.423)
25.	Manikpur *bā ḥavelī*	*Sarkār*-headquarters.
26.	Jais	Well-known town.
27.	Chunar *bā ḥavelī*	*Sarkār*-headquarters, pottery (Mundy, II, p.114).
28.	Mahoba	Famous for its betel leaf (*Ā'īn*, I, 424).
29.	*Kalinjar	*Sarkār*-headquarters.
30.	Korra *bā ḥavelī*	*Sarkār*-headquarters; on the Agra–Allahabad route (Finch, 178–9).
31.	Kara *bā ḥavelī*	*Sarkār*-headquarters; on the Agra–Allahabad route (Finch, 178–9).

(*Continued*)

Appendix 13.A (*Continued*)

	Ṣūba AWADH	
32.	Awadh *bā ḥavelī*	*Ṣūba* capital; *sarkār*-headquarters; manufacture of horn utensils (Finch, 176); coarse cloth (*Remonstrantie*, 252, tr., 7); on the Agra–Jaunpur route; copper-mint (*Ā'īn*, I, 27).
33.	*Gorakhpur	*Sarkār*-headquarters; copper-mint (*Ā'īn*, I, 27).
34.	*Bahraich	*Sarkār*-headquarters.
35.	*Khairabad	*Sarkār*-headquarters.
36.	Chhitapur	Chintz (Thevenot, I, 57).
37.	*Lucknow	*Sarkār*-headquarters; copper-mint (*Ā'īn*, I, 27).
	Ṣūba DELHI	
38.	Delhi	*Ṣūba* capital; *sarkār*-headquarters; chintz; mint (*Ā'īn*, I, 27).
39.	*Badaun	*Sarkār*-headquarters; copper-mint (*Ā'īn*, I, p.27).
40.	Bareilly	On the Delhi–Patna route; later, mint.
41.	Sambhal	*Sarkār*-headquarters; on the alternative Delhi–Patna route; copper-mint (*Ā'īn*, I, 27).
42.	Amroha	Town on the Delhi–Patna route.
43.	Saharanpur	*Sarkār*-headquarters; copper-mint (*Ā'īn*, I, 27).
44.	Rewari	*Sarkār*-headquarters; on the Delhi–Ajmer route.
45.	Hardwar (*pargana* Bhoghpur)	Pilgrim-centre; copper-mint (*Ā'īn*, I, 27).
46.	Hissar Firuza	*Sarkār*-headquarters; copper-mint (*Ā'īn*, I, 27).
47.	*Sirhind	*Sarkār*-headquarters; copper-mint (*Ā'īn*, I, 27).
48.	Thanesar	Sal-ammonia (*Remonstrantie*, 294, tr., 46, Purchas, IV, 49); woven fabrics (*Haft-Iqlīm*, II, 461).
	Ṣūba LAHORE	
49.	Lahore	Second capital of the empire; cloth (*Ā'īn*, I, 106); shawls (*Ā'īn*, I, 104); ship-building (*Ā'īn*, I, 202); cloth (*Remonstrantie*, 278, tr., 31); mint (*Ā'īn*, I, 27).
50.	Kalanaur	Copper-mint (*Ā'īn*, I, 27).
51.	Sultanpur	Chintz & quilts (Purchas IV, 267–8).
52.	Sialkot	*Sarkār*-headquarters; manufacture of muslin, paper, quilts, daggers, spears (Sujān Ra'i, 72); copper-mint (*Ā'īn*, I, 27).
53.	Gujrat	Gypsum plates, etc. (*Ā'īn*, I, 539).

(*Continued*)

Appendix 13.A (*Continued*)

	Ṣūba LAHORE	
54.	Attock Banaras	Ferry point (*Ā'īn*, I, 590); copper-mint (*Ā'īn*, I, 27).
55.	Ruhtas *bā ḥavelī*	*Sarkār*-headquarters; on the Lahore–Kabul route.
56.	Khushab	Well-known town on Jhelam.
57.	Dhankot	Salt mines (*Ā'īn,* I, 548).
58.	Shamsabad	Salt mines (*Ā'īn,* I, 548).
59.	Makhiala	Salt mines (*Ā'īn,* I, 548).
60.	Nilab	Ferry point (*Ā'īn,* I, 590).
61.	*Balda* Multan	*Ṣūba* capital, a big mart on the Qandhar–Multan route; mint (*Ā'īn*, I, 27).
62.	*Uchh	*Sarkār*-headquarters.
	Ṣūba GUJARAT	
63.	Ahmadabad	*Ṣūba*-capital, *sarkār*-headquarters; known for its velvet (*Ā'īn*, I, 486, *Remonstrantie*, 264, tr., 19, Purchas, IV, 167); gold and silver embroidery; inlay work (*Ā'īn*, I, 485, Finch, 173);
64.	*Bandar* Ghogha	Major port (*Ā'īn*, I, 486); ship-building (*English Factories in India, 1634–36*, 95).
65.	Khambayat	Port (*Ā'īn*, I, 486); ivory-carvings; cornelian & agate carving (Thevenot, 18); muslin and quilts (Careri, 164).
66.	Pattan *bā ḥavelī*	*Sarkār*-headquarters; textiles (*Ā'īn*, I, 487); copper-mint (*Ā'īn*, I, 27).
67.	Nadaut *bā ḥavelī*	*Sarkār*-headquarters.
68.	Baroda	*Sarkār*-headquarters, cotton stuffs (*Remonstrantie*, 291, tr., 43).
69.	Bhroach *bā ḥavelī*	*Sarkār*-headquarters; agate and cornelian (Finch, 174); chintz (Pelsaert, 43).
70.	Gandhar	Port (*Ā'īn*, I, 488).
71.	Hansot	Port (*Ā'īn*, I, 488).
72.	Bulsar	Port (*Ā'īn,* I, 488); cotton & silk stuffs (Abbe Carre, III, 767).
73.	Rander	Port (*Ā'īn*, 1, 488); baftas (Pelsaert, 41).
74.	*Champaner	*Sarkār*-headquarters.
75.	Surat *bā ḥavelī*	*Sarkār*-headquarters; port (*Ā'īn*, I, 488, *Remonstrantie*, 286–7, tr., 38–9); ship-building (Fryer, I, 299, 306); cotton and silk stuffs (Tavernier II, 3); mint (*Ā'īn*, I, 27).

(*Continued*)

Appendix 13.A (*Continued*)

	Ṣūba GUJARAT	
76.	Navsari	Ship-building; scented oil (*Ā'īn*, I, 488); bafatas (Finch, 134).
77.	*Godhra	*Sarkār*-headquarters.
	Ṣūba AJMER	
78.	*Ajmer	*Ṣūba*-capital; copper-mint (*Ā'īn*, I, 27).
79.	Amber	*Sarkār*-headquarters, silk stuffs (*Ā'īn*, I, 106).
80.	Sambhar	Salt (*Ā'īn*, I, 512; Br. Mus. Add. 6552).
81.	*Chittor	*Sarkār*-headquarters.
82.	Ranthambor	*Sarkār*-headquarters, copper-mint (*Ā'īn*, I, 27).
83.	Bundi	Chief seat of the Hara principality.
84.	Udaipur	Newly-built capital of Mewar.
	Ṣūba MALWA	
85.	Ujjain *bā ḥavelī*	*Ṣūba* capital; mint (*Ā'īn*, I, 27).
86.	*Raisen	*Sarkār*-headquarters.
87.	*Chanderi	*Sarkār*-headquarters.
88.	*Kotri Pirawa	*Sarkār*-headquarters.
89.	Sironj	Muslin (*Ā'īn*, I, 461); chintz (Mundy, II, 56); betel leaf (Finch, 143); copper-mint.
90.	Mandu	*Sarkār*-headquarters; on the Burhanpur–Agra route; copper-mint (*Ā'īn*, I, 27).
91.	Jalalabad *ba ḥavelī*	*Sarkār*-headquarters.
92.	Handia	*Sarkār*-headquarters, on the Burhanpur–Agra route (Finch, 193–43).
93.	Nadurbar	*Sarkār*-headquarters.
94.	Dhar	Known for its grapes (*Ā'īn*, I, 456).
	ṣūba BIHAR	
95.	*Bihar *ba ḥavelī*	*Sarkār*-headquarters, paper manufacture (*Ā'īn*, I, 417).
96.	Patna	*Ṣūba*-capital; coarse muslin; shields (Pelsaert, 8); mint (*Ā'īn*, I, 27).
97.	*Hajipur	*Sarkār*-headquarters.
98.	*Rohtas	*Sarkār*-headquarters.

Note: Sources are given for most descriptions, unless the facts are too well established to need substantiation. Mints are listed in the *Ā'īn*, I, p.27. References to later mints are derived from coin catalogues. The towns where J/A of rural *parganas* exceeds that of the urban, are marked with an asterisk.

Appendix 13.B
Estimation of Value Added by Manufactures and Merchants' Income on Basis of Taxation Data

In this chapter we attempted a calculation of the extent of non-rural net taxation included in the *jama'* set out by the *Ā'īn-i Akbarī* for various *parganas*. This calculation is on a comparison of *jama'* per square mile/kilometre in urbanised zones with that in adjacent rural zones. In the nature of such comparison the urban taxation detected thereby must be lower than the actual, for no rural zone was likely to be completely bereft of towns. Moreover, high urban taxation could still escape detection if urban settlements were evenly spaced among adjacent territorial divisions. For these reasons, the allowance for urban taxation within the *jama'* needs to be raised from the detected 6.723 per cent of the *jama'* to 10 per cent as a better approximation to the actual.

The resulting figure for *net* annual urban taxation within the Empire, *c.* 1595, was thus set at 40,61,12,358 *dāms* (without deducting *suyūrghāl* figures). To obtain gross urban taxation we need to add tax-collection costs, which were likely to be much lower than in the case of the land tax. We have little tangible to go by here, but it is difficult to imagine, keeping the costs of rural tax collection in view, how it could have been less than 10 per cent of the gross collection. To get the latter, then, we need to increase the figure for net urban taxation by 11.11 per cent, which would yield 45,12,31,441 *dāms*, the cost of collection amounting to 4,51,19,083 *dāms*. The last figure would represent the income of tax-farmers, tax-collectors, etc., who, we may legitimately suppose, were essentially townsmen.

While this figure should be added to the income of townsmen, the major issue addressed in this note is about what the gross collection can tell us about the value of merchandise, manufactures and services on which these taxes were levied.

The major item among these taxes (the *sā'ir jihāt* of our documents) was one called *tamghā*, *bāj* or *zakāt*. It is true that this tax was twice abolished by Akbar, the second time in 1581.[23] But the text of the order issued in 1592–3 shows that the abolition did not extend to 'the *bāj* and *tamghā* on animals, weapons and merchandise'.[24] This is confirmed by

[23] Ārif Qandahārī, 30–2, 35 (*tamghā*, etc.); *Akbarnāma*, Bib. Ind., III, 295–6 (*bāj*, *tamghā*); *Ṭabaqāt-i Akbarī*, II, 327 (*tamghā*, *zakāt*); *Ā'īn-i Akbarī*, I, 204 (*bāj*).

[24] The exceptions (where the *zakāt* was levied) were described as 'horse, elephant, sheep and goat, weapons and merchandise (*qumāsh*)' (*Inshā'-i Abū'l Faẓl*, 67–8, *Mir'āt-i Aḥmadī*, I, 171–2).

the *Ā'īn-i Akbarī*, which adds oxen to the list of the traded animals taxed.[25] On the other hand, goods such as foodgrains, medicinal materials, ghee, salt, sugar, perfumes, cotton (but not apparently textiles), woollen materials, leather goods, firewood, fodder, etc. were explicitly exempted.[26] This means that essentially the *bāj* imposts were levied on urban manufactures and animals traded.

As to the rate or rates followed in assessing the tax, the alternative designation *zakāt* suggests that like the Muslim jurists' levy of this name, the rate was one-fortieth or 2.5 per cent *ad valorem*. The *Ā'īn*, indeed, says that *bāj* collected at the ports was not less than a fortieth (of the value).[27] It is, however, doubtful if an article of merchandise paid *bāj/tamghā* at one point only. Abū'l Fazl states, indeed, that in each *ṣūba* it was levied at one place only.[28] How this rule could be enforced is not easy to understand; but it does leave open the possibility that when a taxable piece of merchandise was moved from one *ṣūba* to another even before reaching its final point in transit, *bāj* could be levied again on it.

Then, there were other taxes on goods involved in local and also long-distance trade. One, levied for a short while under Akbar was called *ṣad-yak*, literally 'one per-cent', and was collected from goods at point of sale.[29] Several kinds of dues, known as *rāhdārī*, were levied by various authorities at stations on routes within their jurisdictions apparently collected roughly according to value of the goods in transit, so as to merit their description as '*tamghā*-like' from Abū'l Fazl. In 1595–6 Akbar had to depute special officers on major routes tasked with the duty of suppressing their collection.[30] There were special levies on cargo of river-boats, known as *mīrbaḥrī*: Abū'l Fazl gives rates of it that seem moderate enough; but none are *ad valorem*.[31] Other 'forbidden' cesses, including those on professions (*peshawarī*), market-levy (*bāzār-nashīnī*), besides *rāhdārī*, were again taxes, whose magnitude relative to values of products concerned remains unknown but must in aggregate have been quite significant.[32]

[25] *Ā'īn*, I, 284. Instead of *zakāt* it uses the terms *bāj* and *tamghā*. The Kotwāl was here asked to prevent this tax being levied on other goods.

[26] *Insha'-i Abū'l Fazl*, 67–8; *Mir'āt-i Aḥmadī*, I, 171–3.

[27] *Ā'īn*, I, 204.

[28] Ibid., 284.

[29] Order dated AH 991/AD 1583 in Blochet, Sup. Pers. 482, f.169a–b. It was soon withdrawn (Blochet, Sup. 482, f.157b). It is mentioned among the remitted taxes in Akbar's *farmān* of 37th Year (1592–3): *Insha'i Abū'l Fazl*, 67–8; *Mir'āt-i Aḥmadī*, I, 171–2.

[30] *Akbarnāma*, III, 670.

[31] *Ā'īn*, I, 284.

[32] For one list of such taxes, see *Ā'īn*, I, 287.

It is difficult to convert these various indications into a general formula for calculating the actual value of merchandise taxed. We can only take the standard rate of *bāj*, viz. 2.5 per cent *ad valorem*, and, taking into account the fact that on part of merchandise, especially that involved in long-distance trade, it could have been levied twice over, we may suppose the actual burden of *bāj* on long distance commerce to have been 5 per cent of the value of merchandise transported. And then there were the other cesses, though formally prohibited, whose yield could yet have been taken into account when the *jama'* was fixed on each territorial unit. All in all, it seems reasonable to assume that an article of merchandise paid about 10 per cent of its total value in total under the heads of various cesses, including *bāj*.

This, as the base of our estimation would put the total sale value of taxed merchandise plus the value of cattle, horses, and elephants traded at (1 × 45,12,31,441=) 4,51,23,14,410 *dāms*, exclusive of the tax.

Now, if we were to make the extreme assumption that the value of cattle traded equalled at least half the entire pastoral income, this would require us to determine the total amount of pastoral income. The most convenient way of determining the latter is to accept the modern statisticians' ratio between pastoral and agricultural incomes. Sivasubramonian put pastoral income at 28.94 per cent of the agricultural income during 1901–10,[33] but reduced it to 20.65 per cent in his revised calculations.[34] Heston assumes the proportion to have been 36.4 per cent in 1899–1900,[35] but this has been shown to be too high by Maddison, who put it at 25.15 per cent.[36] If we assume that the agricultural product in 1595–6 was equal to J′ and so amounted to 10,45,33,32,094 *dāms*, the pastoral income, put at, say, 25 per cent of it, should have amounted to 2,61,33,33,024 *dāms*. The total amount of the value of cattle traded, at half of this amount, should have been 1,30,66,66,512 *dāms*. This, with the further addition of the value of imported horses (Rs 28,47,460.5= 11,38,98,420 *dāms*) (Chapter 16) and of elephants traded, estimated by us at 4,90,30,000 *dāms* (Chapter 18) yield a total of 1,46,95,94,932 *dāms* as possibly the maximum possible to be deducted from the entire value of taxed articles, viz. 4,15,23,14,410 in order to obtain the value of urban manufactures traded and taxed. The total value of the latter would then be 3,04,27,19,478 *dāms*. If labour costs accounted for half of the value of

[33] *National Income,* 1965 (mimeograph), 162.

[34] Ibid., 2000 (printed), 377.

[35] *Cambridge Economic History*, Vol.II, 397.

[36] *Class Structure and Economic Growth: India and Pakistan since the Moguls*, London, 1971, 166–7. For a criticism of Heston's assumptions, "What did Heston do?" (mimeograph) and Irfan Habib, 'Studying Colonial Economy without Percieving Colonialism', *Modern Asian Studies*, Vol.19, Pt.3, 1985, 369–70.

these manufactures we get 1,52,13,59,739 *dāms* for value added by urban manufactures. This has to be compared with our estimated value added in urban manufacture, in the main chapter, viz. 1,90,05,11,588 *dāms* whose larger size may be explained by the fact that it included some goods not traded, and so escaping tax.

In order to calculate the merchants' profits from the above data, we have to go back to the total amount of the value of the taxed trade, we have set at 4,51,23,14,410 *dāms*. To this we must add the trade in agricultural produce, which, as we have noted, was at least formally not subject to tax. A rather rough-and-ready way of estimating its scale would be by considering the trade as one induced wholly by the land tax, which should strictly mean that its annual size was equal to the net annual state revenue of the Empire, *less* the amount of urban taxation. This yields us the figure of (*jama*': 4,06,11,23,580 less urban taxation 40,61,12,358=) 3,65,50,11,222 *dāms*. If we assume that at least 25 per cent of the latter was handled by town merchants (leaving the rest to *banjārās* and 'village *banyas*'), the volume of agricultural trade handled by the town merchatns should have come to 91,37,52,806 *dāms*, taking their total trade volume to 5,42,60,67,216 *dāms*. If we further assume the merchants' net profits to have amounted to 25 per cent of the total volume of trade handled (being at least double the then commercial rate of 1 per cent per month=12.69 per cent. annually compounded) we get a figure of 1,35,65,16,804 *dāms* for profits of the urban merchants.

For the rural merchants and *banjāras* this leaves a volume of commerce 2,74,12,58,417 *dāms*, yielding them an estimated profit of 68,53,14,604 *dāms* at 25 per cent of the volume.

Appendix 13.C
Zamīndārs' Net Income

In order to calculate the *zamīndārs*' income within the territories of the Mughal Empire, we base ourselves on the conclusions reached earlier that the *zamīndārs*' gross income, out of the tax-paying lands was one-third of J (agrarian only) (Chapter 7) that translated into absolute figures, made it equal to (1/3 × 3,65,50,11,222=) 1,21,83,37,074 *dāms*.

In order to get the *zamīndārs*' net income one needs to deduct from this figure the expenditure they incurred on their cavalry and infantry, whose respective numbers, derived from the *Ā'īn*'s statistics, are 3,84,558 and 42,77,057. Assuming their rates of annual pay at 1000 and 100 *dāms* respectively (Chapter 7), the full amounts of expenditure on them would have been 38,45,51,000 *dāms* for cavalry and 42,77,05,700 *dāms*, for the foot-retainers. The total expenditure on their pay would have thus been 81,22,56,700 *dāms*, leaving the *zamīndārs* with a net income of 40,60,80,374 *dāms*.

CHAPTER 14

Prices and Wages

Information on two important subjects—prices and wages—is furnished in profusion by the *Ā'īn*; and this has been studied by V.A. Smith, Moreland, Mukerjee and Desai.[1]

Abū'l Faẓl has a chapter exclusively devoted to listing prices of agricultural and pastoral products, such as foodgrains, vegetables, meat and fowl, spices, etc.[2] A chapter each is devoted to prices of fruits (dry and fresh); perfumes; varieties of silken, cotton and woollen cloth; weapons and armour; and building materials.[3] The prices of chemicals, metals, iron-pegs, horseshoes and a number of other commodities are found scattered in other chapters.

Before making use of these quotations we should be sure about their nature. To begin with, were these retail or wholesale prices, and what place or places were they current at?

The short introductory passage in the '*Ā'īn* of Prices of Provisions' (*Ā'īn-i Nirkh-i Ajnās*) says that these are 'more or less the mean (*miyāna*) prices, though on the march and in the rains, the prices vary substantially'.[4] One can legitimately infer from this statement that the prices that Abū'l Faẓl quotes are those prevalent at the imperial camp, when not on the march and during seasons other than the rainy season. Being those of

[1] V.A. Smith, *Akbar the Great Mogul*, Delhi, 1958, 281–6; W.H. Moreland, 'Prices and Wages under Akbar', *JRAS*, 1917, 815–25, and 'The Value of Money at the Court of Akbar', *JRAS*, 1918, 375–85; R. Mukerjee, 'The Economic History of India, 1600–1800', *JUPHS*, 1941, 41–96; A.V. Desai, 'Population and Standard of Living in Akbar's Time', *IESHR* Vol.IX, 1972, (1) 43–62, and 'Population & Standard of Living in Akbar's Time—A Second Look', *IESHR*, Vol.XV 1978, No.1.

[2] *Ā'īn*, I, 60–6.

[3] Ibid., 68–75, 85–6, 105–11, 119–24 and 167–9.

[4] Ibid., 60.

the imperial camp, they should be retail prices, probably well above the prices (in the case of foodgrains, at least) in the adjoining rural districts.

Yet, while Smith and Mukerjee have taken the *Āʼīn* prices to be retail, Moreland has argued that these are wholesale prices, being those at which provisions were acquired for the imperial kitchen and other departments from various distant places.[5] In other words, the prices were really not those prevalent at the Camp at all. Should one accept this view, one would find it hard to explain why the prices should have altered (as Abū'l Faẓl says, they did) when the Camp was on the move. Prices at distant markets would surely not have been affected by marches of the imperial camp.[6]

That these prices could not have been either wholesale or those prevailing at the market of origin, is shown incidentally by the price of grapes. Abū'l Faẓl says that Kashmir grapes sold at 8 *sers* a *dām* (i.e. 5 *dāms* a *man*) in Kashmir and the cost of transporting them to the imperial camp was Rs 2 a *man* (80 *dāms* a *man*).[7] If then the *Āʼīn* has given prices paid at places of origin, it should have recorded 5 *dāms* per *man* for grapes in its list of prices of fruits. On the other hand, were its price for grapes that of retail at the imperial camp, it should have exceeded 85 *dāms* per *man* (the Kashmir price plus cost of transport). We actually find that the price given in the *Āʼīn*'s list is 108 *dāms* per *man*.[8] It is therefore indisputably the retail price, since it covers the price of grapes at the source of supply, plus the cost of transport and the merchants' (and retailers') profits.

If, then, the prices are retail prices prevailing at the imperial camp, these should relate either to Agra or to Lahore. Agra (with the neighbouring city of Fatehpur Sikri) was the seat of Akbar's court until 1586,[9] when Akbar left it for Lahore. The latter city remained the capital till 1598.[10] Now it seems that much of the material collected in the *Āʼīn-i Akbarī* dates from a

[5] Moreland, 'Prices and Wages', 816.

[6] Cf. Habib, *Agrarian System*, 82*n.* (rev. ed. 90*n*). An argument that Moreland (*JRAS*, 1917, 815–6) puts forward to support his view is that the unit of weight in which the prices are expressed is normally the *man*, suggestive, in his view, of large transactions. But the *man* used here only equals 55.32 lb avdp. and has nothing to do with the British 'maund' of 82.28 lb avdp. It is therefore by no means such a large unit of weight as to have been out of place in retail transactions. Moreover, for certain commodities the *Āʼīn* quotes prices per *ser*; such as for ginger (2½ *dāms/ser*), and sugar of superior quality (*nabāt* and *qand-i safed*).

[7] *Āʼīn*, I, 67.

[8] Ibid., 68.

[9] *Akbarnāma*, III, 494.

[10] Ibid., 748.

period before 1586, while the editing was done mainly when the court was at Lahore.[11] Though Abū'l Faẓl does not clarify which of the two capital cities his prices belong to, he holds that they represent the normal level at the imperial camp over a long period. While there is no explicit evidence to suggest that the prices are those of Agra, it is at least certain that they were not the normal Lahore prices. Abū'l Faẓl tells us in the *Akbarnāma* that with the arrival of the court at Lahore, prices there rose so substantially that Akbar promulgated a 20 per cent increase in the land revenue of the province.[12] This suggests that the normal Lahore prices were well below the normal camp prices.[13] On the other hand, no remission in land revenue apparently occurred at Agra when Akbar left it in 1586.[14] Had such a remission been made, it would surely have been recorded as a notable piece of generosity on the emperor's part. The *Akbarnāma* indeed records remission in land revenue granted in three other *ṣūbas* (Allahabad, Awadh, and Delhi) in the very same year (1586), and this specifically on account of a substantial fall in prices.[15] Neither was any upward revision promulgated when Akbar returned to Agra in 1598,[16] so that one may assume that the level of agricultural prices at Agra was considered to be at par with that of the imperial camp. This does not seem improbable, since Agra was perhaps the biggest commercial centre of the Mughal empire.

There are some other facts which indicate that the agricultural prices in the *Ā'īn* at least are more likely to be those of Agra. A comparison of the prices of foodgrains relative to wheat given in the *Ā'īn*, with those at Agra (in the decade just previous to the firm establishment of the railway network in the region) and in 1894[17] (after the railways) offers us an opportunity of testing whether the *Ā'īn*'s relative prices are closer to those of Agra or Lahore.

The prices of barley and jowar in the *Ā'īn* in relation to wheat, seem to conform to the rates at Agra as well as Lahore; but bajra tilts the similarity decisively in favour of Agra. Bajra is not a crop of the Lahore region: in 1894–5 in district Lahore it occupied only 0.245 per cent of the total cropped area.[18] In relation to wheat therefore its price at Lahore was

[11] See Chapter I.

[12] *Akbarnāma*, III, 747.

[13] Cf. Habib, *Agrarian System*, 82.

[14] *Akbarnāma*, III, 765.

[15] Ibid., 494.

[16] Ibid., 748.

[17] *Prices and Wages*, 1895, Calcutta.

[18] *Panjab District Gazetteers*, Vol.30B, 1916, 50–1.

naturally high, exceeding that of wheat in 1894. There seems no reason to believe that in the sixteenth century bajra was any more widely grown in the Lahore area. Yet the *Ā'īn* rates it much below wheat (66.67 per cent). This on the other hand accords with the position of bajra in the Agra region where it is a widely grown crop. In 1901–2 it covered slightly more than one-fifth of the total cropped area of the Agra district;[19] and its price relative to wheat in the latter half of the nineteenth century fluctuated around 75 per cent, which is pretty close to the *Ā'īn*'s price at 66.6 per cent.

Table 14.1

		Agra		Lahore	
	Ā'īn	1861–70	1894	1861–70	1894
Wheat	100.00	100.00	100.00	100.00	100.00
Barley	66.67	63.54	60.66	64.24	59.03
Jowar	83.33	73.41	60.24	81.23	75.90
Gram	66.67	78.98	62.30	72.42	68.07
Bajra	66.67	76.48	77.46	90.66	121.08

Another indication that the *Ā'īn*'s prices were those of Agra is offered by Pelsaert's statement that during the time Portuguese trade was at its peak (i.e. the last quarter of the sixteenth century), cloves fetched Rs 60 to 80 per *man* at Agra. As Moreland himself notices, this matches well with the price given in the *Ā'īn*, viz., Rs. 60 per *man*.[20]

II

Once we have established the probability that the *Ā'īn*'s prices were the normal retail prices current at Agra during the last quarter of the sixteenth century, we ought to be able to compare them with those collected from modern statistics so as to determine changes in the relative supply of various commodities (after making allowances for changes on the demand side), during the intervening period. The comparison for each commodity can be made by converting all the prices given in the *Ā'īn* into

[19] Nevill, *District Gazetteer of U.P.*, Agra Dist., Volume IV, Appendix, p.VI.

[20] Pelsaert, *Remonstrantie*, 270, tr., 24 & n. If Pelsaert has converted (though this is unlikely) the earlier price in terms of *man-i Akbarī* to *man-i Jahāngīrī*, the range expressed in terms of the earlier weight would be Rs 48–64 per *man*.

[21] Atkinson, Vol.VII, 551.

percentages of the *Ā'īn*'s own price of wheat, and by similarly indexing all modern prices in terms of wheat prices.

For the purpose of comparing modern agricultural prices with the *Ā'īn*'s prices, the averages of annual prices at Agra during the decade 1861–70 seem appropriate. The prices of this decade are the earliest available in the official *Prices & Wages*. The decade had its normal complement of scarcities and good harvests, there being one year of scarcity, 1869, and two of plenty, 1862 and 1863.[21] Moreover, the effects of the railways were yet to be felt, since the railway network was extended into the region only during this decade, and it took time to carry traffic of sufficient volume to alter the price map. There is an additional merit in taking prices of this decade in that the market for wheat was not yet affected by exports. Wheat exports became important only after the opening of the Suez Canal in 1869.[22]

The relative prices of five major food crops have already been compared in Table 14.1 to test the affinity of the *Ā'īn*'s prices with those of Agra. While no great change can be detected in prices relative to wheat, there are still some noticeable variations. The relative price of barley remained more or less the same, while prices of gram and bajra show an increase. The relative price of jowar in 1861–70 was, however, lower than in the *Ā'īn*. These opposite trends in the relative prices of jowar and bajra throw some doubt on the suggestion that there had occurred a decline in the relative area occupied under these crops since Akbar's time.[23]

Pre-railway prices of other food crops are not easily obtainable. *Prices and Wages,* however, quotes prices at which certain commodities were bought for troops at different places, from 1875–6 onwards.[24] taking these prices for comparison with the *Ā'īn*'s, we get the following picture for pulses at Agra.

	Ā'īn (wheat=100)	1875–6 (wheat=100)
Mung	150.00	93.24
Masur	133.33	127.93
Mash	108.33	107.01[a]

[a] The price is that of Aligarh (average for 1861–70) indexed by taking the Aligarh wheat price as=100 during 1861–70

[22] See Z.A. Khan, 'Railways and the Creation of National Market in Foodgrains', *IHR*, Vol.IV, No.2, 1978, 336–46.

[23] A.V. Desai, 'Population in Akbar's Time', *IESHR*, VOl.XV, No.I, 47.

[24] *Prices and Wages*, 1895, 250–1.

Mung is thus rated exceptionally high in the *Ā'īn*, wheareas masur and mash had about the same relative value in the *Ā'īn*'s time as in the 1870s.

The price of oilseeds at Agra for the nineteenth century is not available. However, from a comparison with prices at Aligarh, a city in the vicinity of Agra, we get the following indices:

	Ā'īn (wheat=100)	1861–70 (wheat=100)
Sesamum	166.67	179.78
Mustard	100.00	128.41

The figures suggest a distinct rise in the prices of oilseeds after the *Ā'īn* in relation to wheat.[25] This is not surprising, since these were already becoming important export crops in the 1860s.

A comparison of the prices of sugarcane cannot be made since the *Ā'īn* does not give the price of sugercane. But we can still study prices of the different varieties of sugar. While we do not have the price of sugar at Agra from the 1860s, it is quoted for Aligarh as the average of 1861–70 prices,[26] while we also have prices current at Bulandshahr in the decade 1858–67.[27] The figures below give the prices of 'white sugar' (*shaker-i safaid*) of the *Ā'īn* and 'refined sugar' at Aligarh and Bulandshahr, indexed in all cases with the wheat price as base (=100).

Ā'īn	1066.67
Aligarh 1861–70	642.05
Bulandshahr 1858–67	688.86

There was thus a substantial fall in the relative price of sugar between 1595 and 1870. This is not easy to explain since the metallic crushers which might have contributed to a fall in sugar prices had not come into use before 1870. The cause may perhaps have lain in cheaper methods of refining sugar; but this needs to be studied.

[25] Atkinson, Vol.II, Part I, 479.

[26] Ibid.

[27] Ibid., Vol.III, Part 2, 77.

Abū'l Faẓl furnishes the price for indigo current at Bayana near Agra. Bayana produced the best indigo in India; and Agra was the main market for its crop. According to the *Ā'īn*, the good (*shā'ista*) Bayana variety fetched Rs 10 to 16 per *man*.[28] By the late nineteenth century Bayana was no longer an indigo centre of importance. The price of indigo at Agra was Rs 24.36 per quarter maund in the 1870s.[29] As noted in Chapter 3, the method of extraction of the dye changed form natural evaporation to boiling, and the modern variety yielded a more concentrated extract. The ratio between the price of indigo manufactured by evaporation and by boiling processes has been given by Hadi as 1:1.8.[30] Accepting this ratio, we can convert the prices of '*pakka*' indigo (extracted by boiling), given for Agra for the 1870s into those of '*kachcha*' indigo (extracted by evaporation), which in turn can be compared with the price of the Bayana indigo given in the *Ā'īn*. The price for '*kachcha*' indigo at Agra in the 1870s works out at Rs 36.39 per *man-i Akbarī*. For Aligarh, however, we have a much higher quotation for *gand* indigo (or dye extracted through evaporation), namely, Rs 75 to 105 per maund (i.e. Rs 50.41 to 70.58 per *man-i Akbarī*).[31]

Taking the *Ā'īn*'s indigo prices as base, = 100, we then get the following prices for the 1870s:

Agra	227 to 364
Aligarh (*gand*)	441 to 509

In this case the lower price of *gand* is compared to the minimum price for Bayana indigo recorded in the *Ā'īn*, and the higher to the maximum rate in the *Ā'īn*.

The Agra figures suggest a rise amounting to 2.3 to 3.6 times, which is substantially lower than the magnitude of increase in wheat prices (5 times). But the Agra indigo of the 1870s was probably inferior to the Bayana indigo of the *Ā'īn* and perhaps even to the indigo grown at Aligarh. Even in Akbar's time the revenue rate on indigo for *dastūr*-circle Agra, which was lowest in the *ṣūba*, was 156.5 *dāms*, while for Kol (Aligarh) the rate was 163.12 *dāms*.

[28] *Ā'īn*, I, 422. As pointed out by Habib (*Agrarian System*, 86*n*, rev. ed. 94*n*) the Br. Mus. MSS Add.7652 and 5645 give the price as Rs10 to 16 per *man*, while Blochmann reads Rs 10 to 12 per *man*.

[29] Atkinson, Vol.II, 556.

[30] *A Monograph on Dyes etc.*, 76.

[31] Atkinson, Vol.2, Part I, 476.

On comparing the prices of Bayana indigo with those of *gand* indigo at Aligarh, which was yet likely to be inferior, we find the nineteenth-century prices amounting to 4.4 to 5.1 times that of Bayana indigo in 1595; this suggests, keeping in view changes in the price of wheat, a marginal decline (but no more) in the relative price of indigo by the last quarter of the nineteenth century; such decline does not indeed seem implausible in the face of intense West Indian competition.

We may now pass on from agricultural crops to pastoral products. The comparative price indices (wheat = 100) of *ghī* for Agra during 1861–70 are given below:[32]

Ghī (buffalo)	I sort	1231.08
Ghī (buffalo)	II sort	1161.22
Ghī (cow)	I sort	1313.06
Ghī (cow)	II sort	1239.19

Since the *Ā'īn*'s price for *ghī* is 875.00 (with its wheat price as base, = 100), this table shows a 40 per cent rise in the price of *ghī* relative to wheat.[33]

The rise in the relative value of pastoral produce is further supported by a comparison of the price of goats in the *Ā'īn* and those prevalent at Agra in 1850,[34] indexed with wheat, = 100.

Ā'īn	166.67–222.22
Agra, *c.*1850	232.26–310.18
In the relative price of sheep, the position is however different:	
Ā'īn ('Hindi' sheep)	333.33
Agra, *c.*1850	155.04

This could perhaps be partly attributed to a change in taste, since the price of mutton given in the *Ā'īn* was about 20 per cent higher than that

[32] *Prices and Wages*, 250–1.

[33] It may incidentally be observed that, had the *Ā'īn*'s prices referred to Lahore, the rise in the relative value of *ghī* would have been even more marked. Indexed to wheat (= 100) the 1861–70 prices at Lahore were: *ghī* (buffalo) (I), 1455.60: (II) 1334.70; *ghī* (cow) (I), 1454.55; (II) 1386.36.

[34] Atkinson, Vol.II, 485.

of goat's meat, while about 1850 the price of sheep was about half the price of goat, suggesting a shift in demand in favour of goat's meat. Partly too, the import of European woollens could have depreciated the prices of Indian sheep.

The relative prices of salt offer an interesting picture. The *Ā'īn*'s price is 16 *dāms* per *man*.[35] We may compare this with the average prices we have for Agra and Lahore for the decade 1860–71.[36] With the price of for wheat as the base (=100), the following index is obtained:

Ā'īn	133.33
Agra, 1861–70	256.44
Lahore, 1861–70	203.03

Common salt was thus cheaper in relation to wheat in the last quarter of the sixteenth century than during 1861–70. However, as a result of railway transport, salt prices fell considerably after 1870, hovering around half the price of wheat by 1894: in Agra it now sold at a price 56.86 per cent of wheat, and at Lahore, 52.04 per cent.

Abū'l Faẓl has devoted a full chapter to the price of different varieties of woollen, silken and cotton cloth. For comparative purposes most of these prices are unusable, since these (quoted mostly per piece) are of luxury products which were no longer woven in the nineteenth century. However, the price for an ordinary variety of cotton cloth, namely *salāhatī*, which is given by yard lengths, seem comparable,[37] since *salāhatī* appears to have been a coarse cloth. According to the *Siyāqnāma* it was used for lining tents.[38] Its comparison with two nineteenth-century cheap varieties of 'country cloth', viz., *dhotar* and *gārhā*, therefore, seems reasonable.

Prices for the modern varieties for the period 1858–67 are given for Bulandshahr,[39] a town in the Doāb not far from both Agra and Delhi. We know that the *gaz-i Ilāhī* used in the *Ā'īn-i Akbarī* was equal to about 32 inches,[40] and we can further assume that the width of hand-woven cloth

[35] *Ā'īn*, I, 66.

[36] *Prices and Wages*, 84 & 86.

[37] The price for inferior variety of *salāhatī* was 2 *dāms/gaz-i Ilāhī* while that for the best quality *salāhatī* was 4 *dāms* per *gaz-i Ilāhī* (*Ā'īn*, I, p.109).

[38] *Siyāqnāma*, 176.

[39] Atkinson, III, 78.

[40] Habib, *Agrarian System*, 357–8 (rev. ed. 410); it seems a fair approximation to the tailor's yard of the time as well.

remained the same from Mughal times (being governed by the size of traditional looms). The comparative prices in rupees per *gaz-i Ilāhī* (with those of the *Ā'īn*'s two varieties of *salāhatī* serving as base, = 100) then work out as follows:

*c.*1595	1858–67
Salāhatī I (inferior quality)	*Dhotar*
100	166.50
Salāhatī II (best quality)	*Gārhā*
100	250.00

Clearly cotton prices in real terms fell greatly between 1595 and 1867, because while the price of wheat rose five times, here in the case of *salāhatī* I/*dhotar*, the rupee price increased only by about 67 per cent and, in the case of *salāhatī* II/*gārhā*, by 2.5 times. Such a low absolute increase is perhaps to be primarily explained by a grave depression in the wages of spinners and weavers as a result of the invasion of Indian markets by Lancashire; but the decline in price of coarser quality cloth in real terms is so great that a fall in the price of raw cotton must also be assumed.

Metals such as iron and copper are other commodities whose relative prices fell sharply.

In his chapter on the harness of imperial elephants, Abū'l Faẓl records the prices sanctioned for iron as 2 *dāms* per *ser*.[41] Comparing these prices with the price of Indian iron at Meerut in 1872,[42] we find an increase amounting to 2.42 times. (English iron at the same time and place cost 4.35 times the *Ā'īn*'s price.) The increase in the price of iron was thus less than half that of wheat at Agra (5.04 times); there had therefore been a real fall in the price of local Indian iron before the last quarter of the nineteenth century.

The decline in the value of copper is more spectacular: it is not only relative, but absolute. The price quoted in the *Ā'īn* is 1,044 *dāms* per *man* (Rs 26.10/*man*).[43] The price of copper at Calcutta in 1882 was Rs 31.48 per cwt (Rs15.55/*man*).[44] The price given in the *Ā'īn* was thus nearly 168

[41] *Ā'īn*, I, 141. Moreland, *India at the Death of Akbar*, 150–1, missed this reference and depended upon the price quoted for iron pegs (120 *dāms/man-i Akbarī*) in the *Ā'īn*, I, 143. This naturally led him to suggest a much greater decline in iron price.

[42] Atkinson, Vol.III, Part II, 67.

[43] *Ā'īn*, I, 33.

[44] Watt, Vol.2, 649. The price has been converted into rupees per *man-i Akbarī* by me.

per cent of the price quoted for copper at Calcutta in 1882. In other words, while the price of wheat went up about 5 times, the price of copper fell by 40.42 per cent. A very heavy import of copper during the three centuries is naturally implied.

Changes in the rupee prices of the various commodities that we have established in relation to wheat are set out in Table 14.2. In the last column, the relative prices for 1861–70 have been indexed, taking the relative prices of the same commodities in 1595 as base, = 100.

Table 14.2

Agricultural Produce	*Āʼīn* (a)	Agra, 1861–70 (b)	(b) as % of (a)
Wheat	100.00	100.00	100.00
Barley	66.67	63.54	95.31
Jowar	83.33	73.41	88.10
Bajra	66.67	76.48	114.71
Gram	66.67	78.98	118.46
Mung	150.00	93.24[a]	62.16
Masur	133.33	127.93[a]	95.78
Mash	108.33	107.01[a]	98.78
Sesame	166.67	179.78[b]	107.99
Mustard	100.00	128.41[b]	128.41
Refined sugar	1066.67	642.05[b]	60.02
Indigo	3333.33–5333.33[c]	2423.56–3393.27[d]	63.62–72.71
Ghī	875.00	1161.22–1313.08	132.71–150.14
Goat	166.67–222.22	232.02–310.8[e]	139.31–132.86
Sheep	333.33	155.04	46.51
Minerals and Manufactures			
Salt	133.33	256.44	192.33
Cloth:			
Salāhatī I, per yard	16.67	6.995[f]	41.96
Salāhatī II, per yard	33.33	18.675[f]	56.03
Iron	666.67	505.05[g]	75.76
Copper	8700.00	996.83[h]	11.46

[a] Agra, 1875–6.
[b] Aligarh, 1861–70.
[c] Bayana.
[d] Aligarh, 1872–3.
[e] Agra, 1850.
[f] Bulandshahr, 1858–67.
[g] Meerut, 1871–2.
[h] Calcutta, 1882 (but Agra, wheat, 1861–70, as 100).

III

Abū'l Faẓl records the wages for a number of skilled and unskilled jobs. These are found scattered in the text, except for the wages in the 'Building Establishment', which are set out in a separate chapter.[45] The wages are those sanctioned for employees and workers in the imperial establishments.[46] The majority of servants, especially those tending animals (and birds), or otherwise employed in the animal stables, drew monthly salaries; but for most of the skilled jobs the wages quoted are piece wages.[47] Daily wages were sanctioned only in the building establishment and for some unskilled, low-paid workers such as grass-cutters and boy helpers in the stables.[48]

From such data it is not possible to work out the average wage rates, since we do not know the total number of workers in each category, and the numbers and wages of many categories have not come down to us at all. Moreover, piece wages cannot be compared with time wages. The best course therefore, seems to be to establish the wage level of the lowest-paid, unskilled workers, such as sweepers, water-carriers, bamboo-cutters, grass-cutters, etc., being persons who have traditionally obtained the lowest wages down to modern times. The wages of these workers, recorded in the *Ā'īn*, are given in Table 14.3 (see next page).

These wages give the impression that those tending animals in the imperial stables were more favoured than their counterparts elsewhere. Some stable employees were not only paid by the month, but their wages when converted into implicit daily rates work out to be slightly higher than those paid to similar workers in other establishments. The daily wage of the water-carrier furnishes a clear instance of such favoured treatment for stable staff. Even the water-carrier, Grade I, in the building establishment got less than the ordinary water-carrier in the horse stables. This privileged position seems to have been partly counter-balanced by the higher responsibilities of the stable staff, since any suspected negligence immediately resulted in fines. The sweeper and water-carrier in the stables were liable to lose one-fourth of their (monthly) salary if the horses became lean.[49] On the other hand, there was a system of rewards

[45] *Ā'īn*, I, 170.
[46] Ibid., 134–5, 143–4, 149–50, 151.
[47] Ibid., 12, 14, 16.
[48] Ibid., 135, 144, 150.
[49] Ibid., 164.

Table 14.3

	Monthly Salary (*dāms*)	Implicit or quoted daily wage (*dāms*)
Sweeper in horse stable	65	(2.17)
Water-carrier in horse stable	100	(3.33)
Water-carrier I in building establishment	—	3
Water-carrier II " "	—	2
Bamboo-cutter " "	—	2
Sawyer " "	—	2
Grass-cutter " "	—	2
Meth (supplier of fodder and watchman in elephant stables)	—	3
Meth on march	—	3.5
Helper in stable	—	2

for stable staff; these were given on special occasions such as when the emperor mounted an elephant or horse; but these occasions were likely to be rare in the careers of ordinary staff.

On the whole, then, 2 *dāms* a day seem to represent the lower limit of the range of unskilled or 'menial' workers' wages. For some skilled and semi-skilled workers, however, the sanctioned wages were at an even lower rate (Table 14.4, next page).

These salaries seem abnormally low; and one suspects that they were supplemented by some other forms of payment or advantage.

The lowest wage-rate recorded in the *Ā'īn* can be compared with the wages of corresponding categories in the second half of the nineteenth century. The wages sanctioned for the building establishment can be said with some confidence to be those of Agra, since in the same chapter Abū'l Faẓl refers to Fatehpur as the capital. The wages quoted elsewhere may relate either to Agra or to Lahore—the two capital cities.

Moreland seems to be of the view that since the wages in the *Ā'īn* are those of the imperial establishment, these had an upward bias; and should therefore be held comparable only with the wages prevalent at the 'centre of greatest demand in Northern India'.[50] In northern India one would

[50] W.H. Moreland in *JRAS*, 1817, 822.

Table 14.4

	Monthly Salary (*dāms*)	Implicit or recorded daily wage (*dāms*)
Mahout paid by *faujdār*	40	(1.33)
Mahout of *mokul* elephant	50	(1.67)
Bhoī of female elephant	50	(1.67)
Hāda in *dehbāshī*, emperor's own (*k͟hāṣa*) stable	30	(1.00)
Lowest-paid *chela* (slave)		1.00

expect the greatest demand of labour to have centred at Calcutta and, later on, at places like Delhi and Kanpur.

The wage statistics for the latter half of the nineteenth century available to us are rather limited. The official *Prices and Wages* records wages from 1873 onwards, but the information is inadequate. Wages are given only for 'able-bodied agricultural worker', 'syce' and one omnibus category of skilled workers designated 'mason, carpenter, blacksmith'.

When we compare (as in Table 14.5 below) the wages (money wages as well 'real' wages in terms of wheat) at Calcutta, Delhi, Kanpur, and Agra in 1874, we find that contrary to what one would expect from Moreland's argument, wages at Calcutta[51] were the lowest and those of Agra the highest, with Delhi and Kanpur coming next.

Prices & Wages does not furnish wages for Lahore. The Lahore *District Gazetteer* gives without any specification the highest and lowest wages of skilled and unskilled workers at Lahore in 1870–1.[52] The range for a skilled worker is Rs 9.3–15, or, in terms of wheat, 210.3–336.30 seers.[53] per month; and, for the unskilled, Rs 3.75–7.50, or 84.08–168.15 seers of wheat. This indicates that real wages at Lahore in 1870–1 were at about the same levels as at Agra in 1874. In other words, it should not much matter whether one takes the wages in the 1870s at Agra or at Lahore, to compare with those of the *Ā'īn*.

51 Real wages at Calcutta at that time ought to be measured in rice rather than wheat. But for comparison with the *Ā'īn*, wheat can be the only index.

52 *Panjab District Gazetteers*, Vol.30, Part B, 48.

53 When spelt 'seer', the weight is always that of the official British 'seer'— 1/40th of the 'maund' of 82–2/7 lb. avdp.

Table 14.5

	Horse-keeper		*Mason/carpenter/smith*	
	Money Wages (rupees)	Real Wages (*seers* of wheat)	Money Wages (rupees)	Real Wages (*seers* of wheat)
Calcutta	4–5	49.80–62.25	5–7.5	62.25–93.34
Kanpur	4	69.40	7.50	130.12
Delhi	4	77.08	10.00	192.12
Agra	5	82.00	14.67	240.88

By converting money wages into wheat wages we do not obtain real wages, but only a possible index of real wages, since changes in wheat prices are likely to represent only approximately changes in other food grain prices. (Wheat itself was probably rarely consumed by the poor.) With this reservation, we may attempt a comparison of the 'wheat wages' of several categories of wage earners recorded in the *Ā'īn* with those in the latter half of the nineteenth century.

The nineteenth century wage-data available for Agra cover barely one category of wage-earners; but these may be supplemented by quotations of wages from other western U.P. towns. In Table 14.6, wages for the lowest-paid strata in Agra and other towns are set out, converted into wheat wages, and these are preceded by wheat wages worked out from the *Ā'īn* for the corresponding categories.

Table 14.6 shows that for wages of unskilled labour in the nineteenth century, we get two floor-levels, one true for Muzaffarnagar and the other for Agra, Meerut, Bulandshahr, and Kanpur. The minimum wages in Muzaffarnagar hardly came to 2 seers of wheat a day, which is even less than half the low unskilled-wage in the *Ā'īn* (2 *dāms* or 4.44 seers of wheat). The floor level for the other places, though higher than Muzaffarnagar's is still no higher than 60 per cent of the minimum level of the wages given in the *Ā'īn*, with the exception of the porter's wage at Agra which too barely exceeds 75 per cent of the *Ā'īn*'s wage. The conclusion seems inescapable that unskilled urban wages (in terms of wheat) declined considerably between the close of the sixteenth and the latter half of the nineteenth century.

This conclusion is in accord with the inferences drawn by Smith, that prices went up by 500 to 600 per cent while the wages of unskilled labourers increased by hardly 250 to 300 per cent by the end of the nineteenth century;[54] or in other words, that real wages fell by half during the

[54] V.A. Smith, *Akbar the Great Mogul*, 286.

Table 14.6

Daily wages in seers of wheat
(1/40th of standard maund=82.28 lbs avdp)

	(a) *Ā'īn*	(b) Agra	(c) Bulandshahr	(d) Meerut	(e) Muzaffarnagar		(f) Kanpur
Wage-earner	1595	1871–2	1858, 1863, 1867	1815*	1858–67	1875	1879–90
Sweeper	4.86				1.55		2.68
Water-carrier	4.86–6.68			3.2	1.48		3.09
Labourer/*piyāda* in stable	4.48			3.2			
Herdsmen/*meth*	4.48–6.68		2.53–4.81		2.64		
Coolie, porter/helper in stable	4.81	3.35	2.28–4.05	2.4		2.25	

(a) *Ā'īn*, I, pp.144, 138.
(b) Atkinson, Vol.7, p.550.
(c) Ibid., Vol.3, Part II, pp.77–8.
(d) Ibid., p.303.
(e) Ibid., pp.583–4.
(f) *Prices and Wages*, p.303.
* Wages here are in terms of wheat flour (ordinary variety).

period. Though Smith's estimate of modern wages seems based on a rather rough-and-ready method,[55] his conclusion would seem to be nearer the truth than Moreland's who thought that real minimum wages in 1595 and 1910–14 stood at about the same level.[56]

We may now analyse the information on the wages of skilled and semi-skilled labourers. As stated earlier, for much skilled and semi-skilled work, the *Ā'īn* quotes piece wages, which are very difficult to compare with modern rates. In the building establishment, however, daily rates were sanctioned for *beldārs* ('spademen'), thatchers, carpenters and *gilkārs* (plasterers).[57] Most of the higher-paid attendants of animals, such as mahouts, *bhoi*, *sāī*'s ('syce', horse groom) were paid by the month. For many of these jobs, except for the *sāī's*, comparable official quotations from the nineteenth century are lacking. The *Ā'īn* gives monthly rates too for boatmen and palanquin-bearers; and for these we are fortunate in having comparative rates from modern times. Table 14.7 (next page) gives wages converted into wheat for these various skilled and semi-skilled categories.

The changes in wages in terms of wheat for semi-skilled jobs over the three centuries (seventeenth–nineteenth) appears to be similar to those of wages of the unskilled. The wages of *beldārs* (spademen) and thatchers declined to almost half the earlier level in terms of wheat. This fall was not confined to the building industry only, since the wages of the palanquin-bearers too went down in about the same proportion.

The range of wages of different grades of carpenters given in the *Ā'īn* is very wide, viz., 2 to 7 *dāms* (4.48 to 15.69 seers of wheat a day). The rate for carpenter grade V seems too low, being equal to that of a sawyer and bamboo-cutter. The rate for carpenter grade IV was only 3 *dāms*, the same as for the thatcher. One may, therefore, infer that carpenters of grades IV and V were perhaps not full-fledged carpenters but apprentices. The late nineteenth century rates for carpenters vary from 7 to 12 seers of wheat a day, except in Bulandshahr and Muzaffarnagar where the minimum rates were 4.13 and 4.17 seers respectively, being more consonant with the wages sanctioned for grade V in the *Ā'īn*. We thus discern a decline of 25 to 33 per cent in the wheat wages of the higher grades of carpenters. That is, though wages declined substantially

[55] Smith derived his estimate of nineteenth-century wages from his own experience in paying wages to unskilled servants in U.P. for 30 years (1870–1900). He took the same rates to be true for landless labourers as well.

[56] Moreland, 'Prices and Wages', 284.

[57] *Iṣṭilāḥāt-i Peshawarān*, Vol.1, 84, describes *gilkārī* as plastering; therefore *gilkār* should be 'plasterer'.

Table 14.7

Daily skilled and semi-skilled wages in seers of wheat
(1/40th of standard maund=82.28 lbs avdp)

	(a)	(b)	(c)	(d)	(e)		(f)
	Ā'īn	Agra	Bulandshahr	Meerut	Muzaffarnagar		Kanpur
	1595	1871–2/1874		1815	1850	1875*	1879–90
Beldār (spade-man)	6.72–7.84			3.2		3.74–4.49	
Gilkār/mason	8.96–15.69	8.03	4.80–9.63			7.49–11.98	
Carpenter	4.48–15.69	7.03–10.68	4.13–10.13	7.53	4.7		7.7
Thatcher	6.72					3.74	
Boatman	7.47		3.04–4.81		2.73		
Pālkī-bearer	8.96–11.95			4.80			
Syce	7.62 (minimum)	2.74					

(a) *Ā'īn*, I, pp.170–1, 204, 190, 144.
(b) Atkinson, Vol.7, p.550.
(c) Ibid., Vol.3, Part II, pp.77, 78.
(d) Ibid., p.303; *Price and Wages*, p.303.
(e) Ibid., pp.583, 584.
(f) *Prices and Wages*, p.303.
* Wages here are in terms of wheat flour (ordinary quality).

between *c.*1600 and 1870, the fall is here not as large as with unskilled and semi-skilled categories. On the other hand, the wages of *gilkārs* (plasterers) declined by almost 50 per cent; and we find the same trends in boatmen's wages.

The steepest decline is noticeable in the wages of the 'syces'. Even the lowest paid groom in the imperial establishment received a wage (in terms of wheat) three times that of his counterpart in the last quarter of the nineteenth century. Since modern rates for other animal attendants are not available, it is not possible to see whether the wages of workers tending other animals fell equally sharply. But a steep fall in the wages of this category might be expected, due to the decline in the military importance of elephants and camels, as well as horses.

It seems well-established that urban wages, in terms of wheat, were about 50 per cent higher at the close of the sixteenth century than in the latter half of the nineteenth century. We will now consider whether urban workers in Mughal India were in fact better off than their counterparts in the late nineteenth century in respect of the entire range of essential consumption goods. We have already seen that the prices of various commodities moved in different directions over these centuries. The prices of foodgrains, relative to wheat, largely remained stable, with a margin of ±20 per cent; but there seems to have been a large increase in the relative prices of pastoral products. On the other hand, we observe a substantial fall in the price of industrial products, notably cloth.

To translate these varied alterations in prices into changes in the purchasing power of wages in terms of each commodity, it is necessary to establish the comparable lowest wage-levels. We have seen that two *dāms* a day represent the normal lowest wage of unskilled workers in the *Ā'īn*. The wages of porters and navvies (labourers) (2½ annas a day) are assumed to represent the lowest unskilled wages at Agra in 1871–2.[58] Purchasing power can now be calculated by taking the prices given in the *Ā'īn* and the prices at Agra for 1871–2 abstracted from the official *Prices and Wages*. Unfortunately, *Prices and Wages* does not give the prices for sugar, *ghī* and cloth. As already mentioned, the prices of these commodities are quoted for 1867 in one of our sources for Bulandshahr which also furnishes porters' wages.[59] For expressing wages in terms of sugar, *ghī*, and cloth, I have therefore used the prices at Bulandshahr for 1867, applying them to the porters' wages given for that year.

[58] Atkinson, Vol.VII, 551.

[59] Ibid., Vol.II, 77.

Table 14.8

Commodities	Purchasing Power of Wages of Unskilled Workers (a) 1595 (maunds/yards)	(b) 1867/1871–2 (maunds/yards)	(b) as % of (a)
Wheat	3.36	2.53	75.29
Barley	5.04	3.19	63.29
Gram	5.04	2.49	49.40
Jowar	4.03	2.81	69.73
Bajra	5.04	2.35	46.63
Ghī	0.38	0.20	52.63
Sugar	0.31	0.32	103.23
Salt	2.52	1.08	42.86
salāhatī I/dhotar	26.67	44.40	166.48
salāhatī II/gārhā	13.33	16.00	120.03

Table 14.8 gives the purchasing power of monthly wages in 1595 and 1871–2 (Agra) and 1867 (Bulandshahr); the quantities are stated in maunds (of 82.28 lbs) and in the case of cloth in modern yards.

It appears that the purchasing power of wages in regard to cereals was significantly higher in 1595 than in the latter half of the nineteenth century. It was a quarter more in wheat, while in the case of inferior foodgrains, it was 30 to 50 per cent higher. The unskilled worker in Akbar's time should have been able to buy twice as much *ghī* as his successor could purchase in 1867; while of sugar the worker of Akbar's time could have had just a little less. For salt the purchasing power of his wages was 57 per cent higher (the price of salt was, however, to fall very markedly by the closing decade of the nineteenth century). The unskilled worker in 1595 could, therefore, have had food in much greater quantity than in the latter half of the nineteenth century.

The wage-earner in the nineteenth century was more fortunate in respect of his clothing for the purchasing power of wages in terms of cloth had greatly increased. In respect of the cheapest variety of cloth the purchasing power of the lowest wages in 1867 was 67 per cent higher than in 1595.

To see the trends in the purchasing power of skilled workers' wages, one can compare the purchasing power of wages sanctioned for carpenter grade I in the *Ā'īn* (7 *dāms* a day or 210 *dāms* a month) and the highest wages of the carpenter at Agra in 1871–2 (Rs 15 a month) (Table 14.9) where for *ghī*, sugar and cloth the data are again those of Bulandshahr.

Table 14.9

Commodities	Purchasing Power of Wages of High-Grade Corporates (a) 1595 (maunds/yards)	(b) 1871–2 (maunds/yards)	(b) as % of (a)
Wheat	11.76	8.10	68.88
Barley	17.65	10.20	57.79
Gram	17.65	7.95	45.04
Jowar	14.12	9.00	63.74
Bajra	17.65	7.50	42.49
Ghī	1.34	0.75	55.97
Sugar	1.10	1.20	109.09
Salt	8.82	3.45	39.12
Salāhatī I/dhotar	93.33	166.67	175.58
Salāhatī II/gārhā	46.67	60.00	128.56

The fall in the purchasing capacity of skilled workers' wages in terms of foodgrains appears to be a little more marked than it was in the case of unskilled wages. But the trend in terms of other commodities is similar.

To translate the varied indices of the purchasing power of wages for individual commodities into a single index of real wages, one needs to estimate the quantity of each commodity that the workers actually consumed (as against the quantity of each commodity they could theoretically buy if they spent their entire wages on that commodity). A survey of the conditions of the lower classes in U.P. ('North-western Provinces and Awadh') in 1887–8[60] offers us one means of estimating the amount of food and cloth bought by the lowest-paid workers as well as by those comparatively better off. The data drawn from this survey are set out in Table 14.10 (next page). For calculating the grain consumption of each adult male, out of figures for families, of different sizes and compositions, I have assumed the following weights:

man : woman : boy/girl
100 : 75 : 50

[60] *A collection of papers connected with an Inquiry into the Conditions of the Lower Classes of the Population, Especially in Agricultural Tracts, In the North-Western Provinces and Oudh, Instituted in 1887–8*, Govt. Press, Naini Tal, 73–132.

Table 14.10

	Grain consumed per adult male (seers/day)	Clothing obtained per adult male (yards/year)	Page reference from the 1887–8 *Inquiry*
Cultivator	1.00	14.19	70–1
Cultivator	1.00	12.67	71–2
Labourer & cultivator	1.11	13.85	73–4
Weaver & labourer	0.63	7.71	74–6
Cultivator & labourer	0.89	18.56	81–2
Labourer	1.14	17.27	83–4
Coolie	0.95	14.13	89–91
Cultivator & cart driver	1.38	14.79	93–5
Cultivator & grain weigher	0.94	12.12	97–9
Labourer	0.86	14.54	99–100

For cloth, the assumed weights are:

man : woman : boy : girl
60 : 100 : 30 : 50

It is repeatedly stated in the survey that practically none of the unskilled poor consumed wheat, except on festivals or some very rare occasions, and that their food usually consisted of inferior grains only; cheap vegetables or *arhar* pulses were irregularly consumed. I have converted the money estimates in the survey into quantities by using the Bulandshahr prices of 1867 for foodgrains and cloth.[61]

From the data taken from the *Inquiry*, the average coarse grain consumption comes to 0.99 seers a day or 9.03 maunds a year; and the average cloth consumed by an adult male, to 13.98 yards.

Taking the demographers' conventional size for a family, namely, one adult male, one adult female and 2.5 children, one can calculate the quantity required for the family and can then convert these into amounts in *dāms*

[61] The consumption of cloth has been estimated simply by converting the annual expenditure on cloth into yards of 'country cloth', taking the price of 'country cloth' as 2.75 annas per yard (the average of price of *dhotar*, at 1½ anna/yard, and that of *gārhā*, 4 anna/yard (Atkinson, Vol.III, part 2, 78). We would get a little higher consumption in yards per adult male (by our weights) than the actual because the cost of clothing includes the costs of turning cloth into clothes (tailoring, etc.) which we have ignored altogether.

on the basis of the prices quoted in the *Ā'īn*. Since we have assigned different ratios to men, women and children, for diet and clothing, for obtaining the grain consumption of a family of 4.5 members, the average per adult male should be multiplied by 3, while for cloth the factor should be 4.[62]

The annual grain consumption of a standard family, in this way, comes to 27.10 maunds. The average of the prices for barley, gram, jowar and bajra in the *Ā'īn* is 12.64 *dāms* a maund; the amount spent on 27.10 maunds of these foodgrains (assuming all to have been consumed in equal quantities) should have been 342.64 *dāms* per year. The estimate for cloth obtained per year is 13.98 yards for each adult male or 62.91 yards per family. Taking the average prices of *salāhatī* (3 *dāms* per *gaz-i Ilāhī* or 3.375 *dāms* a yard), the amount spent on cloth should have been 212.32 *dāms*. The total minimum expenditure on foodgrains and clothing would thus have been 554.96 *dāms* per year. The urban worker with minimum wages (2 *dāms* per day or 730 *dāms* a year) therefore had to spend 76.02 per cent of his income on foodgrains and clothing (46.94 per cent on grains and 29.38 per cent on cloth). If we increase it further even by 20 per cent to allow for hut/house-rent, expenses on salt, vegetables, *gur*, etc., the total expenses on food, clothing and housing, that is on 'necessaries', would amount to 90 per cent of the total income. This implies that after paying for 'necessaries' (essential components of diet and cloth) he was only left with 10 per cent of his total income.

On the other hand, if we allow the same amount of grain and cloth to the late nineteenth-century unskilled urban worker (e.g. a porter at Agra who received 2½ annas a day or Rs 57.03 a year) and calculate his expenditure on the basis of prices at Agra in 1871–2, we find that the porter's income was insufficient to buy even these quantities of inferior grain and cloth. His expenses should have come to Rs 55.65 (97.58 per cent of his total income) on foodgrains and Rs 10.81 (18.96 per cent) on clothing. This meant a deficit of 16.54 per cent, with no allowance made for rent or other expenses on diet. It seems, then, that though there was a drastic fall in the proportion of income spent on cloth, the rise in the proportion of income required for the same quantities of foodgrains had gone up by more than 50 per cent (being 97.58 per cent instead of 46.94 per cent).

The average food consumption that we had assumed here is based on rural consumption in 1887–8, and the urban level might perhaps have been comparatively lower than rural (in respect of food at least) in both periods. In that case the urban worker in the late nineteenth century might

[62] We assume:

Diet 1/100 (100+75+50+50+25)=3.0

Cloth 1/60 (60+100+30+50+0)=4.0

not actually have incurred such a large deficit, but the expenditure on other items plus 'savings' of the late sixteenth century worker should, by the same token, have been higher than 10 per cent. It would seem a fair assumption that the late sixteenth century unskilled worker was much better off than his successor in the nineteenth century. Given the data we have, and going only by the proportions of income spent on foodgrains and cloth, the real unskilled urban wages at the close of the sixteenth century seem to have been about 40.5 per cent higher than in the latter part of the nineteenth century.

The position in respect of real wages of skilled workers is difficult to establish, since there is no certain measure for comparing the wages of skilled jobs. Nevertheless one may still hazard a comparison of skilled real wages by taking the wages sanctioned for carpenters grade I in the *Ā'īn* (7 *dāms* a day) and the highest rates for carpenters at Agra proper in 1871–2 (Rs 15 a month). To estimate the consumption level and pattern, I take the average food and cloth consumption of some skilled rural workers and better-off strata in 1887–8 as reported in the official *Inquiry*.

The average consumption of grain per adult male in 1887–8 works out at 1.12 seer a day and of cloth 17.942 yards a year. These persons sometimes consumed wheat also and a noticeable part of their expenses was on purchasing articles of diet other than grain. After paying for their diet and clothing, a large part of their income still remained to be spent on other items or put into savings.

Proceeding on the lines followed for unskilled workers, our estimate for the standard family of skilled workers comes to 30.66 maunds of foodgrains and 80.739 yards of cloth a year.[63] Multiplying these by the averages of the prices for wheat, barley, gram, jowar and bajra in the *Ā'īn* (13.684 *dāms* a maund) and the average price of *salāhatī* (3.375 *dāms* a yard) the expenditure on foodgrains comes to 419.55 *dāms* (16.42 per cent of wages) and on clothing 272.49 (10.66 per cent). This meant that the expenses incurred on the quantity of foodgrains and cloth indicated by the 1887–8 survey amounted to only 27.08 per cent of the total income of the Grade I carpenter in the *Ā'īn*.

But as may be seen from Table 14.11 the skilled worker in the last quarter of the nineteenth century spent nearly 30 per cent of his income on items of diet other than foodgrains. These items included rice (not included in the foodgrains calculated above), pulses, salt, *ghī*, *gur* (raw

[63] The assumed ratio for cloth consumption here is:

Man:	Woman:	Girl:	Boy:	Small child
75:	100:	60:	50:	10

Table 14.11

	Consumption by Skilled Worker		Percentage of Expenditure		
	Grain consumed per adult male (seer/day)	Clothing obtained per adult (yard/year)	on other food items	on other articles	Page reference to *1887–8 Inquiry*
Carpenter	0.80	12.77	30.90	7.90	80–3
Oilman/moneylender	0.86	14.43	49.13	11.87	83–6
Goldsmith	1.72	29.88	39.25	12.13	91–3
Carpenter	1.20	14.85	22.27	3.75	130–2
Carpenter & cultivator	1.00	17.75	7.87	2.92	133–5
Average	1.12	17.942	29.855	7.715	

sugar), oil, sugar, spices, etc. While in the last decade of the sixteenth century, the relative prices of pastoral products were lower than in the late nineteenth, those of semi-manufactured products, such as sugar and oil, were higher. We will, therefore, not go far wrong in assuming that the skilled worker at the close of the sixteenth century too spent about the same proportion of his income on articles of diet other than foodgrains. The total expenditure on food and cloth would thus have worked out at 57 per cent of his income (27.08 + 30.00 per cent). Making an allowance for rents and cesses, repair and purchase of tools and implements and payment for service, such as those of the barber, the expenditure incurred on 'necessaries' should have been 75 per cent of the entire earnings. The balance of income must in bulk have gone to buying or repairing utensils, articles of furniture and payments for services of washermen, potters, etc. This expenditure may fall in the category of 'comforts'. If the life style of the sixteenth-century worker was similar to that of the skilled worker in the nineteenth century, we may allow some amount (say, 5 per cent) as being spent on intoxicants such as opium (partly replaced later by tobacco) and expenses on festivals, marriages, etc. These may be classed as luxuries.

As for the skilled worker's real wages in the latter part of the nineteenth century, these may be compared with those of his predecessor, *c.*1600, by taking into account the expenditure on foodgrains and cloth. The highest-paid carpenter at Agra in 1871–2 must have annually spent Rs 54.57 (30.32 per cent) on foodgrains and Rs 13.88 (7.71 per cent) on clothing if we calculate the values by the same yard-stick. Thus the carpenter at Agra in 1871–2 spent 38.03 per cent of his total income on foodgrains and cloth, while his predecessor at the close of the sixteenth century spent only 27.08 per cent of his wages to obtain the same quantities of goods.

This suggests a distinct fall in the real wages of skilled artisans too. But it could be argued here, that the skilled artisan of 1595 could buy goods other than items of diet, from only a very narrow range of high-priced commodities whereas his late nineteenth-century successor had a larger choice from lower-priced industrial goods. Yet a case in the opposite direction could also be made out by reference to the large amount of unemployment and depressed income of weavers in the nineteenth century. Unluckily, the *Ā'īn* does not furnish any data on weavers' wages. If a comparison of weavers' real wages in 1595 and in the late nineteenth century had been possible, a very marked fall in real wages might have been established even from the percentage of expenditure on the barest necessities.

A fall in real urban wages between *c.*1600 and *c.*1875 may, therefore, be accepted as established. But higher urban wages in 1600 do not necessarily mean that the level of general consumption (rural as well as urban) was also as much higher. Indeed, it is possible that the large extraction of agricultural surplus by way of land revenue, and its distribution amongst an urbanized ruling class placed Mughal towns in a more favourable position with regard to the supply of agricultural produce than the decaying towns of the nineteenth century. If restriction on rural migrations had any practical force,[64] it is possible that the urban labour force did not expand sufficiently to press up prices of agricultural goods in the towns and so lower real wages. Conversely, in view of the drain of supplies to the towns, one might expect a repressed agricultural population, with consumption levels which were quite possibly no higher than those recorded in 1887–8; they might have been even lower. But unless data on agricultural wages in the sixteenth and seventeenth centuries become available, one can do little more than offer words of caution against inferring a higher per-capita consumption for the whole population on the basis of higher urban real wages for *c.*1600.

[64] Cf. Habib, *Agrarian System*, 116–17 (rev. ed. 130–2).

MONEY SUPPLY AND FOREIGN TRADE

CHAPTER 15

Money, Price Changes and Credit

The Mughal Coinage

So far we have focused on the quantitative data at a particular point of time, *c.* 1595–6 and have treated the Mughal economy as if it were a static structure. In large part, this has been a matter not of intention, but of compulsion. For the closing decade of the sixteenth century, we have information, unique in its scale and quality; its very uniqueness inhibits statistical comparison with any earlier or even later period until the nineteenth century. As a result, while the elements of the structure of the economy about 1600 can be studied in quantitative terms, dynamic elements within the economy (tendencies towards change over time) may perhaps be overlooked or obscured. Only in one sphere does it seem possible to study the economy in the process of movement, namely, the monetary system, taking it to embrace both money supply and prices.

Since commodity production and exchange comprised such a large sector of the economy of the Mughal empire, the question of money supply assumes considerable importance. In the absence of official paper-money, metallic coinage represented the totality of money supply (though one must allow for fractional money like cowries, on the one hand, and for paper money concealed in commercial paper, *hundis*, on the other). Since there are no means of establishing the 'velocity' of the coinage, it would not be sufficient to determine (if one could) the total size of metallic coinage in circulation at a particular point of time; one has to be aware of the variations in money supply over time to perceive its actual impact on the economy. I have therefore taken the period *c.* 1556–1630 (our reference year 1595–6 would fall approximately in the middle) to study the changes in the size of money supply over a reasonably extended period.

The Mughal metallic coinage was, in formal terms, 'trimetallic';[1] that is, the mints uttered coins in all the three currency metals; the gold *muhr*, the silver *rūpiya* and the copper *dām*. The value of a coin always equalled its weight in bullion plus the minting charges and seigniorage;[2] the coins were also subjected to a certain discount on account of age. This proximity to the market value of the metal was achieved by maintaining a system of 'free' or open mintage. Any quantity of metal brought to the mint could be converted into coin on payment of minting charges and seigniorage.[3]

Akbar's minting of a pure metallic coinage was a continuation of the measure initiated by Sher Shāh, who introduced a pure silver *rūpiya* or rupee (1540–5). In spite of the introduction of the rupee, the new silver coin could not directly displace the billion *tanka*, large quantities of which naturally remained in circulation. But the billion *tanka* began to be progressively replaced by the pure copper *dām* minted by Akbar.[4] For a number of years the *dām* continued to be minted from a very large number of mints; until the 1580s these exceeded in number the rupee mints, as is shown by Table 15.1, based on the catalogues of various coin collections.[5]

Table 15.1 shows the number of copper mints beginning to decline after 1580, but with a revival in the 1590s. An enormous contraction, however, took place immediately after 1605. The number of silver mints, on the other hand, remained steady from the 1590s onwards and within our period reached its peak in 1626–30, standing at more than nine times the number of copper mints.

[1] For the significance of Mughal 'trimetallism' see Irfan Habib, 'A System of Trimetallism in the Age of the Price Revolution', in: J.F. Richards (ed.). *The Imperial Monetary System of Mughal India*, Delhi, 1987, 137–70.

[2] *Ā'īn*, I, 31.

[3] Irfan Habib, 'Monetary System and Prices', *Cambridge Economic History of India*, Vol.I, 361.

[4] The copper *dām* too appears to have originated with Sher Shāh. Whitehead, *JASB*, NS, XXVIII, 96.

[5] The number of mints has been counted from the coins in (i) *Catalogue of Coins in State Museum, Lucknow*, by C.J. Brown and *Supplementary Catalogue* by C.R. Singhal; (ii) *Catalogue of Coins in the Indian Museum, Calcutta*, by N. Wright, and *Supplement* by S. Ahmad; (iii) *Catalogue of Coins in the Government Museum, Lahore*, by C.J. Rodgers; (iv) *The Coins of the Mughal Emperors of Hindustan in the British Museum*, by S. Lane-Pool; and (v) the coins recorded in the reports of U.P. treasure-troves (to be described presently). The assumption is that if a mint was active during a particular year, at least one coin belonging to that year must have survived in the existing catalogued coin collections or the U.P. treasure-trove reports.

Table 15.1

Number of active mints

	Silver	Copper		Silver	Copper
1556–60	7	9	1596–1600	14	11
1561–5	7	12	1601–5	18	9
1566–70	6	10	1606–10	13	3
1571–5	6	11	1611–15	11	2
1576–80	9	13	1616–20	13	1
1581–5	9	6	1621–5	16	2
1586–90	4	7	1626–30	19	2
1591–5	9	12			

If the number of mints is any guide to changes in the relative size of copper and silver mintage, it becomes obvious that from the 1590s onwards the rupee became the basic unit of currency and replaced the copper *dām*. This is corroborated by sale-deed evidence as well, where the money prices quoted from the 1590s are usually in rupees while previously these were usually stated in billon or copper money (*tanka* or *dām*).[6]

Once the rupee became the principal standard coin, its minting would largely determine the quantity of coined money in circulation. We need, therefore, to form an estimate of the changes in the silver currency output of the Mughal empire to obtain a picture of the changes in money supply. Aziza Hasan devised an ingenious means for it by counting the surviving silver coins with the help of all published museum catalogues.[7] Since each rupee coin bore the name of the mint as well as the year of issue, she made a count of the catalogued coins on the basis of mints and years. She then argued that variations in the number of surviving coins of different years must represent fluctuations in the total currency output. The curve showing the number of preserved coins relating to various years could thus be taken as the curve of the currency output of the Mughal empire, though on an 'unknown scale'. In order to establish geographical comparability over time, Hasan confined her count to north Indian mints.

[6] Irfan Habib, 'Aspects of Agrarian Relations and Economy in a Region of U.P. during the 16th Century', *IESHR*, IV (3), 1967.

[7] 'The Silver Currency Output of the Mughal Empire and Prices in India during the Sixteenth and Seventeenth Centuries', *IESHR*, VI (1), 1969, 85–116.

Hasan's effort must be recognized as a pioneering one; but there was a possible bias in her evidence, which has led to criticism by John S. Deyell.[8] He urges that since there is always an element of selectivity in the coins retained or acquired by museums, which do not aim at possessing more than a pair of coins of the same type (same mint/date/legend), the years in which coins of the more varied styles were minted tend to be more heavily represented in museum collections. Changes in style, rather than changes in quantities of coins minted, might therefore provide a better explanation for the great fluctuations displayed in the number of coins of different periods preserved in the museums.

On the plane of theoretical argument, Deyell's critique is partly unobjectionable; it is also partly overstated since he tends to ignore the fact that most individual museum collections often lack coins of particular mints in some years (though such coins are represented in other collections and therefore were certainly minted), while in other cases particular mints in certain years are practically fully represented in all collections.[9] Clearly, fluctuations in output must be largely responsible for such variations in representation.

In any case, Deyell's principal objection can be met by an elementary empirical check: let us set aside the catalogued collections and go to the records of the coin-finds where no element of selectivity is possibly involved. The Lucknow Museum has one of the richest collections of Mughal coins in the world, and this mostly derives from the large number of coins found in the treasure-troves in U.P.[10] The region is very large and also occupies a central position in northern India; it contained a large part of the core area of the Mughal empire including its capital city, Agra. Coin-finds within it are therefore likely to represent fairly well not only the issues of the entire period we are concerned with, but also the issues

[8] John S. Deyell, 'Numismatic Methodology in the Estimation of Mughal Currency Output', *IESHR*, Vol.XII, No.3, July–Sept. 1976, pp.392–401. Aziza Hasan's effort was earlier commented upon by Om Prakash and J. Krishnamurthy; but they made no fundamental criticism of her method, and their objections, such as they were, were largely met in a reply by A. Hasan herself in the same issue of *IESHR*, Vol.VII, No.1, 139–60.

[9] In Deyell's own Table 2, which he regards as a conclusive demonstration of the weakness of Hasan's thesis, the range of numbers of coins of each type is as wide as 1.60 to 3.00.

[10] Deyell himself refers to the U.P. treasure troves as providing the material from which the Lucknow Museum made its collections on a selective basis; he cites a personal letter from Dr A.K. Srivastava, Numismatic Officer of the Museum, to this effect (*IESHR*, XII, [3], 395–6).

of various parts of northern India without any significant geographical bias. Accordingly, information for all treasure-troves found in U.P. during the period 1882–1968, was abstracted by me from the (unpublished) official reports.[11] The total of such recorded Mughal rupee coins (North Indian mints only) comes to 7,382; this total represents coins belonging to the reigns of Emperor Akbar to Aurangzeb only (Table 15.2). These constitute as random a sample as one can get.[12]

Table 15.2

	Total	Date with mint	Datable by decade with mint	Mintless with date	Dateless with mint	Mintless and dateless
Akbar 1556–1605	2,653	1,719	421	373	86	54
Jahangir 1606–27	1,109	790	0	30	281	8
Shahjahan 1628–59	1,678	1,283.5	9	57.5	80	248
Aurangzeb 1659–1707	1,942	1,696	0	0	246	0

I have excluded (like Hasan) coins uttered by the Deccan mints in order to have the same area to consider during the entire period in question. A noticeable feature of this sample is that the rupee coins from Akbar's reign considerably outnumber those from each of the other reigns. Indeed, in spite of the fact that the number of mints (and hence the coin types) largely increased during Aurangzeb's reign, Aurangzeb's rupee coins in the sample are substantially fewer than those of Akbar. Hasan's count reveals a rather different picture in terms of relative contribution from each reign: Akbar, 1,739; Jahangir, 1,346; Shahjahan, 1,554; Aurangzeb, 2,426.

The smaller number of Akbar's coins in the museum collections is probably owing to the smaller number of mints and early types of Akbar's

[11] For particulars of these reports, see A.K. Srivastava, *Coin Hoards of Uttar Pradesh*, Vol.I, Lucknow, 1981. I have worked from the original reports in the State Museum, Lucknow, since Srivastava does not, unfortunately, record the number of duplicates in each find.

[12] Like A. Hasan, I count 8-anna or 4-anna pieces as 0.50 and 0.25 rupee respectively in arriving at my coin totals. I have also converted Jahangir's heavier rupees into ordinary rupees by taking into account their actual weights: A *sawāi* 'rupee is thus treated as equal to Rs 1.25, a *Jahāngīrshāhī* as Rs 1.20.

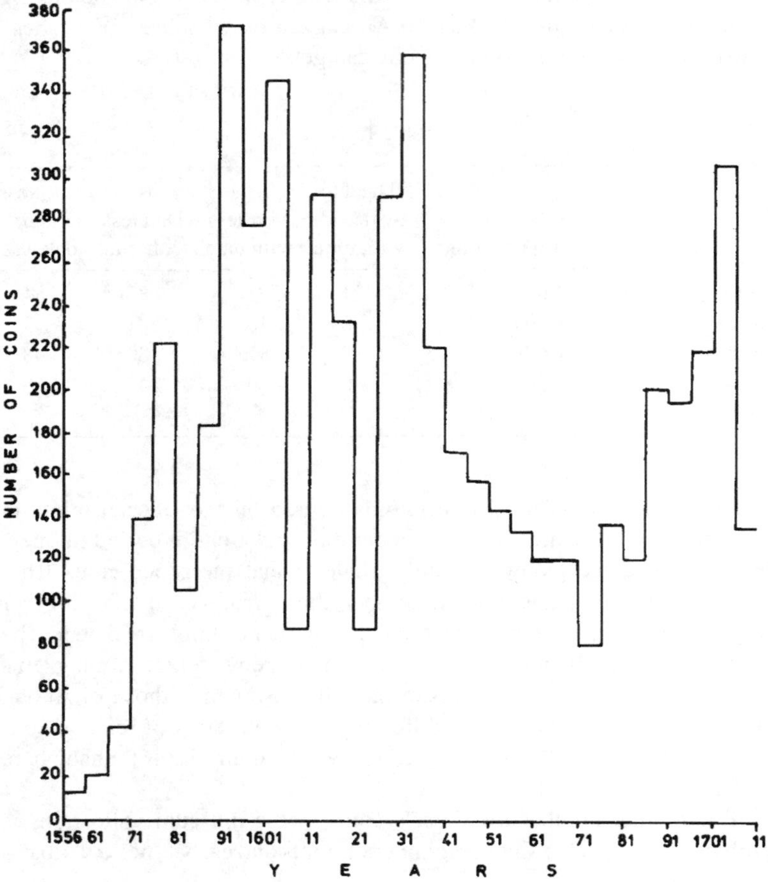

Figure 15.1

Five-yearly histogram of Mughal rupees from North Indian mints. Based on coin finds in U.P.

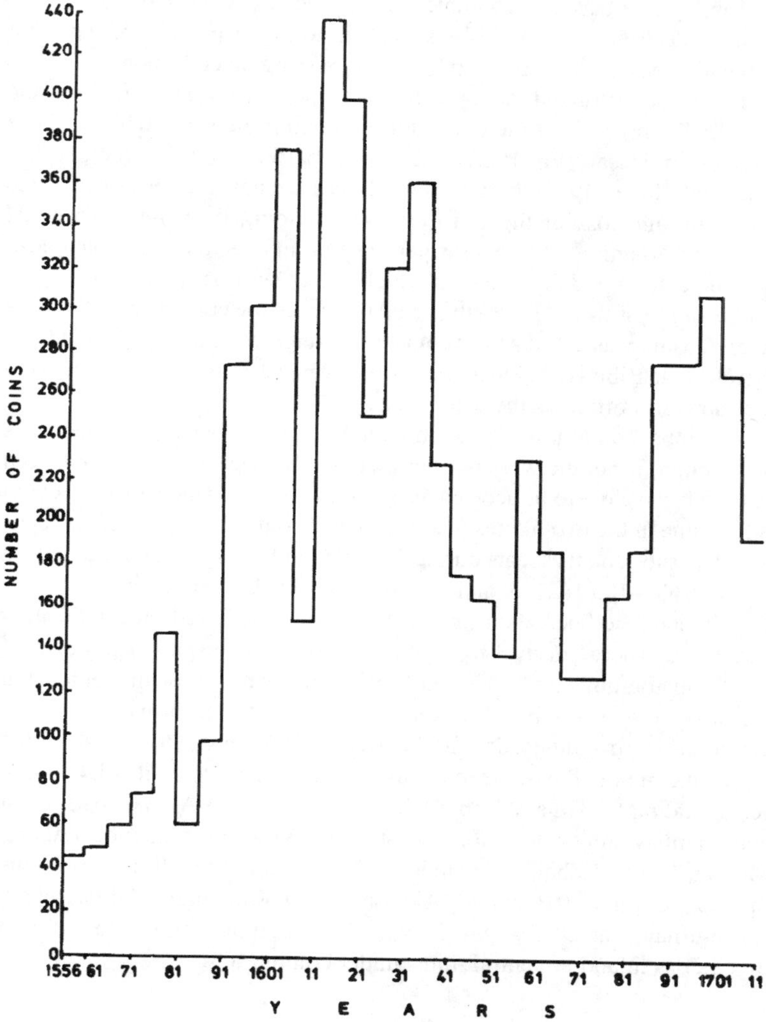

Figure 15.2

Five-yearly histogram of Mughal rupees from North Indian mints. Based on catalogued coins, Aziza Hasan, *IESHR*, VI[1].

rupees,[13] while, conversely, the larger number of mints of Aurangzeb explain the larger contribution of his reign in Hasan's count. There *is*, therefore, the probability of a bias in her sample, whose precise degree is, of course, difficult to determine. It would be safer then to retain Hasan's method, but apply it to the treasurer-trove finds instead of museum collections.

I have constructed a 5-yearly histogram from my own sample (Fig.15.1) drawn from the coin-find reports, on the same lines as those adopted by Hasan (Fig.15.2). The only departure from her method has been that I have also included coins which are datable in terms of decade only (through loss of the last digit), by dividing them into two equal halves for assignment to 5-year periods within each decade. I have also not neglected the dateless coins which are at least assignable to reigns. For example, it would give a distorted picture of the coinage of Jahangir's reign if as may as 281 dateless coins of his reign were disregarded. I have therefore distributed dateless coins among the various five-year period in the same proportion as the dated ones.

A comparison of this histogram with Aziza Hasan's partially vindicates her attempt, if not the whole of her method. The correspondence between the two is too close to be accidental. The trend (towards increase or decline) is the same in the two figures in as many as 25 out of 30 quinquennial periods. The substantial ascents during 1586–90 and 1611–15, and the troughs during 1606–10, 1621–5 and 1636–40, which have been attributed by Deyell merely to fluctuations in coin types, are equally reflected in the treasure-troves where 'survival-by-type' should have had no part to play at all.[14]

Our histogram should theoretically enable us to follow movements in the silver money-supply. In Table 15.3 where the information is converted into terms of decades for the period 1556–1635, an analysis of the regional composition of the total number of coins is also offered. Column 'G', standing for Gujarat, represents the output of the Ahmadabad, Surat and Cambay mints; the North-western ('NW') mints include Lahore, Multan, Thatta, Kabul, and Qandahar. The column headed (B) represents the Bengal mints ('Bangala', Akbarnagar or Rajmahal, Makhsusabad, Jahangirnagar or Dhaka, and Patna). The remaining mints are grouped together as inland or central mints under column 'C'.

[13] I take it that most museums have been concerned with the mint-name and year (*Ilāhī*, regnal, *hijra*) as determinants of the type rather than the *Ilahī* month (when used). If this had not been the case the possible coin-types of Akbar's reign would have been far more numerous than the catalogued types counted by Deyell for his Table II, op.cit.

[14] Thus while Hasan's sample is not perhaps useful for establishing secular trends on a firm basis, it will still be of value for showing changes in short periods within which coin-types are not known to have changed substantially. In some cases, it would appear that coin-types multiplied as silver mintage increased; and this perhaps explains the correspondence between the ascents in Hasan's sample and ours.

Table 15.3

Rupee Coins from Treasure Troves in U.P. (Deccan and South Indian mints excluded)

Decade	Total	G	NW	B	C	Mintless
1556–65	36.0	0.0	2.0	0.0	25.0	9.0
1566–75	240.5	30.0	13.0	0.0	251.5	46.0
1576–85	466.5	97.5	15.0	0.0	228.0	126.0
1586–95	876.5	294.5	47.0	0.0	320.0	215.0
1596–1605	1034.0	592.0	202.0	43.5	165.5	31.0
1606–15	516.5	91.0	139.0	28.0	241.0	17.5
1616–25	432.5	37.0	177.0	43.0	155.0	20.5
1626–35	758.0	118.5	221.5	291.5	92.0	34.5

Table 15.3 is indicative of the relative size of the average annual output (decade-figures in the table divided by 10) of rupee coinage from North Indian mints.[15] It does not of course define the scale and we must seek outside it for such data on mint output as would help us convert its figures into absolute figures of coin output. This might be done if we knew, for example, what the average output of a particular mint in a particular period was, and count its issues in our sample. Luckily, there is such information for the Surat mint during the 1630s.

Statements made by English factors indicate that the Surat mint ordinarily turned out Rs 6,000 a day for the English in 1636, 'when we have the mint alone.' Earlier in 1634, the mint output was said to have exceeded Rs 8,000 daily (coining Rs 5,000 for the English and 3,000 for the Dutch); without the Dutch, the English had been able to obtain as many as Rs 9,000 daily.[16] Apparently by the time the English and Dutch delivered their

[15] There may be a geographical bias in the record of coin-finds in U.P. only—a large region, certainly, but still rather distant from the Deccan, which may possibly be under-represented in it. But there is likely to be no under-representation of any north Indian region; silver coinage must always have had a high degree of mobility. As to Najaf Haider's view that the larger output after 1592 was caused by a new order for remintage of old coins, see my *People, Taxation and Trade in Mughal India*, New Delhi, 2008, pp. 46–7*n*.25, for a detailed argument against this suggestion.

As to Najaf Haider's view that the larger output after 1592 was caused by a new order for remintage of old coins, see my *People, Taxation and Trade in Mughal India*, New Delhi, 2008, pp. 46–7 *n*. 25, for a detailed argument against this suggestion.

[16] *Factories, 1634–6*, 68, 218. Malcolm gives the *maximum* capacity (not average output) of the Central Indian mints during the early years of the 19th century as 10,000 rupees a day (*Memoirs of Central India*, London, 1824, 85).

bullion, the silver brought through the Red Sea and the Gulf had already been coined. These figures then suggest a daily output of more than Rs 8,000 for the Surat mint during the years 1634–6. Now in our sample there are 46 coins of the Surat mint assignable to four regnal years (7–10) of Shāhjahān corresponding to 1634–7.[17] Given an annual output of Rs 8,000 × 365 for the Surat mint, we may take it that each surviving rupee in the U.P. treasure-troves represents 2,53,913 coins actually minted.[18]

Assuming this ratio applies to coins of different years, we can estimate the total coin output of the Mughal empire. In view of the survival rate being presumably higher for the period following 1634–7 and lower for the period preceding, the result would understate earlier coin-production, and overstate the later. Moreover, it would have been better if there had been similar data for mints other than Surat to enable a cross-check. Nevertheless, a minimum output of Rs 8,000 a day for Surat does not seem unreasonable, since in 1676, when the production at the much smaller Rajmahal mint was at an exceptionally low level, the English yet expected to get 10,000 rupees coined there in three or four days.[19]

Converting, then, the number of coins reported from the U.P. treasure-troves as set out in Table 15.3 into absolute figures of coins actually uttered at the rate indicated above, we reconstruct the following figures of the average annual output for each decade (Table 15.4). We can further convert the coin output into metric tons, by allowing 170.88 grains of pure silver for each coin,[20] so that one metric ton of silver may be taken

[17] The number of Surat coins bearing regnal years 7–10 in the U.P. treasure troves is actually 40. But this number has been increased by 6, to allow for the dateless Surat coins of Shahjahan assigned to these years, on the basis (already mentioned) of distribution of dateless coins to different years in the same proportion as the dated coins of the reign.

[18] The Surat mint could not have been kept open all the 365 days. Supposing it was closed once a week, our estimate should be reduced by 1/7. But our estimate of the daily average output is itself very conservative: we have not fixed it at Rs 9,000 but Rs 8,000. Moreover, the English seem to have overlooked petty claimants on the mint other than the Dutch, so that the output might well have been in the region of 9,500. Thus the output ascribed to the closed days can be adjusted against the larger output on working days.

The output of the Surat mint may seem to be rather small in view of a later report (14 October 1672 in Surat Factory Outward Letter Book, V.II, 1663–71/72, 187) (Maharashtra State Archives, Bombay) which gives its daily output as Rs 30,000 (according to Irfan Habib's reading of it in *Essays in Indian History*, 222). But the document shows that minting at this scale was an exceptional measure undertaken by special arrangements with the mint-master; it cannot be used for establishing the *average* daily output of the mint.

[19] Streynsham Master, *The Diaries of Streynsham Master, 1675–80 & other Contemporary Papers relating thereto*, I, ed. R.C. Temple, Indian Record Series, London, 1911, 401–2.

[20] Irfan Habib, 'Currency System of the Mughal Empire', *Medieval India Quarterly*, Vol.IV (1–2), 9. The actual weight of a rupee coin before Aurangzeb was 178 grains; but an allowance of 5.6% is to be made for mint charges and seigniorage.

Table 15.4

	Total Annual Output		Annual Output by Regions (metric tons)			
	(Rupees)	(Metric tons)	G	NW	B	C
1556–65	9,14087	10.12	0.00	0.75	0.00	9.37
1566–75	61,06,608	67.48	10.43	4.53	0.00	52.37
1576–85	1,18,32,346	131.02	37.82	5.78	0.00	87.82
1586–95	2,22,55,474	246.29	109.70	17.50	0.00	119.23
1596–1605	2,62,54,604	290.72	171.12	58.39	12.57	47.84
1606–15	1,31,14,606	145.22	26.49	40.52	8.15	70.14
1616–25	1,09,81,737	121.46	10.92	52.23	12.69	45.75
1626–35	1,92,46,605	213.12	34.91	65.11	85.76	27.27

to be made up of Rs 90,324.80 in coin.[21] In Table 15.4 the tonnage calculated from mintless coins has been added to the tonnage of the different regions according to the proportions established from coins preserving the mints' names.

The statistics of seventeenth-century output of French mints show that between 1631 and 1660 2,259 tons of silver money (including silver equivalent of the gold minted) were issued, giving an average annual output of 75.3 metric tons.[22] Given the size of the Mughal empire relative to France, a silver currency output averaging 159.93 metric tons a year from 1605 to 1635, is, therefore, by no means unreasonable.

The fluctuating quantities of silver minted shown by Table 15.4 may now be considered in the light of silver imports. India did not produce any silver herself;[23] so the entire supply of silver for mintage must have been imported. Imports during the sixteenth century as well as the seventeenth are likely to have originated almost entirely in Spanish America, and to have been channelled mainly through Europe and partly across the

[21] The total for metric tons is directly calculated from the totals of rupees for the respective 5-year periods; a slight difference would be noticed if the regional figures are totalled, owing to rounding.

[22] Braudel and Spooner in *Cambridge Economic History of Europe*, IV, p.444.

[23] It transpires from the *Akbarnāma*, I, 283, that the once famous silver mines of Panjshir in Afghanistan were no longer worked by the mid-16th century (for early medieval descriptions of these mines see G. Le Strange, *Lands of the Eastern Caliphate*, Cambridge, 1930, 350).

Pacific. This is the burden of the statements by a number of contemporary observers.[24]

Influx of Silver through Trade

The Second Half of the Sixteenth Century

Table 15.4 indicates a steady increase in coin output till 1605, which is exactly what one would expect. Akbar's empire from its relatively small core area in the period 1556–65 expanded to embrace the whole of northern India by the 1590s; so the number of mints and the coins uttered grew yearly. In addition, the replacement of copper money by silver which we have already noticed (Table 15.1) required the increase of silver coinage on a far greater scale than what would have corresponded simply to the territorial expansion of the Empire. The source for such increase in coinage must initially have been the internal silver stock which because of the previous prevalence of copper coinage had remained uncoined or had been minted in the form of coarse silver money in certain provincial kingdoms (Malwa, Gujarat, and Khandesh).[25] This perhaps explains the domination of the 'central' or 'inland' mints until the decade ending 1585: these mints provided in that decade as many as 87.82 tons out of a total of 131.02 tons actually coined within the empire. In the next decade too, despite a decline in their relative importance, the Central mints coined nearly 120 tons of silver (Table 15.4).

But in the twenty years following 1585 it was Gujarat which assumed a dominating position. Gujarat (the Ahmadabad mint alone) contributed 109.70 tons a year during 1586–95 out of an estimated total of 246.29 tons of silver minted, and then a phenomenal 171.12 tons out of 290.72 tons during 1596–1605.[26] Gujarat was one of the principal areas of entry of silver, for the Gulf and Red Sea as well as the Cape of Good Hope routes converged there. The province, therefore, had been receiving silver by these channels during the whole of the latter part of the sixteenth century. Some of it must have been previously coined in the coarse silver money (*maḥmūdīs*) minted in Gujarat before the Mughal conquest (1571–2). After the Mughal conquest the Ahmadabad mint must have

[24] Hawkins, *Early Travels*, 112; Bernier, 202–4; Mīr Ghulām 'Alī Āzād Ḥusainī Bilgrāmī, *Khizāna-i 'Āmira*, Nawal Kishor, Kanpur, 1871, p.111.

[25] This domestic stock must itself have accumulated out of previous imports, much of it possibly coming into the country during the 16th century.

[26] If this estimate is correct, the Ahmadabad mint must on an average have coined as many as 40,000 a day during this decade.

had to coin into rupees the large previously-accumulated quantities of silver (whether bullion or *maḥmūdīs*) as well as the silver that entered in the current stream. But even if a major portion of the rupees minted in these two decades was from the silver coin and bullion accumulated previously, the mint output of these decades is still high enough to suggest a very large size of silver imports into Gujarat.

The reader of Hamilton's work on the transfer of American silver to Europe would, of course, not be surprised at the large influx of silver into India at this time, because, as his celebrated histogram of the Spanish imports of American silver shows, this is the period during which the volume of bullion transported from America to Spain achieved its highest scale (undergoing a dramatic rise in 1576–80). The peak was reached in the years 1591–5, and there was only a marginal descent in the next half-decade.[27] That a large part of the American silver was spilling into Asia is recognized by most scholars. Geoffrey Parker estimates the loss of silver by Europe to the East around 1680 at 80 metric tons a year;[28] P. Vilar puts it at 64 tons.[29] Both these estimates seem, however, to understate the amount of silver that was actually entering Asia at the close of the sixteenth century.

Parker suggests, for example, that the annual flow of silver from Europe to the Levant between 1610 and 1614 amounted to 1.5 million ducats, or 39.7 metric tons.[30] But the silver that annually left the port of Ormuz on the Persian Gulf, shortly before 1600, is alone said to have amounted to 2 million cruzados or the equivalent of some 41.7 metric tons.[31] Precise

[27] See Earl J. Hamilton, *American Treasure and Price Revolution in Spain*, Harvard, 1934.

[28] Geoffrey Parker, 'The Emergence of Modern Finance in Europe 1500–1730', *Fontana Economic History of Europe*, ed. Carlo M. Cipola, Glasgow, 1974, 529.

[29] P. Vilar, *A History of Gold and Money, 1450–1490*, London, 1976, 101.

[30] Certain interesting figures for the Venetian exports of silver to Syria during 1593–6 (6.7 tons per annum) and 1610–14 (8 tons per annum) are given in Parker, 'Modern Finance in Europe', *op.cit.*, 529, and Braudel and Spooner, *Cambridge Economic History*, 448 & *n*. The latter apparently consider 37,529 ducats to be equal to one metric ton of silver; Parker puts a slightly higher value on the ducat.

It may be noted that Venetian silver exports to Alexandria are not included in these figures; nor the Genoese exports to the Levant. Moreover, Parker recognizes that Marseilles exported more silver to the Levant than Venice did; but its figures too are not known.

[31] Neils Steensgaard, *The Asian Trade Revolution of the 17th Century: The East India Companies and the Decline of the Caravan Trade*, Chicago, 1974, 199. I have converted cruzados into tons of silver by using values given in ibid., 417–19.

I have used the lower value of the reis of Goa, one mark silver (299.5 grammes) = 4398 reis. One cruzado was worth 400 reis. The values given by Steensgaard are broadly corroborated by those inferable from *Akbar and the Jesuits*, tr. C.H. Payne, London, 1930, 37–8.

information of this kind is unfortunately lacking for the Red Sea route. But Indian trade with the Red Sea was normally brisker than with the Gulf, and whereas the Ormuz trade was connected only with Aleppo, the Red Sea trade was linked to Cairo and Alexandria as well as Aleppo.[32] For the Cape of Good Hope route, Chaunu has estimated that during the sixteenth century Portugal paid for its imports from India by 150 tons of gold, seized from Africa, and an amount of silver far less than the 6,000 tons nominally equivalent to the remaining value of the imported spices.[33] It may then be thought that since Chaunu is speaking of the entire century, imports of silver to the East through the Portuguese by the end of the sixteenth century must have considerably exceeded 60 tons a year.[33a]

Silver also flowed into Asia from the Far East. American silver brought to the Philippines reached enormous proportions during the 1590s, when at one time almost as much silver was transported across the Pacific as the Atlantic. The reported tonnage exceeds 500 tons in single years.[34] If the Portuguese imported only 2 tons of silver from Japan (which itself received American silver) in the 1580s,[35] their silver imports from the Far East must have been considerably more in the 1590s. Moreover, there were direct mercantile connections between the Gujarat ports and South-east Asia; and some bullion must have travelled over this route. Even if a fifth of the trans-Pacific silver reached India, it would have meant something like 30 to 100 tons coming to India annually during the 1590s.

In view of these large quantities of silver entering the Indian Ocean area during the 1590s (probably approaching 150 tons a year), the estimated annual output of the Gujarat and North-western mints, amounting to 178.35 tons during the two decades 1586 to 1605, well matches our

[32] For the connection of the Gulf with Aleppo see a 1640 report from Basra in *English Factories, 1637–41*, 247–8; and for the linkage between Mokha (Red Sea) and 'Grand Cairo', see the report of a visit to Mokha in 1625–6 in *English Factories, 1624–29*, 349–51.

[33] Cited in Wallerstein, *The Modern World System*, p.329 *n*. J.F. Richards, on the basis of P. Vilar's data, estimates the annual imports of gold by the Portuguese at the close of the 16th century at 1.5 tons, a figure which is in accordance with the estimate offered by Chaunu.

[33a] According to Vilar the flow of silver from the West to the East at the beginning of the 16th century amounted to about 20.5 metric tons, while at the end it rose to 64.3 tons per annum.

[34] *Cambridge Economic History of Europe*, IV, 209–10. The quantities sent from Mexico to the Philippines reached 12 million pesos, or the equivalent of 485.765 tons of silver in 1595. In other years it ranged from 3 to 5 million pesos.

[35] J.F. Richards in *Comparative Studies in Society and History*, Vol.23, Part 2, April 1981, 302.

information about silver imports, especially if we allow for the minting of coin of older currencies and of bullion previously hoarded, and if we remember that gold, not silver, was the currency metal in the Deccan and south India, so that silver-minting was now practically confined to the Mughal empire.

Years 1605–30

Immediately after 1605, a decline in the total Mughal currency output becomes noticeable (Table 15.4). The average estimated output fell from 290.72 tons a year during 1596–1605 to 145.22 during 1606-15 and to 121.46 during 1616–25. This decline is almost totally due to a dramatic fall in the output of the Gujarat mints, sliding from 171.12 tons during 1596–1605, to 26.49 during 1606–15 and to only 10.92 tons during 1616–25. The North-western mints that were receiving bullion by overland routes (or the coastal routes form the Gulf to Thatta) continued to maintain their high levels, displaying a steady increase from the decade 1596–1605, until an output of 65.11 tons a year was reached during 1625–34. Clearly, this was due to the brisk overland trade via Qandahar that had developed at this time.[36] This is corroborated by the fact that Venetian exports of silver to Syria did not undergo a decline between the 1590s and 1610s; on the contrary, they tended to increase.[37]

As for the decline in silver mintage in Gujarat, it is possible that the coining of previously-accumulated bullion and coined silver had been completed by 1605. But this alone cannot explain the radical contraction in mintage. The total flow of silver to India seems to have received a setback during the two decades after 1605. This fits in with what we know of the New World silver supply and conditions of the Indian Ocean trade during this period.

For one thing, there was a reduction in the amount of silver entering Spain from America during the period 1601–5 and again during 1611–15; and this could not but have adversely affected the total silver outflow from Europe.[38]

[36] For this development, see Steensgaard, *Asian Trade Revolution,* 206–7.

[37] See f.n. 30 in this chapter for these exports.

[38] In 1621 Sir John Woltenholme estimated the annual outflow of silver from Christendom to Asia at 150 English tons (K.N. Chaudhuri, *English East India Company*, 120). Of these 150 tons, considerable quantities must have been absorbed by the Ottoman Empire and Iran; and, therefore, even if one accepts the estimate, it is difficult to conjecture how much of the estimated quantity reached India. At its face value, when compared with our other indicators (equally nebulous, perhaps) for the 1590s, Woltenholme's estimate would suggest a decline in the annual silver imports into India by the 1620s.

As for the Cape of Good Hope route, English and Dutch exports of silver to India were small, while Portuguese trade was forcibly blocked by the two new intruders. According to the figures given by Balkrishna,[39] and reproduced by K.N. Chaudhari,[40] the English East India Company during the first twenty-three years of the century exported to the East a total of treasure worth £753,336, or 76.84 metric tons of silver. The volume of Dutch trade, judging by its value, was about twice that of the English East India Company during the first quarter of the seventeenth century.[41] If the relative shares of bullion and goods in the Dutch exports roughly approximated those of the English East India Company, the two Companies together should have exported over 230 metric tons of silver, that is, just about ten metric tons a year. During the same period Portuguese trade declined substantially, so that it is difficult to imagine the Portuguese adding even as much as this tonnage to silver imports into India. The Gujarat mints, to the extent that they depended upon silver imports round the Cape must therefore have had their supplies reduced considerably.

Simultaneously, the supply of silver coming from the Levant, through the Red Sea and the Gulf was affected not only by the conflicts between the English and the Portuguese, but also the English raids on Indian shipping, leading to a grave obstruction of Arabian Sea commerce, as Pelsaert noted in 1626.[42] There was therefore a drying up of the flow of bullion over the sea routes;[43] and it was only in partial compensation that an increased flow took place overland through the Qandahar route.

[39] *Commercial Relations between India and England*, London, 1924, 283.

[40] *The English East India Company, 1600–40*, London, p.117.

[41] Based on figures in Balkrishna, *Commercial Relations*, those for Dutch trade stated in florins on p.289 and for the English on p.282.

[42] See Pelsaert's description of the enforced stagnation of this trade (*Remonstrantie*, 187–89, tr., pp.39–4). In 1623 the English seized Indian junks returning from the Red Sea (*Factories, 1622–23*, pp.282, 327, 341). In 1624 the Surat factors recommended a seizure of all Red Sea junks for the most persuasive reason that "they will be rich enough to countervail the English goods ashore ('being per estimate about 26 or 27 thousand pounds sterling'), for often one ship from Jidda is worth more treasure" (*Factories, 1624–29*, p.29). But among the Red Sea junks seized in 1623, the *Shāhī* from Surat was found to have carried only 20,000 rials of eight (less than half a metric ton of silver) (*Factories, 1622–23*, p.327). Another ship (unnamed) carried 40,000 or 60,000 rials, but this vessel was bound for Chaul in Konkan, not Surat (ibid., pp.282, 341).

[43] One must remember that the major immediate source of European silver entering Gujarat must still have been the Levant. In 1618 the Surat ship *Raḥīmī* returning from Mocha, was carrying 29 'tunnes of silver' (John Hatch, 'Relations & c' in *Purchas his Pilgrims*, MacLehose ed., Glasgow, 1905, IV, p.537). The shipping 'tunnes' of that time cannot unfortunately be converted into metric weight.

The Value of Silver and Movement of Prices

The influx of silver as implied in our reconstruction of the silver-currency output (Fig.15.1) is thus backed by the information on silver imports, fluctuations in them corresponding well to fluctuations in rupee coinage. There is little doubt, then, that there was an enormous expansion in silver money-supply during the period 1556–1630. How did this affect the value of silver money? We need first to examine the evidence on the prices of the other two money metals, copper and gold. Data on gold and copper have been put together in tables compiled by Irfan Habib,[44] and the accompanying Fig.15.3 is based on these tables.

Fg.15.3 apparently poses an enigma: when silver was coming in such large quantities and being minted into coin, why should the price of copper

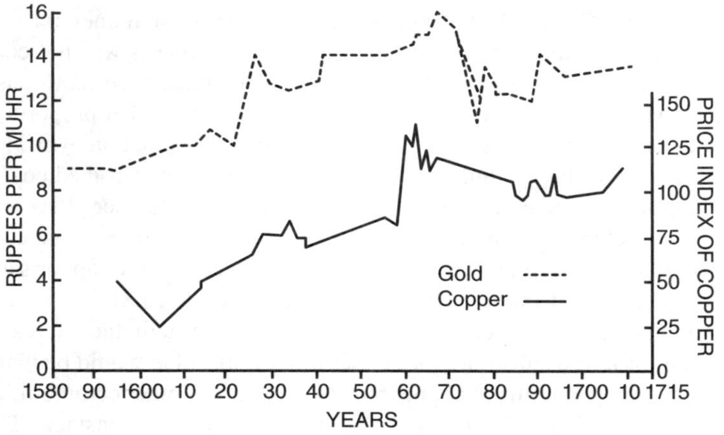

Figure 15.3

The Silver Value of Gold and Copper (to 1640)

[44] In J.F. Richards (ed.), *The Imperial Monetary System of Mughal India*, pp.148–9, checked with data in I. Habib, *Agrarian System,* rev. ed., 432–49. For copper values, I have taken into account the point about there having been no change after Akbar in the meaning of *tanka* and *dām*, that is made by Najaf Haider, 'The Quantity Theory and Mughal Monetary History', *The Medieval History Journal*, Vol.II, No.2, 1999, pp.341–8, noted by Irfan Habib in the 3rd edition of *Agrarian System*, 2014, pp.349–4. Cf. S. Moosvi, *People, Taxation and Trade in Mughal India*, New Delhi, 2008, pp.69–72, esp. p.71*n.* for copper-coin quotations 1605–6 to 1626.

have fallen so heavily between 1595 and 1614? In the beginning, when the pure metallic coinage was introduced, and both the silver rupee and copper *dām* started replacing billon coinage, the silver rupee was reckoned at 48 *dāms*.[45] With the silver influx the rupee seems to have declined in terms of copper, as one would expect, the ratio falling to 1:35 some time prior to 1583.[46] At this point a process of replacement of copper money by silver seems to have begun, partly because copper stocks might have been diverted by the imperial government for manufacturing artillery, but mainly perhaps because of the greater efficiency attained by silver as money metal once its value had fallen to a lower level, permitting coins of reasonable weight of silver to be used in market transactions. Simultaneously, the inconvenience of using copper for medium-level transactions turned people away from copper to silver use. This replacement of copper money by silver, thus begun, seems to have been completed by 1620, when the mints coining copper were reduced to such a small number (Table 15.1) that copper could now furnish money for fractional and petty transactions only. So long as this process was not complete, copper coins being expelled from circulation must have enormously added to the supply of the metal in the market in much higher proportions than those of imports of silver. It was presumably this situation, which, so long as it persisted, continuously threw large quantities of coined copper on the market (to be used as metal) and so forced down its price. A secondary factor behind the rise in silver price in relation to copper in the early years of Jahangir's reign was the contraction in oversea silver imports and the consequent reduction in currency output (see Table 15.3).

So long as silver could maintain its value through the increased demand for it as a substitute for copper money, its value would be maintained not only in terms of copper but also in terms of other commodities, provided the demand-and-supply positions remained constant. This would be naturally true for the silver value of gold as well. According to the estimate offered by Chaunu, Portugal during the sixteenth century acquired spices from Asia by paying 150 tons of gold and less than 6,000 tons of silver.[47] These figures suggest at a maximum the ratio of 1:40 between the quantities of gold and silver entering Asia. This meant that the quantity of gold imported was likely to have been far less in weight than the gold–silver ratio of 1:9. One should, therefore, have expected gold to rise in terms of silver, even if we do not exactly know the ratio

[45] *Ā'īn*, I, p.196.
[46] Ibid., p.176.
[47] Wallerstein, *The Modern World System*, p.329*n*.

between existing gold stock and the quantity of gold imported into India. But this too was for some time prevented by the absorption of quantities of silver, in 'substitute' currency production; the gold–silver ratio of 1:9 could accordingly be maintained right till 1608, when gold broke loose, and began a modest ascent.

The quotations of copper and gold prices show a slow recovery by the former and slow continuing ascent by the latter only late in Jahangir's reign. In 1626 copper was still below its silver price of 1595–6, though gold (which seems to have been on a plateau from 1608–12 to 1621) had reached a level of nearly 56 per cent above that of its value in silver in 1595–6. Copper rose further in value, though slowly, reaching 80 per cent of its former value in 1628 and 83 per cent in 1634. Gold, on the other hand, tended to decline between 1628 and 1634, the gold–silver ratio falling from 1:14 to 1:12.50. It is possible that the latter was due to the fall in imports of silver and the consequent decline in mint output (Table 15.4). Copper rose nevertheless, not only because of the cessation of influx of surplus coined copper, but also owing to rising demand for artillery manufacture, owing particularly to the wars in the Deccan.

When we turn from the inter-metallic values to prices in general, we must remember that, apart from the upward pressure in prices generated

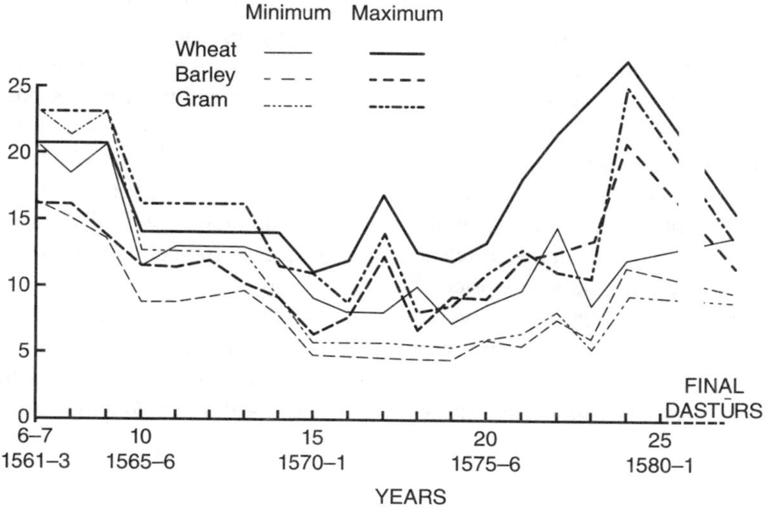

Figure 15.4

Prices implied by *dastūrs* of *ṣūba* Agra

by precious metal imports, there must have been considerable fluctuations in different regions as harvests were good or bad. While we have no direct means of tracing annual fluctuations after 1580, the *dastūrs* in so far as they were based on prices and estimated yields, give us some idea of annual price-fluctuations (in terms of copper money) between 1562 and 1580. Figure 15.4 gives the cash revenue rates for this period for the *ṣūbas* of Agra and Delhi for three crops (wheat, barley and gram). Assuming that rates varied solely according to prices while the standard yields were treated as constant, the curve should broadly represent price movements in this large region.

Prices were apparently very high during the years 1561–4, after which a descent began, continuing till 1568. Between 1568 and 1575 prices fluctuated substantially. From 1575 to 1580 prices rose again, reaching, in 1580, the 1561–2 level. Henceforth while short-term fluctuations must have occurred from year to year, the general stability of prices is reflected in the maintenance of the final *dastūrs* till 1595–6, when they are recorded. We have seen that these were revised only to allow for the change in size of *bīgha*, introduced in 1585. Barring a few exceptions, the conversion did not affect the old schedule.

The first substantial disturbance in price level came between 1608 and 1614, to judge from the rise in gold and fall in copper prices. During this phase silver money supplanted copper in whose terms prices should have risen, but now it was the rupee which became the principal unit of money. We have given reason to show that while silver gained heavily in relation to copper, it declined marginally in relation to gold during the reign of Jahāngīr. Now, this did not mean that a general stability of prices prevailed, since both silver and gold were being imported in large quantities, and so while they maintained tolerably stable ratios between them, their supply increasing in considerable quantity could have pushed up the general price-level. For agricultural products this rise is well illustrated by prices reported in the Dutch accounts at Agra in 1638 and 1639, when compared with the *Ā'īn*'s prices.[48]

Such a rise in the price-level is supported by the increase in *jama'dāmī* figures (which now become really based on the rupee, since the *dām* in which they are stated was a mere money of account pegged at one-fortieth of a rupee). The following figures are indexed, with the *Ā'īn*'s figures as base, = 100:[49]

[48] See I. Habib, *Agrarian System of Mughal India*, rev. ed., 93 (Table 2.1).

[49] The table is based on *jama'* statistics assembled in Habib's *Agrarian System*. For 1595–6, however, I have taken the *jama'* of 1595–6 as calculated in Chapters 1 and 8.

Year	Index
1596–6	100
1605	112
Pre-1627	122
1628–36	126

The *jama'* statistics suggest an upward trend which can only be due largely to increase in prices, since it is hardly possible to argue that population could have increased at this pace.

The price rise that began in 1614 should have had repercussions for the entire Mughal economy, on actual collections of revenue as well as maintenance of the Mughal army through the *manṣab* system. These effects, however, materialized after the period we are concerned with.

The Cost of Credit

The increased money supply with an invisible inflation rate[50] should have affected the cost of credit as well, though the inter-connection between money supply and interest rates is always extremely complex. The level of security, margin of profit, and degree of intensity of economic activity also affect interest rates to an often indeterminate extent; but monetary historians have always tended to find a link between money-supply (as modified by velocity, of course) and the cost of credit.

Unfortunately, information from the latter half of the sixteenth century is very limited. There is in the *Ā'īn-i Akbarī* no reference to interest rates on commercial loans. The *Ā'īn*, however, gives data on the principal and interest to be repaid when loans (*musā'adat*) were given by the emperor to the nobles.[51] The rates calculated per annum on the basis of compound interest, from the additions to principal given by Abū'l Faẓl, are given in Table 15.5 (next page).

It is certain that these rates were lower than those which nobles could obtain from the professional usurers; it is also probable that these are lower than the current rates offered to reputable merchants in the

[50] Shireen Moosvi, 'The Silver Influx, Money Supply, Prices and Revenue Extraction in Mughal India', *JESHO* vol.XXVIII.

[51] *Ā'īn*, I, p.196.

Table 15.5

No. of years	Annual rate of interest (%)	No. of years	Annual rate of interest (%)
1	6.25	6	7.00
2	6.10	7	8.30
3	7.70	8	7.20
4	10.70	9	6.40
5	8.40	10	7.40

commercial world. Otherwise, there would be little point in Abū'l Faẓl's averring that these rates could serve as models to usurers.

If the data on commercial rates that we obtain from Jahāngīr's reign are any guide, Akbar was certainly moderate in the rates of interest that he demanded as a creditor. Table 15.6 (next page) presents monthly rates of interest mainly derived from the English records for Surat, Ahmadabad and Agra, to the end of Shāhjahān's reign, 1658–9.

From these data it appears that interest rates fell during the 1640s at all the places for which we have information. At Surat, rates on loans advanced to the English East India Company or other reputable merchants fluctuated between 1 and 1½ per cent per month from 1624 to 1650, after which there was a considerable fall: from 1651 onwards the rates ranged between ½ and 5/8 per cent per month.

At Ahmadabad a fall of the same magnitude seems to have occurred some time between 1640 and 1647; and in Agra, during 1647. The rates in both these towns otherwise corresponded with those at Surat.

The history of interest rates thus does not corroborate K.N. Chaudhuri's rather superficial judgment that there was no long-term downward movement in interest rates in India.[52] In fact, there is an almost universal fall in interest rates in the mid-seventeenth century, and this requires some explanation.

Unluckily, the rates at which the English East India Company borrowed in England or the Dutch East India Company in Holland have not yet been tabulated. But from the data collected by Sidney Homer it appears that in England there was a fall from about 10 per cent per annum in 1600–25 to less than 6 per cent during 1675–1700.[53] In Holland not

[52] K.N. Chaudhri, *The Trading World of Asia*, p.159.

[53] Sidney Homer, *A History of Interest Rates*, New Brunswick, 1963, pp.125–7.

Table 15.6

Rates of Interest per Month

SURAT		
1624	1	*Factories, 1622–23*, 178
1626	1¼	*Remonatrantie*, 289–9; tr. 41–2
1630	1⅛	*Factories, 1630–33*, 127
1634	1 or 1¼	*Factories, 1634–36*, 35
1635	1	*Factories, 1634–36*, 114
1639	1¼–1½	*Factories, 1637–41*, 116–17
1642	1 or 1¼	*Factories, 1642–45*, 34
1650	1	*Factories, 1646–50*, 316
1651	½	*Factories, 1651–54*, 86
1652	¾	Ibid.
1652	½	*Factories, 1651–54*, 109–10
1652	5/8	Ibid., 119
1654	½ & 5/8	Ibid., 222
1657	5/8	*Factories, 1655–60*, 144–5
1659	5/8 & ½	Ibid., 158
AHMADABAD		
1622	1	*Factories, 1622–23*
1628	1	*Factories, 1624–29*, 215
1628	½	*Factories, 1624–29*, 270
1640	above 1¼	*Factories, 1637–41*, 225
1647	above ¾	*Factories, 1646–50*, 112
1647	13/16	Ibid., 128
1658	¾	Ibid., 163
1658	5/8	Ibid., 163
AGRA		
1626	5/6–1	*Remontrantie*, 274–75; tr., 28–9
1628	2	*Factories, 1624–29*, 239
1645	5/8	*Factories, 1642–45*, 302–3
1645	1–2½	Ibid.
1645	1	*Factories, 1642–45*, 302–3
1645	¾	Ibid.
1645	5/8	Ibid.
1647	¾	*Factories, 1646–50*, 122
1657	¾	*Factories, 1651–54*, 301–2

only were rates lower than in England but there was a steady decline in the first half of the seventeenth century, forcing the rates down from 8½ to 4 per cent and even below in the next half-century, after some temporary fluctuations due to war.[54]

It seems, then, that at the close of the sixteenth century the cost of commercial credit in Europe was a little higher than the cost Akbar laid for his *musā'adat* loans; but it was distinctly lower than rates on commercial loans in India when these are first recorded from the 1620s onwards. The cost of credit in India in subsequent years remained higher than in Europe. Even after the great decline in Indian rates during the 1640s, the English Company's factors stated that the cost of credit in India was double that in England (1650); and that the rate being 7½ to 9 per cent per annum in Surat and only 4 per cent in England, it was even profitable to borrow in England and lend out in India. Indeed, in 1662 it was expressly claimed by the Court of Directors of the East India Company that by sending 'great stocks of money' to Surat they had forced down the interest rates prevailing there to 6 per cent per annum (= ½ per cent per month).[55]

An interesting question thus arises, whether the export of treasure to India was at least in part due to higher profits from usury in India. If so, the import of treasure need not have been fully covered by exports of goods from India (see Chapter 16). Moreover, in such conditions, the downward pressure on the cost of credit in India which we have just examined, would become even more readily explicable.

[54] Ibid., pp.127–9.

[55] Susil Chaudhuri, *Trade and Commercial Organisation in Bengal*, p.117; K.N. Chaudhuri, *The Trading World of Asia*, p.159.

CHAPTER 16

Foreign Trade and the Internal Economy

Though foreign trade indisputably formed an important sector of the Mughal Indian economy, there is little information of any statistical value on this sector in either the *Ā'īn-i Akbarī* or later Indian sources. Whatever data exist come largely from European records. It is therefore not surprising that studies of Indian foreign trade should have remained so largely confined to the trade with Europe.[1]

What follows here is an attempt, in spite of the obvious limitations of data, to assess the magnitude of the entire foreign trade of the Mughal empire. For our purpose, foreign trade is taken to comprise westward overland commerce as well as oceanic trade. The commerce of Akbar's empire with the Deccan and South India, and with Assam is, however, not considered part of foreign trade.[2]

The two outstanding items of import into Mughal India comprised treasure (notably silver) and horses, while textiles dominated exports.

[1] The trend fairly well marked in Moreland (*From Akbar to Aurangzeb*) still continues: Neil Steensgaard, *Asian Trade Revolution of the 17th Century*, Chicago, 1974 offers a example, though there are refreshing departures in M.N. Pearson, *Merchants and Rulers in Gujarat*, Berkeley, 1976, and Ashin Das Gupta, *Indian Merchants and the Decline of Surat, c.1700–1750*, Wiesbaden, 1979.

[2] We assume here that trade with these regions was isolated totally from other sectors of the foreign trade of the Mughal empire, which was not the case. For example, suppose when opium was exported from Gujarat (in Akbar's empire) to Malabar (south India), pepper was there taken in exchange and shipped to the Red Sea; the bullion received in return might then be taken to Gujarat to buy more opium for Malabar. In this case, while the bullion would appear in the imports of the Mughal empire, the opium export made in its return would be excluded since it was sent to Malabar. Wherever possible, I have made some allowance for such cases of interlinked commerce.

In attempting a rough approximation of the size of imports of treasure we may begin by recalling our assumption that the mints in Gujarat, the North-West and Bengal mainly coined freshly-arrived stocks of silver.[3] These mints must also have coined some previously accumulated internal stock and some silver currency brought for re-mintage. On the other hand, some of the bullion entering the Mughal empire could also have been carried past the border and coastal mints and made into coin at the inland or central mints. Yet recoinage in coastal mints might well have balanced the flow of bullion imports inland. On these considerations, the annual silver imports during the two decades 1586–1605 have been estimated at 184.64 metric tons, being the equivalent of Rs.1,66,77,571.[4]

We have already seen that the data of actual silver imports in general corroborate our estimates based on coin evidence;[5] and we may therefore take it that the figure given above is a fair approximation of the silver annually imported into the Mughal empire at the period in question. For purposes of comparison with our other data, we may also take it to be true for the year 1595–6.

If the ratio of 1:40 in weight between gold and silver imports during the sixteenth century, implied in Chaunu's figures of Portuguese exports to Asia, is taken as the basis,[6] the value of gold imports during 1595–6 should have been about 4.616 tons of gold representing, in value, Rs.1,37,94,197.[7]

As for the other chief import, the needs of the Mughal cavalry generated an enormous demand for quality horses from Central Asia and Persia. As seen in Chapter 10 the number of horses in the imperial stables was 12,000, out of which, according to Pelsaert, 3,200 were Persian horses and 5,970 Turkī.[8] *Manṣabdārs* were required to maintain 25,921 horses against their *zāt* ranks, and imperial regulations laid down that of these, 7,299 should be Persian and 5,693 Turkī.[9]

[3] See Chapter 15.

[4] Chapter 15, Table 15.4. Silver imports in the decades 1586–95 and 1596–1605, on the basis of the output of the Gujarat, North-west and Bengal mints, have been estimated at 127.20 and 242.08 metric tons a year.

[5] See Chapter 15.

[6] Wallerstein, *The Modern World System*, 329.

[7] The tonnage of gold is taken as one-fortieth of the quantity of silver estimated at 184.64 tons. The weight of a *muhr* being 169 grains, this weight of gold would be equal to 4,21,566.5 *muhrs*, which, in turn, has been converted into rupees at the rate of Rs 9 to the *muhr*.

[8] *Kroniek*, 120–1 *Chronicle*, tr., 35.

[9] See Chapter 9.

Besides these, there were the horses required by the cavalry troopers. According to Pelsaert, the *aḥadīs* kept 10,736 horses.[10] The effective number of *tābīnān* of the *manṣabdārs*, for which *dāghī* rates were paid, was 1,41,503.[11] Since these were *dāghī* troopers, according to the standard formula for the composition of *manṣabdār* contingents (3 *sih-aspa*, 4 *do-aspa*, 3 *yak-aspa*), they should have kept 2,82,106 horses. On the basis of the *dāgh* documents from Shāhjahān's regin, we may take it that they maintained hardly any horses of Persian breed, but that 55 per cent of their horses or 1,55,158 were Turkī.[12] This might not however have been true of the *aḥadīs*, who received their first horse from the imperial establishment. The horses of the *aḥadīs* were likely to be generally of better breeds; we may, therefore, assume that two-thirds of the horses belonging to *aḥadīs* (7,157) were Turkī compared with a component of foreign horses of over 75 per cent in the imperial stables.

To maintain such large numbers of horses of non-Indian breeds, there was need to import horses continuously, particularly since these breeds could not be raised well in India.[13] The number of horses imported might, then, be determined by estimating the numbers annually needed to replace horses dying or no longer fit for service. Since horses belonging to the imperial stables and the *manṣabdārs* were seldom brought to the battle-field, their average working-life may have been the normal twelve years.[14] On this calculation, 875 Persian and 927 Turkī horses should have been acquired every year to replenish the stables. Horses of the *aḥadī* and *tābīnān* cannot, however, be allowed an equal working lifespan. They saw action much more frequently, and could not have been so well looked after. We might, therefore, take their average working-life as ten years. On these assumptions, about 16,000 Turkī horses must have been required every year as replacements.

Some horses must have been imported to meet the needs of *zamīndārs*, who according to the *Ā'īn*, maintained as many as 3,84,558 horsemen.[15] Obviously, the *zamīndārs*' horses must have been of an inferior quality to those of the imperial army. Supposing that only one-tenth of their horsemen rode imported horses, we get a total figure of 38,4546 horses of Central Asian breeds. If their working life too was ten years, then 3,846

[10] *Kroniek*, 120 *Chronicle*, tr., 35, see also Chapter 11.

[11] See Chapter 9.

[12] Cf. R.A. Alvi's data in *Medieval India—A Miscellany*, II, 73.

[13] See for example P. della Valle, II, 334.

[14] See Chapter 10.

[15] *Ā'īn*, I, 175.

horses must have been bought annually for *zamīndārs* and their retainers.

In addition, there appears to have been considerable demand for horses from the Deccan and south India.[16] Many of these were brought across the Arabian Sea from Hormuz,[17] but a number must also have been taken overland through the Mughal empire.[18] The number of horses thus brought overland should raise the figure of imported horses estimated so far on the basis of the internal demand. Yet since the horses were presumably directly transported to the Deccan, these were in the nature of re-exports and were not paid for by export from the Mughal empire.

Assembling our different estimates, we may say that nearly 1,000 Persian and 21,000 Turkī horses must have been brought every year to supply the cavalry needs of Akbar's empire. The number of horses actually entering the empire would have been somewhat higher to allow for the number of horses that were re-exported to the Deccan.

This estimate is corroborated by Bernier, who puts the number of horses coming from Central Asia ('Uzbec') into India at 25,000 a year.[19] He does not however offer any estimate for the horses coming from Persia and Arabia, and through Qandahar, though he does mention that horses were imported through these channels as well. For an earlier period, before the large demand created by the Mughal army in India materialized, we have an authoritative estimate of 7,000 to 10,000 horses annually taken through Kabul to India, the figure being given by Babur (then ruling at Kabul) under the year 1509.[20] Since Kabul lay astride the main route to Central Asia, these must all have Central Asian or Turkī horses. These figures again, naturally exclude horses imported through Qandahar. In any case, an increase in import of horses from 10,000 to 25,000 in the course of the sixteenth century, owing to the large military organization of the Mughals, does not seem unreasonable.

[16] Nuniz in the 1530s puts the annual demand for horses from the King of Vijayanagar alone at 13,000, though all of these were not imported (R. Sewell, *A Forgotten Empire*, 2nd Indian ed. Delhi, 1970, 61–2).

[17] Tom Pires, I, 58; Caesar Frederick in *Purchas*, X, 93 and 99.

[18] See, for example, *Selected Waqai of the Deccan, 1660–1671 A.D.*, ed. Y. Husain, Hyderabad, 1953, 69, for a reference to merchants taking horses through the Mughal Empire into the Deccan.

[19] Bernier, 203. Thevenot raises the number to above 60,000 ('three score thousand'), *Indian Travels of Thevenot and Careri*, 80; and Manucci (Vol.II, 390–1) to one hundred thousand. But these statements are surely gross exaggerations.

[20] *Bāburnāma*, tr. A.S. Beveridge, Vol.1, 202.

We have already offered an estimate of the total amount of expenditure on purchase of horses by the emperor, the *manṣabdārs*, the *aḥadīs* and the *tābīnān*. These are restated in Table 16.1, along with the average price for imported horses, arrived at by dividing the total expenditure on imported horses by the number of animals. The price of Indian horses is similarly obtained by dividing the remaining expenditure by the number of Indian horses.[21]

Table 16.1

	Expenditure on Purchase of imported horses	Implicit price per imported horse	Price per Indian horse
Emperor	34,000 *muhrs*	44.50 *muhrs*	25.42 *muhrs*
Manṣabdārs	24,300 *muhrs*	22.44 *muhrs*	7.52 *muhrs*
Aḥadīs & tābīnān	2,19,631.5 *muhrs*	13.53 *muhrs*	5.61 *muhrs*

In all probability, the horses of the *zamīndārs*' retainers were generally inferior to those of the *aḥadīs* and *tābīnān*; we should thus not be far wrong in taking the average price of Turki horses, imported for the *zamīndārs*, as ten *muhrs* (just above the average price of the better Indian breeds acquired by the *manṣabdārs* for their stables). The *zamīndārs*' expenses on non-country-bred horses, therefore, may well have been about 38,460 *muhrs*.

The total cost of imported horses thus works out at 3,16,384.5 *muhrs*; this would be the equivalent of Rs 28,47,460½ at Rs 9 per *muhr*.

While bullion and horses constituted the main items of import and must have accounted for the major portion of the value of imports, there were also imports of certain other articles, namely, precious stones,[22] non-precious metals like copper, quicksilver, tin and lead;[23] amber beads, vermilion, Russian hides, pearls, high-quality woollen and silken cloth

[21] It will be seen from the Table that the implied prices for the *manṣabdārs*' horses (imported) fall under the maximum price of Rs 300 set for a horse which was given from the Imperial Establishment to a *manṣabdār* in the Deccan in 1639 (*Selected Documents of Shah Jahan's Reign*, 74).

[22] Linschoten, I, 45, 917; II, 40–1.

[23] Tom Pires, II, 20; *Remonstrantie*, 268, tr., 23; for quicksilver from China see *Factories, 1618–21*, 54–55.

[24] *Remonstrantie*, 274, tr., 28; Pyrard, II, 239.

[25] *Principal Navigations*, III, 206.

from Europe, Persia and China;[24] unprocessed silk from China;[25] spices from South-East Asia and Ceylon;[26] coral, cloves, coffee and ivory from the east Africa coast and the Red Sea;[27] and dry fruit from Central Asia.[28] From across the Himalayas came gold, copper, lead, musk, ginger, borax, woollen stuffs, wooden objects, hawks, falcons, etc. This material was carried upon men's backs and on ponies.[29]

The scarcity of quantitative data makes it impossible to work out any worthwhile estimate of the value of these imports. Some very rough indication, though of the minimum size of imports of cloves, nutmegs and mace may be gauged from Pelsaert. Writing around 1626 he estimated the needs of Agra at 700 *mans* of cloves, 600 *mans* of nutmeg, and 50 *mans* of mace, which according to his calculations were worth Rs 215,000.[30] However, he remarks that earlier about three times this quantity of cloves was supplied by the Portuguese, prices then being lower, viz., Rs 60–80 a *man*.[31] This would have given a total value of Rs 1,26,000–1,68,000 for cloves imported to meet the needs of Agra (and regions served from there) in Akbar's time. We may thus assume that the imports of spices, excluding pepper, into the Mughal empire from non-Indian sources could barely have amounted to a million rupees in value.

Pelsaert also records the quantities of quicksilver, vermillion, tin and ivory brought by the Dutch to Agra.[32] But at the maximum prices expected, the total values were relatively insignificant, viz., quicksilver, Rs 9,000; vermilion, Rs 10,000; tin, Rs 1,200; and ivory, Rs 4,000; a total of Rs 24,000. Of course, these commodities were imported through other channels as well (mainly Portuguese and English), but the total value could have hardly exceeded one or two lakh rupees.

These figures strengthen the assumption that the main imports of the Mughal empire were silver, gold and horses. Other items of import were

[26] Tom Pires, II, 270; *Principal Navigations*, III, 206.

[27] Linschoten, I, 33 & II, 34; Carletti, 220, 221; *Purchas* IX, 559; for coral imported from the Red Sea, see also Khurram's *nishān*, A.D. 1618 Harl. Roll, 43 A. 4; *Factories, 1618–21*, 54–5, for ivory, *Principal Navigations*, III, 206.

[28] *Ā'īn*, I, 67: Bernier, 204.

[29] *Ā'īn*, I, 434.

[30] *Remonstrantie*, 268; tr., 23. The *man* is stated to be equal to 50 lb (Holland) and was thus *man-i Akbarī*.

[31] Ibid., 24*n*. As noted in Chapter 14 Moreland pointed out that prices are in conformity with those given for Akbar's time, viz. Rs 60 per *ser* (*Ā'īn*, I. 65). One may, therefore, take it that Pelsaert's estimate of higher consumption at that time too was not far wrong.

[32] *Remonstrantie*, 274, tr., 28.

of relatively little account,[33] probably accounting for only a tenth of the total imports, in aggregate.

According to our estimates, then, bullion imports into Mughal India at the close of the sixteenth century probably amounted to roughly Rs 2,04,71,768; while the value of horses imported annually was around Rs 28,47,460. Bullion and the value of horses together thus amounted to Rs 2,33,19,228. With the remaining items (taken at one-tenth the total value of annual imports) the total amount of imports would have been about Rs 2,60,00,000 in value.[34]

One has however to make some allowance for re-exports. Fitch says that the Portuguese took 200,000 cruzados annually to China from 'India'.[35] But 'India' here means the Portuguese port of Goa, so that this transport of bullion was only a part of the direct influx of New World silver from Europe to the East. But the payment for Central Asian horses might in part have been made through silver, i.e., through re-export of treasure. The long survival of Mughal coins in the Uzbek dominions as standard money strengthens this supposition.[36] In view of such re-exports, the total value of net imports of treasure might have been somewhat lower than estimated above.

Data on the value of exports are much scarcer. For overland trade however, we have some interesting statements. Steel and Crowther record that in 1615, when trade with Persia through Hormuz was disturbed, 12,000 to 14,000 camel loads were sent from Lahore to Iran via Qandahar, presumably during the course of a year. The value of a camel

[33] The high absorption of precious metals in India was a fact widely recognized by contemporaries. In Hawkins' words 'all nations bring coyne and carry away commodities for the same' (*Early Travels*, 112).

[34] These figures imply that the bullion accounted for 80 per cent of the total imports of the Mughal empire. The proportion is strikingly high but not untenable. In 1629, for example, it was reported that the large 'caphilo' from Cairo carried mainly 'great quantities of monies', and not goods, to exchange for Indian commodities at Mokha (*Factories, 1624–29*, 350). The English East India Company's exports, during the opening decade of the 17th century consisted of 69.72 per cent money; and the percentage of bullion in English exports to India 1601–23 was as high as 68.2 per cent (Balkrishna, 282). The composition of imports by other channels could not have been very different. Treasure seems to have been the major commodity brought from the Red Sea by the Gujarati merchants; the returning Red Sea junks were said to be particularly rich in 'treasure' (*Factories, 1624–29*, 29). The only item mentioned by the English in the seized cargoes from Indian ships returning from the Red Sea was money (Purchas, IV. 537). The value of other goods in the cargo does not even seem to have merited mention.

[35] Tom Pires, I. 17, 58.

[36] A. Burnes, *Travels of Bokhara*, I, 1973, 241–2.

load was estimated at Rs 120 to 130.[37] The total (annual) value of this trade thus would have been Rs 14,40,000 to 18,20,000. Roe in 1616 gave it as his opinion that 20,000 to 30,000 'chourals' (churls) were sent from Agra to Persia and Turkey.[38] Since two churls made a camel load, the volume of trade would, on this basis, have been 10,000 to 15,000 camel loads, giving us roughly the same volume of trade overland to Iran as estimated by Steel and Crowther. Supposing Steel and Crowther to be accurate in their estimate of the value of the load as well, and also that overland trade could not have completely replaced the Hormuz trade, we may put the value of exports to Iran in the earlier years of the seventeenth century at about Rs 25 to 30 lakhs a year.

This figure does not cover the exports to Central Asia, which mainly went through Kabul. The Kabul trade too must have been considerable because the import of horses must have generated returning caravans.

Unfortunately, for the maritime trade to the Red Sea and round the Cape of Good Hope we have no data bearing on value or volume of trade. Clearly, both these channels must have carried far greater quantities of exports than those which went through Qandahar and Hormuz. We may however venture to speak in quantitative terms in respect of indigo. According to Pelsaert's estimate of 1626, indigo production of the Bayana and Doāb tracts during favourable years was 884,800 lb ('4,000 bales') and 221,200 lb ('1,000 bales') respectively. To these may be added the estimated production of the Sarkhej tract, 3,32,000 lb (in 1615), and of Sehwan, 1,32,600 lb (in 1635).[39]

It seems that the bulk of the indigo produced in the Bayana, Sarkhej and Sehwan tracts (15,70,600 lb or 28,391 *man-i Akbarī*) was exported.[40]

[37] *Purchas,* IV, 268–9.

[38] *Letters Received*, IV, 250. The punctuation contributed by the editor may lead a reader to suppose that this quantity is that of indigo only. What Roe really says is that large amounts of indigo as well as other goods were procurable at Agra because of the slump in the Hormuz trade, and he gives the quantities in 'churls' for the alternative overland channel that had developed as a result.

[39] *Remonstrantie*, 259–61; tr., 13–15; *Letters Received*, III, 51; *Factories, 1634–36*, 129. Cf. Habib, *Agrarian System*, rev. ed. 47–9. The estimate of 2,500 chrucls, or 10,000 *mans* (a churle (fardle)=4 *mans: Agrarian System*, rev. ed. 430–1) for the Sarkhej indigo seems to be on the higher side since the production in lean years is reported to have been 6,000 to 8,000 (Gujarat) *mans* only (*Factories*, *1624–29*, 232; Ibid., *1634–36*, 292; Ibid., *1624–45*, 163–4); in years of plenty, it was over 9,000 *mans* (*Factories*, *1634–36*, p.73).

[40] The Bayana indigo was mainly exported to the Middle East and Europe as appears from Pelsaert, *Remonstrantie*, 263, tr., esp. 18; for the Doāb too he says that 'most of its produce is bought up by Armenians, Lahore and Kabul merchants' (Ibid., 260; tr. 15). Only the Mewat indigo, whose production (1,000 bales) we have excluded from our estimate, was bought up locally, 'very little' being exported (ibid).

If we assume that all varieties fetched the price quoted in the *Ā'īn* for the best quality of indigo, namely, Rs 16 per *man*,[41] the value of total indigo exports should have been Rs 4,54,259 at the maximum. The ceiling for the value of indigo exports would constitute a mere fraction in comparison with the total imports of the empire[42]—a rather surprising fact when one considers that indigo looms so large in English and Dutch records of the time.

Besides indigo, other important agricultural and semi-agricultural exports of Akbar's empire were sugar, rice, and opium. Rice was exported mainly from Bengal, with a good variety from Gujarat as well, to ports in the Red Sea and Persian Gulf.[43] Bengal sent sugar in considerable quantities to Pegu and other places.[44] Sugar of various varieties was taken overland via Kabul as well.[45] Mughal India also exported opium.[46] In

The Sehwan indigo was almost entirely exported to Iran and the Persian Gulf; and its production declined heavily when that trade decayed (*Factories, 1642–45*, 136).

Abū'l Faẓl says that the indigo produced in Gujarat was sent to the Ottoman Empire (Rūmistān) and other countries (*Ā'īn*, I, 486). This statement is corroborated by the data of exports relating to the early decades of the 17th century. In 1617 the *Globe*, voyaging directly to England, was laden with 1,167 fardles of Sarkhej indigo (*Factories, 1618–21*, 61) i.e., almost half of the total estimated output of Sarkhej; in 1621 one English ship is shown as carrying 9,000 *mans* of Sarkhej indigo (*Factories*, *1618–21*, 323). The total purchase of Sarkhej indigo by the English in 1615 was 1,273 churcles, *Letters Received*, V, 133). The local demand was not high since the English faced competition mainly from the Dutch (*Factories*, *1633–36*, 73; *1642–45*, 163–4). Indeed, the local consumption of Sarkhej indigo was estimated at 1,000 Surat *mans* only, i.e. one-tenth of the normal production (*Factories*, *1642–45*, 163–4).

41 *Ā'īn*, I, 422 reads Rs 12 but MSS Add. 7652, 6552, 5645 all read Rs 16 per *man*.

42 This was in spite of the fact that indigo was the major item of import, at least by the English, accounting for most of their investment in the Mughal Empire in their early days (*Letters Received*, V, p.323). In the cargo of the *Royal Anne*, indigo accounted for about 90 per cent of the total value (*Factories*, *1618–21*, 16)

43 Tom Pires, I, 30, 43–4; Barbosa, I, 64, 67; *Purchas*, X, 114. Fitch (*Early Travels*, 28) in 1586 found Sonargaon and Bakla in Bengal to possess 'great stores' of rice, large quantities being exported to Pegu, Malacca, Sumatra and many other places. While little is known about the quality of the exported Bengal rice, that of Gujarat was of high quality. Navapur rice was deemed a most acceptable gift in Persia (Tavernier, I, 41).

44 Barbosa, II, 55, 112, 146–7, *Purchas*, X, 103. Caesar Frederick particularly mentions Satgaon in Bengal as a great centre of production and trade (Ibid., 114); Abū'l Faẓl says that sugar was sent to distant places from Agra (*Ā'īn*, I, 244): some might well have been exported. The English factors in Gujarat found it a profitable merchandise for shipment to Persia (*Factories*, *1630–33*, 124).

45 *Bāburnāma*, tr. Beveridge, I, 202.

46 Caesar Frederick in *Purchas*, X, 127.

addition to these agricultural commodities there was some export of iron.[47] But unfortunately no data are available for making even conjectural estimates for the total value of these exports. While the quantities exported, especially of rice, might not have been small, the total value of these exports was probably not very high, owing to the relatively low prices of the items (except opium). The prices given in the *Ā'īn* are: rice, Rs 2.75 a *man*; sugar, Rs 6 a *man*; and iron, Rs 12 a *man*.[48] At such prices the commodities could hardly have absorbed the high costs of long-distance transport.

Malabar pepper was one of the most important items of export from India; but the producing regions and principal exporting ports were in South India, well outside Akbar's empire. In the first quarter of the seventeenth century, it is true, some pepper was re-exported through Surat.[49] But our authorities for the latter half of the sixteenth century do not mention Malabar pepper among exports (or re-exports) from Gujarat. Even if the Gujarat merchants had defied the Portuguese embargo[50] and brought some pepper to Surat, it should have been mostly absorbed within the Mughal empire, the demand here being considerable; and not much pepper would therefore have been left for re-export.

The major portion of Indian exports was accounted for by textiles: their predominant position in Indian commerce has been recognized in almost all modern studies, notably by Moreland.[51]

Indian cotton textiles were also exported by the western overland routes. Babur mentions cotton cloth among the main merchandise brought from India to Kabul;[52] the trade is also referred to at the opening of the seventeenth century.[53] Cotton textiles had an enormous market in the Red Sea countries and Turkey. The English factors at Surat reported in 1630;[54]

> They [cotton goods] are cheifest commodities wherein the Persians and Armenians who takes yearly passage on your shipps invest great summes of money here in India; some of them makeing instance

[47] Ibid.

[48] *Ā'īn*, I, pp.61 (rice), 65 (sugar), 138 (iron); see also Chapter 14.

[49] *Factories 1618–21*, 76; Ibid., *1622–23*. Virji Vora is reported to have offered Deccan pepper worth Rs 10,000 for sale to the English (Ibid., *1624–29*, 90, 94).

[50] Boxer, *Portuguese Seaborne Trade*, 59.

[51] Moreland, *From Akbar to Aurangzeb*, 54.

[52] *Bāburnāma*, I. tr., 202.

[53] *Letters Received*, IV, 250.

[54] *Factories, 1630–33*, 124–5.

> [instant] sale thereof att Gumbroon, from when they are dispersed and sould again to second merchants in Spahan, Balzar, Bagdat, etc., who transport them yet further for a thrid markett at Constantynpole and other places, at extraordinary charges of camel hire, customs and other exaction on the way; and yet every of these, at the first, second, and third hand, doe become great gainers.

Turkey imported Gujarat cloth through the Levant.[55] Quantities of Gujarat calico must thus have been regularly reaching western Europe by the end of the sixteenth century through the Levant as well as around the Cape of Good Hope.[56]

The Red Sea trade indeed absorbed very large quantities of Gujarat textiles. In 1629, an English agent reported that the annual 'caphilo of some 800 or 1,000 cammels' from Cairo returned from Mokha laden with Indian commodities, among which he gives prime place to different varieties of cloth ('shashes, serebasts, allejaes, fine calico, duthy') and only then mentions pepper and cloves. Coarser cloth ('callikeens, coarse calico, chowders') and 'cotton wooll' were first among the Indian goods retained in Arabia itself.[57] In the previous century Barbosa was amazed at the enormous quantities of 'Cambay' cotton used by the people of Aden and Arabia.[58] The Persian demand for Gujarat cloth continued even after the fall of Hormuz; Persian and Armenian merchants carried 'Cambay' cotton goods on board English ships in the seventeenth century.[59]

The export of Indian fabrics to the east African coast was of old standing. Cotton goods from Gujarat were carried to east Africa at the beginning of the sixteenth century.[60] The Portuguese extended this trade to the north-western coast of Africa as well. 'Cambay' cloth, white, painted and printed, was sent to east Africa during the second half of the sixteenth century; the Portuguese mainly carried it from Chaul and Goa.[61] Indian cotton goods were also shipped to Portugal directly, round the Cape of Good Hope.[62]

[55] Linschoten, I, 95.

[56] Carletti, 220.

[57] *Factories, 1624–29*, 350.

[58] Barbosa, I, 56.

[59] *Factories, 1630–33*, 124–5.

[60] Barbosa, I, 7, 15, 154; Tom Pires, I, 43.

[61] *Principal Navigations*, III, 210.

[62] Carletti, 202.

Ceylon and the Maldive islands also imported cotton cloth from Gujarat.[63] Gujarat cloth had still larger markets farther east. Many ships brought to Pegu 'abundance of printed Cambaya and Paleacate (Pulicat) cloth.'[64] In 1563 Caesar Frederick considered Gujarat cloth such a suitable commodity for Pegu that he himself sent it there via Chaul.[65] Tom Pires found 'Cambay' cloth of various kinds exported to Malacca.[66] Later on we find that Portuguese ships sailed laden with large quantities of Gujarat cloth to Malacca, it being mainly sold to the Javanese in exchange for spices.[67] Gujarat ships sailed also to Achin laden with cotton cloth.[68] Later in the sixteenth century when Bantam emerged as a rival to Malacca, Gujarat ships brought cotton goods to Bantam.[69] White and coloured high-quality calico (bafata) was also carried across the Himalayas in return for articles imported.

The impressive scale of cotton textile exports can be judged equally well if we change our focus from the importing areas of the world to the exporting regions within the Mughal empire. In the aggregate, Gujarat seems to have exported enormous quantities of cloth during the second half of the sixteenth century. Caesar Frederick found 'an infinite quantity of cloth made of bombast of all sorts, as white, stamped and painted', being exported from Cambay.[70] Pyrard says that 'every one from the Cape of Good Hope to China, man and woman, is clothed from head to foot' with cotton stuffs made in Gujarat.[71] This, though admittedly an exaggeration, does reflect the large scale assumed by Gujarat cotton cloth exports.

Bengal, the other important exporting region, sent white muslin to numerous markets extending from the Red Sea to China.[72] Caesar Frederick in the 1560s found Satgaon in Bengal a big centre for the manufacture of cotton stuffs.[73] Bengal sent every year to Pegu ships 'laden with fine cloth of bombast of all sorts.'[74] From the port of Chatgaon

[63] Barbosa, II, 117, 164; Tom Pires, I, 86; Pyrard in *Purchas*, IX, 561.

[64] Barbosa, II, 153–4.

[65] *Principal Navigations*, III, 261.

[66] Tom Pires, II, 175.

[67] Pyrard, II, 175.

[68] *Early Travels*, 73.

[69] *Factories, 1618–21*, 93.

[70] *Principal Navigations*, III, 206.

[71] Pyrard da Laval, II. 171.

[72] Barbosa, II, 173.

[73] *Purchase*, X, 114.

[74] *Principal Navigations*, III, 251.

(Chittagong) cloth was dispatched to the 'Indies' along with other merchandise.[75] Bengal cotton cloth was carried by the Portuguese to South-East Asia,[76] and in 1586 Fitch describes Sonargaon and Bakla in Bengal as large manufacturing centres of cotton goods that were shipped to that region.[77]

Sind too produced a 'great store' of cotton stuffs.[78] Various kinds of muslin, perhaps fine calico, were exported from the province to Portuguese India and Hormuz.[79]

Mughal India also exported some quantities of silk. Although Bengal silk exports were such a striking feature of India's trade in the seventeenth century, these do not seem to have been as large at the beginning of that century. Barbosa says that Gujarat silk cloth was exported to East Africa and Pegu.[80] Varthema too mentions silk, along with cotton, as an important item of exports from Gujarat.[81] Later on Caesar Frederick records 'silks of every sort' among the Gujarat exports via Chaul.[82] Alegaes (*alcha*), or striped silk cloth[83] woven in Sind, had a large market in Persia and Turkey.[84] The silk used in these manufactures might well have come from Bengal, though there is no evidence yet of the export of Bengal silk to other countries at this time. Even in the third decade of the seventeenth century most of the raw silk obtained at Patna (brought there from Bengal) was taken to Gujarat, and the remainder to Agra.[85]

In spite of the fact that we have so much information on exports of textiles there is almost no quantitative evidence. All we can do is to endorse Moreland's finding that Indian textile exports were an important fact of the world trade of the time.[86] From this, perhaps, we can assign to textile exports a value estimated by working from the total value of imports, inclusive of treasure, which had to be paid for by exports. The estimate of the total annual value of imports we have estimated for the Mughal empire, *c.* 1600, comes to about Rs 2,60,00,000. This estimate

[75] Ibid., III, 260.

[76] See T. Raychaudhuri, *Bengal Under Akbar and Jahangir*, 103.

[77] *Early Travels*, 28, 34.

[78] Barbosa, I, 107.

[79] Linschoten, I, 55–6.

[80] Barbosa, I, 7–8, 15, 28, 125–7, 153–4, 198.

[81] Varthema, 111.

[82] *Principal Navigations*, III, 210.

[83] *Atlas of the Mughal Empire*, 69.

[84] *Factories, 1634–36*, 130.

[85] *Remonstrantie*, 252–3; tr., 7.

[86] Moreland, *From Akbar to Aurangzeb*, 54.

includes the unknown (though possibly not large) quantity of bullion re-exported to Central Asia to pay a part of the value of imported horses. In addition, some bullion imports, representing a transfer of usurer's capital (see Chapter 15), might not have called for corresponding exports at all. Allowing for these deductions, we may put the net value of imports which had to be paid for by exports of goods at about Rs 2,30,00,000.

In lieu of any hard quantitative evidence we have assumed that all the agricultural, semi-processed commodities, and iron, exported form the Mughal Empire could not have accounted for even a quarter of the net value of bullion and goods imported. The remaining three-fourths of imports could have been balanced only by the export of cotton textiles. One may, therefore hazard the guess that the Mughal empire exported cotton textiles of a total value of roughly Rs 1,75,00,000.

We could now perhaps consider the extent to which exports contributed to increasing the value added by urban manufactures in the Mughal Indian economy. In Chapter 13, we have given calculations based on the estimated value of manufactures that found a market directly within the country, as well as abroad, to the extent that imports for domestic consumption and for hoarding induced such exports. What these calculations left out of account were the net imports of bullion which instead of adding to savings (pure hoard) or into consumption (ornaments and wares), went into additions to the stock of money in circulation. As estimated above, the annual import of bullion around 1595–6 was Rs 2,04,71,768 or 81,88,70,720 *dāms*. In Chapter 12 we offered an estimate for annual savings, which in terms of metallic money meant additions to the hoards of the Emperor, nobility and troops amounting to 37,84,59,557 *dāms*.[87] This has to be deducted from the total import of bullion to give the stock of imported bullion available for entry into circulation as additional money metal (44,04,11,163 *dāms*). We have to reduce this figure further in order to allow, on the one hand, for some re-export of bullion (including coined money) (to Central Asia for example) and, on the other, for internal use in ornaments and for conversion into usurer's capital. It would then perhaps be a reasonable guess that the net annual entry of bullion into circulation was equal in value to about 30,00,00,000 *dāms*. The exports that went to pay for these bullion imports may be assumed to have the same composition as exports in general: that is, these might have consisted of a three-fourths part of textile manufactures and a one-fourth mainly of agricultural goods. If we suppose that urban wages accounted for half the value of textiles (see Chapter 13), we may assume

[87] This is the total of figures entered against savings in Table 12.7.

that 50 per cent of the value of exports against three-fourths of 30 crore *dāms* worth of bullion imports represented additions to value-added by urban manufacture (about 11.25 crore *dāms*).

This figure enables us to compare the value-added by urban manufactures in exports with the total value-added by urban manufactures in the Mughal empire. The latter we have estimated at 1,43,52,60,712 *dāms* by incorporating the figure of 11.25 crores worked out in the preceding paragraph of the value deduced from our investigations of the dispersal of the surplus; this last had already allowed for exports generated by imports of goods and bullion-for-hoard. Given the same ratio of value-added by urban manufactures as has been assumed for exports in return for bullion-for-circulation, viz. 40 per cent of the total value, we may put the total value-added by urban manufactures in exports at Rs 70,00,000 (40 per cent of Rs 1,75,00,000) or 28,00,00,000 *dāms*.

These estimates imply two significant phenomena that require consideration. First, that as much as 21 per cent of all value-added by urban manufactures was contributed by value-added in manufactures of exports. Secondly, since bullion comprised 80 per cent of Indian imports, it follows that nearly 17 per cent of the total value-added by urban manufactures was paid for by bullion imports.

The fact that over a fifth of the total value added by urban manufactures should have been generated by foreign trade does not necessarily put foreign trade as an equally significant factor in the Mughal Indian economy as a whole. The total value added by urban manufactures was apparently no more than 10 per cent of the total value of agricultural production (Chapter 13), so that exports as a whole accounted for about 4.8 per cent of the total value of agricultural production plus value added by urban manufctures.[88]

Nevertheless, in the enlargement of urban manufactures, exports played a more important role than one may have otherwise thought.[89] It needs to be borne in mind, of course, that the manufactures exported must have been goods of high value and skill-intensive, so that their impact on employment might have been far less than is indicated by their high share in value terms. On the other hand, the increasing use of cloth

[88] It may perhaps be best to remind ourselves that exports must have affected high-quality cropping in many localities, muslin-cotton in Bengal, indigo at Bayana and Sarkhej, rice at Navapur, opium in Malwa, and so on. The impact of these could, of course, have only been marginal in terms of total volume of agricultural production.

[89] For example, Irfan Habib, 'Potentialities of Capitalistic Development in Mughal Economy', seems to underrate the role of foreign trade.

printing (substituting for painting and intricate forms of pattern dyeing) might well have been particularly encouraged by the export demand for exceptionally large quantities of cloth.

By 1600, therefore, export markets were already important for urban manufactures in Mughal India, though the degree of importance must have varied with regions and localities. An interesting question arises as to the advantage that the Mughal Indian economy as a whole derived from these exports. No wage-goods and very few raw materials (e.g. unprocessed silk, ivory) were imported into India in return, so that there is little reason to believe that the imports cheapened manufacturing costs to any degree.

The major item of imports was, of course, bullion. A mercantilist view seemingly prevails that bullion imports must have been of great advantage to India.[90] But it seems difficult to understand how simple continuous import of bullion (mainly silver) would in itself have been of use to any economy, especially in view of a steady international depreciation in its value. The silver imported went either into hoards or entered circulation and thereby enlarged money supply within the Mughal empire. Such enlargement of money supply would in normal circumstances have led to a rise in prices. The imported silver-money passing on to the agricultural sector would have raised agricultural prices and so increased in due course the manufacturing costs, in monetary terms at any rate.

Inflation undoubtedly creates additional merchants' profits, since for the time merchants hold on to goods, their value increases. But this particular source of extra profits for merchants was probably not available in Akbar's reign, since silver imports largely went on substituting for copper currency.[91] Moreover, prices in Mughal India were mainly expressed in copper till the last decade of the sixteenth century, and actual inflation accordingly only began in the next century, and that too at a moderate rate.[92]

There was yet a way in which silver imports might have had some impact on manufactures. The replacement of copper by silver as money should have released large quantities of copper for use in manufacturing artillery, muskets and utensils. To this extent, silver imports until *c.*1610 would have had the same effect as imports of copper, an important industrial metal. This role of silver imports would disappear when the copper

[90] For the latest assertion of this, see K.N. Chaudhuri, *Trading World of Asia*, 462.

[91] See Chapter 15.

[92] Cf. S. Moosvi, *People, Taxation and Trade in Mughal India*, 74–5.

component of money supply had been reduced to the lowest possible level, as by the second decade of the seventeenth century.

The portion of silver imports that simply added to usurers' capital could, with some justice, be regarded as inducements to manufactures, since these probably helped to lower rates of interest (Chapter 15). But the positive effects of the import of a small portion of bullion for this purpose are of relatively little consequence when we compare them with the large quantities of the remainder whose retention in India was practically a waste of wealth in the long run.

POPULATION
AND
NATIONAL INCOME

CHAPTER 17

Population

In spite of the variety of statistical information in the *Ā'īn-i Akbarī*, it offers no direct evidence on the basis of which one can estimate of the number of people in either the whole of Akbar's empire or in any portion of it. Abū'l Fazl himself tells us that in the 25th regnal year, the *jāgīrdārs*, *shiqdārs* and *dāroghas* were ordered to record the names and occupations of all inhabitants, village by village.[1] But the results of this census have not come down to us; it may be presumed that either the order was not carried out or the data were incomplete; or, again, that Abū'l Fazl has simply omitted to give us the results. As matters stand, the surviving records of the Mughal empire during its entire period fail to offer us any large-scale census for any region; only returns of houses (enumerated by castes of owners) from some towns have survived.[2] These are supplemented by a few estimates by European travellers for some cities, or general remarks made by contemporaries about the density of population in some regions.

In the absence of any enumerations, one can only resort to the use of indirect information for forming an estimate of the country's population in or about 1600. Moreland was the pioneer in this field.[3] He tried to estimate the population of northern India on the basis of the *ārāzi* figures in the *Ā'īn-i Akbarī*, which he took to represent the entire gross cropped-area. Comparing the *ārāzī* with gross cultivation at the beginning of this century and assuming a constant correspondence between the extent of cultivation and size of population, he concluded that from 'Multan to

[1] *Akbarnāma*, III, pp.346–7.

[2] For example those found in Nainsi, *Mārwār re Pargana ri Vigat*, ed. Narain Singh Bhati, Jodhpur, 1968; also his *Khyāt*. See Moosvi, *People, Taxation and Trade in Mughal India*, 128–9.

[3] Moreland, *India at the Death of Akbar*, pp.16–22.

Monghyr' there were 30 to 40 million people living at the end of the sixteenth century. For the Deccan and southern India, he took as the basis of his calculations the military strength of the Vijayanagara empire. Assuming a rather arbitrary ratio of 1:30 between soldiers and the civilian population, he estimated the population of the region at 30 million. Allowing for the territory lying within the pre-1947 limits of India but not covered by his two basic assumptions, he put the population of Akbar's empire at 60 million, and that of India in 1600 at 100 million.

These estimates received wide acceptance. Nevertheless Moreland's basic assumptions (and therefore his results) are clearly questionable. For estimating the population of northern India he follows two premises. He believes, first, that the *ārāẓi* represents the entire gross cropped-area of that time, which leads to two further assumptions: (a) that measurement was made of the cultivated land only; and (b) that it had been carried to completion everywhere. His second major premise is that the extent of cultivation per capita remained the same around 1600 and 1900.

As for the first assumption, we have seen that the *ārāẓi* of the *Ā'īn* could not have represented the gross cropped-area, but was the area measured for revenue purposes, which included uncultivable waste in varying proportions. Moreover, measurement had by no means been completed everywhere. The *ārāẓi* figures, therefore, were not even an index of the extent of cultivation but give simply the extent of area under measurement.

In deducing the size of population from the extent of cultivation, Moreland implicitly ignores the size of the urban population. But even taking up his own simple assumptions, one would hesitate to agree with his view that the average size of the operational land-holding did not vary over the period 1600 and 1900. Since a comparatively smaller area was under the plough in 1600, the average holding should have been of the optimum size (assuming that agricultural technology remained the same, and peasants had about the same resources per head in terms of cattle, ploughs, etc., as in 1900). At the beginning of the twentieth century, due to the growth of population, the pressure upon land was much greater; and so the availability of virgin land much less. The average holding about 1900 should therefore have been distinctly smaller than in 1600.

With these weaknesses in his basic assumptions, Moreland's estimate of the population of northern India loses much of its credibility. It is weaker still for the Deccan and southern India. The army–civilian ratio is not only arbitrary but undependable; the comparison with pre-1914 France and Germany seems, in particular, to be quite inept, since the military–civilian ratios maintainable in modern states and economies are so variable. None of these can by any stretch of the imagination be used to set limits for the range of military–civilian ratios in pre-modern regimes in the tropical zones.

It is curious too that Moreland has not adopted the same method of counting troops in making an estimate of the population of Akbar's empire. The *Ā'īn-i Akbarī* provides detailed figures for the number of armed retainers of the *zamīndārs*, horse as well as foot. These total 4.66 million.[4] For the year 1646–7, during Shāhjahān's reign, we have Lāhorī's official estimate of the imperial cavalry (1,85,000 cavalry, 8,000 *manṣabdārs*; 7,000 *aḥadīs*; total 200,000) and infantry (30,000).[5] If one were to apply the ratio of 1:30 to these figures, one would get 146 million (not 60 million) for the population of Akbar's empire. The ratio of 1:30 that Moreland had assumed for south India thus undermines his estimate of population for northern India.

Furthermore, Moreland seems to have given inadequate weightage to the areas outside these two regions. To make an appropriate allowance for these regions, Kingsley Davis raised Moreland's figure for the whole of India to 125 million.[6] This modification, reasonable in so far as it goes, does not, of course, remove the more substantial objections to Moreland's method.

Another significant attempt, using different kinds of data, has been made by Ashok V. Desai.[7] This has required rather complex assumptions. Desai compares the purchasing power of the lowest urban wages, on the basis, first, of prices and wages given in the *Ā'īn* and then, of the all-India average prices and wages of the early 1960s. Sher Shāh's *rai'* provides him with a means of measuring the change in agricultural productivity. Assuming that the total food consumption in Akbar's time was one-fifth that of the 1960s, and that cultivation was then concentrated in the areas with highest yields, he finds that productivity per unit of area should have been 25 to 30 per cent higher in 1595 than in 1961. This in turn induces him to estimate the productivity per worker in agriculture twice as high in 1595 as in 1961. Using the statistics of consumption in the 1960s as a base he attempts to extrapolate the level of consumption in 1595 and finds that the consumption level was somewhere between 1.4 and 1.8 times the modern level. He then proceeds to reconstruct the pattern of consumption at the end of the sixteenth century in quantitative terms.

[4] *Ā'īn*, II, p.386.

[5] Lāhorī, II, p.715.

[6] Kingsley Davis, *Population of India & Pakistan*, Princeton, 1951, p.24.

[7] Desai, 'Population and Standard of Living in Akbar's Time', *IESHR*, Vol.IX, No.1, 1972, pp.34–62.

With these figures, and taking into account other relevant modern data, Desai works out the area under various crops per capita. Multiplying these with revenue rates (averages of rates of the last four years from 'The *Ā'īn* of Nineteen Years', for Delhi, Agra Allahabad and Awadh), he computes the per capita land-revenue: this he fixes at between 58.47 and 79.56 *dāms*. Dividing the total *jama'* of the empire, given in the *Ā'īn* by the upper and lower limits, he gets the two limits for the population of the empire, viz., 64.9 and 88.3 million. Desai himself prefers the lower figure of 64.9 millions, confirming thereby Moreland's estimate of 60 millions for Akbar's empire.

Some objections have been raised to Desai's method by Alan Heston;[8] and there has been criticism too of some detailed assumptions involved in his application of it.[9] Heston's main objection is that the modern Indian yields (based on the crop-cutting method) cannot be compared with sixteenth-century estimates of yields which were arrived at by inspection and were influenced by a desire to raise land revenue. But such peremptory dismissal of comparisons of yields seems unjustified, since the estimates of yields down to 1893 were in any case arrived at by the same method and for the same purpose as in Mughal times. Heston's objection cannot thus apply to yield estimates made in the nineteenth century; and yet these do not diverge substantially from later estimates based on crop-cutting.[10] Heston's other objection is not to Desai's method, but to an error (Desai's as well as mine) in converting units of weight, which resulted in highly inflating the purchasing power of urban wages in Akbar's time.

Some other modifications in Desai's method seem called for. Desai used modern all-India statistics to compare with sixteenth-century data. Since the prices and wages in the *Ā'īn* are those of the imperial camp and therefore apply to Agra (and possibly to Lahore),[11] it is inappropriate to compare these with modern all-India averages. In the same way, the *Ā'īn*'s standard crop-rates (*rai's*) applied either to the immediate vicinity of Sher Shāh's capital, Delhi, or at most to the region where the *dastūr-ul 'amals* were later in force, i.e., mainly U.P., Haryana and the Panjab. These are thus not comparable with average all-India yields. Moreover, Desai divided the total *jama'* of the empire by the hypothetical land-tax per capita, without making any distinction between the *ẓabṭ* provinces

[8] Heston, 'Standard of Living in Akbar's Time', *IESHR*, Vol.XIV, No.3, pp.39–6.

[9] Shireen Moosvi, 'Production, Consumption & Population in Akbar's Time', *IESHR*, Vol.X, No.2, 1973. In this paper I myself made some other assumptions which I should now like to withdraw. There are also slips in calculation which need correction.

[10] See Chapter 3.

[11] See Chapter 14.

and other regions, where the tax incidence might have been much lower. Another assumption of his which requires correction is that the *jama'* was equal to total land revenue, whereas it really was an estimate of the *net* income from tax-realization of the *jāgīrdārs* and the *khāliṣa*.[12]

II

In spite of the objections that might be legitimately raised to the estimates of Moreland and Desai, the statistics of area, yields, revenue rates and *jama'* in the *Ā'īn-i Akbarī* are the only data on which we can fall back for estimating the population at the end of the sixteenth century. The methods suggested by Moreland and Desai too remain in essence valid though they can be followed only with certain qualifications and refinements, and with a revised set of assumptions in conformity with the conclusions reached in our previous chapters.[13]

Once we have worked out the relative extent of cultivation based on the *Ā'īn*'s data, though differently from Moreland, this can serve as a basis for working out the population of the period. To translate the extent of cultivation into size of population, data on two other aspects are, however, essential: (a) the ratio of rural population to urban population in 1601;[14] and (b) change in the area of land under cultivation per head of agricultural population between 1601 and 1901.

For (a), we have already argued for a ratio of 15:85 for the relative sizes of the urban and rural populations.[15]

In respect of (b), there is strong case for the premise that the average operational holding in 1601, owing to the lower pressure on land and greater availability of virgin lands, should have tended towards the optimum size, though given the poverty and limited resources of the seventeenth-century peasant, the 'optimum' must have had certain limits. As a rather arbitrary (but not unreasonable) inference, we may take the average operational holding in India, *c.*1601, to be about 10 per cent higher than in

[12] See Chapter 4.

[13] Especially Chapters 2–5, and 13–14.

[14] Since modern censuses in India are undertaken in the initial years of each decade (1901, 1911, 1921, and so on), it has been thought convenient to assign the estimate of population based on the *Ā'īn*'s information to the year 1601, rather than 1595 (the year so far treated by us as the standard for assigning the *Ā'īn*'s statistical information). When one is making a comparison across centuries, the shift of six years is hardly of any significance.

[15] See Chapter 13.

1901. Since the yields as well as the overall agricultural productivity in general remained unaltered,[16] the larger area of cultivated land per head of agricultural population should have implied a higher consumption level. The real wages worked out from the *Ā'īn* do appear to reflect such a higher consumption level: to judge from the *Ā'īn*'s data, urban real wages in 1601 should have been about 35 per cent higher than they were in the latter half of the nineteenth century.[17] But outside the towns consumption levels might have been much lower. For one thing, rural real wages in 1601 might even have been especially depressed, since the rural economy suffered from an enormous drain in the form of land-revenue flowing away to the towns. If we then assume that (a) urban consumption per capita in 1601 was 35 per cent higher than in 1901, but that (b) rural consumption per capita was of the same size in 1601 as in 1901, and given (c) the urban population at 15 per cent of total, we should set 5 per cent for the margin by which general consumption was higher in 1601 over that in 1901. Translated into cultivated land per head of the agricultural population in 1601 we would get 106 per cent for its size relative to what it was in 1901. On the other hand, the higher limit for the size of land in 1601 would be 140 per cent, if we assume that the ratio of urban to rural consumption has remained unaltered down the centuries. But since there are strong reasons for believing that the relative urban level of consumption was much higher than the rural in Mughal India (compared to the ratio in 1901), the actual margin by which general consumption was higher in 1601 than in 1901 should be much nearer to 5 than 35 per cent. This supports our inference that the average operational holding was 10 per cent larger in 1595, since this would imply (with urban population at 15 per cent of the total), a general consumption level per capita equal to 108.5 per cent that of 1901.

With these inferences at hand, one can estimate the population if one can establish the relative extent of cultivation in the closing years of the sixteenth century. Our own analysis and calculations in Chapter 2 suggest that the total area under cultivation in the area covered by U.P., Panjab, Haryana, Multan and Gujarat was between 50 and 55 per cent of what it was in the first decade of the twentieth century. It would be reasonable to assume that the extent of cultivation in the three regions was broadly representative of the extent of cultivation in the whole of India. It is helpful to remember too that the regions comprised areas of full as well as backward cultivation: hardly any extension in cultivation took place in the Doab during the intervening period, since it was already

[16] See Chapter 3.

[17] See Chapter 14.

almost fully cultivated in Akbar's time, while in Multan, due to the introduction of canal irrigation the cultivated area expanded by about three times during the intervening centuries.[18]

The population for 1601 may now, therefore, be worked out on the basis of the relative extent of cultivation we have established. For the sake of convenience the main assumptions are restated below:

I. The total cultivation in 1601 was 50 to 55 per cent of what it was during the first decade of the present century.
II. The ratio of urban population to rural in 1601 was 15:85.
III. The average agricultural holdings in 1601 were 10 per cent larger than in 1901.

The following symbols are used:

A = Area under cultivation
P = Population
a = Cultivated area per head of agricultural population

Subscript 0 refers to 1601 and 1 to 1901. Superscript *r* stands for rural, and *u* for urban:

Now

If $A_1 \propto P_1^r$ and $a_0 = 1.1\, a_1$

$$A_0 \propto 0.11\, P_1^r$$
$$0.5\, A_1 \leq A_0 \leq 0.55\, A_1 \text{ (assumption I)}$$

Or

$$0.5\, P_1^r \leq 0.11\, P_0^r \leq 0.55\, P_1 \qquad (1)$$

$P_1 = 28{,}38{,}70{,}000$
$P_1^u = 0.102\, P_1$ (K. Davis, p.24)

Or

$$P_1^r = 0.8989\, P_1$$
$$= 25{,}49{,}15{,}260$$

Substituting P_1^r in equation (1)

$$12{,}74{,}54{,}750 \leq 0.11\, P_0^r \leq 14{,}02{,}03{,}393$$

[18] See Chapter 2.

Or

$$11{,}58{,}70520 \leq P_1^r \leq 12{,}74{,}54{,}750$$

But $P_0^r = 0.85\ P_0$ (assumption II)
Therefore,

$$13{,}63{,}18{,}310 \leq P_0 \leq 14{,}99{,}50{,}153$$

The population of India in 1601 should accordingly have been between 136 and 149.9 million.[19]

This estimate is achieved by one route. We can take yet another by following Desai's method, though in a modified form. We can, that is to say, proceed from gross land revenue. For this we must work out the incidence of land revenue per capita at that time. To do so, we should continue with some of the assumptions already adopted, and use a few of the conclusions reached in our previous chapters. The basic relevant assumptions are:

1. The yields per unit of area under cultivation remained the same between 1595–6/1601 and 1891/1892 (Chapter 3).
2. The area of land cultivated per head of population was the same in 1595–6/1601 as in 1891/1892. This may be contested on the ground that in Chapter 13 we have held the urban population in proportion to the total in 1595–6 as nearly half as much larger than in 1891. But, on the other hand, India in the latter year exported a large amount of wheat and other agricultural produce which was not the case in 1595–6. It may be reasonable to suppose that the two factors would balance each other.
3. The pattern of consumption of food, and so the relative distribution of land among major food-crops remained largely the same. With less certainty we may make the same assumption about the relative distribution of non-food crops as well.

With these assumptions (some quite different from those of Desai), Desai's method for obtaining an estimate of per capita land revenue can be greatly simplified. The per capita area under different crops in 1601

[19] While the first edition of this book was in press. Irfan Habib in his chapter on Population in Mughal India in *The Cambridge Economic History of India*, ed. T. Raychaudhuri and Irfan Habib, Cambridge, 1982, pp.163–71, pursued Moreland's mode of estimating the population but introducing corrections similar to those suggested by me, arrived at a figure between 107 and 111 million for Akbar's empire and between 140 and 150 million for the whole of India about the year 1600 (p.166).

can now be calculated by simply drawing upon figures of the area of each crop per head in 1892. Assuming that the results obtained for certain districts of U.P. can be applied to at least the five *ẓabṭ* provinces of Lahore, Delhi, Agra, Allahabad and Awadh, the area of each crop per head of population in 1892 can be worked out by dividing the area under different crops in these districts by their total population as counted at the 1891 census (see Table 17.1).[20]

Table 17.1

Crops (a)	Area/Capita (b) (*bīgha-i Ilāhī*)	*Dastūr* (c) (*dāms*)	Land revenue (d)=(b)×(c) (*dāms*)
Wheat	0.337	62.3	20.997
Barley	0.181	41.1	7.439
Jowar	0.150	34.3	5.145
Bajra	0.134	27.9	3.746
Gram	0.182	38.0	6.931
Rice	0.092	49.9	4.574
Other foodgrains and pulses	0.139	30.0	4.167
Oilseeds	0.011	36.3	0.403
Spices	0.008	63.5	0.529
Sugarcane	0.086	132.5	11.410
Cotton	0.149	89.7	13.372
Other crops	0.00185	100.00	0.185
Total			78.898

Multiplying the area under different crops per head with the *dastūrs* (cash rates per *bīgha*) and adding them all, we get the total land revenue per capita in 1595–6. The rates here are the averages of rates for all circles in the *ṣūbas* of Agra, Delhi, Allahabad, Awadh and Lahore, given in the *Ā'īn-i dahsāla*. It is these (and not any of the 19-year rates used by Desai) that were in force at the time to which the *Ā'īn-i Akbarī*'s *jama'* figures relate.

The per-capita land-revenue therefore comes to 78.898 *dāms*. On dividing the gross land revenue of the *ẓabṭ* provinces, by this figure we ought to get the population of that area in 1595–6. The total land revenue is, however, not to be taken as identical with the *naqdī* or *jama'* figures of the *Ā'īn*. As we have already seen, the *jama'* recorded in the *Ā'īn*'s

[20] *Census of India*, Vol.I, p.6.

'Account of the Twelve *Ṣūbas*' is not the total land revenue assessed on the basis of *dastūr*-rates, but the expected net income of the *jāgīrdār*. Making allowances for all expenses of collection (20 per cent) and the share of other claimants (10 per cent for *zamīndārs*[21] and 7 per cent for local potentates), and assuming further that 10 per cent of the *jama'* came from taxes other than land revenue,[22] the *jama'* given in the *Ā'īn* should be increased by 43 per cent or to be more precise 42.857 per cent, to get the gross land revenue based on the *dastūrs* (see Chapter 5).

As we have already noted the per-capita land revenue in regions where the *ẓabṭ* system (with its *dastūrs*) did not prevail might not have been the same.[23] It will, therefore, not be proper to divide the entire gross land revenue of the empire by the per capita land revenue obtained for the *ẓabṭ* provinces. Nevertheless, we can still estimate the population for the five *ẓabṭ* provinces (Agra, Delhi, Lahore, Allahabad and Awadh) on the basis of our data. The total *jama'* of these provinces was 2,12,58,81,769 *dāms*.[24] Reducing it first by 10 per cent to take into account urban taxation and increasing the remainder by 42.857 per cent we get the gross land-revenue: 2,73,32,73,827 *dāms*. On dividing this figure by the per capita land revenue (78.898 *dāms*) we get 34.64 million for the total number of people in these provinces.

Now, supposing we increase the population of the five *ẓabṭ* provinces by the same ratio that the population within the region bore in 1891 to that of the whole of India, excluding Burma,[25] we get a population of 149.07 million for the entire population of India in 1595–6/1601.

[21] See Chapter 7.

[22] See Chapter 4.

[23] Were we to assume that the per-capita revenue rates were the same in both, *ẓabṭ* and *non-ẓabṭ* parts of the empire, the ratio of *jama'* should approximately be the same as the ratio of population of these provinces to the total population of the empire. The total *jama'* of these provinces was 212 crore *dāms* and the total *jama'* of the empire, subtracting half of Kabul (for area beyond the Durand Line), was 510 crore. This gives a ratio of 100:41.569. The ratio of population of the territory corresponding to that of the Mughal Empire (1601 boundaries) to that of the *ẓabṭ* provinces, in 1891, was 100:36.23. Such a difference in the two ratios can be either because the per-capita revenue rates were different, or because of shifts in population. Since a movement of population on this scale since Akbar's time cannot lightly be assumed, we are left only with the former alternative.

[24] The figure is based on the totals of figures given for *pargana*.

[25] We here equate the area of the five *ẓabṭ* provinces with those of the British Indian provinces of the Punjab and U.P. on the supposition that the territory within Punjab that did not belong to the Lahore or Delhi *ṣūbas* would compensate for the territory of Agra and Allahabad *ṣūbas* that lay outside U.P. The figures for the 1891 census are taken from *Imperial Gazetteer*, I, p.490, Table III. In 1891 U.P. and Punjab (both with their states) had a population of 64.97 million as against the total population of India (excluding Burma), 279.59 million.

Thus from two different methods we obtain the following two sets of estimates of the population of India in 1601:

1. Based on cultivated area, 136.3 million to 149.9 million
2. Based on land revenue, 149.07 million

By our second count, the total population of India remains within the range of the first estimate, but almost touches the latter's upper limit. We can, perhaps, reasonably infer from the trend of the second estimate that the population of India lay closer to the upper limit of the first estimate rather than to its lower one, and so take 145 million to be an acceptable round figure for both the years 1595–6 and 1601.

Taking the population of India to be around 145 millions in 1601, and 255 millions in 1871—this being the total counted by the first Census of 1872 (as modified by Kingsley Davis to allow for fuller territorial coverage)[26] the compound annual rate of growth of the country's population for the period 1601 to 1871 works out at 0.21 per cent per annum. Adopting this rate one gets for 1801 a population of some 210 million. This offers a welcome corroboration of our estimates, since the recent estimates for 1801 based on different arguments and calculations range from 198 million to 207 million.[27]

The rate of population growth during the last three decades of the nineteenth century (1871–1921) was 0.33 per cent per annum—a rate higher than the one deduced for the long period 1601–1871, but not in itself a high rate of growth.

An annual rate of growth of 0.21 per cent for a period of two centuries suggests some interesting inferences about the Mughal Indian economy. Population growth has been usually regarded as an index of the efficiency of pre-capitalist economies. Upon this test, the Mughal economy could not be deemed absolutely static or stagnant if the population tended to grow between 36 and 44 per cent in two hundred years. Davis, on the basis of arguments that have now been heavily criticized,[28] had believed in a stable population of 125 millions continuing for practically the two hundred years from 1601 to 1801, thus yielding a zero rate of growth.

[26] *Population of India and Pakistan*, p.24.

[27] Morris D. Morris, 'The Population of All-India, 1800-1951', *IESHR*, Vol.XI, Nos.2–3, p.311 (the population estimate for 1801 here is 198,153,000); Habib, 'A Note on Population' (cyclostyled) (200 millions); D.P. Bhattacharya, 'A Guide to Population Estimates of India' (cyclostyled) (207 million).

[28] Irfan Habib, 'Colonialization of Indian Economy, 1757–1900', *Social Scientist*, No.32, March 1975, pp.34–5.

The rate of 0.21 per cent, on the contrary, suggests an economy in which there was some room for 'national saving' and net increase in food production, although the growth, on the balance, was slow.

It may be of some interest, if only as a historical curiosity, to compare India's rate of population growth with that of some major European countries. Table 17.2 gives population growth-rates (compound) calculated from population estimates in a textbook of European economic history.[29]

Table 17.2

Population Growth Rates in Some European Countries

	1500–1600	1600–1700	1500–1700
France	0.12	0.08	0.09
British Isles	0.43	0.31	0.37
Spain & Portugal	0.19	0.12	0.03
Germany	0.25	0.00	0.11
Russia	0.54	0.12	0.33

According to a recent estimate the average annual growth rate of population in England and Wales between 1700 and 1750 was just 0.2 per cent; it increased, with the beginning of the industrial revolution, to 1.1 per cent, between 1750 and 1801.[30]

Thus the apparently low rate of population growth in India during the seventeenth and eighteenth centuries was by no means exceptional. It would be reasonable to ascribe the sluggishness of growth to phenomena like famines and epidemics, as well as to the immense exploitative pressure upon the peasantry. If one had data for estimating populations for some intermediate points, such as the years 1650 and 1700, one could perhaps have worked out rates of population growth for shorter periods, and obtained a closer view of the efficiency of the Mughal economy within those periods. But unluckily the data from which such estimates could be derived lie un-discovered—if, indeed, they exist at all.

29 *Fontana Economic History of Europe*, Vol.2, ed. Carlo M. Cipola, Great Britain, 1974, p.38.

30 P.E. Razzell, 'Population Change in Eighteenth Century England: A Re-appraisal', reprinted from the *Economic History Review*, XVIII, in Michael Drake (ed.), *Population in Industrialization*, London, 1969, p.131.

CHAPTER 18

The Gross National Product of the Mughal Empire, *c.* 1595–6

Estimates of Indian national income have so far been confined to the period well after 1850, mainly perhaps, since official statistics of prices and wages began only from 1861, while reports of area under crops began to be published from the late 1860s and the first all-India census was held in 1868–72. The data for the latter half of the nineteenth century still remain so incomplete even for British India that a number of assumptions of varying degrees of reasonableness are always needed to sustain any kind of estimation. Partly for this reason, the estimates for the nineteenth century such as those of Dadabhai Naoroji and Fred J. Atkinson have remained subject to much controversy.[1]

Even the series estimates offered for the first half of the twentieth century have failed to receive unqualified acceptance. Sivasubramonian has worked out such estimates of national income for the period 1900–47 based on painstakingly collected statistical data and detailed calculations. These are available in two versions.[2] The earlier mimeographed

[1] The initial estimates by Dadabhai Naoroji made in 1873 for *c.* 1868–9 were attempted for the value of physical product of British India only (*Poverty and Un-British Rule in India*, London, 1901), and so also were those of Williarn Digby in *Prosperous British India: A Revelation from Official Records*, London, 1901, 534. Fred J. Atkinson, 'A Statistical Review of the Income and Wealth of British India', *Journal of the Royal Statistical Society*, LXV (ii), June 1902, offered estimates of national income for British India in 1875 and 1895, Moni Mukherjee has attempted series estimates for the whole of India from 1857 to 1900 in *National Income of India—Trends and Structure*, Calcutta, 1969. He also reproduces almost all 'point estimates' of the period (ibid., 82), and provides a price index for converting his estimates into constant prices.

[2] S. Sivasubramonian, *The National Income of India in the Twentieth Century*, New Delhi, 2000, being a revised version of his 'National Income of India, 1900–01 to 1946–47' (mimeograph of unpublished Ph.D. thesis, Delhi School of Economics, 1965).

version, so much used by the economic historians, now stands superseded by the published version. A. Heston has offered a parallel series by questioning Sivasubramonian's estimates of agricultural production and has postulated a greater increase in the national income during the entire period; but there are good reasons to doubt some of Heston's major hypotheses.[3]

For Mughal India, in spite of the unusual quantitative data in the *Ā'īn-i Akbarī*, no estimates of GDP have so far been attempted. Moreland, basing himself on the *Ā'īn*'s yield statistics and other data, offered a comparison of per-capita production (physical only) as determined by him for about 1605 with what the statistics around the year 1911 displayed to him. The exercise was, however, stated more in impressionistic than quantitative terms.[4] As has been argued in this book, for attempting a quantitative 'national' level picture, we need to build on the statistics given directly by Abū'l Faẓl in the *Ā'īn*, correlated and then tested for consistency and plausibility. True, these are not even remotely comparable to modern statistics; but, then, this is the case with every aspect of pre-modern history in all countries of the world. The *Ā'īn*'s statistics for their time are not only unique but are exceptionally rich; and after our calculation of a number of basic figures for various aspects of economic activity on their basis, it is tempting to go further afield and hazard an estimate for India's gross domestic product in 1595–6.

Calculations of GDP, based on the *Ā'īn*, are admittedly valid only for the area that formed Akbar's Empire in his fortieth regnal year (1595–6), to which most of the *Ā'īn*'s statistics relate. The geographical area thus covered under our estimate is Akbar's Empire excluding the *sarkārs* of Kabul and Qandahar and the territories added after 1595, namely, the *ṣūbas* of Berar, Khandesh and Ahmadnagar and such areas as were claimed but were not under actual Mughal control in 1595, namely *sarkārs* Bakla, Chatgaon, Sonargaon, Fatehabad and Silhat in Bengal and *sarkār* Kaling Dāndpat and Rāj Mahendra in Orissa.[5]

[3] See Heston's contribution on National Income in *Cambridge Economic History of India*, Vol.II, ed., D. Kumar and M. Desai, Cambridge, 1982, 376–86. Heston's estimates have been criticized by Irfan Habib in both his *Essays on Indian History*, New Delhi, 1995, 351–8, and *Indian Economy, 1858–1914*, New Delhi, 2006, especially his thesis of constant agricultural productivity. See also Angus Maddison in 'What did Hesto do?' (mimeograph) which does not seem to have been published.

[4] W.H. Moreland, *India at the Death of Akbar*, London, 1920, 124. In reaction to Moreland's mode of estimation, Radhakamal Mukerji, *Economic History of India, 1600–1800*, Allahabad, 1967, brought up statistical evidence more favourable to Mughal India, especially on real wages.

[5] See Chapter 8.

To maintain comparability with the estimates for the early twentieth century I have accepted the conventional definition of GDP and have included the prevailing value of services as well, without any judgment (as in modern GDP calculations) on their actual degree of utility or contribution to human welfare. I have closely followed Sivasubramonian in his method of treating the value of goods and services under three distinct sectors, namely, (a) the primary sector, comprising agriculture, animal husbandry, forestry, fishery, etc.; (b) the secondary sector, consisting of manufacture, mining, etc.; and (c) the tertiary sector, comprising income from services, mercantile profits, rents, interest and costs of transport. The nature of the data for the close of the sixteenth century, however, warrants some methods and assumptions that are radically different from those of Sivasubramonian.

The Primary Sector

The data relating to agriculture are quite abundant. The average crop yields and market prices are recorded in the *Ā'īn*; the *ārāẓi* (measured area) statistics can be used for establishing the area under cultivation (see Chapter 2), but there is no information at all about crop distribution, except for *dastūr* rates which list taxed crops in different localities. It does not seem possible to compute the value of agricultural produce from the valuations of individual crops. Nevertheless, since the land revenue in Mughal India accounted for a known share of the value of the total produce, the *jama'* (net revenue income) figures given by Abū'l Faẓl can be made to yield the money value of the entire annual agricultural product. The state claim embodied in the revenue rates, by official recognition, accounted for over one-third of the total production.[6] It has been fairly well established that, in fact, the gross land-revenue paid by the peasant amounted to about half of the value of his produce on the average.[7] If, therefore, we know the size of gross land revenue, the value of the agricultural product can simply be computed by multiplying gross land revenue by two.

The problem thus reduces itself to working out the gross land revenue on the basis of *jama'* statistics in the *Ā'īn*. The *jama'* representing net revenue collection, given in the *Ā'īn*, can be raised to the gross land

[6] *Ā'īn*, Vol.I, 300. Abū'l Faẓl, after stating the crop rates worked out under Shershāh on the basis of a claim amounting to one-third, explicitly says that the 'rates at present at every place are higher than these'.

[7] Chapters 4 and 5, see also Irfan Habib, *Agrarian System of Mughal India*, 2nd ed., Delhi, 1999, 230–6.

revenue by allowing for various additions and deductions that our sources tell us about. Out of the gross land revenue 20 per cent was allowed as cost of collection; 7 per cent went to meet the claims of local officials (*muqaddams* 2.5 per cent, *chaudhurīs* 2.5 per cent, *qānūngo* 1 per cent, *patwārī* 1 per cent);[8] and the *zamīndār*'s share was 10 per cent though his actual income was much higher, being about 20.59 per cent of the actual agricultural surplus.[9] The net land revenue incorporated in the *jama*ʻ was thus only 63 per cent of the gross land revenue. On the other hand, the *jama*ʻ being the net revenue income of the Mughal ruling class, it naturally included the yield from taxes other than land revenue as well, though these taxes do not seem to have amounted to more than 10 per cent of the total *jama*ʻ.[10] To get the gross land revenue, the *jama*ʻ should, therefore, be increased by 43 per cent (to allow, as explained in Chapter 5, a deduction of 10% of *jama*ʻ on account of urban and commercial taxation). Incidentally, since the *jama*ʻ as stated by Abū'l Faẓl includes the revenue alienated through *suyūrghāl* (Chapter 6), our figure of gross land revenue takes care of agricultural production from the *suyurghāl* as well.

The agrarian *jama*ʻ of Akbar's Empire (that is, of the area defined by us above) in 1595 totalled 3,65,50,11,222 *dāms*,[11] which gives us a gross land revenue of 5,22,66,66,047 *dām* (J′). This in turn gives the value of total agricultural product as 10,45,33,32,095 *dāms*. Given the nature of Mughal taxation this must be assumed to be the value at local harvest prices and not output multiplied by average market prices; accordingly it excludes transport and marketing costs. Another question that arises is whether seed costs (regarded as annual capital replacement) should be deducted from it. It seems reasonable to accept the finding of the Famine Commission of 1880 that 6.8 per cent of the total agricultural product had to be retained as seed;[12] and this implies a reduction of the value of total agricultural product available for consumption, to 9,74,25,05,512 *dāms*. This we would henceforth call net agricultural product. We do not take into account the other deductions that Sivasubramonian makes for

[8] See Chapter 5.

[9] See Chapter 7.

[10] See Chapter 5.

[11] See Chapter 5. This excludes urban taxes, but includes the amount that was alienated through revenue grants.

[12]. For this estimate of seed relative to output see Sivasubramonian, *National Income*, (printed), 2000, 83. Sivasubramonian himself estimates a far lower percentage, 4.5 per cent for 1900–1 and 4.00 per cent for 1910–11, 88, Table 3.6, but makes other deductions, which we do not, given the nature of our estimation, take into account.

dung, cattle-feed, tool-depreciation, against the stalks and straw and other side-products of cultivation, which, unlike him, we have not counted as part of the crop output.

We may also take into account the income from orchards and gardens while estimating the total share of the primary sector. This has not been considered by Sivasubramonian. The laying out of orchards and gardens was a favourite hobby of the Mughal Emperors and nobility, and of even middle-class men. These were not only meant for their personal pleasure alone but constituted also a profitable enterprise. Orchards were usually rented out seasonally to professional fruit-sellers; even the Imperial orchards were no exception: Finch (1610) informs us that the Imperial orchard at Sirhind was rented out yearly for Rs 50,000, that is, 20,00,000 *dams*.[13] In the countryside village headmen and rich peasants too appear to have maintained orchards.[14] Besides fruits Mughal gardens also provided flowers, specially roses and *keora* flower, for distilled essences. In the late seventeenth century Sujān Ra'i reports that forty *man-i 'Ālamgīrī* (over 18 kg) of roses were daily collected at the imperial gardens at Pinjaur (Panjab) during the spring for distilling rose water.[15] Flowers were also sold, e.g. for temple-use. It will not be unreasonable to put the value of output of orchards and gardens at about 5 per cent of that of the net output of agriculture, i.e., about 48,71,25,276 *dāms*.

In the estimation of pastoral income we are handicapped by the absence of any cattle censuses, but one can legitimately assume a high number of cattle relative to human population in view of the fact that cultivation then covered only one half of the area it covered in the early years of the twentieth century,[16] making a much larger area of forest and waste available for grazing. The fact that, according to the *Ā'īn*, four oxen, two cows and one buffalo were allowed free of tax per plough[17] also suggests that the livestock available to the peasant in Mughal India was considerably larger than what his successor had in the opening years of the twentieth century. Besides being used in agriculture and serving as source of pastoral products such as milk, ghee, meat and hides and skins,

[13] *Early Travels*, 158.

[14] *Tuzuk*, 251–2; Allahabad Docs. No.1198.

[15] For a detailed study see Irfan Habib, 'Notes on the Economic and Social Aspects of Mughal Gardens', *Mughal Gardens—Sources, Places, Representations and Prospects*, eds. J.L. Westcoat, Jr., and J. Wolschke-Bulmahn, Washington, 1996, 127–38.

[16] See Chapter 2.

[17] *Ā'īn*, Vol.I, 287. For a comparison with the cattle maintained by the peasants in various regions of India in the nineteenth century, see Habib, *Agrarian System*, 2nd ed., 59, f.n.149.

a large number of oxen and camels were employed in carrying goods of bulk from villages to towns and in long distance trade. During the seventeenth century the *tandas* of Banjaras carrying grains and salt, laden on 10–, 15– or 20,000 oxen, appear to have been a common sight.[18] Irfan Habib has estimated the number of oxen employed in transporting goods by the Banjaras alone at about 9 million.[19]

The relatively larger number of cattle should have meant lower relative prices for pastoral products. In Mughal India, one finds ghee mentioned as an essential component of even the common people's diet.[20] The price of ghee as reported by the *Ā'īn* was 8.75 times the price of wheat compared to 1866–70 when it ranged between 11.61 and 13.13 times in the same area. The trend in the price of goat has been a similar one; there had been a relative decline in the price of sheep, but that can be attributed more to change in tastes for meat, and a fall in the demand for Indian wool by 1900.[21]

We should also make allowance for the large number of horses bred and reared in the country for use by *zāmīndārs* and their retainers and in the Imperial army, as well as mules for transport in areas like Kashmir.

Since lower values cancel out some of the larger number of livestock, one may assume that the pastoral income relative to agriculture in 1595 was almost the same as around 1900. The income from animal husbandry during 1901–10, according to Sivasubramonian's previous calculations (1965), was 28.94 per cent of agricultural income;[22] he, however, reduced it to 20.65 per cent in his revised version (2000).[23] Heston assumes the proportion to be 36.4 per cent in 1899–1900,[24] an assumption which has been heavily criticized by Maddison who himself puts it at 25.15 per cent.[25] For 1595 it may be safe to put the pastoral income at 25 per cent

[18] Thomas Roe, *The Embassy of Sir Thomas Roe*, 1615–19, ed, W. Foster, London, 1926, 67; *Travels of Peter Mundy*, Vol.11, *Travels in Asia*, 1628–34, ed, R.C. Temple, 95–6; J.B. Tavernier, *Travels in India*, tr., V. Ball, London, 1925, 33–4.

[19] 'Merchant Communities in Pre-colonial India', *Rise of Merchant Empires*, ed. James Tracy, Cambridge, 1990, 376–7.

[20] Father J. Xavier, *Letters, 1593–1617*, tr., Fr. Hosten, *Journal of Asiatic Society of Bengal*, No.XXIII, 1927, 121.

[21] See Chapter 14.

[22] National Income (mimeograph), 1965, 162.

[23] Ibid., (printed) 2000, 377.

[24] *Cambridge Economic History*, Vol.II, 397.

[25] *Class Structure and Economic Growth: India and Pakistan since the Moguls*, London, 1971, 166–7. For a criticism of Heston's assumptions, see A. Maddison, 'What did Heston do?' (Mimeograph), and Irfan Habib, 'Studying Colonial Economy without Perceiving Colonialism', *Modern Asian Studies*, Vol.19, Pt 3.1985, 369–70.

of the gross agricultural product, to allow for the larger relative numbers of cattle at the time. On this basis, it should have amounted to 2,61,33,33,024 *dāms*.

The same assumption (of lower prices balancing higher production) might not be valid for another minor source of income, namely, forestry. Forests were the main source of firewood and timber. Firewood collected for meeting the requirements of the Imperial household alone amounted to 1,50,000 *man-i Akbarī* (3,763 metric tons) per annum, and 600 carts were used for transporting it.[26] Unfortunately, we do not have prices for firewood in the *Ā'īn* to be able to calculate its value in money. In Kashmir we hear of a tax on wood gathered by the villagers.[27] Teak and other good quality timber were, of course, much used for boats, ships and houses. The Himalayan forests and the forests around Dehradun and in Southern Gujarat were the major sources of timber supplies within the Empire.[28] Another forest product, the bamboo was of considerable importance because of its use in providing a great number of people of town and countryside with roof-frames for houses which, being mainly built of mud and straw, had thatched roofs.[29] Other minor forest products were sandal-wood,[30] ebony[31] and gum-lac. The forests of Bengal and Gujarat were the major source of gum-lac that was used as a red dye and a polishing material for furniture as well as for fillings in ornaments. It was much in demand within the empire and for export. In 1609 it fetched Rs 3 to 3.5 a *man* at Surat.[32] Other minor forest products included bezoar, musk, beeswax, honey and cane. Sources of highly valued wild silks (Assam, parts of Orissa and Bengal) had however, not yet been brought under the Mughal empire.[33]

A very important article which forests provided to the Mughal ruling class comprised elephants which were much sought after as war animals,

[26] *Ā'īn*, I, 151–2.

[27] Abū'l Faẓl, *Akbarnāma*, Vol.III, 727.

[28] Irfan Habib, *Atlas of the Mughal Empire*, New Delhi, 1986, Sheets 6B and 7B and corresponding Notes.

[29] *Embassy of Sir Thomas Roe, 1615–19*, ed. W. Foster, London, 1926, 137. He reported 'townes and villages of clay and thatched roofs' between Burhanpur and Surat.

[30] *Ā'īn*, I, 477.

[31] Ibid., 424, Abū'l Faẓl, says ebony was produced in the jungles near Kalinjar in Central India.

[32] *Letters Received*, I, 30.

[33] See for details, Shireen Moosvi, *Man and Nature in Mughal Era*, Indian History Congress Symposia Paper, no.5, Delhi, 1993.

beasts of burden and prestige symbols. They were so much in demand that in the thickly forested eastern regions of *ṣūba* Malwa, tax-money was reportedly paid partly in elephants.[34] A large part of the supply of elephants came from expeditions led into forests, and Abū'l Faẓl provides us with references to major elephant-hunting grounds.[35] His statistics suggest that a total of 14,709 elephants were kept by the ruling class.[36] The natural life of the elephant is very long, but wars and the unruliness of male tuskers took their toll. Elephants breed with difficulty in captivity and the major source of the replenishment of the domesticated stock had to be the wild herds in the forests. I have elsewhere argued that one-thirtieth of the number of elephants had to be replenished every year from the forests and the average value of an elephant was Rs 2,500.[37] The annual value added by Mughal Indian forests on account of elephants alone can, therefore, be placed at about Rs 12,25,750 or 4,90,30,000 *dāms*, which would be above 0.50 per cent of the net agricultural product.

If the income generated by forests on account of elephants collected there was alone so large, it must be concluded that forests contributed from all their products far more to national income in 1595 than they did in 1901, when, according to Sivasubramonian's revised figures they contributed no more than 0.75 per cent of the net agricultural output.[38] We may assume that forests in 1595 generated income that amounted to at least 2.5 per cent of the net agricultural product, or about 24,35,62,638 *dāms*.

Sivasubramonian computes the income from fishery at 1.104 per cent of agricultural income.[39] Our sources for Mughal India do not give any data on the subject. Abū'l Faẓl does not mention fish as part of the royal cuisine nor does he record fish prices. But Jahāngīr refers to fishing and fishermen in Kashmir,[40] and Manrique to those in Agra itself.[41] We may, to be on the safe side, place fishery production at 0.5 per cent of net agricultural product in 1595, i.e., 4,87,12,528 *dāms*.

[34] *Ā'īn*, I, 423–4.

[35] Ibid., 132.

[36] *Man and Nature in Mughal Era*, 21.

[37] Ibid., 22.

[38] *National Income*, (mimeograph), 1965, 162; Revised (printed) 2000, Table 6.4, Col.4, 377. 162; printed (2000), 377.

[39] Ibid., col.5.

[40] *Tuzuk-i Jahāngiri*, ed, Syed Ahmed, Ghazipur and Aligarh, 1863–4, 315.

[41] *Travels of Fray Sebastian Manrique*, 1629–43, Vol.11, tr. C.E. Laurd, Hakluyt Society, London, 1927, 155.

We may now put together our estimates of income from the various sectors of the primary sector as follows (in *dāms*):

Net Agricultural Production	9,74,25,05,512
Orchards	48,71,25,276
Animal husbandry	2,61,33,33,024
Forests	24,35,62,638
Fisheries	4,87,12,528
Total	**13,13,52,38,978**

II Secondary Sector

Much of the calculation necessary for the annual value of **manufactures** has already been carried out in Chapter 13. We may, therefore, recall that our figures for the total value added in urban and rural manufactures were as follows (in *dāms*):

Urban Manufactures (Table 13.1)	1,90,05,11,588
Rural Manufactures	2,46,01,59,782
Total	**4,36,06,71,370**

To this sum we should add the value added in minting and the income from mining.

Minting

While some of the imported bullion went into hoards as uncoined or foreign-coin gold or silver, most of it appears to have been destined for the Mughal mints. In Akbar's later years there was a shift towards silver currency, and heavy minting occurred. This brings us to consider the value added through mintage.

Abū'l Faẓl records in detail the expenses involved in getting silver coined into rupees. The labour charges for minting 1,000 silver rupees came to 102.5 *dāms*.[42] The annual silver currency output during

[42] *Ā'īn*, Vol.I, 31. See also Irfan Habib, 'The Currency System of the Mughal Empire', *Medieval India Quarterly*, Vol.IV, Nos 1–2, 2–6.

1595–1605 has been estimated at Rs 2,62,54,604.[43] The annual wages of mint workers for coining silver currency alone should therefore have amounted to 26,91,097 *dāms*. However, up till 1595 the silver currency had only partially replaced the copper coinage.[44] Moreover, the output of gold coins too was not inconsiderable. To cover the labour costs of minting copper and gold currency, we may quite reasonably double the cost of the coining of silver rupees. The share of coinage in value added by labour in the mints thus should have been about 53,82,194 *dāms*.

Mining etc.

There are no data to make possible even a tentative computation of value of output from mining and quarrying. The scale of building construction and the large use of red sandstone and marble indicates a high level of quarrying activity. In addition to stone quarrying, a large amount of salt was extracted from the famous mines in the Salt Range (Punjab). Since the price of salt, relative to wheat, in Akbar's time, was almost double of what it was in 1861–70,[45] the value of salt production must have been quite significant.

While silver and gold came exclusively from outside the Mughal Empire, copper was extracted from the famous mines of Bairat-Singhana and other mines in Rajasthan, Kashmir and Kumaun (U.P.).[46] Copper was not required only as a currency metal but was also used for making artillery, muskets and utensils. Zinc was extracted from the Jawar (Zawar) zinc mines in Rajasthan.[47]

We have already counted expenditure on buildings as part of expenditure on urban manufactures

To make allowance for mining, quarrying and other uncovered items, I have added 10 per cent of total value added by urban manufactures viz. 19,00,51,159 *dāms*, or 4.17 per cent of the total income of the secondary sector. The share of mining alone in the secondary sector during 1900–1, according to Sivasubramonian's figures, was 5.26 per cent of the total income of the 'secondary sector'.

[43] S. Moosvi, 'Silver Influx, Money Supply, Prices and Revenue Extraction in Mughal India', *Journal of Social and Economic History of the Orient*, Vol.XXX, 58.

[44] Irfan Habib, 'A System of Trimetailism in the Age of the 'Price Revolution': Effects of the Silver Influx on the Mughal Monetary System', *The Imperial Monetary System of Mughal India*, ed., J.F. Richards, Delhi, 1987.

[45] Chapter 14.

[46] For details of copper mines, see Irfan Habib, *Atlas of the Mughal Empire* (Delhi, 1982), Sheets, 3B, 6B and 8B, and Notes.

[47] Ibid., Sheet 6B and Notes.

Our estimates for the various items of value added (in *dāms*) in the secondary sector may then be tabulated as follows:

Manufactures	4,36,06,71,370
Minting	53,82,194
Mining, quarrying, salt collection	19,00,51,159
Total	**4,55,61,04,723**

III Tertiary Sector

The concept of 'services' as part of the national income often takes us into dubious fields, for certain 'services' might not have been services at all. However, it will be surely incorrect to count the activities of the staff of the British administration as 'services' and the salaries of its officials as due compensation for their labour (as Sivasubramonian and Heston do) and ignore the salaries of the Mughal *manṣabdārs*.

The highest charge on the revenues of Akbar's Empire was that of salaries paid to the *manṣabdārs*. The *manṣabdārs* were obliged, in lieu of their pay, to render military and civil services, at the Emperor's direction. Their number in 1595 was 1,823.[48] They were paid salaries for their own maintenance and also a much larger allowance to cover salaries paid to their *tābīnān* (mounted retainers). The emoluments of the *manṣabdārs* varied in accordance with their *manṣabs*. Abū'l Fazl reproduces a detailed pay schedule for the *manṣābdārs*. On its basis we have calculated the total amount of the personal salaries annually paid to the *manṣabdārs* as 82,74,55,200 *dāms*.[49] The emoluments of the *manṣabdārs*' retainers (*tābīnān*) consisted of their personal pay and allowances for horses. We have estimated the total personal pay of the *tābīnān* at 69,01,41,552 *dāms*.[50] The Emperor himself maintained horsemen called *aḥadīs*. According to Pelsaert, the number of *aḥadīs* at the death of Akbar was 4,441.[51] Their personal allowances should have come to about 8,28,57,600 *dāms*.[52] In addition to the *aḥadīs*, foot-retainers performing duties of gate-keepers, palace guards, runners, swordsmen, etc., were employed in the Imperial establishment. For many categories Abū'l Fazl reports their

[48] Chapter 9.

[49] Ibid.

[50] Ibid.

[51] Pelsaert, *Kroniek*, 120; *Chronicle*, tr. 35.

[52] Appendix, 12.A.

numbers and gives their pay scales.[53] These provide us a means of calculating the total amount of their pay. A large number of servants ministering to the needs of stable animals and beasts of burden were also employed by the Imperial establishment. The total amount spent on the salaries of this staff may be set at about 10,45,80,792 *dāms*.[54] The cost of revenue collection was reckoned by the Mughal administration at 20 per cent of the gross revenue. Todar Mal's Memorandum submitted to Akbar in the 27 R.Y.[55] suggests that at least one-tenth of this amount (i.e., 2 per cent of the gross revenue was spent on paying cash salaries to various officials, such as surveyors (*ẕābiṭs*), assessors (*amīns*), etc., the rest being probably appropriated in kind or directly drawn out of the tax collected. All in all taking the gross agrarian revenue collection at 5,22,66,66,047 *dāms*, the cash salaries of the revenue officials and those of the lower staff should have amounted, on this basis, to 1,04,53,33,209 *dāms*. In addition, the emoluments of the tax collectors of taxes other than land-revenue (*sā'ir jihāt*) have been estimated at 4,51,19,083 *dāms* (see Chapter 13). The *pargana* and village officials too were allowed allowances out of the gross revenue collection totalling 7 per cent (the *muqaddam* and *chaudhurī*, 2.5 per cent each and the *qānūngo* and *paṭwārī* 1 percent each).[56] Their allowances thus amounted to 35,58,66,623 *dāms*. We may thus arrive at the following total for the salaries of staff directly or ultimately paid for by the Imperial establishment (except household), in *dāms*:

Manṣabdārs	82,74,55,200
Aḥadīs	8,28,57,600
Tābīnān	69,01,41,552
Other Imperial staff	10,45,80,792
Revenue staff (land-revenue)	1,04,53,33,209
Revenue staff (urban and commercial)	4,51,19,083
Total	**2,79,54,87,436**

The *zamīndārs*, as we have already noted, also maintained armed retainers. Abū'l Faẓl provides us with detailed figures for horsemen and

[53] *Ā'īn*, Vol.I, 187–90.

[54] Chapter 10.

[55] *Akbarnāma*, Br. Lib. Add. 27,247, ff. 331b–332b, summarised in *Akbarnāma*, III, 381–3.

[56] *Ā'īn*, Vol.I, 435, 459, 494–951.

foot-retainers of the *zamīndārs*. The number of horsemen was 3,84,558 and that of infantrymen 42,77,057.[57] In Chapter 7 we have estimated the minimum rate of allowance for horsemen at 1,000 *dāms* per annum and the minimum payment to the foot-retainers at 100 *dāms* per annum. On the basis of these rates the amount paid by the *zamīndārs* to their armed retainers, as already noted, was probably no less than 81,22,63,700 *dāms* (see Appendix 13.C).

The staff in various Imperial departments referred to above has to be distinguished from servants employed in the Imperial household (and the harem). On the basis of data provided by Abū'l Faẓl the total amount paid out in salaries to them has been estimated at 3,81,80,000 *dāms*.[58] Similarly, the Mughal nobles were known for their maintenance of large personal retinues. They also needed attendants for their stables. We have assumed that they spent 24,31,49,411 *dāms* annually to meet the pay claims of their servants.[59] The Mughal cavalryman, too, was a gentleman-trooper: he employed grooms for his horses and servants in order to cook his food and attend to other duties. The total expenditure of cavalrymen (*aḥadīs* and *tābīnān*) on such services has been estimated at 29,83,90,394 *dāms*.[60] The total income of domestic servants in these sectors would thus amount to 57,97,19,805 *dāms*.

The merchants and other 'middle class' or professional groups must also have spent not an insignificant portion of their earnings on servants. In the urban sector we have estimated such payments at 13,68,60,059 *dāms*. In the rural sector, we have not counted the income of the domestic servants, taking it to be subsumed in the amount assigned to *zamīndārs*' foot-retainers, while the landless labourers' and village servants' income is counted as part of the value of harvest left with the peasants after taxation.

There remains the income earned by professional persons such as physicians, surgeons, astrologers, dancers, musicians, minstrels, artists, story-tellers, astrologers, wandering performers, etc., not attached to the court or to nobles' or merchants' establishments, nor divisible into the urban and rural sectors. Then, there were religious divines and their establishments (temples, monastic houses, mosques and *dargāhs*), all employing a considerable number of servants. To make allowances for their earnings and other uncovered wages and incomes, we may perhaps

57 See Appendix 13.C

58 Chapter 12.

59 Ibid.

60 Appendix 13.C.

assign a sum of about 10,00,00,000 *dāms*, though this might well be an underestimation.

In the tertiary sector should also be included the cost of transport and communication and profits of merchants, rents, interest, etc. The total tonnage transported by Banjāras with their pack-oxen has been worked out by Irfan Habib at 281 million metric ton miles for the whole of Mughal India.[61] We may reduce it by one-third to make allowance for our smaller geographical coverage. The cost of carrying goods weighing one *man-i Shāhjahānī* (73.76 lbs) from Thatta to Multan (roughly 500 route miles) by river transport, expressly said to be the cheapest mode of transport, was three-fourths of a rupee.[62] We may, then, take one rupee as the cost of carrying the same weight over the same distance over land by the Banjāras. The cost of overland transport by the Banjāras alone within the Mughal Empire can thus be estimated at 44,79,51,467 *dāms*.

To this we must add the cost of cart and camel carriage, and cart transport was extensively used for goods of higher value and in local trade. Camel carriage was in use throughout north-western India. Much was transported by river: The commodities transported between Bihar and Bengal, for example, were usually carried by river; and 10,000 tons of salt was transported annually by boats from Agra to Bengal.[63] We have no quantitative data for this and coastal transport, the latter being far more important in Peninsular India than in North India. Finally, we should allow for shipping costs in external trade.

In the Mughal Empire the official despatches and newsletters were sent by runners employed by the Imperial administration. Their services were covered under our estimates for salaries. But there were also professional couriers who carried letters, *hundis* and other private despatches on remuneration.[64]

If we regard all other costs of inland transport and communication as equal to the amount we have estimated for the cost of Banjāras (44,79,51,467 *dāms*), we have the figure of 89,59,02,934 *dāms*. If to this added the costs of coastal and open sea transport, we may, by guess-work admittedly, arrive at the round figure of 100,00,00,000 *dāms*.

[61] 'Merchant Communities in Pre-Colonial India', op. cit., p. 10.

[62] *English Factories in India*, 1637–41, ed, W. Foster (Oxford, 1906–27), pp. 135–6.

[63] John Jordain, *Journal*, 1608–17, ed, W. Foster, Hakluyt Society, Second Series, No.XVI (Cambridge, 1905), p.162.

[64] For details, see Irfan Habib, 'Postal Communications in Mughal India' *Proceedings of the Indian History Congress*, 46th (Amritsar) session, 1986.

In Appendix 13.B we have calculated the urban merchants' annual profits as amounting to 1,35,65,16,804 *dāms* and of rural merchants, 68,53,14,604 *dāms*. The incomes of bankers, brokers, money-lenders, and 'village banyas' as well shop and house rents, etc. are all included in both the figures, giving us a total of 2,04,18,31,408 *dāms*. These too need to be counted as compensation for services rendered.

The income of the Tertiary Sector was thus composed of the following (in *dāms*):

Imperial non-domestic employees	2,79,54,87,436
Zamīndārs' retainers	81,22,63,700
Domestic servants including servants of merchants & shop keepers	71,65,79,864
Unattached Professionals	10, 00,000
Transport and communications	1,00,00,00,000
Merchants' profits, house rents	2,04,18,31,408
Total	**7,36,71,62,408**

We now present below our estimates (in *dāms*) for the three sectors:

		Per cent of GDP
Primary	13,13,52,38,978	52.42
Secondary	4,55,61,04,723	18.18
Tertiary	7,36,71,62,408	29.40
Total GDP	**25,05,85,06,109**	**100.00**

To work out the per-capita income from the figure for total GDP as determined above, we need to have the figure for population of the empire as it was in 1595–6. Since we have made our estimate of the population for India (pre-1947 frontiers) in Chapter 17, holding it to amount to 145 million, we may obtain the population of the Empire in 1595–6, by making use of the relative regional population distribution as

[65] For British-period territory corresponding to the Mughal Empire in 1595–6 (as per our Chapter 8), I have taken Bengal which included Bihar and Orissa in 1891 (*less* the districts of Chittagong, Noakhali, Bakarganj, Faridpur, Tippera, Dacca, half of Mymensingh, and Tripura state), North-Western Provinces (U.P.), Punjab, Punjab states, Kashmir, Khairpur, Sind, Cutch, Kathiawar, Gujarat, Rajputana, Ajmer–Merwara, Central India Agency

exhibited by the 1891 census. The ratio of the population of territories not embraced within the Mughal Empire in 1595–6, as counted by the 1891 Census, amounted to 173 million out of a total population of 280 million credited to India as whole (including Burma).[65] If by the ratio between these figures is applied to the total Indian population in 1595–6 as estimated by us (145 million), the population of the Mughal Empire for the territorial limits of which we have worked out the GDP, would amount to 95.056 million. Dividing our estimated GDP by the latter we get 263.62 *dāms* as income per-capita.

To make a very crude comparison with early twentieth century estimates we may convert the per-capita income in 1595–6 and in 1901–10 into maunds (British Indian weight) of wheat at the prices prevalent at the court (1595) and the average prices at Agra for 1901–10 based on the official *Prices and Wages*. The per-capita income at court prices in terms of wheat in 1595 can be estimated at 14.69 maunds as compared to 14.51 maunds being the average of Sivasubramonian's revised estimates of annual per capita income converted at Agra prices for the years 1901–10. This implies that the per capita income for Akbar's Empire in 1595–6 in terms of wheat was marginally higher (1.24 per cent) than that of India during 1901–10. This conclusion is contrary to that of Moreland made on the basis of a comparison of real wages[66] (but not left undisputed),[67] though repeated approvingly by Moni Mukherjee.[68] However, the higher per-capita income worked out for 1595–6 in terms of wheat would have to be revised downwards if we were able to consider not only foodgrains but also manufactured goods, especially clothing. We have already seen in Chapter 14, while considering the purchasing power of money wages that in terms of ordinary cloth the labourers' purchasing power was higher in the latter half of the eighteenth century than in 1595–6. But, compared to food, the amount of per-capita expenditure on clothing must have always been much smaller, so that the picture is not likely to change substantially from what is represented by wheat alone, even if we could work out a comparable basket of goods for both 1595–6 and 1901–10 in whose terms the relative sizes of per-capita incomes of these years might be determined.

and Central Provinces (*less* Berar). The source has been the *General Report on the Census of India, 1891*, London, 1893 (reprint, Delhi, 1985) and the *Imperial Gazetteer of India*, 'new edition', London, 28 Vols. 1907–9, for populations (1891) of particular territories and districts. The main all-India table in Vol.I, 490, has been treated as the basic one.

[66] *India at the Death of Akbar*, p. 203.

[67] R. Mukherjee, *Economic History of India, 1600–1800*, disputes Moreland's findings.

[68] Moni Mukerjee, *National Income*, 366.

We must also note that our estimate of per-capita income is also the minimum possible in that we have used the Imperial camp price of wheat, for stating our money estimate in terms of wheat, though the camp prices were surely higher than the average prices in the rural localities.

Our estimates of income derived from various sectors, when compared with corresponding estimates for the first decade of the twentieth century, raise some interesting points. In the total GDP of 1595–6, estimated by us, the share of the primary sector as a whole is 52.43 per cent. The corresponding estimate for 1900–10 is 64.17 per cent for the entire primary sector. In other words, in both times agriculture played a dominant role in the economy, but its share in GDP was much lower in 1595–6 than in 1901–10.

The share of the secondary sector in GDP in 1595–6 comes to 18.18 per cent as against 11.20 per cent in 1900–10 implying smaller manufacturing sector in the latter year. The tertiary sector in 1595–6 accounted for 29.40 per cent of the total as against 24.63 per cent in 1900–10.

These comparative data indicate essentially that while the service sector underwent little change in its share of the national income between *c.*1600 and *c.*1900, there was a heavy decline in the share of the industrial sector and a corresponding increase in the agricultural sector over the three centuries. The actual shift is likely to have occurred, however, in the nineteenth century, when the twin processes of de-industrialisation and commercialisation of agriculture played themselves out under the colonial regime of Free Trade. We may recall here the conclusions we reached in Chapter 14, regarding the sharp decline in urban real wages between *c.*1600 and *c.*1900, the scale of which is not reflected in the rather marginal decline in per-capita income. This contrast bears out the view that the nineteenth century saw a considerable loss of urban employment based on hand-industry, leading to large-scale deurbanisation, a fact for which we have adduced evidence in Chapter 13.

Such cold statistics, as we have assembled after a long enquiry into the evidence we have been able to gather, present not only a picture of how the Indian economy was constructed and functional around 1600, but also help us to understand what happened thereafter, especially by the time the colonial regime had so extensively reshaped it. Our findings could then be tested not only by checking our evidence for Mughal times, but also by a comprehensive and credible reconstruction of economic statistics of different phases of the nineteenth century.

Abbreviations

The abbreviations are listed alphabetically. The number given against each abbreviation indicates the serial number in the bibliography, where the necessary particulars of the work will be found.

Abbé Carré	78
Add. 6552	2
Add. 6598	4
Add. 6599	7
Add. 7652	2
Add. 27247	17
Agrarian System	149
Agricultural Statistics	92
Ā'īn	2
Akbarnāma	17
Allahabad Documents	40
'Ārif	13
Atkinson	93
Atlas	150
Bāburnāma	12
Badāūnī	16
Bal Krishna	190
Barbosa	51
Bayāẓ-i Khwushbu'ī	33
Bāyazīd Bayāt	14
Bernier	75
Blochet	42
Buchanan, *Journey*	94
Buchanan: Martin	95
Buchanan, *Patna Gaya Report*	96
Caesar Frederick, *Purchas*	64

Carletti	56
Chahār Gulshan	11
Dastūr-ul 'Amal-i 'Ālamgīrī	4
Della Valle	67
Early Travels	57
English Factories	65
Essays	151
Farasnāma	37
Fifth Report	97
Finch, *Early Travels*	57
Firishta	19
Fitch, *Early Travels*	57
Fraser 86	8
Fryer	79
Haft Iqlīm	32
Hamilton	82
Hawkins, *Early Travels*	57
Ibbetson	107
IESHR	254
IHR	255
I.O. 4438	39
Iqbālnāma	22
JESHO	258
JASB	259
JRAS	260
JUPHS	261
Khyāt	6
Khulaṣatu-s Siyāq	10
Lāhorī	24
Letters Received	62
Linschoten	55
Manrique	73
Manucci	80
Maẓhar-i Shāhjahānī	3
Medieval India—A Miscellany	262
Mir'āt	28
Mir'āt-i Sikandarī	20
Monograph on Dyes	106
Monserrate	53
Mundy	72
Nevill	100

Bibliography

The bibliography is confined to documents, books, and articles actually cited in the book. Much material that has been explored but was found to produce little of relevance for the study has, therefore, been excluded.

Section A lists sources, arranged category-wise; within each sub-section a rough chronological order has been followed, based on the date of the original preparation or publication. The reader may consult Chapter 1 for a discussion of the *Ā'īn-i Akbarī*, and other Mughal-period sources of statistical information. Coin-catalogues and treasure-trove reports which may be deemed to present numismatic evidence in the raw, will be found in this Section.

Section B has three sub-sections: the first, comprising works or reports giving statistical information on modern conditions like price and wage data, gazetteers, maps, etc.; the second, giving books and articles concerned with historical matters of relevance to our theme; and the third, journals. In this Section entries are arranged in alphabetical order, according to the surname or last name of the author (or according to the title of the book or journal).

The following abbreviations have been used for certain libraries:

Bodl.	Bodleian Library, Oxford
Br. Mus.	British Museum (now British Library), London
I.O.	India Office Library and Records, London
M.A. Library	Maulana Azad Library, Aligarh

MSS simply designated 'Add.' or 'Or.' belong to the Additional or Oriental Collections of the British Library; 'I.O.' or 'Ethe' to the India Office Library, London; and 'RAS' to the Library of the Royal Asiatic Society, London.

A. Sources

Statistical and Administrative Works

1. Khwāndamīr, *Qānūn-i Humāyūnī*, ed. M. Hidayat Hosain, Bib. Ind., Calcutta, 1940.
2. Abū'l Fazl, *Ā'īn-i Akbarī*, ed. H. Blochmann, Bib. Ind. Calcutta, 1867–77. MSS: Br. Mus. Add. 6552 & 7652. Translation by Blochmann, revised and edited by Phillott, Vol.I, Calcutta, 1927 and 1939; and by S. Jarrett, revised by J. Sarkar, Vols.II & III, Calcutta, 1949. All references to the *Ā'īn* are to Blochmann's edition of the Persian text, unless otherwise stated. See Chapter 1 for criticism of the Blochmann edition, and for my use of the MSS for re-establishing the text of the work as well as its statistics.
3. Yūsuf Mīrak, *Mazhar-i Shāhjahānī*, completed 1634. Vol.II published under the title *Tārīkh-i Mazhar-i Shāhjahānī*, Sayyid Husamuddin Rashidi, Sindi Adabi Board, Hyderabad (Sindh).
4. Anonymous, *Dastūr-ul 'Amal-i 'Ālamgīrī*, *c*. 1659, Br. Mus. Add. 6598.
5. Munhta Nainsi, *Mārwār ra Pargana ri Vigat* (*c*. 1666), ed. N.S. Bhati, 2 vols., Jodhpur, 1968 & 1969. An extremely rich collection of village-wise statistics of Marwar under Maharaja Jaswant Singh.
6. Munhta Nainsi, *Khyāt*, ed. Badri Prasad Sakariya, 4 vols. (Vol.IV contains the index), Jodhpur, 1960, 1962, 1964, 1967. This collection of miscellaneous historical and statistical information in Rajasthani was compiled some time after 1667.
7. Anonymous, *Dastūr-ul 'Amal-i 'Ilm-i Navīsindagī*, post-1676 Add. 6599.
8. Anonymous, *Dastūr-ul 'Amal*. Aurangzeb: Post 1691. Bodl. Fraser 86.
9. Munshī Nand Rām Kāyastha Srīvāstavya, *Siyāqnāma* (1694–6), lithographed, Nawal Kishore, Lucknow, 1879.
10. Anonymous, *Khulāṣatu-s Siyāq* (*c*.1700). Br. Mus. Add. 6588. I have collated this MS with Br. Mus. Or. 2026.
11. Rā'i Chaturman Saksena, *Chahār Gulshan* (completed 1759–60, but statistics relating chiefly to *c*.1720). I have collated the following four Maulana Azad Library MSS to establish the correct text and statistics: Abdus Salam Coll. 292/62; Jawahar Mus. Coll. B1 *jīm, fe*; Abū Muhammad, 69 Farsiya; and University Coll., Fārsiya 78. The work has now been edited by Chander Shekhar, New Delhi, 2011, but its reproduction of the statistics leaves much to be desired.
   The geographical (and statistical) portion was translated by Jadunath Sarkar in his *India of Aurangzeb*, Calcutta, 1901. Sarkar's figures too were not derived from very good MSS.

Historical Works

12. Bābur, *Bāburnāma*, tr. A.S. Beveridge, 2 vols., London, 1921. I have used the Turki text (being the Haidarabad Codex printed by photo-copy method), ed. A.S. Beveridge, Leyden and London. The folio numbers of the

Hyderabad Codex are marked within the Turki text of what is now the standard edition of the *Bāburnāma* by Eiji Mano, Kyoto, 1995, and so specific references to Mano's ed. are not necessary once reference to the Hyderabad Codex is given. For academic purposes W.H. Thakston's translation, New York, 1996, does not supersede Beveridge's well-annotated translation.

13. 'Ārif Qandahārī, *Tārīkh-i Akbarī* (*c.*1579), ed. Muinud-Din Nadwi, Azhar Ali Dihlwi and Imtiyaz Ali Arshi, Rampur, 1962.
14. Bāyazīd Bayāt, *Tazkira-i Humāyūn-o-Akbar*, ed. M. Hidayat Hosain, Bib. Ind., Calcutta, 1941.
15. Nizāmuddīn Aḥmad, *Ṭabaqāt-i Akbarī* (1593), ed. B. De (Vol.III partly edited & revised by M. Hidayat Hosain), 3 vols., Bib. Ind., Calcutta, 1913–35.
16. 'Abdul Qādir Badāūnī, *Muntakhabu-t Tawārīkh* (*c.* 1595–6), 3 vols., ed. Ali Ahmad and W.N. Lees, Bib. Ind., Calcutta, 1864–9.
17. Abū'l Fazl, *Akbarnāma*, ed. Ahmad Ali, 3 vols., RAS, Calcutta, 1873–87. Translation by Beveridge, 3 vols., Bib. Ind., Calcutta, 1897–1921. All references are to the Persian text unless otherwise stated. A variant (earlier) version with valuable additions (e.g. original text of an important memorandum by Todar Mal) is contained in Br. Mus. Add. 27247. Wherever I have used this version of the *Akbarnāma*, this MS has been specifically cited.
18. Rafī'uddīn Shīrāzī, *Tazkirat-ul-Mulūk* (Comp. 1608–12) Br. Mus. Add 23883.
19. 'Abul Qāsim Firishta, *Tārīkh-i Firishta* (original title: *Gulshan-i Ibrāhīmī*), Nawal Kishore, Kanpur, 1874 & 1884; Lucknow, 1905. Pages of all these editions correspond.
20. Shaikh Sikandar, *Mir'āt-i Sikandarī*, 1611, ed. S.C. Misra and M.L. Rahman, Baroda, 1961.
21. Jahāngīr, *Tuzuk-i Jahāngīrī*, ed. S. Ahmad, Gazipur and Aligarh, 1863–4.
22. Mu'tamad Khān, *Iqbālnāma-i Jahāngīrī* (3 vols.), Nawal Kishore, Lucknow, 1870. I have checked the printed text with Br. Mus. Or. 1768 (transcribed in the 17th century, but incomplete) and Or. 1834 (18th century). Or. 1834 adds a statistical conclusion to Vol.II, which is not found in the lithographed text or (apparently) any of the other MSS.
23. Amīn Qazwīnī, *Pādshāhnāma*, Br. Mus. MS Add 20,734, and transcript of MS Riza Library, Rampur, in Department of History, Aligarh.
24. 'Abdul Ḥāmīd Lāhorī, *Bādshāhnāma*, ed. Kabir Al-Din Ahmad *et al.*, Bib. Ind., Calcutta, 1866–72.
25. Moḥammed Wāriṣ, *Bādshāhnāma* (formerly Vol.III of Lāhorī's work), transcript of Riza Library (Rampur) MS in the Department of History Library, AMU. Since this is defective, I have also used notes of certain passages from Br.Mus. MSS Add. 6556 and Or. 1675.
26. Shihābuddīn Tālish, *Fatḥiya-i 'Ibriya*, Bodl. Or 589, *c.*1666.
27. Sujan Rāi' Bhandārī, *Khulāṣatu-t Tawārīkh*, 1695, ed. Zafar Hasan, Delhi, 1918.
28. 'Alī Muḥammad Khān, *Mir'āt-i Aḥmadī* (1761), ed. Nawab Ali, 2 Vols. & Supplement, Baroda, 1927–8 and 1930.

Other Works in Persian & Arabic

29. Jalāluddīn Thānesarī, *Risāla dar Juwāz-i (bai'-i)ārāẓi*, MS. In Maulana Azad Library, Shaifta Collection, Arabic: Fiqh 24/26. This interesting tract, written exclusively from the point of view of revenue-grantees, has been edited and translated into Urdu by Said Ashraf Nadvi under the title, *Taḥaqquq-i Ārāẓī-i Hind*, Karachi, 1963. Jalaluddin Thanesari died in January 1582 ('Abdu'l Ḥaqq, *Akhbaru'l Akhyār*, Delhi, A.H. 1322).
30. Abū'l Fatḥ Gīlānī, *Ruqa'āt-i Ḥakīm Abū'l Fatḥ Gīlānī*, ed. Muhammad Bashir Husain, Lahore, 1968.
31. Abū'l Faẓl, Letters: Two collections: (a) *Inshā'-i Abū'l Faẓl,* collected by Abdus Samad, lithographed, Nawal Kishore, Kanpur, 1872. Recognized as authentic. (b) *Ruqa'āt-i Abū'l Faẓl*, Lithographed ed., printed at the Alawi Press of Ali Bakhsh Khan (place not stated), A.H. 1270. The genuineness of this collection is open to some doubt (see Chapter 9).
32. Amīn Aḥmad Rāẓī, *Haft Iqlīm*, Vol.I, ed. Ross, Bib. Ind., Calcutta, 1918.
33. Anonymous, *Bayāẓ-i Khwushbu'ī*, a text on aristocratic household management, with recipes, plans of gardens, etc., written before 1647, MS. I.O. 828.
34. Ānand Rām '*Mukhliṣ*', *Mir'āt-al Iṣtilāḥ* (1745), Or. 1813.
35. Munshī Tek Chand 'Bahār', *Bahār-i 'Ajam* (1739–40). Lithographed edition, Nawal Kishore, 1916.
36. Mīr Ghulām 'Alī Azād Ḥusainī Bilgrāmī, *Khizāna-i 'Āmira* (1761), Nawal Kishore, Kanpur, 1871.
37. Anonymous, *Farasnāma*, Maulana Azad Library MS. Subhanullah Collection 616/3 (17th century). A tract on horses and their maintenance.
38. Khwāja Yāsīn, Glossary of Revenue and Administrative Terms (late 18th century) (Persian) Br. Mus. Add. 6603.

Documents

39. *Madad-i ma'āsh* documents (*farmāns* and *parwānas*), chiefly relating to the *pargana* of Batala (Panjab). Originals in India Office Library, I.O. 4438: (1) to (70). The dates of the documents range from A.H. 933 to 1171 (AD 1527 to 1758).
40. Documents in the Central Record Office, Allahabad. The documents used by me are those accessioned in the first series (accessioned till 31 March 1958). These include an original copy of Akbar's *farmān* ordering consolidation of *madad-i ma'āsh* grants in villages reserved for them, dated 7 Rabi' II, A.H. 986 (13 June 1578); its accession number is 24. All documents in this collection are cited as Allahabad Documents, with accession nos. immediately following; reference to the first series is to be assumed.
41. Revenue grants and other Persian documents, texts ed. & tr. by B.N. Goswamy and J.S. Grewal, *The Mughals and Jogis of Jakhbar*, Simla, 1967.
42. Documents mostly relating to Surat, ranging over the period 1583–1648, Bib. Nat. Blochet, Suppl. Pers. 482.

43. Shāhjahān's *nishān* regarding English trade in corals, 1618–19 Br. Mus. Har. Roll. 43A.
44. *Selected Documents of Shahjahan's Reign*, ed. Yusuf Husain Khan, Daftar-i Diwani, Hyderabad, 1950.
45. Shāhjahān's *farmān*, 4th RY (1630–1) Br. Mus. Add. 3582.
46. *Selected Waqai of the Deccan*, AD 1660–71; ed. Y. Husain, Hyderabad, 1953.
47. *Taksim* (*taqsīm*) documents in Rajasthani, Rajasthan State Archives, Bikaner, entitled *Taksim pandrahsala pargano Antelo Bhabhro sarkar Alwar subo Akbarabad* Sambat 1706–20. I have used a microfilm copy of these documents available in the Library, Department of History, A.M.U.
48. *Arhsattha* Documents in Rajasthani, Rajasthan State Archives, Bikaner. I have used the following: *Arhsattho mujmili pargana Lalsot babat Sambat 1744*; *Arhsattho pargano Malarna Sarkar Garh Ranthambhor Sambat 1747*; *Arhsattho pargano Amber Sambat 1747* (Seal, A.H. 1098); and *Arsattho mujmili, sarkar Alwar, Subah Akbarabad*, V.S. 1748.
    I was able to read transcripts of these documents (available on microfilm in Library, Deptt. of History, A.M.U.).

European Sources

49. Ludovico di Varthema, *The Travels of Ludovico Di Varthema* (1503–8), ed. J.W. Jones, Hakluyt Society, Old Series, No.32, 1863.
50. Tome Pires, *The Suma Oriental of Tome Pires (1512–15)*, 2 vols., ed. & tr., Armando Cortesao, Hakluyt Society, London, 1944.
51. Durate Barbosa, *The Book of Durate Barbosa* (*c.*1518) tr. M.L. Dames, Hakluyt Society, New Series, nos.44 & 49, 1918–21.
52. The accounts of Domingo Paes (1520), and Fernao Nuroz (1535) translated in Robert Sewell, *A Forgotten Empire*, London, 1924.
53. Fr. A. Monserrate, *The Commentary of Father Monserrate, S.J. on his Journey to the Court of Akbar*, translated by J.S. Hoyland & annotated. S.N. Banerjee, London, 1922.
54. Fr. J. Xavier, Letters, 1593–1617, tr. Hosten, *JASB*, NS. XXIII, 1927, pp.109–30.
55. J.H. van Linschoten, *The Voyage of John Huyghen van Linschoten to the East Indies*, from the old English translation of 1598, ed. A.C. Burnell (Vol. II), Hakluyt Society, Nos.70–1, London, 1885.
56. Francesco Carletti, *My Voyages around the World*, (1594–1605) tr. Herbert Weinstock, London, 1965.
57. *Early Travels in India (1583–1619)*, ed. Foster, London, 1927. Gives the narratives of Fitch (pp.1–47), Mildenhall (pp.48–59), Hawkins (pp.60–121), Finch (pp.122–87), Withington (pp.188–233), Coryat (pp.234–87), and Terry (pp.288–332).
58. Richard Hakluyt, *Principal Navigations, Voyages, Traffiques & Discoveries of the English Nation*, Everyman's Library Series, 5 vols. London, undated.
59. *Letters from the Mughal Court: The first Jesuit Mission to Akbar (1580–83)* tr. and ed. by John Correia-Afonso, Bombay/Anand, 1980.

60. Du Jarric's account of the Jesuit missions at the court of Akbar, translated by C.H. Payne, under the title *Akbar and the Jesuits*, London, 1926.
61. Francois Pyrard de Laval, *The Voyages of Francois Pyrard of Laval to the East Indies, the Maldives, the Moluccas and Brazil (1608–9)*, tr. and ed. A. Grey, assisted by H.C.P. Bell, Vol.II, Part 1, Hakluyt Society, 1888.
62. *Letters Received by the East India Company from its Servants in the East, 1602–17*, 6 vols: Vol.I, ed. Danvers; Vols.II–VI, ed. W. Foster, London, 1896–1902.
63. John Jordain, *Journal, 1608–17*, ed., W. Foster, Hakluyt Society, Second Series, No.XVI, Cambridge, 1905.
64. Samuel Purchas, *Hakluyutus Posthumus or Purchas his Pilgrimes* (orig. pub. 1613–26) James MacLehose & Sons, Glassgow, 1907, 20 vols. These volumes have not generally been used for travellers' accounts that are available in more extensive translations, or modern editions. However, references occur in our book to the narrations of Caesar Frederick, Linshoten, Pyrard da Laval, Steel and Crowther and Sir Thomas Roe that are contained in different volumes of Purchas's compilation.
65. *The English Factories in India, 1618–69*, ed. W. Foster, 13 vols. Oxford, 1906–27. Individual vols. are indicated by years covered by them, and are so cited.
66. Sir Charles Fawcett, *The English Factories in India*; New Series, 4 vols. Oxford 1954.
67. Pietro della Valle, *The Travels of Pietro Della Valle in India (1623–24)*, 2 vols. The Hakluyt Society, No.84, tr. G. Hovers (1664), ed. Edward Grey, London, 1892.
68. W. Forrest (ed.), *Selections from the Letters, Despatches and other State Papers Preserved in the Bombay Secretariat*, Home Series, Vol.II, Bombay, 1887.
69. Francisco Pelsaert, 'Remonstrantie', *c.*1626, published in *De Geschriften van Francisco Pelsaert over Mughal Indie, 1627 Kroniek en Remonstrantie* eds. D.H.A. Kolff en H.W. Vansanten, The Hague, 1979, 243–335, tr. Moreland and Geyl, *Jahāngīr's India*, Cambridge, 1925. Reprint, Delhi, 1972.
70. ———, 'Chronicles', in *De Geschriften van Francisco Pelsaert over. Mughal Indie, 1627, Kroniek en Remonstrantie*, eds. D.H.A. Kolff en W.H. Vansanten, The Hague, 1979, 59–241, tr. Brij Narain and S.R. Sharma, *A Contemporary Dutch Chronicle of Mughal India*, Calcutta, 1957. There is strong reason to believe that this is a free translation of an unidentified Persian chronicle.
71. de Laet, *The Empire of the Great Mogol*, tr. J.S. Hoyland and S.N. Banerji, Bombay, 1928.
72. Peter Mundy, *The Travels of Peter Mundy in Europe and Asia*, Vol.II: *Travels in Asia*, ed. R.C. Temple, Hakluyt Society, 2nd Series, No.35, London, 1914.
73. F.S. Manrique, *Travels of Fray Sebastian Manrique, 1629–1643*, tr. C.E. Luard, Hakluyt Society, London, 1927.

74. Jean de Thevenot, *Account of India,* in *Indian Travels of Thevenot and Careri*, tr. & ed. S.N. Sen, National Archives of India, New Delhi.
75. Francois Bernier, *Travels in the Mughal Empire, 1656–68*, tr. A.Constable, revised V.A. Smith, London, 1916.
76. Jean-Baptiste Tavernier, *Travels in India*, tr. V. Ball, ed. W. Crooke, 2 vols., London, 1925.
77. Collections of English records compiled by C.R. Wilson, *Early Annals of the English in Bengal*, 2 vols., London, 1900.
78. The Abbé Carré, Journal, tr. Lady Fawcett, *The Travels of Abbé Carré in India and the Near East*, 1672–4, ed. Sir Charles Fawcett & Richard Burn, 3 vols., Hakluyt Society, 2nd Series, No.95–97, London, 1947 & 1948.
79. John Fryer, *A New Account of East India and Persia being Nineteen Years' Travels, 1672–81*, ed. W. Crooke, 3 vols., Hakluyt Society, 2nd Series, 19, 20 & 39, London, 1909, 1912 & 1915.
80. Nicolao Manucci, *Storia do Mogor*, 1656–1712, tr. W. Irivine, 4 vols., Indian Text Series, Government of India, London, 1907–8.
81. Streynsham Master, *The Diaries of Streynsham Master*, 1675–80 & other contemporary papers relating thereto, ed. R.C. Temple, Indian Records Series, 2 vols., London, 1911.
82. Alexander Hamilton, *A New Account of the East Indies*, ed. W. Foster, 2 vols., London, 1930.

Coin Catalogues

83. Mughal Coins in U.P. Treasure Troves:
    Unpublished official reports (signed by Secretary, Coin Committee, U.P./ Curator, Lucknow Museum) of the treasure troves found in U.P. during the period 1880–1968 (deposited with the State Museum, Lucknow). The reports give the places and years of finds and offer a reasonably detailed account of each coin in the treasure trove. In the case of Mughal coins, the names of mints and dates of minting, when legible are invariably mentioned.
84. S. Lane-Poole, ed. S. Stuart Poole, *The Coins of the Mughal Emperors of Hindustan in British Museum*, London, 1892.
85. Nelson Wright, *Catalogue of Coins in Indian Museum, Calcutta*, Oxford, 1907.
86. C.J. Rodgers, *Catalogue of Coins in Government Museum, Lahore,* Punjab Government, Lahore.
87. C.J. Brown, *Catalogue of Coins in the Provincial Museum*, Lucknow Oxford, 1920.
88. Shamsuddin Ahmad, *Supplement to Volume III of the Catalogue of Coins in Indian Museum, Calcutta*, Delhi, 1939.
89. V.P. Rode, *Catalogue of Coins in the Central Museum, Nagpur*, Bombay, 1969.

90. C.R. Singhal, *Supplementary Catalogue of Mughal Coins in the State Museum, Lucknow*, Lucknow, 1965.
91. A.K. Srivastava, *Coin Hoards of Uttar Pradesh*, Vol.I, Lucknow, 1981.

B. Modern Works

Statistical Information: Gazetteers, Surveys, Maps

The following list includes works containing information on modern conditions, which I have used essentially for comparative purposes.

92. *Agricultural Statistics of India*, initially issued by the Department of Revenue and Agriculture, Government of India, Annual volumes since 1884–5 (Calcutta/ Delhi).
93. Edwin T. Atkinson, *Statistical, Descriptive and Historical Account of the North-Western Provinces*. Each District portion separately paginated within volumes devoted to particular Divisions. Some volumes such as XIV (Benares Division) were issued under a different editor. Allahabad, 1875–94.
94. Francis Buchanan, *A Journey from Madras through the Countries Mysore, Canara and Malabar, & c.*3 vols., London, 1807.
95. ———, District Reports (1806–12), ed. & abridged by Montgomery Martin, *The History, & Antiquities, and Statistics of Eastern India*, 3 vols., London, 1838; Indian reprint, 1976, 5 vols., but with the same pagination.
96. ———, *An Account of the District Bihar & Patna in 1811–12* (Patna–Gaya Report), Bihar & Orissa Research Society, 2 vols., Patna, n.d.
97. *Fifth Report from the Select Committee on the Affairs of the East India Company with an Appendix and Glossary to the Report, 1812–13*; Irish University Press Series of British Parliamentary Papers, Colonies: East India 3, Shannon, Ireland, 1969.
   This volume is an offset reprint of the original *Fifth Report* and so must supersede all other editions of that celebrated work for reference purposes.
98. Donald Butter, *Outlines of the Topography and Statistics of Southern Districts of Oudh, and the Cantonment of Sultanpur Oudh*, Calcutta 1839.
99. *Census of India* (1911), Calcutta, 1913. Besides the main volume of the Census giving all-India figures, various provincial volumes of the 1911 Census were consulted. This series of the Census volumes conveniently also gives figures for the four Censuses of 1872, 1881, 1891, and 1901, besides those of the 1911 Census.
100. *District Gazetteers of the United Provinces of Agra and Oudh*, ed. (most vols.) by H.R. Nevill and (a few) by D.L. Drake-Brockmann. Series of district vols., pub. Allahabad, 1909–30. Cited either as *Dist. Gazetteer* or as Nevill's *Dist. Gazetteer*, with name of District.

101. H.M. Elliot, *Memoirs of the Races of North-Western Provinces*, ed. J. Beams, 2 vols., London, 1869.
102. H.F. Evans, *Final Report of the Settlement of Farrukhabad District*, Allahabad, 1875.
103. *Gazetteer of the Bombay Presidency*, ed. James M.Campbell & others, dist. vols., Bombay, 1874–84.
104. Government of North-Western Provinces, *A Collection of Papers Connected with an Inquiry Into the Conditions of the Lower Classes of the Population, Especially in Agricultural Tracts, in the North-western Provinces and Oudh, Instituted in 1887–8.* Govt. Press, Nainital, 1888.
105. Government of N.W. Provinces, *Permanent and Temporary Settlements, N.W. Provinces*, 1872, Allahabad, 1873.
106. S. Muhammad Hadi, *A Monograph on Dyes and Dyeing in the N.W. Provinces and Oudh*, Allahabad, 1896.
107. D. Ibbetson, *Panjab Castes*, Lahore, 1916.
108. *Imperial Gazetteer of India*, Government of India, Oxford, 1910.
109. *Prices and Wages* (1861–95). Government of India, Calcutta, 1895. The prices and wages are quoted for district headquarters on the basis of monthly average; the coverages varied considerably over time.
110. *Punjab District Gazetteers*, series of vols., each devoted to a District or a Native State or groups of Native States, in two parts: 'A', text and 'B', statistics. Series issued from Lahore in various years. Very uneven in content.
111. James Rennel, *Bengal Atlas*, London, 1781.
112. W.H. Smith, *Final Settlement Report of District Aligarh*, Allahabad, 1882.
113. John Augustus Voelcker, *Report on the Improvement of Indian Agriculture*, London, 1893.
114. G. Watt, *Commercial Products of India*, London, 1908.
115. ———, *The Dictionary of Economic Products of India*, 6 vols. (Vol.VI in 4 parts), London, 1889–93.
116. Zafaru-r Rahman, *Istilahat-i Peshawaran* (Urdu), 7 vols., Delhi, 1940 & c.

Books and Articles

The works included here are chiefly those concerned with the history of Mughal India or of other parts of the world during the 16th and 17th centuries, including the history of contemporary international commerce.

117. M. Athar Ali, *Mughal Nobility under Aurangzeb*, Bombay, 1966.
118. Fred J. Atkinson, 'A Statistical Review of the Income and Wealth of British India', *Journal of the Royal Statistical Society*, LXV(II), June 1902.
119. R.A. Alvi, 'New Light on Mughal Cavalry', *Medieval India—A Miscellany*, Vol.II.
120. Abdul Aziz, *Mansabdari System and the Mughal Army*, London, 1945.

121. ———, *The Imperial Treasury of the Indian Mughals*, reprint, Delhi, 1972.
122. J. Beames, 'On the Geography of India in the Reign of Akbar', *JASB*, LII, Part i, 1884, pp.215–32.
123. Neeladri Bhattacharya, 'Introduction', *Studies in History*, N.S. Vol.14(2), 1998, 165–71.
124. D. Bhattacharya, 'A Guide to Population Estimates of India' (cyclostyled).
125. C.R. Boxer, *Portuguese Seaborne Trade*, London, 1969.
126. Fernand P. Braudel, *Mediterranean and the Mediterranean World in the Age of Philip II*, 2 vols., London, 1972–3.
127. ———, and F. Spooner, 'Prices in Europe from 1450 to 1750', *Cambridge Economic History of Europe*, Vol.IV, ed. E. Rich and Wilson, Cambridge, 1967.
128. A. Burnes, *Travels into Bokhara and a Voyage on the Indus* (originally printed 1834), reprint, Karachi, 1973.
129. *Cambridge Economic History of India*, Vol.I, ed. T. Raychaudhuri & Irfan Habib, Cambridge, 1982.
130. *Cambridge Economic History of India*, Vol.II, ed. Dharma Kumar & M. Desai, Cambridge, 1982.
131. Satish Chandra, 'Some Aspects of the Growth of Money Economy during the 17th century', *IESHR*, Vol.III, No.4, 1966.
132. K.N. Chaudhuri, *The English East India Company, 1600–40*, London, 1965.
133. ———, *The Trading World of Asia and the English East India Company, 1660–1760*, Cambridge, 1978.
134. Susil Chaudhri, *Trade and Commercial Organisation in Bengal, 1650–1720*, Calcutta, 1975.
135. B.S. Cohn, 'Structural Changes in Rural Society', *Land Control and Social Structure in Indian History*, ed. R.E. Frykenberg, London, 1969.
136. W. Crooke, *The Tribes & Castes of the N.W. Provinces*, 1896.
137. Kingsley Davis, *Population of India and Pakistan*, Princeton, 1951.
138. A.V. Desai, 'Population and Standard of Living in Akbar's Time', *IESHR*, IX, 1972, pp.43–62.
139. ———, 'Population and Standard of Living in Akbar's Time—A Second Look', *IESHR*, Vol.XV, No.I, 1978, pp.53–79.
140. John S. Deyell, 'Numismatic Methodology in the Estimation of Mughal Currency Output', *IESHR*, Vol.XIII, No.3, 1976, pp.375–92.
141. William Digby, *Prosperous British India: A Revelation from Official Records*, London, 1901.
142. Charles Elliott, *The Chronicles of Oonao*, Allahabad, 1862.
143. A. Fuhrer, *Monumental Antiquities & c. in the North Western Provinces*, Allahabad, 1891.
144. B.R. Grover, 'Nature of Land Rights in Mughal India', *IESHR*, Vol.I, p.I, 1963–4.
145. B.R. Grover, 'Raqba-bandi Todar Mali 1001 Fasli wa Tappahbandi', *Indian Historical Records Commission Proceedings*, Vol.XXXVI, Part ii, pp.35–60.

146. Ashin Das Gupta, *Indian Merchants and the Decline of Surat c.1700–1750*, Wiesbaden, 1979.
147. S.P. Gupta, 'The System of Rural Taxation in Eastern Rajasthan', *Proc. IHC*, 1972.
148. S.P. Gupta and Shireen Moosvi, 'Weighted Price and Rate Indices of Eastern Rajasthan (*c.*1665–1750)', *IESHR*, XII, No.2, 1975.
149. Irfan Habib, *Agrarian System of Mughal India (1556–1707)*, Bombay, 1963. Second revised ed., New Delhi, 1999. The page references to second edition also apply to 3rd edition (2013), since despite making many changes in text, the author has maintained the same pagination.
150. ———, *Atlas of the Mughal Empire*, Delhi, 1982.
151. ———, *Essays in Indian History: Towards a Marxist Perception*, Delhi, 1995.
152. ———, *Indian Economy*, 1858–1914, New Delhi, 2006.
153. ———, 'Currency System of the Mughal Empire', *Medieval India Quarterly*, IV, Nos.1–2, 1957.
154. ———, '*Zamīndārs* in the *Ā'īn-i Akbarī*', *PIHC 21st session* (Trivandram), 1958,
155. ———, 'Banking in Mughal India', *Contributions to Indian Economic History*, I, ed. Tapan Raychaudhuri, Calcutta, 1960.
156. ———, 'Usury in Medieval India', *Comparative Studies in Society and History*, Vol.VI, No.4, 1964.
157. ———, 'Social Distribution of Landed Property in Pre-British India', *Enquiry*, NS, II, 3, 1965, reprinted in *Essays*.
158. ———, 'Aspects of Agrarian Relations and Economy in a Region of U.P. During the 16th Century', *IESHR*, Vol.IV, No.3, 1967.
159. ———, 'The *Mansab* System, 1595–1637', *PIHC, 29th session* (Patiala), 1967.
160. ———, 'Potentialities of Capitalistic Development in the Economy of Mughal India', *Enquiry*, N.S. Vol.III, No.3, 1971, reprinted in *Essays*, 180–232.
161. ———, 'A Note on the Population of India, 1800–1872', Seminar on Colonialization of the Indian Economy, Aligarh 1972 (cyclo-styled).
162. ———, 'Colonialisation of Indian Economy, 1757–1990', *Social Scientist*, No.32, March 1975, reprinted in *Essays*, 296–335.
163. ———, 'Economy of the Delhi Sultanate', *IHR*, Vol.IV, Part II, 1978.
164. ———, 'Mansab Salary Scale under Jahāngīr and Shāhjahān', *Islamic Culture*, Vol.LIX, No.3, 1985.
165. ———, 'Studying Colonial Economy without Perceiving Colonialism', *Modern Asian Studies*, Vol.19.
166. ———, 'A System of Trimetalism in the Age of the Price Revolution: Effects of the Silver Influx on the Mughal Monetary System', *The Imperial Monetary System of Mughal India*, ed., J.F. Ricahrds, Delhi, 1987.
167. ———, 'Akbar and Social Inequalities', *PIHC 53rd session* (Warangal), 1993.

168. 'Notes on the Economic and Social Aspects of Mughal Gardens', *Mughal Gardens—Sources, Places, Representations and Prospects*, eds., J.L. Westcoat, Jr., J. Wolschke-Bulmahn, Washington, 1996.
169. ———, 'Postal communications in Mughal India', *PIHC 64th session* (Amtisar), 1986.
170. Najaf Haider, 'Precious Metal Flows and Currency Circulation in the Mughal Empire', *JESHO*, Vol.XXIX No.3, 1996.
171. ———, 'A Note on the Alf Coins', *Akbar and His India*, ed. Irfan Habib, New Delhi, 1997.
172. ———, 'The Quantity Theory and Mughal Monetary History', *Medieval History Journal*, Vol.II, No.2, 1999.
173. Earl J. Hamilton, *American Treasure and Price Revolution in Spain, 1501–1650*, Cambridge, 1934.
174. Aziza Hasan, 'Mints of the Mughal Empire: A Study in Comparative Currency Output', *PIHC, 29th session* (Patiala), 1967.
175. ———, 'The Silver Currency Output of the Mughal Empire and Prices in India during the 16th and 17th Centuries', *IESHR*, VI, No.1, 1969.
176. S. Nurul Hasan, *Thoughts on Agrarian Relations in Mughal India*, Bombay, 1973.
177. ———, '*Zamīndārs* under the Mughals', *Land Control and Social Structure in Indian History*, ed. R.E. Frykenberg, London, 1969.
178. ———, K.N. Hasan and S.P. Gupta, 'The Pattern of Agricultural Production in the Territories of Amber', *PIHC, 28th session* (Mysore) 1966.
179. A.W. Heston, 'The Standard of Living in Akbar's Time—A Comment', *IESHR*, Vol.XIV, No.3, 1977, pp.391–6.
180. S. Hodivala, *Historical Studies in Mughal Numismatics*, Calcutta, 1923.
181. Sidney Homer, *A History of Interest Rates*, Part Two, New Brunswick, 1963.
182. W. Irvine, *The Army of the Indian Mughals: Its Organization and Administration*, London, 1903.
183. Iqtidar Alam Khan, 'The Middle Classes in the Mughal Empire', *PIHC, 36th session* (Aligarh), 1975.
184. Jan Kieniewicz, 'Portuguese Factory and Trade in Pepper', *IESHR*, Vol.VI, No.1, 1969, pp.61–84.
185. A.R. Khan, *Chieftains in the Mughal Empire during the Reign of Akbar*, Simla, 1977.
186. S.U. Khan, 'Status of Vegetation and Agricultural Productivity: Pargana Haveli Ahmadabad', *Studies in History*, N.S. Vol.14, No.2, 1998.
187. Z.A. Khan, 'Medieval Archaeological Remains in Uttar Pradesh—A Geographical Study', read at I.H.C., Aligarh, 1975 (cyclostyled).
188. ———, 'Railways and the Creation of National Market in Food-grains', *IHR*, Vol.IV, No.2, 1978.
189. Pir Ghulam Husain Khuyhami, *Tārīkh-i Hasan* (in Persian), 2 vols., J. & K. Government Publications, Srinagar (J & K), n.d.

190. Bal Krishna, *Commercial Relations between India and England*, London, 1924.
191. Frederic C. Lane, 'The Mediterranean Spice Trade: Further Evidence on its Revival in the 16th Century', *Crisis and Change in the Venetian Economy*, ed. Brian-Pullan, London, 1968.
192. A. Maddison, *Class Structure and Economic Growth: India and Pakistan since the Mughals*, London, 1971.
193. Vittorino Magalhaes-Godhinho, *L'economie de l'empire Portugais au xve et xvie siecles*, Paris, 1969. I regret I have not been able to make use of this work directly.
194. John Malcolm, *A Memoir of Central India including Malwa and Adjoining Provinces*, 2 vols., London, 1824.
195. McAlpin, Michelle B., *Subject to Famine*, Princeton, 1983.
196. ———, 'Railroads, Cultivation Pattern, and Foodgrains Availability: India 1860–1900', *IESHR*, Vol.XII, No.1, 1975.
197. Roger Mols, 'Population in Europe 1500–1700', *Fontana Economic History of Europe*, Vol.II, ed. Carlo M. Cipola, London, 1974.
198. Shireen Moosvi, *People, Taxation and Trade in Mughal India*, Delhi, 2008.
199. ———, 'Production, Consumption and Population in Akbar's India', *IESHR*, X (2), 1973, pp.181–95.
200. ———, 'Magnitude of Land-Revenue Demand and Income of Mughal Ruling Class under Akbar', *Medieval India—A Miscellany*, Vol.IV, 1977.
201. ———, 'Note on Professor Alan Heston's 'Standard of Living in Akbar's Time—a comment', *IESHR*, Vol.XIV, No.3, 1977.
202. ———, 'Evolution of the Mansab-system under Akbar', *JRAS*, London, No.2, 1981.
203. ———, 'The Silver Influx, Money Supply, Prices and Revenue Extraction in Mughal India', *JESHO* XXVIII, 1987.
204. ———, *Man and Nature in Mughal Era*, IHC Symposium No.5, Delhi, 1993.
205. ———, 'Domestic Service in Precolonial India—Bondage, Caste and Market', *Domestic Service and the Formation of European Identity—Understanding the Globalization of Domestic Work, 16th–21st Centuries*, ed., Antoinette Fauve-Chamoux, Bern, 2004.
206. ———, 'Charity Objectives and Mechanism in Mughal India (16th–17th Centuries', *PIHC, 73rd (Mumbai) session*, 2012.
207. W.H. Moreland, *India at the Death of Akbar*, London, 1920.
208. ———, *From Akbar to Aurangzeb*, London, 1923.
209. ———, *Agrarian System of Moslem India*, Cambridge, 1929.
210. ———, *Notes on the Agricultural Conditions of the United Provinces and of its Districts*, Allahabad, 1913.
211. ———, 'The *Ā'īn-i Akbarī*—A Possible Baseline for the Economic History of Modern India', *Indian Journal of Economics*, I, 1916.
212. ———, 'The Prices and Wages under Akbar', *JRAS*, 1917.

213. ———, 'The Value of Money at the Court of Akbar', *JRAS*, 1918, pp.375–85.
214. ———, 'The Agricultural Statistics of Akbar's Time', *JUPHS*, Vol.II, Part I, Lucknow, 1919.
215. ———, 'Ranks (*Mansab*) in the Mughal Service', *JRAS*, London, 1936.
216. ———, 'Sher Shāh's Revenue System', *JRAS*, London, 1926.
217. Morris D. Morris, 'The Population of All-India, 1800–1951', *IESHR*, XI, Nos.2–3.
218. Moni Mukherjee, *National Income of India—Trends and Structure*, Calcutta, 1969.
219. R. Mukerjee, *Economic History of India, 1600–1800*, Allahabad, 2nd ed., 1967.
220. Dadabhai Naoroji, *Poverty and Un-British Rule in India*, London, 1901.
221. Hamida Khatoon Naqvi, *Urbanisation and Urban Centres under the Great Mughals, 1556–1707*, Simla, 1972.
222. Geoffrey Parker, 'The Emergence of Modern Finance in Europe, 1500–1730', *Fontana Economic History of Europe*, Vol.II, ed. Carlo M. Cipola, London, 1974.
223. V.I. Pavlov, *Historical Premises for India's Transition to Capitalism*, Moscow, 1979.
224. M.N. Pearson, *Merchants and Rulers in Gujarat: The Response to the Portuguese in the Sixteenth Century*, California, 1976.
225. Om Prakash, 'Bullion for Goods: International Trade and the Economy of Early 18th Century Bengal', *IESHR*, XIII (2), 1976.
226. ———, *The Dutch East India Company and the Economy of Bengal, 1630–1720*, Delhi, 1988.
227. Brian Pullan (ed.), *Crisis and Change in the Venetian Economy in the Sixteenth and Seventeenth Centuries*, London, 1968.
228. A.J. Qaisar, 'Note on the Date of Institution of *Mansab* under Akbar', *PIHC*, 24th Session (Delhi), 1961.
229. ———, 'Distribution of Revenue Resources of the Mughal Empire among the Nobles', *PIHC*, 27th session (Allahabad), 1965.
230. T. Raychaudhuri, *Bengal under Akbar and Jahāngīr*, Calcutta, 1953.
231. Tapan Raychaudhuri, 'Agrarian System of Mughal India', *Enquiry*, N.S. II (1), 1965.
232. P.E. Razzell, 'Population Change in Eighteenth Century England: a Reappraisal', reprinted from the *Economic History Review*, XVIII, in Michael Drake (ed.), *Population in Industrialization*, London, 1969.
233. J.F. Richards, 'Mughal State Finance and the Pre-modern World Economy', *Comparative Studies in Society and History*, Vol.23, Part 2, April 1981.
234. Kaviraj Shyamaldas, *Vīr Vinod*, 2 vols., Udaipur, 1886.
235. R. Swell, *A Forgotten Empire*, 2nd Indian ed. Delhi, 1970.
236. V.A. Smith, *Akbar the Great Mogul*, Delhi, 1958.
237. O.H.K. Spate and A.T.A. Learmonth, *India and Pakistan*, 3rd ed., London, 1967.

238. Niels Steensgaard, *Asian Trade Revolution of the Seventeenth Century*, Chicago, 1974 (previously published under the title *Carrcks, Caravans and Companies*, Copenhagen, 1973). I have used the Chicago edition.
239. G. Le Strange, *Lands of the Eastern Caliphate*, Cambridge, 1930.
240. S. Sivasubramonian, *The National Income of India in the Twentieth Century*, New Delhi, 2000, being a revised version of his 'National Income of India 1900–1901 to 1946–47' (mimeograph of unpublished Ph.D. thesis, Delhi School of Economics, 1965).
241. Sanjay Subrahmanyan, ed., *Money and the Market in India, 1100–1700*, Delhi, 1994.
242. R. Swell, *A Forgotten Empire*, 2nd ed., Delhi, 1970.
243. Edward Thomas, *Revenue Resources of the Mughal Empire in India, from A.D. 1593 to 1707*, London, 1871. Reprinted in Edward Thomas, *The Chronicles of the Pathan Kings of Delhi*, Delhi, 1967.
244. R.P. Tripathi, *Some Aspects of Muslim Administration*, Allahabad, 1959.
245. K.K. Trivedi, 'Changes in Caste Composition of the Zamīndār Class in Western Uttar Pradesh, 1595, *c.*1900', *IHR*, Vol.II, No.1, 1975.
246. ———, 'Movement of Relative Value of Output of Agricultural Crops in the Agra Region, 1600–1900', I.H.C., 1975 (cyclostyled).
247. ———, 'The Share of Mansabdars in State Revenue Resources: A Study of the Maintenance of Aniamls', *IEHSHR* Vol.XXIV, No.4, Oct–December 1987.
248. ———, 'Estimating Forests, Wastes and Fields, c. 1600', *Studies in History*, N.S., Vol.14(2), 1998.
249. H.C. Verma, *Medieval Routes to India—A Study of Trade and Military Routes*, Calcutta, 1978.
250. P. Villar, *A History of Gold and Money, 1450–1490*, London, 1976.
251. ———, 'Problems of the Formation of Capitalism', *Past and Present*, No.10, 1956.
252. Immanuel Wallerstein, *The Modern World-System—Capitalist Agriculture and the Origins of the European World-economy in the Sixteenth Century*, New York, 1974.
253. H.H. Wilson, *A Glossary of Judicial & Revenue Terms of British India*, London, 1875.

Journals

254. *Economic History Review*, Hertfordshire, England.
255. *Enquiry*, Delhi.
256. *Indian Economic and Social History Review*, Delhi.
257. *Indian Historical Review*, Delhi.
258. *Indian Journal of Economics*, Allahabad.
259. *Islamic Culture*, Hyderabad.
260. *Journal of the Economic and Social History of the Orient*, Leiden.
261. *Journal of the (Royal) Asiatic Society of Bengal*, Calcutta.

262. *Journal of the Royal Asiatic Society*, London.
263. *Journal of the U.P. Historical Society*, Lucknow.
264. *Medieval India—A Miscellany*, Aligarh/Bombay.
265. *Medieval India Quarterly*, Aligarh.
266. *Modern Asian Studies*, Cambridge.
267. *Past and Present*, Oxford.
268. *Proceedings of the Indian History Congress*, vols. cited by place and year of annual sessions.
269. *Proceedings of the Indian Historical Record Commission.*
270. *Social Scientist*, Trivandrum/New Delhi.
271. *Studies in History*, New Delhi.

Index

For the sake of the reader's convenience, the index includes technical terms, which have been italicized, and provides brief definitions of terms or explanations as well. Some abbreviations for terms used in the book have also been indexed and the terms they stand for have been given against them.

The following abbreviations have been used to indicate territorial divisions: 'dist.' for district; '*p.*' for *pargana* and '*s.*' for *sarkār*.

Delhi, City, 320, 324, 344–5; urban taxation 318
Delhi, *dastūr*-circle, 49; cropped area, 67; value of crop output, 90; *dastūrs*, 102; *dastūr* indices, 117, 124; price indices, 117; revenue incidence, 136, 140–1; *zamīndārs*' expenditure, 147
Delhi, dist., 91; yields, 76, 81; *dastūr* indices, 115; price indices, 115; yield indices, 115
Delhi, *s.*, 40, 119, 163, 186; *ārāẓī*, 25; *jama'*, 30; *suyūrghāl*, 34, 172, 176; *zamīndārs*' expenditure, 184, 186, 190
Delhi, *ṣūba* (province), 12, 48, 59–61, 170, 184, 186–7, 198; *ārāẓī*, 25; *jama'*, 30; *suyūrghāl*, 34, 163, 170, 172–3, 176; *parganas* in, 18; measured area, 48*n*; *dastūrs*, 102–5, 107; revenue incidence, 147–8; *zamīndārs*' retainers, 180; *zamīndārs*' expenditure, 183, 185, 190; urbanization, 318–19; urban taxation, 318; urban centres, 324
Delhwara, *dastūr*-circle, *dastūr* indices, 128
Deoband, *dastūr*-circle, cropped area, 67; *dastūr* indices, 117, 125; price indices, 117; incidence of revenue, 136, 140; *zamīndārs*' expenditure, 147
Deorana, *p.*, *jama'*, 173; *suyūrghāl*, 173
Deoria, dist., 169
Desai, A.V., 331; on *ārāẓī*, 146 and *n.*, on population, 407 ff
Deyell, J.S., 22, 364
Dhangot, *p.*, 316, 325; urban taxation, 315; commerce in salt, 316
Dhar, *p.*, 326; urban taxation, 316
Dharab, *p.*, *ārāẓī* worked our from *jama'*, 72
Dholpur, *p.*, 316, 322; urban taxation, 318
Dilawarpur, *p.*, 130
Dilwara, *p.*, *jama'*, 174; *suyūrghāl*, 174
Dipalpur, *dastūr*-circle, *dastūr* indices, 128
Dipalpur, *s.*, 13, 62, 174; *ārāẓī*, 25; *jama'* 31; *suyūrghāl*, 35
dīwān, official concerned with finances; imperial finance minister, of *aḥadīs*, 226
Dodot, *p.*, *ārāẓī* worked our from *jama'*, 72
Doon Nakur, *p.*, *ārāẓī* worked our from *jama'*, 71

East India Company (English), 376, 384ff
elephants, imperial, 237–8, 212; kinds of, 291; expenditure, 238–10, 247, 283; number, 239; of *zamīndārs*, 179; of *manṣabdārs*, 209–12, 391
England, 384
Erach, *dastūr*-circle, *dastūr* indices, 123
Erach, *p.*, 323
Erach, *s.*, 172; *ārāẓī*, 23; *jama'*, 28; *suyūrghāl*, 32, 175; *zamīndārs*' expenditure, 190
escheat of nobles' property, 198, 203, 267
Etah, dist., 81; yields in, 76
Etawah, dist., 81; yields in, 76, 84, 86–7; crop distribution, 92; *dastūr* indices, 115; price indices, 115; yield indices, 115; value of crop out put, 90
Etawah, *dastūr*-circle, 40–1, 47; cropped area in 67; value of crop output, 90; *dastūr* indices, 117, 123; price indices, 117; revenue incidence, 136
Europe, 279, 374, 390
exports, 392–8

Faizabad, dist., 167

About the Author

Shireen Moosvi, former Professor of History, Aligarh Muslim University, India, has published widely on Mughal India and the economic history of colonial times. Her previous publications include *People, Taxation and Trade in Mughal India* (Oxford University Press, 2008) and *Episodes in the Life of Akbar: Contemporary Records and Reminisces* (1994). Her edited works include *Facets of the Great Revolt: 1857* (2010) and *Capitalism, Colonialism and Globalization: Studies in Economic Change* (2011).